THE YUGOSLAV EXPERIMENT
1948–1974

THE ROYAL INSTITUTE OF INTERNATIONAL AFFAIRS is an unofficial body which promotes the scientific study of international questions and does not express opinions of its own. The opinions expressed in this publication are the responsibility of the author.

The Institute and its Research Committee gratefully acknowledge the comments and suggestions of the following who read the manuscript: Stephen Clissold, Professor Hugh Seton-Watson and Professor Marcus Wheeler.

THE
YUGOSLAV
EXPERIMENT
1948 – 1974

BY

DENNISON RUSINOW

*Published for
the Royal Institute of International Affairs, London,
by the*
UNIVERSITY OF CALIFORNIA PRESS
BERKELEY AND LOS ANGELES

UNIVERSITY OF CALIFORNIA PRESS
Berkeley and Los Angeles

ISBN: 0-520-03730-8
Library of Congress Catalog Card Number: 76-20032
Copyright © 1977 by Royal Institute of International
Affairs, London

First Paperback Printing 1978

Printed in the United States of America

1 2 3 4 5 6 7 8 9

To Alison and Tamara,
the only good reasons,
and to Mary,
the reason for reasons

PREFACE

For more than three decades Yugoslavia has attracted and sustained a level of international interest disproportionate to the size and economic and military importance of a backwater Balkan State with a population of 20 million. Initially inspired by the romantic and dramatic Yugoslav resistance to Axis occupation during World War II, this interest has since 1948 been focused on a remarkable and still unfinished voyage of exploration, otherwise known as 'the Yugoslav road to socialism', which is the subject of this book. The proclaimed destination may not exist on any of the headings which have been tried; the vessel or its navigators may ultimately prove inadequate to the enterprise; or the landfall, if one is ever made, may prove to be only a small, rather ordinary and sadly familiar island still half a world away from the shores of Communist Cathay. The story of the great adventure nevertheless remains worthy of the attention it has received, both for its intrinsic drama and for its wider significance.

In 1948 Yugoslavia became the first Communist-ruled State to defy Soviet domination. It then became the first and for many years the only such State to deviate from the Soviet model in order to experiment with market mechanisms inserted into and gradually replacing a command economy and with decentralised decision-making, wider personal freedom, novel forms of political participation, and open frontiers and 'integration into the world division of labour'. In the process the Yugoslavs boldly and imaginatively confronted, if they seldom solved, a series of central dilemmas of our times. These have included the problem of achieving rapid economic and social modernisation without institutional or social breakdown; the relations between freedom and development and between national and individual liberty; the nature and limits of independence and influence for small States in the contemporary world; and the capacity of a revolution from above to create and then to acknowledge the existence of social and economic preconditions and popular acceptance of values appropriate to self-sustaining further modernisation based on broad popular participation in the making of rational and effective public choices. Meanwhile, the experiment was at times facilitated and at times frustrated or distorted by Europe's most acute case of multinationalism, making the Yugoslave story again of wider significance in a world ubiquitously perplexed by the problem fashionably known as 'community-building' and by the conflict between ethnic diversity and the ideology of the nation-State.

As this odyssey enters its fourth decade, with Yugoslavia now armed with a new Constitution and a political redefinition which clearly mark the opening of a fresh chapter, with or without a leader whose longevity has already defied normal expectations, it seems an appropriate moment to attempt a preliminary and tentative analysis of the meaning of the first thirty years. This is cast in the form of a political history, laying emphasis on the dynamics of the complex, two-way relationship between a specific style of deliberately engineered social and economic modernisation and the engineers and engines of the process.

The focus and the largest portion of the text concern the years since 1961 and, to a lesser extent, the period from 1949 to 1953. There are two reasons. First, these two periods are the ones in which the vital political and ideological struggles, which were to transform the regime and Yugoslav society, took place. The rest of the history of postwar Yugoslavia is in this sense prelude, interlude and epilogue. Although they are also undoubtedly important and deserve more detailed analysis, reasons of space and the author's personal preferences provide a good excuse for calling them relatively less significant and passing them by with brief summaries. Secondly, since it was during the later of these two periods that I was resident in Yugoslavia and a close observer of the Yugoslav scene, from 1963 to 1973, I have more to say about these years, at least pending an opening of archives which will permit a scholarly revision of present perceptions (and existing studies) of preceding phases.

Contemplating the decade of residence, observation and study on which this book is based, I am humbly aware that it and I owe an enormous debt to numerous Yugoslavs who generously offered me their knowledge, their insights and often their friendships, and without whom it would contain far more errors of fact and faulty judgements than it does. To name even the chief of them would be impossible without either excessive length or invidious selection. I must trust that both those who saw me officially more often and lengthily than official duty required and those who shared with me their professional and personal lives and intimate thoughts and hopes will understand that my tribute is nameless also because the list would do me far more honour than it would do them, and would occasionally be indiscreet. They include our own *kumovi*, many other friends and acquaintances in high and low places in academic, journalistic, political and professional circles in Belgrade, Zagreb, Ljubljana and Rijeka, and those numerous villagers of Croatia,

Serbia, the Vojvodina, Dalmatia and Montenegro with whom we have had the privilege of frequently sharing bread and *rakija* in their homes and ours.

Among other foreign observers to whom I owe debts of almost equal magnitude, special mention must be made of Sir William Deakin, who first inspired and has continued to encourage my interest, of those perceptive Balkan journalists David Binder and Paul Lendvai, and of the remarkable group of scholar-diplomats who staffed the British and American embassies in the days of Ambassadors Sir Terence Garvey and Burke Elbrick. For the text itself, I owe many thanks to Mary Rusinow, Dines Björner and Karen Rautenstrauch, without whom it would never have been ready, to Lloyd Hickman for the map, and to Hermia Oliver of Chatham House, whose patience and tolerance are exceeded only by her editorial acuteness.

I am also immensely indebted to my colleagues, the American Universities Field Staff, who made this book possible by according me the privilege of serving as AUFS Associate for Southeastern Europe since 1963, by permitting me to make extensive use of my *Fieldstaff Reports* from Yugoslavia, and by tolerating the time I have stolen in writing it. Among these colleagues I owe a special debt to E. A. Bayne, Director of the AUFS Center for Mediterranean Studies in Rome, for his useful and encouraging comments on the manuscript. And to an unpaid AUFS colleague, my wife, who understands Yugoslavia better than I ever shall and whose understanding so pervades and illuminates these pages that she really is the author of the best that is in them.

April 1975

D. R.

CONTENTS

PRINCIPAL ABBREVIATIONS*

CPY   Communist Party of Yugoslavia (to 1952)

FEC   Federal Executive Council (the Yugoslav cabinet after 1953)

GIF   General Investment Fund (the principal source of investment credits, 1954-64)

LCY   League of Communists of Yugoslavia (after 1952, but still commonly and in this text called 'the Party')

OZNa   *Odeljenje za zaštitu naroda* (Department for the Protection of the People), name for internal security or 'political' police until superseded by UDBa (q.v.)

SAWPY   Socialist Alliance of the Working People of Yugoslavia

UDBa   *Uprava državne bezbednosti* (State Security Administration).

* Excluding internationally recognised abbreviations and those confined to specific chapters, where they are spelled out at the first occurrence.

FOREWORD

Yugoslavia was born of an idea, a century-old aspiration which held that the South Slav peoples, the *Jugoslaveni*, should be united in one State. It was a vison of liberty and modernisation which sought to reconcile the prevailing ideology of the nineteenth century with the reality of the ethnic map of south-eastern Europe: positing national emancipation and the nation-State as prerequisites of individual freedom and social progress, an especially appealing idea for peoples living under oppressive alien regimes and in poverty, but perceiving the unity of diverse but related nationalities as the only viable answer to the problem of small nations living in an ethnic patchwork and in a place where great power imperialisms intersect. Among its symbols perhaps the most poignant and graphic is the fresco which one of its first and greatest Croatian protagonists, Bishop Josip-Jurai Strosmajer of Djakovo, ordered to be painted in the neo-Gothic cathedral which he built for his Slavonian see. There, on the wall of the south transept, the South Slav nations, represented by a Serb, a Croat, a Slovene, a Dalmatian and a Bulgarian, come to present their Epiphany gifts. These, the simple fruits of South Slav peasant agriculture, are regionally diverse in kind but together offer the Christ child all that he might need. The site is also symbolic of the vision's rationale, for Slavonia is an historically Croatian land peopled in modern times by a mixture of Croat and Serb peasants who had already spent up to 700 years under alien rule, alternately Magyar and Ottoman, when Strosmajer built his church.

The State created in 1918 through the amalgamation of the previously independent kingdoms of Serbia and Montenegro with sizeable fragments of the former Habsburg, Ottoman and Venetian empires was ostensibly the nearly complete fulfilment of this dream. Only the Bulgarians, with a State of their own, and a few compact or scattered minorities of other South Slavs in five other neighbouring States were left outside its frontiers. Its history, however, was in essence to be a history of conflict between the Yugoslav idea and the stubborn fact that the South Slav peoples, never before joined politically, had little in common except the aspiration for unity and the similarities of language, of myths of historical origin and of centuries of alien rule on which that aspiration was based. Everything else that has happened to the Yugoslavs, in the sixty years since World War I began on Yugoslav soil and as an immediate consequence of an incident in the struggle to realise the Yugoslav idea, happened in the context of the manifold political, economic, cultural and psychological dimensions of this historic problem.

It was not just that the Yugoslav peoples had lived under various, usually foreign masters before 1918, as had the Italians before 1860, or the Poles after the partitions of the eighteenth century. The Yugoslavs had lived in effect on two different continents, for the Habsburg Empire was a European power and a distinguished centre of European culture, while the Ottoman Empire was an Asiatic despotism with an entirely different heritage. If Asia did not quite begin on the Landstrasse Hauptstrasse at the eastern gates of Vienna, as Metternich is supposed to have said that it did, it certainly began as late as the mid-nineteenth century along the line of the Sava and Danube rivers. Beyond that line, already in Maria Theresa's day the world's first and here literal 'cordon sanitaire', with a strictly enforced quarantine to protect Europe against Asian plagues, lay Turkey and the Balkans, names which were once household words for obscurantism, corruption, anarchy and violence.

The geography of the region, externally accessible in almost all directions but with internal movement from one part to another seriously impeded by some of Europe's most difficult terrain, has been more conducive to invasion than to commerce or internal cohesion. This is one reason why the inhabitants have often excelled as warriors but seldom as merchants, and for the stubborn persistence of the extraordinarily complex ethnic patchwork created by successive invasions and migrations. Their lands have been a permanently disputed frontier zone: between the Eastern and Western Roman Empires, between Catholic and Orthodox Christianity, between Christian Europe and Islamic Asia, between a Germanic *Drang nach Südosten* and a Pan-Slav push towards warm seas, between Eastern Europe's Bolshevism and Western Europe's bourgeois democracy or fascism. As Tito himself once observed: 'Historians have recorded the disastrous fact that not one of fifty generations on our territory has been spared the devastation of war and heavy losses'.[1]

Independent powers have existed in this situation only as buffer States between rival empires or upon the ruins at the edges of decaying ones. Thus one may explain the medieval Bulgarian and Serb empires, the early Croatian and later Bosnian kingdoms, the Republic of Ragusa (Dubrovnik), the nineteenth-century creation and expansion of Serbian and Montenegrin principalities, or in our own day the establishment of an independent and non-aligned socialist Yugoslavia.

More frequently, however, all or most of the Yugoslav peoples have lived under foreign rule. The Slovenes, in the far north-west, never had an independent State but formed a part of a German empire from Charlemagne's day until 1918, under Habsburg rule from the thirteenth century to the twentieth. The Croats were joined with the Magyars from the year 1102 until 1918, first under Hungarian and then after 1526 under Habsburg kings—except that many of them also lived under Ottoman rule for nearly two centuries. The Dalmatian Croats passed from Hungarian to Venetian or Ottoman and then Habsburg hands. The rest—Serbians, Bosnians and Herzegovinians, Macedonians and the non-Slavic Albanians of 'Old Serbia' in Kosovo and Metohija—came under Turkish rule in the fourteenth or fifteenth centuries and remained there until their gradual and progressive transfer during the nineteenth, either into independent buffer States or (in the case of Bosnia and Herzegovina) into the Habsburg Empire. The last Yugoslav lands—Macedonia, Kosovo and the Sanjak of Novi Pazar—emerged from the Ottoman Empire in 1912-13, as a result of the First Balkan War. Only diminutive Montenegro and Ragusa preserved a tenuous independence during most of this period, the former because its terrain was effectively unconquerable and the latter by means of skillful diplomacy and a formal acknowledgement of Turkish suzerainty; but even the Ragusan Republic vanished from the map, at Napoleon's insistence, a few years before the rebirth of Serbia.

These various experiences made a deep impact on the culture and ethos of the South Slavs. Those who were longest under Byzantine and Turkish influence and rule inherited a Greek Orthodox or Islamic tradition and were unmistakably 'Balkan'. Their brethren in the north and west, who received Christianity from Rome and authority from Vienna, Budapest, or Venice, belonged to Catholic Central or Mediterranean Europe. Thus it was, in the most fateful case of all, that the Serbs and Croats, speaking variants of the same language, said by some to have been one people in origin, and living next door to each other, developed strikingly different social and value systems and political cultures. The differences are symbolised by their use of two different alphabets—Latin by the Catholic Croats and Cyrillic by the Orthodox Serbs—to write a common language in which the Croatian literary variant is closer to the spoken language of a majority of Serbs and Montenegrins than to that of most Croats. The disruptive potential of these differences in a common State and in the many regions in which the two nations are intermingled is further symbolised by a common Yugoslav saying born of post-1918 experience: 'the very way of life of a Serb and a Croat is a deliberate provocation by each to the other'. Another and self-complimentary Serbian stereotype, which holds that in a conflict with authority 'the Serb reaches for his sword and the Croat for his pen', focuses metaphorically on an essential difference in inherited political styles. That of the Serbs remembers the tradition of the *hajduk*, the patriotic bandit in the hills offering the only possible answer to the oppressive anarchy of the Ottoman Empire's last two centuries, while that of the Croats reflects lessons learned from highly legalistic and often legally answerable infringements of national and individual freedoms under Habsburg rule.

United at last by the collapse of the Habsburg and Ottoman Empires in 1918, the Yugoslavs remained disunited by nationality, religion and diverse Habsburg, Ottoman and Venetian influences on such basic features of their way of life as urban forms, rural settlement and landholding patterns, legal systems, levels of economic and social development and modes of perception. Their State, however logical, desirable, and desired such a union might be, was a multi-national anachronism in an age characterised by the triumph of the ideology of the nation-State which had created it in 1918. Its official name until 1929, the Kingdom of the Serbs, Croats and Slovenes, bore formal witness to this fact. No single nationality comprised a majority of the population, then about 14 million. Serbs were most numerous, with about 41 per cent of the total, followed by Croats with about 24 per cent and Slovenes with 8·5 per cent. Macedonians, Bosnian Moslems and Montenegrins brought the share of South Slavs in the total population of the South Slav state to about 83 per cent.[2] The rest consisted of nearly two dozen ethnic minorities, among whom more than 500,000 Germans (until their flight or expulsion after World War. II) and nearly as many Magyars and Albanians were numerically and in political potential the most important. The presence of these last and of unredeemed Yugoslav minorities in Italy, Austria, and elsewhere, all symbols of the impossibility of drawing ethnic frontiers on the ethnic map of south-eastern Europe, also added to the fragility of the new State, as irredentists on one side or the other challenged its frontiers with six out of seven neighbours.

The situation was further complicated by an acute maldistribution of both economic and political power, which was rendered socially and politically more dangerous by their respective polarisation in ethnically as well as geographically different parts of the country. As a result of different histories, the peoples of the ex-Habsburg lands of the north and west—Slovenia, Croatia and the Vojvodina—enjoyed higher living standards, most of the little industry, industrial tradition and modern communications which existed, higher literacy and lower birth rates, and more complex social stratification than the peoples of the Balkan and ex-Ottoman provinces, where between 80 and 90 per cent of the people were still dependent on subsistence peasant agriculture for their livelihood in 1918. At the same time, however, ruling groups in Serbian Belgrade, exploiting their nation's numerical preponderance and the political and psychological consequences of the Serbian Kingdom's role in the war and in the founding of the new State, succeeded in imposing themselves and a highly centralised political system on other nationalities whose leaders usually, and especially in Croatian Zagreb, would have preferred a federation.

While economic power was therefore concentrated in more developed Slovenia and Croatia, political power came to be held almost exclusively by Serbians.[3] The Croats, Slovenes and other non-Serbs in the south as well as the north, the majority of the population, found themselves living in what was really a Greater Serbia, with a Serbian king, a Serbian capital, Serbian prime ministers throughout the inter-war period (except for a few months in 1928) and Serb domination of the officer corps of the army and bureaucracy.

In such a situation all significant political parties were ethnic parties except an initially pan-Yugoslav Communist Party, which was driven into illegality and impotence after 1921 and which later and for several years, conforming to Comintern directives, favoured the break-up of Yugoslavia. The political system founded on such parties fluctuated between instability and deadlock until, in frustration, a Serbian royal dictatorship was imposed in January 1929. One of its first acts was to change the name of the State to 'Yugoslavia' and to redefine Serbs, Croats and Slovenes (the first category already subsuming Montenegrins, Macedonians and Bosnian Moslems) as 'tribes' of one 'Yugoslav nation', which seemed to be indistinguishable from the Serb nation in most of its culturally salient characteristics. The dictatorship and perceptions of progressive Serbianisation in turn spawned or spurred militant and sometimes fascist separatist movements, especially among Croats and Macedonians, whose fascist Ustaša and terrorist IMRO[4] combined their talents to assassinate King Aleksandar Kara-djordjević in Marseilles in October 1934. In these muddy waters expansionist foreign powers—first Mussolini's Italy and then Hitler's Germany—fished with considerable skill and profit.

Yugoslavia's economic history, meanwhile, was similar to that of most of its neighbours. There was a brief and hopeful if modest developmental boom in the 1920s, largely financed by foreign capital and therefore leaving most Yugoslav extractive and manufacturing industries under foreign ownership. Then the Great Depression brought its usual social and political as well as economic consequences. In Yugoslavia these included a reluctant but unavoidable slide into economic dependency on Nazi

Germany, which alone was able and prepared to take Balkan agricultural and raw materials in return for growing influence and an ability to dictate terms of trade designed to keep these States in a condition which a later age would describe as neo-colonialism. Despite notable progress in some areas, Yugoslavia remained one of the poorest countries in Europe. Per capita national income in 1938 has been variously estimated at between US$60 and $70, compared to then levels of $521 in the USA, $337 in Germany and $236 in France. Manufacturing accounted for only 26·8 per cent of national income, an increase of 6 per cent since 1923. The agricultural population, almost entirely peasant smallholders, still represented 75 per cent of total population. The peasant problem was if anything more acute than it had been earlier, with man–land ratios growing progressively worse: from 131 peasants for every 100 hectares of arable land in 1921 to 144 per 100 hectares on the eve of the war. Only 30·1 per cent of children of primary school age were actually in school, and 44·6 per cent of the population was illiterate.

The fragile vessel of such a Yugoslavia broke apart on the rocks of World War II. Under the impact of an Axis invasion in April 1941 the State collapsed and was divided by its conquerors into a patchwork of puppet States and occupied zones, with borders and definitions which emphasised ethnic differences and invited civil strife.

Out of this debris and out of the fires of an extraordinary combination of an epic national liberation struggle, an inter-ethnic civil war and a social revolution there arose the phoenix of a new Yugoslavia, wearing the red star of communism. The unsolved basic problems of the old Yugoslavia remained: how to achieve effective independence for a sensitively located small country; how to achieve rapid economic and social modernisation in a poor country endowed with little appropriate social infrastructure and less capital and trained manpower, and with sharply differing regional levels of backwardness which coincided with the distribution of mutually suspicious ethnic communities; and how to achieve, along with such modernization, the brotherhood and unity of these diverse peoples. Solutions were now to be sought by a group of inexperienced, dogmatically-trained but eager and frequently intelligent and flexible Balkan Communists, who had just proved themselves to be motivated at least as much by patriotism as by Marxist ideology. In principle they would seek to answer the national question with federalism and cultural autonomy under the umbrella of a one-party but multinational dictatorship, the developmental question with socialism, and the problem of independence with a rash but successful defiance of the logic of their own and their country's weakness.

MAP

1

THE BIRTH OF A NEW YUGOSLAVIA

The Axis invasion of Yugoslavia began on April 6, 1941, with a savage bombing of Belgrade and ended on April 17 with an armistice which was in effect an unconditional surrender. King Peter II and his Government, newly installed on March 27 by the military coup d'état and anti-Axis demonstrations which precipitated Hitler's decision to attack, had already fled the country, en route to form a Government in exile in London and later in Cairo. The collapse was more than a military defeat, which was inevitable considering the overwhelming military supremacy of the Axis powers. It was, as one of its chroniclers describes it, 'the total disintegration of a ruling system, a disintegration after which it looked as if the Yugoslav state as a unified political entity would never recover'.[1]

Yugoslavia in fact ceased to exist. In Zagreb an 'independent State of Croatia' under Italo-German protection had already been proclaimed, with the enthusiastically fascist Ustaše of Ante Pavelić in charge. It included Bosnia and Herzegovina, an old dream of Greater Croatian nationalists, but not a large part of Dalmatia and the Adriatic islands, which were annexed by Italy. The Ustaša regime took as its first task the ethnic and religious purification of their domains, which meant the extermination of the Serbs—15 per cent of the population of Croatia proper and more than a third of the population of Bosnia-Herzegovina—through forced conversions and massacre. Slovenia disappeared from the map, the southern two-thirds annexed by Italy and an economically more important northern third by the German Reich. Montenegro was declared a kingdom again, its crown united with that of its Italian occupiers; the Kosovo region, with its Albanian majority, became part of an Albania already under direct Italian rule since Easter 1939. The Bulgarians occupied and anticipated annexing Yugoslav Macedonia. The Hungarians annexed Prekomurje and Medjimurje, Baranja and the Bačka. The remainder of the Vojvodina, the Yugoslav Banat, was administered directly by the Germans, primarily through its large *Volksdeutsch* minority. The rump of Serbia, virtually reduced to the Principality of 1878, was occupied by the Germans and administered by local collaborators under their tutelage. Its head, a Balkan Pétain in contrast to super-Quisling Pavelić in Zagreb, was General Milan Nedić, a man typical of those throughout occupied Europe who did the enemy's bidding in the tragic hope of saving their peoples from a still worse fate.

On November 29, 1943, less than thirty-one months after this total disintegration and in the midst of a holocaust of resistance, reprisal, and inter-ethnic civil warfare unprecedented even in Balkan annals, Yugoslavia was reborn in a new form in the medieval Bosnian capital of Jajce. The occasion was the second session of an Anti-Fascist Council of National Liberation of Yugoslavia (AVNOJ), the formally supreme political organ of a National Liberation Movement, loosely but better known as the Partisans, created and led by the Communist Party of Yugoslavia (CPY).[2]

AVNOJ had been established one year earlier, when 54 representatives of the Partisan movement from all regions except Slovenia and Macedonia held a first session at Bihać, another Bosnian town, to create a political roof organization for the civil administrations, called People's Liberation Committees, which the Partisans had established in each 'liberated territory' temporarily or permanently under their control. These committees in turn, already described in October 1941 as 'provisional organs of government',[3] now constituted the discreet nuclei of a new State apparatus being built on the ruins of the old. They also represented the gradual maturation of a decision that the war of liberation should also become a social revolution, led by the Communist Party and designed to lay the foundations for a socialist transformation of Yugoslavia. But this was not said at Bihać, partly from deference to Soviet instructions.

Now, while still specifically denying any intention of imposing a Soviet type of system, AVNOJ stepped forward at Jajce as the self-proclaimed legitimator of a Provisional Government for all of Yugoslavia. In the presence of officers from British and American military missions to the Supreme Headquarters of the Army of National Liberation, it established a National Committee of Liberation of Yugoslavia as its executive organ, with all the attributes of such a government. The head of the Committee was to be Josip Broz, called Tito, a 51-year-old Croat of peasant and partly Slovene origins who was supreme commander of the National Liberation Army and Secretary-General of the CPY. AVNOJ had also just proclaimed him Marshal of Yugoslavia.

The second session further proclaimed that the new Yugoslavia would be a federal State, one which would recognise the autonomy as well as the brotherhood and unity of the South Slavs, now defined as constituting five distinct nations. Each of these, Serbs,

Croats, Slovenes, Macedonians and Montenegrins, should have a republic of its own, while Bosnia and Herzegovina, a historical rather than an ethnic unit with a mixed population of Serbs, Croats and Serbo-Croatian-speaking Moslem Slavs, would constitute a sixth republic. Proclamations annexing wholly or partly Yugoslav-populated districts belonging to Italy under treaties of 1920 and 1924 (Istria and Rijeka, Trieste, Gorizia, Zadar and some Adriatic islands), recently issued by the Liberation Front of Slovenia and the Regional Anti-Fascist Council of National Liberation of Croatia, were confirmed. King Peter was prohibited from returning to the country until a postwar plebiscite should determine the fate of the monarchy, and the right of the Royal Government in exile to represent Yugoslavia or to make international agreements in its name was denied.

The epic story of the complex and bloody struggles and sacrifices which led to the meeting at Jajce and beyond, turning a self-proclaimed Provisional Government into an internationally recognised and revolutionary regime with absolute authority in a re-established, expanded and devastated Yugoslavia, has been told many times in monographs, memoirs, and Homeric ballads in dactylic hexameter to be sung by the *guslari* who still occasionally roam the mountains where the great battles were fought.[4] The tale is in its first and simplest dimension one of popular resistance and guerrilla warfare, with its mobility, sudden reversals of fortune and greater scope than most forms of modern warfare for daring acts of individual heroism or deceit and for darkest intrigues, especially in the Balkans. All is then infinitely complicated by the fact that the forces arrayed on all sides—in the resistance, among the occupiers and among collaborators with both—were composed of elements pursuing various and in part contradictory aims. There were in effect three wars waged concurrently and by shifting combinations of persons and groups—a national liberation struggle against German, Italian and other occupiers, and two civil wars, one among the Yugoslav nationalities and another between those who would restore the old and those who would establish a new regime and political-economic system. As such the tale contains elements of a Homeric-Balkan epic, of a Greek tragedy for some leading actors on all sides, and of a case-study textbook for a successful socialist revolution in an underdeveloped country.

The second session of AVNOJ and its timing were more than a merely symbolic watershed in this complex chronicle, although the proclamation issued at Jajce at the time seemed absurdly pretentious and a wild gamble. The Germans still exercised effectively uncontested control over all Yugoslav cities, most major towns, and all important lines of communication and densely populated areas. They were still able to chase Tito and his headquarters back into the woods when they chose, as they chased him out of Jajce six weeks after the AVNOJ meeting. Alternative, anti-Communist solutions continued to muster impressive popular and armed support in most parts of the country and especially in Serbia. Finally, and of equal importance, all the Allies, including the Soviet Union, continued to recognise the Royal Government in exile and its 'army in the homeland', the Serbian royalist Chetniks of Draža Mihailović, the Partisans' domestic arch-rivals. The British, with tacit Soviet approval, had only recently made one final effort to bring about Partisan-Chetnik co-operation, and Tito's sensitivity concerning Soviet attitudes to the Royal Government and to his own political pretensions was evident in his calculated failure to notify Moscow of what he planned to do at Jajce—a breach of international Communist discipline.

Nevertheless Jajce had in fact taken place at the end of a phase in the struggle which had already eliminated any realistic possibility—except putatively through German destruction of Tito and his staff, an 'accident' which did almost happen six months later at Drvar—that the regime envisaged by AVNOJ would not be in power after the war.[5] Any other alternative was now based either on the premise of a German victory, already clearly impossible, or on an Anglo-American willingness to invade the Balkans in strength, taking on the Partisan army which had just been recognised as an Allied force and possibly the Russians as well. This option also did not exist, although some continued to imagine or to hope that it did. It was so militarily, politically and, in terms of Allied public and staff officer opinion, psychologically impractical that even Winston Churchill (falsely accused of advocating what he may have wished he could) never proposed it. With characteristic realism and perhaps prescience, Churchill chose instead to display a much-quoted complacency, in sharp contrast to his usual attitude to extensions of Communist and Soviet power, when the chief of his mission to the Partisans told him bluntly that Tito intended to set up a Soviet type of system in Yugoslavia.[6]

The British Prime Minister thereafter confined his efforts to continuing and increasing British aid to the Partisans, to encouraging Roosevelt and Stalin to do the same, and to forcing King Peter II to recognise and include them in his Government. While primarily designed to create a unified and more effective Yugoslav front against the Germans, these policies had or developed another and secondary function. They might also build a foundation for postwar Western political and moral credit with the future Yugoslav regime, a motive confirmed by Churchill's subsequent probing of Stalin's intentions in the Balkans with his famous and 'cynical' suggestion of 'fifty-fifty' Soviet and Western influence in Yugoslavia after the liberation.[7] In fact the principal result of Britain's Yugoslav policy after mid-1943 was very substantially to help the Partisans to achieve their aims. While Western military aid was of only marginal if welcome importance, Churchill's advocacy of the Partisans and the King's reluctant acquiescence gave the nascent regime a much needed international recognition and legitimacy. It also weakened Mihailović's Chetniks, whom the King was forced to disown and whose collaboration with the Italians and Germans was now publicised by the Allies. Churchill's other and for him more important purposes were not realised. Unity in the Yugoslav resistance was achieved only when and because all except the Partisans were discredited or eliminated, while the credit which the British had hoped to bank with the future regime was only acknowledged much later and because other events had dramatically altered that regime's perspective.

What had meanwhile made a Partisan regime run by Yugoslav Communists increasingly inevitable was in part the evolution of the wider war and the impressive military successes of the Partisan army. The latter had grown from a General Staff without an army in July 1941 and a force of about 80,000 at the end of that year to some 230,000 organised in 'divisions' and 'corps' (therefore not including smaller guerrilla units) by the autumn of 1943. Escaping increasingly massive and co-ordinated efforts to encircle and exterminate their main striking force—at one point, during 'Operation Weiss' and 'Operation Schwarz' in the spring of 1943, involving a combined force of about 117,000 Germans, Italians and various Croatian and Serb collaborators against some 19,000 Partisans[8]—they survived, carrying their wounded with them in incredible odysseys, and then regrouped to strike again. With the help of arms captured and territory won (and sometimes lost again) after the Italian capitulation in September 1943, they controlled and had established People's Liberation Committees in 'liberated territory' which by the time of the Jajce meeting included the larger part of the Alpine and Dinaric highlands from Slovenia and Istria to the Sanjak. By mid-1944 they would have more than 350,000 under arms.

Underlying these successes were on the one hand the strategic and tactical political as well as military brilliance of Tito and his Party comrades, including their definition of their goals, and on the other the continuous blunders of their domestic opponents, beginning with disparate and contradictory motives and goals which could never appeal to more than a fraction of the populace. In combination these factors accounted for the growth and morale of the Partisans, which also made their military successes possible, and for their opponents' shrinkage, demoralisation and eventual isolation and dependence on the doomed forces of the 'Nazi-Fascist' occupiers.

As well as their military talent, the Partisans enjoyed three comparative advantages. The first was a better and more disciplined organisation, combining hierarchical links with flexibility and generous room for autonomous local initiative. Such a structure was made possible by the availability of a core of dependable persons, synonymous with the inner leadership of the Communist Party, who had been trained to operate in such a context, who knew and generally trusted one another, and who usually had personal bonds of loyalty to the leader who had handpicked most of them. On the basis of a June 1941 decision to transform the Party's central organs into a supreme command for a then non-existent Partisan army, these men could be dispersed throughout the confused countrywide battle zone of a guerrilla war with confidence (occasionally betrayed, as in Montenegro in 1941[9]) that their autonomous actions and decisions would conform to and promote the strategy decided at headquarters. The second advantage was consistent implementation of the decision to fight the enemy constantly and everywhere (if not always as uncompromisingly as Partisan mythology later claimed), disregarding reprisals against the civilian population and defining the enemy as the forces of all the occupiers and of all Yugoslavs who fought with them. The third was their solution to the national question, blazoned in the slogan 'brotherhood and unity' and in the promise of a federal State and manifested in the all-Yugoslav composition of their own leadership.

This last, probably the most important of the three, made the Partisans the only group which could appeal to people of all nationalities throughout the country. The appeal of 'brotherhood and unity' nevertheless requires explanation, since the old 'Yugoslav idea' had manifestly died in the bitterness of interwar experiences, leaving only a transparent mask to be worn by Greater Serbian nationalism. It was the war itself which gradually created a propensity to accept a rebirth of the idea in a form which promised national equality and autonomy in a federal framework. Disintegration had brought foreign domination and the hideous fratricide of inter-ethnic civil war. The lesson, paraphrasing a slogan from an earlier revolution on the other side of the Atlantic, seemed to be that if the Yugoslav peoples did not hang together they would end by hanging each other. The number of people from all the nationalities willing to fight for a federal Yugoslav State under a new leadership grew progressively as the war continued. To such people the Communist leaders of the Partisans, partly as a calculated device and partly out of a deep conviction, preached reconciliation among the nationalities and a new order based on federalism, equality and mutual understanding. It was a message of hope which no other party to Yugoslavia's triune war offered.

Thus armed morally and politically—and better armed in the literal sense after their massive capture of Italian weapons in September 1943 and more substantial Western military aid in the following months—the Partisan supreme command felt itself ready to challenge all domestic opponents to a final showdown. This challenge, which included a further challenge to the Allied great powers to recognise their political as well as military legitimacy, was the essential meaning and purpose of Jajce.

That the CPY should have been capable of playing such a role was remarkable. The Party's notorious factionalism and the fecklessness of most of its leaders during the interwar years had made it the despair of the Communist International in Moscow and an easy target for Royal Yugoslav police in the homeland. Membership in the early 1930s was down to about 500, many of them and the Party's headquarters long in exile and out of touch with developments at home. Even after the Party became a rallying point for anti-fascist sentiment after 1935 membership climbed only slowly, to 1,500 by 1937. The Secretary-General since 1932, Milan Gorkić, was summoned from Paris to Moscow in July 1937 to disappear in Stalin's Great Purge, which eventually accounted also for 100 other Yugoslav Communists from the apparatuses of the Comintern and the Party in exile. A new Secretary-General was not appointed for over fifteen months, and in 1938 the Comintern apparently considered dissolving the CPY, even as the Polish Party was dissolved that same year. Instead, but only after long hesitation and disagreements in Moscow, it was decided to confirm as Secretary-General Josip Broz, who had been co-opted as Organisational Secretary in 1936 and who had been acting Yugoslav Party head since Gorkić's purge the following summer. He was usually known by a variety of Party aliases, among them 'Walter' and 'Tito'. Whatever his shortcomings in Comintern eyes, his appointment was recommended by his non-involvement with the old factions, his circumspect loyalty and his sound peasant and working-class origins at a time when Party intellectuals were regarded with great suspicion by Moscow. He had also displayed an impressive efficiency as Organisational Secretary.[10]

Tito had first encountered Bolshevism as an Austro-Hungarian prisoner of war in Russia during the Revolution and subsequent civil war. He became a Communist soon after his return to his native Croatia, where he initially combined a job as a machinist with trade union agitation as a Party worker. He was imprisoned for Communist activities for over five years, from late 1928 to March 1934. Sent abroad by the Party organisation in Zagreb after his release, originally to re-establish contact with Party headquarters in exile, he attracted attention in higher quarters by his energy and devotion and his willingness to undertake what most of the then leadership was not willing to do, which was the risky business of reorganising and revitalising the illegal Party inside Yugoslavia. Co-opted as a member of the Central Committee and then as Organisational Secretary, he was sent to Paris in October 1936 to organise the transport of Yugoslav volunteers to fight with the Republicans in the Spanish Civil War, but managed to spend most of 1937 inside Yugoslavia on what he considered his basic mission. During this period he also handpicked those who were eventually to comprise his own Politburo and wider inner circle. All except those who were to fall in the coming war were to play important roles in postwar Yugoslavia. Chief among them were Edvard Kardelj, a Slovenian schoolteacher and janitor's son, Milovan Djilas, a fiery young Montenegrin and Communist agitator at Belgrade University, and Aleksandar Ranković, a tailor's apprentice of peasant origin from Šumadija, the Serbian heartland. Others with whom Tito established or renewed contact at this time included the Slovenes Boris Kidrič, Boris Ziherl and Miha Marinko, the Croat Vladimir Bakarić and the Serb Ivo Lola-Ribar, whom Djilas and Ranković brought to him as a candidate to revitalise the Communist youth organisation (SKOJ) and whose promising career as a Tito favourite and potential successor was to be cut short when he was killed in 1943. Moša Pijade, Tito's friend and instructor in Marxism during his prison days and the only Jew on the early postwar Politburo, was then still in gaol. Of this future inner group the only ones with Soviet experience were Tito himself, Kardelj and the Montenegrin Veljko Vlahović, who had come to Moscow after losing a leg in the Spanish Civil War and who returned there to act as wartime CPY liaison with the Comintern.

Tito, Djilas, Kardelj and Ranković, along with Franc Leskošek (another Slovene, who was to remain a quiet member of the Party summit until he retired in 1964) and two men who were to fall in the war (Rade Končar, a Croatian Serb, and Ivan Milutinović, a Montenegrin) comprised the new Politburo presented to a secret all-Yugoslav Party Conference which was brazenly held under the noses of the Royal police, in a Zagreb suburb in October 1940, to bear witness to the Party's revival and its new leadership. By that time membership had already quadrupled since 1937 and stood at 6,455. SKOJ now had 17,800 members and was the dominant political movement in Belgrade University. By the time the uprising was proclaimed in July 1941 the Party had between 8,000 and 12,000 members and SKOJ had 30,000.[11] The cadres of these two organisations were to supply the Army of National Liberation with its political and fighting cores. They included some 300

Spanish Civil War veterans, who brought invaluable military experience; one of these was Koča Popović, son of a Belgrade millionaire and a sometime *rive gauche* surrealist poet, who commanded the Partisan army's proudest unit, the First Proletarian Division. Of those who were Party members in the spring of 1941 only 3,000 were to survive the war. From their ranks, the 'club of '41', came the inner élite of the new regime, undiluted by later arrivals for more than two decades.

The still modest growth of the Party and SKOJ since 1937 was only in part attributable to the energy, morale and organisational abilities of the new leadership. Many young Yugoslavs joined or became 'fellow travellers' because they saw the Communists as the only staunchly and uncompromisingly anti-Fascist and anti-imperialist political party in the country, or as the only party now favouring a united Yugoslavia in a form which was not a Greater Serbia in disguise.[12] The importance of such motivations, which only rarely included serious study and comprehension of the ideology of Marxism-Leninism-Stalinism, was to become evident after 1948. In addition, reasons for becoming and the duties and risks of being Party members meant that the CPY, despite still miniscule membership, contained a disproportionately high number of Yugoslavia's most talented, politically and ethically motivated, daring and often fanatic youth. This too was to be important both in the war and afterwards.

These, then, were the strengths and potential advantages which the Communists brought to the Partisan movement. But their triumph was ensured as well because their domestic opponents made mistakes which overwhelmingly enhanced the Partisans' comparative advantages. Among these opponents—discounting those like the Ustaše, who were doomed by their initial and enthusiastic identification with the power, policies and ideology of the losing side in the wider world war—the most important and only other potential victors were the Chetniks, who looked for leadership to Draža Mihailović, a colonel on the General Staff of the prewar Royal Army. Mihailović and his followers had in fact been the first Yugoslavs to continue the fight against the Germans and Italians after the collapse of April 1941. Initially a small group of Royal Army officers and soldiers who refused to accept the capitulation and took to the hills, they consciously modelled themselves on the classic tradition of the Serbian *četnici* (from *četa,* a band or a company of soldiers), irregular troops who had harassed the earlier Turkish plunderers of their land. Similar bands of guerrilla fighters sprang up spontaneously throughout the country and were often in unco-ordinated action against the occupiers before the CPY, responding to orders issued by the Comintern when the German invasion of the Soviet Union began on June 22, 1941, issued its own call for a popular rising. For several months there was sporadic co-operation and no clear line of demarcation between the two resistance movements, although isolated clashes also occurred. Urged respectively by the British and the Russians, both then desperately eager to promote unified resistance fronts throughout occupied Europe, Mihailović and Tito met twice, in September and October 1941. At the October meeting Tito offered to place his forces under Mihailović's military command, but insisted that they should retain their own units and political infrastructure. Mihailović rejected the offer, and the struggle between the two movements soon took precedence over the battle with the common enemy.

The Chetniks were in essence an ill-disciplined and ill-organised anti-Axis resistance force which aspired to recreate the old Yugoslavia, but with an even stricter Serbian domination to prevent any future repetition of the Croat 'betrayal' of 1941. They were therefore an almost exclusively Serb formation. Their leaders, including Mihailović, quickly perceived the Communist-led Partisans to be a greater long-run threat to their concept of Yugoslavia than the occupiers of the country, and the German system of mass reprisals as a threat to the physical existence of the Serb nation if the Germans were provoked too much and too soon. Hence the Chetniks adopted a passive attitude towards the occupiers, an attitude which they always considered temporary, and determined to destroy the Partisans in the meanwhile. The first of these policies took them out of the anti-Axis firing line and the second gave them and the occupiers a common interest. Together they constituted a slippery slope which led the Chetniks gradually, piecemeal, and almost always reluctantly into *de facto* collaboration with first the Italians and then the Germans against the Partisans.[13]

The understanding of the situation which led them to adopt this course was as faulty and the results as disastrous to their cause as their initial logic was impeccable. If their passivity may have been welcome to the majority of the Serbians, wanting peace and personal security above all, it demoralised the Chetnik forces. It also stunted their growth because it was unattractive to potential recruits who wished to fight the foreign foe—including most of the Serbs of Croatia and Bosnia, who had reason to hate and usually preferred to fight rather than await death by massacre. Chetnik collaboration with the Axis further eroded their domestic support and, when it became known abroad, deprived them of that of the Allies. Of equal importance, their ethos, their pronounced anti-Croatianism and their goal—the restoration of the old Yugoslavia, which was not only Serbian dominated but had a poor record as a sponsor of economic development and social welfare—could not appeal to more than an insignificant number of non-Serbs or to those with the aroused expectations of change and social mobility which are one of war's frequent side-effects.

Basically the same defects and dilemmas also affected all other non-Communist but essentially or potentially anti-Axis political and military forces in the country: Slovene nationalists and Christian Populists; leaders of the Croatian Peasant Party, individually perplexed and often paralysed by the problem posed when their dream of an independent Croatia became a nightmare clothed in Ustaša bestiality; and leaders and followers of those other prewar parties which had opposed both the Royal dictatorship and the Axis, and which might therefore have claimed a legitimate place and popular support on the postwar political stage. All were prisoners of their own histories, without an appeal which could transcend their respective ethnic frontiers and with programmes which either sought to perpetuate the breakup of Yugoslavia or promised that a new one would be like the old, subject to the same inter-ethnic disputes which had taken on new meaning for people confronting attempted mutual genocide.

In a civil war, especially one as multi-dimensional and all pervasive as that which the Yugoslavs suffered during World War II, many or most people may profoundly wish to be left out but find it increasingly difficult not to take a stand. By the winter of 1943-44 this was tantamount to a stand for one of three parties: those fatally compromised by identification with the retreating occupiers; the Chetniks, whose solution was the restoration of the old Yugoslavia, and who were also compromised or the Partisans, allies of the Allies and protagonists of a new, federal, but clearly Communist-dominated Yugoslavia. Individuals, families and groups who had attempted to reinsure through multiple contacts or distributed participation—Montenegrin clans with both Partisan and Chetnik sons, some of the Nedić forces in Serbia and the left wings of the Croatian Peasant and Slovenian Populist parties were examples—gradually sought to make the increasingly obvious choice and with varying degrees of conviction. As most could at least dimly perceive, the consequences would be of enormous personal and group importance which went beyond short-range postwar prospects of participation or prison. Twenty-five years later it would still be easy to distinguish 'Partisan' from 'Chetnik' or 'Ustaša' towns, villages and even individual peasant homesteads in regions like Bosnia-Herzegovina and Montenegro, and if one did not perceive the difference there was always someone eager to point it out. To the victors belonged the spoils and a subsequent generation of privileges and pork-barrelling.

The Partisans meanwhile pursued their road from Jajce to Belgrade. Its milestones included more battles, formal recognition as an Allied force by the Teheran Conference which was held the same week as Jajce, final British abandonment of the Chetniks, the belated arrival of a Soviet mission to join British and American missions at Tito's headquarters in February 1944, and Tito's narrow escape from a German paratroop and glider attack on his Drvar headquarters in May. Then came a new Royal Government in exile, imposed on the King and his advisers by Churchill, headed by Ivan Šubašić (the first Croat prime minister of Yugoslavia), and ready to recognise and deal with Tito. Its formation was followed by Tito's meetings with Churchill in Naples in August and with Stalin in Moscow in September 1944, the latter to prepare for a joint Partisan-Red Army liberation of Serbia which ended with the capture of Belgrade on October 20. Only then, during the advance on Belgrade, did the Partisans again dominate the scene along the valley of the Morava river and its tributaries, where their Supreme Command had started the uprising in 1941, but where large-scale Partisan activities had been embarrassingly conspicuous by their absence since Tito's ouster from Užice that November. Now, however, the Serbian Chetniks quickly disintegrated.[14]

A new Yugoslav Provisional Government was created on March 7, 1945, after Stalin, Churchill and Roosevelt, meeting again at Yalta in February, had pressed Tito and Šubašić to implement and extend their agreements of the preceding summer. Tito became the last Royal Yugoslav prime minister and minister of defence and accepted Šubašić and two other members of the Government in exile in his Cabinet. Yugoslavia again had a single Government, for the first time since Jajce, and the Partisan regime had achieved the international legitimacy which had been one of Tito's primary concerns during the preceding fifteen months. When AVNOJ met for the third and last time in August 1945 it was expanded to include sixty-eight members of the last prewar parliament who were not 'compromised by collaboration with the enemy', but that was the extent of Tito's compromises. His was for the moment a Royal Government, formally installed by a Partisan-approved Regency of three in the name of the exiled King, but the first act of the Constituent Assembly, which convened with deliberate appropriateness on November 29, 1945, was to abolish the monarchy and declare Yugoslavia a Federal People's Republic. The three non-Communist ministers had already resigned to protest their exclusion from all effective decision-making, and all prewar parties not included in a Communist-dominated People's Front (a peacetime metamorphosis of the People's Liberation Front) boycotted the elections for the Constituent Assembly in reasonable anticipation of an inability to campaign freely. Ninety per cent of the 7·4 million Yugoslavs who voted cast their ballots for the single list presented by the People's Front.

Of the three stages in the model for Communist takeover in Eastern Europe described by Hugh Seton-Watson,[15] the CPY had entirely skipped the first, a 'genuine coalition' with non-Communist parties, and had paid only passing respect to the second, the 'bogus coalition', in order to achieve international recognition and formal legitimacy. With all legal opposition destroyed or emasculated in the People's Front and a few non-Communist deputies temporarily tolerated in the new Federal Assembly, Yugoslavia was theirs. They had won it largely by their own remarkable efforts.

Yugoslav Stalinism

The new regime had in its own eyes four sources of legitimacy, three of which were of kinds which most of the populace would recognise. The first was power *per se*, already almost entirely in Communist hands before the war ended and a total and all-pervasive political monopoly within the following year. The second was international recognition and legal continuity with the *ancien régime* and hence with old Yugoslavia, achieved with the most minor and transient of compromises with the Allies and the Government in exile. The third, which was for an entire generation the most significant and seminal dimension of the regime's popular and self-image, was the Partisan war as a myth of political founding and of two kinds of solidarity, that of the Yugoslav nations who had united to fight the enemy and recreate their common state, and that of the Partisan veterans, the *stari borci*, who had done the actual fighting.[16] The fourth, which was relevant only for Communists, was the legitimacy bestowed by Marxism's historical imperative and incarnate in the Communist Party as the vanguard of the proletariat, hastening and implementing the next and last turn of history's inherent dialectic. It, too, had a popular variant, for built into it was the promise of rapid economic development which Lenin and Stalin had added to the definition of 'building' socialism' in adapting it for use in underdeveloped countries.

The third of these legitimisers and also the first—because it was based on the Yugoslav Party and army's own strength and conquests and not on Soviet power and the Red Army—made the Yugoslav regime unique among the Communist regimes of postwar Eastern Europe. So did the fact that the majority of the Party's 141,066 members at the end of the war, like that of the Partisan army from which almost all of them had been recruited, were peasants and under thirty years of age. Equally important was the leadership's consciousness of their uniqueness and of their feat in creating a victorious army and revolution out of unarmed and illiterate peasants, alone and against huge odds. It endowed the members of the inner circle, most of them still in their 30s, with a reckless and often arrogant and fanatical self-confidence which blithely ignored the country's glaring unpreparedness for what they were about to do and their own total inexperience in State administration, economics, or almost anything except conspiracy, organisation and war. It also if contradictorily made them hyper-sensitive to any suggestion that they might not be quite as unique as they thought they were.[17]

It is in the nature of legitimacy that its perceived sources commit as well as strengthen a regime. If they include the rule of law, for example, a Government which violates its own laws too often and publicly will lose its legitimacy in the eyes of important segments of the public and of its own officers. In Yugoslavia the way in which legitimacy was articulated and the personalities of the leaders committed the new regime to four historic and enduring tasks. The first, which most of the leadership became clearly aware of only after 1948, was independence, the right of the regime to chart Yugoslavia's own way, right or wrong, despite the country's exposed position on the geographic and ideological frontier of the Cold War. The second was 'brotherhood and unity', the need to mould often antagonistic nations with diverse experiences and traditions into a unified State. The third was modernisation, the transformation of a largely primitive society, dependent on peasant farming for its livelihood, into a literate and prosperous industrial society. And the fourth, for the regime the mode in which all else was to be accomplished, was the evolution of socialist political, economic and social forms and 'consciousness', by means of which the Yugoslav peoples were to move through socialist democracy towards communism.

Thus armed and committed, the new rulers faced a set of more immediate and corollary tasks: to implement and enforce their solution to the national question; to feed their people, revive economic activity and make good the devastation of war; and to establish mechanisms and modalities, based on the Soviet model of a command economy run by the State, for rapid industrialisation through coercively induced and centrally controlled mobilisation of human, natural and financial resources. To these were added two subsidiary preoccupations: the western frontier of the State, where annexations decreed at Jajce were being challenged by the postwar Italian regime and in the Trieste area by the Western Allies as well, and the liquidation of all remnants of past or potential opposition to monopolistic Communist power and plans for social recon-struction.

The last was most easily accomplished, since all such opponents were already politically destroyed, disintegrated or demoralised by four years of war and by the nature and completeness of the Communist take-over and were incapable of effective, organised resistance. It was nevertheless done with thoroughness, cynicism and brutality—consequences of bitterness accumulated during the war, of Communist doctrines concerning 'the sharpening of the class struggle during the transitional phase', and of a genuine concern that opposition might revive and reorganise with the covert help or even the open intervention of the now militantly anti-Communist Western powers. The campaign began with the harassment and arrest of non-Communist politicians who still presumed to play an independent political role, of 'collaborators', including both genuine ones and anyone whose property or silencing the regime desired, and of 'imperialist agents', a category susceptible to equally broad definition. A still disputed but large number of all three kinds were executed after often farcical trials, usually by military tribunals, and thousands went to prison or to forced labour camps. After an olive branch which Tito gingerly offered to the Yugoslav churches was rejected by the Roman Catholic hierarchy and its Primate, Archbishop Aloysius Stepinac of Zagreb, who perceived it to be full of thorns, sporadic harassment and arrests of Catholic (and of a smaller number of Orthodox and Moslem clergy who opposed the new order) also developed into a systematic campaign. In October 1946 Stepinac himself was tried for wartime collaboration with the Ustaša regime in Croatia and sentenced to sixteen years in prison.[18]

The leading role in all of this was played by the security service which Ranković had organised in 1944 under the name OZNa (*Odeljenje za zaštitu naroda*, Department for the Protection of the People), later renamed UDBa (*Uprava državne bezbednosti*, State Security Administration). Its mission, as defined by Tito, was 'to strike terror into the bones of those who do not like this kind of Yugoslavia',[19] and it did. In 1951, in the first of a series of campaigns for 'stricter legality', Ranković himself was to admit that during the previous year, when the terror had already shifted its focus to 'Cominformists' and abated for others, 47 per cent of arrests had been 'unjustified' and 23 per cent were for crimes of 'minor significance'. The entire judicial system, he said, had been guilty of 'converting ordinary crime into political criminal offences', indiscriminately and wrongly depriving people of their liberty.[20]

On the western frontier the conflict with the Anglo-Americans over Trieste in May and June 1945 was the new Yugoslavia's first serious clash with the Western Allies, with whom relations had cooled since the preceding September and would become worse during the next three years. The Yugoslavs had won the race to liberate Trieste, beating by one day a New Zealand corps speeding east from Venice and when the city was in fact already in the process of being liberated by its own competing Italian and Slovene resistance movements. Eventually, after forty-five days of escalating tension and an Anglo-American ultimatum, Yugoslav forces were withdrawn from Trieste, from Pula at the tip of the Istrian peninsula, and from the Soča valley to the north. They continued to occupy the rest of what they claimed until the Italian Peace Treaty of 1947 granted them all of it except some districts in eastern Friuli and the ill-fated Free Territory of Trieste, where they continued to administer but could not formally annex 'Zone B' in the north-west corner of Istria. The conflict, apart from its intrinsic importance as a political and territorial issue which would compli-cate Yugoslavia's relations with Italy, Britain and the United States until the London Agreement of 1954 and occasionally thereafter, also affected Yugoslav relations with the Soviet Union. The Yugoslavs had acted on their own in attempting to defy the British and Americans, one more example of both independence and recklessness to annoy the Russians, who feared that the Western powers would assume that Yugoslav claims and sabre-rattling over Trieste represented a Soviet initiative and a probe to test Western reflexes. The Russians were right, for the Western powers did treat Trieste as the first military confrontation of the developing Cold War. At the same time Soviet support for the Yugoslav position was in the eyes of the Yugoslav leaders at most lukewarm and an ominous confirmation of their growing suspicions concerning great power spheres of interest and 'percentage agreements'.[21]

On the national question, Yugoslavia's paramount question, the regime's response took the form of a sometimes contradictory set of policies and legal arrangements, only some of which were directly addressed to the problem. The net effect was merely the first of many postwar Yugoslav examples of that 'unity in contradictions' which is dear to Marxist theory and sometimes perversely appropriate in Balkan practice. In this particular case, the synthesis of opposites was successful in suppressing the question for several years but did not answer it.

Federalism as the CPY's formal solution, foreshadowed by the formation of autonomous Slovenian and Croatian Communist Parties in 1937 and of provincial or regional Party committees for Serbia, Kosovo and other districts in subsequent months, had been confirmed by the organisational structure of the wartime Liberation Front and in the proclamations issued from Jajce. Now the Constitution of the Federal People's Republic of Yugoslavia, adopted by the Constituent Assembly on January 31, 1946,[22] and in this and other respects modelled on the Soviet Constitution of

1936, formally institutionalised the six people's republics promised at Jajce. It also established within Serbia, the largest of them, an autonomous province (*pokrajina*) of the Vojvodina and an autonomous region (*oblast*) of Kosovo-Metohija, usually abbreviated as Kosmet. These sub-units recognised the mixed population and concentration of the 'developed' Magyar minority in the south-east corner of the Pannonian Plain and the numerical preponderance of the 'underdeveloped' Albanian majority in 'Old Serbia'. Both, however, were significantly if not publicly more than that. The creation within the Serbian Republic of an autonomous Vojvodina, including the Bačka, the Yugoslav Banat and Syrmia, was also a compromise between Serbian claims to all these territories, in which the populations are partly to largely Serb, and Croatian historic and ethnic claims to Syrmia. The dispute among Communists which led to this compromise, concerning which only vague hints reached the press,[23] was a reminder that the Serbo-Croat problem was not only alive but could infect the higher ranks of a Party supposedly imbued with an internationalist spirit. As for the Kosmet, the autonomous region created there might one day and in due course become the nucleus of another republic in an enlarged Federation including presently independent Albania. This was not a wildly improbable prospect: the new Albanian Communist regime under Enver Hoxha had grown out of a Communist-led resistance front which Yugoslav emissaries had helped to organise and was in many ways already a client regime of the one in Belgrade.

Meanwhile, in one of the new Yugoslav Constitution's few departures from its Soviet model, the six republics were endowed with slightly greater fiscal powers than were republics in the Soviet Union, the thin end of a wedge which would one day lead towards confederation. Central Government departments, as in the Soviet Union, included both federal and federal-republic ministries. By 1948 each republic also had its own Communist Party and Central Committee. At the top of the Party pyramid the Central Committee of the CPY, which before the 1948 Party Congress consisted of twenty-six survivors of the 1940 Zagreb Conference and new members co-opted during the war, was a careful if not proportional mixture of all the South Slav (but not the minority) nationalities. So too was the Federal Government.[24]

On the other hand, both State and Party were in practice highly centralised and hierarchical. In the former such centralisation was in part sanctioned by the Constitution, which declared the republics to be the sovereign possessors of all residual powers but then granted most of those of any importance to the Federation. There, although one chamber in the bicameral Federal Assembly was composed of delegates from the republics and autonomous regions, most effective legislative and executive powers were vested in the Assembly's Presidium and in the Government. In the Party, which mattered far more, concentration of power was achieved more informally, primarily through the mechanism of 'democratic centralism'.[25]

In addition, Montenegrins and Serbs were in proportion to their share in total population over-represented in both Party and State apparatuses at all levels. That this was so was almost inevitable, since the regime was based on a Partisan movement and Party in which Montenegrins and Bosnian and Croatian Serbs had been similarly over-represented. In part this had been because the former are a nation of traditional fighters and the latter, as noted, had nowhere else to go if they preferred fighting to passively awaiting massacre, and in part it was simply because Partisan operations and hence recruitment were until late in the war centred in the Dinaric highlands, where most of the inhabitants are Serbs, Montenegrins and Moslems. For basically the same reasons the same nationalities also dominated the officer corps of the army and the security police, both OZNa and its subsequent reincarnation as UDBa.[26] While therefore in essence representing the rule of highlanders over lowlanders,[27] the ethnic dimension of such over-representation created a potential for the restoration, in reality or in popular belief, of 'Greater Serbian' domination.

Finally, and also of symbolic as well as practical importance, Belgrade, the Serbian capital associated in popular consciousness with Serbian domination in old Yugoslavia, remained the capital of the new Federation. Some Party leaders, sensitive to the implications of this choice, had suggested that Sarajevo, nearer the geographic centre of the country in ethnically neutral Bosnia, would be a better solution. Tradition, the recognised importance of not humbling the Serbs more than had already been done, and Sarajevo's geographic isolation and lack of communications and other infrastructure triumphed.[28]

Centralism and Serbo-Montenegrin preponderance in State and Party bureaucracies and in UDBa would pose major problems in the future. Meanwhile, the modest real effects and the psychological impact of even the formal creation of the republics and of all-Yugoslav ruling apparatuses, added to popular revulsion against ethnic nationalism after the horrors of civil war, acted to pacify inter-ethnic tensions, temporarily. Where this was not enough the regime, implementing its principles and proclamations, ruthlessly suppressed any display of what it chose to define as 'nationalist' rather than acceptable 'national' sentiment.[29] At the same time generalized and therefore ethnically non-discriminatory harassment, arrests, nationalisation, forced labour, compulsory deliveries by peasants and other oppressive acts by a multinational regime gave those who suffered a set of basically non-national grievances which at least temporarily took precedence over national ones in their consciousness. For a time it was therefore possible for both outside observers and many Yugoslavs to imagine that the national question really had been solved.

The regime's other immediate tasks—feeding the people, restoring a ravaged economy to prewar production levels and creating a Stalinist apparatus for planned and rapid industrialisation— were undertaken simultaneously and treated as a whole. In their eagerness and confidence the new leaders were unwilling to take the time to treat them sequentially.

Yugoslavia had suffered 1,700,000 dead in the triple holocaust of 1941–45, 11 per cent of the total prewar population and a proportionate loss second only to that of Poland. Especially hard hit were age-groups on the threshold of their productive years and those with skills and education: the average age of the fallen was 22 years and they included an estimated 90,000 skilled workers and 40,000 'intellectuals'. Some 822,000 buildings had been destroyed, 3·5 million people were homeless, and an estimated 35 per cent of prewar industry, 289,000 peasant homesteads, between 50 and 70 per cent of various categories of livestock and 80 per cent of ploughs and harvesting equipment had been lost or put out of operation. Over 50 per cent of railway trackage, 77 per cent of locomotives and 84 per cent of goods waggons had been destroyed.[30] Mass starvation was avoided in 1945 and 1946 primarily through aid from the UN Relief and Rehabilitation Administration (UNRRA), and the first factories and railways were put back into operation with the help of volunteer and forced labour, both largely unskilled, and reparations in equipment and cash from defeated enemies. By the end of 1946, however, 90 per cent of the prewar rail network was back in use and the index of industrial production had recovered to 79 per cent of the low 1939 level. In 1947, according to official statistics, industrial output was 120·6 per cent of 1939 levels and agricultural production was back to the level of that year. These achievements, which Yugoslav officials were later to claim had established a world record for speed of postwar recovery, served to increase the regime's self-confidence.[31]

Most of Yugoslavia's prewar industries and mines and a large part of the commercial and banking network had been foreign owned and by the end of the war was in German hands, either originally or through wartime confiscation or purchase. Most of the remainder was owned by Yugoslavs who could with greater or lesser credibility be accused of wartime 'collaboration', if necessary merely because they had kept their factories open and had sold to the occupiers. Property in both categories could be confiscated, under a decree issued in November 1944, and generally was. As a result, fully 80 per cent of Yugoslav industry, a number of banks and the entire wholesale network had already been nationalised before the first Nationalisation Law, covering industries 'of national importance', transportation, banking and wholesale trade, was passed in December 1946. A second Nationalisation Law was enacted in April 1948, affecting remaining industries, the retail trade, insurance companies and cultural and health institutions; this, too, was largely an *ex post facto* legalisation of measures already taken, since 'all industries of federal or republican importance and 70 per cent of local industries ... all transport ... and 90 per cent of the retail trade' were in State hands by mid-1947.[32]

With prewar production levels achieved and the entire economy nationalised, except for agriculture, the regime was ready to begin 'building socialism' with the classic Soviet formula of electrification and industrialisation.

Already, in early 1946, a decision had been taken to proceed with rapid and extensive industrialisation on the Soviet pattern, complete with five-year plans. It was opposed in the inner circle by Andrija Hebrang, a controversial personality who had been removed as Secretary of the Croatian Party late in the war, possibly for 'nationalist deviations', but whose considerable administrative talents had been put to use by making him minister of industry and chairman of both the Economic Council and the Planning Commission. He seems to have viewed crash industrialisation as adventurous or at least premature until the problem of agricultural production had been solved through collectivisation and mechanisation, and to have had the support of Sretan Žujović, the minister of finance and later of transport. Hebrang was overruled and removed from the Politburo and as chairman of the Economic Council and minister of industry, but remained head of the Planning Commission and a member of the Central Committee.[33] His successor in the posts he lost was Boris Kidrič, a man whose considerable talents did not yet include practical economic experience, and who was therefore sent to Moscow to study Soviet planning before drafting Yugoslavia's first Five-Year Plan. The Plan was officially inaugurated in April 1947 and with it Kidrič's position as the principal architect of Yugoslav economic policies until his early death in 1953.

Kidrič's Plan was fantastically ambitious and was criticised on this ground by some of the Yugoslav leaders, again apparently including Hebrang and Žujović, and by their Soviet advisers. On the basis of 1939 levels, it called for a fivefold increase in gross industrial output, a 66 per cent increase in labour productivity, a fourfold increase in electric power output and production of a large number of often highly sophisticated articles never previously made in Yugoslavia. Investment would consume 27 per cent of Social Product by the final year of the quinquennium.[34] Following Soviet precedents, it concentrated on basic industries like iron and steel and on big factories and big hydro- and thermo-electrical schemes requiring large initial investments and long periods of construction. The Plan also placed the bulk of projected new plant in the less developed regions, particularly in Bosnia-Herzegovina, Montenegro and Macedonia. It thereby simultaneously conformed to accepted Soviet doctrines of the spatial distribution of economic activities, sought to begin fulfilling Partisan pledges to equalise prosperity and opportunities in all regions, and provided 'jobs for the boys' from the backwoods who had contributed so much manpower to the Partisan army and the new regime. In its ambitiousness, which Djilas claimed would enable Yugoslavia to catch up with England in per capita production of goods within ten years, it was an outstanding symbol of the naiveté of the leadership and their 'ecstasy of big ideas and goals'.[35] More than enthusiasm and the 'voluntarism' of the mass support of which the regime boasted, it needed large and centralised apparatuses to plan, to control, and to coerce when enthusiasm flagged without the material incentives which low production and high investment rates could not supply.

At the same time the Politburo decided to continue to go slow on the agricultural front, a second point of conflict with Hebrang and some others in the leadership. An agrarian reform in 1945 had restricted the size of private holdings to between 35 and 45 hectares of arable land, but there were not many holdings larger than this after the post-1918 land reforms in the ex-Hungarian parts of the country. The total pool netted by the 1945 reform, including land confiscated from fleeing or expelled ethnic Germans, was a little over 1·5 million hectares. About half of this was distributed to landless peasants, primarily Partisan veterans from the Dinaric highlands transported to abandoned German villages in the Vojvodina. The rest was organised in State farms and Peasant Work Co-operatives (*Seljačke radne zadruge*, SRZ), the Yugoslav equivalent of Soviet collective farms. These were further subdivided into four categories, only the fourth and 'highest' of which was a true *kolkhoz*. Otherwise the land was not even formally nationalised, and by 1948 the entire socialist sector accounted for only 6·2 per cent of the country's arable land. Conscious of the peasant origins of their revolution and of fully half the members of their Party, the rulers of Yugoslavia felt it to be impossible to act otherwise, as they were to tell Stalin in the correspondence which led to the break in 1948. It was a lesson which they shortly thereafter temporarily forgot. Meanwhile, the bulk of Yugoslavia's peasants suffered and resisted compulsory deliveries of part of the fruits of their labour to the new State at fixed, low prices, sold the rest to the hungry cities for what they could get, and did what they could to avoid highly discriminatory taxation, all of which generally meant a retreat back into pure subsistence farming.[36]

With the reorganisation of federal, republican and local government to cope with the Five-Year Plan, the Yugoslav political-economic system came even closer to its Soviet model and became a single, giant, countrywide and monopolistic trust. In the words of a contemporary Yugoslav scholar, it was a 'centralist global social system', an 'unfissured monolith ... divided into sectors or subsystems and founded on an all-inclusive State-ownership monopoly over the means of production, what ends they served, and at whose behest'.[37] And those who presided over the monolith, the all-powerful Politburo, were as though in some arcane mythology hidden in the clouds and invisible to ordinary human eyes. With the CPY's peculiar penchant for clandestinity even when in power, the names of the members were never published until a new Politburo was chosen at the 5th Congress in 1948. Even today lists of the first postwar rulers of Yugoslavia do not agree, in part because some of them were themselves not sure whether they were attending meetings as permanent or ad hoc members.[38]

The break with Stalin

Yugoslavs and foreigners who write about Yugoslavia, behaving like divorce lawyers seeking evidence of irreconcilable incompatibility from the first days of the marriage, have since 1948 pushed the origins of the Soviet-Yugoslav quarrel back into the prehistory of both Communist Parties or at least to the troubled relations between the Comintern and the CPY in the interwar period. The exercise has its utility, especially when it deals with mutual annoyances during the war years. Like most lovers' quarrels, however, even they would probably only have been harbingers of a permanently troubled and temperamental relationship, unlikely to lead to divorce, if both partners had not undergone a change of mind or personality on the way home from the war. At most the wartime disagreements and disappointments which became public knowledge after 1948 provided a background and a context for the great rupture and excommunication of 1948, a set of accumulated puzzles and resentments temporarily shoved into their subconscious by the CPY's inner group and a dossier of Yugoslav troublesomeness and insubordination to be pulled out of the Kremlin files when the time came.[39]

It was three postwar developments which put these earlier events in focus for all the protagonists, making a crisis eventually inevitable and shaping its seriousness and outcome. Chronologically the first of these, in some of its dimensions causally related to the others, was increasing Yugoslav emphasis on the uniqueness of their revolution, Soviet denials of it, and growing awareness on both sides of what the claim and the denial implied. The second consisted of Tito's international activities and initiatives, which suggested that he was aspiring to become an autonomous viceroy of south-eastern Europe under Soviet suzerainty and perhaps to play Mehemet Ali to the ageing and increasingly suspicious Sultan in Moscow. The third was Stalin's decision to proceed to a *Gleichschalting* of the East European people's democracies and to the forging of a monolithic socialist bloc under firmer Soviet control, a decision taken in the course of 1947 and possibly a previously unplanned response to the escalating Cold War, to his own senile paranoia, or to both.

The story of the break and of its background has been told too often and additional details added by more recently published testimony and documents have clarified too few of the several remaining mysteries to warrant detailed repetition here.[40] For present purposes what is relevant from the wartime phase of this saga is the series of real or imagined grievances and grounds for suspicions which each side collected and would not forget.

The Partisan high command, for example, resented the failure of the Russians to send them any material assistance in the early years of the war, which was basically unreasonable but additional evidence of their technological innocence and naive faith in Soviet power.[41] Even more important grounds for Yugoslav resentment were repeated Soviet objections to their premature political pretensions, to their attitudes to the Chetniks and the Royal Government in exile and even to provocative symbols like the red stars on Partisan caps. Tito also resented Stalin's high-handed 'deals' over Yugoslavia—with Churchill in Moscow, when he learned of it after the war, and with Churchill and Roosevelt at Yalta. On the other hand, Comintern messages to the Partisan high command and other evidence clearly document continuing and increasing Soviet annoyance over Tito's repeated and deliberate ignoring of Soviet advice and his pursuit of political aims which were contrary to Soviet policy, at that time eager to avoid splitting resistance movements in occupied Europe or damaging inter-Allied relations with any sign that Communists intended to use the war for revolutionary purposes. Stalin then or later may also have imputed more than just pretentious Yugoslav impudence to Tito's insistence that the Red Army was welcome to help the Partisans liberate Serbia and Belgrade but should then leave Yugoslavia. It would not have escaped Stalin's naturally suspicious mind that their negotiations on this point, which took place during the first

Tito-Stalin meeting in Moscow in September 1944, had come just after Tito's independent initiative in meeting Churchill in Naples and just before Churchill's suggestion of 'fifty-fifty' Western and Soviet influence in postwar Yugoslavia.

Most incidents of otherwise normal and predictable disagreements in the first postwar years similarly assumed importance only in the context of occasional signs that each regime was indeed pursuing policies diametrically opposed to what the other considered its vital interests, a then unthinkable proposition in the international Communist movement. Such indications included Tito's Trieste policy, which the Russians opposed in secret communications and threatened to oppose publicly because they were not ready to risk confrontation with the West, and his later policy of support for the Communist insurrection in Greece, which alarmed the Russians for the same reasons. They also included Tito's travels to and enthusiastic reception in other new people's democracies, culminating in an increasingly clear intention to unite Albania with Yugoslavia, negotiations looking towards a Yugoslav-Bulgarian federation, and statements by Bulgarian leader Georgi Dimitrov and others anticipating a Balkan federation or East European confederation. Although Stalin himself had initiated or approved plans of this kind, the Yugoslavs and Dimitrov were again being rash and precipitant when American military preponderance, and the readiness to use it suggested by American intervention in Greece, recommended caution. On the other side, the Yugoslav leaders, too inexperienced and arrogant to understand Stalin's reasons for caution, deeply resented his objections where they expected active support for their contribution to advancing the frontiers of the Socialist bloc. They were also 'discovering' the Soviet Union's propensity to behave like an arrogant and imperialist great power, rather than a comradely Communist one, in the behaviour of the Red Army *en passant* and of Soviet military and technical advisers in later months, in negotiations for the establishment of joint Soviet-Yugoslav companies like those already established in Hungary and Romania, and in attempted penetration of the Yugoslav People's Army and the UDBa, State and Party bureaucracies by recruiting Soviet agents in all of them.

The cumulative effect of such developments was a determining factor of even greater psychological than political importance, at least for the Yugoslavs. While Tito kept his thoughts and conclusions born of his Soviet experience during the Great Purge to himself, at least some members of his inner circle and others close to it—far younger, often 'true believers', and on both counts particularly 'susceptible to the full bitterness of betrayed idealism'[42]—suffered their separate moments of doubt and disillusionment through involvement in one or another of these incidents before the spring of 1948. For Vladimir Velebit, for example, it was in negotiating the creation of Soviet-Yugoslav joint-stock companies—negotiations which he dared to break off because he found the conditions intolerably exploitative of a comradely and sovereign Yugoslavia, thereby earning special mention as a 'British spy' in Stalin's accusatory letters two years later. For others, like Djilas, it was as members of delegations to the Soviet Union. It was significant that attempted Soviet penetration of the Yugoslav army and other agencies, considered normal by the Russians and presumably expected by Tito, seems to have been resented by other senior Yugoslav Communists initially only as an unwarranted impugning of their loyalty to the Soviet Union and was only later interpreted as threatening. On the other side, because they considered it normal and necessary, the Russians found Yugoslav objections and resistance to such penetration equally ominous.

The basic issue in the great quarrel of 1948 was very simple: whether Tito and his Politburo or Stalin would be dictator of Yugoslavia. What stood in Stalin's way was Tito's and hence the Yugoslav regime's autonomous strength, based on the uniqueness in Eastern Europe of Yugoslavia's do-it-yourself and armed Communist revolution and its legacy: a large Party and People's Army recruited primarily on the basis of patriotic rather than socialist slogans, and the independent source of legitimacy as well as power which came from the Partisan myth of political founding.

It was thus that the most important of the often irrelevant or unimportant charges hurled at the Yugoslavs during the spring of 1948 was the accusation that they had greatly, absurdly and arrogantly exaggerated the role of their Party and Partisan army in liberating the country and establishing the new regime. The Yugoslav leaders, according to the Soviet letter of May 4, 1948, were indulging in a boundless self-praise which ignored the equal merits of other Communist Parties and the fact that the Red Army had in fact liberated Yugoslavia by coming to the rescue of the Partisans after Drvar.

It seems highly probable that Yugoslav boastfulness, the irritation it caused the Russians and the arrogance of both in late wartime and early postwar encounters were initially only manifestations of post-victory exuberance and competitive personal and national pride in the remarkable accomplishments of both armies. Stalin, however, soon grasped the political and also ideological significance of the boast. Then Yugoslavs like Tito and Djilas were prompt in following his line of thought, as is clear from the emphasis they placed on Soviet slurs on Partisan heroism in their early public reactions to the anathema of June 1948, an emphasis which was an indistinguishable mixture of honest outrage and political calculation (see Chapter 2). In fact Stalin's emphasis on this point, however ideologically sound, proved a boomerang, for insults to the Yugoslav Partisan ego provided Tito with a perfect device for mobilising domestic support. It also made it difficult for those in the Yugoslav leadership who might have chosen to side with Stalin to do so.[43]

The ideological dimension at this stage was so subtle as to be almost unnoticed both by most of the protagonists and by later analysts. The initial Yugoslav definition of their 'people's democracy' did not differ significantly from that proposed by other East Europeans and by Soviet academics in 1945-46. It was these others and not they who spoke of 'separate roads to socialism' in those years, when this was in fact the Soviet line as well. By the second half of 1947, however, the Yugoslav Communists' definition of their State, of their regime's legitimacy and its own independent roots in the Partisan war, and of their consequently special status in the socialist world, was increasingly and significantly in conflict with an emerging Soviet line.[44] This line, rationalising the reality of externally imposed Communist regimes in the rest of Eastern Europe—a possibility unforeseen by Marxist-Leninist theory—and seeking to justify the *Gleichschaltung* and consolidation of their satellite status which was now to take place, had not yet taken clear shape, so that the Yugoslavs could not technically be accused of failing to conform. It was nevertheless implicit in increasing Soviet emphasis on the principal or exclusive role of the Soviet Union and the Red Army in creating the regimes of the people's democracies, on the imperfect nature of a transitional stage which was not yet fully a dictatorship of the proletariat, and thereby by implication on these countries' dependence on and subordination to the Soviet Union and Soviet experience in building socialism. Its symbol was the creation in the autumn of 1947 of the Communist Information Bureau (the Cominform), with the Communist Parties of the Soviet Union, Eastern Europe, Italy and France as members. Ironically, the CPY was the only founder other than the Soviet Party to be really enthusiastic about the new body, which was within the year to be the instrument of the Yugoslav Party's excommunication, and its headquarters were at Stalin's personal suggestion located in Belgrade.

The first sign the Yugoslavs had that their relations with the Soviet Union were moving towards a serious crisis came at the beginning of February 1948, when Stalin abruptly summoned high-level Yugoslav and Bulgarian delegations to Moscow for what turned out to be a bullying at the Kremlin. Dimitrov came himself, but Tito, apparently anticipating trouble, sent Kardelj and Bakarić to join Djilas, who was already there (with Koča Popović and Svetozar Vukmanović-Tempo) for talks about Albania and Soviet military aid to Yugoslavia. Stalin and Soviet Foreign Minister Vyacheslav Molotov took the Yugoslavs and Bulgarians sharply to task for pursuing policies which were 'inadmissible either from the Party or the state point of view' and for not consulting the Soviet Union in foreign policy matters. This last was not true except for the latest Yugoslav moves in Albania, as Molotov admitted when pressed, but Kardelj was forced to sign a formal agreement promising prior consultation in foreign policy before he left Moscow. The principal objects of Stalin's wrath were Yugoslav and Bulgarian initiatives looking towards a wider Balkan federation and Yugoslavia's Albanian policy. (On the other hand, he displayed an apparent inconsistency, which has never been satisfactorily explained, by demanding an 'immediate' Yugoslav-Bulgarian federation; only a few days earlier he had flabbergasted the puritan Djilas by urging Yugoslavia to 'swallow Albania', dramatising the suggestion with appropriate gestures.) There were also hints that larger issues were involved. 'Your trouble is not errors', Stalin said when Dimitrov humbly admitted that some had been made, 'but that you are taking a line different from ours'.[45]

While the stunned Yugoslav delegation was on its way home, pictures of Tito were removed in Romania and he was publicly insulted by the Soviet chargé d'affaires in Tirana. Events thereafter moved rapidly towards a climax. The Russians suspended until December the negotiation of a renewal of the Soviet-Yugoslav trade agreement on which fulfilment of the Yugoslav Five-Year Plan was predicated. At this point Tito took the conflict before his Central Committee, on March 1, the first time it had been discussed outside his inner circle, and the first time the Central Committee had met in full session since its election at Zagreb in 1940. There the Politburo received a vote of confidence for their rejection of Soviet demands, including federation with Bulgaria. Although the members were sworn to secrecy, the Soviet Embassy received a full report, apparently from Žujović, who was purged from the Party and then jailed, along with Hebrang, in May. On March 18 the Yugoslavs were informed that all Soviet military advisers and instructors were being recalled 'because they were surrounded by unfriendliness and treated with hostility'. Civilian advisers and specialists were recalled the next day. On March 20, Tito sent to Moscow the first letter in the exchange of correspondence with Stalin and Molotov which the Yugoslavs later published.[46]

Many specific Soviet accusations in Stalin's letters were certainly true enough: that the Yugoslavs had obstructed the recruitment of Soviet agents inside Yugoslavia and the supplying of information to Soviet representatives except through official channels; that they had failed to nationalise the land or press collectivisation of agriculture while pursuing a 'left extremist' policy in other fields; that they had 'hidden' the Communist Party behind the People's Front and continued to behave as though they were still an illegal, conspiratorial organisation; that the Party itself was undemocratic, all decisions being made by a closed, self-recruiting Politburo; and that they had disdained the importance of Soviet experience, particularly in retraining the People's Army, and had bragged constantly about the uniqueness of their achievements in war and in laying the foundations for building socialism so quickly. Such charges were also generally irrelevant, and many blithely hypocritical, except for those which referred to the central issues: refusal to take orders and to facilitate the creation of an apparatus for more direct and efficient transmission of those orders and the information on which they should be based, and insistence on the unique and autonomous origins and legitimacy of the Yugoslav regime. The generally restrained and cautious Yugoslav replies, denying each new accusation in detail, were also basically irrelevant except for the audacity of denial and one point. It came in the key Yugoslav answer which committed the regime to stand or fall on its refusal to submit, and which was submitted to and amended by the Central Committee during a two-day meeting on April 12 and 13. In this long letter one sentence stood out as both an important truth and a calculated rallying point for popular as well as Party resistance to Stalin's pressures: 'No matter how much each of us loves the land of socialism, the USSR, he can in no case love his own country less.'[47]

But if Tito knew that they were irrelevant and already at the beginning of April wished to 'say clearly what it is about,... a struggle concerning the relations between one state and another', he was also right in fearing that others, 'uninformed and under Russian pressure', and including members of the Central Committee, would treat the accusations seriously.[48] As news of the conflict and some details of the Soviet charges reached wider Party circles, many reacted on the well-indoctrinated assumption that Stalin could not be wrong and that action must be taken to remedy Yugoslav 'errors'. One result was the hastily drafted second Nationalisation Law of April 1948. Dedijer describes the consequences of this and similar reflexive acts based on the feeling 'that we must accept some of the Soviet criticism':

The cheque was paid by various hotels, vendors, small retailers, taverns and cafes. All nationalised overnight! And one of my good friends from the Partisans, also a high functionary, gave a speech in Šumadija, his native region, and accused the peasants: 'You, kulaks, you've got us into a conflict with Stalin.' I told him afterwards: 'Don't cut off the branch we're sitting on....'[49]

Another act which belonged in this category, but which was at the same time a bold device for mobilising and demonstrating support for the regime, was the decision, formally approved by the Central Committee at a meeting on May 25, to convene a Party Congress as soon as possible. 'This meant', Dedijer recorded, 'accepting the gauntlet which Stalin had thrown down' by accusing the Yugoslav Party of hiding its face and of undemocratic procedures and by implicitly inviting 'healthy elements' in it to depose their leaders.[50]

Meanwhile the conflict with Stalin ran its now appointed course. An amendment introduced by the Central Committee into the draft of Tito's letter of April 14 invited the Soviet Party to send representatives to see how misinformed they were about conditions in Yugoslavia. In their reply, which brought new accusations including 'militarism' in the Yugoslav Party and an ominous comparison between the Yugoslav leaders and Trotsky, Stalin and Molotov rejected this invitation and said that the matter should be taken up by the Cominform, to whose members copies of their earlier letter had already been sent. The Yugoslavs in turn refused to attend the Cominform meeting. While they would not 'flee from criticism', Tito and Kardelj wrote on behalf of their Central Committee, 'in this matter we feel so unequal that it is impossible for us to agree to have this matter decided now by the Cominform'. They also categorically refused a Soviet demand that Soviet representatives be allowed to attend the trials of Hebrang and Žujović, a demand which reminded Pijade of Austria-Hungary's ultimatum to Serbia in July 1914.

The Cominform met at Bucharest, without the Yugoslavs. The assembled Parties unanimously condemned the CPY and declared that by refusing to attend the meeting the Yugoslav Communists had placed themselves 'outside the family of fraternal Communist Parties, outside the united Communist front, and consequently outside the ranks of the Information Bureau'. The Resolution repeated Soviet charges, adding that recent Yugoslav measures had been 'leftist', 'adventurist', and 'demagogic and impracticable'. It then addressed itself to Yugoslav Party members, inviting 'healthy elements, loyal to Marxism-Leninism' to force their leaders to rectify their mistakes and, if they would not, 'to replace them and to advance a new internationalist leadership of the Party.... The interests of the very existence and development of the Yugoslav Communist Party demand that an end be put to this regime'.[51]

The bomb which was to shake the world Communist movement had exploded. The date was June 28, 1948, Vidovdan, a day on which an uncanny number of events of importance in South Slav history have taken place. The battle of Kosovo Polje in 1389, which began five centuries of Ottoman domination, and the murder of the Habsburg Archduke Franz Ferdinand, which precipitated world war in 1914, were among them.

One month later the Party Congress which had been summoned in May assembled in Belgrade. It was the first Yugoslav Party gathering to bear that title since the 4th Congress in Dresden in 1928. Hebrang and Žujović were in jail with other 'Cominformists', whose numbers would eventually reach 14,000.[52] Tito's former Army Chief of Staff, Arso Jovanović, had been killed by border guards while attempting to escape to Romania. Others had made good their escape or had defected while abroad. With these relatively few exceptions the Yugoslavs, Communist and non-Communist alike, would have agreed, had they been asked, with the ovation the Congress gave to Tito and to those whom the Cominform was now calling his 'renegade clique'. By their defiance of the Soviet Union and defence of Yugoslav independence Tito and the regime had won back a large part of the popularity they had lost, particularly among the non-Communists who comprised 94 per cent of the population, during the past three years.

The quarrel with the Cominform was nevertheless mentioned at the Congress only occasionally and almost incidentally and was never identified with Stalin himself. There would be no deviation from Yugoslavia's Marxist-Leninist and Stalinist road to socialism, Tito and others speakers declared. The quarrel with the Soviet Party and the Cominform was based on misinformation, as was proved by the demonstrable falsity of the charges against the CPY, and could be resolved if the fraternal Parties would only send a delegation to see the true situation for themselves. At the opening ceremony on July 21, the entry of the Politburo was greeted by chants of 'Long live Comrade Tito', 'Long live the renowned Communist Party of Yugoslavia', 'Long live the fraternal Soviet Union', 'Long live the leader and teacher of progressive humanity Comrade Stalin', and finally 'Long live the heroic Yugoslav army and its supreme commander Comrade Tito'. Eight days later Tito closed the 5th Congress by proclaiming: 'Long live the Great Soviet Union with the genius Stalin at its head!'. An hour earlier the final plenary session had acclaimed a Resolution rejecting all accusations made by the Communist Party of the Soviet Union and the other members of the Cominform and calling on the new Central Committee 'to do everything in its power to liquidate the misunderstanding' with these Parties.[53]

On this note of gradualist public defiance, which did not yet openly include Stalin, which insisted that the quarrel was a mistake which could be remedied, and which reaffirmed an uncompromising Stalinism in speeches and in the first programme adopted by the CPY since 1920, Yugoslavia and its Communist regime began a new chapter, friendless in a hostile world.

2

THE BREAK WITH STALINISM

The Yugoslav experiment with an independent and novel 'road to socialism' was born of necessity, not of conviction. In June 1948, and for a year thereafter, the Party élite could not imagine and did not attempt to imagine that socialism could be built in any way that differed essentially from their understanding of the Soviet model. Even the break with Stalin did not seem to them, at first, to be irremediable. When they were finally forced to re-think their institutions and their ideology, the content of their response was in large measure dictated by circumstances. These included isolation from and increasingly bitter polemics with the Soviet bloc, rendered more acute by a Cominform economic blockade and political and military pressures; a breakdown of the domestic Stalinist economic machinery under the triple impact of the blockade, of over-ambitious and often badly calculated plans, and of a poverty of resources, infrastructure and technological cadre; a consequent dependence on Western aid and trade for survival, bringing extensive contacts with Western ideas, technology and institutions; and a need to broaden their base of consent within the country if they were to survive as a Communist regime without the support of the Soviet Union. It also included an imperative need to criticise both the Soviet system and its ideology and to distinguish their own practice and theory from Soviet precedents, in order to justify to themselves and to other Marxists their defiance of Stalin and the Soviet Union.

All this emerged only gradually and to some degree consecutively during 1949-50, giving members of the élite time to adapt themselves, psychologically and ideologically, to their new and unprecedented situation.

Time was important, even necessary. Yugoslav leaders, including Tito himself, were later to claim that their year-long reluctance to criticise Stalin personally or the Soviet Union generally, like the praise of both and the many quotations from Stalin with which they all larded their speeches at the 5th Party Congress in July 1948, reflected a conscious and prescient policy decision, a strategy to cope with the Party rank and file's carefully inculcated love of the USSR and Stalin. 'We dared not give free rein to indignation and reply to all the lies and slander coming from the Soviet Union', Tito told his biographer Dedijer in 1952. 'It was necessary to allow Stalin time to do such things to Yugoslavia as would move the people themselves to say: "Down with Stalin", instead of estranging ourselves from the masses by being the first to raise this cry....'[1] This was, in part at least, an *ex post facto* rationalisation. If ordinary Yugoslav Communists needed time to unlearn love of the Soviet Union and faith in Stalin's benevolent omniscience before they could comprehend what had happened and learn to think for themselves and experiment with novel ideas and solutions, so did their leaders, with a far longer and deeper commitment to the cause, its rationale, its accomplishments and its crimes. These were men who 'were defying not only one of the greatest powers of all time but also their own past and the belief which had been their only religion and occupation for most of their adult lives'.[2] Tito himself, fundamentally non-ideological and with an 'instinctual, ever vigilant sense of danger' based on Moscow experience,[3] may have been an exception. His delay in attacking Stalin and his system may therefore have indeed been calculated, but for most if not all of the rest it was not. Only prolonged, uncompromising and increasingly vicious attacks by their erstwhile mentors would drive them finally to riposte, and only the logic of this critique and a disastrous economic crisis at home were to force them to draw domestic conclusions from their criticism of their external enemies.

Dedijer, in his later, retrospective book on the conflict, is one of the most sensitive witnesses to the distress, the confusion, the personal traumas and the continued 'dogmatism that infected us all, some more and some less', as well as to the unevenness of the cure.[4] His own reflections at the time of the 5th Congress in July 1948, as he recalled them twenty years later, were probably typical for most of those in or near the Party's inner circles: 'At that moment it seemed to me that we must do everything possible to stop that conflict.... But is that at all possible? Hasn't it already gone too far? Is there no turning back?'[5] The intensity of the psychological trauma was also manifest in the psychosomatic illnesses which Tito, Kidrič and others suffered at the time.[6] Louis Adamic, who had many long and revealing conversations with most members of the Politburo during the first half of 1949, was also impressed by the pervasive sense of isolation and insecurity, reflecting more than cold calculation of the political and economic odds and projected in the form of a continuing desperate yearning for compromise or reconciliation with the Soviet Union. 'Without having anything specific to go on', Tito told him in April, 'some of us continue to hope—against hope, if you like—that this nightmare will pass somehow.' During succeeding months, Adamic adds, 'while I had many ... meetings with Tito, Kardelj, Pijade, Ranković, Djilas, Kidrič and others, I sensed every once in a while that vestiges of the old hope-against-hope sentiment clung on. In Tito and Kardelj they lasted until the end of June.'[7] While Adamic may have been wrong about Tito, he was too keen an observer and judge to be wrong about those whom he saw more frequently and knew better.

The quarrel was also bound to assume ideological forms, sooner or later, because of Stalin's success in insisting that the basic issue was ideological from the beginning: the Yugoslav Party's misapprehension or misapplication of Marxist-Leninist principles. Tito himself had immediately sensed the inappropriateness and the dangers of such a formulation. At the vital Plenum of April 12, 1948, he had warned his Central Committee that 'the issue here, above all, concerns the relationship between one state and another.... It seems to me that they are using ideological questions to justify their pressure on us, on our state ...'.[8] The final paragraph of his draft reply to the Soviet Central Committee's letter of March 20, which he was putting before the Plenum, apparently contained essentially the same argument. It was precisely this paragraph, however, which was deleted during the Plenum's editing of Tito's draft, to be replaced by one inviting the Soviet Central Committee to send a delegation to see for themselves what good Stalinists the Yugoslavs really were.[9]

This Yugoslav acquiescence in Stalin's choice of battlefield, despite Tito's misgivings, had two ultimately contradictory effects on the further evolution of the quarrel. In the longer run it was to make the movement from attacks on Stalin to attacks on Stalinism both logically consistent and quicker than it might have been. In the short run, which lasted as long as the Yugoslav Party leadership hoped for some form of reconciliation, it increased the pressure to prove each (basically irrelevant) Soviet accusation wrong by adopting corrective measures which at times made the Yugoslav Party *plus Staliniste que Staline.*

The Russians had accused the Yugoslav Party of continuing to hide its face from the people, of continuing the 'conspiratorial' style of operation appropriate to an illegal revolutionary movement, not a Party in power. The 5th Party Congress was designed in part at least to prove that this was not so; Fred Neal appropriately called it 'the first public appearance, as it were, of the Yugoslav Party'.[10] The Yugoslavs were accused of letting their Party be absorbed in the People's Front, in violation of Leninist principles. In reply, at the Front's 3rd Congress in April 1949, it was made clearer than ever that the People's Front was only a subservient tool and transmission belt for the Party, even as

Kardelj had argued vehemently at the Party Congress that it had always been.[11]

Yugoslav foreign policy also continued to follow the Soviet line, and the consequent behaviour of Yugoslav delegations to the United Nations and at the Danubian Conference, which met in Belgrade on July 30, just after the end of the 5th Congress, lent spurious credibility to Western speculation that the whole Soviet–Yugoslav quarrel was artificial, kind of subtle Communist plot.

Most indicative of all was the line taken at the 2nd Central Committee Plenum, in January 1949. The economic situation was becoming serious. The 1948 harvest had been poor and fulfilment of the ambitious Five-Year Plan was now being seriously undermined by the beginnings of the Cominform economic blockade. The negotiation in December 1948 of a new Soviet trade agreement, in which the volume of exchanges was cut to one-eighth of 1948 levels, abolished any lingering hopes that the blockade, already indicated by non-deliveries of promised equipment, would not be complete and of long duration.[12] The response of the Central Committee was completely orthodox. The Plenum called for greater discipline, effort and sacrifices to fulfil 'the basic tasks stipulated in the Five-Year Plan', mentioning specifically the need for greater efforts to effect savings, to plan the distribution and expenditure of labour, foodstuffs and raw materials, to support socialist competition, and to depend on one's own resources. As for the Party itself, the Plenum stressed the need 'to strengthen the Party apparatus'. It also 'set as a task the ever firmer harmonisation of the work of Party and State organs in economic and other questions and the strengthening of Party control over the work of State organs'.[13]

Thus no changes in the economic system were contemplated, despite suggestions by some participants that some aspects of the existing system might already be proving dysfunctional, while the only formula offered to cope with lagging production and enthusiasm was tighter, more centralised Party control and more 'agitation and propaganda'.

Still more important was the one new and in the event nearly disastrous policy adopted by the 2nd Plenum. Overruling apparent objections by Bakarić and possibly by Kardelj,[14] the Plenum agreed that collectivisation of agriculture was to proceed 'with more boldness and increased tempo'. The drive was supported by reference to the backwardness of Yugoslav agriculture, the critical lack of adequate food supplies to meet growing demand in the rapidly expanding urban sector and the impossibility of increasing productivity and marketable output with the existing pattern of subsistence smallholdings, all making rapid collectivisation the 'only solution' consonant with accepted Communist doctrine. Yet both later Yugoslav and foreign writers agree that the primary motivation was a desire to answer Soviet criticism of earlier agricultural policies by doing it the Soviet way, quickly and energetically. They also agree that in taking this decision the 2nd Plenum represented the apogee of Stalinism in Yugoslavia—a full seven months after publication of the Cominform anathema and the break with Stalin.[15]

The immediate results were dramatic, resembling the first years of Stalin's collectivisation drive in the Soviet Union in terms of numbers of collectives founded, the magnitude and methods of peasant resistance and the pressures used by the Party and State apparatuses. Before this the total number of SRZs, the Yugoslav collective farms, had grown slowly: from 454 in 1946 to 779 in 1947 and 1,318 in 1948. In 1949, after the Plenum, the number jumped fivefold, to 6,626, and in 1950, before the retreat began, the total reached 6,797, with 2 million co-operative members and 2·3 million hectares of land—about one-fifth of the country's total of agricultural land.[16] Peasant motivations in joining varied from occasional cases of ideological conviction (either personal or under the influence of relatives in the Party) or awareness of material advantages (landless or nearly landless peasants), to a desire to escape the compulsory delivery system, discriminatory taxation, and other economic and administrative measures deliberately designed to penalise and discourage private holdings, or finally to direct political and even physical pressures and threats.[17]

Peasant resistance, expressed through decreased production, slaughter of livestock, evasion of compulsory deliveries, etc. became epidemic. The consequences were aggravated by a severe drought in 1950 (a Soviet diplomat in Belgrade at the time told a Western observer that the drought proved that 'God is on the side of the Cominform'),[18] and were not helped by failure or inability to exploit the potential advantages of large farms through rapid mechanisation and improved techniques. Grain production fell to 41 per cent and overall agricultural production to 73 per cent of prewar average levels. Starvation threatened the cities.

Meanwhile, although difficulties with the Five-Year Plan, intensified by the Cominform blockade, were causing concern by the time of the 2nd Plenum, there was as yet no serious alarm at the Politburo level. A fortnight before the Plenum, Kidrič told Adamic (still 'strictly off the record') that the blockade was indeed 'giving us serious trouble' and that there had been and would have to be 'minor changes' in the Plan as a result. But the Plan was going forward and there would be 'no essential changes, at least none I can foresee at this time'.[19]

For some time, even after the break with Stalin and the

beginnings of the economic blockade, the Party leadership had been shielded from a clear view of the economic future by encouraging if temporary successes. The speed with which wartime destruction had been made good led to claims of a world record in postwar reconstruction. Many large new factories dedicated to the Communist deity of Basic Industry were under construction, as were a dozen new hydro-electric installations. By 1948 the physical volume of industrial production had already reached 150 per cent of 1939 levels; the total employed in the socialist sector rose from 461,000 in 1945 and 721,000 in 1946 to 1·5 million in 1948 and just under 2 million in 1949; national income surpassed the 264,200 million dinars of 1939 to reach 441,100 million in 1948. The populace had accepted, without significant resistance, the hard work without visible return in the form of rising living standards which was necessary to support a 1947–49 gross investment rate of 32 per cent of gross national product, most of it for the construction of big factories and electrification schemes from which only long-run returns could be expected.

Yugoslav historians and social scientists of the Partisan and post-Partisan generations, looking back at this period from the later perspective of a revised ideology which condemned the Stalinist system as inherently inefficient, have attempted to explain these early successes largely in terms of the social psychology of a revolutionary epoch and of the temporary survival of revolutionary élan. Some specific policies reflecting the same ethos must also have had a positive impact on attitudes and effort. These included the first postwar agricultural reforms and their effect on peasant expectations, the privileges granted to industrial workers (special prices for and guaranteed minimum access to rationed foodstuffs, etc.) and a near approach to 'egalitarian socialism' through low wage differentials (with a ratio of one to 3·5 in the early years). At the same time rapid reconstruction, extensive industrialisation and a consequently massive expansion in non-agricultural employment lent a momentary credibility to the regime's boast that full industrialisation and modernisation, with all their benefits, would be achieved after two or three Five-Year Plans and that equal and virtually unlimited opportunities for personal economic and social mobility were already at hand. Finally, the kind of decentralised local initiative and willingness of lower echelon officials to assume high-risk responsibility which had of necessity characterised the wartime Partisan movement survived for a time and were only gradually suffocated by the new regime's dogmatic dedication to centralised hierarchical decision-making and increasingly effective control from the centre.[20]

An additional and important role was played by the ubiquitous and often ruthless use of the coercive power of local State and

Party apparatuses in mobilising those not infected with revolutionary enthusiasm or visions of a better future. The paved highway from Belgrade to Zagreb, one of the proud accomplishments of the period, was built not only by volunteer youth brigades, as advertised, but also with extensive use of prison labour, especially that of 'class enemies' from the former bourgeoisie, which may be one reason why it is so badly built. Similarly, much of the manual labour involved in the reconstruction of war-ravaged cities and factories or the early work on new urban developments like Novi Beograd was indeed performed by the 'voluntary', unpaid efforts of ordinary citizens, but their voluntarism was usually based in fact on the old army principle.[21] Such methods nevertheless made a distinct contribution to the successes recorded in these years. Yugoslav industrialisation was still, after all, at the 'pyramid-building' stage, when forced labour can be as productive as any other, and economic development was still at the stage in which producing something is better than producing nothing for a starved market which would absorb almost any goods of any quality produced at any cost.

However effective in the short run, a development strategy based on such a combination of factors contained implicit longer-run disadvantages which were beginning to be felt by 1949. Central control and coercion required a bureaucratisation which was beginning to suffocate the remnants of the local initiative, enthusiasm and risk-taking on which early successes had partly depended and which were also a central aspect of the Partisan ethos.[22] With declining enthusiasm, continued mobilisation could only be achieved through material incentives or increasingly massive coercion. But it was not possible to provide sufficient material incentives without either large-scale foreign aid (the Five-Year Plan had been predicated on such aid from the Soviet Union and the people's democracies) or such a drastic cut in investment that continued economic growth would be minimal. Coercion on a scale adequate to replace voluntarism or material incentives also had enormous disadvantages. Difficult and costly to administer, it would alienate what was left of the regime's mass support. It was a system which could build pyramids, or even an *autoput* or a steel mill, but it was a difficult way to run a steel mill and an impossible way to run a modern economy. And as a long-term policy it was repugnant to the fundamental principles and honest beliefs of at least many of the Party élite as well as to the theoretical values of the revolution. Either the élite and its original values must be corrupted by the system or the system must become one which minimised coercion.

Twenty years later a controversial young Belgrade sociologist ruminated about this dilemma and came to the same conclusions:

It is not possible to live long exclusively on revolutionary enthusiasm. The attempt of the revolutionary élite to perpetuate primitive communism and enforce it as a *permanent* social state, comes soon into conflict with life and with human inclinations towards individual differences, initiative, adequate material reward and a more comfortable and normal life. Suppression of human nature provokes revenge: general indifference towards work, low productivity, material poverty, and intellectual inertia....

Hence the necessity to use force, yet 'those who do it, being themselves human, share the same inclinations they want to suppress in others'. They too would thus have to be restrained by force, but

this process cannot be carried on *ad infinitum*. So the revolutionary avant-garde gratifies the human inclinations of *its own* members, and forces the primitive-Communist way of life upon all the other citizens. When such an adjustment to reality takes place, the oligarchic-étatist Thermidor of revolution soon follows.[23]

The problem before the rulers of the new Yugoslavia in 1949–50 was thus complex as well as critical. Locked in a struggle with the Cominform for political and even physical survival, without a foreign friend in the world, they could look for help to only two sources: on the one hand, a disciplined and loyal Party apparatus in unchallenged, monopolistic, and fear-inspiring control of the country; on the other hand, a populace ready to acknowledge the legitimacy of the regime and defend its existence with more effort and better results than sullen fear alone could ever invoke—i.e., if not with love, at least with the conviction that this was the least of possible evils. But was it possible to maintain both of these supports, and could the regime and system survive if either were lost? The loyalty of the Party, State and military apparatuses, purged of their surprisingly small Cominformist minorities, had been tested and found true in the first months after June 1948.[24] The continued monolithic unity of these institutions and monopolistic centralised Party control over all of them seemed more essential than ever in the face of mounting external pressure and attempted internal subversion by the Cominform, as well as in defence of the new order against residual 'anti-socialist' elements. This was basic Leninism and also basic practical politics, and in one form or another it was to remain one of the strands of the Yugoslav political dialectic in future years as well. But to some of the leadership it was becoming increasingly apparent, even in 1949, that the policies and the behaviour of these apparatuses were alienating what was left of the considerable mass support which the regime had once enjoyed. In Yugoslavia's situation, isolated and besieged, such support mattered.[25]

The peasantry's dogged resistance to forced collectivisation urgently sharpened the Party élite's awareness of their dilemma. The regime boasted of and apparently believed in the broad mass support their revolution had enjoyed; Tito and others were already fond of noting that no other Communist regime, including the Soviet, had come to power with such wide support.[26] That support had been peasant-based, not only because 75 per cent of the population at the time of the revolution consisted of peasants but because the nature and locale of the combined national liberation and social revolutionary struggle, and the relative passivity of most urban classes, had dictated that the Communist-led Partisan army and subsequently the new élite would be manned and officered largely by peasants and ex-peasants. In 1948 the social composition of the Party still reflected these origins, with 50 per cent of Party members registered as of peasant origin.[27] Resistance to the regime's agricultural policies not only threatened to starve the country into collapse. These policies were also destroying what was left of the regime's mass support, with unpredictable repercussions among the rank and file of a still peasant-based Party. But accepted doctrine about the only correct way to build socialism, especially in a predominantly agrarian society, made it quite clear that only such a radical programme of introducing socialist relationships in the countryside could ensure the success of the revolution.

The conflict between received dogma and reality, most dramatic in agriculture, was increasingly felt in other sectors of the economy and in the political mood of the country. 'Bureaucratism', repeatedly condemned in principle, spread as revolutionary enthusiasm waned; in the absence of effective material incentives, more and more administrative regulations covered an even larger sector of economic and social relationships, further stultifying initiative and ad hoc problem-solving. The postwar boom ground to an end. National income, which had grown by 23 per cent in 1948, grew by 9 per cent in 1949 and then actually declined in each of the following three years. Centralisation as a general line led to State administration and control of all systems, from the economy to culture and the arts, while Tito himself and others worried, uncomprehendingly, about the failure of Yugoslav writers and artists to produce anything of quality, worthy of their new 'socialist freedom'.[28]

Responsibility in the new and expanding apparatuses carried privileges, both legal and extra-legal, and power and privileges corrupted, while sanctioned use of coercion tended to brutalise the users. Adamic found that many of the senior officials he talked to in the spring of 1949 were concerned about the 'moral-political' consequences of such phenomena, while Dedijer quotes an old childhood friend and fellow Communist as saying at the time that they were quickly beginning to lose the moral capital earned during the prewar illegal struggle and in Partisan times: 'Our people are not stupid. They are watching what we are doing now.'[29]

It was this realisation that affected not only popular support but also Party morale, especially in the upper echelons and among the veterans of the war and revolution, who still comprised one-third of the membership in 1949. Every system and regime is to some degree the prisoner of its own ideology and proclaimed values, and the new Yugoslav regime was also the prisoner of its youthfulness. Formally bureaucratised, in loyal emulation of its Soviet model, its bureaucracies were still largely staffed by revolutionaries, many of whom had not yet had time to lose their idealism and revolutionary élan under the corruptive influences of routinisation and privileges. For those who had not succumbed, or who felt guilty about the privileges and power which they simultaneously enjoyed, values still mattered.

To say this is not to idealise the Yugoslav revolution and its protagonists. Idealism, faith and youthful enthusiasm, all instructed by a special quality of naiveté, are essential ingredients of any credible explanation of their performance in the Partisan war, of their 'left extremism' of the Stalinist years with its brutality and naively ambitious Five-Year Plan, and of their defiance of Stalin. Leaders with these qualities, here largely ex-peasants with a salting of intellectuals, dizzy with power and now living in a separate closed world of special houses, special shops and resorts and limited communication with ordinary people, are particularly susceptible to brutalisation and to corruption by power and privilege. Yet the same conditions may also produce incorruptibles and eternal romantics, or an uncomfortable combination of corruption and guilty puritanism not necessarily as pharisaical as it appears. The Yugoslav élite contained examples of all of these. Those among them who still cared—either permanently or on alternate days—must try to do and be what they had fought (and killed) in order to do and be, or else they felt that they had no right to be where they were.[30] This spirit circumscribed the limits and in part dictated the direction of future policies and actions. The myths of the revolution, which included 'electrification and industrialisation' and 'applied Partisan ethics', defined the minimum expectations which the regime must at least be seen attempting to fulfil if it hoped to retain legitimacy in the eyes of key elements of its own élite as well as critical sections of the non-Party populace.

Faced with increasing problems of such magnitude and complexity, fettered by inexperience in running a State and an economy and by a dogmatism which supplied only the existing set of increasingly dysfunctional answers, Tito and his colleagues hesitated, perplexed, until the growing urgency of their predicament forced them to act. As late as July 1952, for example, Tito himself could still see no alternative to collectivisation in some form, although he recognised, in a singularly revealing exchange with his biographer, that 'we committed a capital error when we went the Russian road in creating co-operatives' and that large-scale and now regrettable coercion had been used. (When Dedijer protested that 'there wasn't such pressure as in Russia', Tito answered that 'There was out there, in the field, everywhere', and when Dedijer said 'But there was no Siberia', Tito responded: 'We don't have a Siberia, but if we had one, we would have sent people there ...'.)[31] Such uncertainty, a growing consciousness that serious mistakes had been made and a groping for viable new solutions were typical of the thinking going on in the Politburo and other leading Party circles, beginning in early 1949 and gaining in focus and conviction in subsequent months. The quarrel with Stalin and Tito's successful defiance of him had set the Yugoslavs free to choose alternative ways of doing things. The economic isolation and crisis of the next three years were making it imperative that they should so choose. But to make such choices they still had to free themselves from ideological rigidity; in the process they were to open their own ideology and practice to modification, evolution and eclecticism.

Between Cominform and the West

The ideological emancipation of the Yugoslav Party leadership was made easier and given a focus as well as added urgency by the evolution of the quarrel with the Cominform. The viciousness of the Soviet bloc's anti-Yugoslav propaganda intensified beginning in the early spring of 1949 and possibly related to alleged peace feelers from both sides which had aborted when each found the price of a compromise acceptable to the other too high.[32] Purges, trials and executions of alleged 'Titoists', some of them leading figures, became epidemic in several of the people's democracies during the summer and autumn. The Albanian 'Titoist' Koçi Xoxe was executed on June 11, 1949. In September Laszló Rajk and his 'accomplices' were hanged in Budapest after a trial which was reminiscent of the Russian great purge of the 1930s and in which they were accused of arranging with Ranković for Yugoslav troops in Hungarian uniforms to invade the country and install them in office as Yugoslav puppets. In Bulgaria Traicho Kostov, arrested in June, had to undergo a similar show trial in November, charged like Rajk with plotting a coup in association with the Yugoslavs. In the Polish purge, though it was gentler, even the Party First

Secretary, Wladyslaw Gomulka, was anathematised as a 'Titoist'. There were countless lesser victims. While the real issues involved were complex, including the settling of a variety of domestic and bilateral Soviet-client State scores, the common denominator was anti-'Titoism', ominous even when the specific charges were so incredible that the trials often seemed a macabre theatre of the absurd.

Cominform propaganda was distributed inside Yugoslavia, while Ranković's UDBa was kept busy pursuing Soviet agents and breaking their networks, which purportedly included extensive use of Yugoslavia's White Russian émigré community. By August 1949 Yugoslav Party leaders were actively fearing a Cominform military intervention, a possibility which they had considered as early as July 1948 but then dismissed as unthinkable. When Molotov on August 18, 1949, delivered a sharply-worded protest about the arrest of Yugoslav White Russians, many of whom had taken Soviet citizenship, a nervous leadership considered the protest tantamount to an ultimatum.[33] Troop movements by Soviet and satellite forces were reported along the northern and eastern frontiers. Kardelj viewed the situation as very serious, Tito, telephoned on his Brioni island retreat, agreed, and Vukmanović ordered a state of alert for the units he was designated to command in case of attack.[34] At the same time, in September 1949, the Russians exploded their first atomic bomb. The situation was so tense that the Presidium of the Federal People's Assembly approved a secret proclamation ordering a preliminary defence alert.[35]

In late September and early October the Soviet and East European Governments abrogated their postwar treaties of friendship and mutual aid with Yugoslavia, thus formalising the economic and diplomatic blockade. Earlier, in June, the Soviet Government had abandoned its support of Yugoslav territorial claims to part of the Austrian province of Carinthia without even consulting the Yugoslavs. This act seems to have played a decisive role in persuading the Yugoslav leadership that the quarrel really was both total and irremediable—perhaps because it was taken as final proof that the Soviet Government would not support them even in a dispute with the capitalist West.[36]

The Cominform met again in November 1949, this time in Budapest, to call on Communists both inside and outside Yugoslavia to overthrow Tito and to suppress the Yugoslav heresy wherever it might be found. The meeting heard reports by Mikhail Suslov, Palmiro Togliatti and Gheorghe Gheorghiu-Dej, and published a resolution which bore the title of Gheorghiu-Dej's report, 'The Communist Party of Yugoslavia in the Power of Assassins and Spies'.[37] In this document, which entered Yugoslav history as the Second Cominform Resolution, the invective heaped on the Yugoslav renegades reached new heights, reassembling and sometimes coining phrases and slogans which were common currency in subsequent Cominform propaganda until Stalin's death: 'the Belgrade clique of hired spies and assassins'; 'the Tito clique of fascism'; 'a political gang consisting of reactionary, nationalist, clerical and fascist elements'; 'the Tito-Ranković clique, direct agents of imperialism and abettors of the warmongers'; a 'brutal Gestapo-type terrorist regime'; and 'Tito's regime of terror'. The Resolution further declared that 'the fight against the Tito clique ... is an international duty for all Communists and workers' parties'. It was published on November 29, anniversary of the Jajce meeting of AVNOJ and Yugoslavia's official birthday. Thus the Cominform had again chosen, deliberately or not, a date of special symbolic significance for the Yugoslavs.

The Yugoslav regime at last reacted with counter-invective and an attempt to break out of their diplomatic and economic isolation, which had concerned the leadership since at least the beginning of the year; they were informally exploring the possibilities of a rapprochement with and possible support from the Western powers, in conversations with unofficial Westerners, as early as January,[38] but had then seen no hope of a breakthrough and were reluctant to take risks as long as some of them hoped for reconciliation with Moscow. By mid-year, however, the entire general line of Yugoslav foreign policy was in flux. In July they abandoned their support of the pro-Cominform Communist rebellion in Greece. By September, when they feared Cominform military intervention, they 'discovered' the UN, breaking with the Soviet bloc line in the General Assembly, bringing their complaints before that body for the first time, and pushing their own candidacy for a non-permanent seat in the Security Council against frantic and somewhat undignified Soviet opposition.[39]

Meanwhile, the first tokens of Western diplomatic and material support were materialising, introducing a new factor into both foreign and domestic political equations. The process was a gradual one, but the decisive symbolic moment came, like the Second Cominform Resolution one year earlier, on Yugoslavia's National Day. On November 29, 1950, President Harry Truman sent a letter to Congress supporting a Yugoslav Emergency Relief Act. Truman's argument, which made no reference to the nature of Yugoslavia's political system, was to remain the rationale of American (and other Western) policy towards Yugoslavia throughout a decade of Cold War:

The continued independence of Yugoslavia is of great importance to the security of the United States. We can help preserve the independence of a nation which is defying the savage threats of the Soviet imperialists, and keeping Soviet power out of one of Europe's most strategic areas. This is clearly in our national interest.[40]

The passage of the Act regularised US economic aid to a Communist regime and ended a period in which both sides had gradually, if still only partially, overcome intial caution, suspicions and embarrassment in the face of their respective ideological principles and public (or in the Yugoslav case Party) opinion.[41] The first US loan to Yugoslavia, $20 million, had come in September 1949; it was ostensibly a 'normal business transaction', but both sides recognised that it was basically a political loan. The two Governments spent the next year moving gingerly together. American policy was based on strategic considerations, with frequent reference to the geopolitical map of Europe and to Tito's 33 divisions, the strongest army in Eastern Europe, and on hope that the example of a Communist regime independent of the Soviet Union might prove infectious; in deference to militant American anti-Communism it was explicitly designed to 'keep Tito afloat', not to help him 'build socialism'. Yugoslav policy was based on desperate need and an initially disbelieving discovery that American aid really had no politically or ideologically unacceptable strings attached to it. It was nevertheless only the disastrous drought of 1950 and the prospect of famine the following winter which forced the Belgrade regime finally to abandon its scruples and officially seek aid on a scale which required Congressional approval. While a number of Yugoslavs nursed ideological reservations, the only political casualty of the rapprochement was former Serbian prime minister Blagoje Nešković, who in 1952 quixotically abandoned politics, resigning from the Politburo and as a deputy prime minister, in protest.[42]

Military aid was a more delicate matter. It too passed through a stage of 'half-secret, improvised, and legally questionable'[43] devices which soon proved unsatisfactory. The legal obstacles to more formal arrangements were overcome by a modification of US legislation which had not foreseen assistance to a Communist regime, and by the somewhat unexpected ease with which the Yugoslav regime accepted the remaining conditions, which included an American Military Assistance Advisory Group (MAAG) in Belgrade.

For a time it also seemed, at least to US Secretary of State John Foster Dulles, 'that this informal alliance might become a formal one, bringing Yugoslavia into NATO in at least an associated status. In February 1953, less than a week before Stalin's death, the Yugoslavs signed a Treaty of Friendship and Co-operation with Greece and Turkey which included mention of informal consultations among the three general staffs. The Americans continued to press for its conversion into a full military alliance, and on August 9, 1954, at Bled in Slovenia, the three countries signed a second and stronger Balkan Pact. It defined an act of aggression against one as an act of aggression against all, created a permanent secretariat for collaboration, and called for continuing military staff discussions and regular meetings of the three foreign ministers.[44] In October a new crisis over this stillborn Free Territory of Trieste, provoked by American diplomatic ineptitude, was resolved in the London Memorandum, the product of a full year of painstaking diplomacy by Vladimir Velebit, Manlio Brosio (for Italy), Llewellyn Thompson (for the US) and Geoffrey Harrison (for Great Britain). The London agreement authorised *de facto* but not *de jure* Italian absorption of Zone A, including the city of Trieste, and Yugoslav absorption of Zone B, slightly enlarged and with a tripartite credit to help build an alternative Slovene seaport at Koper as a sweetener.[45] With relations between Yugoslavia and its third NATO neighbour at last normalised, the way seemed clear for a plugging of the one remaining gap in Dulles's grand scheme for a NATO-CENTO-SEATO chain of alliances encircling the Sino-Soviet bloc. But by this time the Yugoslavs were already normalising their post-Stalin relations with the Soviet bloc. The Balkan Pact became a dead letter, never denounced or abrogated but quietly ignored.[46]

Meanwhile, Britain and France had in the spring of 1951 joined the United States in a tripartite grant programme designed to cover Yugoslavia's anticipated balance-of-payments deficit in the coming year. The programme was renewed in 1952 and 1953, after which the Americans carried on alone. By 1955, when the first phase of massive Western aid ended, American economic assistance to Yugoslavia had totalled $598·5 million and the official price tag on military assistance, which included surplus and second-hand equipment with depreciated values, was $588.5 million. Only $55 million from the first category was in the form of repayable loans.[47]

The new relationship between Yugoslavia and the West was of triple importance. Politically it ended the country's isolation and the frightening consciousness of isolation which had sometimes almost paralysed the leadership; it soon led to diplomatically useful contacts and later concerted action with the new States of the 'Third World'; and in both these dimensions it created helpful bargaining cards for future use vis-à-vis the Soviet bloc.[48] Economically it enabled the country to avoid starvation in 1950-52, to reorient its foreign trade from East to West and obtain the machinery, technology and raw materials essential to any hope of industrialisation, and to afford rapid economic growth without lowered living standards in later years. Thirdly, it had an important impact on institutions and ideology.

As already noted, one of the leadership's basic problems in 1949–50, when they became painfully aware that new roads must be sought, was lack of knowledge about alternatives. Inexperienced as administrators and economic managers, they were also woefully ignorant of the outside world. While some of them had spent some time in the Soviet Union, particularly between 1945 and 1948, very few had been to the West except for brief trips on Party assignments in conspiratorial underground work.[49] As early as 1945 Tito himself had complained to a Western visitor about the limitations which this provincial upbringing imposed on his team. Now the wider international contacts open to many Yugoslavs in the 1950s were to have a dual impact on the evolution of Yugoslav theory and practice. Directly there was the influence of early, immediate access to non-Marxist (or semi-Marxist socialist) economics, political science and sociology, and earlier and wider personal experience of post-Marxian capitalism, political democracy and democratic socialism in the West. If the admission that one can learn from non-Marxist social scientists later became commo nplace among Soviet bloc as well as Western Communists, it had a head start in Yugoslavia. In addition, primarily because of the relatively larger number of all kinds of decision-making Yugoslavs who were to enjoy such contacts, information from a variety of sources was available to more levels and sectors of the political and economic establishments than in other Communist-ruled States; in Yugoslavia it was not just a strictly selected élite who had access to such influences.[50] Indirectly and subsequently there was the effect of the introduction into the Yugoslav system of Western and non-Marxist (but not necessarily anti-Marxist) principles of business organization, marketing, indicative planning, fiscal instruments, etc., with a consequent need to integrate these novelties into Yugoslav socialist theory.

In other words, extensive intercourse with the West, rendered possible and then necessary by the quarrel with the East in 1948, made available to the Yugoslavs alternative solutions to their problems—theoretical and technical, political and economic. At the same time isolation from the East and from Soviet dictation freed them to choose among these alternatives, if they should so desire, with a remarkable minimum of external restraint.

To the 'Yugoslav Road'

The shift from defence to offence in polemics with the Cominform and in propaganda which took place gradually during 1949 was a prerequisite and animator of the equally gradual but increasingly self-confident breakthrough to new solutions of urgent domestic problems which was the beginning of the novel Yugoslav 'road to socialism' that the West called 'Titoism'. As long as the Soviet Union could not be attacked ideologically, Yugoslav propagandists had had to defend the Yugoslav position in the quarrel only by denying the justice of Soviet accusations concerning 'deformations' in Yugoslav socialist thought and practice. The restriction inhibited critical thought as well as propaganda. Once the Soviet Union was open to direct attack and criticism, however, both propagandists and ideologists could instead look for the mote of 'deformations' in their adversary's eye and thus impugn the validity of Soviet socialism. As a Yugoslav historian noted:

Yugoslav Communists posed to themselves a dilemma: either there exist real Communists and true socialism in the USSR—in which case the Soviet Communist Party is right in the clash with the CPY—or else socialism there is deformed and Communists there are no longer Communists, in which case the CPY is the true Marxist Party and Stalin and the CPSU leadership no longer stand on true socialist positions.[51]

Once the logic of this argument had been discerned and stated, Yugoslav polemicists and serious political thinkers moved on with alacrity to 'discover' wherein the Soviet deformations of socialism consisted and what had led to them. If their 'discoveries' were not always as original as they seemed to think they were, it was not the first time that Yugoslavs have indulged in 'discovering America' for themselves—as their frequent, self-ironic use of that phrase, in many contexts, suggests.

Thus they embarked on that amazing voyage of exploration, of critical thought and of institutional innovation which characterised the Yugoslavia of 1949 and the early 1950s. The South Slavs, whatever their other talents, had never been renowned as philosophers or original political thinkers. Yugoslav Marxists, with the possible exception of Svetozar Marković, had never before made a contribution to socialist thought that the outside world had deemed worthy of remark. The latest State and Party leadership, although they included the usual Communist embarrassment of 'intellectuals', had seldom if ever tried their hands at serious theoretical writing. Now, from this thin soil, there came a remarkable flowering of criticism, theory and experimentation—originally often ideologically unsophisticated and politically naïve, but with growing self-confidence and a curiously sure instinct for the politically possible. Moreover, because the 'theorists' who in these years contributed so prolifically to the pages of *Partijska izgradnja, Komunist*, the Party's other theoretical journals and *Borba* were also at the pinnacle of power in a highly centralised apparatus, responsible for a political and economic system in crisis, their thought and the institutions they devised reflect a relationship between changing theory and practice which resembled that of the chicken and the egg, making it difficult if not impossible to say which came first.

Ideology, like power, remained highly centralised, and the inner 'establishment' of Titoism in its formative years was still the small group of men, personally recruited by Tito after 1937, who had run the Partisan war and revolution. Their cohesiveness and exclusiveness, forged by shared experiences and dangers of such intensity, made them a remarkable group of close friends as well as colleagues. They met at work and they met at play, they telephoned one another in the middle of the night, and they talked incessantly. Ideas were bounced from one to another until original authorship became undiscoverable as well as unrecorded. The articles and speeches of each included the thinking of others, with selection and emphasis the only reliable clues to particular personal interest, or individual value preferences. Decisions reflected a consensus reached informally, by obscure processes rooted in inter-personal intimacy, shared values and experiences, and a complicated and fragile web of mutual respect and trust in which the strands were of varying thickness, durability and quality. Tito presided over the whole tumultuous and often confused process as a non-intellectual final arbiter and ultimate decision-maker, his great authority vested in him by his institutional role and by his personal role as 'Stari', the loved, respected and feared 'old man' of a curious, close-knit family of former conspirators and comrades-in-arms.

Those engaged in this great debate included some of the Party Politburo and very few others. Even most of the other members of the Central Committee (63 full members and 42 candidate members elected at the 5th Congress) played a relatively small role. There were only four Central Committee Plenums in the ideologically crucial four years before the 6th Congress in November 1952, and the only one held in the period of gestation of 'workers' self-management'—at the very moment that the first workers' councils were being constituted—does not seem to have dealt with the subject.[52]

In 1949 the Politburo consisted of Tito and eight colleagues: Ranković and Djilas (Secretaries of the Central Committee, with the former doubling as minister of the interior and the latter as minister of propaganda); Pijade (First Vice-President of the Presidium of the National Assembly and chairman of its Legal Commission); Nešković (a deputy prime minister and chairman of the State Control Commission); Kardelj (foreign minister and a deputy prime minister); Kidrič (chairman of the State Planning Commission); Leskošek (minister of heavy industry); and Ivan Gošnjak (deputy minister of war). Of these, Kardelj, Djilas and Kidrič were particularly active in re-thinking Marxism-Leninism

and the Yugoslav road to socialism, as were a few others, like
Vladimir Bakarić on agrarian problems and the non-intellectual
but irrepressible Svetozar Vukmanović, who formed part of the
informal inner circle without being Politburo members.[53] In one
sense and in part this represented a kind of natural division of
labour based on personal function in the élite. Djilas, as
propaganda minister, had both time and a specific mandate to
undertake theoretical work, but one reason he held that particular
job was his personal predilection for theory. Kidrič, in charge of an
economy in deep trouble, was also specifically motivated to search
for new solutions as well as intellectually inclined to enjoy the
exercise. Kardelj was a born (and often pedantic) theoriser and
needed no special incentives. Pijade acted as the true Moses of the
period, the law-giver who as chairman of the Assembly's Legal
Commission turned theory into draft legislation, but made little
contribution to ideology *per se* after 1948. Ranković produced a
theoretical discourse only when the occasion required it of him as a
Marxist chieftain; he preferred the role of a practical man of
politics and 'conscience of the Party', as his colleagues liked to call
him.[54]

It was thus a personalised, intimate and even private undertaking by a small group. It was carried out, however, in the
broader context of the influence of foreign and domestic developments and of a wider circle of friends and colleagues who moved
on the fringe of the inner circle, sharing ideas in endless discussions
and acting as a sounding board for the reactions of those beyond
the fringe, in the wider Central Committee or *na terenu*, in the
countryside. In other terminology, the 'role-set' of the principals in
the drama consisted of three concentric circles of diminishing
importance: their own peer-group of less than a dozen intimate
colleagues; a larger group, varying in numbers, basically informal,
and consisting of those (Dedijer is a good example) whom the
inner group saw frequently on a basis of personal friendship and
wartime comradeship; and finally, both impelling action and
drawing the limits of the politically possible, 'noises off' in the form
of events and popular reactions to them in the country as a whole,
with this information transmitted to the inner circle both through
Party and People's Front channels and through extensive travel
and personal contact.

Djilas's account of the genesis of the idea of self-management is
suggestive. Soon after the Yugoslav Party was expelled from the
Cominform, he says, he started 'to re-read Marx's *Capital*', but this
time 'with much greater care, to see if I could find the answer to
the riddle of why, to put it in simplistic terms, Stalinism was bad
and Yugoslavia was good'. In the process he rediscovered the
Marxian principle of social self-management, with its anti-

bureaucratic and anti-étatist implications. Here was not only a basis for criticism of Soviet practice, but also an echo and rationalisation of the emotional reaction which Tito and his colleagues were already feeling as they contemplated the system they had created in Yugoslavia, a reaction which found them 'in the grip of rage and horror over the incorrigibly arbitrary nature of the party machine they had set up and that kept them in power'. Djilas continues:

One day—it must have been in the spring of 1950—it occurred to me that we Yugoslav Communists were now in a position to start creating Marx's free association of producers. The factories would be left in their hands, with the sole proviso that they should pay a tax for military and other States' needs 'that remained essential'.

Djilas explained his idea to Kardelj and Kidrič, he says, 'while we sat in a car parked in front of the villa where I lived'. They liked it, although Kidrič at first thought it was too soon for such a step. The issue was debated for months in closed circles including trade union leaders before it was presented to Tito in the lobby of the Federal Assembly. His first reaction was: 'Our workers are not ready for that yet!' Djilas and Kardelj pressed their arguments, emphasising the value of the idea as a 'radical departure from Stalinism' which would appeal to the international workers' movement.

Tito paced up and down, as though completely wrapped up in his own thoughts. Suddenly he stopped and exclaimed: 'Factories belonging to the workers—something that has never yet been achieved!' With these words, the theories worked out by Kardelj and myself seemed to shed their complications and seemed, too, to find better prospects of being workable. A few months later, Tito explained the workers' self-management bill to the National Assembly.[55]

Whether or not these details and attributions of authorship are strictly accurate, Djilas's description of the style of élite functioning in this period and of the process of idea generation and decision-making rings true. Both instinctively and because they knew no other reliable sources, Yugoslavia's leaders looked first to the classics of Marxism-Leninism for guidance in their hour of need. Indeed, as other reminiscences and the evidence of published articles confirm, one of the minor remarkable features of the enterprise is that these men did find time in 1949-50, amid the press of their day-to-day duties, to indulge in a thorough re-examination of their prewar prison textbooks. One pictures them in their studies, immersed in Marx, Engels and Lenin—Marx's *The Civil War in France*, Engels's *Anti-Düring* and Lenin's *State and Revolution* were the texts which they found most fruit-ful—searching for properly theoretical answers to the riddle of

where the Soviet Union went wrong. Outside the window starvation threatened the country and the new factories which they
had built ground remorselessly to a halt for lack of raw materials,
technical knowledge and appropriate incentives. This conjunction
of scholasticism and reality produced new slogans and
theories—'debureaucratisation', 'decentralisation', and 'workers'
self-management'—and these in turn produced new institutions
and an ideology with a life and logic of their own which were not
always what their authors had anticipated or even desired.

The process of primary emancipation from dogmatism, of
re-thinking, and of preliminary conclusions reflecting a new
theoretical approach, or more accurately a new style, occupied
most of 1949. At the beginning of the year Tito and the inner
circle, although still 'hoping against hope' for a compromise
reconciliation with Moscow, were already becoming preoccupied
with the question of where the Soviet Union had 'gone wrong'.
They had no clear answers, but were already certain that it was not
Stalin alone, not just what would later be called the 'cult of the
personality'. 'Something has happened in the Soviet Union', Tito
told Adamic at their first meeting in mid-January:

What happened? For one thing, the Bolshevik revolutionary mind, which
Lenin exemplified, was supplanted by the bureaucratic and police mind, if
it can be called a mind.... I suppose her leaders' primacy in the
International Communist Movement, their being rulers of a vast land and
a great power, and winning a tremendous military victory, all this has
blinded them, and they've blundered into the rankest type of nationalism:
into Great-Russianism, which always had imperialistic over-tones.[56]

The Soviet leadership, he suggested in another conversation the
following day, had 'meandered into revisionism', and one of those
present—who included Kardelj, Ranković, Pijade, Djilas and
Kidrič—argued that 'perhaps the weight and involutions of
Russia's internal problems created tensions within the Politburo of
the Central Committee of the Bolshevik Party that pulled everything askew'.[57]

The same week that these conversations took place Kidrič
published an article on 'The Character of Commodity-Monetary
Relations in the FPRY' which was generally orthodox, but in which
the careful analyst could perceive the first seeds of some new
ideas.[58] Because the socialist 'transitional period' is still marked by
'the existence of commodity-monetary relations', Kidrič argued,
the 'law of value' would still apply to the State as well as to the
private sector, implying a continuing role for the market as an
indicator of the shape of supply and demand curves. At the end of
the month, in his report on his agitprop work to the 2nd Plenum of
the Central Committee, Djilas warned that the conflict with the
Soviet Party was not after all based on 'misunderstandings' but on

Soviet 'revisionism on a whole series of questions', and that it would therefore 'inevitably sharpen'.[59]

The 2nd Plenum nevertheless represented the apogee of Stalinist orthodoxy in Yugoslavia, as we have seen, and Djilas's report was not included in its resolution or carried in *Komunist* with other Plenum reports; it was relegated instead to the pages of a new Party journal concerned with cadre problems.[60] The Yugoslav leadership's effective intellectual and policy break with Stalinism clearly postdates that meeting and as clearly antedates the 3rd Plenum in December of the same year, when the new style is clearly discernible.[61]

In the interval occasional measures were adopted to combat some 'negative phenomena', like bureaucratism, the abuse of power and privileges and excessive centralisation, which could be attacked without ideological innovation or deviation from the ideal type of the Soviet model, under which they also stood condemned. However orthodox in substance, these measures pointed in the same direction as the re-thinking of principles going on at the top. The policy balance-sheet for 1949 thus presents a picture of contradictory currents: alongside measures tending to further centralisation, to tighten the command structure and to extend Stalinism to the countryside through forced collectivisation, there were other initiatives and 'agitprop campaigns' (for example, against 'bureaucratism as the cancer of socialist society') which represented or anticipated the first steps towards a revival of local authorities and a reduction in the size and powers of the central apparatuses.

The most important in retrospect was a new law on local government organs (the *narodni odbori*, or people's committees), drafted by Kardelj and Pijade and adopted in May 1949. It permitted the people's committees to propose their own budgets for the first time and gave them a modest degree of fiscal autonomy by permitting them to form part of their income from the profits of economic enterprises located on their territories. Recognising the work already done towards the formation of citizens' commissions and advisory councils designed to enlarge popular participation in local social services, the 1949 law also required the people's committees to report on their activities at least once every two months to public 'meetings of voters' (*zborovi birača*), another innovation with a potential for future development. Finally, despite continued direct State control over the activities and even the internal administration of the people's committees and continued immediate Party control through the habitual appointment of the local Party secretaries as their chairmen, the law is credited by Yugoslav historians with creating a new atmosphere, one in which the people's committees would gradually come to be regarded—and to assert themselves—as a unit of autonomous local self-government rather than as the lowest-level administrative organs of the central Government.[62]

That this was the intent of the law was emphasised by Kardelj in the characteristically marathon speech with which he submitted it to the Assembly on May 28. The speech, expanded and published with the title 'On People's Democracy in Yugoslavia', represents a major landmark in the emergence of new Yugoslav theories concerning the nature of the socialist State and socialist democracy and the first fruits of intensive restudy of Marxist classics. It also bears the imprint of Kardelj's excited rediscovery of Marx's writings on the Paris Commune of 1871 and Lenin's *State and Revolution*, which he quotes at length.

Kardelj was particularly concerned with the necessity 'to safeguard the revolution—as Marx said—from its own bureaucrats'. The basic thesis of the speech is that defence against bureaucracy and the further development of socialism depend on the extension of 'socialist democracy':

It should never be forgotten that no perfect bureaucratic apparatus, even headed by an inspired leadership, can develop socialism. Socialism can be developed only from the initiative of the millions, with the proletariat in the leading role. Therefore the development of socialism cannot proceed in any other way but through the constant strengthening of socialist democracy, in the sense of increasing the self-management of the peoples' masses, in the sense of their greater inclusion in the work of the state machinery from the lowest organs to the highest, in the sense of their increasing participation in direct management in each individual enterprise, institution, etc.[63]

Language of this sort had of course been heard often enough before, even from the lips of Stalin himself. But as the Yugoslav critique of the Soviet system gathered momentum, born aloft by an increasingly effervescent enthusiasm which soon verged on ideological recklessness, these themes gained in purposefulness and assumed institutional, if not yet practical and wholly unhypocritical, forms.

One of the earliest direct attacks on Soviet 'deviation', Djilas's essay entitled 'Lenin on Relations among Socialist States' which appeared in September 1949,[64] is a reminder that the starting point of this voyage of intellectual discovery was a search for a Marxist explanation of the Soviet Union's un-Marxist, imperialist behaviour in Eastern Europe and a justification of the Yugoslavs' insistence that each State must find its own road to socialism. The same month, in the context of the Rajk trial and its echoes of the Stalinist purges of the 1930s, Pijade published a series of articles in *Borba* which for the first time publicly suggested that the sources of the Soviet Union's international deviations should be sought in

Soviet domestic history and the Soviet system.[65] Some members of the Politburo, including Djilas, apparently objected that Pijade was at least being premature in attacking the system which Yugoslavia's so closely resembled,[66] but the theme was taken up again before the end of the year.

By 1950 the dictatorial nature of the Soviet regime, its imperialism, its tyranny over and exploitation of the Soviet and East European peoples were all seen as consequences of the Russian Revolution's fatal incompleteness, which had left all political and economic power concentrated in the hands of a highly centralised Party-State apparatus—a 'State capitalism' worse than the private kind[67]—responsible to neither the people nor the Party itself and inevitably bureaucratised, corrupted and brutalised. The revolution, the Yugoslavs concluded, could be saved from such an otherwise inevitable degeneration only by immediate steps to fulfil the rest of the Marxian socialist programme: the State must begin to 'wither away' as soon as its 'last independent act', the nationalisation of the means of production, had been completed, and it must be replaced—gradually but quickly—by 'direct social self-management' by a 'free association of producers' in all public and common affairs. The process must begin with the economic base, with the 'production relations' on which all social superstructures rest, and thus should begin with an early implementation of a one-time tactical slogan of the Russian Revolution: 'the factories to the workers'.

In such an atmosphere of intellectual ferment and against a background of declining industrial production, with a dourly resistant peasantry presaging worse to come in agriculture, the Central Committee assembled again at the end of December 1949, eleven months after the 2nd Plenum. The session was primarily dedicated to two subjects, and the conclusions in each case reflected both the new style of thought among the leadership and the pressure of reality.

Considering the problem of the school system, the Plenum declared that 'the goal of education must be the formation of an all-around educated, free builder of socialism, to whom bureaucratism and rigidity of thought are alien'. To this end there must be not only a uniformity of pedagogical theory but also greater initiative and independence on the part of local school systems and individual teachers, a general 'debureaucratisation and decentralisation' of education and culture. Turning to agriculture and analysing the results of the collectivisation campaign, on the basis of a report by Kidrič, the Plenum warned against 'violations of the voluntary principle' in forming SRZs 'at any price and without concern as to whether or not there exist the necessary political and economic preconditions'. With no dramatic improvement in growth rates to be expected for several years, a stabilisation of the number of collectives was considered desirable.[68]

The Plenum's warnings against over-zealousness in collectivisation might seem no more than a pathetic repetition of Soviet experiences at a similar stage, of Stalin's 'dizzy from success' warning to his collectivisers in 1931, but in Yugoslavia they marked the first step in a permanent and total retreat, however reluctant and gradual, from the concept of the *kolkhoz*. The new trend was confirmed in January 1950, when the Executive Committee of the People's Front 'recommended' that for the time being further efforts to advance socialism in the countryside should be focused on the development of General Agricultural Cooperatives (*opšte zemljoradničke zadruge*, OZZ), the more traditional form of marketing and technical assistance cooperatives known in the West and prewar Yugoslavia.[69] The rate of formation of new SRZs rapidly dropped to zero, which was a relief but not a solution. For three more years, right through the killing drought of 1952, the regime struggled to find some way of avoiding surrender to indefinite private ownership of agricultural land. While Kardelj continued his dogged search for some way of employing the OZZs to this end, the imaginative thinking was done primarily by Bakarić. Starting with an eight-month study of ways to make existing SRZs efficient (published in early 1950), the Secretary of the Croatian Party moved gradually, over a two-year period, to advocacy of their dissolution.[70]

In industrial enterprises, meanwhile, experiments with workers' participation had already begun in the form of informal consultations with workers' representatives concerning 'the organisation of production, business and various problems in the field of labour relations, health and safety protection, cultural activities and holidays, housing problems, etc'.[71] In some enterprises these consultative bodies were assuming the status of permanent councils. Once again theory and practice were evolving along parallel paths, with practice at times ahead of theory. Now, in the autumn of 1949, it was decided to introduce formal elective workers' councils on an experimental basis in a group of selected enterprises. To this end discussions were held between representatives of the Central Committee of the Trades Union Federation, some of whom seem to have opposed the idea, and the Economic Council of the Federal Government.[72] On December 23 the heads of these two bodies, Djuro Salaj and Kidrič, signed a joint 'Recommendation on the Founding and Work of Workers' Councils in State Economic Enterprises', which was dispatched to the 215 large enterprises selected for the experiment. The Central Committee of the Party, which held its 3rd Plenum that same week, does not appear to have been consulted. Perhaps, however, no one yet imagined that the experiment would soon grow into the principal unique feature of the 'Yugoslav road to socialism'; for if Djilas is reliable, it was only in the following spring that Kardelj had the idea of marrying their joint proposal for 'workers' self-management' to the originally merely consultative device of 'workers' councils'.[73]

In the six months before the experiment was confirmed, expanded in concept, and made universal by law, a number of other 'decentralising and democratising' measures were introduced. A new Law on Elections of People's Deputies, in January 1950, abandoned the list system for candidates and introduced direct nomination by voters' meetings (*zborovi birača*). This was a modest enough step towards wider participation in selecting political representatives, since the Party leaders had no intention of permitting full effective control of nominations to slip out of their grasp. It nevertheless reflected a new degree of self-confidence in their ability to control political processes throughout the country with a lighter touch and yet without risk of awkward incidents or the reappearance of an effective opposition. It was in this sense a sign that they were at last convinced that both the old opposition of anti-Communist parties and the new opposition of pro-Cominformists were powerless to oppose them on a public battlefield.

The State administration was reorganised to reduce the number of federal 'bureaucrats'—a process which had already begun in 1949—and groups of federal economic ministries were liquidated, their functions transferred to the republics.[74] Federal councils for individual economic sectors were established to replace these liquidated ministries and to co-ordinate all-Yugoslav economic activities. By July 1950 about 100,000 jobs in State and Party bureaucracies had been abolished.

A concerted but still largely ineffective attack on privileges and attendant corruption waited until the autumn and initiation by a Central Committee 'Recommendation', which formally dismantled the special shops with lower prices and guaranteed supplies and the special villas and vacation resorts of the Party élite. The legal position of Communists was declared to be the same as that of non-Communists.[75] But it was easy to bypass the abolition of legal privileges—villas, for example, could be presented to leading personalities by grateful constituents—and merely declarative statements about egalitarian status could be ignored by those who had always ignored them. The high living of many members of the new élite continued to invoke the cynical disdain of their non-Communist countrymen and the despair and embarrassment of more ascetic or at least guilt-ridden fellow-Communists.

Meanwhile, on June 27, 1950, the National Assembly approved

what remains the most famous legislative act of the postwar era in Yugoslavia, a Basic Law on the Management of State Economic Enterprises and Higher Economic Associations by the Work Collectives, generally known as the law on workers' self-management.[76] Tito, who presented the new law personally, justified the proposed legislation on the basis of the Party's position on three questions facing Yugoslav socialist society: the law was necessary to inaugurate the process of the withering away of the State (here he poured scorn on Stalin's argument that the State must instead become stronger in the 'transitional phase'); it was necessary in terms of Party awareness of the danger for its own integrity as a progressive and ideological force inherent in tendencies to integrate the Party with the State apparatus—and both with the economic system—in a monolithic, hierarchical way; and thirdly, since genuine Marxist-Leninists held that national-isation and State ownership of the means of production represented only 'the first and lowest form of socialism', the new law marked a transition to 'a higher form' and a return to 'true Leninism' from Stalinist deviation. 'Therein', Tito said, 'lies our road to socialism.'[77]

With the introduction of the law the State ceased to be the formal owner of the means of production, which became 'social property'. The workers in each enterprise became, in effect, trustees of the share of this socially owned property committed to their hands in the form of machinery, buildings, etc., exercising their trusteeship through elective organs: workers' councils consisting of between 15 and 120 members (or of all the workers in small enterprises with less than 30 employees) and management boards of less than two dozen members, selected by the workers' councils and including the director of the enterprise as an *ex officio*, non-voting member.[78]

The powers of these organs, as enumerated in the law, appeared to be extensive:

The workers' council ... approves the basic plans and annual balance sheet of the enterprise; adopts conclusions regarding the management of the enterprise and the fulfilment of the economic plan, elects, recalls and relieves of duty the board of management or its individual members; enacts enterprise rules subject to approval by the board of management of the higher economic association or appropriate State agency; reviews reports on the work and individual measures of the board of management and adopts conclusions regarding the approval of its work [Art. 23]. ... The board of management ... prepares drafts of the enterprise's basic plans, lays down its monthly operational plans ... decides on the appointment of staff to executive posts, decides on workers' and office staff's complaints against decisions on dismissal and internal assignment to jobs, ... [and] is responsible for the fulfilment of the plan and for the efficient operation of the enterprise [Art. 27].

In fact, however, these were merely formal powers, largely devoid of meaningful content. Effective control remained in the hands of the director and of the State whose appointed agent he continued to be. The director was legally responsible for production and business affairs, operating within the framework of the economic plan. He represented the enterprise 'before State agencies and in legal matters concerning third persons, natural and juridical'. He retained control over the hiring, dismissal (subject to a complicated appeals procedure), and transfer of workers, and was legally bound to veto any decision of the self-management organs that he considered at variance with the law or with the plan, which still had the force of law (Arts. 8, 37–40). He was appointed and removed by the 'Higher Economic Associations' referred to in the law, and these, while formally controlled by 'self-management' organs or their own, were in reality 'a new name for old organs: the General and Principal [Economic] Directorates which had operated as the operational organs of the [State] ministries and councils'.[79]

The new dispensation did not affect the centralised, administrative system of planning, of quantitative production targets, and of central allocation. The State continued, as long as a Soviet-type command economy remained in effect, to control the quantity and assortment of inputs and outputs, income distribution and investment. Workers' councils were duly elected and consulted but played no real management role; they had no money to dispose of on their own initiative. Management boards had somewhat wider effective powers, but were too small, too indirectly elected and usually too dominated by the director to be truly representative or autonomous. Yugoslav historians and economists themselves no longer date the beginning of the transition from the 'administrative period' in the economy from 1950.

Two conclusions are possible. The new law was a manoeuvre in the propaganda war with the Cominform and its allied Communist Parties across the world and with the Yugoslav people, who might be induced to accept an illusion of popular power in place of the reality they had been promised.[80] Alternatively, it was a very cautious first step, which recognised the force of the arguments of those who had opposed the whole idea as impractical, a dangerous, or at least premature, leap into the unknown, pointing out that an underdeveloped and largely still primitive country, in which only centralised, forced savings and planned economic control could ensure development and in which most workers (and even most directors) were still illiterate or semi-literate ex-peasants, was hardly ready for anything like genuine workers' control. As the councils grew in experience, they would gradually be given increased real power over a maturing economy.[81]

Probably both interpretations are valid, the first for some and the second for others of the decision-making élite, while still a third group must have stood between the two views, welcoming the law and its slogans as immediately useful in the propaganda war and adopting a wait-and-see attitude towards the real future potential of the idea. There was also, however, an urgent, practical, and immediate reason for going slow with radical institutional reforms or expanded individual freedom. The law on workers' self-management had been adopted at the very moment of worst economic crisis. Industrial production was falling, and it was already clear in June that the harvest, dealt a double blow by drought and collectivisation, would be a disaster. The impact of the Cominform blockade was at its maximum, reducing the total value of foreign trade in 1950 to 115·5 million dinars (about $385 million), down 35 per cent on the 1948 level; Western trade and aid had not yet materialised in the quantities which would significantly help after 1951–52. National income was back below the level of 1948, while increasing expenditures on armaments had raised the cost of national defence to nearly one-quarter of this inadequate and dwindling total. By the end of the year inflation in Western Europe and the United States induced by the Korean War was further aggravating the situation; prices of Yugoslav imports (now exlusively from the West) rose by 41 per cent. In December the National Assembly extended the Five-Year Plan for one year, to run to the end of 1952. This was really only a meaningless gesture of defiant determination; the Plan was already dead, the victim of its ambitiousness, the blockade, disrupted supplies and rescheduled priorities.[82] 'Planning' had long since given way to ad hoc decisions hastily adopted under the pressure of events.

At this nadir in the fortunes of postwar Yugoslavia, which was to last for three years of economic stagnation, near starvation and unremitting Cominform pressure, the basic question before the regime was its simple survival, which its leaders put in terms of the survival of an independent State. To this end they asked of the people continued loyalty and greater effort, with lowering living standards. If a positive response to these demands could be facilitated by an illusion of participation through workers' councils, with no real decision-making powers which might undermine existing instruments of mobilisation and enforcement, well and good, but in a time of crisis a new device of untested worth must logically be considered a marginal and in the eyes of many a risky auxiliary. The primary reaction to such a crisis by such a regime, if not by any regime, was rather to look to 'strengthened instruments of force, of the power and position of the State apparatus, of the police, the military, and other power factors, and a weakening of democratic relations'.[83]

Thus the critical thinking, the rhetoric, and the legislation of the year in which the CPY broke with ideological Stalinism did not mean a break with an essentially Stalinist system. They did, however, lay the basis for further ideological and institutional development, and they brought the process of ever further centralisation of functions and power to an end in most sectors. In addition, extensive propaganda and exaggerated claims for the workers' councils created an atmosphere in which this came to be seen as *the* pillar of the regime's pretensions to uniqueness and even of its legitimacy, so that the institutions and expectations created in June 1950 could not be abandoned, whatever else might be. The Communist regime in Yugoslavia was now based on two untouchable 'founding myths': the Partisan war and 'workers' self-management'.

Hence further and genuine changes became increasingly unavoidable. The mere pronouncement and formal institutionalisation of the idea of factory administration by workers was in blatant contradiction with the existing, 'étatist' system. The conflict with the Cominform, growing in intensity until Stalin's death in March 1953, provided a continuous spur to ever more vigorous and profound criticism of the Soviet system, a criticism which strengthened with new arguments the concept that the revolution could be saved only by undoing 'étatism' and realising 'socialist democracy'. And because the Yugoslav system was still basically a Soviet one, these arguments contributed to an ever more critical attitude towards and analysis of existing domestic practices. At the same time the multinational structure of Yugoslav society, institutionalised in the federal Constitution, produced additional motives as well as appropriate bodies for decentralisation. In the economy the continuing crisis, while it could be used to argue against any dismantling of existing coercive and normative · incentives, also provided the basis for counter-argument: that the visible effects of the present, non-stimulative system—slowness, irresponsibility, disinterest, inefficiency—had made new kinds of incentives a matter of urgency, and that these could best be provided by the independent and innovative initiative and cost-consciousness which rewards for profitability in a competitive free market could provide. Fundamental changes in the economic system could thus be advocated both in the interest of reviving economic activity and as a political affirmation of new social theory. The result was the creation of a social climate ready to welcome further radical reforms, both political and economic.

'Market Socialism' and 'Socialist Democracy'

The dominant historic task of the regime, henceforth and for the next fifteen years, was to be the search for appropriate and politically acceptable mechanisms capable of translating this expectant climate into fulfilled expectations. In view of the technical complexity and originality of the problem, the backwardness of the country, the stubborn heritage of Stalinism in institutions and thought and the doubts and covert opposition of many or most members of the State's only powerful political organisation, this was no easy task.

The first important technical problem to be solved was not primarily organisational but the construction of a new economic model, one which would endow socially-owned enterprises with the autonomous decision-making power and voice in income distribution (especially distribution of profit, the Marxists' 'surplus value') without which workers' self-management must remain an empty shell. This meant, in effect, dismantling a Soviet-type command economy and replacing it with something else, equally or more perfectly socialist. In such an undertaking there was no historic precedent to learn from; no one had ever attempted it before. Some theoretical help could be found in the work of occasional Marxist economists like the Pole Oskar Lange, who had discussed the idea of a socialist market economy, and later (when the Yugoslavs decided that such theories were ideologically harmless) in some non-Marxist economic theory, but they had not discovered these sources in 1950-52 and even Lange had not considered the special problems of transition from a rigid (and collapsing!) Stalinist model to a market one.[84]

The first eighteen months after June 1950 were marked by a series of administrative and legal changes which were individually of minor significance but which reflected and also reinforced the new approach. They included further hesitant steps which were to lead along the road to abandonment of collectivisation: abolishment of Machine Tractor Stations in September 1950, gradual abandonment of compulsory deliveries in 1951 and the Central Committee's 'Recommendation on Means of Socialist Development in the Village' of November 1951, which again emphasised only improvement of existing SRZs and otherwise concentration on expanding OZZs. Measures affecting the economy adopted in 1951 included the elimination of the State Control Commission in February; the suppression of the Federal Planning Commission and most remaining federal-republican economic ministries and directorates-general in April; no less than three laws (in January, May and September) attempting to free price formation in consumer goods; and the liberation of the consumer from restrictions on his choice of market and an 'administered supply' of agricultural products. All, and particularly the last two, were seen as the first step towards a free market. Voters' meetings were instituted as tribunes for general complaints in December 1950, and the 'transmission belt' concept was declaratively abandoned at congresses of the women's, youth and other organisations gathered in the People's Front. The 4th Plenum of the Central Committee, in June 1951, was primarily concerned with the system of justice, hearing Ranković's confession of UDBa excesses and issuing calls for stricter observance of 'socialist legality', improvement in the Criminal Code, a more independent judiciary and greater respect for individual rights by police and judges.[85]

Whatever their cumulative importance, all of these acts left the central problem untouched. Only at the end of December 1951 was a more comprehensive and meaningful effort made to give substance to the great experiment. The Law on the Planned Management of the National Economy, which was passed at that time and gradually implemented during 1952, was still a very cautious act which was only to be in effect for two years,[86] but it was in fact as important historically as the law which created workers' councils. Representing a further evolution in the thinking of Kidrič, the bill's author, it marked the decisive first step in the transition from a command to a market economy, and it thereby laid the foundations for the second of the complementary twin pillars of 'workers' self-management' and 'market socialism' on which Yugoslavia's unique economic system was to rest.

The Soviet system of planning was abandoned. In its place the Yugoslavs introduced annual (and later medium-term) 'Social Plans', which at the enterprise level were no longer directive and compulsory, but indicative. The new planning system was based on the setting of 'basic proportions', through which the State would continue to plan and control the general and basic parameters of economic growth. In the 1951 law there were three 'basic proportions' which were to fulfil this function: the minimum rate of utilisation of capacity by industrial sector and republic (i.e. the minimum expected aggregate supply); the total volume of 'basic' (State-financed) investment by value, sector and republic, to be distributed through a General Investment Fund (GIF) and Republican Investment Funds (RIFs)—a new device actually established by 1953—rather than through the budget; and the fund needed to meet payrolls at the level of minimum capacity utilisation (i.e. the total minimum wage bill). The remaining 'basic proportions' were instrumental and were intended as temporary measures through which the first three would be implemented: the 'rate of accumulation'—in effect the rate of contribution to Investment Funds and some budgetary 'social funds'—for each sector and for each enterprise in 1953 only, determining and determined by the wage fund (thus dictating by sector the primary distribution of national income into consumption and savings); the distribution of these 'contributions' to the community among Investment Funds and State budgets at various levels (including communal people's committees, thus strengthening the role of local government), etc.[87]

Four elements of the new system require particular comment, for they indicated the direction of future evolution. With 'Social Plans' the State was out of the business of micro-economic planning and of direct, 'command' control over enterprise behaviour. It remained in the business of macro-economic planning through control of primary distribution (savings and consumption) and investment, which for the enterprise meant indicative planning. It therefore no longer wrote production plans, it wrote investment plans. As Pejovich points out, the difference is manifest in a change in planning terminology: after 1953 the language of the Social Plans vis-à-vis the enterprise no longer commands, it anticipates.[88]

The enterprise now enjoyed, for the first time, a degree of genuine autonomy. Instead of implementing detailed production plans prepared and dictated by State agencies, it was itself to determine the type, quantity and quality of its output, its own production processes and the source and kind of inputs. Materials and equipment would be bought and products sold competitively, on the market. Thus the enterprise still could be told, and was extensively told, what it could *not* do (raise wages on its own initiative, raise prices except for certain commodities under certain circumstances, control its own profits, etc.), but it could not be toldwhat it *must* do in the course of normal entrepreneurial activities (buying, producing, selling). It unavoidably became market-oriented, for it now produced to sell, not to fulfil a quota.

Thirdly, what enterprises got from the GIF and other investment funds were credits, to be repaid with interest, and not grants. The Yugoslavs therewith parted company with another dogma, but not without soul-searching. Vukmanović, who was to succeed Kidrič as chairman of the Economic Council when the latter died in 1953, tells the credible story of what happened when he suggested such repayable credits during the discussion before the law was drafted. Kidrič immediately responded: 'That would be returning to capitalism!' After a heated discussion Vukmanović spent a sleepless night reconsidering. He eventually decided that Kidrič had been right and telephoned him in the morning to say so, only to discover that Kidrič had decided that Vukmanović was right: 'But no!', Kidrič said, 'I too spent the night worrying. It doesn't at all mean a return to capitalism. On the contrary, we must accept the principle of credits for investments.'[89]

At the same time real incentives—to productivity, quality, cost-cutting and improved efficiency and competitiveness in general—were still missing, and these had been one of the primary purposes of the exercise and of 'workers' self-management' as a whole. The State guaranteed 90 per cent of the payroll fund, in case the firm could not pay its workers, but through the tax system (the 'contributions' to the Investment Funds and federal, republican and local budgets) and through its integral philosophy 'the State took almost the whole income above the salaries prescribed by the central organs'.[90] To increase salaries it might therefore be useful to heed the suggestions of State organs and to argue for a corresponding reduction in fiscal obligations to the community, but it was not useful to increase enterprise income through greater efficiency. Enterprises could increase their total revenue by increasing sales, but the division of these returns was decided elsewhere, in the political system. Investment policy also remained a State monopoly, and since it was already widely believed that political influence was more likely to win an investment credit from the GIF than a well-documented plan for profitable expansion, this too was a stronger incentive to cultivate well-placed Party or State officials than to efficiency and profitability.

During 1952, with its repeat of the disastrous drought of 1950, the economic situation was again more critical than ever—national income fell to 1,282 billion dinars (at constant 1960 prices), below the 1948 level. In 1953, however, the economy at last escaped from stagnation: national income grew by 18 per cent, to 1,511 billion dinars, and employment, which had fallen by 100,000 in 1951 and by 110,000 in 1952, was up 102,000. It was the beginning of a boom which was to last, with one brief interruption, for a decade. Foreign aid, largely American, was arriving in growing volume and having a major impact.[91]

The Yugoslavs were encouraged by these results, which they interpreted as proof that their economic system was on the right track. They were also, however, bedevilled by problems resulting from lacunae in the law of 1951, by unsuccessful experiments and by a tendency of workers' councils to 'eat accumulation' by raising wages at the expense of investment funds whenever they could. With this multiple motivation, therefore, they embarked on yet another end-of-year economic reform, adopted as a Government Decree in December 1953 and implemented in 1954. The primary target this time was the distribution of enterprise income between the enterprise and the State. The 'system of State determination of rates of accumulation and funds' (as the cumbersome device of 1952-53 had come to be known) was abandoned, to be replaced by 'the system of profit-sharing'—that the word was now acceptable, despite its capitalist connotations, was another indicator of the weakening hold of ideological dogmatism. As defined by the new law, 'profit' was enterprise net income remaining after the following had been paid out of gross income: material costs of production; depreciation; interest rate on fixed assets (the standard rate was 6 per cent, in principle a payment to 'society' for the use of socially-owned capital goods, and in practice a primary source of investment financing through the GIF); interest on credits; turnover taxes; other federal, republican and communal taxes; annuities; and the wage fund. 'Profit', so determined, was then subject to a final federal and republican tax, and the remainder was divided between the local commune and the enterprise itself, with the communal government deciding the proportions. The workers' council of the enterprise then disposed of its share: to the workers as additional wages, to reserve or investment funds, and to collective uses (factory amenities, an enterprise holiday camp or *odmaralište*, workers' housing, etc).[92] This residual share understandably tended to be a very minor or even non-existent share of gross profit, and even where it did exist there were further regulations restricting the proportion which could be shared out in salaries. In 1954, the workers' share amounted to 4·8 per cent of the net profits of the enterprise, a figure which gradually rose to 9·2 per cent in 1957; in proportion to fixed wages it usually amounted to the value of one monthly wage payment (called the 'thirteenth pay-cheque'), but sometimes to two, three or even more.[93]

Thus the 'new economic system' of 1954, although it facilitated more rational book-keeping and created a more rational and predictable tax structure, left the Federal Goverment as the most important single economic actor, actually reduced the power of enterprises to set wages and control the division of their profits and did little to increase incentives. It did, however, further increase the power of the local commune over local enterprises (which now 'elected' their own directors, but on the basis of nominations by a commission to which the communal government elected two-thirds of the members and the workers' council one-third) and strengthened the links between them. The profit-sharing system itself was also subject to annual alterations 'in a game of hide-and-seek between the Federal Government, the local authorities, the management of enterprises, the workers' councils and the workers themselves, all competing for better gains from the profit-sharing legislation'.[94]

The regulations of December 1953 were to be the last significant changes in the economic system for four years, a remarkably long period by Yugoslav standards. As they were being implemented, the Djilas crisis was engaging the full attention of Party leaders, and in its aftermath further liberalisation was unthinkable for some time.

Paralleling the experimental, frequently ill-planned or merely declarative and abruptly revised economic reforms of these exuberant years,[95] political philosophy and the political system also experienced changes, affecting the organisation and style of both State and Party organs.

In particular, the change in the role and status of local government was to prove of long-run importance. The process of progressive emasculation of these organs was stopped, as has been seen, with the Law on People's Committee's of May 1949. In April 1952, after a full year of preparation and three months after the adoption of Kidrič's first significant reform of the economic system, another Law on People's Committee's was presented to the National Assembly by Kardelj, whose province of special interest was now the reform of political institutions. Kardelj utilised the occasion to present another lengthy theoretical discourse, which merits particular and detailed attention. A useful summary of the theoretical position reached by the leadership in its analysis of what had gone wrong in the Soviet Union and could go wrong in Yugoslavia, it was also a relatively complete and early statement of an emerging and specifically Yugoslav theory of the political institutions of a genuine 'socialist democracy', a theory which was to bear more significant fruit in the following decade.[96]

Kardelj began with the by now familiar Yugoslav explanation of monolithic autocracy in the Soviet Union. It was the result of the creation of a centralised bureaucracy with a monopoly of political and economic power, 'inevitably' breeding a bureaucratic 'caste' with more arbitrary, irresponsible power than any 'class' Government in the bourgeois-democratic West, where such a concentration of power is prevented by the growth of political and the survival of economic pluralism. The secret of this continuing autocracy lay not only in economic monopoly under the control of the Party-State bureaucratic apparatus but also in the political 'superstructure', in the suppression of autonomous local government by workers' and peasants' elective organs (the soviets) and their replacement in the 1936 Soviet Constitution by a 'formal' parliamentary system of a Western type, but without a Western multi-party system: 'Thus the Soviet system truly became a "one-party system" in the negative sense of the word.' So long as the working masses have independent organs through which they can express their will and influence higher State organs,

such a system will guarantee them more democratism than any multi-party system. But once such a system is abolished ... and a centralised bourgeois State system enforced, but without its multi-party system, it is then that any talk of democracy becomes downright buffoonery. And that is how matters stand today in the so-called Soviet democracy.[97]

To escape this fate, Kardelj argued, the Yugoslavs must effectively implement three 'basic guiding principles'. The first was a genuine 'leading role of the working class', not as in the Soviet Union through a fictitious 'dictatorship of the proletariat' which was in reality the dictatorship of a few men in the name of the proletariat, but through workers' control of the economy in the system of workers' councils and a workers' share in political decision-making through representation *qua* workers in legislative and administrative bodies. Then there must be genuine decentralisation, the only certain guarantee against a political monopoly by a few at the centre, to be achieved by giving real power to local government organs, with higher State organs controlled by deputies responsible and responsive to them. With the help of these two, the remaining principle—'a clear and consistent course of socialist democratisation in our entire social life and development'—would be achievable. Kardelj now had a vision of the political form this 'socialist democracy' would gradually assume: in effect a hierarchy of 'supreme workers' councils' in which delegates of workers *qua* workers (producers), alongside delegates of the same workers *qua* citizens (consumers), would make decisions on matters of wider communal interest.

This concept had another advantage, Kardelj thought. He had already argued, as we have seen, that a 'bourgeois' parliamentary system without a multi-party system made a mockery of democracy, as in the Soviet Union. Some countries might build socialism and still avoid this danger by retaining a multi-party system, he said, but this was not possible in Yugoslavia. Here any party 'created outside the People's Front' would 'inescapably become the rallying point' for all kinds of anti-socialist forces, both counter-revolutionary and pro-Soviet. They therefore represented a potentially serious threat to the kind of socialist system the Yugoslav revolution was building, and any revolution has the right to defend itself by any means against vital threats to its central values.[98]

In this situation the Yugoslavs must find an alternative to the political institutions of that 'bourgeois form of democracy' which 'presupposes the existence of a. multi-party system'. This, too, could be achieved by the kind of representation the Party was now proposing: 'an organisational mechanism of our socialist democracy which suits its social-economic bases', founded on the twin pillars of local political self-government through people's committees and local economic self-management through workers' council. The goal was 'a new partyless system, in which each individual citizen will even directly, without the mediation of parties, take a conscious part in the functions of social management'.[99] If it was not yet clear, in Kardelj's exposition, why the Party leadership thought that such a system would institutionalise the pluralism of effective participants in public-decision-making which they had come to believe essential to any kind of real 'democracy' (and there is no reason to suppose that they had thought it through in this form at this stage), it did become clear a decade later, when the Constitution of 1963 established multi-chamber parliaments based in part on functional representation: decision-making through public contest among parties based on class or agglomerations of individual interests would be replaced as the guarantor of effective political pluralism by decision-making through a consensus publicly reached among institutionalised functional interest groups.

The new Law on People's Committees which he was introducing was not ideal, Kardelj said, and would have to be replaced 'when our socialism has become still stronger socially-economically', but he hoped that it represented a step in the right direction. An administrative reorganisation of local government units was designed to strengthen them through enlargement to achieve a viable economic base. The existing 7,104 local people's committees were replaced by 3,834 communes (*opštine/opčine*) grouped in 327 counties (*srezovi/kotori*), plus 24 cities without county affiliations. The former executive committees of local government were abolished and political executive functions were vested in the officers of the people's committees. These drew up their own budgets, as they had done since 1949, but now they had the added advantage of a legally stipulated minimum income, independent of the whims of higher administrative organs, in the form of a percentage of enterprise taxes ('social contributions') determined by the Social Plan—an aspect of the December 1951 economic reform which had anticipated the new Law on People's Committees.

The people's committees themselves were now divided into two chambers: a political one, elected by direct, universal suffrage, as before, and a 'Council of Producers', elected by 'working men' in their place of work in the socialist sector of the economy. This was the first step towards realisation of that new concept of functional representation for producers *qua* producers which Kardelj had articulated. In electing delegates to the Councils of Producers, voting power was to be proportional to an economic sector's contribution to national product, a provision which gave significantly greater voting power to industrial workers than to farmers, while 'non-producers'—meaning anyone not employed in productive enterprises in the socialist sector or a member of some kind of agricultural co-operative—did not participate. Kardelj, admitting that such a composition 'cannot, of course, be considered ideal or lasting', attempted to defend it on the ground that it 'accentuates the leading role of the working class'. This was a good Marxist principle, but he also admitted: 'This is the instrument ... by which our working men can prevent deformation of our socialist revolution.'[100] The underrepresentation of the peasantry, who had proved their 'conservatism' and unreliability by their resistance to socialism through collectivisation, was to last for a decade, while privately employed persons were never represented in the Councils of Producers.

The trend towards larger and thus economically stronger communes and counties continued through amalgamation of smaller ones, rationalising the structure of the basic units now that they were politically significant; by 1955 there were 1,479 communes and 107 counties. The fiscal position of the communes, and with it their control over local enterprises, also continued to grow and in fact took a great leap forward with the new economic system of 1954: the people's committees now exercised full control over the profit of their enterprises, as noted above, and could even take it all. This, plus power in appointing enterprise directors, meant that the people's committees and the local organisations of the Party, which controlled them, had acquired a dominant voice in the local economy and in enterprise decision-making, the workers' councils notwithstanding.[101] They also had acquired a strong incentive to have tax-paying enterprises on their territory, a factor of growing and not always healthy importance for national investment policy.

Constitution and Congress

A partial and interim codification of all these new Yugoslav views of the socialist State and economy, in what was in effect a new Constitution, and their extension in theory to the definition of the Communist Party and its role constituted the next and last chapters in the turbulent first phase of the Yugoslav departure from the Soviet model of socialism.

During 1952 a parliamentary commission headed by Pijade drafted an act containing 115 articles and cumbrously entitled a 'Constitutional Law on the Bases of the Social and Political Structure of the Federal People's Republic of Yugoslavia and on the Federal Organs of Power'. Passed by the People's Assembly on January 13, 1953, it replaced most provisions of the now clearly obsolete Constitution of 1946, which was formally retained until 1963 as a kind of appendage, usually referred to as 'the Constitution of January 31, 1946 (Parts which have not been abolished)'. The reason for this curious arrangement, Kardelj explained, was that it was too soon in a period of fundamental political and institutional changes to attempt a complete overhaul of the existing Constitution.[102]

The Party élite's momentary obsession with more extreme forms of decentralisation, their euphoric belief that the national question really had been solved and that a 'Yugoslav socialist consciousness' was taking firm roots, as well as a realistic tendency to ignore a republican autonomy which had been little more than a legal fiction combined to bring a formal down-grading of the status of the republics. These were no longer defined as 'sovereign' (giving rise to a portentous debate between Serbian and Croatian constitutional lawyers),[103] and references to their right to secede were also deleted. Sovereignty was now ascribed to 'the working people'. The 1946 Constitution had assigned to the republics all residual powers not explicitly vested in the Federation or local communities. Under the 1953 law all such powers also belonged to 'the working people' and were vested in their organs of local government—the people's committees—and in their workers' councils and associations of citizens formed in sectors like education, culture and the health services. With these provisions an important new concept, 'social self-management', far broader in scope than 'workers' self-management', had been enunciated.

At the federal level the Chamber of Nationalities of the People's Assembly, in which the republics and provinces were directly represented *per se* and a primary aspect of federalism, was absorbed into the Federal Chamber as a semi-automomous body with few separate competencies. The Federal Chamber thus assumed a split personality, which it was to retain until 1968: most of its deputies represented traditional single-member constituencies, with one deputy for every 60,000 Yugoslavs, but 70 additional deputies were delegated by the republican and provincial assemblies and met separately under specified circumstances.[104] The second chamber in the Federal Assembly (and in the assemblies of the republics and provinces) was now to be a Chamber of Producers, the solution anticipated at the local level by the 1952 Law on People's Committees. The Kardeljian concept of functional or corporativist representation and a 'hierarchy of supreme workers' councils' was thus extended to the republican and federal levels.

The Constitutional Law envisaged direct election of deputies to all of these assemblies and to both kinds of chambers. In 1954, however, members of Chambers of Producers at all but the local level were elected indirectly, by the local people's committees, and after 1957 all assembly chambers above the communal level except the Federal Chamber were indirectly elected. This was an additional measure of practical caution and concern to retain Party control which corresponded nicely with Kardelj's evolving theoretical preference for total abandonment of 'bourgois concepts' of political representation.

Other important changes included the institution of a President (in place of a Presidium of the People's Assembly as a collective Head of State), a post to which Tito was duly elected. The Federal Government was transformed from a traditional Council of Ministers into a Federal Executive Council (FEC), which was supposed to be a collegial political executive without administrative functions or individual ministerial responsibilities. Another characteristic Kardeljian idea, the attempt to separate political and administrative organs and functions as an 'anti-bureaucratic' device was to be tried again and in various forms in later years but never worked.[105] The President of the Republic was to be the FEC's presiding officer. In the federal administration, the 1953 arrangement (already amended in 1956 and frequently thereafter) called for the establishment of only five 'State secretariats', corresponding to five major areas of federal responsibility and headed by State Secretaries appointed by the FEC. In other sectors like health, education and culture, ministers were replaced by 'councils' as a further token of their removal in theory from the State to the 'self-management' sector. Like many other reforms of the period, the concept embodied in this arrangement began to assume practical significance only a decade later.

With an eye on the eternally sensitive national question, the Constitutional Law also specified that the FEC must include members from all the republics and that the presidents of the republican executive councils would be *ex officio* members of the FEC, but it was not stipulated that the regions and nationalities must be proportionately represented—a further step taken only in 1971. On one calculation, for example, the FEC in 1959 was composed, by republic of origin, as follows:

	No.	Per cent		No.	Per cent
Serbia	10	29	Bosnia-Herzegovina	4	12
Croatia	2	6	Macedonia	3	9
Slovenia	6	18	Montenegro	9	26

The most dramatic over- and under-representation respectively was that of Montenegro (3 per cent of the total population) and Croatia (22 per cent).[106]

The possibility that the State institutions which the Constitutional Law had rearranged might actually come to play a genuine political role had already been significantly enlarged two months earlier, at the 6th Congress of the CPY, through a dramatic redefinition of the function and role of the hitherto only really important political institution, the Party. Like the redefinition of the socialist State, that of the Party was rooted in the Yugoslav critique of 'what had gone wrong' in the Soviet Union and might also go wrong in Yugoslavia, and in the implications of the theory of social self-management.

Tito's first recorded suggestion that total identification of Party and State in the Soviet Union was a major factor in the exploitation of the working class there occurred in his speech introducing the Law on Workers' Councils to the People's Assembly in June 1950. That same week a Central Committee directive ordered an end to the almost universal practice of Party secretaries also serving as presidents of district people's committees in order to prevent excessive and direct Party interference in State matters.[107] By early 1952, the problem of the definition and role of the Party in a socialist democracy, already discussed at the second regional conference of the Communist Party of Croatia in December 1950 and at Plenums of the republican central committees in the spring of 1951,[108] had become a dominant theme in the theoretical writings of the Politburo ideologists.

In the course of this debate the rulers of Yugoslavia for the first time confronted and then sought to evade the central ideological and political dilemma of their concept of socialist democracy. Their view of the problem was summarised in Tito's statement, made during the Brioni Plenum which purged Djilas in January 1954, was to appear again in—different circumstances— among the slogans of the Belgrade University student revolt of 1968: 'There is no true democracy without socialism or socialism without democracy'. If this were true, how could one speak of democracy without transparent hypocrisy—or a stipulative definition like the Soviet one, which the Yugoslavs had now joined the West in condemning as hypocrital—if a closed and self-recruiting Party élite or even an internally democratic but Leninist cadre Party continued to exercise a monopoly of all political power? But if it did not, who would guarantee that genuinely democratic decision-making processes would produce genuinely 'socialist' decisions, especially in a still largely traditional society in which the socialist values of the élite (called 'socialist consciousness' in the Party vocabulary) had not been accepted and internalised by everyone or even by a majority?

The Yugoslav answer which emerged in the course of the debate, to be sanctioned by the 6th Congress, was that the Party must separate itself from the State and from day-to-day political decision-making *per se,* but must continue to act as 'an ideological and political leading force'. It would square this particular circle by sacrificing *power,* exercised by monopolising political participation and by fusing State and Party apparatus, in favour of *influencing* open and democratic decision-making on specific issues through education, propaganda and the active participation of individual Communists in the life and politics of enterprises, workers' councils, local government organs, etc. The policies which these individual Communists would advocate in turn would be the product of a free intra-Party debate by internally democratic Party organisations and a democratically elected hierarchy, with the decisions binding on all members through the rules of democratic centralism. In addition, although some members of the inner élite now for the first time also considered reintroducing a multi-party system as part of democratisation,[109] the rejection of this possibility tacitly endowed the Yugoslav Party's redefined leading role with another political weapon of vital importance. While the Party was in principle to abandon its monopoly over the political decision-making process, it would not abandon its monopoly of explicitly political *organisation*. Thus as long as they maintained internal unity and discipline through strict enforcement of the rules of democratic centralism, this monopoly would almost always, if not invariably, give Communists an insuperable advantage over the unorganised forces of the country's non-Communists in elections to leading posts and in decision-making in the People's Front, the trade unions, municipal governments and enterprise organs of management. As added insurance, although not an explicit public part of the new scheme, steps would be taken to ensure that members of the inner Party élite would themselves continue to occupy the key posts in key institutions like the People's Front, the trade unions, and the federal and republican executive councils. Nominations to other important but lower-ranking executive positions would at least be subject to the *nihil obstat* of appropriate Party organs. The Soviet device of the *Nomenklatura*[110] would thus remain in a modified and unofficial form.

The 6th Congress met in Zagreb during the first week of November 1952. Tito devoted a large part of his keynote speech to a sharp attack on Soviet international and domestic policies and to their roots in the nature of Soviet 'State capitalism' and other 'revisions' of Marxism–Leninism. He thereby put the seal of the 6th Congress on the Yugoslav revision of Stalinism and of the fulsome praise which had been heaped on the Soviet Union and its leader at the preceding Congress. Kidrič, already dying of leukaemia and making his last public speech, indicated the direction in which the last turn in his own rethinking of socialist economic theory was taking him and the Yugoslav economy. 'The new economic system', he said, 'must be based on objective economic laws and must to the greatest possible degree avoid administrative smothering of those laws.' There should be interference with them only where absolutely necessary to 'prevent the appearance of capitalist anarchy' and to 'give a general direction' to economic development. The alternative of State-planned quantities and assortment and investment grants out of central budgets, which sought to ignore these laws, had been tested and found wanting, for they had led to arbitrariness, irrationality and economic stagnation.[111]

The most important business of the Congress, the redefinition of the Party which it was to endorse, was symbolized by a change of name. The CPY became the LCY, the League of Communists of Yugoslavia. Djilas claimed later that the new name was his idea, and that he only remembered afterwards that it was what Marx himself had called the First International a century earlier.[112] The Congress as a whole has often been identified with Djilas and his ideas; he drafted the Resolution, and Vukmanović and Dedijer recalled much later (when they had every reason not to) that Djilas's speech at the closing session was for them the highlight of the meeting.[113] The decisions which it endorsed nevertheless again represented a consensus of the top leadership, reached through the subtle process which has already been described. It was Tito (and Kardelj), not Djilas, who in 1951 had first referred to 'the withering away of the Party',[114] as Tito was to recall somewhat ruefully at the Brioni Plenum which expelled Djilas for taking the suggestion seriously and insisting that it should happen at once.[115]

The Resolution and Statute adopted by the 6th Congress redefined the role of the Party. The 'basic duty and role of Communists' was 'political and ideological work in educating the masses'. The LCY 'is not and cannot be the direct operative manager and commander in economic, State, or social life'. Primarily by means of persuasion it was to influence all other bodies and institutions to adopt 'its line or the views of its individual members'.[116] Significant changes in the wording of the Statute included a description of the LCY as 'the conscious and most progressive organised section of the working class' rather than its 'vanguard'. Instead of the 'leading role' of the Party, Kardelj spoke of its 'conscious role'.

Party meetings in basic (local) organisations were henceforth to be public and non-Communists should be encouraged to attend, a provision which Fred Neal successfully tested by attending Belgrade Party meetings in 1954.[117] Political bureaux in basic organisations were replaced by a single Party secretary or a three-man secretariat in larger organizations. The principle of separation of Party and State was expressed in the abolition of Party organisations in the State bureaucracy and in non-governmental public organs; Communists in such bodies were to work only as individuals or members of an *aktiv*. Basic Party organisations would henceforth be founded on functional and territorial divisions like factories, urban communities and villages. Higher

Party organs would no longer have authority to assign specific operational tasks to lower one, but would only prescribe general policy and suggestions for implementation. Regional and local Party organisations were given more autonomy; the Central Committee was no longer to appoint Party organisers to take over their affairs and basic organisations were authorised to enrol or expel their members without reference to higher authority. An eighteen-month period of candidature before full membership was no longer required.

At the top of the pyramid the Politburo, its name changed to Executive Committee as another token of the break with Stalinist precedents, was expanded to thirteen members. Tito was re-elected as Secretary-General, and all eight members of the old Politburo were elected to the new Executive Committee.[118] Three of the new members, significantly, were the Party and governmental heads of their respective republics: Bakarić of Croatia, Djuro Pucar of Bosnia-Herzegovina and Lazar Koliševski of Macedonia. With Leskošek resident in Slovenia, four members of the new Party summit would not live in Belgrade or play primarily federal roles. This, too, was a more important real harbinger of future developments than the formal downgrading of the status of the republics in the Constitutional Law. The other new members were Vukmanović as the dying Kidrič's heir-designate in the economy, and Salaj as head of the trade unions.

While divorcing the Party from the State and intra-Party decentralisation and democratisation were thus the dominant themes of the Congress, Tito and Ranković (the latter interpreting the new Statute in his capacity as the Politburo member responsible for organisational matters) emphasised that democratic centralism was still the basic rule of Party life. Tito further insisted that 'the League of Communists not only does not reduce its role in and its responsibility for the successful development of socialism, but further increases its role and responsibility'. Ranković made the same point and warned that preoccupation with 'the danger of the bureaucratic method of work' had in many cases 'led to the other extreme'. Many Party members had understood the new line to mean that Party organisations

should be engaged only in some general and highbrow political problems, not delving into basic problems of the enterprise, village, institution, school, etc. The result has been that some Party organisations remained passive during elections of workers' councils and leaderships of certain mass organisations, as well as during the solving of certain very important political and economic problems in some towns, villages, enterprises and universities.[119]

How Tito's and Ranković's emphasis on democratic centralism and the Party's increased responsibility—or the continuation of the practice of putting individual Party Executive Committee members in charge of all key 'sub-systems'—could be reconciled with the Resolution and the new Statute's emphasis on divorcing the Party from power and on its own decentralisation was not answered. Those who had invented the new definition did not have an answer. Neither did perplexed Party members in the field, who were now told in one and the same breath that their responsibility for the making and implementation of 'correct' socialist decisions had increased but that their power to fulfil that responsibility must diminish. Their dilemma and that of their leaders was to dominate Yugoslav political life in the decades to come.

Later, after his fall from power, Djilas was to conclude that even this version of the role of the Party defined at the 6th Congress, or anything short of a multi-party system, would inevitably corrupt Communists into a ruling caste and socialism into at least a modified version of Soviet autocracy.[120] Even without this extreme conclusion, the vision which Djilas himself had helped to articulate in 1952-53 was dogged by another cardinal weakness—the quality of the Party's membership. The Party had grown by another 68 per cent since the 5th Congress in July 1948, to reach a total of 780,000 members at the end of 1952. Many if not most of these and earlier postwar additions consisted of the kinds of careerists, opportunists and thugs who are inevitably attracted by an apparatus exercising such power. Such people, added to the primitivism and 'low ideological level' of the peasant-based Party of 1945, helped to make the LCY an increasingly inappropriate instrument for the implementation of the principles enunciated by the Politburo's intellectual ideologists and endorsed by the 6th Congress.[121] Most Party members and leaders either honestly did not know how or were disinclined to attempt to substitute the subtle practice of ideological and political persuasion for simpler and surer methods like holding positions of power and issuing orders backed by coercive sanctions. 'Confusion in the ranks', characterised by demoralisation or stubborn resistance to change, was already widespread before the 6th Congress and became endemic in subsequent months.[122]

In February 1953, delegates of the now 7 million members of the People's Front assembled for their 4th Congress and changed its name to the Socialist Alliance of the Working People of Yugoslavia (SAWPY). At the Party Congress Tito and Kardelj had admitted that the People's Front had suffered a 'certain stagnation' since the end of the war, its role confined largely to mobilising 'voluntary' labour projects. Now, at the Front's own Congress, Kardelj's keynote speech seemed to herald a new day of vastly increased political importance for the organisation. The Alliance, he said, 'should be the political foundation of all State and social self-governing bodies; in extensive discussion and criticism these bodies will here be under the supervision of the masses.' To this end, he said,

It will be necessary to put an end ... to the practice whereby the Party organisations at their meetings decided all political and other questions and then simply forwarded these decisions to the People's Front organisations for approval. The tasks of the League of Communists should primarily be turned to ideological questions ... and to similar matters, while concrete political and other social questions should be settled directly in the organisations of the Socialist Alliance.[123]

It never turned out that way. It is nevertheless unclear whether the declaration of intent was never serious and merely a feeble domestic and international obfuscation of Communist dictatorship,[124] or whether events of the following eleven months caused a retreat from a genuine might-have-been.

One other statement in Kardelj's speech meanwhile heralded another policy change of real and lasting importance. At some point in the weeks since the Party Congress, at which the Party line on agriculture was not modified, Bakarić and other opponents of collectivisation had finally won the day with their colleagues on the Executive Committee. As Kardelj told the SAWPY delegates:

Practice has shown us that the existence of a strong socialist sector in the economy—if economic relationships between it and agriculture are laid down correctly—must encourage the socialist transformation of agricultural production, naturally, gradually and in forms corresponding to economic requirements. Practice has also shown that compulsion—and there has been compulsion in our country in spite of Comrade Tito's unceasing warnings—and the creation of artifical structures in this area as well yielded only negative economic results.[125]

One month later, on March 30, 1953, an FEC regulation sanctioned the dissolution of the SRZs. Peasants could leave, taking their equipment and land with them, and the entire SRZ could be dissolved if all its members voted to do so; clearly unprofitable ones had to be dissolved.[126] The effect was predictable: by the end of 1953 only 1,152 SRZs were left, with 192,582 members. In the Vojvodina, where the largest concentration had been found, two-thirds of the peasants abandoned the collectives within nine months. The number of SRZs continued to decline until a bare two dozen were left in the mid-1960s; by 1957 the share of the entire socialist sector in Yugoslavia's total arable land had sunk to 9 per cent from a 1952 record of 25 per cent. For a decade after 1953 the regime had no real agricultural policy beyond vague and largely inneffective promotion of general co-operatives, the OZZs, as a gradualist road to 'socialist relations' in the countryside.

Besides residual dogmatism and lack of any guidance from the

Marxist classics on which reforms in other areas were based,
political reasons why the surrender to the peasants had come so
tardily and reluctantly included the problem of some 100,000
landless peasants in the SRZs, most of them Bosnian and
Montenegrin ex-Partisans resettled in the Vojvodina after the war,
and the even greater problem of morale among Party activists in
the countryside, whose main task had been promoting collectivisation and then attempting to rationalise the existing SRZs. As a
gesture towards mitigating both these problems, but in theory to
prevent the growth of 'capitalistic tendencies' in the countryside,
the Vojvodina Party leader, Jovan Veselinov, proposed a further
restriction in the maximum permitted size of individual holdings,
from the 25–35 hectares of cultivable land allowed by the 1945
agrarian reform to 10 hectares. The restriction was apparently
opposed by a group within the Party, again headed by Bakarić,
who denied that a peasant owning 25 hectares could exhibit
'capitalist tendencies', and who argued that the measure would
only add to the difficulty of increasing agricultural production.
Veselinov's proposal nevertheless received the backing of key
leaders, including Kardelj, who saw the importance of the political
issues involved, and became law on May 27, 1953.[127] It in fact
affected only 275,000 hectares belonging to 66,459 households, 3·7
per cent of the total arable land and 2 per cent of the peasant
population,[128] but its more important effect, as Bakarić had
foreseen, was to prevent the development of household farms of an
economically efficient size. Despite periodic and at times serious
efforts to increase the legal limit after 1965, the 10-hectare
maximum was still law, modified only by a concession to mountain
farmers in 1970, more than two decades later.

  The 6th LCY Congress, the 4th SAWPY Congress, the economic
reform decreed in December 1953 and the surrender to the private
peasantry represented the high point and the end of the first phase
of liberalisation and emancipation from Soviet precedents. On
March 3, 1953, just after the SAWPY Congress and as Tito was
about to embark on a State visit to Great Britain which symbolised
the high level achieved in Yugoslavia's rapprochement with the
West, Stalin died. In June the new Soviet leaders proposed and the
Yugoslavs agreed to exchange ambassadors again, and a gradual
'normalisation' of relations with the Soviet bloc began. At the same
time the Yugoslav economy at last emerged from its prolonged
crisis, as already described, and began an eight-year period of
uninterrupted and unprecedented growth. Meanwhile, the
demoralisation and confusion of the Party rank and file after the
6th Congress and the final abandonment of collectivisation—a
demoralisation therefore particularly marked in the countryside[129]—became a matter of increasing concern at the Party

centre. Others in and outside the Party, encouraged by all these developments, excitedly discussed the maturity of Yugoslav society for further 'democratisation', a discussion which sometimes included reconsideration of a second socialist party, possibly based on a further evolution of the Socialist Alliance.

The net effect of all these developments on Tito and some of his chief lieutenants was to induce a cautious reappraisal. Tito was to declare eighteen years later that he 'had never liked the 6th Congress' (see Chapters 7 and 8). His emphasis on democratic centralism and Party responsibility at the time and his reaction to almost all later moments of stress or crisis suggests that this was true, or at least that he always nurtured doubts and reservations about the line adopted in November 1952. Now his response to post-Congress developments—expectations of further reforms which seemed to him dengerous, the revival of the economy and decreased dependence on Western aid, the possibilities which he perceived in the Yugoslav-Soviet rapprochement and especially the demoralisation of his Party—led him to summon his Central Committee to decree a hesitant and small step backwards from the implications of the 6th Congress. Within seven months the writings of one member of the inner circle, Milovan Djilas, and the aggravation of the Party's confusion which Djilas's articles caused were to lead to a further step backwards and a freeze in that posture. It lasted, where the role of the Party was concerned, for more than a decade.

The Yugoslav system after 1954 nevertheless differed radically from that of 1949, when the first great debate about the nature of a socialist State and economy began. A number of basic ideological doctrines and the rhetoric of self-management now distinguished Yugoslav theory and political style from those of the Soviet Union and all other Communist-ruled States. If these had not yet had much effect on 'real life' and ordinary people, the permanent legacy of the reforms of 1950-53 also included one fundamental change in the very nature of the system which would eventually have such an effect. In Yugoslavia the role of the State in the economy and of the Party in the State were both now indirect. The deeper significance of this fact, however intimately the economy, the State and the Party might remain interconnected and controlled by the last, was that these three basic 'sub-systems' had been definitively disaggregated and given separate formal structures with inherent capacities for autonomous growth. The 'monolithic global social system' of 1949 was no more.

3

CONSOLIDATION AND DEVELOPMENT

The Djilas crisis

The Brioni islands, just off the south-western tip of Istria, were developed under Italian rule between the world wars as a luxury resort of villas scattered along narrow lanes winding through a parkland of meadows, ancient woods and seaside Roman ruins. After the Yugoslavs took possession in 1947 they became a resort for the very top level of the new Communist élite and Tito's favourite personal retreat. In June 1953, he summoned the LCY Central Committee to meet him there, the first time a postwar Central Committee had met outside Belgrade and the 2nd Plenum of the one elected at the 6th Congress. Djilas, already beginning to move beyond his comrades in the radicalism of his criticism of the Party's tendency to become a privileged and exclusive 'bureaucratic caste' when in power, did not like the implications of the choice of setting and said so, but 'Kardelj replied that this was of no importance, and the others kept a downcast silence'.[1] Consciously or not, Tito was setting a significant precedent. A Plenum held at Brioni in the years to come, beginning with the 3rd Plenum of January 1954, usually signified a major decision or moment of crisis at the Yugoslav Party summit.

The purpose of the 2nd Plenum was to analyse and pass judgement on the performance and morale of the Party since the 6th Congress. The judgement was on both points nervously critical. 'In carrying out the decisions of the 6th Congress', a letter addressed to all Party organisations by the Plenum stated,

two basic negative tendencies have appeared: *first*, in various conceptions that Communists are now freeing themselves from responsibility for the future development of socialism; that the role of Communists is now reduced to holding lectures; that the development of democratism means that it is no longer necessary to struggle against anti-socialist phenomena and tendencies, that the positions taken by organisations and leaderships of the League of Communists on questions of the political struggle and socialist development no longer obligate Communists; that abolishing the methods of command in the work of Communists means that Communists are renouncing the struggle for their conceptions and goals; that they no longer need to have their own positions, etc.; and the *second* negative tendency [is] in the conception that nothing has changed in the method and way of work after the 6th Congress; that work continues in the old way; that democracy is our agitation-propaganda tactic, and so on.[2]

It was further said that 'all kinds of uncertainty and anti-Marxist theories are starting to appear', that many Communists were becoming passive and adopting 'petty-bourgeois-arnarchist ideas of freedom and democracy', and that 'the struggle for ideological and political unity is very weak'. The concept of 'the withering away of the Party' had been generally misunderstood; this idea concerned only the distant future, when the final liquidation of class enemies and contradictions meant that strong, unified ideological leadership would no longer be required.

Djilas did not like this either. As he recalled many years later:

On the following day, on the road through Lika on our way to fish for trout, I told Kardelj that I would not be able to support the course we were now adopting. He, very wisely, avoided the issue, remarking merely that I was exaggerating what was a transitional stage in 'our socialist development', not an essential feature of it.[3]

Djilas returned to his writing desk convinced, as he told the 3rd Plenum which condemned him seven months later, that the Brioni Plenum 'had been one-sided, that it had forgotten the struggle against bureaucratism, and that this Plenum had somehow to be corrected'.[4]

During the next months several articles he wrote stressing the need to fight for more democracy and against bureaucratism and other relics of Stalinism[5] were well received, and he determined to step up his campaign. In mid-October he began to publish in *Borba* the series which was to precipitate the crisis. He consulted Tito, who thought that what he had published so far reflected 'what many of us had already said or written about the matter'. As for the present series, 'There are some things I do not agree with,' Tito said, 'but in the main there are good things in them.... Go on with it.'[6]

Djilas did. Until the summer of 1953 he had if anything lagged behind Kardelj and some others in the intimate inner circle in the timing and intensity of his criticism, but now, having taken the bit between his Montenegrin teeth, he pushed this criticism to its logical conclusion. He did so with the blithe disregard for the political consequences of a pure intellectual and of the only member of the inner circle who did not hold an administrative job to keep him in touch with Yugoslav backwoods opinion, with the turbulence of rapid and frightening social change and with popular as well as Party unpreparedness for what he was proposing.

The Yugoslav Party's evolving social and self-critique had always been an intimate and private undertaking by a handful of men at the Party summit, as we have seen. Now it was explosively concentrated in the ultimate intimacy and privacy of the mind of one man, who was first unconsciously and then consciously cutting himself off from his comrades, sometimes deliberately slighting or insulting them when they met, as he gradually realised that he was parting company with them and perversely wished them to know it too.[7] The psychological dynamics of this fact, both within Djilas and in his relationships with his colleagues, were as important to the course of events as what he wrote, and were intimately connected to the evolution of his thought. Djilas had broken the unwritten rules of the process of collective thinking and consensus-building among old comrades. He was criticising as though from the outside (Vukmanović and others noted and reacted to the significant slip which now led him occasionally to refer to the inner élite as 'they' rather than 'we'), an act which the inner circle never learned to tolerate, even in later decades. And he was unprecedentedly doing this in public, in the pages of *Borba*, without—except for his cursory conversation with Tito—having done it first in private, within the group.

By midway in the process it could no longer be otherwise: during the night of December 7-8, Djilas tells us, his conversion was complete and he knew what he had to do. He discovered that the liberty of the individual human spirit, not communism, was his one ultimate and uncompromisable value, and he embraced it with the same fanatical devotion which he had once given to his earlier god. His description of that night suggests two images: one of Saul of Tarsus on the Damascus road and the other of Prince Lazar on the night before the battle of Kosovo, offered a choice of a heavenly or an earthly kingdom and choosing the former. It was characteristic and significant that Djilas, unlike Saul of Tarsus, deliberately avoided making any effort to organise support for his views. The true prophet bearing witness converts by the passion and truth of his words, not by mundane politicking, and Djilas's purpose, although he went about it in a remarkably inept way, was the conversion and not the manipulation or overthrow of his friends. In this tortured introspective mood, having made his struggle a purely intra- and inter-personal and no longer a social and political one, it had also become literally impossible for him to do what very numerous Party and non-Party Yugoslav supporters of his views have ever since bitterly criticised him for not doing. This was to remain in power by only slightly moderating the expression of those views and so remain in a position, as one of the four most powerful men in the country, to work for their more gradual realisation.

Until the end of November, the *Borba* series, written in Djilas's complex and obscure ideological style, had said little that was new or startling in the 1953 Yugoslav context.[8] Then the articles gradually became sharper and more focused. Beginning with attacks on 'bureaucratism' and advocacy of greater freedom as largely abstract concepts, and with references to Soviet practice which were implicit attacks on the 2nd Plenum in the name of the 6th Congress, he passed on with quickening steps to increasingly specific attacks on the survival of Stalinist thinking and Leninist forms of organisation and command in the Yugoslav Party. These for Djilas had become the chief remaining impediments—along with those who could not or would not see that it was so—to the immediate realisation of a genuine socialist democracy, to a society of workers and peasants freely debating and accepting or rejecting the advice of the LCY. As for the League itself, its role should become that of a ginger group, a band of progressive 'Communist-democrats' generating and offering pioneering and progressive socialist ideas and policies to that free society. The selfless and progressive content of these ideas would be guaranteed by the motivations on which membership carrying neither power nor privileges would be based. Although he claimed that he was not advocating 'the dissolution of the League of Communists', which he called 'a ridiculous suggestion', his proposal must seem to others to be just that:

Thus the League of Communists would change from the old Party into a real and vital union of ideologically united men.... The present League of Communists would 'weaken', 'wither away' as a classical party.... [It] would gradually take on the character of a strong, ideological, widely-diffused nucleus, but would lose its party character. It would merge with the Socialist Alliance, and the communists would merge with ordinary citizens ...

By the time he arrived at this conclusion, in an article published on January 4, 1954, he had been warned that Tito, secluded in his winter retreat in a castle near Ljubljana, was 'very angry' and that other old friends like Kardelj (with whom he had had a long talk on December 22) were aghast at the implications of the later articles. Kardelj and Ranković again confronted and argued with him at length, but he would not withdraw.[9] Instead he rushed into print, in *Nova misao*, with another and different article, titled 'Anatomy of a Moral'. It was an undigested mixture of sensitive, poetic writing and crude political caricature. It used an actual case, the social ostracism of the beautiful actress bride of the Partisan hero and Yugoslav chief of staff Peko Dapčević by the preten-tiously *arriviste* ex-Partisan wives of the élite—names were not used, but everyone could identify the persons—as a vehicle for a scathing attack on the degeneration of a band of revolutionaries into a narrow caste corrupted by power and privilege. It was a strangely suicidal act; Djilas must have realised that making enemies of the wives of one's friends is extremely dangerous.

At this point Kardelj informed him that a Party commission had been appointed to initiate proceedings against him. It was headed by Bakarić, 'presumably', Djilas wrote later, 'because his opinions were close to mine'.[10] On January 10, *Borba* announced that Djilas's articles were 'contrary to the opinion of all other members of the Executive Committee' and would be considered at a Central Committee meeting the following week. The Party rank and file and editors of the Party press, assuming that Djiilas was still speaking with Tito's authority, had been reacting to his articles with a wave of enthusiasm which was sometimes dutiful but often genuine.[11] Alarmed by this reaction, Tito moved.

Djilas was arraigned before the Central Committee, again summoned to Brioni for its 3rd Plenum, on January 16 and 17. The proceedings, unprecedently, were broadcast live to the country. The method and the penalty invoked were in calculated contrast to those of purge trials in the Soviet Union, but the function was, *ceteris paribus*, the same: the public isolation and disgrace of one who had grievously erred, if possible to end with his confession and recantation.

Tito led off with a political condemnation of Djilas. Kardelj followed with a tortuous ideological refutation of his ideas. It was not the chief court ideologist's best performance, and it was the non-ideological Tito, not Kardelj, who pinpointed the vital ideological 'error' underlying Djilas's conceptions. In one of his last *Borba* articles, published on December 31, Djilas had poured scorn on continuing insistence on the 'class struggle' in Yugoslavia, pointing out its insidious consequences:

… the class structure of society has changed, but the theory remains more or less unchanged. The bourgeoisie is in every respect a vestige of a former class, and in the big cities, even the petty-bourgeoisie is gone. Continuing the struggle against the bourgeois reactionaries … must now deviate into bureaucratism, into conflict with plain people because they hold differing opinions…. Stories about intensifying the class struggle above the law and in spite of the law undermine legality and democracy.

Not so, said Tito:

For Djilas there are no longer classes, there is no longer a class enemy, all are now equal. But his case proves precisely how dangerous the class enemy still is. The class enemy exists … in the very breast of the League of Communists and assumes the most varied forms.

On this basis Tito re-emphasised what had already been said at the 2nd Plenum:

I was the first to speak of the withering away of the Party, the withering away of the League. However I did not say that that ought to happen within six months or a year or two, but that it would be a long process. Until the last class enemy had been rendered incapable of action, until socialist consciousness has penetrated all layers of our citizenry, there can be no question of the withering away of the League of Communists or of its liquidation.[12]

This was a theme, a rationalisation of renewed Party control, and even phrasing to which Tito would return twenty years later, when the 'class struggle' had all but disappeared from the Party's vocabulary.

Djilas responded, rather confusedly, and for two days the other members of the Committee heaped ideological, political and moral scorn on him. In the end Djilas spoke again. It was an almost complete and almost abject recantation, from which he soon retreated and which has been the subject of many contradictory and unsatisfactory explanations, including his own. But he also stubbornly repeated that the Party was 'the chief obstacle in the way of democratic and socialist development', which was the main point. He was purged from the Central Committee and given a 'final warning', a Party punishment just short of expulsion. He was soon stripped of all his State offices, including the Presidency of the Federal Assembly to which he had just been elected, ironically while the last of the *Borba* series was appearing. Three months later he resigned from the Party on his own initiative. With that act he began his lonely road to isolation and then prison, to contemplation and literary works of better stylistic quality and human insights than his writings as a Party or anti-Party polemicist ever revealed, and eventually to a quiet life of mature philosophical reflection in a modestly comfortable flat on Palmotićeva street in Belgrade. It is a few yards from the parliament building ... *za svaki slučaj* (just in case), he tells his visitors with a self-ironic smile.

At the Brioni meeting the only people who defended Djilas were his ex-wife Mitra Mitrović, somewhat indecisively, and Vlado Dedijer, with characteristic courage and emotion. The latter was to join Djilas in ostracism, and then go into voluntary exile instead of prison until he worked his passage home ten years later, because he violated the unanimity of condemnation which was supposed to characterise the meeting by telling the Plenum the truth:

Milovan Djilas's postulates in *Borba* were more or less adopted by the majority of us sitting here.... All of us, if we put our hands on our hearts, would admit it.... All at once the very same people who approved these articles are attacking Djilas fiercely.... How can we think one thing today and all of a sudden change our opinions overnight?[13]

Tito had already offered one answer, when he told the Plenum that he had realised that Djilas's ideas would lead 'to anarchy, to a terrible uncertainty. If we permitted this, in a year's time our socialist reality would not exist. It would not exist, I tell you, without a bloody battle.'[14] But Djilas himself had already provided another if less dramatic argument in his last important article before he began the fatal *Borba* series. 'To renounce power', he wrote in August 1953, 'is possible and progressive and socialist, but only in so far as that renounced power does not come into someone else's hands, in so far as simply nobody (no other class, party) seizes it.'[15] It was when they realised that he was proposing such a renunciation immediately, and when they paused to list those other hands which would seek to seize the power relinquished by the Party—some may genuinely have thought of 'class enemies' but it must have occurred to others that only UDBa and the army would then be left as organised forces with a political potential—that even those who agreed with Djilas's criticism shrank from his conclusions. Their addition to the ranks of those eager to find any excuse for not relinquishing power left Djilas virtually alone at the only political level which mattered.

Tito and Khrushchev

'Djilas did us a great disservice because he stopped progress for a decade', a commonly heard remark among Yugoslav Communists of liberal persuasion in the early 1960s, proved an unexpectedly accurate estimate of the time it would take for the Party pigeons, sent into alarmed flight by the cat which his ideas had set among them, to come back to where they had been when he did it. Djilas had at most, however, intensified a process of retrenchment and reappraisal which had begun before and indeed inspired his famous series of articles, as we have seen. It had many other causes. These, to recapitulate, included the behaviour of the economy, demoralisation and resistance at all Party levels to the challenge to their power and privileges, and fear at the Party summit (to which Djilas's ideas and widespread positive response to them seemed to add further justification) that the Party's grip on the vital levers of power had already been relaxed too far too soon, encouraging the revival of liberal or anarchic 'bourgeois' democratic conceptions for which there was still fertile soil in Yugoslav social structures and popular attitudes. They also included the international situation in general, the evolution of Soviet domestic and East European policies in particular, and the way these were perceived by Tito and others in the Yugoslav leadership.

The last of these factors did not play the almost exclusive or unidirectional cause-and-effect role ascribed to it by those who have seen periods of Yugoslav liberalisation as a simple function of quarrels with the East and dependence on the West, and periods of 'tightening up' as a necessary, and for many in the leadership an enthusiastic, sacrifice on the altar of a sequence of rapprochements with the East.[16] A relationship existed, but it was more subtle, complex and at times contradictory than is suggested by the simple notation that the 2nd Plenum took place during the same month in which Belgrade and Moscow began 'normalising' relations, or that intensified efforts to tighten internal Party discipline and political authoritarianism occurred during the high tides of the first and second rapprochements in 1956 and 1957.

Despite gradual 'normalisation' of diplomatic and commercial relations, mutual criticism in the press continued at close to its wonted level of violence during most of 1954, suggesting that the improvement in relations was merely part of the overall diplomacy of détente being pursued by the new Soviet leadership. There were some indications from Moscow in October and November that more might be contemplated, but a statement by Molotov in February 1955 saying that a further improvement in relations mainly depended on Yugoslavia brought a sharp rejoinder by Tito. This was taken to mean that an ideological reconciliation, if ever really contemplated, had misfired. Hence a sudden announcement on May 14, that a high-level Soviet delegation headed by Party First Secretary N. S. Khrushchev and Premier N. A. Bulganin would make an official visit to Yugoslavia before the end of the month, took the world by surprise. It only later became apparent that the visit had been in preparation for six months, and that Molotov's speech had signalled opposition by some members of the Soviet leadership.[17]

The scene at Belgrade airport on May 27, 1955, has been described many times: Tito standing rigid and unsmiling in his immaculate Marshal's uniform while Khrushchev, a Party leader significantly heading what was ostensibly a State delegation, shuffled to the microphone in his rumpled summer suit to read to the world the Soviet Party's abject apology and confession of its historic guilt for the quarrel with Yugoslavia.[18] 'We sincerely regret what happened', Khrushchev said. Since Stalin was not yet under attack, he blamed it all on 'the now unmasked enemies of the people, Beria, Abakumov and others.' After thorough study, he said it was clear that 'the grave accusations and insults' levelled against the Yugoslav leaders had been based on 'material ... fabricated by enemies of the people, the contemptible agents of imperialism, who had fraudulently wormed their way into the ranks of our Party'. Now, however, all that was over. The Soviet leaders were ready to 'take all necessary steps' to remove the obstacles to 'completely normal relations between our States' and to strengthen friendship between their peoples. He also spoke of the 'desirability' of establishing 'mutual confidence between our

Parties as well'. Tito continued to scowl, and when Khrushchev had finished, the Yugoslav President brushed the microphone aside and silently led his guest to a waiting Rolls Royce. With Khrushchev's speech and Tito's ostentatiously grim silence the Russians had accepted exclusive responsibility for a quarrel which they now described as unjustifiable.[19]

At the end of the visit eight days later, after negotiating sessions in Belgrade and on Brioni and the obligatory tour of countryside and factories by the Soviet delegation, a document known to history as the 'Belgrade Declaration' was signed by Tito and Bulganin. It formally confirmed the Yugoslav position on separate roads to socialism. The two Governments affirmed their 'respect for sovereignty, independence, territorial integrity, and for equality between the States in their mutual relations' and pledged

mutal respect and non-interference in internal affairs for any reason—whether of an economic, political or ideological nature—since questions of the internal structure, differences of social systems and differences of concrete forms of developing socialism are exclusively a matter for the peoples of the different countries.[20]

Tito and the Yugoslavs had defied the living Stalin and won, and Stalin's heirs had now dramatically conceded the point. The Yugoslavs had been helped to victory by Stalin's over-confident miscalculations, which always led him to do too little too late: first 'shaking his little finger' in the expectation that the Yugoslav Party would rise against Tito at his order, only to discover that the CPY was loyal to Tito and not to him; then invoking a crippling economic blockade, only to find that the West was unexpectedly willing to 'keep Tito afloat' without demanding impossibly compromising political and ideological concessions; and at last indulging in sabre-rattling when that was also too late to be credible because a still unchallengeable NATO nuclear umbrella had in the meanwhile been tacitly but effectively extended to cover Yugoslavia. That Stalin had thus contributed to his own defeat in the only major conflict he ever lost did not, however, mar the quality of the Yugoslav victory or depreciate its enormous significance in Eastern Europe and the wider world. The second most powerful State in the world had been publicly humiliated by a small country. Even more importantly, the nature of that great power's surrender set a precedent which challenged the ideological and political lynchpin of its hold on other Communist-ruled States and Parties: if Yugoslavia could be genuinely independent of the Soviet Union and pursue its own 'different road to socialism', and do both with Moscow's blessing, why could others not do the same? The myth of a Communist's primary loyalty to 'the first land of socialism' and to one centre dictating doctrinal truth and political strategy, still essentially intact despite many blows, was shattered for ever at Belgrade airport on that afternoon in May 1955. Soviet military and economic power and special prestige as the senior as well as most powerful socialist State remained. But the Belgrade precedent and the process of Khrushchevian domestic and international de-Stalinisation to which it was intimately linked would force the Soviet leaders to make increasingly and embarrassingly naked use of the first two of these—the very thing that Khrushchev was hoping to avoid—in order to maintain hegemony in a looser version of Stalin's empire.

The Belgrade Declaration made no mention of Party relations; it would have been inappropriate if it had, since this was an agreement between Governments at the end of what was then officially only a State visit. In any case the open re-establishment of such relations seemed in Yugoslav if not in Soviet eyes premature. A year later, however, Tito returned the Bulganin-Khrushchev visit, the first time he had been to the Soviet Union since 1946, was received as a hero, and signed a 'Moscow Declaration' which made good this lacuna.[21] In the intervening months de-Stalinisation had taken on greater significance with Khrushchev's 'secret speech' to the 20th CPSU Congress denouncing Stalin and his crimes and specifically including his post-1948 Yugoslav policies among them. The Cominform was formally dissolved in April 1956. Molotov, co-signer with Stalin of the correspondence of 1948, was dismissed as Soviet foreign minister on the day before Tito's arrival in Moscow in June. 'Titoists' in the satellite States were being rehabilitated, dead or alive, and Eastern Europe was in ferment.

For seventeen months after May 1955 Tito was dazzled by the prospect, opening up before his eyes, of the conversion of the entire Soviet empire to principles advocated by Yugoslavia and of a leading ideological and political role for himself, particularly in Danubian and Balkan Europe. The dream of 1945-47 was revived in a new and happier form. By the summer of 1956 Poles and Hungarians were excitedly discussing workers' councils and other aspects of the Yugoslav system. Palmiro Togliatti, the head of the Italian Communist Party and a Comintern official in the interwar years, was following the road taken by the Yugoslavs five years earlier, but still not taken by the Russian de-Stalinisers, by attributing the evils of the Soviet system to its 'bureaucratic degeneration' and not simply to Stalin's 'cult of the personality'. In September, Khrushchev came secretly to Brioni to consult Tito about developments in Hungary and took Tito back to Yalta with him to meet and approve a new Hungarian leadership. It was to be headed by Ernö Gerö, a faithful deputy of the outgoing Stalinist leader Rákosi, and not by the Yugoslavs' candidate, Imre Nagy (an advocate of a more liberal line and of special relations among

Hungary, Yugoslavia and neutral non-Communist Austria, an idea with interesting potential), but this could reluctantly be accepted as a transitional formula. What was important was that Khrushchev seemed to have recognised and accepted the special influence of Tito in Danubian Europe which Stalin had denied in 1948.

In November 1956, however, Tito's hopes, the Soviet-Yugoslav rapprochement itself, and much else besides lay shattered on the barricades of Budapest. Nagy, who had become prime minister during the lull between the first and second Soviet military interventions, sought asylum in the Yugoslav embassy in Budapest, while his quondam liberal ally and Gerö's successor as Party head, Janos Kadar, invited the Red Army back to restore order and stop Hungary's defection from the Warsaw Pact and return to a multi-party system. As the guns fell silent a week later Tito, who had made his own tactical miscalculations and now saw his grand strategy in tatters, attempted to clarify the Yugoslav position in a speech at Pula on November 11. He was in a difficult situation: he had been notified of the second Soviet intervention on the night that it began and had reluctantly approved what he could not prevent, a fact which seemed likely to become public knowledge sooner or later, but he also feared the consequences of the events in Hungary both internationally and inside Yugoslavia, where his people and a large part of his Party were sympathetic to Hungarian aspirations and enraged by the Soviet action. The interpretation with which he attempted to reconcile contradictions and save the saveable, and which was incidentally so consistent with his reaction and attitude to other events in his career that it must have been honest as well, only annoyed both the defenders of Hungarian independence and its violators.[22]

Tito scoffed at Soviet claims that the Hungarian revolution had been initiated by reactionaries and outside influences. It was begun, he said, by 'progressive forces' fighting Stalinism. Soviet policies had greatly aggravated the situation by supporting Hungarian Stalinists too long, by picking and imposing an inappropriate successor (Gerö), and by responding to Gerö's appeal for armed assistance. Tito described this first Soviet intervention, on October 23, as unwarranted by events and disastrous in its consequences. It 'still further enraged the people' and thus permitted 'reactionaries to turn a justified revolt against a clique into an uprising of the whole nation against socialism and the Soviet Union'. Once the revolution had taken on this anti-socialist coloration, however, the choice became one between Soviet intervention and 'chaos, civil war, counter-revolution and a new world war', in which case the second Soviet military intervention, while deeply regrettable, was clearly the lesser evil.

The Soviet leadership (or part of it) had already demonstrated their concern about Yugoslavia's role in early September, despite Khrushchev's continued wooing of Tito, by sending to the East European Parties a confidential letter calling for solidarity under Soviet leadership, warning against Tito's influence, and questioning the Leninist nature of Yugoslav socialism. Now they reacted sharply to Tito's Pula speech, accusing the Yugoslavs of 'sowing disunity' and of claiming that 'the Yugoslav road to socialism is the more correct and only possible road'.[23] Soviet and other East European credits to Yugoslavia granted in 1956 were unilaterally postponed in February 1957, and the slanging match of earlier years revived in the media on both sides. Tito compared the situation to that of late 1948. This was not in fact the case, because neither side wanted it to be. Vanity and hope seem to have blinded Tito to the lesson of Hungary, which was that Khrushchev's 'socialist commonwealth' would continue to be based on effective Soviet hegemony, while Khrushchev apparently believed that the Yugoslavs would ultimately return to the bloc on his terms. After August 1957, when Tito and Khrushchev met secretly at Bucharest to talk out their differences, another rapprochement seemed to be in full swing. Tito spoke of the Soviet Union and of 'proletarian internationalism' in strongly positive terms and of NATO in equally negative ones; Djilas, who had already been imprisoned at the end of 1956 for publishing articles in the West condemning the Soviet intervention in Hungary, had his term extended for ten years when *The New Class* (printed from a manuscript mysteriously smuggled out of Yugoslavia) appeared; and Yugoslavia became the first non-Soviet-bloc country to recognise the German Democratic Republic, causing West Germany to break relations with Belgrade. The Soviet bloc credits which had been postponed in February were reinstated in July.[24]

The second rapprochement did not last long. In preparation for the celebration of the fortieth anniversary of the October Revolution in Moscow in November 1957, the Soviet Party circulated the draft of a resolution on Communist unity which the heads of other ruling Parties would be asked to sign while there. 'Revisionism ... under the pretext of national peculiarities' was said to be the principal contemporary threat to the Communist movement, and there was repeated reference to 'proletarian internationalism' and the leading role of the USSR. In the words of a quasi-official history of the Yugoslav Party, the draft contravened the principles proclaimed in the Belgrade and Moscow Declarations: 'With this declaration the conception of a camp with the leading role of one country was revived, and the invitation to a struggle against revisionism was above all directed against Yugoslav socialist practice and foreign policy.'[25]

Tito, who had announced his intention to attend the anniversary celebrations, pleaded illness and did not go to Moscow. The LCY was represented instead by Kardelj and Ranković, who refused to sign the declaration. Khrushchev's angry and threatening reaction was reported in the Yugoslav press, and Soviet-Yugoslav relations teetered on the brink of a new quarrel. Then, when the LCY circulated to the Soviet and other Parties the draft of the Programme which was to be approved at their 7th Congress in April, they fell over the brink. The Soviet Party sent detailed and extensive criticism of the draft Programme. The Yugoslavs made some changes, none of them substantive, in a last gesture of 'socialist solidarity'. Three days before the Congress opened the Soviet Party's theoretical journal *Kommunist* published the substance of the Soviet criticism and announced that the Parties of the socialist bloc would not accept Yugoslav invitations to attend. At the Congress itself Ranković made a strong and defiant speech, and the ambassadors of the Soviet and East European countries demonstratively walked out of the diplomatic gallery. The only one who did not was the Pole, which caused a momentary sensation until it was noticed that he seemed to be asleep.

Anti-Yugoslav polemics in the socialist bloc press began again and took on a sharper note than at any time since 1954. This time, significantly, the most violent attacks came from the Chinese Party, whose own independent and peasant-based revolution had once led the Yugoslavs to expect their strongest ally there. Those off-again-on-again Soviet bloc credits were off again, suspended for five years. Khrushchev, addressing a Congress of the Bulgarian Party in neighbouring Sofia on June 3, 1958, called Tito a 'Trojan horse' and said the Cominform resolution of June 1948 was 'fundamentally correct'. He referred sarcastically to 'some theoreticians who exist only because of the alms they receive from imperialist countries in the form of leftover goods', and added that 'socialism cannot be built on US wheat'. Tito, in a speech at Labin in Istria a few days later, replied that 'those who know how can do it, while those who do not know how will not even be able to build socialism on their own wheat'.[26]

The new quarrel was to last for three years. In retrospect it is clear that the Soviet position was intimately connected to the separate story of the developing Sino-Soviet dispute, but it was also a consequence of Tito's and Khrushchev's misapprehensions of one another's position during the flirtation of 1957. Each had overestimated his importance to the other and set his price too high. Khrushchev seems to have persuaded himself that the Yugoslav leaders, whose concern about Western influences and excessive economic dependence on the West had been manifest in word and deed since the Djilas crisis, were so eager for socialist legitimation and a counterpoise to Western ideology and credits that they would accept a 'Polish solution': recognition of their right to determine their own domestic policies in return for solidarity with Soviet foreign policy and renunciation of the right to pronounce on matters of Marxist dogma. Tito, on the other hand, had created and then accepted a myth that Soviet policy towards Belgrade was a key issue in the struggle for power being waged inside the Kremlin between Khrushchev and neo-Stalinists, and that by supporting Khrushchev's faction through meeting its demands he could again play a major role in the liberalisation of Soviet internal and bloc policy and within the bloc. Both were wrong.

Economic growth, political stagnation

The weight of this sequence of external events as a factor in Yugoslav domestic policies is difficult to determine, but common sense suggests that it operated in complex, multi-dimensional ways. Hope of reconciliation and efforts to translate the original Soviet surrender into increased Yugoslav influence in the world and power in Eastern Europe recommended careful conservation of Yugoslav independence (and with it both intensive promotion of 'active peaceful coexistence', growing into a 'non-aligned' alignment with other neutral States in Asia and Africa, and quiet maintenance of economic and political bridges to the West, the latter battered by each rapprochement).[27] But it also recommended an ideological stance and domestic policies which were not too ostentatiously at variance with those of the post-Stalin bloc. This was in addition, however, an argument which could be used by those, like Ranković and Tito himself, who for quite separate and domestic reasons wished to limit the extent of Yugoslavia's internal reforms and postpone fulfilment of pledges already made.

Conversely, each new quarrel with the Soviet Union strengthened the position of those within the Belgrade leadership who wanted further liberalisation at home, or at least no further retreat from the level achieved in 1953. It enabled them to argue that domestic ideological and political 'concessions' to the Russians were embarrassing and had done no good, because the Soviet rulers would be satisfied with nothing less than Yugoslavia's complete return to the bloc, that they were damaging relations with the West which were important to Yugoslavia's economic development and ability to resist pressures from the East, and that they were again undermining the regime's domestic support. At the same time both the ebb and the flow of this basic tide tended to produce a rip-tide, further complicating the net effect: periods of alienation from the East and intimacy with the West induced some in the ruling élite to seek firmer control of Party and populace in order to minimise contamination by 'alien Western ideas', while periods of rapprochement provoked others into more watchful efforts to hold or at least save the saveable from the last high tide of liberalisation. Finally, a more intimate, psychological dimension must also have played a role: the equally complex and often internally contradictory reaction to Soviet blandishments and bullying of those, particularly in the top Yugoslav leadership drawn from the prewar Party generation, who were simultaneously Communists, Slavs and patriots, and who found themselves still involved in a love-hate relationship with the State which was simultaneously the fatherland of the Revolution, Mother Russia and the intolerable oppressor of smaller East European nations.

That the international situation was a factor which could cut either way domestically was clearest in its effect on the level and kind of police intimidation of ordinary Yugoslavs. High tides for basically political arrests and harassment in the 1950s came during the 'second quarrel' stage of Soviet-Yugoslav relations in late 1956 and 1957 and after the third quarrel began in 1958, not during periods of rapprochement, and coincided with periods of generally tighter control and surveillance of the populace than at any time between 1950 and 1973. The reason in 1956-57 was clearly the lesson of Hungary: if liberalisation in Budapest could turn into what Tito and UDBa considered counter-revolution, against Tito's expectations, it just might happen in Yugoslavia too. The Yugoslavs must therefore be made aware, by demonstrative arrests and convictions, that their different and more liberal road did not mean any softness towards 'the enemies of socialism'. In 1958, it may have been Ranković's nervous reaction to the damage done to Tito's personal and by extension to the regime's popular prestige by the failure of the gamble on Khrushchev.[28]

In the Party itself, the 'tightening up' began in the summer of 1953, as has been seen, and primarily as a response to confusion and apathy in the ranks and the alarming spread of 'bourgeois democratic' ideas and expectations in the country. The dazzling possibilities offered by de-Stalinisation in Eastern Europe in 1955-56 were too distant a gleam on the horizon to be considered an important factor for more than another year. They may have played a role in renewed efforts to reassert Party discipline and authority in 1956, but even then there were powerful domestic motives.

Party membership dropped sharply after the 2nd Plenum, partly as a result of expulsions of purge proportions and partly through voluntary resignations and deliberately curtailed recruitment. In 1953, 72,067 members were expelled from the LCY and more than 32,000 resigned, most of them during the second half of the year.

During the next two years there were an additional 273,464 expulsions, while 136,887 new members joined the Party. By mid-1956 total membership, which had been over 780,000 at the time of the 6th Congress, was down to 635,984. Some basic organisations had lost nearly half their members. Of those purged nearly 25 per cent were workers, 54 per cent were peasants and 18 per cent were white-collar employees. With the highest proportion of new members belonging to the last category, the LCY had ceased to be a predominantly peasant Party without becoming a working-class one.[29]

If the drop in total membership was not in itself disturbing, because the policy of the period involved a partial return towards a Leninist 'cadre party', the changing social structure and a drop in the percentage of youth among new members were. So were reports indicating continued ineffectiveness and apathy, now blamed on the organisational reforms carried out under the rubric of the 6th Congress. Disbanding Party organisations in State and other institutions, except economic enterprises, was said to make it difficult for Communists to be effective as an organised force and reduced most meetings of the remaining communal organisations, with no focused interest and responsibility, to listening to lectures. This had admittedly been the explicit purpose of the reforms, but times had changed.

In March 1956 Tito summoned the Central Committee to its 6th Plenum to take action against 'various negative phenomena', which he blamed on 'the decline in Party discipline and responsibility, the weakening of the united action of Communists, and increasingly frequent instances of breaches of the principles of democratic centralism'. The list of problems which the Plenum was to discuss was suggestive, including hints that the national question, re-emerging in the costume of republican economic interests, was involved. 'Negative phenomena', the Plenum agreed,

were particularly found in the economy, in which they were assuming the proportions of an outbreak of negative localistic and technocratic tendencies. Instances of investments beyond planned levels, evasion of regulations, surrender to technocratism and to practicism in conducting economic policy and passivity towards localism and republican parti-cularism, alleged to be 'in the interest of the economy', were among the deformations.... This had a destructive effect on Communists as socio-political workers and converted them into economic 'managers' who closed themselves up within local or republican contexts and 'swam down the stream of spontaneity'....[30]

To deal with these problems the Plenum, in addition to rapping the knuckles of those guilty of 'deformations', decreed several changes which further undid the intentions of the 6th Congress. '*Aktivs*' of politically engaged Communists were established in factory sub-units and all institutions in which 'basic organisations' had been abolished in 1952. The number of professional Party workers in Party organisations, cut back drastically in the early 1950s, was to be increased again, and the Party schools for training them which Djilas had liquidated were to reopen. Youth work projects would be reinstituted, a special Party organisation would devote its attention to propaganda among youth, and Party organisations were re-established in universities and other higher schools. Communists from the army should be more extensively engaged in local government, in the Socialist Alliance, and in other 'socio-political organisations'.[31]

By 1958 these measures had been so successful in reasserting ubiquitous and direct Party control, leading to 'abuses', 'monopoly of responsibilities' and 'usurpations of power by a narrow circle', that signs of workers' unrest and inefficiency in the economy led to a retreat. It coincided in timing, once again, with the renewed deterioration in Yugoslav-Soviet relations following circulation of the draft of the new Party Programme. In a Circular Letter to all Party organisations in February 1958 the Executive Committee of the Party warned that many Communists were using dictatorial methods, accumulating privileges and indulging in corrupt practices. Ethnic particularism was again cited as a specific culprit. 'Very often', the Letter said, 'members on the leading bodies of the League of Communists fall under the influence of the petty-bourgeois intelligentsia and ... are guilty of nationalist and chauvinist influences'.[32]

While the freeze on ideology and on any redefinition of the role of the Party was in these years virtually total, there were two areas in which proposals for decentralisation or liberalisation were still legitimate. One was in local government, where Kardelj's particular personal fascination with the subject granted adequate authority, and the other was in the economy, where authority was derived from the now sacrosanct theory of workers' self-management.

Changes in local government were nevertheless largely proclamatory and in practical effect minimal, except that they sanctioned a phenomenal flowering of communal bureaucracies and of the number of paid employees working in them. The 'communal system' which was introduced in September 1955, after elaborate public discussion and with much fanfare, redefined the commune (*opština* or *općina* in the Serbian and Croatian variants) as 'the basic political-territorial organisation of self-administration by the working people and the basic socio-economic community of the population on their territory', a formulation in accord with Kardelj's concepts of community and self-management.[33] Except that the communes (and the counties—the *srezovi* or *kotori*) were again increased in size and reduced in number to create economically more viable units, the new dispensation did little to increase their power or competence. They continued to be characterised by the two dominant and contradictory features already imposed by the local government law of 1952 and subsequent Party reforms. The first was extensive economic and political power over economic enterprises located on their territories, which was both an important measure of genuine decentralisation and pluralisation of power and an incitement to the kind of 'localism' condemned by the Party in 1956 and 1958. The second was ultimate control over their affairs by Party and police organs, ostensibly subject to a rigid hierarchical discipline which was obviously not imperative enough to make local Party bosses heed verbal injunctions against such localism. In a sense this contradiction at the local level mirrored an emerging personal division of labour at the Party summit: Kardelj, the ideologue, decentralising the administration, while Ranković, the guardian of the system, used the hierarchical Party apparatus, his control of appointments, and UDBa to maintain whatever he at a specific period considered the appropriate minimum of centralised Party discipline and control.

The behaviour of the economy, as we have seen, also militated against further changes in the system after 1954, and again for contradictory reasons. The boom which began in 1953 and continued (with a brief pause in 1956) until the end of the decade suggested that reforms already introduced—workers' councils and a quasimarket economy with continuing direct State control of saving and investment and indirect State control of other macro-economic instruments—had gone far enough to achieve their primary purpose, the stimulation of work, growth and greater rationality. High growth rates were also in themselves a disincentive to tampering with a system which worked. At the same time, the first experience in economic liberalisation after 1952 had produced enough instances of workers' councils seeking to do unacceptable things, like raising prices instead of productivity and wages at the expense of investments, to persuade those who had always predicted this that the State must strengthen and certainly not weaken its remaining instruments of control over them. Progressive taxes on 'bonus' wages in 1953, administrative control of wages after 1954, and the step-by-step imposition of price controls, which by 1955 covered 50 per cent of the total value of industrial raw materials and semi-fabricates, were small retreats from the 1952 level of workers' council autonomy which generally remained in force until 1961 or after.

Growth rates after 1952 were in fact among the highest in the world. Taking 1952 as a base year, in which output was 2 per cent below the level of 1947, the index of industrial production was 111 in 1953, 126 in 1954, 147 in 1955 and 162 in 1956. Employment expanded accordingly, but more selectively than in the first postwar years, from over 1·8 million in all economic enterprises in 1953 to nearly 2·4 million in 1957. The biggest production gains were recorded in 'industries which build industries': the output of machine tools and of iron, steel and other metals tripled between 1947 and 1955, that of construction machinery was seventy times larger, and production of road vehicles, electrical machinery and modern agricultural machinery was begun. Per capita national income (at 1956 prices) was 83,000 dinars in 1955, compared to 63,200 in 1939.[34]

On the other hand, the production of consumer goods lagged behind, so that living standards in the mid-1950s did not rise as fast as output or provide rewards for additional effort. That the increase in total wages from more employment and higher per capita wages was larger than the increases in the supply of consumer goods was also generating inflationary pressures. In addition, high industrial growth rates were due more to the completion of many new factories begun in the previous period, to a better supply of domestic and imported raw materials (the latter reflecting the impact of Western aid, as did an otherwise insupportably high investment rate) and to improvements in infrastructure (railroads, roads, power lines, mines and supporting facilities) than to a genuinely better allocation of resources, which subsequent developments indicated had not taken place. Funding the high rate of investment on which 'global industrialisation' depended was also becoming increasingly difficult. The peasants, deprived of incentives to increase holdings or productivity, could no longer provide sufficient savings to meet the increasing demand for industrial development funds, while Western aid was dwindling in reaction to successive rapprochements with the East. Means of accumulating such funds must somehow be transferred to industry.

Another chronic and major problem, far from being on the way to solution, was gradually worsening and could not fail to aggravate the national question. This was Yugoslavia's 'dual economy', the great disparities in per capita national income, productivity, social services, opportunities and 'development' in general between the ex-Habsburg regions (and the Belgrade area) and the ex-Ottoman ones. In 1953 Social Product per head of population in the more developed regions of the north was 110 per cent (and in Slovenia 182 per cent) of the countrywide average, while that of the underdeveloped republics south of the Sava-Danube line (therefore including Serbia proper and the Belgrade area) was 71 per cent and in Kosmet, the poorest region, only 53 per cent. By 1957 Social Product per head in the developed regions had increased to 116 per cent and that of the underdeveloped regions had fallen to 67 per cent (and in Kosmet to 42 per cent) of the Yugoslav average.[35] These trends continued with only a few local exceptions through the following decade, despite numerous efforts to find a solution and a redistribution of income, primarily by redirecting savings generated in the north into investments in the south, which was massive enough to cause increasing dissatisfaction in Slovenia and Croatia. Gross productive investments in the underdeveloped regions, for example, amounted to 43·5 per cent of their Social Product (in Montenegro the figure was 99·1 per cent!) in 1953 and to 36·9, 29·4, 26·5 and 22·8 per cent in the following four years. Comparable figures for the developed areas were 22·6 per cent in 1953 and 21·6, 20, 20·1 and 18 per cent in the following years.

One reason for the failure to achieve better results lay in the higher rate of natural increase in the south,[36] which meant that a larger increase in gross Social Product was needed to produce an increase in per capita Social Product than in the north. Output per worker was also strikingly lower in almost all sectors. Both factors were indicative of deeper problems of inherited social backwardness and lack of social and technical infrastructure. There was an obvious correlation, for example, between differences in output per worker and cultural levels as measured by literacy; in 1953 40·4 per cent of the population of the underdeveloped regions was classified as illiterate, compared with 19·1 per cent in the developed regions. In the best of circumstances time would be needed to solve these problems.

Policy nevertheless also played a role in the failure to move faster. If investment is measured on a per capita basis rather than as a percentage of Social Product, more was still going to Slovenia, Croatia and Serbia proper than to the south. Bosnia was no longer getting the privileged treatment which it had enjoyed during the struggle with the Cominform, when its isolated valleys were considered the right place to put strategic industries, and was left with new (and often unfinished) factories established in splendid isolation from markets, roads or skilled manpower. This last was also true of Montenegro. There Yugoslavia's outstanding example of a mis-located industry was the steel mill at Nikšić, which began production in 1953, waited eight years for a rail connection to the nearby Adriatic, more than ten years for a paved highway to anywhere, and until 1975 for a standard-gauge rail line to the rest of the country. While many of these absurdities could be blamed on primitive planning and the 'megalomaniacal ambitions' of the republics concerned, they also suffered from the ad hoc and annually changed nature of assistance designed by federal planners.[37]

By the end of 1956 a combination of official enthusiasm engendered by success and awareness of these residual or emerging problems was generating renewed discussion of further liberalising economic reforms and was determining the form which they would take. This, and the special ideological protection enjoyed by proposals in this sector (already described), meant that the stagnation in creative and critical thinking imposed by the events of 1953 was ended here several years earlier than in other sectors. International factors again played a role. The American reaction to Tito's flirtation with Khrushchev was posing a threat to continuing Western economic aid, still an important substitute for inadequate domestic savings, exports and agricultural production; there were signs, particularly in Hungary and Poland, that the consumer revolt which had started in Western Europe in the late 1940s was spreading to Eastern Europe; and the lesson of the Hungarian October and its brutal suppression had its impact on Yugoslav thinking about economic as well as political policy.[38] As in 1949–53, the initiative and most of the thinking about these problems would at first come from a narrow circle at the top of the Party élite. This was not only because only these people were licensed to think independently, although this was still largely true. It was also because, as Bićanić points out,

the process of decentralising party control from the top, but not transferring power to the lowest levels created a middle layer of State and party officials, who were very anxious to preserve their positions and therefore became pillars of dogmatism and the establishment. As a rule, more liberal opinions and critical attitudes were found at higher levels. The struggle for legality was fought mainly by the top leadership of the League of Communists, and was chiefly directed against the State bureaucracy.[39]

The reopening of the debate on the economic system was preceded and affected by two important decisions. In October 1955 the Party Executive Committee, meeting with economic experts on Brioni, recommended that the share of investment in Social Product should be reduced and that a higher proportion of investment funds should go to consumer goods and to agriculture. The official explanation was that a basic industrial infrastructure had now been created, making it possible at last to concentrate on raising living standards, but the new policy was in fact designed to kill two birds with one stone. By giving priority to economic sectors which could accumulate income quickly and which were easily taxable, it was seen as a better way to provide resources for the development of new industries while simultaneously raising the standard of living. The shift in priorities did not begin to have a serious impact on output assortment and living standards until after 1961, for a variety of reasons which included timelags in construction and the burden of continuing commitments to the completion of existing projects, often large and primarily still basic industries. It nevertheless marked a major watershed in the evolution of postwar Yugoslav economic policy, the effective abandonment of the principle of 'global industrialisation' for the principle of 'accumulative industrialisation'.[40]

The following year, again in response both to enthusiasm generated by success and to continuing or new problems, the regime decided to abandon exclusively annual Social Plans and to draft a new Five-Year Plan which would give them and the country's socialist entrepreneurs a broader, longer-range view on which to base annual decision-making. The writing of such a medium-range indicative plan, in which fulfilment would depend on how well macro-economic parameters and the instruments selected by the planners took into account the role of the market and how micro-economic decision-making in enterprises would react to the combined dynamics of plan and market, was a more complex task than Yugoslav planners had yet undertaken. Drafting consequently required a year of work at all levels, from Federation to commune and by economic chambers and enterprises as well as Government bodies, and the Five-Year Plan for the years 1957-61 was finally adopted only late in 1957. It set high targets: national income should increase by 54·5 per cent, industrial output by 70 per cent. and agricultural output by 42 per cent; the increase in personal consumption was projected at about 35 per cent. The underdeveloped regions—now momentarily defined as including only Macedonia, Montenegro and Kosmet—were offered a system of Federal Government guarantees of credits for economic investments, grants from the GIF repayable to the RIF rather than to the Federal Fund (a device already adopted in 1956), some tax benefits and direct budgetary assistance to 'non-economic' investments in social infrastructure.[41]

Despite its ambitiousness, the Plan's global and almost all sectoral targets were fulfilled in four years. Social Product in the years 1957-60 rose by 62 per cent, or 12·7 per cent per annum at a compound rate, compared to a planned rise of 9·5 per cent per annum. Private consumption of goods and services rose by 49 per cent, or 10·5 per cent per annum, compared with the Plan's anticipated 7·3 per cent per annum. Imports grew by 67 per cent, less happily also twice the planned rate, but exports also did better than foreseen, growing by 65 per cent in value. It was a phenomenal achievement by any standards and the second highest growth rate recorded anywhere in the world in those years.[42]

These continuing successes and the broad participation which preparation of the Plan had required gave additional impetus and legitimacy to a public rather than purely private Party discussion of the economic system and the future evolution of self-management. The idea of a Congress of Workers' Councils, first mooted in 1954 and then a victim of the intervening freeze on risky initiatives, was revived. The Congress met in Belgrade for three days in June 1957, and its debate and Resolution suggested that such consultations might prove an interesting way of evading the opposition to economic reform by middle-level apparatuses. The main themes were 'freer income distribution' and 'the strengthening of enterprise independence'. The Resolution called for changes in the wage system and 'equal conditions of economic activity for all work collectives', significantly defined as including equal capital taxes for all and fiscal and other policies which would ensure that 'greater or smaller participation in income distribution is the result of production achieved and labour productivity as well as of the success of the total economic activity'. A number of reforms to this end were urged and included what seems to have been the first mention in an offical document of the possibility that investment ('expanded reproduction') might also be transferred, at least in part, from the State to the self-management sector.[43]

A platform for further reforms of the economic system and a climate of public expectation, in part deliberately engineered and in part spontaneous, had thus been created. The adoption of the Five-Year Plan obviously provided an appropriate moment to fulfil these expectations. The mountain of the appropriate apparatuses laboured and at the end of 1957 gave birth to a mouse. Hailed as a major step towards real self-management, the changes which came into effect on January 1, 1958, had a minimal immediate practical effect.

The reform of 1958 proclaimed an entirely new principle of income distribution. This had theoretical importance and an interesting potential for future evolution. In place of 'profit-sharing', the system of 1954–58, the reform introduced 'income-sharing'. After 1958 there would technically be no such things as wages and salaries in Yugoslavia, but only 'personal income' as a part of the 'net income' of individual enterprises. This net income was in turn defined as what was left of gross income after deduction of 'business expenditures' (material expenses, depreciation, capital tax, interest on credits and other funds, rates and 'contributions'—but no longer as before including wages), and of turnover and other State taxes. Such net income was for the first time theoretically at the entirely free disposal of the enterprise, to be divided into personal incomes, investment and general funds, reserves, etc., as the workers' council should decide.

Once again, however, the principle of freedom was promptly undermined by a series of qualifications and subsidiary regulations which gave back a large measure of *de facto* control to State organs. This time it was done primarily by establishing a schedule of 'minimum personal incomes' (MLD in the Serbo-Croatian acronym), initially set at 80 per cent of 1957 wages and salaries, and by permitting stiffly progressive supplementary taxation of all personal incomes above that level. According to one calculation, an enterprise which attempted to authorise personal incomes amounting to 140 per cent of the MLD would after taxes actually pay its workers only 109 per cent of their previous year's income.[44]

Caution was still the watchword of reform. This time it was based not only on fear of 'excesses' by workers' councils and management if they were left to decide for themselves, but on concern for the living standards of workers in enterprises in which 'net income' might be too small to permit 'personal incomes' to constitute a living wage. If an enterprise could not pay its workers their MLD, the difference would be made up out of a communal reserve fund, in effect an insurance fund to which all enterprises in a commune contributed, and if it did not resolve its difficulties within a specified period it would be placed under a 'compulsory management' appointed by the commune. This was a fair point—in later years, when principles had prevailed and such paternalism was abolished, workers in many enterprises were to suffer payless paydays, sometimes for several successive months—but more was at issue. 'Some people' (a favourite establishment phrase for anonymous obstruction) had other reasons for defending the *status quo* in the economic system. For the time being, as long as the boom lasted, they had their way.

The 7th Congress

Preparation of the Five-Year Plan in 1957 coincided with preparations for another LCY Congress, the seventh since its founding as the CPY. The Congress should have been held in 1956, according to the Party Statute, but the situation in the Party and the ups and downs of its relations with what was euphemistically called 'the international workers' movement' led to repeated postponements, first to the autumn of 1957 and then to the spring of 1958. When it finally convened, on April 22, 1958, in Ljubljana, Yugoslav-Soviet relations were again strained (in part because of the draft programme to be presented to the Congress, as has been seen), but the Party itself had regained membership and self-confidence. The LCY now boasted 755,066 members and some improvement in its social and age structure: those officially registered as workers accounted for 32 per cent of the total, an all-time high, and 63 per cent of new members enrolled during the preceding year were classified as youth. On the other hand, the proportion of peasants and women had continued to decline, to 17 and 16·4 per cent respectively. Fully 46 per cent of all members were registered as clerical staff, engineers, technicians, economists, physicians, teachers, professional politicians or in other non-proletarian categories.

Following tradition, the first half of Tito's marathon report to the Congress dealt with the international situation and with Yugoslavia's relations with the outside world.[45] This time he began with and devoted special attention to events in the Afro-Asian world and Yugoslavia's relations with other non-aligned States, a symbol of the growing importance of non-alignment in Yugoslav foreign policy—and in Tito's continuing efforts to maintain his own role and image as a major international statesman. On the again delicate subject of Yugoslavia's relations with the Soviet bloc, he virtually ignored the renewed deterioration which had taken place since the preceding November, portraying the second rapprochement as still alive but marred by 'certain comrades in some of those countries'. Such people were 'displaying a tendency towards lack of faith in and an erroneous treatment of internal developments in our country' and were absurdly insisting that 'we are not internationalists because we are not in the camp'. Relations with the Soviet Union and other socialist States, Tito concluded, should be based on the Belgrade Declaration of 1955; he did not mention the Moscow Declaration of 1956, which had called for relations between Parties as well. It was left to Ranković to take the sharper line which led to the walk-out of the 'camp's' ambassadors.

The main business of the 7th Congress was the adoption of a new Party Programme, replacing the long obsolete one of 1948 and only the third since the founding of the CPY. It was an enormous document which had been a year in preparation and which took up 230 pages in the printed version of the Congress' proceedings. Discussing everything from 'social, economic and political relations in the contemporary world' and the historical significance of the National Liberation Struggle in Yugoslavia to the principles of the Yugoslav system, its problems, and the role of the LCY and other 'socio-political organisations', it was simultanously a survey of the status of Yugoslav theory, a vision of 'socialist democracy' and occasionally a platform for political action.

The new Programme was in a sense a return to the *status quo ante* Djilas, almost as though nothing dramatic or important had happened since the 6th Congress except an economic and social modernisation which had brought the vision of socialist democracy a little closer to the foreseeable future. The text and the report with which Kardelj introduced it defined the Party and its role in much the same terms that had been used at the 6th Congress, complete with the caveats about its continuing 'responsibility' and the validity of democratic centralism which had been temporarily undermined in 1953. There was even a cautious reference to the Party's eventual 'disappearance', which would 'proceed in tandem with the objective process of the withering away of social antagonisms and of all forms of coercion which historically grew out of these antagonisms.'[46] That there should be no renewed misunderstandings about this, Kardelj explained:

We would of course be indulging in hypocrisy if we did not openly say that in the present period Communists in our country have and must have a direct influence on certain key positions of power, those on which the stability of the political order depends and which ensure the ever freer development of socialism.[47]

The Programme repeated now traditional concepts of the necessity for an immediate 'withering away of the State' during the socialist transition, a process said to have begun in Yugoslavia with the creation of workers' councils in 1950. 'In the sphere of economic relations', it was further said, 'that process at the same time means a process of overcoming the remnants of State capitalism'. Socialism was defined as 'a social order based on socialised means of production, in which the associated direct producers administer social production'. It would be achieved when 'the entire social community becomes a community of producers'. Soviet deviations from all of these principles were criticised, as they had been in 1952, although post-Stalin improvements were carefully mentioned.

The Programme also turned its attention to the national question. After repeating familiar theses about 'the individuality, equality and the right of self-determination of all the Yugoslav peoples', it struck a new note. The future of national relations, it said, lay in the development of socialist relations and of 'a socialist, Yugoslav consciousness, in the conditions of a socialist community of peoples'. This statement in such a document represented the high point of a shortlived campaign for 'Yugoslavism' (*Jugoslavenstvo*), a socialist patriotism superimposed on separate ethnic consciousness and leading eventually to a 'Yugoslav culture'. Although it was carefully and specifically stated that there was no intention of creating a Yugoslav 'nation' to replace the existing ones, the concept of a 'Yugoslav culture' inevitably involved more specific questions—for example about the language in which a 'Yugoslav literature' would be written—and these in turn were bound to stir unpleasant memories and grave suspicions in the minds of non-Serbs.[48]

Except for such marginalia, the Programme and the Congress brought no significant changes. Neither did the composition of the Executive Committee which the new Central Committee of 135 members approved at its first session just after adjournment. All fourteen members of the outgoing Executive Committee, which now included the secretaries of each of the six republican central committees, were duly re-elected and only one new member (Veljko Vlahović) was added.[49] The Committee now consisted of 4 Serbs, 4 Croats (including Tito), 3 Slovenes, 3 Montenegrins and 1 Macedonian. Tito was re-elected as Secretary-General, and Kardelj and Ranković were named as secretaries of the Central Committee, the latter with special responsibility for 'organisational-political work'. This Party role and his continuing effective control of the UDBa which he had founded made Ranković clearly the second most powerful man in Yugoslavia.

The very fact that the 7th Congress and the new Programme repeated the principles enunciated at the 6th Congress was nevertheless significant in the light of all that had happened in the intervening years. Failing to bring Yugoslav theory and proclamations of intent into line with existing institutions and practice, the Congress, like the recent economic mini-reform and the Congress of Workers' Councils, had recreated a climate propitious to further liberalising changes, a climate which had not existed since 1953.

For a time, however, nothing happened. The Central Committee elected at the 7th Congress did not even meet again for more than a year. When it did, in May 1959, it paid lip service to the fact that 'there is still much to do in adding on to the system', but when it came to specifics it exuded satisfaction with the *status quo*, especially the state of the economy and the level of effective workers' self-management achieved with the 1958 mini-reform. And why not? The 'system' was working.

4

THE GREAT DEBATE RESUMED

Reform and recession

The Yugoslav regime entered the new decade of the 1960s in an ebullient mood. Economic growth rates, the levels of production and consumption which had already been achieved, domestic political stability and relations with the outside world were all incomparably better than ten years earlier, the country's postwar nadir. Completion of the 1957-61 Social Plan a year ahead of schedule seemed an appropriate symbol of a remarkable success story.

If there were clouds on the horizon, some were perceived as receding and others were overlooked by all but a few economists and particularly disadvantaged or ambitious groups. To be sure, relations with the Soviet Union and its client States and Parties were still apparently in the 'third quarrel' stage that had begun in 1958. The Moscow Declaration by 81 Communist Parties in December 1960 even seemed to presage a new outburst of polemics. It unanimously condemned the Yugoslavs for 'betraying Marxism-Leninism' with their 'anti-Leninist revisionist programme' and accused them of conducting 'subversive work against the socialist camp'. Tito, however, chose to consider such statements a 'rotten compromise' with 'Chinese dogmatism' which could not last.[1] With the wisdom born of many years in the international Communist movement, he waited patiently for the Sino-Soviet quarrel to break out again, as it did the following year, thus paving the way to a new and more durable Yugoslav—Soviet rapprochement.

The clouds which were ignored were economic in nature. The boom of the 1950s, now in its eighth year, had been achieved in part by means of an unexpectedly high rate of investment expenditure. Productive investment in fixed assets at constant prices, increasing at 13·4 per cent per annum instead of the planned rate of 8·5 per cent, had risen faster than total output, while social investment in housing, schools and hospitals had also been larger than anticipated. Gross investment in 1960 was 29 per cent higher than in 1959 and 32 per cent of Social Product; a significant proportion of it, despite the shift in investment priorities after 1956, was still earmarked for major industrial and infrastructure projects which would contribute to production and productivity only in future years. The inflationary pressures inherent in these rates and types of investment, reinforced by the rapid rise in personal consumption permitted in the last years of the Five-Year Plan, were already making themselves felt by the end of the 1950s. Further burdens were added by bad harvests in 1960 and 1961, as two successive years of unfavourable weather again exposed the weakness of the perennially neglected agricultural sector.

In addition, and as a consequence of all of those factors, the balance-of-trade deficit, which had grown consistently but at an acceptable rate in each recent year except 1959, was displaying an alarming upward trend: from 32 billion dinars in 1959 to 72 billion in 1960 or to 78 billion if American grain surpluses acquired under Public Law 480 are also counted as imports. The greater part of these continuing deficits had been covered, as described, by Western aid and 'soft' credits which had reached a total of over $2,000m by 1960. Since 1955, however, the relative roles of these two kinds of external assistance had been reversed. While until that year grant aid covered 52·2 per cent of the deficit on current account and foreign loans only 16·2 per cent, since 1956 non-repayable aid had covered only 10·7 per cent and credits nearly 43 per cent of the gap.[2] Although significant amounts of American assistance were again available since the renewed quarrel with the Soviet Union in 1958 and would total $511 million in the four years 1960–64, almost all of it was also in the form of credits, however 'soft', which must be repaid in dinars or dollars.[3] Future high investment and growth rates would presumably continue to depend on additional injections of such external funds, but repayment of earlier loans was already placing new burdens on the balance of payments and a larger deficit on current account would jeopardise the country's international creditworthness.

To make matters worse, the highest growth rates, and therefore the principal stimulants in the boom since 1957, were in the processing industries, whose rapid expansion was facilitated not only by favourable prices but by the easy availability of imported raw materials, again largely bought with foreign credits and doubly attractive because artificial exchange rates and low import duties made them seem cheap. Now these particular credits were running out and the balance of payments made it difficult to foresee new ones on the same scale, while domestic prices for raw materials offered Yugoslavia's own producers little possibility or incentive to fill the gap through expanded production, which would in any case require time. As foreign credits ran out, so did the processing industries' supply of raw materials.[4]

Encouraged by their recent successes and ignoring these signs, the regime launched a new Five-Year Plan in January 1961, slightly more modest than their latest achievements but still more ambitious than the former Plan. It was accompanied, more in ignorance than in contempt of the inauspiciousness of the moment, by another attempt to liberalise the economic system. Introduced with great fanfare, the new reform was hailed as the most important since 1950. The decline in the growth rates in several sectors during the second half of 1960 was dismissed by the Government and the Federal Planning Institute as 'within the framework of normal fluctuations'.[5]

The State abandoned its control over distribution of the net income of enterprises, which were thereby free for the first time to determine for themselves how much should be reinvested, how much consigned to reserves and how much distributed as personal incomes. The tax structure was rationalised and (except for an excess profits tax, one of several compromises in the reform package) reduced to flat rate rather than progressive taxes as an additional incentive to profitable enterprises. A reform of the banking and credit system, designed ultimately to transform the banks from *de facto* Government disbursement agencies into autonomous credit institutions, had the initial effect of permitting rapid expansion of short-term credits and their misappropriation for capital investment purposes. Important changes were also introduced in the foreign trade system, partly under pressure from the US, West German and other Western creditors who supplied loans in support of the reform, partly as a step both towards Yugoslav full membership in the General Agreement on Tariffs and Trade (GATT) and towards free international competition—for foreign goods on the Yugoslav market and for Yugoslav goods abroad—which the regime believed would eventually be necessary to make domestic production more efficient and to counterbalance domestic monopolies. The dinar was devalued, multiple rates of exchange were to be abolished and the proportion of imports subject to quantitative restrictions was reduced.[6]

Whether or not these reforms had had time to add to existing inflationary pressures, as some were later to argue, the gross investment rate, wage levels and the foreign trade deficit were all thoroughly out of hand by the middle of 1961. The Government was forced to intervene with emergency measures, including a wage freeze, a moratorium on new investment and a partial reversal of the latest liberalisation of foreign trade. Other classic deflationary devices followed these temporary decrees: wage rises were tied to prior rises in productivity and compulsory blocked reserve funds were created to siphon off a portion of enterprise investment funds.

By the second half of 1961 the boom had turned into recession and by mid-1962 the new Plan and the hopes that had accompanied it had been discarded. The growth rate for industrial production, which had been 15 per cent in 1960, declined to only 7 per cent in 1961 and an annual rate of 4 per cent in the first half of 1962. Labour productivity showed a similar decline and per capita real wages, which had risen by 13 per cent in 1959 and by 8·2 per cent in 1960, actually declined in 1961-62.[7]

An alarmed Tito, who had virtually ignored domestic affairs in recent months, leaving his lieutenants to mind the home front while he concentrated on foreign affairs, turned his attention once again to the internal scene. In March 1962, he called a three-day meeting of the Party's Executive Committee 'with augmented complement' and sternly said that the fault lay in 'subjective shortcomings'—lack of discipline and 'of unity in action and thought, first and foremost among leading Communists and those in the highest positions'.[8] But the only immediate results were some personnel changes of subsequent importance—placing Boris Krajger of Slovenia and Miloš Minić of Serbia in key economic policy-making positions and replacing the director of the Institute for Economic Planning—and a strongly-worded circular letter of April 3 to Party leaderships at all levels, inveighing against private enrichment, bureaucratic malfeasance and indiscipline, and calling on them to combat individual, 'localist' and 'nationalist' abuses of the existing system.[9] These slender results only thinly disguised the basic disagreements which had been aired at the March session and were the beginning of a 'papering over' of a fundamental split at the Party centre which Tito was publicly to regret four years later.[10] For the moment, however, his own political instincts were distinctly inclining him to blame excessive liberalisation. In May he went before the country with an angry speech at Split, attacking the narrowly selfish, profit-seeking and un-Communist behaviour of socialist and private entrepreneurs so uncompromisingly that it was widely interpreted as signalling a victory for advocates of a return to central planning and control.[11] When the reactions to the letter and the speech were in, the Central Committee was convened, its 4th Plenum since the 1958 Congress.

The agonising reappraisal had begun. Before it was over the political as well as the economic compromise of the 1950s was in tatters and even the supremely delicate question of the role of the Party in a 'self-managed' socialist democracy, unasked since Djilas had answered it too boldly in 1953, had been raised again.

New actors to articulate old interests

The recession of 1961-62, exposing the weaknesses of the compromise economic model of the 1950s, did not create the bewildering array of proffered solutions, or the Party and other interest groups, and the differing interpretations of ideology supporting each of them, which characterised the confusion and growing social and political tensions of following years. All of these were latent and occasionally openly expressed in the debates preceding the adoption of the Second and Third Five-Year Plans and the mini-reforms of 1958 and 1961. But the recession did have the effect of making a thorough rather than another superficial reform of the entire system seem urgent. It thereby posed again with equal urgency the prior problem of the basic direction and strategy of socialist Yugoslavia's future economic development, a problem evaded through compromise in each previous mini-reform because any coherent solution presupposed a non-existent and increasingly evasive ideological and political consensus.

The recession therefore acted like a chemical precipitant on a Yugoslav political establishment within which evanescent factions on specific issues had formed and dissolved for seven years without clear or enduring divisions. It inaugurated a process of polarisation in which it was increasingly legitimate to speak of two factions and to define the social, economic, and regional or ethnic interests backing each of them. For convenience, one group can be called 'conservatives', for they wished to conserve (if also to improve upon) the partly de-Stalinised quasi-market economy and loose-reined, largely indirect but still politically monopolistic Party control which constituted the operational essence of the existing system. The other, *pace* their own Marxist and historically conditioned dislike of the term, can with technical and also historical accuracy be called 'liberals', for they sought an expansion of entrepreneurial and civil liberties, a diminishing role for the State, and a (usually limited) extension of the effective franchise. Some of the latter, to complete the historic analogy implicit in the metaphorical use of this label, were in the course of a decade to pass, like ghosts out of nineteenth-century Central Europe, from liberalism through national-liberalism to nationalism.

The process was initially confused because so were the actors and most of the immediate if not the underlying issues. It remained confused, even in the second phase after 1966, because of an enduring feature of the rules of the political game in socialist Yugoslavia, one which would be challenged only after 1966, and still only gingerly and hazardously, as a relic of Stalinist dogmatism. This was the Party's residual claim to historic infallibility in matters of doctrine, enforceable by Party sanctions tantamount to exclusion from political participation. While

Yugoslav doctrines protected by such sanctity were relatively few in number and usually so general that they easily countenanced various and changing interpretations, the inhibitions imposed by the rule meant that usually only secondary or specific issues could be openly debated but not the underlying doctrinal or programmatic principles that were often being challenged. At the same time, the need to phrase every criticism or proposal in terms of subtly different definitions of unchallengeable concepts like 'self-management', 'social ownership' or the Kardeljian definition of 'socialist democracy' often reduced (or elevated) the argument to the level of obscure scholasticism.

Some of the classic doctrines of Marxist economics were subjected to the same process. For example, the old slogan 'to each according to his work' was ritually repeated and even used as a polemical weapon by both sides to the Yugoslav debate but with quite different meanings. The 'conservatives' appeared to construe it in accordance with the labour theory of value—to each according to his contribution to the physical volume of production under equal conditions of work—but for the 'liberals' it was now in effect redefined to mean to each according to his contribution to the market value of production, or as one foreign scholar was to phrase it, 'to each according to the factors of production supplied by the human agent or to which the human agent has access, as valued on the (imperfect) market'.[12] Similarly, everyone was in favour of 'equalisation of conditions of work' because it also meant two different things: to the conservatives that a ton of coal produced by a Bosnian mine should earn the same as a ton produced by a Slovenian mine, and that the 'surplus' earned by the higher productivity of the Slovenian mine should be taxed away and given to Bosnia to help raise productivity there by further investment; to the liberals, who noted that such a policy was a disincentive and even a penalty for more efficient, lower-cost operation, the same phrase was coming to mean equal obligations to the community for both mines, with the rich getting richer and the poor forced to become efficient or go out of business.

As an additional complication, the participants in the dialogue, whether consciously or not, were reflecting in the positions they adopted an ill-digested mixture of concerns and motivations. Some were almost purely economic in scope: was one more frustrated by inefficiencies in the existing system or by almost annual changes which made it extraordinarily difficult to plan ahead? was the existing system or one or another of the proposed changes in it perceived as advantageous or disadvantageous to one's own enterprise, economic sector, region or nationality, or institutional or personal role? Some were ideological: if such things mattered, was one more distressed by the manifest gulf between the real state of affairs and the normative or programmatic principles of self-management, or by the growing gulf between both theory and practice and the 'real' socialism of orthodox Marxism-Leninism? did one give greater priority among sometimes contradictory Yugoslav principles to the doctrine of self-management, to ideological aspects of the problem of reconciling planning and market mechanisms, or to the doctrine of the leading role of the Party and its corollaries? The answer in each case had political implications because each of the questions concerned the locus of power, whether monopolistic or pluralistic, over a significant range of public decisions. And because the men involved were simultaneously economic, ideological and political animals, the position that each of them ultimately assumed was the composite function of sometimes contradictory positions on each of these questions and others, further coloured by the rules of the political game and by conceptual frameworks shaped by the vocabulary of that game.

Concern over misallocation of investment resources and other negative effects of an awkward combination of market and planning mechanisms had been expressed by a number of leading economists for several years. Instead of the best of both worlds, Yugoslavia appeared to them to be having the worst of both, with what Rudolf Bićanić described in 1957 'as an ambivalent system, partly governed by the laws of imperfect competition, and partly administratively controlled, so that it is very difficult to make this system work'.[13]

A Congress of the Yugoslav Association of Economists, in May 1958, had been preoccupied primarily with this problem.[14] The first frontal attack and the only significant one prior to the 1961 recession came, however, from a different and somewhat surprising source: the Federation of Yugoslav Trade Unions. Still largely unnoticed, a new institutional actor was moving from the nondescript ranks of the obedient chorus of the Party's preemptive organisations to a downstage position where its voice, while still fundamentally in harmony, would be separately heard.

Yugoslav trade unions, like their counterparts farther to the east, had hitherto behaved like the passive 'transmission belt' for the Party word that they were designed to be. Their last recorded gesture of independence had been Djuro Salaj's alleged resistance to and then reluctant co-operation in setting up the first workers' councils in 1949-50. Now, in the context of continuing dissatisfaction with the meagre expansion of enterprise control over enterprise revenue introduced by the 1958 reforms, their Central Committee was suddenly showing signs of pretensions to a role in the formation as well as the execution of policy. The change in behaviour was directly attributable to a change in leadership which was in turn the regime's characteristic reaction to the shock of

Yugoslavia's first serious strike since nationalisation. An apparently spontaneous two-day work stoppage had paralysed the important Trbovlje coal mines in Slovenia at the end of 1957 and its spread to the rest of the Republic was narrowly averted. An investigating commission concluded that the strike represented a breakdown in self-management and was therefore basically justified.

The matter was considered serious enough to merit a meeting of the top Party leadership, at which Tito declared that the primary responsibility lay with the passivity of the trade unions, which had failed in their watch-dog function by not taking timely preventive action. Union leadership must therefore be changed 'from top to bottom'. The man chosen to carry out this task and replace an ageing Salaj was Svetozar Vukmanović-Tempo.

Vukmanović's appointment was an astute choice. It removed from the key position in the economy an eager primitive spirit and self-confident economic illiterate who was generally held responsible for many of the wilder, more expensive mistakes and abrupt systemic changes of the 1950s. It put him instead into a role where his real talents could be more fully exploited: the ebullient energy that had earned him his Partisan *nom-de-guerre* and a happy combination of fierce Party loyalty and an independent mind, intense personal ambition operationally limited by simplistic belief in proclaimed principles and extreme tactlessness, and a special quality of bull-headedness, simultaneously endearing and infuriating his colleagues, but which guaranteed that the desired shake-up would be thorough. Now, resentful at his demotion,[15] he brought all these qualities to bear in an effort to make his new fiefdom both a principal agency in bringing Yugoslav practice into line with Yugoslav theory and an active new personal power base. In the process the trade union organisation become first the essential, if seldom recognised, ally of the liberal faction in the Party and then its nascent critic and even potential rival, a role which eventually led in 1969 to another and this time definitive removal (to the largely honorific Council of the Federation) of the irrepressible character whom someone once called 'the Yugoslav George Brown'.[16]

The first focus of attention on the part of the revitalised trade union leadership was the question of income distribution, both within the enterprise and between the economy and 'society' in the form of the State. Their starting point was the inadequacy and even hypocrisy of the 1958 reforms, incidentally also resented by Vukmanović simply because they were adopted without his participation, while he was out of the country.[17] The reforms had declaratively freed the enterprises to determine for themselves how much should go into personal incomes and how much into investment and social funds, but then had effectively denied them this right through the modality of State-dictated minimum personal incomes and through progressive taxes which left very little net income to distribute in any case. They had therefore failed to satisfy the demands put forward at both the Congress of Workers' Councils in 1957 and the 7th Party Congress in 1958, or to provide the incentives that should have been a cardinal virtue of self-managed market socialism. On the basis of this argument the trade union leaders, unprecedentedly refusing to co-operate with the FEC in working out the details of the minimum personal income scheme, elaborated their counter-proposals. The tax system should be strictly limited to (1) the existing capital tax on the book value of 'socially owned' fixed and working capital, at variable rates by economic branch, (2) a turnover tax designed exclusively to expropriate income based on monopolistic positions, (3) a rent to be paid for privileged access to scarce natural resources, and (4) proportional rather than progressive taxes levied against net income to finance public administration, defence, the health service, education, etc.[18]

Superficially a technical question and one logically within the purview of the trade unions, the 'battle for the law of incomes' on which they were now embarked clearly had far wider economic and political implications. Tito perceived this immediately when he warned Vukmanović, who presented the draft proposals with a request for advice and political support, that he would face more serious opposition than he imagined, 'because you've come to grips with the basic problem of socialism'.[19]

The crux of the matter, as Tito was aware if Vukmanović was not, was that by including 'the means for expanded reproduction' in the class of residual income which the enterprises should control and distribute, the trade unions and others who shared their views had in fact challenged the foundation stone of the compromise system of the 1950s. This was the explicit division of labour between plan and market (and hence between the State and the economy) which had left control over the volume and sectoral distribution of most investment funds to the State as an ideological and practical necessity, essential to socialist planning, to effective 'social ownership', to the avoidance of an 'anarchic' market and uncontrolled economic development no better than capitalism, and even to the preservation of the delicate political balance of the 1950s.

Debate on these proposals and related intrigues continued throughout 1959 and 1960 and occasionally surfaced in the press or in parliament. The rationale of enterprise control of investment funds and a revamped tax system was again and more forcefully argued in the pages of a reorganised and suddenly militant *Rad*, the central trade union newspaper, and at the 4th Congress of the Trade Union Federation in April 1959. Joint commissions of leading figures from the trade union organisation, the Government, the Federal Economic Chamber, and/or economists' associations were formed on two occasions to prepare concrete proposals. Both times, however, and despite the apparently firm support for the project of Kardelj as vice-president of the FEC, the mandates and composition of these commissions were arbitrarily changed and they were abruptly dissolved.

Opposition at this stage seems to have come from several sources and was based in part on pragmatic considerations and in part on political caution and bureaucratic jealousies. As long as growth rates remained high, there was good reason to argue that too frequent changes in the system were more damaging than existing distortions and disincentives. This was the view expressed by Mijalko Todorović in presenting the 1959 Social Plan to the Federal People's Assembly on behalf of the FEC. It is probable, however, that some of those at the Party-Government summit also resented the unwontedly independent assertiveness and meddling of the trade union Central Committee and the Federal Economic Chamber in this previously sacrosanct area and at a time when their own drafting of the 1961 reforms was already under way. Others resented this assertiveness on principle. Their views were pressed within the trade union Central Committee by Dragi Stamenković, the president of the Serbian Trade Union Federation and generally considered to be close to Ranković. According to Vukmanović, it was Stamenković and then Ranković himself, ultimately backed by Tito, who insisted that Vukmanović withdraw from the draft of his report to the 1959 Trade Union Congress a section in which the unions were said to have the right and duty 'to form their own positions on all social problems'.[20]

Underlying all of these arguments for at least many of the participants was a lively awareness that any further serious reform, and particularly one affecting the role of central political authorities in investment, would necessarily bring about a significant interregional (and in Yugoslavia therefore inter-ethnic) redistribution of capital, of economic growth rates and of national income, further implying an eventual shift in the primary geographic and ethnic locus of political power as well. This awareness was a factor in the attitude taken by many of those involved in the 'battle for the law of incomes' in 1959–60, but it interested other if partly overlapping sets of actors even more directly, and with greater long-run importance. These were the regional authorities, in both Party and Government, and the local economic interests which stood to gain or to lose with any such redistribution.

Again, there was nothing new in this awareness of what was really at stake, or in regionally different preferences arising from conflicting interests. What was new was an increasing willingness and ability to insist that these interests be heard from and counted, initially expressed (in the logic of things) by those who wished to alter the *status quo* and then, in reaction, by those who wished to maintain it. For the moment this insistence was based primarily on the exploitable gulf between proclaimed principles and observable practice in 'self-management' and on growing self-confidence engendered by the discovery, in small conflicts and victories, that decentralisation in the 1950s (and their own awareness of the contradiction) had weakened both the will and the ability of the central authorities to keep taut the reins of central authoritarianism. When this still amorphous basis proved inadequate to the achievement of reform, as it soon did, new institutional means for the aggregation and expression of these regional and particular interests would be found or invented.

It was thus that the regime, which had sowed decentralisation, economic and social modernisation and a myth of participant socialism, reaped the whirlwind of newly mobilised social forces and demands. The first result was the creation of an effective pluralism in which consensus was to prove peculiarly evasive, primarily because the regional element in the conflict of interests would be perceived by most of the participants as an ethnic conflict and thus elevated to a transcendent and emotional level which made mutual understanding and compromise extraordinarily difficult. Thus it also was that the Yugoslav 'national question', relatively dormant since the war, again became Yugoslavia's central question.

The interregional dimension of the dispute was phrased in terms of the conspicuous failure of fifteen years of economic development under socialism to fulfil one of its basic promises by narrowing if not eliminating the great economic and social differences between the relatively developed northern republics and the desperately underdeveloped southern ones. All parties agreed that the failure existed but disagreed profoundly about the reasons and therefore about future strategies.

As has been seen (pp. 99f.), the search for a more rational method of assisting the underdeveloped regions, at minimum cost and with maximum effect, had been a dominant theme of the 1950s. That one had not been found was reflected in the continuation of ad hoc and repeatedly changed modes of assistance, the widening gap and increasing frustration openly expressed on all sides. The difficulty lay not only in the complexity of the problem, which was simultaneously baffling the equally determined and at least as sophisticated planners of other ethnically more homogeneous countries with similar 'dual economies', most notably in neighbouring Italy.[21] It also lay in deep mutual suspicions that the other side was getting or seeking more than its fair share of the cake. Such suspicions, rooted in the history of the Yugoslav national question, had been reinforced since 1953 by an economic localism which was encouraged by a system in which initiative and decision-making were decentralised but most funds were not.[22]

In this area the 1961 reforms constituted yet another compromise which would not be implemented. The system of guaranteed investments to encourage speedier economic development and grants-in-aid to equalise social services and finance administration in the country's underdeveloped regions, which at least had had the advantage of permitting longer-range planning since 1957, was abandoned in principle. It was to be replaced by a federally-financed Special Fund for the Development of Underdeveloped Areas, similar to the Cassa per il Mezzogiorno in Italy, but the actual establishment of the Fund was postponed for another four years because of continuing disagreement about how it should be financed. An ambitious new classification of eligible underdeveloped regions represented a further concession to the 'developed' republics, especially Croatia: in addition to all of Macedonia, Montenegro and the Kosmet, specified districts in southern Serbia, large parts of Bosnia-Herzegovina and the Croatian districts of Lika, Banija, Kordun and the Dalmatian hinterland were now included.[23] The new tax system was also a compromise among regional interests, as well as a partial acceptance of the tax proposals drawn up by the Trade Union Federation. Flat-rate, proportionate taxes by economic sector favoured profitable enterprises with already favourable prices, which usually meant the processing industries concentrated in the north and west, but the addition to the package of a progressive super-tax on 'excess' profits partly righted the balance. It also largely eliminated the incentives to greater productivity which had motivated the turn to flat-rate levies.

It was at this point that the recession of 1961–62 raised to the level of an urgent reappraisal of the entire system all of these previously somewhat academic or apparently marginal debates about regional development priorities, the relative merits of centrally planned or decentralised, market-dictated allocation of resources and the economic role of the State under market socialism. The reappraisal began with a grand debate among rival schools of economists, initially about the reasons for the recession and at first largely restricted to professional meetings and journals. The line-up, predictably if with some exceptions, reflected regional interests. As a result, highly technical and sometimes ideological arguments about economic issues often seemed a transparent mask for that other, bitterer debate about ethnic domination or subordination and the basic form and purpose of the Yugoslav State. This was in a sense true but also misleading. Both sets of issues were real, and although they were logically and even psychologically inseparable, the question of the economic system for the moment took precedence and could be treated as though separate, albeit for primarily political reasons. Given the existing balance of forces within the Party centre and the Party's continuing monopoly of organised political activity, it was still only in the economy that significant reform could take place, but such a reform was now highly possible. As one of the Party's leading social scientists observed in retrospect, after 1961

one could easily 'attack' the old economic system in the name of rationality and an economic economy. That is, a 'socialist' bureaucracy, which makes a fetish of production, would find it difficult to resist the liquidation of economic instruments and relations which visibly gave rise to, multiplied, and stimulated people to irrationality, and there were many such instruments.[24]

The economists' debate

Public 'debates' in Yugoslavia during the decade after 1954 tended to follow an observable pattern. They normally waited for a cue given by a senior official, often Tito himself, usually a sign that the private debate on the issue within the inner Communist establishment had been concluded at least temporarily. Then the winning side's case would be presented to the public and almost invariably debased by the primitiveness and over-eagerness of lower-rank exegesis into an over-simplified 'campaign' which was carried to extremes and soon induced some vigorous backpedalling at the top. From the arguments offered it was often possible to extrapolate the opposition's case. Nor was the opposition entirely silent and inactive. The discipline of 'democratic centralism' tended to break down in the face of (1) issues on which the central authority had not spoken unequivocally and thus implicitly declared to be questions of confidence; (2) issues which were sufficiently complicated to be subject to challenge or sabotage on points of detail; and (3) decentralisation, which really had dispersed power into a number of semi-autonomous centres capable of acting independently when conditions (1) or (2) were also fulfilled.

All of this happened in the debate on the economic system which began in 1962, but in a curiously extended fashion. The original 'cue' was apparently given by Tito in his May 1962 speech at Split, which was interpreted as signalling a pro-centralist hard line. Such a line had already been anticipated by emergency anti-inflationary measures at the end of 1961, by the Executive Committee's letter of April 3, 1962, and by the adoption that same month of a law creating a network of commissions to oversee implementation of the FEC's new rules for the distribution of enterprise net income. All together these measures were equivalent to a return to the pre-1958 system. After the Split speech a characteristic 'campaign' was mounted against private craftsmen, who were so hard-pressed that they closed their shops by the thousands, ultimately bringing about a grudging retreat by authorities who could no longer find anyone to repair their own TV sets, cars and plumbing. Observers who liked discovering a correlation between Yugoslav domestic politics and fluctuations in Soviet-Yugoslav relations noted that the latter had again been improving since the summer of 1961, bringing Soviet Head of State Leonid Brezhnev on an official visit to Yugoslavia in September 1962 and allegedly sending Djilas back to prison that autumn because the publication abroad of his *Conversations with Stalin* had offended the Russians.

This time, however, such judgements were premature. The debate, both public and private, had only begun.

In July 1962 the Central Committee of the LCY assembled for its 4th Plenum, an occasion which would normally produce a definitive statement. It produced instead, at the end of the discussion, a complaint by Tito that he had 'expected this Plenary Session to mark a turning point in our economic policy', but that, on the contrary, 'I do not find in the reports an answer to the question as to how we should overcome our present difficulties and how the Yugoslav economy should develop in the future'.[25] Despite some acute analyses of the economic problem by Krajger and Minić in their reports and by Tito himself in his concluding remarks, the discussion and the conclusions adopted at the end of the Plenum were unambiguous on only three subjects: some unexceptionable recommendations on short-run reflationary measures to get the economy moving again, a continuing belief that increased agricultural production must come primarily from the small socialist sector and a firm statement that decentralisation and economic integration to achieve economies of scale through mass production were not incompatible goals. The second of these was of primarily negative significance and the third was not new, although its restatement at this time did act as a 'cue' to launch a renewed 'campaign' for more amalgamations of enterprises as an antidote to the uneconomic fragmentation of the 1950s. As usual, the campaign quickly led to extremes and to political pressures on workers' councils to accept unwanted integrations. Entrenched localism found an answer to the problem of how dutifully to integrate something without violating local frontiers by promoting often absurd and irrational combinations of enterprises with nothing in common except location on the territory of the same commune or district.[26]

Ranković's lengthy report, as Organisational Secretary, surveyed what the Party had and had not done since the April letter and the Split speech. Noting that 'there has been sharp criticism of particularism and localism, of chauvinistic trends, of republics' sealing themselves off and of local national complacencies and other tendencies which run counter to all-national integration', he called for disciplined and active implementation of the Plenum's conclusions.[27] These, however, offered no clear line on any fundamental issue. Even Tito's sharp remarks about the waste and wider negative consequences of assisting underdeveloped regions by building 'political factories' were moderated to meaninglessness in the conclusions as adopted. Specific references by several speakers to the key issue of an enlarged role in investment for enterprises or republics and communes were similarly reduced to the non-commital statement that 'constant attention should be paid to the further strengthening of the material basis of workers management.'[28] The tenor of the debate and of the adopted conclusions indicated that divisions were not yet clear or that there was no viable majority, and that the 'papering over' of differences which had begun in March would therefore continue, presumably in the hope that a consensus would somehow eventually emerge.

Tito's own concluding remarks, full of inconsistent arguments which could be interpreted as supporting contradictory solutions, confirm this interpretation but also suggest that his own position had become ambivalent. Perhaps the most revealing came in a somewhat rambling section in which he seemed to endorse the major plank in the 'liberal' platform and then admitted that opinions were divided and postponed a decision. Turning again to the crucial question of investment funds, he complained that the reports before the Plenum still 'do not say where these funds should be situated and who should dispose of them'. There were references, in general terms, to the republics and communes but not to the enterprises, although 'we have taken everything away from them so far'. Tito agreed that 'we must ensure correct decentralisation and a proper distribution of resources, so that people ... should be able to dispose freely of their resources', but he did not agree that this should be done 'entirely through decentralisation to the republics and communes'. He repeated that he would prefer to lay emphasis on the enterprises, but added: 'I think some comrades will perhaps not agree with me and I do not insist that this should be adopted here today'.[29]

These remarks, full of hesitations, were consistent with later reliable reports that Tito's initial reaction, when he returned to the country and was confronted by the economic situation, had been to blame decentralisation of investment funds for the excess demand which had destroyed the boom and to opt for rigid recentralisation, but that he was then shown evidence that about 80 per cent of investment funds remained under effective but financially irresponsible central control, despite formal decentralisation. By the time of the 4th Plenum he was therefore no longer willing to support the centralist position, but was still unwilling to take the other side and countenance an open split for the sake of republican contenders for existing federal power.[30]

Meanwhile, and exploiting the absence of a decision at the centre, reinforcements for both sides appeared in the form of the unserried ranks of the country's economists. In December 1962 a conference of the Yugoslav Association of Economists was convened to discuss the economic implications of the new Constitution, then in the final drafting stage. While several points of view were expressed, the dominant one held that the recession was primarily the consequence of excessive liberalisation, which was also encouraging disintegrative localism, unequal rates of regional development and insupportable increases in personal incomes. The answer implicit in this line of criticism was at least partial recentralisation, with improved planning and a reduced role for the market.[31]

A month later the economists met again, this time in Zagreb, on January 17–19, 1963, under the joint sponsorship of their Association and the Federal Institute for Economic Planning. It proved to be the most heated and important confrontation of the extended debate.

The basis for the Zagreb discussion was provided by two at times contradictory studies of the sources of Yugoslavia's present economic problems, subsequently known respectively as the Yellow Book and the White Book.[32] The first was prepared by a group of economists associated with the sponsoring Federal Planning Institute and under the supervision of Branko Horvat, its director (since March 1962) and himself an outstanding but often controversial economist whose independent views, never clearly either centralist or liberal, were appropriately symbolised by his position as a Croat in charge of the federal planning agency. The authors were a regionally and ethnically mixed group, two of whom also contributed to the White Book, and the Yellow Book took a fundamentally middle-of-the-road position. It discovered immediate causes of the recession in the hasty and ill-considered nature of both the liberalising reforms of 1961 and the restrictive measures of that autumn and the following year, as well as in serious defects in the structure of investments, which did not necessarily reflect defects in the basic system. The White Book was more clearly partisan, both regionally and in argument. Croatian Party Secretary Bakarić called himself its 'co-initiator', and the authors were all leading Croatian economists, several of whom were to play important political as well as economic roles in the coming decade. They included Savka Dabčević-Kučar, Croatian prime minister and then Party boss from 1966 until December 1971; Ivo Perišin, later governor of the National Bank and Croatian prime minister after January 1972; and Jakov Sirotković, vice-president of the FEC for economic affairs after 1969.

The White Book was thus the first comprehensive statement of an emerging Croatian version of a 'socialist model for a developed country'.[33] The basic argument was that central planning might be the best principal allocator of resources in the early stages of economic growth (because it is good at mobilising labour and resources and at enforcing a higher rate of saving than would otherwise occur in a poor society, and because the market functions badly in such circumstances), but that it thereafter becomes increasingly dysfunctional, if only because the number and complexity of allocative decisions becomes greater than any planning system can cope with, while the market becomes increasingly capable of efficient allocation. The higher the level of economic development, therefore, the more freedom for market forces and the fewer interventions by planners or politicians there should be.

The Zagreb discussions were sharp and at times acrimonious. While the principal confrontation was between 'centralisers' and 'decentralisers', or between proponents of more planning and proponents of more market, there were in fact four distinct views, as Deborah Milenkovitch points out. Among the 'decentralizers', who all agreed that present difficulties 'were attributable to over-centralization, mismanagement, and meddling, the "legacies" of a central planning psychology', there were those who wished 'to free the enterprises from the morass of regulations and to allow them to make decisions, including investment decisions, on the basis of market forces', and those for whom 'decentralization was used to express an opposition not to planning as such, but to planning done at the national center instead of at the republican or local level'. There were also two kinds of 'centralizers': those who advocated more central planning and greater control over the enterprises, and those who accepted the existing limits of the market economy but did not wish to see them enlarged.[34]

The economists' debate continued throughout 1963 and into 1964, when (significantly) it ceased to be confined largely to professional meetings and small-circulation professional journals and was taken up by the mass media and in public speeches. It was also influenced by the context in which it was conducted, the post-recession behaviour of the economy.

Essentially what the regime did in 1963, as we have seen, was to turn the clock back to 1956, cutting out significant if still marginal enterprise and communal control over investment decisions by blocking their funds, putting the lid back on the rise in personal incomes, and extending price controls. To these moves were added some minor but helpful reforms of the foreign trade and credit systems and the psychological impact of the Split speech and a display of Government and Party energy. The economy responded accordingly, and the last months of 1962 and all of 1963 saw a renewal of the rapid expansion of the 1956-60 period. At the end of 1963, in presenting the annual Plan for 1964 in his capacity as chairman of the FEC's Committee for the Social Plan, Minić was able to point to an encouraging list of accomplishments: Social Product had grown by 12 per cent during the year, the third highest postwar growth rate, industrial production by over 15 per cent and agricultural production by 7 per cent; exports were up 16 per cent, realised investments by over 17 per cent, real personal consumption in the socialist sector by 13 per cent and labour productivity by 9·5 per cent, an all-time record.[35]

Lurking in this same list of happy socialist growth statistics there were, however, two ominous notes. Demand, in the form of personal consumption and especially of investments, was again growing more rapidly than supply; and the cost of living, which had been stable for many months, began an upward movement which abruptly picked up speed early in 1964. The trade gap widened to help finance booming consumption by means of the deficit, and another devaluation appeared increasingly inevitable. News that industrial production during the first six months of 1964 was 18 per cent higher than a year before, and the value of investments 50 per cent higher (!), was no longer considered grounds for self-congratulation.[36] The new boom was accompanied by the same distortions which had led to the collapse of the old one in 1961.

Thus the recession of 1961-62 had given way to growth restarted by stop-gap measures of short-run effectiveness. The economy's structural weaknesses, so intensively but inconclusively discussed in the meanwhile, were still virtually untouched, but could not remain so much longer without at the very least an unacceptable repetition of a very unsocialist and unsettling business cycle. Perhaps this realisation led to the political decision to bring the economic debate into the open air of the Federal Assembly and the mass-circulation daily newspapers—a move which took place, after several false starts, at the end of January 1964. The date coincided with a public admission that 'work stoppages' (only three years later freely called 'strikes') were occurring in a number of industries, especially in Slovenia and Slavonia, and with a now public acceptance of their legitimacy as a sign that workers' self-management was not functioning as it should.[37]

The debate becomes public

It was clear that some decisions of long-range significance had been made somewhere and also that they were still being challenged, now on specific issues rather than on general principles, by an unreconciled opposition. *Komunist*, commenting on April 23, hinted that this was the case and for the first time publicly admitted the existence of both past and present differences. Noting that 'agreement on certain essential changes' had now been reached, the writer added: 'It may seem superfluous to put extra stress on that agreement. But it is a fact that, a year ago, there was no such unanimity and determination.' And later: 'It is necessary, though, to state that despite this unanimity concerning the most general matters, there are still differences of views about certain very important details.'

The case for economic reform presented to the public in 1964 contained the same list of themes discussed by Tito and others at the 4th Plenum in July 1962, subsequently refined, elaborated and in some cases reduced to practical proposals for structural reforms which bore the imprint of the Croatian views expressed in the White Book of January 1963. In the process, the argument had become more precise and had undergone some significant changes in emphasis and preferred slogans.[38]

The liberal attack was now concentrated quite specifically on three major target areas: existing proportions in the distribution of national income between investment and consumption, political control of the investment system, and the existing price regime, with the first and third treated primarily as functions of the second. In their style of attack the liberals had also shifted their ground slightly but significantly. The key word was no longer 'decentralisation' (*decentralizacija*) but 'de-étatisation' (*de-etatizacija*), while in recent months they had discovered that implicit in their programme was a slogan with great popular appeal, 'a low tension Plan for higher living standards'.[39] In part these shifts were a tactical move to get on to firmer ground—to avoid, for example, the accusation that through decentralisation they were advocating local and national (specifically Slovene and Croatian) interests against all-Yugoslav ones—but in part they also reflected a discovery of what it was that they really did not like in the existing system and what they thought had gone wrong with earlier attempts at liberalisation.

In its mature form, as in the White and Yellow Books of 1963, the liberal argument began by agreeing that the mixed system evolved during the 1950s had expedited economic growth at the time. The then remaining instruments of State control, including a dominant role in saving and investment, might even be necessary for rapid and sustained growth in any underdeveloped society, but only until the achievement of economic 'take-off'—simplistically defined as a per capita national income of $500, the magic threshold of 'development' posited by many Western economists and by happy chance the level approached by Yugoslavia in 1964—and a certain minimum of technological and political experience by a larger sector of the population.[40] The liberal economists and politicians might also agree that the liberalisation of 1961 had been imposed too quickly and without short-term cushioning, but their basic argument was that what went wrong then was a failure to carry liberalisation far enough. The retention of ubiquitous administrative interventions and of centrally determined and inevitably political allocation of investments in the post-take-off period, they insisted, introduces a series of distortions which must fatally compromise both the economic goals and the socio-political principles of Yugoslav socialism.

These distortions, it was argued, were particularly evident in three fields. The first was in the investment-consumption ratio, which had been unchanged for a decade, with the share of national income allotted to personal incomes stagnating at around 42 per cent, while gross investment had absorbed as much as 35 per cent of Social Product (compared by the Yugoslav press with 16 per cent in the United States, 23 per cent in Italy and Poland, 19 per cent in Hungary, etc.). Looked at another way, Social Product had grown by 120 per cent in the decade 1952-61; in the same period investment consumption grew by 142·4 per cent and personal consumption by only 99·1 per cent.[41] Yugoslavia had passed beyond the stage at which such a suppression of the standard of living was necessary or useful. Not only did people deserve a larger share of the cake (38 per cent of wages in the social sector were still less than 25,000 dinars—then $33—a month), but their getting it, and preferably in the form of direct income which they could themselves decide how to spend, would contribute to the building of a more rational demand structure and a better balanced and healthier economic growth.

The second and basic source of distortions lay in the investment system, in principle based on a division of labour in which the Plan was responsible for the sectoral distribution of the total investment fund, therefore involving political factors, while the market was responsible for allocation to final users (the enterprises) within each sector. The malfunctioning of this system was said to account in large part for both the size and the inefficient use of investment's share in national income.

Earlier reforms, it was pointed out, had genuinely decentralised the initiative in making investment decisions—by 1961 exercised by a multitude of enterprises, banks and communal governments, as well as by the Federal Government—but not control and real responsibility for mistakes or miscalculations. Although business banking criteria, profitability in particular, were supposed to be used in distributing investment and short-term credits, the banks in such a system were inevitably more susceptible to political pressures than to economic criteria in making their decisions. Their funds, after all, came through political channels (the State) and not from the economy itself. Furthermore, the system left no one ultimately responsible for the economic employment and repayment of these funds. The banks did not care if they were lost, for these were not 'their' funds; in fact their own income was largely dependent on the volume of business they did, creating an incentive to make as many loans as possible. Nor was the Government responsible for decisions made by others. So enterprises in trouble could ask for debts to be wiped out, or for a moratorium, or (and most frequently the case) for just one more credit to get them over the hump to profitability.

Such possibilities bred another, specialised, form of irresponsibility, the essential ingredient of the now universally condemned vice of economic localism. It was obviously a good thing for a commune to have a factory, paying taxes and creating employment, on its territory. With a blueprint for a nice, cheap little factory a credit could be obtained. And once the plant was started it could be discovered that costs had been drastically underestimated, so that additional credits were needed. As the commitment by commune and bank grew, so did the difficulty of calling a halt, especially when it was not they but the Federal or republican Government which must provide the means to keep an unprofitable enterprise in business.

Thanks to these and other abuses, actual investments always exceeded planned investments, sometimes by a multiple of the plan, unbalancing the savings-investment equation and breeding inflation. And all over the country, but especially in underdeveloped areas, 'political' factories sprouted up, so-called because of the 'political' decision that a commune should have a factory and the later 'political' decisions that a factory, once there, could not be allowed to close—or even to merge with a stronger enterprise located somewhere else and therefore under the control of another communal government and tax regime.[42]

The third distortion resulted from controlled prices affecting 70 per cent of all industrial commodities, the need for which was dictated by inflationary pressures now in turn considered primarily a function of the excessive level and inefficient use of investments. The particular problem presented by these controls was that they tended to preserve a structure of price ratios inherited from and designed to meet the requirements of a command economy and later altered ad hoc and without planning, in response to unco-ordinated individual needs. As a result, Yugoslav prices still only rarely and coincidentally reflected relative scarcity values and therefore could not provide the rational 'signals' essential to the functioning of a market economy.[43] In a Soviet-type command economy, for example, the prices of raw materials and producers' goods are kept low and those of consumer goods are pegged at a high level in order to increase demand for the former and restrict demand for the latter. In Yugoslavia's quasi-market economy of the 1950s this relationship was maintained, with negative effects on the structure of supply. Sectors like mining, forestry, metals and machine tools appeared unprofitable because of low prices, required concessions and had little incentive to expand. On the other hand, consumer goods enjoyed misleading windfall profits from high prices; enterprises in this field were induced to expand output excessively and hence to overinflate the demand for raw materials which were not being produced in sufficient quantity because their prices were too low.

The consequences of such a system, the liberals concluded, involved more than an enormous wastage of national income, unnecessarily low personal consumption levels and the creation of much unutilised industrial capacity which could never be used profitably. They also provided a massive disincentive to workers and management in profitable factories, who had seen their earnings taxed away for investment in, or subsidisation of, unprofitable enterprises and regions—the preferred critical phrase had become 'fiscal "seizure" of accumulation'[44]—and for redistribution as 'indirect income' in the form of subsidised housing, holidays, travel and social services in no way related to individual ability or diligence.[45] The apparent profitability of even these enterprises was rendered virtually meaningless, because no one in such a system of irrelevant prices and other misleading signals, where profit depended less on market factors than on political connections which provided access to funds and favours, could calculate his real costs of production or where real relative cost advantages lay. The consequences also included an appalling fragmentation of industry, founded by the eager and self-interested response of local authorities to the slogan of competition and competing as the market theory said they should, but without suffering the penalties of unprofitability which can make a market economy an efficient allocator of resources. They created, in short, an economy foundering between crippled central planning and a too imperfect, distorted market, a totally but inefficiently politicised economy.

The correct answer, now allegedly accepted in principle but with unresolved 'differences of views about certain very important details', was a further and this time major and definitive retreat from intervention in the economy by Government and other political organs. In particular, the State at all levels should get out of the investment business, except for public works and major infrastructure projects to which business banking criteria could not be applied and responsibility for the still unestablished Fund for the Development of Underdeveloped Areas. Taxes and 'contributions' could then be reduced and 'accumulation' left in the hands of the profitable enterprises which had earned it. These would presumably also know best how to invest these funds, either in their own modernisation or expansion, in subsidiaries or in other enterprises and regions through a banking system designed to respond to economic, not political, criteria. The banking system itself should therefore be overhauled, with its depositors (primarily the profitable enterprises) as in effect shareholders, jointly deciding on investments and sharing the profits.

Thus individual enterprises, in collaboration with the banks, would be given control over a larger share of their earnings, plus real responsibility to prosper or perish according to the soundness of their judgements. Enterprises in the underdeveloped areas, deprived of State aid except when eligible for help from the Special Fund, should come to depend more on partnership agreements or credits from related industries in the developed republics. Under such a regime, with a lower investment rate reducing inflationary pressures, prices too could be gradually freed of administrative control. Production in general, thus rationalised, would register the statistically lower but more realistic and balanced growth rates appropriate to an intermediate level of development at which intensive rather than extensive industrialisation should be the rule.

Counter-arguments and the national question

All of these arguments and policies, whatever their economic merit, were clearly viewed as benefiting primarily the more developed republics and regions. Although this was not to prove entirely true in fact,[46] the perception was what mattered, and it was right enough in principle. The liberal argument began, as has been seen, with the assumption that 'take-off' had been achieved and that this condition demanded the revised economic strategies and new institutional devices now being recommended, including especially an increased dependence on market mechanisms for macro- as well as micro-economic allocation. But if it could be maintained that Slovenia, Croatia and northern Serbia with the Vojvodina had achieved take-off, the south manifestly had not. Its economists and politicians could reasonably argue, on the basis of accepted Marxist (and perhaps even Rostowian) views of the development process, that a high and somewhat forced investment rate must be maintained a little longer for their sakes, and that it must continue its concentration on the economic and social infrastructure which they still lacked—implying political control and central redistribution, not bankers' criteria, in allocating resources. They could also maintain that the liberal counter-argument, which held that interregional, inter-enterprise economic investments in the underdeveloped areas would largely compensate for their loss of centrally-determined 'political' investments, was either wishful thinking or hypocrisy. Economic localism, ethnic particularism and the principles of self-management (which prevented one enterprise from maintaining control over or taking profits from funds invested in another enterprise) would continue to prevent such investments from taking place on an adequate scale.

This opposition line, now under the rules of Yugoslav debates heard only *sotto voce* or in the context of those 'differences about important details',[47] included several arguments which were to prove prophetic. One was that the economy could not bear the economic or the social consequences of the collapse of enterprises and sectors whose solvency depended on subventions, subsidies and continuous injections or yet more 'political' investment funds. Nor could a regime with Welfare State commitments, and one founded on the protests of backward regions against neglect, accept the social and political consequences of the unemployment, restricted social services and widening gap between developed and underdeveloped which were certain to come. A corollary of this second objection took cognizance of the claim that a shift in emphasis from investment to personal consumption would bring a double blessing, for it would raise living standards while also structuring total demand in such a way as to provide the best balance of incentives for optimum economic growth. It was clear that in making this claim the reformers were thinking primarily of demand for consumer durables and services. But to obtain an upward adjustment of demand curves in these sectors implied larger personal incomes for those already at the top of the scale, since higher minimum wages would tend to increase demand for more expensive, higher-quality foodstuffs like meat, for low-cost housing and for other classes of goods with particularly inelastic supply curves or other reasons which made increased demand for them undesirable.[48] Was a Communist regime therefore prepared to accept the social consequences of enlarging personal income differentials at a time when rising food prices and a threat to curtail social services and 'indirect income' were already making things worse for those with lower incomes?

More specifically, it was argued that the existing system had not in fact discriminated against the developed regions, taking from them in order to invest wastefully in underdeveloped areas, as was alleged. The statistical evidence in support of this claim was complex and controversial, and was typified by the conservatives' emphasis on per capita investment, which showed the developed republics doing better than the underdeveloped (except Montenegro), while the liberals preferred data on investment as a percentage of Social Product, which put the underdeveloped areas above the Yugoslav average.[49] The claim could nevertheless be credibly made and added to other, older and purely economic arguments in favour of real future (in contrast to fictitious past) preferential treatment for the less developed regions.

The most important of these arguments was that the rapid development of the south was and would remain the most rational long-run development strategy because these areas were richest in the natural resources appropriate to an industrial society, especially minerals, and in unexploited labour reserves which it would be cheaper to use *in situ* than to move. This fact had been hidden by the historical accident which had given the south far less social overhead capital and by the postwar structure of controlled prices which discriminated against raw materials, and these together were responsible for the admittedly lower rate of short-run return on investment in the south. Preferential treatment to overcome this inheritance should therefore be regarded not as aid but as a compensation for inequities imposed by history and by faulty price policies, which would pay handsome economic as well as social dividends in the long run. More significantly, such an argument also constituted a powerful case against greater or perhaps any serious reliance on market mechanisms. Free play for the market would only increase the regional polarisation of the economy, while even limited use of market indicators in the recent past had produced an economically as well as socially undesirable distribution of industry. Such results were inevitable because the market, which calculates only direct economic costs, underestimates the true social cost of investment in developed regions, including the costs of migration and higher per capita costs for communal services, housing and other social infrastructure.[50]

These, too, were powerful arguments, backed by ideological exegesis and statistics as impressive in quality (and quantity!) as those mustered by the liberals, so that Bakarić was led to cry in despair: 'Who *does* receive something in Yugoslavia if we are all plundered?'[51] More importantly, since the issue would surely be decided on the basis of political strength and not on the relative merits of opposing arguments about 'exploitation' or the appropriateness of different socio-economic models, they were arguments which apparently bespoke the interests of the majority of the Yugoslavs, of the republics, and of Party members at key levels. The failure of 'centralists' or 'conservatives' to capitalise on this potential was one key element in their ultimate defeat.

The attempt to impose a centralist solution in 1962-63 was thwarted by a combination of circumstances, some of which have already been examined. The inability of the Party conservatives to command a majority in the Executive and Central Committees or Tito's firm support, at least after the middle of 1962, left their opponents free and with time to muster new arguments and allies without risking the penalties of a violation of Party discipline. The subsequent performance of the economy, where recentralisation to cope with the recession led to the reappearance of the inflation, the investment excesses and the foreign trade problems of 1960-61, further discredited centralism and demoralised its advocates. At the same time the tendency ever more openly to transfer the dispute from the economic to the national plane, while it confused the issue because economic and ethnic interests were in reality not always served by the same solutions, operated for the moment to strengthen the hand of the liberals.

The increasingly open discussion of the republican and frankly ethnic dimension of economic disputes which took place in the early 1960s, after fifteen years of public pretence that such 'bourgeois' nationalist and in Yugoslav history dangerous rivalries did not count under socialism, could be either exhilarating or alarming. It could even have foreign policy implications, as for example in an apparently subsidiary debate which attracted the attention of the national press as well as economists in 1963. The subject concerned the relative advantages of a 'Danubian concept' or an 'Adriatic concept' of the future prime focus of economic development, the one based on river and the other on maritime transport. The Adriatic is largely Croatian and beyond it lies the West; the Danube and its navigable tributaries flow through Serbia towards the East. The Croats said that this was a false dilemma and that their coast linked East and West and was non-aligned, as was proved by growing East European transit traffic through their ports. The Serbs replied that this was not the issue, but that population, arable land, industry and the future lay along the broad river valleys, not on the rocky coast.[52]

Ethnic rivalries emerged equally clearly, and with more immediate importance, in current competition for investment funds and other centrally distributed favours. Sea ports as competitive symbols of Slovenian, Croatian, Bosnian or Serbo-Montenegrin national pride and interests were an outstanding and obvious case. A 1963 visitor found in a series of interviews, from Koper to Bar, a universal, sometimes happy and sometimes bitter, but almost always open recognition that the national sentiments of the appropriate political authorities were more important than economic and geographic considerations in determining which ports would grow and hold or expand their hinterlands and which would not.[53]

Similar perceptions, with repercussions directly related to the great debate, surfaced in public as well as private discussions of the allegedly disproportionate number of major infrastructure projects, requiring federal financing, which were to be built in Serbia under the defunct 1961-65 Social Plan and which now supplied a highly important practical reason for continuing, stubborn Serbian support of (and Croato-Slovenian opposition to) the disputed federal role in investment. The list included the great Yugoslav-Romanian hydro-electric and navigation system at the Iron Gates of the Danube, on which engineering work began in 1963, and the Danube-Tisa-Danube canal system in the Vojvodina, begun shortly after the war but long neglected and unfinished for lack of money. But the most controversial and patently 'nationalistic' project, however sound the developmental and social arguments for it, was the Belgrade-Bar railway, the pan-Serb route to the sea which Serbian and Montenegrin politicians had dreamed of since 1879 and the only route which completely avoided non-Orthodox lands and dependence on Croatian or foreign sea ports. Although it had figured in every postwar development plan, only two brief sections at each end, from Belgrade to Valjevo and from Bar to Titograd, had so far been built. The construction of the rest, through extraordinarily difficult mountainous terrain, was clearly the main purpose of an unprecedented formal agreement on inter-republican co-operation in economics, culture and education signed in December 1963 by the Serbian and Montenegrin Party Central Committees (not, it is interesting to note, by the formally more appropriate republican Governments). The agreement was inevitably interpreted by others as evidence of a Serbo-Montenegrin conspiracy by 'Greater Serbian nationalists' whose short-run objective was to forestall the abolition of and pre-empt the use of centralised investment funds.[54]

Its long-run objectives might be far more sinister, since the preceding year had also seen a modest but in the present context significant revival of the polemics about *Jugoslavenstvo* which had first troubled the political scene in the late 1950s. This 'Yugoslavism' was still carefully defined as no more than a vague, eventual merging of separate national cultures into a single Yugoslav culture or as a (socialist) Yugoslav patriotism superimposed on but not replacing separate national identities and loyalties, but for most non-Serbs it still smelled like a modern version of King Aleksandar's 'Yugoslav nation', which had turned out on closer inspection to mean Serbianisation. The sensitivity of the issue had again been revealed by the publication in December 1961, and in *Borba* of all places, of an unsparingly and unprecedentedly blunt exchange of polemics on the subject between Serbia's most famous living writer, Dobrica Ćosić, and the Slovenian poet Dušan Pirjevec.[55] Three months later, however, Tito himself had seemed to support the campaign, for his Split speech contained, among its other pro-centralist bombshells, a clear reference to the need for 'a uniform socialist Yugoslav culture'.[56] With this encouragement, articles in favour of 'Yugoslavism' had continued to appear, particularly in publications like the journal of the Serbian Writers' Association, *Književne Novine*.[57] By September 1962, Tito and Kardelj themselves felt obliged to offer public reassurances. 'When we speak about integration', Tito told a joint meeting of the Federal Assembly and the Federal Committee of the Socialist Alliance, 'we do not think of the integration of nationalities, of their assimilation or negation'. Kardelj, speaking from the same platform, was more explicit: 'our Federation is not a frame for making some new Yugoslav nation, or a frame for the kind of national integration which various advocates of hegemonism or denationalising terror have been daydreaming of'.[58] But suspicions lingered on.

The open admission of the ethnic dimension in economic disputes was potentially and would prove to be a double-edged weapon. For the moment, however, it was being used with more skill by the Slovene and Croatian liberals, unwittingly assisted by renewed references to *Jugoslavenstvo* and by Serbian conservatives who over-exposed the element of republican and ethnic self-interest in their position, forgetting the special burden of suspicion they bore as members of the most numerous and historically dominant nation, whose capital was also the capital of Yugoslavia and symbol of centralist autocracy. They thereby failed to consolidate the position as patrons and spokesmen of the underdeveloped majority of the country to which they were now aspiring. With this unintended help and some success in distracting attention from the equivalent element of republican self-interest in their own position by their adroit shift of focus from *decentralizacija* to *de-etatizacija*, the liberals were able to manipulate and profit from an ever clearer popular identification of economic centralism with Greater Serbian nationalism.

For other nationalities like the Macedonians, with basically pro-centralist economic interests but with suspicion of the Serbs already rearoused by the apparent revival of the campaign for 'Yugoslavism', the reaction to this identification assumed the form of an agonising conflict between fear of Serbian domination on the one hand and the advantages of central redistribution of national income on the other. The choice for many of them was made easier by the Zagreb liberals, who assembled statistical evidence indicating that among the underdeveloped only the Montenegrins, with their special political influence, had really done consistently well out of central redistribution. They also dropped subtle hints that additional revenues left in the hands of wealthy northern enterprises would surely find their way south in response to profitable economic investment opportunities, compensating for the loss of 'political' investments.[59] Whether or not this was the deciding consideration, by 1964 younger Macedonian leaders like Krsto Crvenkovski and Kiro Gligorov—the former a rising star not hitherto counted as a liberal and the latter already with a reputation as a bright and liberal economic specialist in the Federal Government—were as outspokenly in favour of *de-etatizacija* as any Slovene or Croat. Even the Albanians of the Kosmet were growing more audibly restive under a Serbian and UDBa domination which had brought them few economic benefits.[60]

The conservatives thus lost the initiative they had held in 1962 and failed to achieve the solid bloc of Serbia and the underdeveloped regions which had been their apparent strategy in the succeeding months. But the liberals, despite their reinforcements and success in frustrating a centralist solution, were still not in a political position to impose their own. The elevation of the dispute into a national question which was bringing them new allies, including those whose economic interests were pro-centralist, had an analogous effect on those numerous Serbs whose ideological position or political or economic interest (the last including at least as many in enterprises in Belgrade and northern Serbia as in Croatia) should have pushed them towards the liberals. They now tended instead to unite behind the Serbian conservatives or at least to remain silent. Three other factors were, however, of far greater importance. The liberals, like the conservatives, commanded no stable or effective majority among the fifteen members of the Party Executive Committee, several of whom had divided allegiances or were in some degree non-aligned.[61] Tito's position was pivotal but remained equivocal. And the central Party, State and police apparatuses were still dominated by Serbs, while the first two were increasingly dominated by the last, the chosen instrument of the country's leading conservative, Aleksandar Ranković.

The liberal solution which emerged piecemeal during the

eighteen months from early 1964 to July 1965 was therefore not the
result of a prior victory for the liberal faction at the Party centre,
where every major decision in postwar Yugoslav history had so far
been made. It emerged instead out of a complex process involving
the interplay of a number of separate elements and actors. There
was the ever more urgent need for some kind of solution as
economic problems due to flaws in the existing system resisted
indecisive tampering and were aggravated by inaction. There were
also the stalemate at the summit, which continued to preclude the
imposition of a centralist solution, and the activities of several
other and sometimes new centres of political initiative, freed by the
decision-making vacuum at the Party centre and impelled by
collective frustration, ambition or the perception of a long-awaited
opportunity to articulate and pursue their own policy preferences
in a new, open and autonomous way. Then there were the
dynamics of social and economic change and of the quality,
cumulative impact and 'internal logic' of previous reforms and
their ideological rationale, which together all served to define,
constrain and ultimately focus these formally separate and unco-
ordinated aggregations of preferences. If the turn to the market in
the ensuing reform seemed almost inevitable, the way it happened
was portentous. Yugoslavia no longer had an effective single locus
of primary political power and only the unworkability of the
emerging *de facto* pluralism or a conservative *coup de main* could
henceforth restore one.

5

LAISSEZ-FAIRE SOCIALISM

The dialectics of development

The high road to the reform of 1965 passed through a series of political events in which the effect and the convergence of diverse elements, actors and preferences can be identified. These included the drafting of a new Constitution in 1961-62 and its adoption in the spring of 1963, significant innovations in the procedure by which the Social Plan for 1964 was adopted, some changes in the economic system which could be accepted by centralists as neutral tampering but could also constitute preliminary steps towards a comprehensive liberal reform, and a trade union congress and a parliamentary debate and resolution which were unambiguously pro-reform. The Party Congress which put a final and essential seal of approval on the liberal solution in December 1964 was in effect responding to an accumulation of demands and accomplished facts rather than to a clear-cut decision by its Executive Committee. In the crucial period, it is also worth noting, the Central Committee of the LCY met only once, on March 16, 1964, and only for the second time since the inconclusive Plenum of July 1962.

The principles of the reform had been drafted, as we have seen, by economists in the service of political and economic leaderships in the developed northern regions and the liberal faction at the Belgrade centre, who together had been able to frustrate the imposition of any alternative solution but who lacked the power at the centre or the modalities outside it to impose their own. It was these modalities for the aggregation of pro-reform preferences that were now being created, either *ex novo* or in the perversion to new purposes of existing institutions like the Trade Union Federation, where the beginning of this process as early as 1959 has been described. And it was the products of the style and quality of social change during the decade between the first and second rounds of the great debate that were staffing these new instruments of reform and providing the liberal faction with a politically effective constituency—significantly increasing the number and classes of active or potential supporters of one of the parties to the debate while leaving the other largely untouched.

Supporters of a centralist solution in the struggles of 1962–66 were still essentially the same kinds of people who had been troubled by the declarative reforms of 1950–53 and relieved when Djilas's extremism led to a quasi-centralist compromise. Then and now they included most Party activists and members of the bureaucracy—some of them Marxists who saw the revolution betrayed, others job-holders jealous of their power and privileges and many (including Ranković himself) primarily practical political men who feared that the devolution of power implicit in the proposed reforms would lead to anarchy, loss of direction and quite possibly the disintegration of the multinational State. They also included, although in marginally but significantly declining numbers, as we have seen, most of those who had been getting more out of centralised, politically administered funds than they were putting into them, which meant enterprises and communes dangerously concentrated in less developed parts of the country largely inhabited by specific nationalities. But if the supporters of a centralist and 'conservative' solution were essentially the same in kind and in numbers as they had been, both the quantity and the quality of those with an interest in one or another variant of a 'liberal' solution had undergone a change of fundamental importance with the years. The missing alternative to the League of Communists as an instrument with which to implement the ideals evolved in 1950–53 had been created by the successes of the compromise model of the following decade.

By 1965 the Yugoslavs numbered nearly 19·5 million, about 4 million more than at the end of the war. At the end of a second decade of bewilderingly rapid social change they were for the most part and with significant regional exceptions a different people, in demographic profile, in social stratification and in standards and styles of living. Some of their expectations of the mid-1950s had been fulfilled, many were still frustrated and new ones had been aroused even in those who had still traditionally or rationally refused to hope ten years before.

It was around 1965 that someone defined Belgrade as the only Communist capital with a parking problem. In 1966 an American anthropologist, Joel Halpern, returned to the village of Orašac, where the first Serbian revolt had begun in 1804 and where he had pioneer anthropological fieldwork in 1953–54. There he such profound changes underlying a superficial appearance ᴨeness in even this relatively remote and untouched corner of ᵢja that he described the difference as 'part of a marked n in human life ways ... a revolution characterized by the ᵢᵃ. ʲut perceptible disappearance of traits which have made and town patterns of life socially, culturally and economically distinct'. Social mobility for some and changing values for most were documented in new interviews with those whom he had first surveyed twelve years before. Even more telling are the anecdotes, one in particular:

> One old villager who used to love to talk about the glories of Serbia's past now points his cane skyward and proudly identifies a 'karavel' as the Yugoslav Air Transport's daily jet from Belgrade to Titograd passes overhead. He delights in describing his first plane trip, at age seventy, when he flew to Montenegro to visit his son, a factory manager who is building a summer home on the Adriatic.[1]

In 1953, Halpern notes, he and his family arrived in Orašac by oxcart and in 1966 by automobile, but the dirt road to the village had been better maintained in 1953. The present writer's favourite village, across the Danube in the Banat, had had the same problem but had just solved it. Also in 1966, despairing of State help, the villagers built their own paved access road, replacing a wide dirt track across the cornfields, with voluntary contributions of money and labour and with equipment borrowed from a nearby fertilizer plant. As one of them explained it: 'We have lived here for 250 years. Pashas, princes and commissars have come and gone, but the mud remained, so we decided to do something about it ourselves.'

For individual Yugoslavs, social change in the 1960s was measured in happenings like these. It was also measured in the arrival of clean, piped water in one's village, or in cash, after agricultural prices were raised, to build an indoor bathroom and toilet in anticipation of piped water next year or the year after. It meant a job in town, for a brother or a cousin if not for oneself, or an increased interest in cash income to fulfil an urgently felt need which was less likely to be another bit of land and more likely to be secondary or vocational training for a child. It meant more frequent abortions, either because one could only afford to educate one or two children or because more were now perceived to be a burden rather than an asset in any case, since the household could not own more than ten hectares and mechanical cultivators, now available, were demonstrably cheaper than offspring and less ungrateful. Or it might mean the recovery of the kind of social status that one's parents had known before the revolution, this time with the satisfactions of a professional career as an engineer, a doctor or a scientist rather than those of a 'capitalist'. It might be measured in terms of a cottage on the coast or on the banks of the Sava, or of a trip abroad which was no longer just to Trieste for things which could now be bought at home, but further and as a real tourist. It certainly meant, even in remote provincial towns by the mid-1960s, the marvel of a supermarket or a self-service 'superette' to supplement the still ubiquitous peasant market, bringing the convenience and more varied diet which come with the packaging and modern food-processing that were a market economy's response to the demand created by the mere existence and nature of supermarkets.

Yugoslavia's population profile, as usual with regional exceptions, was already that of a West European country. The crude birthrate, declining in Slovenia, parts of Croatia and eastern Serbia since at least the 1890s, now ranged from 14·4 per thousand population in the Vojvodina to 37·9 in Kosovo (which had the highest birthrate in Europe), and the rate of natural increase in the country as a whole was down to 1 per cent per annum and still falling.[2] The phenomenon of 'demographic transition', characterised by falling death and birth rates and important changes in the age distribution of the population, was thus virtually complete or well under way in most of the country, although just beginning in Kosovo and some other mountainous regions.

A decade of rapid economic development had also had its impact on the profile of employment and education and on where and how many Yugoslavs lived. By 1966 nearly 3·6 million were employed in the socialist sector—an addition of 1·2 million in nine years—with 3 million of these in the economy and 1,358,000 in industry and mining. Those so employed were different in quality as well. According to official statistics, 59 per cent of the total labour force in 1966 (excluding private farmers and artisans) had completed some form of schooling, compared to 20·7 per cent as recently as 1958. Employees in industry and mining with a university degree or its equivalent had increased by 65 per cent in four years—to a still modest 15,328—although 175,000 workers in this sector were still said to be without necessary skills. Between 1963 and 1968 the number of industrial enterprise directors with only primary schooling declined from 33 to 14·4 per cent. These changes reflected the gradual impact on the economy of an impressively growing if still inadequate school system and output.[3] More Yugoslavs were also living in communities defined as urban than ever before—28 per cent by 1961, an addition of 1·5 million (precisely absorbing natural increase) since 1953, and 35 per cent by 1971—although the rate of urbanisation was curiously lower than in most rapidly developing societies and Yugoslavia remained the least urbanised country in Europe except Albania.

The new kinds and quality of contacts with the world implicit in these changes provided only some of the expanding channels of information which were having a major impact on the horizons, values and life styles of all Yugoslavs, urban as well as rural. Some of the others derived from the very nature of a Marxist approach to development and a Communist system of administration and control, which probably has at least the technical capacity to raise the level of 'cultural availability' of the populace of an underdeveloped country to near totality more rapidly than any other existing system. The hierarchical Party and an ubiquitous network of socio-political and cultural organisations make it possible for all kinds of directives, 'guidelines' and information to be passed to the most remote communities and brought to the attention, superficially at least, of all but the most determined citizens. Moreover, the Marxist concept of development, despite a theoretical belief in the primacy of economics, displays in practice a better grasp of the totalistic nature of the process than most if not all competing models for modernisation. What is communicated through the various 'transmission belts' therefore concerns wider aspects of social change—culture, education, family mores and value systems—as often as it does economic and political matters as such. These have their effect, even when the citizens of such States, including Yugoslavia, exposed to a continuous barrage of often spasmodic but repetitive 'campaigns' mounted by these interlocking networks on behalf of this or that policy, value or programme, tend to develop a protective layer of deafness and apathy which makes them less 'available' than the technical effectiveness of the system suggests.

Other important sources of information and potential political mobilisation were provided by a widening range and greater availability of mass media. There were 21 radio stations in Yugoslavia in 1962 and 77 in 1966, during which time the number of registered radios rose from 2 to 3 million; one-half of the owners in the latter year put themselves down as workers, 373,000 as peasants. There were 126,000 registered TV sets in 1962 and 777,000—one for every 25 inhabitants—in 1966. Four TV stations broadcast a total of over 4,000 hours that year, of which 776 hours were devoted to 'news and the broadcasting of political and other current events', and 389 hours to 'current themes and commentary'. The former included more hours taken from 'Eurovision' than by any other member country,[4] and the latter included programmes like Jovan Šcekić's *Aktuelni Razgovori* (Topical Conversations), a series of weekly face-the-nation interviews of startling frankness with leading politicians and others. By 1967 there were to be 1 million TV subscribers and by 1971 2 million, or one for every 2·8 households in the country.

Newspaper circulation was less impressive, especially in the countryside, where the regime as well as publishers frequently lamented the lack of readership, and was suffering a further decline with the rapid spread of radio and TV sets. The total circulation of daily newspapers, of which there were 23 in the mid-1960s, rose to 1·7 million copies in 1964, sank to under 1·5 million by 1966 and regained the 1964 level only at the end of the decade. But the quality, freedom and liveliness of the reporting improved progressively, especially after 1966. This was particularly true of Belgrade's leading daily, *Politika*, which had the advantages of a public image of relative independence and outstanding reporters and was probably one of Europe's best newspapers in the late 1960s, but the domestic news columns of Zagreb's *Vjesnik* and Ljubljana's *Delo*, both with special national missions, made increasingly worthwhile reading.[5] Among more than 150 weeklies the most popular serious newsmagazines were Zagreb's *VUS* (*Vjesnik u Srijedu*), which had the highest circulation of all by 1970, and *NIN* (*Nedeljne Informativne Novine*), published by *Politika* in Belgrade. Other types of periodicals of social significance included popular and serious literary and professional journals and the in-house newspapers of several hundred enterprises of various sizes. Finally worth noting for their influence on élites, although with very limited circulations, are the journals which concentrated on ideological and theoretical matters, and which fell roughly into two categories: 'establishment' organs like *Socijalizam*, and independent and often anti-establishment ones like *Gledišta* and *Praxis*. The weekly *Komunist* occupied a special place of its own, as the only really official Party journal and ostensibly required reading for all Party members.

One other highly significant aspect of social change, which was also the only completely inevitable one, was for the moment having only a muted and delayed and therefore sometimes perverse influence on two key social groups, so that the delay became as politically and socially important as the inevitability. This was the impact of the passing of the years, of the ageing of the Partisan generation and the coming of new ones, on recruitment to and the structure of political and economic élites.

Generation gaps and succession problems exist in every society. The special Yugoslav problem, already alluded to several times, was that the older generation in charge of the Party, the State and the economy was not really old. Those who had led the National Liberation Struggle and in consequence taken over the country while in their late 20s or early 30s, and who had run it ever since, were still only in their 50s and reluctant to retire. Waiting with growing impatience after twenty years were the eligibles of the next generation, which in the Yugoslav political context meant those who had been in SKOJ at the beginning of the war or teenage Partisans at the end, now in their 40s. Close behind them came what in effect constituted a third generation, if the term is construed to mean another age-group with significantly different formative experiences: those who had known the war only as children and who had not participated in the founding of a new Yugoslavia, but who had lived in it and gone to its expanding schools, absorbing or reacting to its values, and who were now pushing upwards along career ladders in politics and the economy, often with far better education and professional qualifications to reinforce youth's natural disdain for the incompetence and failures of its elders. In this situation the middle generation of eligibles, relatively few in numbers but significant because they currently manned many of the most important posts just below the top level, were in serious danger of being squeezed out, of never having their day at the top if they did not get there soon, before the pressure from below became too great.[6] With the promotional logjam of the senior Partisan generation still largely unbroken in 1965, both of the generations behind them suffered from career frustrations which could easily become political, but those of the middle generation were for the moment more acute. One of the functions of the economic and political reforms launched in 1965-66, even if only dimly perceived by most of those who supported them, was to break the logjam.

In the economy it had already begun to happen. The improving educational profile of enterprise directors reflected the infiltration into their ranks of a growing number of younger and frequently better educated men (or even, very occasionally, women). Of the 1,269 directors re-elected or elected for the first time in 1966, 14 per cent were aged 30-39, 48 per cent were aged 40-49 and 35 per cent were aged 50-59, with two of the re-elected directors under 30 and 32 of them over 60 years old. Of the 262 directors who were elected for the first time, however, 45 per cent were in the 30-39 age bracket, 40 per cent were aged 40-49, and only 8 per cent were over 50 years of age (compared to 60 per cent of those whom they replaced). Fifteen of the new directors, nearly 6 per cent, were under 30.

As for the Party, its composition could be regarded in either of two contrasting ways. It was an ageing Party, as we have seen. With a progressive decrease until 1965 in the proportion of young people in the total number of new admissions and with existing members moving into older age categories, the number of Party members less than 26 years old declined from nearly 40 per cent of total membership in 1950 to 11·5 per cent in 1966. The proportion of those over 40 years of age rose correspondingly to 29·7 per cent, while the 26-40 age-group consistently accounted for the majority, with 58·8 per cent in 1966.

In terms of seniority, however, the LCY was now numerically a new Party, belonging to the era of reforms and of self-management as official ideology. Of its 1,046,018 members at the end of 1966, only 2,900 (0·3 per cent) were veterans of the prewar CPY, while an additional 63,756 (6·1 per cent) had memberships dating from the wartime years. Of the rest, 169,660 (16·2 per cent) had received their red books since 1963, and 447,759 (42·8 per cent) since 1958.

The sum of all who had joined before the break with Stalinism now accounted for 25 per cent and of those who had joined later for 75 per cent of total membership. In terms of the period in Party history in which they had been motivated to join, the two largest classes in 1966 consisted of the 187,000 (17·9 per cent) who had become members during the 'administrative period', 1945-48, and the 278,095 (26·6 per cent) whose membership dated from the 1958-62 period, the years of liberalisation and renewed quarrel with the Soviet Union after the 7th Congress. On the other hand, membership declined absolutely in 1962-63, as it had in 1953-55, both periods of rapprochement with the Soviet Union abroad and of conservative retrenchment at home.

Recent changes in the Party's occupational and educational composition carried on, with slight variations, trends observable ever since it had come to power. The decline in the number of workers had in fact accelerated in the mid-60s, with nearly 5,000 fewer in 1965 than in 1964 and 11,500 fewer in 1966 than in 1965, bringing the proportion of those so registered down to 33·9 per cent of total membership. More of these were now highly skilled or skilled and fewer were semi-skilled or unskilled workers than earlier or than equivalent ratios in the labour force as a whole. In the same two years the number of pensioners and unclassified 'others' rose by 14,000 and 15,000 respectively. There had also been an absolute and relative increase in the number of engineers, technicians, lawyers, economists and educational and health workers, and a drop in the number of clerical and other lower-grade employees. The number of peasants in the Party, constantly declining since the war, had temporarily stabilised at around 7 per cent of total membership. The educational profile of the Party reflected all of these changes.[7]

Generalisations based on such statistics are hazardous. The most that can be said with certainty is that the Party was in composition very different from the CPY of 1945 or even the LCY of 1955, that by 1965 over 70 per cent of the rank and file and most middle-grade officers had not been adults during the war, that 75 per cent of them had not been members at that time or before the break with Stalin, that the top leadership by virtue of longevity in power had survived and might be presumed to have learned from a greater variety of revolutionary and post-revolutionary experiences than in any other socialist State except China, that fewer youth were moved to join, and that the Party was less proletarian and better educated than it had ever been. But the behaviour of both rank and file and leaderships, then and in the following years, was a reminder, *inter alia*, that younger Communists or those who joined in periods of liberalising reforms are not necessarily and always more 'liberal' or less likely to display 'the subservient mentality of clerks' than older ones, including prewar and wartime veterans whose motives in becoming Communists were also mixed and whose outlooks had as often as not been dramatically altered by sometimes traumatic experience. It was also a reminder that institutionalised procedures and expectations may be more important in determining behaviour than the social or personal composition of the organisations which embody them.

From the social strata created, significantly enlarged or newly mobilised by rapid economic development and social modernisation came the new kinds of support and the potential for its articulation which were shaping the reforms of 1965. The growing army of actual or potential supporters of part or all of the reform programme included a wide variety of people who had any of a number of strong reasons for objecting to political control of the economy in general or by Belgrade in particular, or to political control of any kind by Belgrade or by the Party at one or another or all levels, and whose jobs or status in society put them where these sentiments could be aggregated and articulated. This meant a large part of a genuinely new class of socialist entrepreneurs and many members of a vastly enlarged proletariat, particularly those in both categories employed in profitable enterprises or wealthier regions, and with them those who directly and consciously shared in the wealth generated by this entrepreneurship and labour. It also meant many of the increasing number of those whose education, achieved social status or migration to or increased contact with urban centres had exposed them to either nationalist or democratic socialist doctrines which made either a Belgrade-based semi-autocracy or existing restrictions on political participation in general seem evil. And it meant ambitious persons in the rapidly expanding ranks of the employed or the potentially employed whose career or personal frustrations could be projected, rightly or wrongly, as the fault of 'bureaucracy', centralism, the Party or the State.

The same dynamics of development and changes in the political system had at the same time created new or modified existing institutions in ways which made them appropriate places in which this potential could be mobilised. There were, first of all, the institutional consequences of political decentralisation since 1950. However gradual and partial, decentralisation had produced a network of semi-autonomous republican and communal apparatuses with their own planning functions and with direct fiscal and other links to economic organisations on their territories, including considerable influence over appointments and personnel policy in enterprises, banking and social services. These links in turn meant significant independent fiscal powers which local politicians could use to increase their autonomy, because they could do a growing

number of things without needing to seek funds and therefore
approval from higher up, and which they were interested in
protecting against encroachments from hierarchically superior
political units. Of equal importance, local apparatuses and
individual leaders were thereby provided with improved means, in
the form of a growing capacity to grant or withhold favours and
funds, which they could use to create their own networks of clients.
These in their turn constituted a system of discrete power bases
which strengthened the bargaining positions of those who
controlled them. Finally, the fact that local and republican
Governments did have considerable and with the years more rather
than less power, patronage and money at their disposal, reinforced
by ethnic or other prejudices against moving to Belgrade, meant
that local government tended to attract and hold a higher
proportion (and federal apparatuses a correspondingly lower
proportion) of ambitious and/or talented people than would have
been the case in other circumstances.[8]

Ethnic particularism played an important but two-edged role in
this emerging pattern of elementary geographic political pluralism.
It provided regional politicians, who were themselves far from
immune to national sentiments and prejudices, with additional
personal justification for their pursuit of regional and hence ethnic
interests and for their suspicion of the intentions of fellow-
Communist spokesmen for other ethnic groups and of a Belgrade
which was identified with Serbian interests by all except some of
the Serbs themselves. More importantly, ethnic particularism
provided them with a potential for genuine popular support,
which, if mobilised, would further strengthen their bargaining
position and their autonomy. To arouse this kind of support they
only needed to defend regional interests with vigour and effect,
which they were doing, and then to be seen to be doing it,
identifying these interests with national ones and with themselves
as national as well as Communist leaders. These things, too, were
easily done, and the need to be seen defending local and ethnic
interests had the additional effect of helping to bring about more
public political debate and conflict, leading to a better informed
populace, another prerequisite of increasing pluralism and participation. On the other hand, the greater the success of this strategy
in any one republic, the greater the suspicions it would arouse or
confirm in others and among that republic's own minorities, and
the greater the fear among many people everywhere, both ordinary
and élite, that national passions might get out of hand and lead
once again towards separatism and civil strife—or at least
dysfunctionally closed local economies and politics. Such a
reaction would surely prove a recipe for the reimposition of the
centralism which was presently in retreat. In any case, the strategy

itself, consistently implemented everywhere, could at best only reproduce the existing national question in a series of microcosms, since only Slovenia and perhaps Montenegro could really lay claim to being the ethnically (almost) homogeneous nation-State which the strategy and the ideology implicit in it assumed.

Still other actual or potential rallying points for the mobilisation of anti-centralist and anti-étatist sentiments, individually of minor importance but collectively significant, were being generated in the latter half of the decade by further and intrinsically interesting experiments in extending 'direct social self-management' and the liquidation of the role of the State in communal and social services which are State or private functions in almost all societies. In local 'communities of education' and 'health communities', for example, directly elected representatives of suppliers and consumers of these services (teachers and school administrators or doctors and other health workers; parents, older pupils and those who paid local school taxes or subscribers to health insurance funds) negotiated about their funding, administration and quality. These bodies were manned by people who had or who tended to develop an interest in defending and expanding their new and self-satisfying roles in decision-making about matters of direct concern to themselves or their families.[9] In later years and after further growth in kinds and in jurisdiction, the device of such 'communities of interest' (*interesne zajednice*), negotiating 'social contracts' (*društveni dogovori*) among themselves, would become a central feature of the system, in theory at least, and of hopes for further socialist 'de-étatisation' (see below, pp. 284, 328).

Additional and more immediately relevant centres for the aggregation of particular and autonomous group interests, by definition therefore pluralistic and anti-monopolistic if not necessarily anti-centralist, were now being created along the road to reform. The most important of these, transforming the parliamentary system in ways that would have surprising and significant consequences, were products of Yugoslavia's third postwar constitution, in the drafting stage since November 1960.

From Constitution to Congress

The Constitutional Law of 1953, replacing most of the Constitution of 1946, had been clearly and in the declaration of its authors an unfinished work—an interim stocktaking of basic changes in political and economic theory and institutions which were themselves too unfinished to warrant anything like definitive codification. The Constitution of 1963, while again carefully termed a transitional statute for a society and system in transition and moving rapidly along a long road called 'building socialism', was both a clearer codification of the normative and institutional consequences of the distance already travelled and a map (albeit hard to read in places!) for the next stage. Because of other changes in Yugoslavia's political and economic systems, theory and style during the intervening years, it was also somewhat less a deliberate obfuscation of political reality or a pious wish than one had learned to expect of Communist-made constitutions: the institutions and normative rules that it created or modified and even some of the principles it enunciated were to have an active and effective life and genuine if sometimes unanticipated impact.

The new Constitution presented for public discussion in the autumn of 1962 had been in preparation for nearly two years. A special Commission for Constitutional Questions under Kardelj's chairmanship was assigned the task of writing a preliminary draft, with Jovan Djordjević as chairman of a sub-committee for legal questions. Other standing or ad hoc sub-committees were established for particular sections; a group from the Trade Union Central Committee, for example, prepared first drafts of the clauses dealing with the communal system and with 'work units', a refinement in the organisation of workers' self-management advocated by the trade unions since 1960 in the context of the struggle for the 'law of incomes'. Of the republican leaders Bakarić was most intensively involved, contributing among other things a theoretical study which argued that with the establishment of appropriate 'socio-economic relations', which should be a concern of the Constitution, there was no danger that workers would 'eat up accumulation'. They could then safely be left in charge of savings and investment, a measure of 'de-étatisation' which should also find its place in the new charter.[10]

Most of this little-publicised preliminary work, which included intensive study of constitutional systems in other countries, took place in the privacy of the retreats for the élite at Bled and on Brioni. The principal theses of the preliminary draft were submitted to and approved by the 4th Plenum of the Central Committee in July 1962 and the completed draft was presented for public debate, amid massive publicity, at a two-day joint session of the Federal People's Assembly and the Federal Committee of the Socialist Alliance on September 20-21. After six months of often genuinely lively public (and private) discussion, a revised draft incorporating a number of changes was placed before the Federal Assembly in March 1963. It was adopted, and the new Constitution was officially proclaimed on April 7. Republican and provincial constitutions and communal statutes were rewritten to conform and elections followed in early June. The reorganised Federal Assembly was convened on June 29, Kardelj became its President and a new era in Yugoslav parliamentary life began.

The new Constitution was extraordinarily long and complex. The text as finally adopted consisted of nine 'basic principles', presented as an Introductory Part running to sixteen printed pages, and 259 articles grouped in three Parts subdivided into fourteen chapters.[11] Hondius describes the Introductory Part as 'a rambling collection of whatever principles did or should apply in the Yugoslav universum', while Part One ('The Social and Political System') 'elaborated the principles into general rules for man, social bodies, the economy and the State'.[12] Only Part Two ('The Organisation of the Federation') bears a recognisable resemblance to more conventional federal Constitutions like that of the United States or the Yugoslav Communists' own first effort of 1946.

The rest bears witness instead to the Yugoslav concept of the State, which 'withers away' as its functions are gradually taken over by society through the mechanism of 'social self-management'. The new Constitution therefore preferred the terms 'social community' and 'socio-political community' (*društvena zajednica* and *društveno-politička zajednica*) to the term 'State' (*država*) and purported to serve as a body of rules for society as a whole as well as for its formal political institutions. It was also therefore modestly and avowedly a transitional document, sharing the lack of clarity of the still evolving concept and practice of 'social self-management'. It was thus to be seen, Kardelj told the September meeting, as an attempt to codify the experience in enterprise and communal self-management of the preceding decade, to provide for the wider and more genuine application of this experience in a larger sector of public life, and to ease the way for further political changes to accompany the further maturing of the 'social structure'.[13]

To these ends the 1963 Constitution placed great emphasis on 'social self-government' as a general system and 'inviolable right' (Art. 34). The Chapter on 'Socio-Economic Organisation', which dealt with self-management *per se*, bore the stamp of now familiar trade union and liberal theses. It incorporated the formula for income distribution—to each in proportion to his own work, that of his work unit, and that of the enterprise as a whole—for which the Trade Union Federation had been pressing for three years (Art. 12) and gave constitutional sanction to the most important single plank in the platform of the Croatian and Slovenian economists and political leaders, a role for enterprises in the allocation of investments proportionate to their profitability (Art. 11). Although on balance the republics were not strengthened vis-à-vis the Federation, the enterprises, other self-managing associations and the communes were. The Constitution as a whole represented a new apogee of self-management as a normative principle in Yugoslavia, and this was the *Leitmotiv* of the liberals since their tactical switch from decentralisation to de-étatisation in the struggle against economic and political centralism.[14]

The same principle was extended to the parliamentary system, where the 'Councils of Producers' created in 1953 already represented a step in this direction and where the new Constitution's most remarkable and politically significant institutional experiment was now to be tried. The Federal Assembly (formerly the Federal People's Assembly), of which Kardelj was to be President, became a unique legislative body consisting of no less than five chambers, four of them representing citizens aggregated by economic or social function. Election in every case was to be indirect, by communal or republican and provincial assemblies rather than by citizens, but with nomination by open meetings of constituents.

The Federal Chamber, with 120 deputies representing traditional territorial constituencies,[15] remained the basic political chamber. It still contained within it the Chamber of Nationalities, which was now to consist of ten delegates from each republic and five from each autonomous province.[16] Its primary task—apart from exclusive jurisdiction in a few areas, most importantly in electing and dismissing the FEC—was to discuss and approve legislation and other acts of the Assembly in conjunction and on a basis of equality with one or another of the four specialised 'chambers of work communities': an Economic Chamber, Chambers of Education and Culture and of Welfare and Health, and an Organisational-Political Chamber. Each of the four consisted of 120 deputies nominated by and from 'a work organisation or work community in the relevant spheres of activity' and elected by the communal assemblies.[17] Usually called corporate or vocational chambers by foreign scholars, they represented an extension of the concept and an expansion of the constituency on which the Council of Producers, created as a second chamber in 1953, had been based: four functionally distinct chambers in place of one and an (indirect) electorate which included all 'working people in work communities' and not only those employed in 'productive' enterprises. Each acted, in conjunction with the Federal Chamber, on matters defined by the Constitution as relevant to its own corporate interests; the five-chamber Assembly therefore functioned like a bicameral parliament on each bill or resolution.[18]

With republican and provincial assemblies similarly reconstituted and with one or more corporate chambers in each directly-elected communal assembly, the Yugoslav voter now usually enjoyed, formally and (above the communal level) indirectly, a triple representation: as a citizen-consumer in the political chambers; as a citizen-producer in the corporate chambers (but only if employed in a 'working community', i.e. not if he were a private peasant who was not a member of a general co-operative, or a private artisan, an independent lawyer, etc.); and at the federal level, in the Chamber of Nationalities, as a member of an ethnic nation, institutionalised in a republic or province.

Kardelj claimed that the new assemblies represented a radical departure from the bourgeois-democratic concept of a parliament. He himself had first argued the need for such a departure in 1952 and now, as he explained the rationale of the new system, some of the same phrases recurred. The retention of a bourgeois type of parliament in a one-party State makes a mockery of democracy. It may be acceptable in the first years after the socialist revolution, when the dictatorship of the Party is necessary to defend the new order, but it must then be abandoned if the one-party and eventually non-party socialist State is to become truly democratic. The representative institutions appropriate to such a socialist democracy must reflect and be capable of resolving the legitimate 'contradictions' of the socialist 'transitional period', which will assume the form of conflicts of interest among communities of workers and also the conflict within each citizen between his interests as a consumer and as a producer of commodities, services or other values. Therefore these institutions should not aggregate men and their interests by class, as in a bourgeois democracy, but by function. The Yugoslav model was designed to do this, to represent legitimate socialist interests and to mediate conflicts among them through a combination of the Federal Chamber, as a 'general political body with all the legislative and political competencies granted to the Federation' working together with the corporate chambers understood as 'primary organs of social self-government, i.e. kinds of supreme workers' councils in individual spheres of work and self-government'.[19] The corporate chambers of the republican and provincial assemblies and the expanded Councils of Producers in the communes, similarly understood, completed an inclusive hierarchy of such 'supreme workers' councils', functioning in respective juxtaposition to and collaboration with republican, provincial and communal chambers as lower-level 'general political bodies'.

Whatever the authors of this system may have expected, the behaviour of the new federal and some republican assemblies promptly surprised nearly everyone else. Yugoslav parliamentary life became, virtually overnight, more exciting and effective than in any other Communist single-party State. By the winter of 1963-64 Government bills were being rejected or substantively amended, ministers had been criticised on the floor of the chambers, and parliamentary correspondents, in doubt as to what they should tell their readers about such unprecedented scenes, were summoned and told to report the debates as they had occurred.[20] Most importantly, if not as dramatic as the rejection of a bill, the Social Plan for 1964 was submitted in preliminary draft for extensive and critical debate and amendment by the FEC, appropriate assembly committees and the Federal and Economic Chambers. This was the first time that the Assembly had not merely given formal approval to the final draft of a Plan. The particular target of much of the criticism at every stage of a stormy passage was the Plan's manifestly interim quality. It was designed, its sponsors frankly admitted, to dovetail with any conceivable variant of a delayed Seven-Year Plan which was still not ready for presentation seventeen months after it had been called for at the 4th Plenum. Where was the medium-term plan, the deputies asked angrily and repeatedly, and where were those decisions about basic reforms which were obviously the reason for the delay and for which the economy had been waiting with growing desperation since 1961?[21]

The deputies who behaved this way were members of the same formerly monolithic and highly disciplined Party as the ministers whose decisions they rejected and the very senior Party officials whose indecision they criticised. They had arrived through indirect and still usually uncontested elections and carefully 'filtered' candidacies: in 1963 a total of 647 candidates were nominated by voters' meetings, but only 603 were 'confirmed by electoral commissions' to run for the 600 seats in the Federal Assembly.[22] These deputies therefore were not and should not have felt themselves to be effectively responsible to their ostensible constituents, who had not really put them where they were, but rather to those who had, the Party and Socialist Alliance officials and organs in charge of 'cadre policy'. These in turn were ranked from commune to Central Committee in a hierarchy which was loose and ill defined but usually capable of effective transmission of orders from above. At the top sat the Organisational Secretary of the LCY, Ranković, whose other role as the now informal but still undisputed chief of the State Security Service more than doubled his ability to control appointments and candidacies which happened to interest him. But Ranković and UDBa were simultaneously the Party-annointed guardians of obedience and discipline, especially for Party members, and the self-appointed guardians of the *status quo*, the political and economic systems forged in the early 1950s. Such men could be expected to note challenges to all these things, and to their own power as well, in the behaviour of the assemblies and in the principles of the Constitution which had created them.

These considerations raise two obvious questions. The first is why (and therefore also which) parliamentary deputies behaved as early as 1963-64 in ways which could be expected to irritate those whom they should have considered capable of removing them. The explanation, both in these and in other increasingly autonomous structures, involves a number of factors. In the first place, the representation of particular group interests and public disagreements with other Communists in other, even superordinate bodies, including the Federal or a republican Government, were in many cases no longer really acts of defiance against a Party which had specifically sanctioned such things, admittedly within uncomfortably shifting and ill-defined limits. In addition, the Party itself, as frequently noted, was no longer monolithic. Even before the fall of Ranković, cadre policy and the Security Service in several republics had remained or become partly independent of his control, permitting the emergence of significant shades of differences in Party policy on other matters. The scope for such differences was then enlarged by the stalemate on basic policy issues at the Party centre after 1962, which left a vacuum, marked by ambivalent or contradictory directives from above, which could be exploited and which also thereby facilitated the building of local clientage systems founded on open patronage of local interests.

At least as important was a subjective, psychological factor which derived from the ethos as well as the organisational forms of Yugoslav socialism, and which was based on a generally observable if far from universal human tendency to adapt to and attempt to perform the role(s) to which one is assigned. All of these people might be members of the wider Communist Party establishment, but most of them also functioned in other roles, political or economic, which dominated their consciousness because they dominated their time and which were, in design and in some of their sanctions, derived from a specific, anti-étatist concept of a Communist society. Then, in attempting to perform in accordance with these role descriptions and in response to these sanctions, they encountered continuous frustrations because political and economic realities differed sharply from those presupposed by the theory.

Yugoslavia's socialist entrepreneurs, for example, had been told to build socialism by making profits and had been put into jobs in which this injunction was enforced by social expectations, peer group pressures, anticipation of pecuniary and status rewards and punishments for success or failure and even political sanctions. They found, instead, that the 'system', with its administrative and price controls, disincentive tax structures and a market too imperfect to give rational signals, made it almost impossible to perform satisfactorily (to make profits) while playing by the rules. One could react to this situation in several ways which involved establishing and playing by other rules, usually meaning illegal operations, the use of political influence to circumvent legal norms or to obtain funds, and other corrupt practices. But one could also become a deputy to the Federal or a republican Chamber of the Economy in order to fight for changes in the system which would enable one to function as a director in accordance with social and normative expectations. Similarly, members of workers' councils and trade union leaders had been told that the enterprises belonged to them or that they were to protect the interests of the working class and had been put into offices in which they were expected to behave as though these things were true, only to find that they were not. They, too, frequently attempted to play the roles in which they found themselves, however unreal and therefore frustrating, and by the very act of performing them they made the roles a little more real and the institutions in which they were played a little more like their normative descriptions.

It was thus that the existing system, which had created such roles, staffed them and then created conditions which made expected performance impossible, encouraged in yet another way a revolution against its reality in the name of its ideals. This is a major part of what Paul Lendvai means in one of his best insights:

When the Yugoslav leaders decided to find an ideological alternative and felt compelled to bridge, partially at least, the gulf between the rulers and the ruled, they offered the people working in the economy the illusion of power. The irresistible logic of the economic and social forces, however, transformed the illusion of power into a power of illusion that gradually became a prime mover of developments, animating them from below.[23]

That the primary locus of this power of illusion and associated revolution was to be found in the parliamentary chambers and certain other institutions and not in the Party itself was principally because the former were now appropriate, accessible and viable vehicles of reform while the Party, the least changed of Yugoslavia's instruments of change, was none of these. As one triumphant pro-reform Communist told the present writer after the battle: 'When we realised that we would never be able to count on the Party machinery, we put our boys into the assemblies'.

The second question, which also helps to answer the first, concerns the apparent failure of Ranković and his friends to take timely action, when they must have had the capability, to prevent the drafting and adoption of a Constitution which was in essence contrary to their views and which legitimised principles, institutions and procedures which were to be used against them.

The Constitution of 1963 was the work of Kardelj, of Bakarić and the liberals, and of sometimes or consistently liberal constitutional lawyers like Jovan Djordjević and Leon Geršković. The preliminary draft represented their views with a consistency which is initially surprising in view of the deep divisions in the Party leadership. There is, however, no evidence that any leading conservative figure participated in its preparation; changes introduced into the adopted version which were apparently the result of conservative objections or amendments were with one significant exception of marginal importance. The only explanation which makes sense is that Constitutions, parliamentary institutions and the proclamation of popular political participation had never meant much in any Communist-ruled State, including Yugoslavia, and that Ranković and his lieutenants, well aware of this from their early study of the Soviet prototype and later practical experience with their own system, drew appropriate conclusions. They therefore paid little attention to what seemed a harmless game of Constitution-writing which might even be useful if it distracted the attention and energies of those whose ideas they despised as impractical, but who had recently displayed a dangerously able determination that they should be tried.

What mattered, in the eyes of the conservatives and in the light of experience, was control of the apparatus through cadre control, which they held and expanded. The one important change in the draft Constitution which was clearly their doing was the creation of the new post of Vice-President of the Republic, to exercise functions delegated to him by the President and to deputise during presidential absences (Art. 223).[24] The job was created for Ranković, who was duly elected and thereby widely regarded as Tito's chosen heir apparent. Another Serbian, the pliant and then dutifully conservative Petar Stambolič, became Head of Government as President of the FEC, also formerly Tito's post and reasonably assumed to be more poweful than the presidency of a presumably powerless parliament.[25] With these two most important new offices in their hands, Ranković, Serbia and Yugoslav Communist conservatism were satisfied.

Ranković's attitude as suggested by his behaviour at this juncture—disdain for Constitutions, parliaments, ideologues and idealists, but intense interest in identifying and controlling key positions in the Party and State apparatuses—was both reasonable and consistent with his political style throughout his career, which had so far been extraordinarily successful both personally and in the service of Yugoslavia's separate road to socialism. Through his control and manipulation of Party cadre and the security service he had achieved eminence and special recognition for performing a vital role in protecting the revolution from its enemies during the war, Yugoslav independence from the machinations of the Cominform in 1948-49, and the power of the Party and purity of Yugoslav socialism from both Stalinist and 'anarcho-liberal' deviations thereafter. In origin a Serbian peasant and tailor's apprentice, with a Šumadinian countryman's shrewd common sense, anachronistic combination of simplicity and subtlety and suspicion of cant and the urban intellectuals who preach it, he had grown into an extremely competent political operator who instinctively understood the people and the relative political weights of the institutions he was dealing with, and who thought that he understood the only correct way to rule and serve the unruly peoples of the Balkans. He was uncritically loyal to a simple version of socialism, to the Party as the most effective vehicle to achieve the Balkan peasant's aspirations for national emancipation, relief from poverty and social mobility, and to Tito as the man and friend who had recognised his talents, promoted him and made him the strong right arm and 'conscience' of the Party.

His philosophy, if that is not too grand a word for native shrewdness, suggests an amalgam of lessons learned from the style of ruling the Serbs developed by Nikola Pašić, from the political essence of the Leninism-Stalinism to which Yugoslav Communists were exposed in prewar prison 'schools', and from his own wartime and postwar experiences. His style combined a ruthless firm hand when necessary with paternalistic populism when possible, a keen recognition of the importance of Lenin's insistence on a disciplined, cadre Party and a Serbian Radical's intuitive comprehension of the means and uses of the politics of clientelism. In addition, his wartime experience in building OZNa seemed to confirm the prejudice that comes easily to any Serbian, the conviction that his fellow Serbs were the most reliable instruments for the building of a strong, independent Yugoslav State and for the protection of socialism as he understood it. With no pretensions to interest or competence in ideology and theory he was, in brief, a good Leninist and a good Serbian Radical but not much of a Marxist, which is to say a sociologist, and so he failed to realise that Yugoslav society in the 1960s was no longer, in crucial ways, the society that Pašić had known and ruled.

These failings he himself admitted at the time of his fall, in a statement which was derided at the time as hypocritical but which in fact suggests honest self-awareness:

Some comrades may remember that I have often said that many things were beyond me and that I could not do them, or at least not as I had done them in certain periods of our development ... I have always thought and I still think today that I can only be an executor and perhaps to a certain extent an interpreter of the line and of policies, because I do not have the capability to participate in the working out of policies ... in creating policies on broad social questions.[26]

The principals whom Ranković failed to oppose over the Constitution, Kardelj and Bakarić, differed sharply from him and from each other in personality and in political values and styles. Kardelj, generally regarded outside Yugoslavia as the paladin of consistent 'liberalism' jousting with Ranković as the guardian of 'dogmatism', has never been so regarded inside the country. Both labels are misleading. If Ranković in a sense always remained a peasant of Šumadija, it is even truer that Kardelj remained a Slovenian schoolteacher, looking and speaking the part. His advocacy of decentralised and liberalised communism after 1949 was certainly genuine and frequently very important after he inherited Djilas's role as chief court ideologist, but it was always as pedantic, academic and even dogmatic as the 'left extremism' of his earlier years. The usual result was an abstract intellectual exercise in which the logical (Marxist) conclusion seemed more important than the practical consequences of its application to real (Yugoslav) life; attempts to implement his extreme, dogmatic definitions of communal and enterprise autonomy as prerequisites of self-management, for example, certainly contributed to the absurdly uneconomic fragmentation of industry and services which was as much to blame for the country's woes in 1962 as the centralism which he now considered the principal evil. Nevertheless, and perhaps because they *were* intellectually sound, his basic political and sociological insights and general principles happened to be on the side of the emerging social forces and the more pragmatic liberal politicians who knew how to use them.

Bakarić, although also an intellectual with an abiding interest in Marxist theory, belonged primarily to the latter group and has undoubtedly been the ablest politician, aside from Tito, produced by Croatia in the past century. A man of fertile but impenetrable mind who preferred to operate quietly from behind the scenes but who was among the first to recognise the potential political uses of the mass media in a changing Yugoslav society, he has always been an enigma, even to his closest friends from the days of prewar clandestine Party activity.[27] A stout quasi-invalid who frequently retires in illness or for contemplation to his retreat on the island of Hvar and a man who knows how to conserve his limited energy, he was the undisputed master of Croatia from the end of the war until the late 1960s, a member of the all-Yugoslav Party Executive Committee since 1952 but shrewdly defying repeated offers of high federal posts (reportedly including the Presidency of the FEC in 1963) which would have required Belgrade residence and separation from his Croatian power base.[28]

At every crucial moment in Yugoslavia's history since 1948, his considerable weight and his keen but fallible political instinct for what could be achieved and the best way of achieving it at a particular moment have been thrown in the scales on the side of pragmatism and liberalisation. His role in the decollectivisation of agriculture in the early 1950s has already been described, as has his subtler role in switching the focus of Croatian agitation from decentralisation to de-étatisation after 1961 and in suggesting ways in which both could be to the advantage of previously centralist but non-Serb underdeveloped regions. The same insight displayed in the latter key contribution to the liberal cause inspired him consistently to take the lead in attacking ethnic nationalism, particularly in Croatia. As an anti-nationalist, if also a consciously Croatian Communist who believed in what he was saying, he perceived more clearly than most of his countrymen that Croatian national interests could in fact be equated with non-national, anti-étatist economics and political liberalism, that emphasis on the national aspect would isolate Croatia and strengthen the hand of conservative centralism as it had always done in the past, and that emphasis on anti-étatism and laissez-faire economics provided a platform on which many allies could be assembled. Many men in many places joined to make the reform of 1965 and to destroy Ranković in 1966, but Bakarić was the first and possibly the only one who set about doing these things with a comprehensive political strategy based on a vision of a viable coalition which he did more than anyone else to bring into being.[29]

The actors were now all present and accounted for. There were those managers, 'technocrats' and local political magnates with reasons to dislike central redistribution and those spokesmen for ethnic groups with anxieties about Serbian domination, all of whom were finding in the new spirit of parliamentary responsibility to autonomous group interests, sanctioned by a new Constitution, a means of articulating their preferences which was politically far more effective than impotent congeries of economists or the pages of *Ekonomska politika*, *Delo* and *Vjesnik*. There were, with particular and timely potential among these new devices for the aggregation of interests, the Economic Chambers as the chartered voices of socialist enterprises with an accumulation of grudges against the existing system. There was the Trade Union Federation defending what it claimed were the interests of all workers but were primarily the interests of workers (and managers) in profitable and potentially profitable enterprises. There were also republican political bureaucracies, exploiting paralytic dissensions at the Party centre to build their own empires as eagerly as the Nemanjids had exploited the Latin conquest of Constantinople and finding much to interest them in the platforms of the trade unionists and the vociferous advocates of laissez-faire socialism in the Economic Chambers. And there were the ideological liberals of Yugoslav communism, those lonely generals who had spent a decade searching for any army with which to impose the ideals of the 6th Congress, and who were now discovering that social, economic and political changes had created, if not an army, at least a motley array of forces with a common interest in attacking the same citadel.

The stormy passage through the Federal Assembly at the end of

1963 of an apparently still indecisive annual Social Plan was quickly followed, at the turn of the year, by two developments which indicated that a decision was emerging after all and however piecemeal. The liberal side of the 'economists' debate' passed into the public domain of the mass media, as has been seen, with the admission that agreement on the principles of reform had now been achieved but that the details were still in dispute. On January 1, 1964, the principal agency of federal control of savings and investment, the GIF, which had handled between a third and a quarter of gross investment financing, was abolished along with corresponding republican and local investment funds. Their assets and liabilities were transferred to the banks which had administered them.[30] 'Contributions' to these funds were thereby also abolished, as was the federal tax on 'surplus' profits. Federal levies against enterprise income were thus reduced to the capital tax and personal income taxes. The initiative for these changes was Boris Krajger's, and Vukmanović wryly noted that they constituted a belated implementation of reforms agreed upon at a high-level meeting of economists and politicians summoned by Kardelj three years earlier, in January 1961.[31]

On March 16, the Party Central Committee assembled for its 6th Plenum, the main purpose of which was to set the date and begin preparations for the 8th LCY Congress. The leadership had before them a document entitled 'Basic Directives for Pre-Congressional Activities', which was sent to all Party organisations for guidance, and a report on 'current ideological problems and the role of the LCY' by Vlahović, who seemed to be assuming the mantle of chief court ideologist after Kardelj's attention had turned to constitutional, parliamentary and economic questions.[32]

Both dealt somewhat gingerly with recently revived criticism of internal decision-making and the external role of an authoritarian Party in a more open society and democratic polity in which 'direct social self-management' was said to be an increasingly realistic and immediate goal. Old clichés and euphemisms were repeated, a signal that the Party would continue as vaguely as ever to seek the elusive golden mean to which it had declaratively aspired since the 6th Congress: neither 'an outside factor which acts from above ... and is authorised to issue orders', nor a 'pseudo-liberalistic underestimation and negation of the leading role of the League of Communists'.[33] This was all very well but not very specific. A proposition like Vlahović's re-definition of Party 'unity' for a more democratic age—'under conditions of decentralisation of economic and social affairs the unity of the League of Communists is a vigorous concentration of political consciousness in which individual and social consciousness are integrated'—might have ideological significance but did not offer much practical guidance to Party Secretaries in the field or even to ordinary members of the Central Committee. It was perhaps inevitable and certainly revealing that one of the latter should ask a little plaintively, during the debate on the Basic Directives, whether the message of this document was that 'a campaign for the living standard should be waged'. Tito replied with patient paternalism: 'I think that it is not a question of a campaign, but of the need to grasp the problem, which is now at a stage when it must be solved. The question, however, is how to do this.'

The possibility and 'obligation' to raise standards of living by raising the share of personal consumption in national income, a slogan of the reformers, was in fact only one if the most easily comprehensible and popular of ten economic subjects treated by the Basic Directives. Particular emphasis was placed on the need to enlarge the portion of enterprise gross income under the direct control of the workers (i.e. the enterprises), although there were only three passing references to the now crucial issue of the inclusion of investment funds in this category. The reformers' favourite code word 'de-étatisation' did not occur. The document approved by the Central Committee still lagged behind the mood of the Federal Assembly and was less specifically reformist than recent or forthcoming legislation, but it did indicate a considerable evolution since the pro-centralist 3rd or the indecisive and ambivalent 4th Plenum.

The 5th Congress of the Trade Union Federation, held on April 20-25, 1964, provided a timely forum for the mobilisation of additional support. Preparations had lasted a full year and, according to Vukmanović-Tempo, had aroused opposition by unspecified persons who objected 'that we were "too ambitious", that we wanted to make the [Trade Union Federation's] Central Council into a "second Central Committee" [of the Party], that we were creating "a shadow government" '. He later recalled that he reported these accusations to Tito, who replied bitterly and in the presence of a delegation from the Central Council: 'So you are forming a Central Committee! Well, if the people who are supposed to form one can't do so, you might as well.'[34]

Whether or not these conveniently remembered words were actually said, Tito's brief welcoming address to the assembled trade unionists on the opening day of the Congress seemed to endorse their activities and the principles of the reform. He had already spoken twice (briefly in a speech at Niš on March 7 and again at the 6th Plenum) in favour of 'low tension' plans and higher living standards, a slogan of the liberal reformers, and now he repeated the commitment to a larger and particularly appro-priate audience. This time he added a plea, typical of his rhetorical style on such occasions but in the present context noteworthy, for pressure from the workers, 'from below', to force the political leadership to make the necessary changes in the economic system. He also told them: 'It's not only that things don't always work as they should among you below, in the enterprises and the economy, but among us at the top things are not as they should be either.'[35]

Vukmanović's 72-page presidential report and others read to plenary sessions of the Congress vigorously supported those planks of the reform programme which coincided with trade union positions and which also happened to be the central issues of the reform: a smaller proportion of GNP for investment and more for consumption, and the primary role in investment shifted from the State to the economy. Vukmanović himself had already elaborated these themes in a series of characteristically aggressive pre-Congress articles in *Borba* and he repeated his views in off-the-cuff remarks to Congress commissions which were so blunt that they were deleted from the report of the proceedings. Others eagerly followed suit, while delegates from individual enterprises submitted examples to prove that

the considerable material resources at the disposition of state organs and other social factors outside the economy are irrationally invested and expended, and that this would be avoided only if the direct producers and their organs of self-management were to become the principal agents of savings and investment.[36]

Meanwhile, the Federal Assembly had devoted two days to a major discussion of the economic situation, on April 16–17, during which the same themes were stressed and the ground rules for the 1965 reform were in effect established.[37] The leading spokesmen, significantly, were Slovenes like Boris Krajger and Croats like Miko Tripalo and Mika Špiljak; the first of these was already an important federal spokesman in economic matters, the last was now prime minister of Croatia and recently Vukmanović's vice-president in the trade union Central Committee, and all three were to play weighty if different roles in post-Reform Yugoslavia. Their chief support in the debate came, equally significantly, from back-bench deputies from the industrial and business world like Norbert Veber, the manager of the important Sisak Steelworks. The managers and 'technocrats' of market socialism were standing up with growing confidence, and with their Party cards tucked safely in their pockets, to demand lower taxes and fewer State regulations so that they could get on with the business of building socialism by making profits and investing them sensibly. The debate was followed, on May 20, by the adoption of a 'Resolution on Basic Guidelines for the Further Development of the Economic System' which faithfully repeated the same themes and those of the Trade Union Congress.[38]

In July came two further steps to reduce the economic role of the Federation. Abrupt increases of up to 29 per cent were announced in the retail prices of formerly subsidised basic commodities like flour, bread, milk, electricity and coal, a first step in eliminating subsidies and establishing price ratios more appropriate to a genuine market economy. And on July 9, the Federal Assembly passed a new 'Basic Law on the Financing of Socio-Political Communities', redefining the division of responsibility and resources for social services and interventions in the economy among the Federation, the republics and the communes.[39] The communes were henceforth required to finance these services out of their own means, with the role of the Federation reduced to supplying grants-in-aid to republics whose resources were inadequate for the satisfaction of 'minimum needs' in these fields—a level now for the first time precisely defined as a per capita income, by commune, which was lower than the Yugoslav average.

The 8th Congress

The stage was now set for the 8th Congress of the LCY, which met in Belgrade from December 7 to 13, 1964. The international context, except for minor shadows cast by the fall of Khrushchev two months earlier and by the anti-Yugoslav stance of the American Congress since the Belgrade non-aligned conference, was unusually propitious. Not since the summer of 1944 had Tito found himself so simultaneously accepted by both East and West as during the preceding two years—a status symbolised by the bonhomie of Khrushchev's two-week visit to Yugoslavia in August 1963 and the cordiality of President John Kennedy during Tito's first official visit to the United States two months later. A second conference of non-aligned Heads of State and Government, in Cairo in October 1964, had perhaps not been quite the triumph of the Belgrade conference of 1961 and was marred by a Tito-Sukarno duel over coexistence, but it had demonstrated that non-alignment was alive and growing in adherents and had reconfirmed Tito's own status as one of the three most respected leaders of the movement. At the same time and with the chronic exception of Albania, relations with all of Yugoslavia's neighbours had never been better, no mean achievement for a country which at one time or another in the previous eighteen years had been at daggers drawn with each of these countries—claiming territory from Italy and Austria, promoting Communist insurrection in Greece, and quarrelling violently with the Warsaw Pact.[40]

Of all these external relations, it was the rapprochement with the East which most immediately concerned the Yugoslav Party and which was manifest in the presence at their Congress, for the first time since the war, of representatives of the Soviet and other ruling Communist Parties of Eastern Europe.

The new détente in Soviet-Yugoslav relations had begun in 1961, apparently at Soviet initiative and as a by-product of the Sino-Soviet quarrel, which became dramatically public at the Soviet Party's 22nd Congress that November.[41] The immediate issue which led Chou En-lai to walk out of the Congress was Albania, but the wider issues included a struggle for hegemony in the world Communist movement and for influence in the Third World. On all three scores the sympathy and support of Yugoslavia, the still unique tri-borough bridge connecting Eastern, Western and Third Worlds, would be of use to an embattled Soviet leadership. Careful soundings on both sides began even before the 22nd Congress and included a visit to Moscow by Yugoslav Foreign Minister Koča Popović in July 1961 and kind words for the Soviet Union by Tito at the Belgrade non-aligned conference in August. Then Khrushchev himself stumped Bulgaria and Romania in May 1962 to tell the other Balkan comrades that the Yugoslavs were 'also building socialism'. In September the Soviet Head of State Leonid Brezhnev paid an official visit to Yugoslavia (which was not an unmitigated success), and in December Tito travelled to the Soviet Union for a busy 'holiday', his first visit since 1956. Granted the rare honour of addressing the Supreme Soviet, the still unrehabilitated heretic carefully referred to Yugoslavia as socialist but non-aligned and spoke highly of its peculiar institutions, like self-management, which were still anathema to the USSR. But Ranković, also in the delegation and speaking in Kiev, referred to 'the working class of the entire world together with all progressive forces, led by the Soviet Union', the first time a Yugoslav official had pronounced that litany since 1948. Then Tito himself, back at home in January 1963, lashed out against abstract art, *Kitsch* and other 'decadent foreign influences' in Yugoslav culture. His language echoed Khrushchev's recent attacks on the same phenomena in the Soviet Union and appeared to be an effort to bring Yugoslav policy into line with Soviet in at least one relatively marginal sphere.[42] During his August 1963 visit Khrushchev returned the favour by unprecedently calling workers' self-management 'a positive phenomenon' (although he worried about its implications for 'the Leninist principle of unity of leadership'), and it was announced that Yugoslavia would be granted observer status in Comecon, the Soviet bloc's common market. An intensified series of lower-level exchanges of economic and cultural delegations began in 1962 and continued throughout 1963, while licence for Yugoslav relations and influence with other Warsaw Pact countries 'reached a peak unknown since the 1956 explosion in Hungary'.[43]

By mid-1963, however, the pace of rapprochement had already slowed down, accompanied by a series of small indicators that the Yugoslavs had gone as far as they intended to go, if not a little farther.[44] In May, the Central Committee met to consider 'the position of the LCY on current international questions and tasks of the international workers' movement in the struggle for peace and socialism', i.e. the Party's position on the crisis in international communism provoked by the Sino-Soviet dispute. Tito's report hinted at another and domestic reason—in addition to the leadership's own caution born of experience and their awareness of the risks to still important economic and political links with the West—for hesitation and oscillation in the new relationship with the Soviet Party. Almost all of the 1 million members of the LCY and most middle-rank cadres, who mattered more, had joined since the war, most of them since the Cominform excommunication. They had grown up in an age of violent dispute with Moscow, and many were apparently having difficulty in adapting to an age of rapprochement. Tito in his report issued a plea to these younger Communists to 'forget misunderstandings' which were 'now a thing of the past', and to 'grasp the tremendous positive significance of establishing not only normal but good relations between our country and the USSR and other socialist countries'.[45]

One ideological justification, directed at least in part to these doubtful domestic comrades and a popular theme in the press in subsequent months, was found in an updating of the Yugoslav principle of 'active peaceful coexistence'. For years Yugoslav theoreticians had based this principle on the argument that the world was not divided into naturally and inevitably antagonistic capitalist and socialist blocs (the traditional Soviet thesis), but was a world of States in each of which, West or East, the struggle for socialism was going on with varying degrees of success. It was therefore nonsense and inimical to the interests of socialism to speak of a possible 'just' war or to deny the possibility of coexistence between 'capitalist' and 'socialist' countries, as the Chinese were doing in their current polemic with the Russians, if these were really non-existent categories. Now it was further argued that today's crucial struggle was between forces of peace and forces of anti-peace, with the latter consisting of an unholy alliance between the extreme right (Cold Warriors and other reactionaries) and Chinese and other 'dogmatists' of the extreme left. In this struggle there should be no non-alignment, and Yugoslavia could with good conscience align itself with a Khrushchevite Soviet Union against Maoist revolutionary dogmatism.[46]

All of these themes found their places in Tito's opening address to the 8th Congress on December 7, 1964. They were accompanied by a diatribe against the Chinese and by a careful eulogy of the deposed Khrushchev's understanding of these matters and of the importance of good relations with Yugoslavia—both apparently directed at the Soviet guest delegation.[47] But Tito's main concern, and that of the Congress, was the forthcoming economic reform and the forging of a Party consensus in support of it. For once those foreign observers who had always found a consistent correlation between the state of Soviet-Yugoslav relations and oscillations in the domestic political pendulum were to be confounded.

The historic function of the 1964 Congress was to place the seal of approval of the Party's formally supreme authority on the most far-reaching and significant changes in the system since 1953, a set of reforms which Tito himself was later to call a social and economic 'revolution'—a strong term for an old Bolshevik to use—and one with revolutionary political implications as well. Approval by the Congress, while in one sense a ritualistic formality after it had been advocated by Tito, Kardelj and other spokesmen for the Executive Committee,[48] was in another sense of vital importance. Under the rules of the Yugoslav political game it formally ended the period of legitimate debate and opposition inaugurated by the ambiguity and indecisiveness of the 4th Plenum, and under the rules of democratic centralism it required that the opposition should now loyally support the reforms they disliked, beginning with verbal support at the Congress itself. Failure to do so could henceforth be considered grounds for disciplinary action, including dismissal from office or the Party. Ranković himself pointed this out in his own report to the Congress, albeit as a general principle of Party unity and without specific reference to the forthcoming reforms, and so did his deputy and friend in charge of UDBa, Svetislav Stefanović, whose intervention in the general debate dealt with the 'responsibility' of Communists in the more difficult circumstances created by social modernisation and political diversification.[49]

It is in this light that the 8th Congress marked the effective if still qualified ascendancy of the 'liberal' coalition which had been forged by Bakarić and others and which now included Communist 'Whigs' at the Party centre, economic liberals in charge of viable but frustrated enterprises and branches concentrated in the northern half of the country, anti-centralist or anti-Serbian regional politicians and the disinterested or interested ideologues of self-management among intellectuals and in the trade unions.

Their ascendancy was also reflected in debates or conclusions relating to non-economic subjects, notably the national question and some aspects of 'cadre policy', to both of which the Congress devoted as much or more attention than it did to economic reform.

Tito, Kardelj and Vlahović all dedicated long sections of their reports to the first of these, which was the subject of fully one-quarter of Tito's keynote address and which received the frankest airing it had ever had at a Party Congress. While both 'particularist' (non-Serb) and 'centralist' (Serbian) nationalisms were again declared to be equally pernicious, the focus in all of these reports and in the Resolution was on the latter variety. Especially to be condemned were those advocates of 'integral Yugoslavism' whom Tito had so recently seemed to support but whom he now described as 'certain people' who had

the confused idea that the unity of our peoples means the elimination of nationalities and the creation of something new and artificial, that is a single Yugoslav nation, rather on the lines of assimilation and bureaucratic centralisation, unitarism and hegemony.[50]

It was generally held that local nationalisms and what Vlahović called the 'Communist provincials' who fed on them were a reaction against such views and against the allegedly related phenomenon of economic centralism, especially in the investment system. This last led to interregional and hence inter-ethnic competition for scarce funds, mutual recriminations about exploitation, attempts to 'territorialise' funds at a regional and ethnic rather than a federal and therefore (Serbo-)centralist level and other problems. Thus the reform and the national question were linked because, as Kardelj noted, only a thorough depolitisation and 'de-territorialisation' of investment by transferring control to the economy would simultaneously destroy the 'material basis' of 'centralist hegemony' and undermine the position of those whom Tito described as 'often arrogating to themselves the right to become self-styled "protectors" of the national interests of one or other of our nationalities'.[51]

Tito's own remarks about the economic reform itself were relatively brief—only eight pages out of a 58-page report which devoted more space to international affairs and to the national question. Casting himself in one of his favourite roles on such occasions, that of a simplifier and populariser of an intrinsically popular position, he emphasised the pressing need for a shift in the consumption-investment ratio, favouring more consumption and higher living standards, as a rationale for the proposed changes in the investment system. He also conceded that

some of our comrades, primarily those from the underdeveloped areas, have associated the development of the underdeveloped regions with the existing socio-economic system, believing that changes in our present practice might jeopardise this accelerated development.

Now, however, 'awareness is growing that the retention of administrative-centralistic methods would be a brake not only on further progress in the less developed regions but also on the entire economy'. There had been 'enough compromises'; in the future 'we cannot allow the non-implementation of the decisions and policy lines of the Central Committee on the part of individual Communists holding executive positions'.[52]

Kardelj spelled out the leadership's analysis and recommendations in a long report entitled 'Socio-Economic Aims of Economic Development in the Forthcoming Period'.[53] The ground he covered was by now familiar. De-étatisation of savings and investment ('expanded reproduction') was necessary to achieve true 'socialist production relations' and 'self-administration', for the sake of more efficient investment and the avoidance of a situation in which 'every investment problem automatically becomes a political problem as well', and for a more consistent application in the framework of a market economy of the principles of 'distribution according to work' and 'equal conditions for the acquisition of income'. Less but more efficient investment would then make possible a more rapid rise in living standards, a reform and then a freeing of prices, a more rapid and rational inclusion in the international division of labour, and other desirable fringe benefits. The socialist State would still be necessary as the 'custodian' of 'socialist economic relations', armed with suitable but largely indirect and fiscal rather than administrative 'social instruments and measures of intervention' with which to correct the 'spontaneous' action of the market, but the market would be 'the first and decisive factor ... by which fundamental income distribution is effected'.

Kardelj also recognised that new devices would have to be found to attract and mobilise, within a reformed credit and banking system, sufficient capital for larger or longer-term investments. While he even said that this was 'of such importance that the functioning of the whole system of expanded reproduction actually depends on the solution', he was ominously vague about how it should be done: 'above all in the banks, and also in the utilisation of funds from economic and other organisations, funds from insurance institutions and social insurance, reserve funds, etc'. Like the special problems of the underdeveloped regions and the probable impact of the reform on employment rates, which he also noted, his anticipation of the problem was to prove prophetic, viable solutions would be indefinitely delayed for political as well as technical reasons, and the consequences of these and other lacunae were to bring the reform and the reformers to the brink of failure within three years.

In the plenary debate it was Boris Krajger, one of the authors of the impending reform, who was willing to admit that the road they were about to follow would not be an easy one. Raising the level of personal consumption, he said, was not just a question of changing the existing consumption-investment ratio, as popularisers of the reform had sometimes suggested. A far-reaching restructuring of Yugoslavia's fragmented and inefficient industry and a dramatic change in the structure and quality of the labour force (its 'qualification profile') would be required. The impact of abandoning existing redistributive instruments, like high taxation on enterprise profits to finance large-scale subsidies, would be as severely disruptive in the short run as it would prove healthy in the long run. Exports would have to increase rapidly to pay for raw materials for the production of more consumer goods, and this would increase the pressure on producers to move away from extensive production of everything and into intensive production of those Yugoslav articles which enjoyed potential comparative advantages on the world market. Unemployment would certainly rise generally, and the underdeveloped regions would suffer particularly, unless there were increased emphasis on the tertiary (service) sector, where unexploited opportunities were numerous and new employment cost less than in industry. The underdeveloped regions would profit from the shift from a turnover tax on production to a sales tax on consumption, but would still need a (rationally administered) federal Development Fund. All of these things would require very hard work and a readjustment of business attitudes, but the only alternative was to continue with the old investment system, the greater evils of which were now manifest.[54]

Also worth noting were those delegates who had the courage or the mandate to express continuing reservations publicly. Most were from the underdeveloped regions and followed the example set by Djoko Pajković, secretary of the Montenegrin Central Committee and a member of the Yugoslav Central Committee since 1948. He adopted a 'yes, if ...' stance: the reform was very welcome in the less developed regions like Montenegro, but only if the special difficulties faced by newly created industries were kept in mind, more appropriate prices for raw materials and producers' goods were accepted, and measures were adopted to ensure the territorially free circulation of capital.[55]

A warning of a different kind was sounded by a young protégé of Bakarić. Miko Tripalo, Secretary of the Zagreb Party and a member of the Croatian Executive Committee, noted that there had already been two years of intensive discussion and agreement by a variety of authoritative institutions, but without any consistent action. Instead, enterprise taxes which had been repealed as a first step towards reform had been replaced in 1964 by an 'obligatory loan' to the Federation which in turn had not been used. What most bode ill, he thought, was that the draft

Social Plan for 1965, now ready for approval, included another obligatory loan but did not include a further promised tax relief and 'thus continues the old tendency towards an increase in investments and a further centralisation of funds'. If the Seven-Year Plan were to display the same features, centralised funds would be committed to such an extent and for such a time period that reform would be impossible. It was therefore a question of reform in 1965 or never, and it was consequently high time to finish with 'discussions only in principle'.[56]

The Resolution adopted at the end of the week was unequivocal, reiterating and even plagiarising the same set of ground rules for reform proposed by the Federal Assembly eight months earlier. There was even a confession that 'leading bodies of the League of Communists have not been sufficiently determined' in their efforts to find answers to questions posed as early as the 4th Plenum, and an implicit admission that the initiative had therefore come from parliament, so that the Party was in effect merely endorsing the stand taken there—a remarkable reversal of gears on one of the traditional 'transmission belts' of a Communist-ruled State.[57]

Ranković's report, meanwhile, had been concerned with the organisational and disciplinary matters appropriate to his own Party function. His main theme was the maintenance of Party control in an ever more complex social and political environment:

We need to make even greater efforts in the future to establish a method of work which will ensure that Communists are kept at the hub of activity in society, which will enable them to follow social processes in the most direct way possible, to react quickly to various phenomena, to distinguish between what is and what is not socialist, and to deal comprehensively with relations between people, and one which will ensure that they do not allow themselves to be ousted to the periphery of problems by bureaucracy and other detrimental tendencies.

He also insisted that the principle of democratic centralism had not become 'obsolete' in an age of self-administration, as some were claiming, and that 'advocacy of the legalisation of "minority rights" ' in the Party was not acceptable.[58] Such statements were of course not new and had long been the Party line. However, their restatement at this time, not only by Ranković but by Vlahović as a spokesmen of more moderate views, constituted a warning to those who in the renewed ideological ferment of the preceding year had again queried the appropriateness of the existing level and quality of Party control and the continuing validity of democratic centralism, and who had wondered aloud whether the time had not come to legitimise intra-Party, 'minority' oppositions or even a second party.[59] The conservative wing of the Party had lost some battles, but not this vital one.

They did, however, agree to an enlargement and rejuvenation of the Party leadership and to a further separation of Party and State functions which were on balance to the advantage of their opponents. That they did so was in part because they, too, were concerned about the continuity of a regime based on a Party which had lost its appeal to youth—the number of Party members under 25 years of age had declined from 23·6 per cent of total membership in 1958 to 13·6 per cent in 1964—and whose leadership was ageing and too full of primitive ex-Partisans ill equipped to cope with the more modern and subtle political style which the times required.

There was also another consideration. Ranković and the conservatives had as much reason as the liberals to be dissatisfied with the existing Central Committee, which they were inclined to blame for a large part of their own present difficulties. The Committee had been conspicuously inactive as such and its members had failed in their traditional role of enthusiastic collective endorsers and individual executors of policies decided by the Executive Committee and interpreted and administered by Ranković's Organisational-Political Secretariat. Ranković and the Report on the Work of the Central Committee which was submitted to the Congress blamed this performance primarily on the fact that members of the Central Committee had been overburdened with other jobs and distracted by the conflicting role expectations and interests which these represented,[60] but awareness that a stalemated Executive Committee had contributed by failing to produce operationally unambiguous directives was also reflected in the changes which they proposed.

The same logic which was forcing the conservatives to agree to an economic reform which they disliked was now imposing on them the cadre who advocated that reform. As Communists they had made a fetish of rapid economic growth. The system and the people they preferred had manifestly failed, for a variety of reasons which included the obstruction of the liberals, to maintain that growth without insupportable side effects. And so they were forced to permit those other people who promised a way out with another system to have a try. With determination and control of the apparatus they no doubt thought that they could keep that try and its political implications from getting out of hand, and if the reform failed their own reservations would be vindicated and they would be back in charge with a strengthened mandate for centralism.

The Central Committee was enlarged to 155 members (from 128 survivors of the 135 elected at the 7th Congress). Of these 71 were elected for the first time; 44 members of the old Central Committee were dropped, some of whom went voluntarily and others despite their bitter objections.[61] But omission did not always mean demotion—several who were dropped were senior Government officials whose departure was part of a new campaign to separate Party and State functions. The average age of the Central Committee declined from 52 to 45 years and for the first time some were too young to have participated actively in the National Liberation Struggle. The Executive Committee was meanwhile enlarged to 19 members, of whom 6 were Serbs, 4 were Croats, 3 were Slovenes, 4 were Montenegrins and 2 were Macedonians. Of the fifteen members elected at the 7th Congress, Djuro Salaj had died and the veteran Slovene Communist Franc Leskošek, 67, now asked to be relieved because of failing health; the others were all re-elected. The six new members were Krsto Crvenkovski (Macedonian), Boris Krajger (Slovene), Cvijetin Mijatović (Bosnian Serb), Djoko Pajković (Montenegrin), Mika Špiljak (Croat) and Mijalko Todorović (Serb). Ranging in age from 44 (Crvenkovski) to 51 (Mijatović and Todorović), they brought the average age of the Executive Committee down from 57 to 54. All except Pajković and Mijatović, the Yugoslav ambassador in Moscow, had been associated with the reform movement and were considered liberals. Tito was re-elected as Secretary-General. Vlahović joined Kardelj and Ranković as Secretaries to the Central Committee.

The reforms of 1965

That the economic reforms inaugurated during the following seven months were less uncompromisingly liberalising and decentralising than the mandate given by the 8th Congress was initially and ironically as much for economic as for political reasons. The general economic situation had not improved with the delay in changing the system. Demand in both the investment and consumption sectors continued in 1964 and early 1965 to grow far more rapidly than the supply of goods. So did production bottlenecks in some sectors, surpluses in others, and perceptions of 'unjust' income differentials because differences in profitability ratios among economic branches and regions still bore no relation to the structure of demand, to the logic of a market economy or to the Yugoslav definition of the principle 'to each according to his work'. In foreign trade differences in the effective rate of exchange for the dinar applicable to various importing and exporting sectors, where parities now ranged from 750 to 1,300 dinars to the US dollar, had reached a point of dysfunctional complexity as great as that of 1960, before the last reform which was supposed to introduce a single, uniform parity.

The consequences by early 1965 included a rate of inflation which then seemed intolerable and a deficit on current account in the balance of trade and balance of payments which was clearly unsustainable. The volume of State interventions in the form of subsidies, rebates or special tax relief to compensate for distorted differences in rates of profitability or to promote exports was rising alarmingly. The federal Secretariat for Finance calculated that without major changes in foreign exchange rates and domestic price ratios it would be necessary to allocate an additional 100,000 million dinars for export subsidies in 1965. Import pressures would continue to grow, the railways and the electric equipment industry would have deficits of 90,000 million and up to 25,000 million dinars respectively, numerous enterprises would operate at a loss which could only be covered by an estimated 200,000 million dinars in new taxes for additional subsidies, and earnings from tourism and other non-commodity sources of foreign currency, lately of increasing importance, would stagnate or decline.[62]

The nature of these problems made it unavoidable that emergency measures which were tantamount to a further centralisation of control over the economy would have to precede decentralisation and liberalisation. In the spring of 1965 the FEC introduced by decree a deflationary package which had this effect. It included a total price freeze, measures to reduce investment demand and slow down the rate of new employment and restrictions on consumer credits. That these decrees were treated as though they were an integral part of the general reform of the system led to contradictory interpretations which complicated the political situation the following year.

At the same time, in March 1965, the Federal and Economic Chambers of the Federal Assembly passed a new Law on Banks and Credit Transactions which constituted an essential first step towards the creation of a radically different investment system.[63] The Law sought to 'de-étatise' the banks by making them responsible to all of their institutional depositors rather than to the State alone. It also contained provisions to induce enterprises to deposit and thus make available through the banking system a significant portion of the additional funds which lower taxes and the liquidation of social investment funds were to leave in enterprise coffers, and without which the economy as a whole would lack an adequate pool of free investment capital. Both were of cardinal importance to the revised Yugoslav concept of market socialism and represented the first serious attempt by a socialist State to find a viable alternative to either traditional capitalist or traditional socialist methods of capital accumulation and mobilisation. Its inadequacies were to prove of equal importance to the political as well as the economic difficulties which Yugoslavs were to encounter in coming years.[64]

Since the 1961 reforms all Yugoslav business banks had in theory been entitled to grant both long-term (investment) and short-term credits, although the activities of the republican and communal banks, of which there were 200 in March 1965, were restricted to their own territories. In fact only the three federal banks and to a minor extent the six republican ones disposed of enough capital to engage in granting investment credits, and even so they were almost entirely dependent for this purpose on the social investment funds which they administered. From 1958 to 1961 a mere 1·7 per cent of total investment credits were financed by banks, although their share jumped to 20·4 per cent in 1963. In addition to the indirect political control over investment decision-making which derived from the political source of these funds, the State at various levels exerted direct control by appointing the management boards and directors of all banks. This power remained when the social investment funds were abolished in January 1964 and their assets were transferred to the appropriate federal and republican banks.

Under the new law the banks became autonomous economic organisations charged 'on behalf of the community' with 'the management of social capital earmarked for investment and the expansion of production'. The sources of this capital included deposits (with major institutional depositors sharing both profits and risk, another innovation), money obtained through borrowing at home or abroad and repayments and retained earnings from credits granted. The last category also incidentally included a gigantic and later highly controversial windfall for the three formerly 'federal' and now essentially Serbian banks in Belgrade—the Yugoslav Investment Bank, the Yugoslav Agricultural Bank and the Yugoslav Foreign Trade Bank—which had administered and then in 1964 inherited the assets of the former GIF. They now retained these assets for lack of a political agreement about how they might otherwise be distributed, and so became by far the strongest banks in the country.

Territorial restrictions on banking operations and hence also on the choice of bank by a depositor or a borrower were eliminated. All banks were entitled to operate throughout Yugoslavia, although a specified minimum capital fund was required to engage in granting long-term investment credits. Banks could also now be founded 'jointly by enterprises other working organisations and socio-political communities', not as formerly only by the last (i.e. only by the government of a commune, a district, a republic or the Federation). The State at various appropriate levels retained the right to indicate 'basic guidelines' for investment policy through social plans or other general acts, to appoint the directors of banks founded under federal or republican law (a provision abolished three years later), to earmark their own deposits for specific investments and in special cases 'to arrange with banks to extend credits for specified purposes at lower charges and under other privileged terms, in which case they are bound to compensate the banks for the difference in interest charges'. A consultative Council of Banks under the chairmanship of the governor of the National Bank was instituted. The Federal Government, acting through a reformed National Bank or directives of the Federal Assembly, also continued to manipulate normal monetary controls like the setting of minimum reserve levels and maximum interest rates or the terms under which the National Bank would act as a 'bankers' bank'. Finally, the National Bank was to continue to control and supervise all foreign exchange activities on behalf of the central Government, and until 1967 only the three former 'federal' banks were authorised to effect payment transactions and to contract credits with foreign countries.[65]

Otherwise operational control over each bank was to be vested in its own Assembly, a new body including representatives of the bank but primarily—the law stipulated at least 90 per cent—representatives of the enterprises and other legal persons, including political units, which had invested in the bank's capital. These now became in effect shareholders (even the term was used unofficially), with voting power proportionate to the amount invested but restricted to a maximum 10 per cent control per depositor.

The dual purpose of the law was manifest in the composition and function of a bank's Assembly and Executive Committee. By controlling the banks and their investment policies in proportion to their contribution to banking capital, enterprises and other depositors would in theory collectively control the distribution and have a major role in determining the size of gross national investment, while the amount of control they exerted individually would be proportionate to their contribution to national income, or more accurately to national savings. Ideologically consistent with the socialist principle according to which 'the producer should decide about the distribution of the value created by his work' and with the Yugoslav concept of social self-management, this control was also expected to mean economic rather than 'political' investments, since the depositor-shareholders would have a vested interest in seeing to it that their savings were invested where earnings would be maximised and not in 'political factories'. At the same time it was to be hoped that interest earned on idle capital plus voting power in a banking system from which one would sooner or later want to borrow would attract, in sufficient volume to satisfy the lower goals of national investment policy, the kind of funds which had formerly been extracted by the State through the tax system as a form of obligatory saving.[66]

Meanwhile, last-minute political difficulties were threatening to surface from an unexpected source. According to an admission by Bakarić made a year after the event, a growing number of Croats were at last doing their sums, discovering the losses which proposed changes in price ratios would impose on Croatian industry, and demanding that the Croatian Central Committee should oppose or at least demand major changes in the proposed reforms. The Zagreb leadership, already concerned because pro-reform propaganda was fuelling the fires of Croatian nationalism with its emphasis on statistics 'proving' the exploitation of Croatia under the existing system, became seriously alarmed. 'That', said Bakarić, 'was why we agreed to launch the reform quickly and to express strong support for it.'[67]

Fearing that with such additional complications the tide might turn against them, the sponsors of the reform, with Boris Krajger their chief technician, proceeded to draft legislation with a haste that the economists whom they had failed to consult and they themselves were later to blame when foreseeable but unforeseen difficulties arose. The package was submitted to the LCY Central Committee at its 2nd Plenum on June 17 and approved. On July 24 Krajger presented it, in the form of a dozen laws, decisions, regulations and orders, to a joint session of the Federal and Economic Chambers of the Federal Assembly. All were passed, signed by President Tito and promulgated the same day.[68] Other related legislation had already been approved, including a revised Basic Law on Enterprises[69] as well as the new banking law, but July 24, 1965, was henceforth treated by Yugoslav historians and the Yugoslav public as the day on which the Reform was launched.

This reform with a capital 'R' was designed to effect major changes in three all-encompassing sectors: in primary distribution and in secondary redistribution of national income and in foreign trade. The goal was to increase the role of the market in the first sector, to reduce the scope of secondary redistribution by the State and to simplify and rationalise foreign trade and increase its impact on the domestic market. It was also explicitly declared to be a 'social' as well as an economic reform, which would bring about a radical enlargement in the decision-making role of ordinary citizens as 'self-managing' producers and require a major change in the role and operating methods of the Party.

The principal instrument for reorganising primary distribution was a drastic revision of existing price ratios through highly differentiated increases in all prices. Within the framework of an overall 24 per cent rise (over 1964 average levels), prices in industry and mining generally were increased by 14 per cent, in agriculture by 32 per cent, in transport by 26 per cent, in the construction industry by 22 per cent and for basic raw and semi-processed materials (ores, minerals, timber, pig iron, lead and zinc, electrolytic copper, aluminium, etc.) by as much as 59 and an average of 45 per cent. In the processing industry, on the other hand, price increases averaged only 8 per cent. The basic criterion in most cases was the so-called world market price for the item, translated in accordance with the new parity for the dinar. In presenting these changes to the Federal Assembly, Krajger admitted that many of the new prices were still arbitrary, that some represented concessions to special interest pleading and that numerous adjustments would no doubt have to be made. The market, he said, would not really function efficiently as an allocator of national income until prices could respond freely to supply and demand, which he hoped would happen soon but could not happen yet.

To reduce the role of the State in secondary redistribution of national income the tax system was subjected to a general overhaul designed ultimately to reduce the State's share in the net income of the country's enterprises from 49 to 29 per cent. Such a change, Krajger said, 'represents a great revolutionary act'. Turnover tax was reduced to a sales tax on final consumption. It would be variable and manipulable by sector or product (and thus still an important fiscal means of State intervention in the market) with a general level not to exceed 20 per cent, including a 12 per cent federal, a maximum 6 per cent local sales tax, and a temporary 2 per cent republican levy for disaster relief in Croatia-Slavonia and neighbouring Bosnia, which had recently suffered unusually severe flooding, and in Macedonia, where the reconstruction of Skopje after the 1963 earthquake was still in its early stages. Corporate income taxes were eliminated entirely. The capital tax, henceforth virtually the only source of funds for State-financed investments in the economy, was reduced from the existing statutory 6 per cent per annum to 4 per cent but with fewer exceptions, so that some branches which had lately paid little or no capital tax would now pay more.[70] Taxes on gross personal incomes and social insurance contributions were reduced, the former from 17·5 to 10·5 per cent.

These tax reductions were to be made possible by the virtual elimination of the State's role in investment and of subsidies and rebates for exports or in support of weak industries or sectors whose unrealistically low prices had made them artificially unprofitable, and by a reduction in 'indirect income' (subsidised holidays, travel, housing, etc.) and other forms of centralised redistribution. Krajger noted, however, that State budgets in other fields and at all levels would also have to be cut back, and that this would not be easy at the federal level—where national defence, veterans' pensions and the servicing of foreign debts accounted for 75 per cent of all non-redistributive expenditures—or in services financed by social insurance. In fact they were not cut back at all, despite persistent nagging by the Economic Chamber of the Federal Assembly in particular, and this became one of the points at which the objectives of the Reform were to be eroded from the beginning.[71]

To support all these changes and to liberalise and simplify foreign trade a major change in the already highly unrealistic official parity of the dinar was required. It was devalued in two quick stages, from 750 to 1,250 to the US dollar, a figure changed at the end of the year to 12·50, for psychological reasons, through a reissue of the currency at a rate of 1 new dinar for 100 old dinars and a resurrection of *para* (cents) for fractions thereof. Most quantitative restrictions on imports were removed, average customs duty was reduced from 23 to 11 per cent, and Krajger and others spoke for the first time of a convertible dinar by the 1970s. International support had already been sought—one technical reason for final delays in announcing the reform—and the response had been favourable. The International Monetary Fund had approved the changes and was supporting them with an additional $80 million in drawing rights, the Soviet Union and three of its European allies had offered credits for the modernisation of Yugoslav industry and similar negotiations were under way with the Governments of the United States, Britain, Italy and France.[72] Foreign assistance in support of the reforms eventually totalled $140 million,[73] and in August 1966 Yugoslavia finally achieved full membership in the GATT.

The total reform package also included several other important features. It was decided in November 1965 to abandon annual Social Plans as inappropriate under the new system. The Fund for the Development of Underdeveloped Regions was at last established, in February 1965, although the precise mode of its financing remained in dispute. The housing sector received special attention. Property in this category was revalued as of August 1, 1965, and rents were raised sharply and in stages until they approached 'economic' rents which would at least cover depreciation and maintenance. A new device for pooling these funds in amounts large enough to pay for major repairs and to undertake new housing construction in larger cities was eventually found in the form of 'housing enterprises' as authorised and exclusive rent collectors, which quickly gave rise to blatant new forms of porkbarrelling, graft and corruption, but to little improvement in the maintenance of existing residential buildings.

In agriculture private peasants were for the first time granted access to new mechanised equipment and to bank credits on terms of equality with the socialist sector. The first major concession to the private sector since the abandonment of collectivisation in 1953, these last measures implicitly recognised the failure of the socialist sector to attract the peasant and to utilise his land to an economically significant degree. They also explicitly recognised the importance to the fulfilment of the Reform's other goals of more marketable agricultural surpluses and of a richer peasantry, capable of consuming more industrial goods.

Aftermath: resistance and Ranković

Reform had been proclaimed and the reformers, armed with clear mandates from Party and parliament, were ostensibly in charge. Within a matter of months it was nevertheless clear that little was happening, beyond the initial and in many sectors negative impact of changed price ratios and devaluation, and that even this little tended to be either a feeble echo or what was soon termed 'a mechanical and primitive execution' of the bold intentions announced in July. Individual measures were frustrated, sometimes mysteriously, or else pushed to ridiculous extremes. The most visible results of a characteristically much publicised 'campaign', urging enterprises to find and exploit material, organisational and human 'internal reserves' in order to adapt to the new conditions, was to provide good material for suddenly sophisticated Yugoslav caricaturists and cabaret satirists.

There were always sound reasons for deviations, vehemently and sometimes apparently unwittingly argued by politicians and an increasingly disputatious and regionally or functionally partisan press. Certain major investment projects could not be postponed without serious damage to the future economic wellbeing of this or that republic. Certain economic sectors had been unfairly penalised by altered price ratios or other reform measures and must be supported. Despite promises to the contrary, unemployment was growing and the standard of living, particularly for the least well paid, was falling, requiring concessions or the restoration of curtailed social services. Workers' councils were taking the easy way out when belts had to be tightened by sacking a handful of needed engineers and technicians instead of a hundred surplus unskilled workers and by cutting out research and development or scholarship funds, economically dysfunctional and sometimes socially unjust measures which only State directives or budgetary interventions could prevent. Cries for help were coming from the developed northern republics as well as from the south. The Croats and Slovenes were now discovering in practice the implications of changed price ratios for the processing industries in which they specialised and were demanding help (Tripalo specifically suggested a lower capital tax rate) for this beleaguered sector.

By early October, when the Federal and Economic Chambers of the Federal Assembly debated the first effects of the Reform, demands were being made for reflationary measures to stop the decline in growth rates and to relieve enterprises beset by illiquidity. Boris Krajger, replying for the Government with a firm 'no', said investment levels and also the State's share in national income were still grossly over-inflated, and that to retreat now from the July measures would be disastrous. He also told other deputies demanding free price formation that this too was still quite impossible. On October 21, *Komunist*, in an authoritatively unsigned front-page editorial entitled 'Through the Back Door', sombrely described attempts to evade or distort the Reform's intentions. That same week a survey of 425 enterprises employing 225,000 persons found that 12,574 workers had already been dismissed and that they were expecting to sack another 19,000.[74]

By mid-winter prominent liberal politicians and economists were at least privately deeply discouraged. 'It's like punching a rubber wall', one told the present writer; 'you seem to make an impression, but then it's just like it was'. 'The Reform is dead', another said bluntly in January 1966. A month earlier Bakarić had plainly told the Croatian Party Executive Committee where the political source of the trouble lay: 'We have sought to mobilise the masses as never before, and this must cause conflicts *even where we have had our chief support in the past*'.[75]

It was increasingly clear, although difficult to demonstrate as long as everyone played by the rules of the Yugoslav political game, where the epicentre of resistance was to be found, and that this resistance was more important than the inadequacies of the reform programme or the complexity of the problems it was exposing. Those in leading or middle-rank positions in the Party, State and economic apparatuses who had felt deep-seated reservations before the new course was adopted were not willing to wait to be proved right when the Reform failed without their assistance. In a situation in which no one could openly oppose the accepted policy they were a doubly powerful group because they occupied the best institutional positions from which decision-making at all levels could be informally and surreptitiously influenced in one direction while dutiful public statements gave lip-service to its opposite.

Most of them were also Serbians, men like Ranković for whom a preference for strong centralised Government, instilled by history and a primitive Communist vision of economic development stressing conspicuous and expensive investment projects, were more important than a mundane cost-benefit analysis of the potential impact of the Reform on the Serbian economy, which might have made them into ardent supporters. Although a number of important Serbian leaders, including Todorović and Milentije Popović, did not share these views and said so,[76] they tended to be involved primarily with federal rather than republican politics. It was therefore men like the Serbian Party Secretaries Jovan Veselinov and Vojin Lukić—the latter one of Ranković's closest collaborators and recently in direct control of the police apparatus as federal Secretary for Internal Affairs from 1963 to 1965—who dictated the Serbian Party line. They gave the Serbian position a strikingly recalcitrant tone, particularly on the subject of the range and type of still permissible Party 'interference', which contrasted sharply with the Croatian position.[77]

It was therefore also increasingly clear that the Reform would never really be implemented unless the citadels which these people commanded, in particular the central and Serbian Party apparatuses and the State Security Service (renamed *Služba državne bezbednosti* in November 1964 but still invariably called UDBa), could be disciplined or broken. It was equally clear that relations among the nationalities and the question of who really ruled Yugoslavia were both intimately involved.

For a time Tito and the reformers still confined themselves to vague diatribes, which never named names, against 'bureaucratic and étatist forces' and a 'revival' of prewar 'café politics' in which groups of Communists who had just repeated their support of the Reform at an official meeting gathered informally to conspire against it. Meanwhile, behind the scenes, the Party's Executive Committee held a series of meetings between November 1965 and February 1966 to discuss failure to implement the reforms and the national question. In describing the last of these sessions, *Komunist*, on February 3, referred specifically to Serbia as a centre of anti-Reform resistance. It was also announced that a special Party investigative commission was being formed, including members of the Executive and Central Committees, to look further into 'inter-nationality relations in the field of the economy'.[78]

When these warnings failed to have any noticeable effect, the reformers, with Tito's backing, reached for an old Party weapon, which proved to be pathetically ineffective in the new circumstances: they demanded with increasingly strident voices a return to Party discipline and to rigid observance of the principle of 'democratic centralism', according to which a decision once adopted must be loyally and actively supported by all Party members. An expanded 3rd Plenum of the Central Committee of the LCY was convened in Belgrade on February 25 for this express purpose. To make its meaning absolutely clear, Tito proposed in his opening remarks that the meeting should be held in two stages, with an interval between them to allow all members to consult their regional constituencies and return prepared to make binding commitments involving the assent of all higher Party organs. The Plenum was duly adjourned on the evening of February 26, after two days of debate. It reconvened on March 11, to discuss, amend and adopt a Resolution[79] which reiterated in more specific language than usual the commitment of all Communists to unreserved and active support of policies adopted at the 8th Congress and the 1965 reforms. The committee of seventeen appointed to draft the Resolution was comprised almost exclusively of prominent pro-reformers, including at least three of the four Serbian members.

Speeches at the 3rd Plenum produced the usual rash of self-criticism and appeals for unity and loyalty. These included a strong statement by Ranković, with whom Tito had apparently had an unusually blunt and critical private conversation on the eve of the meeting,[80] and who now made his last public attempt to align himself with official Party policy, assuming in addition the burden of making the principal attack on Serbian nationalism. There was also a mildly self-critical statement by Serbian Party Secretary Lukić, who blamed half-hearted support of the reform in Serbia on 'objective difficulties' like inflation and declining living standards. These, Lukić said pointedly, were making it difficult for Communists to understand the Reform, much less explain it to others.

Tito's own opening address, on February 25, contained one revealing curiosity which gave rise to considerable debate and varying interpretations even before the Plenum ended. He was specific enough about the responsibility borne by Party members and particularly by 'top circles of our League of Communists' for failures to implement agreed decisions and the economic reform, but he repeatedly claimed that the real source of disorientation and disunity and of the resurgence of ethnic nationalisms and 'coffee-house politics' lay with a category of persons all but forgotten in current Yugoslav ideology. 'All of this', he said, 'has one single background: the class enemy is behind it all.' And later, apparently to make his meaning clear, he referred to the international situation: 'The class enemy, personified in the imperialists and the capitalist bourgeois class, is now on the offensive on all fronts.'

When the Plenum reconvened on March 11, both Vlahović and Kardelj felt obliged to agree with this Titoist warning but managed to give the term a different twist by redefining it. Vlahović, noting that 'we had not used this term "class struggle" for many years', until Tito mentioned it, explained that besides the residual influence of the bourgeoisie and their ideas, even within the Party, 'the class struggle is also expressed in preventing the working people from realising their rights, in bureaucratic self-will'. This, with its unacknowledged resemblance to Djilas's theory of the 'new class', was also Kardelj's interpretation, but Tito in his closing remarks stuck to his original meaning. The class struggle in

Yugoslavia was of course not what it once was, he said, because the revolution had deprived the class enemy of his authority, 'but physically he has not disappeared, he is still present and has connections with all possible factors of the class opponent abroad'.

Differences of opinion were as usual on such occasions a matter of nuance, although Boris Krajger noted wryly on the first day that while Dragi Stamenković of Serbia and Miko Tripalo of Croatia were both in favour of Tito and of consistency in implementing the reform, 'that "consistency" was interpreted in a very divergent manner' in their respective speeches. Crvenkovski was the bluntest of all of those whose interventions were made public. At the final session on March 11, he said:

It has been established that there are still some disagreements over certain matters, that we have not discovered a common language, and moreover that we are not going to arrive at unanimous conclusions, or that in adopting conclusions there will be no unanimity of action.

He was right. Party forums at all levels dutifully met to discuss implementation of the conclusions of the 3rd Plenum. The diligent observer might detect varying degrees of disguised defiance in the words and acts of some of them, for example in Serbia and Montenegro, or find it significant that in these republics it was at first only the Party executive committees and not, as elsewhere, the central committees which assumed this task.[81] What really mattered was that the results of the Plenum's call for discipline were negligible. There was no longer a monolithic Party in Yugoslavia.

There was, however, an organised force within the Party which had proven that it had the will and the ability effectively to defy the official Party line. It was clear to Tito himself, as an astute politician trained in Marxian dialectics, that if that force could not be disciplined it must be broken or it would replace the Party as the effective ruler of Yugoslavia. Not because he really believed in the Reform or the reformers but to save the Party as he understood it, and sadly conscious of the human and political implications of what he was doing (as several remarks after the event reveal), he was now to destroy the man and the apparatus which had done so much to make and to protect his revolution, the strong but now hopelessly insubordinate right arm of the very Party and system which he would save. As he seems to have anticipated, the future was sorely to test the ability of both to survive this mutilation.

To Brioni: The 4th Plenum

On July 1, 1966, the Central Committee of the LCY met at Brioni, even as it had for the fall of Djilas twelve years before. It was the

4th Plenum since the 8th Congress. There had been persistent rumours that important decisions would be taken, but few had expected them to be so dramatic. Now, while the meeting was still in progress, the island's teleprinters broadcast the news of the resignation of Ranković, the denunciation of UDBa and elements in the Party leadership alleged by Tito himself to have been part of a 'fractional group' engaged in a 'struggle for power', the promise of a purge of Communists opposed to the Reform and a reorganisation of the Party, and the publication of a report by a special Party-State commission investigating responsibility in high places for insubordination, illegal wire-tapping and worse.

While details about the final political manoeuvring which led to Brioni are still obscured by contradictory and partial accounts,[82] the basic outline is clear enough. Tito's attitude and willingness to take action were crucial. As long as Ranković retained the confidence of the Secretary-General who was 'Yugoslavia's only historic personality' (as one speaker at Brioni described Tito), he and the apparatus he controlled were untouchable. Dobrivoje Radosavljević, the Serbian member of the Party-State Commission, in effect admitted this when he explained to the Plenum why the Commission had deemed it inappropriate, as late as the second half of June, to ask Ranković to testify before them, although his failure to do so must be considered 'an abnormal thing':

Ours is a situation in which Ranković held such a position that he thinks that he does not need to come before the Commission and we likewise thought it unnecessary to call him before the Commission. Supposedly this was his business which he should settle with Comrade Tito.[83]

In the weeks before and after the 3rd Plenum, however, Tito's growing disenchantment with his Vice-President and Organisational Secretary was becoming known to other close collaborators. Emboldened by this knowledge, and possibly also exploiting Ranković's departure on March 26 for a two-week visit to the Soviet Union (where he represented the LCY at a Soviet Party Congress), these opponents began to move against him. Bakarić, always a significant bell-wether, was in one of his politically active phases again, after some months nursing his health on Hvar, and now moved out of his Croatian fortress to lecture Belgrade television's general audience (on March 24) and Party activists there (May 18) and in Sarajevo (May 29) about the need to reform the Party's organisation and mentality for a more democratic age, to facilitate implementation of the 1965 reforms, and as a barrier to nationalism.[84] The public phase of his offensive began with an interview published in *Borba* on March 6, after the first session of the 3rd Plenum. A correspondent had commented that 'in spite of everything, it seems to me that at the present moment nationalism is not even a number two question for our socio-political and economic development', to which Bakarić replied:

... at the present moment I should say that it is at least question number two. The question is whether we will be able, by carrying out our reform, to win our struggle against nationalism as well. If we do not win it, our progress in the reform will be much slower, and then it may indeed happen that the question of nationalism will from a question number two become question number one.

In Serbia itself, to judge by the ambivalent attitude of the Central Committee and other Party forums in April and May, other leading politicians were beginning to reinsure by edging gingerly towards the more liberal and implicitly anti-Ranković position of men like Todorović and Milentije Popović.

The obvious place to begin the search for incriminating evidence was with UDBa, whose agents' ubiquitous and arbitrary misuse of their great powers in the service of 'centralist conservatism' and of what they assumed to be Ranković's will was well known and made them popular, convenient and at least partly genuine scapegoats. A key role at this point seems to have been played by Milan Mišković, a Croat who had succeeded Ranković's man Lukić as federal Secretary for Internal Affairs in 1965. Although Mišković had held important posts in OZNa and UDBa in Croatia and Macedonia after the war and had once been Under-Secretary for Internal Affairs, he was an outsider to the Serbian group at the UDBa centre and soon found that he was being by-passed by subordinates. These were reporting instead to Svetislav Stefanović, Ranković's closest associate, co-founder and long-time operational chief of UDBa and now a member of the FEC and chairman of its Commission for Internal Affairs. On the other hand, Mišković had privileged access to UDBa's important and independent institutional rival, the army's Counter-Intelligence Service, in which his younger brother Ivan was a colonel-general. A complex intrigue followed, allegedly involving army counter-intelligence wiretapping of UDBa and belated efforts by UDBa to add army counter-intelligence to its own wiretapping network, which already included its own minister and every other political leader of importance, apparently not excluding Tito.

The UDBa wiretaps on senior Party officials and the discovery of a microphone (or microphones) in Tito's own residence (in his office and/or bedroom, depending on the version) provided the anti-Ranković forces with the last straw for which they had been hoping and which they eagerly laid on Tito's back. Tito had in any case apparently been moving towards a decision of some kind, since on April 28 he had summoned the Party .Executive Committee to a meeting, hastily convened between presidential

visits to Romania and the United Arab Republic, at which it was
decided that the business of the forthcoming, 4th Plenum of the
Central Committee would be 'cadre policy' (Ranković's preserve)
instead of the previously announced discussion of the resurgent
national problem. When news of UDBa's unauthorised wiretapping
reached him, he acted with dispatch and firmness.

The wiretapping of Tito's residence was apparently discovered
on June 9, also incidentally the last day that Ranković's official
activities were mentioned in the press. A 'technical commission'
was promptly appointed to investigate and uncovered the extent of
wiretapping among top Party officials. When its preliminary report
was in, the Party Executive Committee was summoned, on June
16. The evidence was presented and the Committee voted to
appoint a six-man special Party-State Commission, with one
representative from each republic and Crvenkovski as chairman, to
carry out a more official and thorough investigation. Ranković
voted for the appointment of the Commission and offered his
resignation. Six days later, on June 22, the Executive Committee
met again to hear a preliminary report, decided that it contained
enough damaging information to justify political action against
Ranković, Stefanović and UDBa, and called the meeting of the
Central Committee held at Brioni on July 1.

Vukmanović in his memoirs adds some credible and illuminating
human details to this part of the story. Tito summoned him, he
says, a few days before the meeting of June 16 and announced
bluntly that he was being wiretapped and that it was being done
'by Marko and Ćeća' (Ranković and Stefanović). Vukmanović was
incredulous, to which Tito responded: 'By the way, your house is
bugged too.' Later, shortly after the meeting of June 16,
Vukmanović happened to enter the same lift at Party headquarters
with a visibly shattered Ranković and as the lift rose could not
forbear embracing him, whereupon both began to cry and
Ranković murmured brokenly: 'Oh, Tempo, Tempo!' He got out
at his own floor, leaving Vukmanović to contemplate sadly 'the
fate of revolutionaries whom time has passed over'. On the eve of
the 4th Plenum, however, he received and read a copy of the
Crvenkovski Commission's detailed report, discovered that his
telephone had been tapped as early as 1950 and was less inclined
to be sympathetic.[85] A similarly credible and revealing story is
retold by Paul Lendvai:

During a debate about the Ranković affair in the small circle of Tito's
closest collaborators, Kardelj is reported to have remarked, 'I had noted
years ago that my telephone was being tapped.' 'Why didn't you tell me?'
snapped Tito. 'I thought *you* might have ordered it ...', Kardelj said
quietly.[86]

At the 4th Plenum Ranković and Stefanović both spoke twice.

They attempted to concentrate attention on the wiretapping episode and then to deny that they had had anything to do with it, although Ranković in his first statement accepted 'moral responsibility' for what had happened and in his second and in response to criticism expanded this to 'moral and political responsibility'. Stefanović bluntly denied that UDBa had tapped Tito and said that someone else had done it. On that point at least, in the Byzantine complexity of the affair, he may have been telling the truth, especially since one of the first dismissals recorded after June 9 was that of Tito's personal military aide-de-camp, one Luka Vožović, apparently in connection with the microphone planted in the President's home.[87] Proof in this and other wire-tapping incidents was in any case hard to find, since alarmed UDBa officials had apparently begun destroying incriminating records before the beginning of June.

For this and more pertinent political reasons, the Central Committee refused to focus on wiretapping and insisted on treating it as a marginal aspect of the problem, if also a deplorable and revealing one. Two larger issues were involved. The first was the overall behaviour and role of UDBa, which had created a state of affairs that led Tito to ask the Plenum, 'Does this not somehow remind you of what was going on under Stalin?' Here, while Ranković and Stefanović were directly responsible, the Executive and Central Committees must assume indirect responsibility: the latter (again in Tito's words) 'had made a mistake in having virtually left our Security Service to go its own way for more than twenty years'. The second issue concerned the implications of this behaviour and of the permissiveness of the Party leadership in this area for the mentality, organisation and role of the LCY as a whole.

The picture of UDBa's operations which was made public by the Crvenkovski Commission and through a veritable plague of post-Plenum 'revelations' in the popular press exposed a pattern of purposeful meddling in personnel policy and in decision-making which ranged from the Foreign Office and other federal ministries down to the communal and enterprise level. Some of it was clearly done to impose 'conservative' views or to sabotage official Party policies, and by implication to build support (with or without his knowledge and approval) for Ranković as Tito's heir apparent. Much of it, however, was simply designed to assure prestigious and remunerative jobs for otherwise unqualified people in the Partisan-UDBa old boy network. Even more discreditable to UDBa's image as 'the sword of the Party' was the exposure of widespread corruption of a non-political kind, including organised trans-Adriatic smuggling and other illegal international as well as domestic economic activities, kickbacks from those whom UDBa had helped to appoint, misappropriation of public property for private uses, private gambling casinos and forced labour by prisoners in the construction of villas for UDBa officials. Finally, the ethnic prejudices of those who manned the Serbian and federal security apparatuses were publicly exposed in articles which described in detail the pattern of intimidation and calculated police brutality which was still being inflicted on the Albanian majority in Kosovo-Metohija nearly twenty years after such methods had been generally abandoned in the rest of the country.

If most Yugoslavs found little that was surprising in all of this, the mere fact of the authorised public revelation of such activities on such a scale by the security police of a one-party State was unprecedented and in itself had an enormous impact on political behaviour and popular attitudes. In other countries deposed police chiefs like Beria or individual security officers had been accused by the regime they served of grossly abusing their authority, but here it was the entire apparatus which was under attack. Only those republican branches which could claim with some hope of credibility that they had resisted effective penetration by 'the Ranković group', as in Croatia and Slovenia, could escape the disgrace and the impending purge.

Another significant point emphasised in the Crvenkovski Commission's report was that UDBa, legally licensed to spy only on known or suspected foreign agents and the 'class enemy', had in fact created an ubiquitous network for gathering and processing all kinds of information about the attitudes of ordinary Yugoslav citizens and Party members, including what were scathingly described as 'primitive' and 'non-modern' methods of sampling public and Party opinion on specific issues like the economic reform. The results, purposefully interpreted or distorted to convey conclusions consonant with the policy preferences and prejudices of UDBa's bosses, were then passed on to the central Party apparatus, where it was now said that these reports comprised virtually the only detailed information available to that apparatus, including its Executive Committee, about Party cell activities and popular opinion in the countryside.

It was this last aspect, a sudden insight into the full implications of depending on a single, closed, self-recruiting, basically autonomous and self-interested channel for vital political information, which genuinely disturbed the more perceptive members of the Central Committee, however hypocritical the shock and disapproval they displayed over the 'revelation' of UDBa's 'illegal' information-gathering operations. To make this monopoly of information doubly dangerous, it was joined through the person of Ranković to an almost equally monopolistic control over all political appointments and candidacies. Vukmanović summarised the consequences when he pointed out to the 4th Plenum that

Ranković, as the organiser of the State Security Service and Organisational Secretary of the Party, 'in practice, from the organisational point of view, had the entire Party in his hands'. The result was that 'although we have taken correct political positions, the fact is that the Party is not organisationally capable of putting them into practice'.[88]

Later in the debate, Radosavljević pointed out that exclusive dependence on UDBa for 'the transmission of information and misinformation' also had equally serious implications for relations among the republics, although this had not been mentioned in the Commission's report. In Serbia, he said, events happening in Slovenia were known through UDBa, while in Slovenia it was similarly known what was happening in Belgrade. But this was not accurate, objective information; it had 'a certain special interpretation'.

It is not normal practice for the Secretary of the Central Committee of one republic to telephone the Secretary of the Central Committee of another republic and tell him: we have received such and such information about some phenomena in your territory, phenomena which concern us; what is correct in this information? But if it is not done in this way, then the information circulates, is refabricated, while the Secretaries do not talk about these things among themselves. Excuse me if I put it this way.[89]

For Tito himself, the present crisis, which no longer seemed as critical as he had feared it would be, was also a result of the failure to 'pursue things to the end' at the March 1962 session of the Executive Committee, 'when we had already established approximately what these anomalies, distortions, etc., were all about, but we failed to pinpoint their source'. For this he assumed personal responsibility. The leadership had 'stopped halfway' then, he said, 'because of certain tendencies to compromise, lest the whole affair might reflect on the unity of our party, the unity of our leadership, which had in fact even then already been undermined'. He did not mention that the Crvenkovski Commission had also discovered the tapes which UDBa on Ranković's orders had surreptitiously made of the March 1962 session, a meeting which was supposed to have been highly confidential and unrecorded, or the additional speculations that this discovery inevitably aroused.[90]

While popular attention was understandably focused on the drama of Ranković's fall and the humbling of UDBa, and while Tito was denying with annoyance the interpretation placed on the 4th Plenum in the Western press—'I did not join up with any liberals', he told a delegation of Partisan veterans on Brioni three days after the session ended[91]—the leaders of the anti-Ranković coalition were busy drawing and implementing the political conclusions of their triumph. The Brioni Plenum endorsed a series of recommendations made by the Crvenkovski Commission. The

Security Service should be thoroughly reorganised, separated from direct association with the Party, confined in scope to 'the activity of the class enemy and threats from abroad', and placed under the effective supervision of 'representative bodies and their executive organs', which in due course meant parliamentary commissions overseeing the work of secretariats of internal affairs. Meanwhile, 'political functionaries' should immediately replace professional security officers in UDBa's executive posts. The investigation should continue in order to ferret out 'the real intentions behind and meaning of individual instances of abuse of office and power'. Ranković's resignation from his Party offices was accepted and his resignation as Vice-President was recommended to the Federal Assembly. Stefanović lost not only his offices but also, because of his 'unco-operative attitude', his Party membership. Ranković was replaced by Todorović as Secretary of the Central Committee and Milentije Popović took his seat on the Executive Committee. Radosavljević was co-opted to the Central Committee in place of Stefanović. On July 14, the Federal Assembly accepted Ranković's resignation as Vice-President of Yugoslavia and elected Koča Popović in his place. In each case the new office-holder was also a Serb, a pattern carefully followed at lower levels as the purge was extended.

Looking further to the future, the Plenum approved a motion by Vlahović appointing a forty-member special commission under Todorović's chairmanship to consider and make proposals for 'a radical change' in the organisation of the LCY. Vlahović's report, which in effect set guidelines for the Todorović Commission, was in itself a firm restatement of the principles of the liberal wing of the Yugoslav Communist establishment. The Party's failure to define and adapt itself to a role appropriate to 'conditions of far-reaching social change and the democratisation of society' was blamed on obsolete organisational forms and attitudes. The former included 'the organisational set-up and methods of work of the LCY leading bodies, which have too long clung to old methods of work and the old character of power'. The latter included 'a civil-servant relationship and mentality' in the Party and 'a practice of tolerating, for the sake of formal unity ... forces in the League of Communists which openly advocate a "strong-hand" policy'. All of this 'has given rise to vacillation and ideological disorientation, and has blurred the idea of the danger which the abandoning of the system of self-government and direct democracy would constitutute for our society and for socialism'.

In seeking an answer the report was impatiently specific in restating an eternally unfulfilled principle of the 1952 Congress and in once again negating its negation at the 2nd (Brioni) Plenum of June 1953. All discussions and proposals to date, it was said, were based on the conviction ('and this has already been debated several times') that

the leading bodies in the League of Communists should not concern themselves with those issues which fall within the jurisdiction of elected, responsible bodies, but should rather concern themselves with questions of relations among people, and should channel the work of members towards essential problems of self-government in practice and the role of the working man in society.

This must become 'the guiding principle' for all central and executive committees.[92]

With the difficult if not impossible mandate for a reform of the Party and of the personality of Party members inherent in this analysis and prescription, a new chapter in the Yugoslav political odyssey had opened. It ended five and a half years later when the same charges about faulty organisational forms and the inappropriate 'mentality' of Party members, and the same description of the consequences in terms of a 'Party not organisationally capable of putting [correct political positions] into practice', were applied with equal accuracy to the single most important unit of the now triumphant liberal coalition, the central apparatus of the League of Communists of Croatia.

6

THE LIBERAL ASCENDANCY

The new polyarchy

The events of the summer of 1966 opened the door to further political and social changes and to a consolidation of the anti-centralist coalition's control of important decision-making organs. There were also more such organs, more widely distributed, after the destruction of the principal citadel of centralised authority and the consequent weakening of the political centre in general. If Yugoslavia in the years after 1966 was still far from the non-party socialist democracy based on direct social self-management to which the official ideology aspired, the regime had at least been transformed from a centralised Party oligarchy into a kind of multi-storied polyarchy of particular and institutionalised regional and functional interests. This emerging polyarchy was also, however, so inchoate and ill-defined, with power so unevenly distributed within it, that it became increasingly and ominously difficult to say where effective primary power and therefore responsibility had found new homes.

Four kinds of centres, each backed by shifting coalitions of individual or group interests and ideologies, participated in the scramble to inherit all or a major part of the legacy of disintegrating central control. These were the republican and provincial Party–State apparatuses, those of the 500 communes which are Yugoslavia's basic territorial-political units, the 'managerial-technocratic élites' in the national economy and the broad-based proletarian élite which Yugoslav theory calls 'self-managers' (or sometimes in this context 'the working class'), in most functions synonymous with those employed in the socialist sector. In addition, the presently humbled federal apparatuses comprised a potential fifth candidate, either as an unreformed residual legatee which might be left with more than anyone else intended, or in a new form, which might or might not be less authoritarian than the old.

It is also worth noting that only primary power in the hands of the fourth of these contenders was fully consonant with the principles of functional aggregation and 'direct social self-management' embodied in Yugoslav theory and the 1963 Constitution. A victory for any of the others would mean instead the continued existence of forms explicitly rejected by official Yugoslav Marxism, of a State or States with the usual mix of traditional and modern functions, ruled at worst by autocracy and at best by a 'bourgeois-type' representative democracy based on territorial, ethnic or class constituencies. However narrow or wide the effective franchise, the principle of aggregation and modes of representation would be fundamentally different.

This last was more than an abstruse point of political philosophy or an index of the seriousness and executability of the Yugoslav variant of Marxism. It concerned the basic and eternally unre- solved question of the real nature and purpose of the Yugoslav State. Was this the incarnation of a once already transient idea (originally the idea of the natural unity of the South Slavs, for which the present regime had substituted the idea of international socialist solidarity writ small); or was it a community of nations held together primarily by force, a federation in the process of becoming a confederation of nation-States, a community of perceived and institutionalised common economic and political interests, or (as Yugoslav theory in its most pretentious moments claimed) a totally new kind of social organisation in the process of becoming? The answer, or lack of one, would determine how ordinary Yugoslavs lived and were ruled.

In 1966 this question seemed to be entirely open-ended or slightly weighted towards one of the last two solutions. That this was not quite accurate was because three additional factors—apart from the risks if the new system and its leaders should fail to produce promised results, particularly in the economy—were temporarily overlooked or underestimated.

The first of these was a consequence of the fact that the decisive element among the forces which were making the emasculation of centralist State and Party apparatuses possible, both before and after the fall of Ranković, was not the strength of the ideologues and interest groups of 'self-management' but, as we have seen and will see, the growing ability of increasingly autonomous regional and national leaderships to frustrate action at the centre.[1] As a result, and for the moment at least, the autonomous power and mutual jealousies of these national leaderships provided the firmest guarantee of no return to the quasi-centralism of the 1950s, a role which made their perceptions of their situation and future behaviour of particular importance. It was perfectly possible, for example, that such people might honestly consider the consolidation of their own power in a sub-State within a confederation to be a necessary precondition of a genuinely 'de-étatised' and democra- tised socialist social order, but might find that the means had become an end in itself and even, perhaps, that they liked it that way.

There were also other ways that the national question could influence or even determine the outcome and with it the fate of the fragile new polyarchy. The events of 1966 might generate a Serbian nationalist backlash which would unite all or most Serbs, 40 per cent of the country's population, on a 'conservative' platform understood or disguised as the defence of Serbian national interests and as revenge for a Serbian national humiliation. All of the precautions taken after the 4th Plenum—the replacement of every purged Serb by another Serb; the use of Serbs to make almost all speeches denouncing UDBa (with its Serb majority) and the Ranković 'fractional group'; threats and rumours of *quid pro quo* purges on the other side, of 'pseudo-liberal' and 'anarcho-liberal' elements in Zagreb and elsewhere—could do little to dissuade those, including most Serbs and nearly all Croats, who were inclined to view Ranković's fall, the reform and the purge of UDBa as a Serbian defeat. On the other hand, there was an equal danger that some of the other nationalities, intoxicated by what they considered their own national triumph and either incompetently or irresponsibly led, might indulge in provocative displays of national sentiment which could also bring about a conservative backlash, or even invoke a *coup de main* to restore strong central control as a defence against local chauvinism and the spectre of separatism. For anyone who was in Zagreb in the summer of 1966, experiencing the euphoria over the fall of Ranković and the almost universal tendency to interpret it as primarily a victory for Croatian interests, it was obvious that it would take a team of extraordinarily level-headed and able leaders to forestall such a development and to channel enthusiasm in the officially desired direction of mobilisation for further reforms.

Secondly, the 'liberal coalition' of 1965-66 might break up into its component parts when the process of redistributing the former power of a common centralist enemy exposed important differences in their own interests and objectives. There was already a hint that this might happen within three months of the Brioni meeting, in a sharp exchange between Vukmanović, speaking for trade union and ostensibly for working-class interests, and two Belgrade newspapers, *Ekonomska politika* and *Politika*, the former traditionally and the latter at least for the moment expressing the views of the people described in this study as socialist entrepreneurs.[2]

The third factor of indeterminate weight and later increasingly underestimated potential was the Party itself, which is to say the Party in its traditional function as ultimate and ultimately centralised arbiter of the system and 'with Tito at its head', as a ritual phrase from the Party catechism reminded the faithful.

The proper role of the League of Communists in a society and State based on 'social self-management' had been defined in theory more than thirteen years earlier, before the Djilas crisis, and had recently been repeated and refined by the most authoritative ideologists. The Party should become progressively less an instrument of power and more an instrument of influence based on a prestige born of superior knowledge and proven consistency as a progressive force. For thirteen years, however, even those who had sincerely wanted to do so had not known how to translate this theory into practice. They agreed that the League, as an association of 'the most progressive elements in society', equipped with special wisdom based on schooling in scientific socialism (and more recently also in an eclectic modern social science), must continue to exercise a 'leading role', as a mentor and a mediator among conflicting but legitimately 'socialist' inter-group, inter-personal and intra-personal interests. But the most sophisticated among them had so far failed to define this modernised leading role and solve the riddle of effective influence without effective power in a way that ordinary Communists could understand and use, simultaneously avoiding both of the hazards which Kardelj was now describing as Yugoslav Communism's Scylla and Charybdis: impermissible interference and political impotence. Either Communists would remain in a position and be individually obliged to see to it that essential principles as defined by the Party were transformed into policies, or they would not. Either the Party's recommendations could not be disregarded by the executive, the legislatures and the enterprises, or they could. If they could be disregarded, Yugoslav institutions and policies might be diverted into paths which the Party considered unacceptable. At the very least the Party would be little more than a debating club, shorn of dynamism as well as power, and liberal establishment theoreticians like Kardelj, Vlahović and Bakarić had again specifically said that they did not intend to reduce it to that. But if the Party could not be disregarded, it would not have divested itself of power and the theory would remain empty rhetoric.[3]

After 1966 a resolution of this dilemma seemed to be emerging *de facto*—imposed 'by life itself', in the words of another favourite Party phrase—and only partly in accordance with the aspirations of this still unclear theory. The Party had already ceased to be a monolith directed from one centre and had now ceased to enjoy a fully effective monopoly of political power. By 1969, as will be seen, central authority was almost completely paralysed by disagreements among republican Party barons, and even parliamentary elections were bringing an increasing number of surprises in the form of contested seats won by those who did not have the approval of official leaderships. Local politics were increasingly characterised by open conflicts openly resolved, in which local Party committees, individual Party *aktivs*, communal assembly organs and erstwhile 'transmission belts' like the local executive committees of the Socialist Alliance, the trade unions, the Youth Federation or the association of war veterans took opposite sides in shifting coalitions reflecting differences among personalities or group interests. It seemed ever more reasonable to conclude that a genuine polyarchy, if not 'self-management', had taken such deep roots in a firm soil of diverse, powerful and now conscious and articulate group interests that only a coup d'état could overthrow it, and that the ensuing damage to the economic and social subsoil which such a blow might be expected to entail would seriously inhibit such an event. This appeared to be particularly true of the 'federalisation' of the Party itself. In May 1971, only seven months before events proved him wrong, a politician as knowledgeable and engaged as Krsto Crvenkovski told a small group which included the present writer: 'We have evolved to a stage at which it is no longer thinkable that a republican Party leadership could be removed by the federal Party centre.'

This conclusion ignored the fact that the Party's partial abdication of centralised and to a certain extent even of decentralised control, essential to the kind of pluralisation of decision-making and expansion of participation currently taking place, was only partly a function of the dynamics of largely or entirely irreversible social change and the strength of anti-centralist republican Party barons. Three other at least quasi independent reasons for the changing role of the Party were still subject to arbitrary or accidental change or removal. One was the predominance in the LCY Executive Committee and other key central Party organs of those who for various reasons were encouraging or acquiescing in such an abdication—a predominance inaugurated by the 8th Congress and reinforced by the 4th Plenum and subsequent Party reforms but still both relative and tenuous. The second, intimately related to the first, was the deep division within these central organs since at least 1962, a division which still existed and which had partly paralysed them and thereby permitted other centres to increase their autonomy, uncontested except by Ranković and his apparatus. A change of personnel in these organs, gradual or sudden, or a change of mind by a number of those at present in charge—perhaps in response to economic or nationalist troubles—could eliminate both of these barriers to an attempt to reimpose centralised Party authority. At that point the outcome of a struggle between a Party apparatus newly determined to regain control and Party members and others with newly institutionalised and entrenched interests in the existing level of pluralism would be moot, their relative strengths impossible to calculate *a priori*. The balance might then be tipped by the third and perhaps most important removable or changeable factor, which was Tito himself. At the time of the 4th Plenum he was 74 years old, and for the moment and for reasons of his own the reluctant and possibly only temporary ally of anti-centralist and liberalising forces. When the crunch came, he and only he had made the removal of Ranković and purge of UDBa possible. It was a formidable power, which could turn in other directions and might or might not diminish with the years he had left, making it also incalculable.

Finally, as if this were not enough, external influences, particularly Soviet interests and policies in Eastern Europe and the eastern Mediterranean, might come to play a role which had not been built into present estimates. So too might the way in which the domestic and international situations were perceived by one vitally important and presumably pro-centralist agency which had so far been a non-factor, the officer corps of the Yugoslav Peoples' Army.

Yugoslavia's unstable polycentric political system, and with it the ideals, the expansion of participation and the enlarged civic and entrepreneurial liberties which were both cause and effect of that system, faced an uncertain and still hazardous passage.

The Party reforms of 1966-67

While popular attention continued to focus on the further details of UDBa misdeeds which were filtered through the mass media during the summer of 1966, the Todorović Commission set to work on the proposals to reform the Party which had been promised at Brioni and through which the anti-centralist coalition hoped to consolidate their victory. By the end of September a preliminary report and set of organisational changes had been drafted, debated by appropriate leaderships and approved by the Executive Committee. Meanwhile and to the delight of the non-Party public, the journalists who had whetted their appetites as serious investigative reporters on UDBa were proceeding to a series of exposés of Party privileges and corruption reminiscent of Djilas's lone attack on Communist morals twelve years earlier.

The Central Committee, meeting in Belgrade on October 4 for its 5th Plenum, approved the proposals for reorganisation and agreed that these changes could be carried out under the existing Party Statute. It would therefore be unnecessary to run the risk of convening a special Party Congress, which had been mooted since July, before the leadership had decided what further changes it wanted and had prepared the membership for them. All changes carried out until the next regular Congress, then scheduled for late 1968, would thus be considered provisional and experimental.

Leaving the Central Committee's composition and formal competences untouched, the reform approved by the 5th Plenum abolished the hitherto powerful Secretariat and drastically altered the composition and function of the Executive Committee. It was now to become a purely executive and administrative organ and was reduced in size to eleven members—with the secretaries of the six republican executive committees as *ex officio* members—and totally reconstituted. The senior Party functionaries who had inevitably made it into a powerful policy-making body, in defiance of Party Statutes, were excluded. All members of the new Committee except the Secretary, a post assigned to Todorović, were to be younger (the oldest was then 48) and previously less well known and powerful. They were not simultaneously to hold other political executive posts; nor could they be members of the new supreme policy-making body created by the reform, a 35-member Central Committee Presidency, which incorporated all the former 19 members of the Executive Committee except Todorović. Central Committee members were assigned to five commissions which took over the competencies previously divided among the three Secretaries. To crown the new edifice the Central Committee created a new post for Tito as President (formerly Secretary-General) of the LCY. Republican central committees were advised to undertake reorganisations of their own along the same lines. All did so during the next six weeks.[4]

Tito in his closing remarks confirmed that the initiative for these changes had come from him, some months before the Brioni Plenum, and said that they had represented his own initial reaction and solution to the Ranković problem. This he had characteristically interpreted in terms of faulty organisation, which had encouraged passivity in both the Central and Executive Committees and permitted power without responsibility to concentrate in the Secretariat as a whole and in Ranković in particular. The consequences, he said, included a 'cult of the personality' and a 'factionalist grouping' around the heir apparent.

Tito's own limited purposes were clear enough. He wanted institutional devices which would prevent power from accumulating, as Ranković had accumulated it, in any one else's hands. He also wanted a limited but more representative consultative basis for decision-making at the Party summit and an executive organ which would be energetic, effective and reliable, but without pretensions to autonomous power or a major role in making policy. All of this he hoped to achieve by separating policy-making (the Presidency) from administration (the reformed

Executive Committee), and through the number and quality of those chosen to staff both bodies. The new Presidency, for example, would be larger and therefore more representative and perhaps less pretentious and prone to 'personality cults' than the old Executive Committee, but it should also still be small and authoritative enough to function effectively, unlike the 155-member Central Committee.

Others had more in mind. Hints were evident in the widespread objections already made (according to Tito and Todorović) to the creation of a Presidency the majority of whom were still the authoritative veterans who had ruled Yugoslavia since 1945. What these others sought was a real reduction in the political power exercised by the Party centre in any form, to be achieved either through a 'genuine democratisation' of decision-making or through a loosening of the hierarchical connections so far considered essential to a Leninist cadre party. Some viewed even this as a minimum objective, seeking the reduction in the power of the Party as a whole that had been a declarative principle since the 1952 Congress.[5]

Because the motives and objectives of the reformers were not always the same, which could not be admitted, and because there was still strong opposition to more than the 4th and 5th Plenums had already accomplished, the debate took longer than anticipated. Publication for Party-wide discussion of the draft 'Theses for the Reorganisation of the LCY' produced by the Todorović Commission after the 5th Plenum, originally promised by the end of December 1966 and then by the end of March 1967, did not take place until April 27. Even after that, only its specific proposals for further 'provisional' organisational changes were accepted by the Central Committee's 7th Plenum, on July 1, 1967; its political and philosophical sections were non-committally termed 'a good basis for further discussion'. This discussion in turn continued until the delayed 9th Congress finally met in April 1969, by which time both the domestic and the international context had undergone important changes. It was already significant, at the 5th Plenum, that while Todorović in his report was primarily concerned with reforms to adapt the Party to 'conditions of self-management', Tito's primary concerns were different. In his closing remarks he expressed anxiety that criticism of UDBa might go too far since it was still needed, that people outside the LCY had begun to deal with Party questions, and that 'various alien elements have started to present their views on Marxism and to create various lines of philosophy'. He also thought that press exposés of Party privileges were going too far, since this was an internal Party matter that the Party could and should handle for itself. Reforms should strengthen and not weaken the Party's 'leading role'.[6]

The further organisational changes accepted by the 7th Plenum, on the first anniversary of the fall of Ranković, were nevertheless potentially important and consonant with the more radical hopes of the reformers, despite the cautious reception given to the 'Theses for Reorganisation'. Fragmentation of Party members in small cells was to be ended with the creation of single Party organisations in each enterprise and commune. The latter were to include all Communists resident on the territory of the commune, which meant that most of them would be members of two basic organisations at the same time, i.e. of their commune or local community and of their enterprise or army unit. The supreme organ of a communal or enterprise organisation was to be its Conference, elected every two years. Party committees were to be considered purely as executive organs of the Conferences.[7]

The declared purpose of these changes was to provide greater opportunities for Party members to concern themselves with 'real questions' of direct concern to their enterprises and communities while retaining a 'wider view' through dual membership, and at the same time to enable the Party's basic organisations to escape the trap of purely hierarchical linkages. The reformers hoped thereby to solve both of their principal problems at one blow. With larger organisations built into enterprises and communes as the basic decision-making units of 'self-management socialism' and horizontally linked to one another, individual Communists would be in a position to play by the new political rules and still win, influencing solutions through their day-to-day activities rather than imposing them as an 'outside force' and mere 'transmission belt' for hierarchically superior Party organisations.

On the public evidence of local Party behaviour during the five years that this scheme was in effect, it succeeded in fulfilling some but not all of the hopes of those who devised it. Political life in many districts was increasingly characterised by basic organisations defying one another and superior Party bodies, including republican executive committees, on issues which were often of more than local significance. Flying squads sent from republican headquarters, on appeal or on their own initiative, were only sometimes successful in imposing their will. Because their potential, based in large part on continuing control of many appointments and promotions, was nevertheless still considerable, 'connections and protection' (*veze i protekcija*, often abbreviated as VIP) remained as important as ever. The growing relative independence of local Party organisations therefore reinforced the significance of those clientage networks shaped by patronage under the investment system of earlier years. But there was little evidence that this partial pluralisation of Party power was being accompanied by much 'democratisation' in the form of increased participation in policy- or decision-making by rank-and-file members. What had been enlarged was the ability to defy policies made higher up, which is not the same thing as the ability to make policy, and even that defiance was usually by a local Party committee or 'informal group' and only occasionally by a more directly representative body like a Conference. A Party committee and/or its secretary were usually (but not always) more powerful than the Conference to which they were ostensibly subordinate or its president. As political life became more open and exciting, it tended to assume forms reminiscent of the 'machine politics' of local 'bosses' and 'ward-healers' known to other mixed or transitional polities. A particularly Yugoslav form of shifting coalitions of impermanent 'informal groups' based on specific interests and personalities, already a dominant characteristic of local Party life before the reforms,[8] gained rather than lost in significance. The new emphasis on Communist participation in an 'open struggle of opinions in self-management bodies' was a licence to carry conflicts among these groups out of the Party meeting and into workers' councils or communal assemblies, further agitating the political climate in these bodies. As for the new politics of Party influence and manipulation in place of Party directives and coercion, only the most sophisticated operators occasionally learned the skills necessary for its successful implementation. The rest either ignored a theory they did not know how to apply and stuck to old and tested techniques, or else they lost or in discouragement even abdicated control.[9]

The Plenum of October 1966 had meanwhile considered one other item of business. At the request of the Montenegrin, Macedonian and Bosnian Central Committees, it was agreed to deprive Ranković of Party membership. Some Party organisations thereafter began to demand his arrest and trial. Proceedings began, but in December a presidential decree, approved by the Federal Assembly, pardoned him and seventeen of his closest collaborators. The official justification was that 'the strength of self-management, humanism and past services rendered by Ranković and some of the other accused' made their further punishment unnecessary and undesirable. A few weeks later, on New Year's Eve 1966-67, Djilas was released from prison after serving slightly more than half of the sentence imposed on him in 1962. Earlier in the same month, the Slovene Government had resigned after a bill to raise social insurance taxes was defeated by a 44 to 11 vote in the Chamber of Social Welfare and Health of the Republican Assembly. Although the 'crisis' was resolved by compromise, it caused a considerable stir at home and abroad. Never before, to anyone's knowledge, had a Communist Government in a one-party State chosen to interpret a parliamentary defeat as a vote of no confidence and felt obliged to resign. Each of these three events was in its own way indicative of a changed political atmosphere since the Brioni Plenum.

The economy after the Reform

With the reforms of 1965 the Yugoslav economy entered a long and difficult period of readjustment, many features of which could be interpreted as evidence that the opponents of a market economy had been right after all. The first three post-reform years were marked by a decline and in 1967 by complete stagnation in growth. The consequences included growing unemployment and emigration, stagnant or declining real incomes for most people, political unrest and instability and a temporarily more stable currency than at any previous period since the war. After these phenomena led to another reluctant, ad hoc and ill-planned series of orthodox reflationary measures, the succeeding three years were characterised by renewed if irregular growth in investment, production and employment, and by the now familiar concomitants of such measures: a high rate of inflation, a booming balance-of-payments deficit and a weakening of the dinar which eventually led to ill-timed devaluations. Occasionally it seemed as if the only goal of the reform to be fully realised was its politically least desirable one—the growth in individual, sectoral and regional disparities in income which the reformers had reluctantly accepted, despite socialist abhorrence, as an inevitable side effect of an otherwise desirable genuine market economy.

After growing by 12 per cent in 1963 and again in 1964, the Social Product grew by only 1·4 per cent in 1965. It recovered to 6·6 per cent in 1966, primarily because good weather and the initial effects of higher agricultural prices and associated reforms raised agricultural production by 16·4 per cent, and then slumped to a bare 1 per cent in 1967, the year in which industrial output did not grow at all while agriculture fell back by 2 per cent. The average yearly growth rate for the four years 1964-67 was 2·9 per cent, compared with 9·7 per cent in 1961-64 and 12·7 per cent in 1957-60. By the end of 1967 the value of industrial production in constant prices was only 9·1 per cent larger and that of Social Product only 11·3 per cent larger than in 1964, another sad comparison with the cumulative growth rates of the 1950s or with 1963-64, a two-year period in which industrial production had grown in value by 27 and Social Product by 21 points.[10]

Total employment by 1967 was 1 per cent less than in 1964, down from 3·61 million to 3·56 million; in the socialist sector it was in fact down by 3 per cent, partly compensated by a rise of 42 per cent in the small private sector (largely crafts, services and catering), which accounted for only 3 per cent of the total employed. To make matters worse, this slump occurred not only in a society accustomed to rapidly growing employment in industry and more recently in the tertiary sector but also at a moment of maximum demographic pressure on the labour market, since the postwar population bulge had matured and was seeking employment. The number of registered unemployed in 1968 was 47 per cent larger than in 1964, despite massive temporary emigration to find work in Western Europe. An increasing proportion of those seeking work consisted of persons with secondary, advanced vocational or university training.[11]

The employment problem and the state of the economy in general were not helped by the regime's continuing failure to find an adequate solution to what earlier Balkan generations called 'the peasant question'—a social as well as economic problem. With rapid expansion of employment outside agriculture, outstripping natural increase everywhere except in Bosnia-Herzegovina and Kosovo, the agricultural population had continued to decline relatively and then absolutely until the post-reform recession. From 1953 to 1961 nearly 2 million and by 1967 an estimated 2·5 million Yugoslavs had transferred from agricultural to non-agricultural sources of livelihood, bringing the number still dependent on the land down from 67 per cent of total population in 1948 to about 48 per cent. The flight of these usually younger people to industry and the towns left a progressively older farming population everywhere and abandoned fields in some districts, threatening agricultural productivity in general and undermining the tax base and hence locally financed social services, including education, in rural communes.[12] At the same time, the recent and continuing magnitude of the exodus was confronting politicians and planners with a dilemma familiar to many developing countries and not faced by the reforms of 1965.

A social revolution led by Communists crying 'electrification and industrialisation' and manned by peasants with high expectations, followed by a period of rapid, extensive industrialisation with jobs for all comers and special social status for 'workers', had contributed to the widespread acceptance of industrial and urban values as aspirations towards which all ambitious men and women should strive. The migratory influx came faster than industry and town could absorb. Back on the farm, neglected by the regime, agriculture suffered not only because of an ageing population but because departing manpower, however underemployed it had been, was not replaced rapidly enough by mechanisation and improved land use. Now the economic reform was bringing a drastic cut in the number of new jobs in non-agricultural sectors, affecting primarily unskilled and semiskilled categories. The country's politicians, with the sociological ignorance or irresponsibility common in their profession, talked blithely of sending surplus labour back to the farms. Instead, as in many other Mediterranean countries, the surplus migrated to Western Europe in search of the urban employment it could not find at home, partly relieving the pressure at the critical moment but not solving the problem.

There was no sign that the creeping socialisation of the countryside on which the regime had counted since the retreat from collectivisation would be more successful in the future and of more help in solving the rural employment problem than it had been so far. The relics of collectivisation were irrelevant: by 1963 only thirty-nine Peasant Working Co-operatives (SRZs) were left in existence and by 1966 a pathetic seven, together farming 11,000 hectares of land. The General Co-operatives (OZZs), the regime's great hope in the 1950's, had stagnated or declined in number of members (1·5 million in 1964 and 1·3 million in 1966), in the total agricultural and arable land they owned (890,000 and 444,000 hectares respectively in 1966), and in the number of co-operating peasants (fluctuating at around 1·2 million since 1963). Since 1960 official emphasis had shifted to another device, large agricultural-industrial combines engaging in everything from crop and livestock raising to slaughtering, food processing and canning, sugar production and even retailing. There were 262 of these in 1966 (down from 348 in 1963 as a result of generally economical amalgamations), together owning over 1 million hectares of agricultural land, 841,000 hectares of it arable, and employing 142,000 persons. Land owned or farmed by the socialist sector as a whole had meanwhile increased through purchase or lease to nearly 13 per cent of total agricultural land (*vice* about 9 per cent after collectivisation was abandoned), but the rate of growth remained very slow and seemed unlikely to accelerate; older peasants and those departing to the cities were already offering more than the sector was prepared to take.

The agricultural-industrial combines and the sector as a whole therefore could not be expected to do much more for either agricultural output or employment. Socialised agriculture was in any case still not setting an exactly brilliant example for presumably watchful private peasants. The largest Yugoslav farm of all, the agricultural-industrial combine 'Belje', occupying most of the fertile if flood-prone Baranja region at the junction of the Sava and Drava rivers, suffered a loss of about 2,000 million dinars in 1963. That same year another such combine, at Bečej in the Vojvodina, was said to possess 15,000 hectares of good agricultural land, several industrial plants, 3,500 employees and 'some 3,500 million dinars of uncovered losses' as a result of 'wrongly placed investments and unsuccessful experiments'. Higher agricultural prices after mid-1965 temporarily improved the financial condition of such farms, but by 1968 Belje's profitability ratio was plunging again and by 1971 the combine's economic problems had developed, as happens in Yugoslavia, into a major local Serb-Croat political dispute.[13]

The dilemma remained. If the exodus from the farm could not be absorbed, it must be slowed down or stopped. If it were, the problem of rural overpopulation would not be solved. In addition and of importance to the legitimacy of a socialist system, a new class division with semi-impermeable boundaries would be created between a closed proletarian aristocracy of those who had made it into the city and the factory while the doors were open, and a residual peasantry still too large to get rich and condemned to stay where they were.

Nor was it at all clear how one could persuade people to stay down on the farm, much less go back there, once the dam of traditional rural values had been irreparably breached, as was now the case in Yugoslavia. Not only the fact of rapid industrialisation and the opportunities it had offered, but other policies and the regime's success in propagating at least some of their own values had done their work well in this area. The 10-hectare limit had made it impossible to become a *gazda*, a rich peasant with much land, the traditional aspiration of most rural Yugoslavs. At the same time twenty years of both deliberate and incidental indoctrination, now including TV and school textbooks portraying almost exclusively urban and industrial scenes and values,[14] had glorified these values with cumulative effect and dramatised the contrast between the eight-hour working day, the higher incomes and the urban delights which were depicted and the daily reality of dawn-to-dusk labour, low incomes, mud and boredom which were the peasant's lot.[15]

Recession, unemployment, emigration and an eternally unsolved peasant question were accompanied by the equally unpalatable growth of what in Yugoslavia were now called 'social differences', i.e. growing income disparities. By 1968, while about 40 per cent of the employed were still receiving monthly incomes of less than 600 new dinars (then US$48), others were receiving six times that amount or more. These included some senior functionaries in State, Party and related organs, but also a growing number of managerial and technical categories, persons in the free professions, small private entrepreneurs and most people employed in particularly profitable sectors like banking, insurance, the State lottery (!), some foreign trade enterprises and the electrical industry. The press gleefully cited cases in which janitors in one enterprise or sector were better paid than highly qualified workers or university graduates in another. With the sharp cutback in State-directed redistribution of national income from richer to poorer regions, interregional disparities in income also increased.

One of the main goals of the reform, as has been seen, was to alter the structure of national income in two ways, enlarging personal incomes at the expense of investment and changing the distribution of control over savings and investment ('accumulation') in favour of the socialist enterprises ('the economy itself') and at the expense of State organs at all levels. For a time there was impressive movement towards these goals. From 1964 to 1967 the share of net personal incomes in national income in the socialist sector grew from 33 per cent to nearly 40 per cent. The role of economic organisations in the distribution of national income grew, according to one calculation, from control over 45 per cent in 1961 to 49 per cent in 1964 and nearly 58 per cent in 1967. Their share in the financing of investments in the economy reached a peak of 39·4 per cent in 1966.

In 1967 and subsequent years, however, these trends were reversed, until economic enterprises found themselves with control over proportionately very little more disposable income than before the reform. This time the redistribution favoured the State less than it did a new economic power on the Yugoslav scene, one which was to prove as independent of and non-responsible to the enterprises as the State had been. This was the banking system, and especially the three former federal banks in Belgrade which had inherited the assets of the General Investment Fund in 1964. By 1970 bank funds would account for 51·2 per cent of all investment in the economy and in housing, coming ever closer to the 61·7 per cent of such investment financed by the State in 1961, when bank funds had provided only 0·9 per cent of total investment. By the same year the share of economic organisations would fall to 26·8 per cent, less than their 29·5 per cent share in 1961.[16]

There were many and often mutually reinforcing reasons for such a disappointing performance. The heritage of the past counted in several ways. First there was the burden of irrational investments under both preceding economic models, leaving more 'political factories' than could be allowed to close and serious imbalances in the assortment and quality of production. There was the additional burden of the commitment to major, expensive and slow-maturing investment projects, primarily in infrastructure, which had been made on the eve of the reform and on the assumption of continuing high growth rates, and which now had to be honoured in a period of recession and then of inflation-derived cost overruns. These commitments consequently took an ever larger rather than smaller portion of the total investment pie.

Because they represented commitments by the State and were too large and too slow-maturing to be interesting to banks or enterprises with free funds, they also helped to keep the State in the investment business on a scale contrary to the intent of the reform. Finally, there was the heritage of an economy as well as governments and a Party staffed primarily by those who were incompetent or who lacked ability to think and do business in terms of a genuine market economy.[17]

There was also the burden of at least one piece of bad luck. The Yugoslavs had opened their economy to the competition of the outside world to a greater extent than ever before and with the optimistic zest of nineteenth-century free-traders just when their principal trading partners, the EEC countries in particular, were moving back towards protectionism. Yugoslav countermeasures were slow in coming, contrary to the laissez-faire spirit of the reform, and in any case of limited potential effectiveness in view of Yugoslavia's small share in the total foreign trade of these partners.[18]

In addition, the ethnic and regional prejudices of all those involved in investment decision-making—whether enterprises, banks or State organs—continued severely to restrict interregional free circulation of capital and pooling of investable resources. These, too, had been primary goals of the reform, essential both to the creation of a genuine, all-Yugoslav capital market and to any hope that backward regions, poor in capital but often rich in natural resources, would ever catch up with the relatively developed north and west.

The consequences of more immediately political factors, of the haste with which the reforms had been drafted and implemented, were as important. The results included many defective provisions and the postponement for later resolution of several politically sensitive and disputed but fundamental issues. Of the sectors in which decisions were dangerously postponed, the foreign currency system was technically perhaps the most amenable to solution but became politically the most passionately disputed. Essentially the question was how to reconcile a non-convertible currency with the aspiration for free trade in foreign as well as domestic economic relations and with appropriate export incentives. The reform regime, committed to work for convertibility as a definitive solution but underestimating the time needed to achieve it, found a temporary device in the form of 'retention quotas' introduced in 1967 to encourage exports: exporting and tourist enterprises were entitled to keep an average of 7 per cent of their hard foreign currency earnings, the precise amount varying by sector from 4 per cent up to 20 per cent in tourism, to be used as they saw fit. The rest had to be sold for dinars to a specially authorised bank, of which there were seventeen at the end of 1967, the five strongest in Belgrade. These banks then resold these currencies to importers and other claimants, including the enterprises that had originally earned them, and with demand always exceeding supply.[19]

The device was clearly open to the charge that it was a relic of the old system of central redistribution, which took from those who earned (in this case desirable hard currencies) to give to those who did not. This argument was pressed by politicians and businessmen from regions or sectors that earned the most foreign currency. The issue became a particular concern in Croatia, whose industries, Dalmatian tourism, and large number of migrant workers in Western Europe now produced 40 per cent of all Yugoslav hard currency earnings. In the political atmosphere of the late 1960s the resulting dispute was unresolvable and was even aggravated when a renewed high rate of inflation and an explosive trade deficit after 1968 made it clear that a convertible dinar was more remote than had been hoped in 1965.

More complex political as well as economic problems were generated or at least unsolved by the 1965 Law on Banks.[20] The new banking system failed to evolve as its authors had intended, into a socialist substitute for a capitalist capital market responsible to enterprises, in turn presumably responsive to market-dictated investment needs and through the banks in control of most of gross national investment. For while the banks were assuming the dominant role in the investment system, as we have seen, the enterprises and other legal persons who had subscribed to banking capital, and who therefore controlled the Bank Assemblies (to which the banks were formally responsible), were finding it as difficult in practice to control the banks' decision-making as their own workers' councils had found it difficult to control their enterprises. The same reasons included the power to intimidate inherent in professional expertise and specialist information possessed by a bank director but not usually by a Bank Assembly. More importantly, while representatives of the 'shareholders' formally dominated its Assembly, each bank's credit committee, which actually made the investment decisions, was comprised exclusively of bank employees, with the bank director as chairman. In any case, the Assembly included representatives of a large number of varied and often conflicting business interests, which tended to cancel each other out. The 'shareholders' were also usually debtors of the bank they 'owned', often in amounts greater than their subscriptions to its capiital (total 'accumulation' by all Yugoslav businesses in 1968-70 was only 2 per cent larger than their repayments of investment credits in those years), which also tended to weaken their influence over its decision-making. All these factors were further reinforced by a trend towards concentration in the banking system, imposed by the need for larger concentrations of capital. By June 1967 mergers of small banks or their fusion with larger ones had reduced the number of Yugoslav banks from a pre-reform total of 217 to 102. The power of an individual 'shareholder' was necessarily smaller in a larger bank.

A different kind of limitation on the power of both enterprises and the banks' own credit committees over gross savings and investment was imposed by the considerable part of the investment funds of larger banks which represented the repayment of credits granted from State investment funds before these were abolished in 1964. Under the 1965 law the State had retained the right to earmark these funds for uses of its own choosing, a power strengthened by a 1966 amendment. The Federal Government in particular made extensive use of these 'extra-budgetary accounts' (*vanbudžetski bilanci*) to finance incentive subsidies and old and new investment programmes of its own, for example in tourism. Added to the trend back towards an increasing tax burden on enterprises after 1967, continued State control of these funds further restricted the proportion and absolute value of the investment funds actually controlled by either enterprises or the banks. The result was a *de facto* recentralisation of a portion of national savings for redistribution by the State and thereby a partial reversion to the pre-1965 system.[21]

Meanwhile, the power and behaviour of big banks, like that of enterprises and 'socialist conglomerates' enjoying a monopoly or a dominant position on the domestic market or in foreign trade, was suggesting that in this sector, too, laissez-faire socialism would tend to display most of the vices as well as some of the virtues of its capitalist counterpart. This, added to economic stagnation, unemployment, illiquidity and 'social differences', swelled the ranks of the discontented and of those demanding a reform of the reform. Such demands were invariably interpreted by the reformers as attacks on their own political position and disguised demands for a return to the pre-1965 economic system. They themselves could find no third solution. They therefore clung to what they had so far accomplished with a stubbornness unusual in a system hitherto better known for too frequent changes. Problems remained unsolved and continued to grow in magnitude and political potential, as will be seen.

Between neo-imperialism and neo-Cominform

While the economy was stagnating and the Party anguished over its own reform, events beyond Yugoslavia's borders and the way they were viewed in Belgrade were having a serious effect on the regime's attitude to domestic policies. The world of 1963, reasonably viewed as the heyday of non-alignment, Soviet-American détente and non-intervention in domestic affairs of other States and good relations with all Yugoslavia's neighbours, had in Yugoslav eyes been turned upside-down. Communists aspiring to ideological and political independence were again being subjected to Soviet pressure; the non-aligned, especially those professing socialism, seemed to be subject to renewed and increasingly militant US pressure; the cold war and its arms race had penetrated the Mediterranean; and the security of Yugoslavia's own borders against Bulgarian and even Italian irredentism was more doubtful.

The Yugoslav press, foreign affairs officials and Tito himself professed to believe that American public and clandestine interventions in the affairs of other States betokened a new aggressive response to Communism and non-alignment, imperilling peace and inciting reckless responses. Yugoslav lists of such interventions included the continuing Vietnam war, the June 1967 war in the Middle East, military pressures on Cambodia and frustrated 'national liberation movements' in various Third World countries, most blatantly in the Dominican Republic. Nearer home there were renewed Italian hostility in a dispute over a trade pact and a mini-crisis over the ex-Zone B of the Territory of Trieste, the April 1967 military coup in Greece and aggravation of the Cyprus question and an American ban on further sales of wheat surpluses to Yugoslavia in 1966.[22]

While many Yugoslav officials were ready to admit privately that talk of an 'imperialist conspiracy' was undoubtedly an oversimplification, the impression remained that there had been a basic change in American and therefore Western policy, that now it was US pressures and the unrelated revival of protectionism in Western Europe which were more worrying than Soviet pressure, which might even be turned to good tactical use. On the other hand, although the Soviet Union had not intervened militarily in the affairs of smaller States since 1956, unlike the United States, Yugoslavia's relations with the Eastern bloc had taken a turn for the worse since mid-1966. Two specific issues were involved: Soviet reactions to Ranković's fall and to the Yugoslav economic and Party reforms, and preparatory meetings for a world Communist conference, which the Yugoslavs could not have attended even if they had been invited, which they were not.

It seemed for a time during the spring of 1967 that the Russians might resort to open polemics against the Yugoslav reforms, particularly the reorganisation of the Party and restatement of its political role, both seriously contravening Leninist political doctrine. However, after both sides had launched a few polemical trial balloons, the public debate died down. The Yugoslavs declined to attend the Karlovy Vary Conference of European Communist Parties in April 1967, but they did send a member of the Party Executive Committee and former diplomat, Nijaz Dizdarević, to explain why and to restate the Yugoslav view that multilateral Party discussions might be acceptable in certain other contexts.[23] Then, in June, the Arab-Israeli Six-Day War provided both a distraction and an unexpected opportunity for Tito to co-ordinate his foreign policy with that of the Soviet bloc (excepting Romania) on an important issue; indeed, the common cause of diplomatic support for the Arabs even brought the Yugoslav President to Moscow for the first multilateral consultation by all European Communist Heads of Government and Party that he had ever attended.

However, Eastern misgivings about the Yugoslav domestic reforms obviously remained and were intimately connected—in internal ideological if not in external political logic—with the question of the Yugoslav attitude to preparations for a new world Communist meeting. The Yugoslavs had several reasons for viewing such a meeting and the preparatory conference which assembled in Budapest in February-March 1968 with serious misgivings. If the meeting were to condemn the Chinese Party for its domestic policies, even without formal 'excommunication', it would constitute a renewed precedent for interference in the internal affairs of 'fraternal Parties' and for dogmatic assertions about 'correct' and 'incorrect' roads to socialism. So, too, would any attempt to set a 'general line' for the domestic or foreign policies to be followed by individual parties. Yugoslav commentaries noted that such moves, even if they were to be stated in general terms, would create a situation in which 'one form of guidance—on the part of a centre—is replaced by another form of guidance—on the part of international conferences'.[24] There was also the sponsors' insistence that the meeting must be considered a continuation of the 1957 and 1960 international Communist conferences, and that the conclusions reached at the 1960 meeting were therefore still valid. These conclusions, as the Yugoslav press noted in every commentary on the subject, had included a strongly worded condemnation of the Yugoslav Party and its programme as opportunistic, revisionist, subversive and a betrayal of Marxism-Leninism. Finally, while the Yugoslavs, like the Italian Communists, were in favour of a meeting which would bring together all Communist Parties and 'other progressive forces' on a common platform of anti-imperialism and anti-colonialism, they had expressed repeated doubts that a conference confined to Communists would materially assist the cause. If its theme was really to be anti-imperialism, they argued, it was meaningless to include inconsequential parties or factions from the underdeveloped world, which called themselves Communist but which had done little or nothing for the cause of 'national liberation' in their homelands, and to exclude the non-Communist but 'progressive' movements—often ruling Parties—which had done far more.

Eager to avoid a new quarrel, and apparently genuinely concerned lest the chance of a 'Popular Front' of Communist and other 'progressive forces' in Europe and the Third World should be jeopardised, the Yugoslav Party leaders phrased their position carefully. They were not invited to the Budapest preparatory conference because invitations were based on attendance at the 1960 Moscow conference. They could not have gone, even if they had been invited, as long as the proposed new conference was formally based on and had not formally repudiated the anti-Yugoslav clauses in the Declaration signed by the 1960 conference of 81 Parties. But the Yugoslav Party was not against 'constructive' multi-Party Communist consultations in principle (although preferring a broader front including non-Communists), and would therefore 'support any views by the consultations in Budapest which it assesses as useful'.[25]

Bilateral relations with Yugoslavia's immediate Warsaw Pact neighbours reflected the downturn in relations with the Soviet Union: cooler with Hungary and Bulgaria, for the same reasons, and marginally cooler even with Romania, where Gheorghe Gheorghiu-Dej's April 1964 'declaration of independence' from Soviet tutelage and Yugoslav-Romanian co-operation in building the Iron Gates hydroelectric and navigation project had created the basis for particularly close bonds between the two countries—now equally dedicated to a combination of national independence and socialism—and between their leaders.[26] In the past two years, however, Tito had failed to establish the same kind of personal rapport with Nicolae Ceauşescu, Georghiu-Dej's successor. Then, in 1967, Belgrade and Bucharest found themselves on opposite sides on two important issues: the Middle East crisis, where Tito stood with the Russians and the Romanians played odd man out, and preparations for the world Communist conference, in which the Romanians reluctantly participated while the Yugoslavs did not. Meanwhile, the unkindest comradely cut of all came from Sofia when the Bulgarian press, in an apparently co-ordinated campaign in anticipation of the 90th anniversary of the Treaty of San Stefano, once more raised the Macedonian question. The Yugoslav response was even angrier and more fretful than usual. It seemed unlikely that the Bulgarian regime would have played this particular card at this time without at least the acquiescence and quite possibly the initiative of Moscow, a consideration which gave rise to more ominous speculations by Yugoslav diplomats and public opinion.[27]

Whether the Yugoslav reactions were exaggerated or not, reminders of Bulgarian irredentist claims to Macedonia and of Italian irredentist claims in the Julian Region, like the accession of a militantly anti-Communist military dictatorship in Greece, renewed the Yugoslavs' sense of being under attack from all sides. Four years earlier they had boasted of unprecedentedly good relations with six of their seven neighbours. By 1967 only relations with Austria were still as good as they had been then.

Yugoslav diplomatic reactions displayed an uncertainty and ambivalence which were not unrelated to domestic political developments and the confused process of pluralisation through which the political system was passing. The Foreign Ministry took pains to signal both superpower blocs that Yugoslavia was eager to maintain good relations, despite disagreements on issues like Vietnam or a world Communist conference. The Socialist Alliance, whose less official status made it a more useful vehicle for experimental approaches, was assigned the task of exploring the regional or wider potential for a clearly 'anti-imperialist' but also non-aligned (i.e., non- but not anti-Soviet) front of independent Communist, socialist and other 'progressive' forces, but its first major effort was a fiasco.[28] Its place on the front pages was taken by Tito's appeal, issued during a press conference in Cairo on February 7, 1968, and after soundings taken with President Nasser and Emperor Haile Selassie, for 'a new conference not only of non-aligned but also of countries supporting the policy of peaceful settlement of international conflicts'. The Yugoslav press and Government, apparently taken by surprise, hastened to agree but also interpreted Tito's cautionary additional remark about the need for thorough preparation to mean (as *Komunist* put it) 'that the path to this conference is naturally long, intricate and tedious'. In fact it proved so calculatedly long that the Lusaka Conference of the non-aligned, successor to the Belgrade and Cairo conferences of 1961 and 1964, did not meet until September 1970.

Passive opposition to initiatives and showmanship of this kind was now coming from those within the Yugoslav establishment who apparently believed that Yugoslavia had been living beyond its diplomatic means in pursuing an ambitious, world-wide foreign policy, at least since 1965. For these people Yugoslavia was in the last analysis a small, semi-developed country in southern Europe, and its foreign policy should be tailored accordingly. Their primary concerns were therefore with bilateral and economic relations with neighbours and important trading partners, particularly including a commercial treaty with the EEC, and with attracting foreign investment and expanding joint production arrangements with foreign firms made possible by a still controversial law passed in 1967.[29] While they too thought non-alignment important, it was primarily as a useful if limited device for recruiting diplomatic support from others who shared their interest in the struggle of small countries to resist the pressures of more powerful ones. Thus they also voiced demands for a 'democratisation' of foreign policy formation as a natural corollary to the democratisation of the economic and political systems. By this they meant a growing influence for local and republican interests, as well as a greater role for the Federal Assembly, in setting the style and focus of a foreign policy which might thus be less susceptible to delusions of grandeur. One of them, Foreign Secretary Marko Nikezić, was to break all precedents and commit what turned out to be an unpardonable sin by telling the President, on Tito's return from the Moscow summit meeting of June 1967, that he should not have gone or committed Yugoslavia to the Soviet line on the Middle East crisis without first consulting his colleagues.[30]

The new ideological debate

An initially cautious reopening of the debate on sensitive issues like culture and society under socialism, the changing role of the Party and democratic centralism under self-management, or the changing nature of the Yugoslav class structure and its political implications had antedated the fall of Ranković by several years. Non-establishment Marxists and non-Marxists had probed the boundaries of the permissible in often ephemeral journals and in avant-garde plays and films since the beginning of the decade, sometimes getting into more or less serious trouble which occasionally involved arrests.[31] Meanwhile, first in the context of private intra-Party and then in public discussions focusing on the drafting of the 1963 Constitution, the struggle for the economic reform, and preparations for the 1964 Party Congress, establishment theorists again began to debate the same issues with parallel if more directly self-serving freedom. A new quasi-official Party theoretical journal, *Socijalizam*, was created in 1964 as a major vehicle for such efforts. The re-entry into the lists of these people in this way inevitably stretched the boundaries for others as well.[32]

On both sides of the dialogue the vocabulary and conceptual frameworks had become noticeably more eclectic, reflecting the impact of years of exposure to a variety of Marxist and non-Marxist influences. The Marxism of academic philosophers now bore the imprint of existentialism, particularly in Ljubljana, of symbolic logic and latter-day logical positivism, especially in Belgrade, and of what one of them called 'a marxistically-oriented philosophical anthropology'[33] centred in Zagreb. Towards the end of the decade social science terminology, primarily Western and sometimes debased and detached from its academic origins and meaning, had found its way into the vocabulary not only of intellectuals and students but also of ordinary politicians. It was no longer uncommon for a local Party or State official, addressing an audience of workers or peasants, to use such phrases as 'a pluralistic society', 'socialist pluralism', 'broadening the basis of consent', 'social stratification', 'élites' or 'conflicts of interest groups', in a kind of terminological counterpoint to continued use of the equally esoteric and popularly incomprehensible jargon of traditional Marxism.[34]

There were still limits, including one absolute taboo, at least in public discussion. In Ljubljana a group of young Slovene intellectuals, most of them sons of prominent Communists of the Partisan generation, founded a literary and political review called *Perspektive* as a successor to two previously suppressed journals. They began with a controversial, but in the then Slovenian atmosphere permissible, sociological analysis of the 'open structures' created by self-management, the laws of the market, and the partial rehabilitation of the peasantry. From there they went on, by way of an attack on the 'cultural bureaucracy' and demands for greater political representation for the peasantry, to a thinly disguised attack on the Party bureaucracy as a whole. Then, despite repeated warnings from younger and more liberal members of the Slovene Party establishment, they took the final and fatal step, openly advocating a two-party system. In May 1965 *Perspektive* was suppressed. The Party offical most involved in trying to persuade the young editors to stay within bounds and save the magazine had been Stane Kavčič, who admitted, in discussing the case with an ex-Communist Italian journalist, that some of the top Party leadership had themselves reconsidered—and again rejected—the possibility of a two-party system.[35] Then the 44-year-old chairman of the Slovenian Party's ideological commission, Kavčič, was to become the republic's leading political figure in the era of the reform, only to fall from power in 1972 accused of 'technocratism' and 'anarcho-liberalism'.

Two years after the *Perspektive* case the regime was forced, somewhat reluctantly and in special circumstances, to repeat the lesson. A young instructor in Russian literature at the faculty of philosophy in Zadar, Mihajlo Mihajlov, himself of Russian origin, had been tried in 1965 for spreading 'hostile propaganda' through a series of articles—published in a Belgrade literary journal and based on a summer of research among avant-garde writers in Moscow—which were eloquently critical of contemporary Soviet cultural policies and oppression of freedoms and which even suggested that Lenin rather than Stalin had created the first Soviet concentration camps. Although prosecution had begun after a strong protest by the Soviet ambassador and condemnation by

Tito himself, he was given a one-year suspended sentence. Apparently influenced by the wide and sympathetic publicity given to the case in the Western press, he wrote a series of articles and open letters to Tito denouncing the lack of freedom of expression in Yugoslavia. Then, in July 1966, he announced that he was going to found an 'opposition journal' as a nucleus for a second party. He was arrested again and this time went to prison, beginning a career as Yugoslavia's most publicised political martyr since Djilas. The precedent, had he been allowed to continue with his journal and party, was evidently considered dangerous, even if he himself was not.[36] The multi-party solution nevertheless continued to crop up from time to time and insistently enough to oblige regime spokesmen to repeat that it was still excluded.

With only one other exception, a tacit because never challenged prohibition on the expression of doubts about the principles of self-management, there seemed to be no untouchable subjects in the re-examination of Yugoslav Marxist ideology and its implications which now preoccupied Yugoslav intellectuals. Because the immediate occasion was provided by first steps towards the reorganisation of the Party and by the apparently disputable premises of the Todorović Commission's 'Theses', these issues, involving the relationships of Party and State to each other and to society, constituted the initial focus of the debate.

The Ranković crisis had been a fresh reminder that such questions had a practical and immediate political dimension as well as theoretical implications for a political philosophy of 'direct socialist democracy'. The central problem, as Kardelj stated in his own first contribution to the new debate,[37] was the need to evolve a system, based on self-management and democracy, which would

make it possible to resolve the objective contradictions in our society, and along with them the differences of interests, views and opinions, in the most democratic and normal way, as painlessly as possible and with the least friction.... This means that we, Communists, must pose the question of how, in what way and by what expedients, we can overcome that historical practice ... under which every political change imposed by the course of events in a socialist State, be it a change of government or of practical policies, is always attended by political disturbances which are reminiscent of a coup d'état.

In the same article Kardelj advanced several other postulates, which together covered most of the main subjects being debated. The LCY was not the 'only creative factor' in Yugoslav socialism. A majority decision was not always necessarily a progressive one. The League must 'have concepts and principles, and be ready to defend these, but flexibly' and without worrying unduly if they were not always proved right. 'We have given up the illusion of formal unity'; the problem now was how to forge a genuine one. And finally, a more categorical restatement of an old theme:

> The internal decision-making and acts of the assemblies and of the bodies of self-management in working organizations must not be interfered with by Party organizations and their bodies except by means of political action, i.e., by persuasion, help, by providing information to the public, education, and similar methods.

Statements like these clearly put democratic centralism and the question of 'Divorcing the Party from Power' (the title of an early 1967 Crvenkovski article[38]) 'on the agenda' in a more radical way than since 1954. Meanwhile, discussion of these matters logically led to a reconsideration of class structures in present-day Yugoslavia. Was it true, for example, that as a result of modernisation (according to the 'Theses'), the working class 'in the old sense of the word' was beginning to 'become fused with the technological intelligentsia and indirectly also with the working people in non-material activities, with intellectual workers'?[39] If it were true, then Marxist logic dictated that certain practical consequences affecting the organisation of decision-making in enterprises and communes and the role of a redefined working class in the Party should follow. It was similarly important how one defined and classified 'socialism's own bureaucracy', which some were discussing as a separate social entity capable of becoming a 'new class'. Not only was that 'Djilasism', and for that reason alone politically suspect. If 'bureaucracy' were indeed capable of becoming a 'class' replacing the bourgeoisie as the working class's opponent, Bakarić wrote, Marxists would be duty bound to seek to destroy it. This was clearly absurd, he said, since a modern society cannot function without a group which performs the functions of bureaucracy; a new one will always come into being if an old one is destroyed. The problem—as Marx had recognised in warning the working class to beware of its own bureaucracy under socialism—is rather who the 'bureaucrats' are, to whom they are responsible, and how to keep them responsible. The critics of establishment views replied that a bureaucracy which had escaped control by an ostensibly ruling class (in socialism theoretically the working class), and which therefore administered people and things like surplus value on its own authority, had acquired all the attributes of a 'class' as defined by Marx. If it was not then a class, what was it?[40]

Always at the centre of controversy on these and other subjects was the bimonthly journal *Praxis*, founded by a group of philosophers at the University of Zagreb in 1964 and thereafter constantly with one foot outside the boundaries of the hitherto permissible, testing the ground beyond. *Praxis* began with an ostentatious and in establishment eyes arrogant dedication to 'criticism of everything that exists' in the light of 'creative Marxism' and 'Marxist humanism', and to the proposition that philosophers, as disinterested seekers after pure truth, must of necessity oppose and counterbalance politicians, whose function required that they distort truth to serve political interests, even when they also thought of themselves as Marxist theorists. Accused of intellectual élitism and of making neo-scholastic use of youthful Marxian tests to destroy not only Lenin but also the mature Marx, *Praxis* and its contributors were subjected to continuous and often threateningly sharp attacks, which began as early as 1965 and included full-dress public criticism by the Zagreb Party organisation and the Republican Chamber of the Croatian Sabor in May and June 1966.[41] Prominent among the critics, who included Tito himself, were Party theorists like Bakarić, Kardelj, Vlahović and members of the younger generation like Miroslav Pečujlić, Miko Tripalo and Budislav Soškić, all usually considered liberals and with published opinions which to the layman closely resembled most of the *Praxis* platform. Such attention brought the journal wide international publicity and sympathy and almost annual—but until 1975 always premature—obituaries in the Western press.[42] A highly significant exchange during the Sabor's 1966 discussion of *Praxis* remained virtually unnoticed. One of the discussants had asked petulantly: 'What I want to know is who is subsidising this rag?' Bakarić, in an apparent non sequitur in the middle of his own sharp attack on the journal, responded: 'Comrade Gaće has posed the question, who pays for it. We have subsidised and we are subsidising *Praxis*'.

The ideological debate had by then already shifted its focus from a clearly 'policy-oriented' discussion to become instead another of those interminable, wordy, bitterly personal and tiresomely scholastic Marxist dialogues which the uninitiated find largely incomprehensible and boring and in which it is often difficult to understand why the participants have become so angry with one another over apparently fine and unimportant differences of phrase or emphasis. Why, for example, did it matter so much whether State and Party bureaucracies were described as 'a social stratum' or 'a class' in a specific historic case in which both sides agreed that functionally these bureaucracies had emancipated themselves from control by any other class or stratum and were exercising monopolistic control over the means of production, appropriating surplus value for use or redistribution by themselves? Or whether the 'étatism' which Kardelj had described, and which clearly meant the Soviet system, should be defined as a distinct third kind of socio-political system, alongside capitalism and socialism, or as a 'degenerate socialism'? It was nevertheless precisely on these kinds of points that the most violent and sometimes personally vicious polemics developed, ranging *Praxis*, its only slightly more circumspect Belgrade equivalent *Gledišta*, and other non-conformist journals on the same 'anti-establishment' side against *Socijalizam, Komunist* and occasionally *Borba* as preferred 'establishment' media.[43]

The answer is in part, of course, that such apparently esoteric details can matter greatly and have enormous political implications and consequences, as the histories of the Second and Third Internationals and their member parties bear witness. There were, however, other and also interesting reasons.

During a later phase of the debate the astute editor of *Komunist*, Gavro Altman, commenting on a dispute between a Belgrade University student newspaper and a group of older Slovenian writers in which the latter had been called 'Stalinists' because of their published criticism of some 'new left' writings in Ljubljana, suggested sadly 'that in a political polemic … one must look at who says *what* and not only *who* is saying what'.[44] The fact that many Marxist, most Central European, and nearly all Yugoslav political polemics fail to do this and tend to become personal provides a useful clue for an understanding of both the causes and effects of such a style. The latest Yugoslav Marxist dialogue was occurring in a specific historic and cultural context and among members of a numerically small and both intellectually and literally endogamous cultural community of a kind characteristic of smaller nations and 'face-to-face' societies. Its style of argument and of personal abuse was true to a Central European political tradition which has not been confined to parties of the left but seems to be part of the 'political culture' of the region.[45] The participants in the present dialogue had also grown up and studied together, either as young prewar *SKOJevci* and in the underground Party or in the universities of socialist Yugoslavia (or both), and they had often fought on the same or opposite side of earlier wartime or ideological barricades. They had frequently intermarried, formally or informally, even as officials of the new regime had frequently intermarried with members of the classes they had overthrown. Both tradition and personal reasons therefore led them, on both sides, to extensive use of *argumenta ad hominem* that easily became personal attacks in which revenge for past personal or political wrongs and *a priori* assumptions concerning the 'real' intentions of another participant were more important than what was actually said.

There was also a form of personal and group betrayal which each side perceived in the words or acts of the other. For the 'humanist intelligentsia' the politicians were betraying mutually shared youthful ideals and true democratic socialism. For the politician-theorists, the 'humanist intelligentsia' were betraying the post-1965 economic and political reforms, at this moment the maximum politically realisable steps towards a similar vision of socialist democracy. They were doing this both by insistently pointing out abuses and deficiencies like unemployment and inequality, which could be avoided at the present stage of development only by a return to more central control and redistribution by apparatuses still imbued with 'Stalinism', and by a noisy and radical criticism which could only play into the hands of 'forces condemned but not destroyed at the 4th Plenum'. Worst of all, with their frank discussion of the necessary role of 'élites' (with or without their own pretensions to being the wisest one), theorists like the *Praxis* group were implicitly if seldom explicitly saying what everyone else, and especially the reformers presently in power, did not dare to say: that the emperor had no clothes on. The basic theoretical premise of the system in general and of the reforms in particular was that the working class should make all public choices, directly and without intermediaries, and that social change and education had by now created a politicised working class large and sophisticated enough to do the job without any kind of élite. The authors of the reforms, of the 'Theses' and of 'establishment' contributions to the ideological dialogue knew that this was not true, and in practice acted accordingly, but they consistently said that it was. To do otherwise would be either to surrender anew to momentarily defeated advocates of centralised paternalistic Party-State authoritarianism or to admit that someone else, not the workers, would step into the vacuum which their destruction of that authority was creating. It was unpleasant, politically and emotionally, to have their sincerity on this point challenged, especially by people whose credentials as Marxists and social scientists were as good as their own. They therefore preferred to go on repeating the liturgy of the need to bring more workers into the Party and meanwhile to seek to discredit the credentials of the 'humanist intelligentsia' on both Marxist and scientific grounds, accusing them (for example) of 'substituting the thesis of C. Wright Mills for the thesis of Marx' in their discussion of élites.

At the same time, however, the establishmentarian liberals who so uncompromisingly attacked the ideas and ideological integrity of the academics continued quietly to protect their right to work and publish their opinions, as Bakarić had admitted *en passant* during the 1966 Sabor debate on *Praxis*. This was not as anachronistic as it seemed. A grudging respect for the persons and ideas of these opponents in the debate may have played a role, but those who had conspired against Ranković out of a self-interested or ideological commitment to greater pluralism and liberty were also being true to their principles. If Yugoslav society was held to be mature enough for a genuine, free 'struggle of opinions' (always of course within the limits, increasingly broadly defined, of a choice among 'socialist alternatives'), then *Praxis* and *Gledišta* and the professorial activities of their contributors must also be tolerated. Freedom of opinion, in the view of these protectors, meant that they and Party organs also had a right to have and voice opinions, which they were doing, and to undertake political action to assist these opinions to prevail. But it no longer permitted the Party to take 'administrative' action against those with other opinions.[46] While this definition of freedom conveniently begged the vital question of the Party's continuing insistence on its monopoly of organised political action, it gave rise to impassioned panegyrics of the importance of freely expressed minority views which were worthy of J. S. Mill.[47]

Meanwhile, the principal immediate political effect of an esoteric debate had been to split the reform coalition along another of its natural fracture lines. The drama of the battle between the Party and the intellectuals also distracted attention from the quieter and largely intra-establishment discussion of more obviously and immediately significant issues. One of these, centred on the proposition that the League must become 'an essentially new type of political organisation, its basic feature being the function of ideological guidance', concerned precise ways of really moving decision-making on specific issues and problems from Party organs to those of self-management without unduly reducing the Party's influence and thereby risking too many decisions which in the Party's view could 'lead backward'.[48] Another concerned democratic centralism, with regional spokesmen like Crvenkovski and Tripalo and central apparatus theorists like Šoškić taking the lead in urging formal recognition of the right of members of a Party minority to continue to argue their case after a decision had gone against them or to withdraw from an executive position, without suffering discredit or Party sanctions, rather than execute a decision with which they disagreed.[49]

Also virtually unheard in the clamour of the disputing Scholastics and the enthusiasm of the moment was the warning issued at an early point in the debate, on the eve of publication of the 'Theses', by an otherwise non-participating Tito: 'The consciousness of our people is still far below the required level, the level at which the Party could gradually begin shedding its attributes and diminishing its role'. Until that time, he said, the 'lesson of 1948', which was unity and discipline through strict enforcement of the rules of democratic centralism, must remain of central importance for the LCY.[50]

Dissent and reaction

By 1968 the prevailing atmosphere in Yugoslavia was one of insecurity, drift and a rising tide of dissent. The real legitimacy of the regime in the eyes of the people rested on its proven ability in four fields: defence of the precarious independence of a small State on the East-West frontier and of the equally precarious 'brotherhood and unity' of its quarrelsome ethnic groups, and the promotion of rapid economic development and of at least some visible advance towards a stable economic and political democracy. On all four fronts it was manifestly faltering. The post-reform recession had become acute. In the aftermath of the Greek military coup and the June War, and with the deterioration of relations with the Soviet Union, which had begun in 1966, taking a sudden turn for the worse after mid-1968, the security and independence of Yugoslavia seemed more precarious than at any time since Stalin's death. Both the Federal Government and the central Party apparatus were increasingly paralysed by the inability of regional leaderships to agree on key issues, and there was an associated escalation of distrust, mutual recriminations and incidents among ethnic communities. It began to seem to many people that a divided Communist élite which had lost its sense of purpose and ability to act decisively might be worse than one that had not. The universities provided a seismograph of dissent: 'new leftist' in Ljubljana, predominantly nationalist in Zagreb and a bit of everything in Belgrade.

For more than two years the basic reaction of the regime, now largely in the hands of the anti-centralist reform coalition, was virtually to ignore the rising tide except when it urgently threatened to undermine and topple one of the pillars of their platform or public order. The reformers had what an American Government a few years later would call 'a game plan', and they pursued it with a dogged determination unprecedented in postwar Yugoslav politics. It was based, in the coinage of Rudolf Bićanić, on 'four Ds': decentralisation, de-étatisation, de-politicisation and democratisation.[51]

In the elections held in April 1967 for half the members of the federal, republican, provincial and communal assemblies, for example, the voters were on Party instructions offered a choice of candidates for more seats than ever before. The hitherto informal role of the Socialist Alliance as principal organiser of the nomination and election procedures was made a formal responsibility, and Party members and organs were given strict instructions to influence the choice of candidates only through the Alliance, in accordance with the new rules for Party behaviour, and not to 'impose' their own lists as they had always done.[52] The results were to suggest that Communists in many areas had either genuinely attempted to obey these instructions and were not up to the job, or else had withdrawn in bitterness or confusion from any effective role in the campaign.

In the directly elected communal chambers, where half the seats had been contested even in 1965, an average of 2·3 persons stood for each seat in 1967. While all chambers of assemblies above that level were indirectly elected (by the communal assemblies), a curious provision of the 1963 Constitution, requiring 'confirmation' by popular ballot of those elected to the Federal Chamber of the Federal Assembly and the republican and provincial chambers of the republican and provincial assemblies, made it technically possible for communal assemblymen to let the voters in on the selection process by proposing more than one candidate for each seat in these most powerful chambers. Both the system and political habits had operated against such a course, however, and in 1963 the voters were asked to confirm 120 candidates for the 120 seats in the Federal Chamber. After criticism by some liberal Party leaders, the electoral law was amended in 1964 to encourage the proposal of more names. Even so, only three Federal Chamber constituencies out of the 60 in which elections were held in 1965 nominated two candidates. It was here, in the new spirit of 1967, that the most remarkable results were achieved: the communal assemblies sent 82 candidates to the voters, again for 60 seats in the Federal Chamber. To the surprise of most observers, all but four out of the 14 multiple-candidate constituencies thus created were in Serbia, where the voters were offered 41 candidates for 25 seats (six with two candidates each, three with three each, and one with five).[53]

It was the results of these contests, and of contested elections for local or republican seats in some other, primarily underdeveloped regions, which gave members of the reform coalition one of the first of a series of shocks which were to force some of them to reconsider the appropriateness of direct and freer elections or even the 'ripeness' of Yugoslav society for more democracy. In most of the contested Serbian constituencies for the Federal Chamber, one of the candidates represented the Partisan and Party 'old guard', typically a much-decorated hero of the National Liberation Struggle. His opponent was usually a man of the reformed and 'liberalised' post-Ranković Party machine, proposed by that machine. It was the old Partisans, the 'wild' and unwanted candidates labelled as Communist 'conservatives', who won over the younger, 'official' candidates and men of the reform.

In one election district in south Serbia, for example, the liberal federal Secretary for Foreign Trade, Nikola Džuverović, was unexpectedly defeated by one Obrad Lazović, a retired Partisan major-general and holder of the highest decoration bestowed for

Partisan heroism, a 'People's Hero'. In the Western Morava constituency of Čačak another People's Hero and retired general, Sredoje Urošević, defeated a member of the Serbian Central Committee in a performance he was to repeat more dramatically in the 1969 elections.

The most notorious such contest of 1967 took place in Lazarevac, a largely rural commune in Šumadija. The victor here, over a record number of four competitors, was Radivoje Jovanović, called 'Bradonja' (the Bearded One), a prewar royal army officer, later a Partisan People's Hero and lieutenant-general, who had come to the Partisans wearing the full beard usually characteristic of the Chetniks. He later served in UDBa. In the campaign he employed what the Party called 'demagogic practices': promising the peasants paved roads to their villages, higher prices for farm products, and a better deal vis-à-vis industrial workers, while muttering darkly about the neglect of Serbian interests during the last year or two.

In winning, Jovanović also carried his personal friends into office in the commune. With their help and that of the Partisan veterans' organisation (SUBNOR), also formerly a Ranković fiefdom, he then proceeded—according to the charges later made against him—to circumvent, isolate and finally attack the local Party organisation. In addition, to keep his campaign promises, he pressured the only important industrial enterprise in his constituency into donating machinery for farm road-building; for this he was charged with violating self-management and using 'outmoded methods of authority and command'.

In the autumn of 1967 local and republican organs of the LCY launched a co-ordinated campaign to unseat him and drive him out of the Party. To the above-mentioned charges a more serious one was added, that his campaign and present power rested on a curious coalition of Party and non-Party opposition forces which was coming to be known as 'the political underground': former Ranković men, ex-Cominform supporters, ex-Chetniks and others, all with a common platform of 'Serbian chauvinism'.

By the end of the year Bradonja's recall as a deputy had been engineered and he was expelled from the Party, but similar if less dramatic cases continued to reach the press or the Belgrade rumour mill from various parts of Serbia, Bosnia-Herzegovina and some places in Croatia.[54]

This last republic had already produced another and more immediately dramatic shock, widely interpreted at the time as the most serious public incident in Serbo-Croatian relations since the war. On March 17, 1967, Zagreb's leading literary weekly published a 'Declaration on the Name and Position of the Croatian Literary Language' which had been signed in the name of 19

Croatian literary groups, including the distinguished Matica Hrvatska, by 130 prominent Croatian intellectuals. Eighty of the signatories were Communists and one was Miroslav Krleža, Croatia's most famous living writer, Tito's personal friend and a member of the Croatian Central Committee. The 'Declaration' denounced the Novi Sad agreement of 1954, which had proclaimed 'Serbo-Croatian or Croato-Serbian' to be one language with two scripts (Latin and Cyrillic) and two variants (*ijekavski* and *ekavski*). It called for complete official and constitutional recognition of two separate languages, an end to alleged discrimination against the Croatian variant and its exclusive use in Croatian schools, press, official documents, etc. A political uproar and almost hysterical campaign against nationalism followed. The signatories were anathematised and some of the Communists who refused to recant lost their Party memberships. The same treatment was meted out to forty-five Serbian writers, half of them again Party members, who drafted a reply in the same terms, 'A Proposal for Reflection', which demanded among other things the use of Cyrillic by Belgrade television and that the 700,000 Serbs of Croatia should be educated in their own language.[55]

In the shadow of these events the outgoing Federal Assembly passed a first set of six amendments to the 1963 Constitution, proclaimed on the eve of its dissolution in April. The amendments represented the first impact on the structure of the Federation of the changed balance of political forces created by the fall of Ranković and subsequent Party reforms. Four of them affected federal-republic relations, always to the advantage of the latter, while the fifth abolished the office of Vice-President of the Federation which had been created for Ranković in 1963. Amendment I, an initiative by the Republic of Bosnia-Herzegovina after a dispute over the allocation of development aid from the Federal Fund in December 1966,[56] significantly broadened the competences of the Chamber of Nationalities, buried in the Federal Chamber since 1953. The list of subject areas on which this chamber was now to meet 'mandatorily' and to decide 'on terms of equality' with the Federal Chamber and 'from the viewpoint of the equality of the republics, nations and nationalities and the safeguarding of the constitutional rights of the republics' included almost all economic and other matters which had lately proved to be sensitive in inter-nationality relations. Although still formally within the Federal Chamber, the Chamber of Nationalities was now in effect separate and on the way towards its establishment as the Assembly's most powerful chamber in the next package of amendments only one year later. Amendment IV, directly reflecting the lessons of the Ranković case, made the republics co-responsible for public order with the Federation, which had previously enjoyed full powers in this field, and stipulated that republican public prosecutors should be appointed by the republican assemblies and no longer by the federal Public Prosecutor. Although in fact the package as a whole was at most a first small and reversible step in that direction, 'some Yugoslav scholars and politicians even ventured that their country was changing from a federation into a confederation'.[57]

On May 11 the new Federal Assembly convened to elect its officers and a new FEC and to re-elect Tito as President of the Republic. The principal concern of Kardelj's farewell speech as outgoing Assembly President was with the electoral system, and his remarks reflected the lessons of Lazarevac and similar 'cases'.[58] For Kardelj this was an opportunity to revive another of his pet ideas: the present Assembly and electoral systems and the trend towards more direct, contested elections still retained too many relics of 'bourgeois democratic' theories about political representation, a system in which the voter's interests are imperfectly aggregated and filtered 'through political parties as general representatives—or their top leaders as is the case under the parliamentary system'. He said that the latest Yugoslav elections had again suggested that 'an uninformed or inadequately informed citizen certainly becomes an unqualified elector', and it was questionable whether under the present electoral system it was possible to improve the provision of information without 'giving rise to various forms of political struggle for power which characterise the bourgeois political system'. The question was whether the time had come to discard 'with increasing speed' the system of formal political representation, 'a system which is based on abstract citizens deprived of the concrete social labour relations characterising them, and to take a more resolute course towards the delegate system?' The time had not yet come, as events were to prove. It would take another seven years, a different set of circumstances, and a clearer definition of 'the delegate system' before this particular pet piece of Kardeljiana would become constitutional.

The composition of the new FEC and other administrative organs approved by the new Assembly was consistent with the downgraded competences and powers of the Federation and the principles of the reform. Except for Tito and the State Secretaries for Foreign Affairs (Marko Nikezić) and Defence (Colonel-General Nikola Ljubičić), the turnover was virtually total. Only the President and one vice-president of the 17-member FEC and none of the State or federal secretaries, now only six in number, would also be members of the Party Presidency, although another nine of them were on the Central Committee. In the person of the President of the FEC the new team was even weaker than had been intended, since the President-designate, Boris Krajger, had been killed in a traffic accident in January. In his place the Assembly elected Mika Špiljak, lately president of the Croatian Executive Council and earlier Vukmanović's deputy at the Trade Union Federation, as successor to the moderately conservative Serb Petar Stambolić.[59] During his two years as federal Prime Minister Špiljak was to become the butt of many jokes impugning his intelligence and ability because he ran a 'do-nothing' Government. Although Krajger would undoubtedly have been a stronger President, Špiljak was in fact only fulfilling his mandate, which was to be the Calvin Coolidge of a Yugoslav laissez-faire epoch.

In the Party the power to appoint and dismiss higher and middle-rank functionaries, ostensibly elected but in fact for twenty years the prerogative of Ranković as Organisational Secretary, had now passed entirely to republican organs.[60] This directly strengthened the overall powers of these organs and at the same time shifted the focus of loyalty of members of the federal apparatus away from the centre towards these new, plural mandators and masters of their professional fates and the plural and often divergent policies which these mandators were pursuing. A further consequence concerned the quality of the personnel manning first and second rank positions in the federal apparatuses, both Party and State. A federal appointment was now regarded as one phase in an otherwise republican career, to which one expected to return. There were obvious disadvantages in being away from the base where the real action and one's real electors were to be found, engaged in and identified with decisions and policies which could not always fully satisfy those electors. The effect on an already inefficient federal administration, as described by a member of the Croatian Central Committee and a social scientist who was himself seconded to the federal Party apparatus in 1969, was that

the quality of its operation continued to decline further. Outstanding personalities went to work unwillingly in the federal administration; they turned instead to centres of new political power, and these continued to grow in the republics. It even became difficult to put together a Federal Government, to which the republics generally sent only second-rank persons.[61]

The process of eroding central Party and State authority continued as further organisational or policy changes, which were symbols and effects of an already accomplished shift in the locus of prime power, acted in their own turn to accelerate the rate of transfer. One was a decision taken in the autumn of 1967 to hold republican Party Congresses before rather than after the next Yugoslav Party Congress. The Federal Congress had always been the first to meet, had determined the composition of central Party organs, and had set policy for subsequent republican congresses to accept and adapt to local circumstances. Now this would be reversed: the republican Parties would draft their own political platforms and name their own officers, including their representatives on central organs, the composition of which would then merely be confirmed by the later Federal Congress.[62]

In the State sector another and more significant package of thirteen additional amendments to the 1963 Constitution, promulgated in December 1968, confirmed the trends signalled by the 1967 amendments. The Federal Chamber of the Federal Assembly was abolished, its competences and others passing to a fully independent Chamber of Nationalities (twenty deputies from the assembly of each socialist republic and ten from the assembly of each autonomous province), which now became by far the most powerful chamber in the Belgrade parliament. It was explicitly stipulated that the deputies must faithfully represent the views of the assemblies which had sent them. The legislative competence of the republican assemblies was also enlarged at the expense of those of the Federal Assembly, whose tax powers were now explicitly restricted to the capital tax, the turnover tax and ('if necessary for the purpose of ensuring the unity of the market or preventing or eliminating market disturbances') setting limits within which lower-level governments could fix their own taxes. Other amendments redefined the nature, origins and competences of the Autonomous Provinces of Vojvodina and Kosovo, making them the equal of republics in most respects except name, and extended to all ethnic minorities ('nationalities') all rights which had earlier specifically been guaranteed only to 'the nations of Yugoslavia'. The supremacy in the Yugoslav concept of federalism of 'the nations and nationalities' and of the republics and provinces which were supposed to be their nation-States was thus confirmed.

The old Organisational-Political Chamber, a curious body of bureaucrats and managers, was replaced by a Socio-Political Chamber comprised of 120 deputies directly elected from single-member constituencies by universal adult suffrage. This was a clear rejection, for the moment, of Kardelj's objection to 'relics' of bourgeois-democratic principles of representation and a compromise with those who were beginning to urge that all assembly chambers should be directly elected in a true socialist democracy. Where the latter were concentrated became clear when the Croatian Sabor defiantly amended its republican Constitution to require direct elections for four of its own five chambers.[63]

One amendment in the package (XV) concerned the organisation of self-management in enterprises and faithfully reflected the continuing importance of technological and managerial efficiency for those who had made the reforms of 1965. Management boards became optional; the 'organs of management' of an enterprise could now be shaped and staffed as each enterprise should determine, including the right to delegate 'specific executive functions' to individuals or bodies chosen by and responsible to the workers' council. It thus became possible to establish boards of professionally qualified people—managerial staff, engineers and other trained experts—and to 'delegate' to them the power to run the enterprise effectively unencumbered by interference by non-experts except in the form of ultimate formal responsibility to the workers' council and thus to the collective. The importance of this change was to become clear when it and its authors were later condemned on grounds of 'anti-self-management managerial-technocratic élitism'.

Before this second package of amendments was adopted, barely in time for the 1969 elections, the liberal regime had been buffeted by more and sometimes violent criticism of its economic and social policies from a growing number and assortment of people. Among these the students of Belgrade University, who sparked a country-wide student strike in June 1968 which was to shake the liberal coalition seriously for the first time, and the Albanians of Kosovo, who took to the streets of Priština the following November, presented the most critical and immediate challenges. They and the reactions to them were also, in their different ways, symbols and omens of three oppositional forces in search of coalitions of their own: 'firm-hand conservatism', ethnic nationalisms of various hues and aims and 'new leftist' disgust with what was seen as the *embourgeoisement* of Yugoslav socialism.

Of economists, students and the 'political underground'

During the last months of 1967, paralleling the continuing ideological debate, articles by two of the country's leading economists precipitated a new discussion of the 1965 reforms, of the intelligence or at least the literacy of their drafters and of the motives and consequences of criticism. The implications of the ensuing polemics went well beyond the boundaries of economics *per se*.

It began when Branko Horvat, the director of the Federal Institute for Economic Planning in Belgrade, published a series of articles in the Zagreb daily *Vjesnik*, in September, discussing the relationship (or the lack of one) between economic science and economic policy in Yugoslavia. The articles suggested that if Yugoslav policy-makers had been better educated in contemporary economics, including particularly Western post- and neo-Keynesian economics, they would have been more successful in timing their reforms and in damping the oscillations in growth-rates which had been induced or exaggerated by their own

'stop-go' policies. Six weeks later *Vjesnik* published another series
by Aleksander Bajt, professor of economics at Ljubljana University. Bajt agreed with most of Horvat's analysis but was also
concerned lest pessimism about the current economic situation,
combined with continuing popular and governmental ignorance of
how a market economy really functions and can be controlled,
might lead to a reaction against the principles of the 1965 reform
instead of minor modifications to introduce appropriate control.
The same week another *Vjesnik* organ, the popular weekly *Vjesnik
u Srijedu* (*VUS*), published a more dramatic article by Horvat,
entitled 'The Price of Slowed-Down Growth'. Seeking to drive his
earlier point home with a popularly comprehensible and alarming
statistic, the Belgrade economist calculated at 7,200 billion old
dinars, or the value of total output in 1966, the 'loss' of production
in the past three years because of theoretically avoidable non-
growth.[64]

However critical of specific reform measures, neither economist
had challenged the basic virtues of a properly controlled market
economy and the tone and purpose of both were clearly 'pro-
reform'. The articles were, however, a serious attack on the abilities
of the reformers. The *VUS* article in particular, written in popular
and dramatic language for the weekly with the largest circulation
in the country, could also be construed as dangerously subversive
to the morale of people, who were in effect being told by respected
authorities that the efforts they had been asked to make for the
sake of the reform had been misguided, that the deprivations they
had suffered in its name had been largely if not entirely
unnecessary, and that ignorance and mismanagement at the
highest level were to blame. The undesirable effect of the critique
on public opinion and morale was indeed the central message of a
prolonged series of attacks on the two economists and on *Vjesnik*
and *VUS*, most of them in *Borba* or in *Svet*, a popular weekly
published by the *Borba* house, but also in *Ekonomska politika*,
usually the authentic voice of Yugoslavia's socialist entrepreneurs.
Borba's commentators wondered what 'objective interests' were
being served by criticism which 'demobilises and demoralises'
because it 'irresponsibly' accuses the country's leaders of being
'unscientific, amateurish, technocratic and ineffective' and of
thereby pursuing 'a catastrophe-bound policy'. There was even
room for doubt about the 'subjective' motives of certain editors if
not about those of the professors: why, one writer in *Borba* asked
suspiciously, were all these criticisms published in Zagreb when
Bajt lived in Ljubljana and Horvat in Belgrade?[65] What had begun
as a debate between economists and politicians thus became a
sullen Belgrade-Zagreb war of words conducted between the

Borba and *Vjesnik* publishing houses perceived as exponents of ethnocentric or even chauvinist Serbian and Croatian views.

In the middle of this dispute the Party's Central Committee assembled in Belgrade for its 8th Plenum, on November 23, 1967, with 'ideological-political problems of the reform' as the principal item on the agenda. The Horvat–Bajt criticism was specifically mentioned in the discussion, and the resolution adopted by the meeting responded somewhat defensively: 'The League of Communists will as always shape its policy and practice on the basis of the results and discoveries of progressive social thought and scientific research'. On this basis it would 'carry on the struggle against any attempts made under the guise of being "scientific" at imposing conservative and bureaucratic-statist concepts of social development'.[66]

While claiming success in many fields, particularly in the adaptation of the 'business mentality' in many enterprises and sectors to the pressures of a freer, more competitive market, the Central Committee admitted that the reform was still beset by major problems and deficiencies. The shift from investment to consumption and to decision-making by 'the economy itself' had stagnated with rising taxes, new grandiose investment schemes and too much residual political control over the banks; modernisation of existing plant and development of underdeveloped regions were not going as planned; and illiquidity and unemployment, especially of educated cadres, were posing increasingly serious problems. Another souce of concern was the 'excessive' level of personal incomes being realised in certain sectors, 'in banks, Chambers, the electric power industry, foreign and wholesale trade, business associations, insurance companies, housing enterprises, trade agencies, lottery, some sports clubs, etc.'—a significant list including later prime targets of both Croatian liberals and their neo-centralist opponents.[67] It was also admitted that there had been difficulty in achieving 'unity of views among the Leagues of Communists of the constitutent republics' on what should be done.

Despite these implicit confessions that the critics had a point, the discussion and resolution were on balance optimistic and defiant. There would apparently be no turning back or wavering in the basic commitment to muddling through with laissez-faire socialism. Intervention by the State in the economy must be further reduced. As for those like the humanist intelligentsia or Party 'conservatives' who worried about technocracy, big enterprises, and socialist conglomerates undermining self-management or Party control, the resolution did not mention them but gave their concerns a sharp answer:

Communists in work organisations will fight for the establishment of self-management relations and an atmosphere in which the creative abilities, initiative and responsibility of specialised services in charge of technology will come to fuller expression,[68]

The complacency displayed by those who had set the tone of the Plenum contrasted sharply with the seriousness of the recession and with the mood of the country as registered in the recent elections, nationalist 'incidents', a bolder press now increasingly preoccupied with the growth of 'social differences' and evidence of the growing strength of the 'political underground'. It continued, however, until a serious shock was administered by one group which had never before given the regime any significant trouble: university students, formerly a reliably passive part of a generation so often chastised by Party spokesmen for being apolitical. This, it was now to become apparent, was not or at least no longer true. That fact and diverse establishment reactions to it were revealing as well as important.

For some time before the explosion of June 1968 it had been evident that the traditional apathy of young Yugoslavs was likely to give way to internationally fashionable activisim and protest. A combustible collection of ingredients had been assembled: ideological disorientation in the Party and ideological ferment in both halves of Europe; the regime's effort to encourage politisation of the masses, leading to increasingly public debate and a sense, at least in urban centres, that effective participation in political processes might now be possible; and the recession and growing unemployment, extensively discussed in the press. More specifically affecting students were overcrowded universities, poor housing and too few scholarships, especially limited employment prospects for young graduates, a 'conflict of generations' advertised by vigorous denials that one existed in Yugoslavia, and the televised example of rebellious youth in other countries.

During the spring there had been several anticipatory signs that students and other young people were unhappy and becoming vocal about it. In April and May student groups in various parts of the country met to discuss 'inequalities in socialism' and again criticised a reform which seemed to include enrichment of a few, rising unemployment and unavoidable emigration of workers and technicians. At a symposium at the Belgrade law faculty on May 8, addressed by professors of the now notorious 'humanist intelligentsia', one faculty member advised the students to demand 'a free university, a critical and progressive university', adding 'there is only one step between the demand for the reform of the university and for the reform of the whole of society'. Students should be critical, he said, although in socialist society criticism 'is sometimes identified with opposition to socialism'.[69]

The revolt itself began with a banal incident, a street fight on a warm summer evening between Belgrade students and voluntary youth brigade workers over admission to a free variety show. City riot police intervened with excessive zeal, inciting a massive student reaction which quickly became political. By the next afternoon two serious confrontations had occurred between the police and ultimately some 4,000 student marchers, who already carried posters making political demands. At the second of these a police charge left at least 169 persons injured seriously enough to need treatment, some for gunshot wounds.

So far the student revolt and official reaction to it had resembled events in other university cities in Europe and North America. But after the second battle with the police there was a marked difference. There was no more noteworthy violence, either in Belgrade or in other university cities as the movement spread to Zagreb, Ljubljana and Sarajevo. Instead, both students and the regime displayed a significant willingness to pass from confrontation to a dialogue based on mutually accepted ground rules. Five days after the Belgrade students and their supporters had shifted from street demonstrations to a remarkably disciplined sit-in strike and prolonged discussions inside university buildings, there was a moment when local and Serbian authorities seemed about to yield to those who were demanding a 'firm hand'. Then Tito himself intervened with a dramatic television address, apparently siding with the students and recalling his ministers to their earlier policy. The strike promptly ended on a note of euphoria, with the students dancing the *kolo* in the streets of Belgrade.

The wider significance of the June 1968 student strike was, first, that it marked the emergence of students as a new factor in the Yugoslav political equation. The factor itself might prove to be short-lived, but the programme of the movement revealed much about the values and attitudes of a new generation of educated Yugoslavs, the first to have lived entirely in the environment of Yugoslavia's 'separate road to socialism'. Secondly, a spontaneous movement, which was remarkably self-disciplined in rejecting anti-socialist slogans and which did influence policy, had demonstrated that political initiatives could now come from below as well as from above. That fact in turn accelerated the polarisation within the Yugoslav Communist establishment between those who were willing to accept its implications as socialist and democratic and those who were not. Also significant, but generally overlooked then and later, was the success of certain Party officials at the university and their protectors in higher Party organs in first capturing and subsequently demobilising and disintegrating the movement without resort to 'administrative methods' (which were occasionally used, but always against their will).

The Belgrade student programme evolved during the week of

the strike, becoming more specific, moderate and sensitive to the limits of what then seemed ideologically acceptable and politically possible.[70] Even so, the final version still retained the essential elements of the demands and slogans with which the students had festooned the walls of university buildings on the first day, along with pictures of Marx and Tito, and which epitomised their original, spontaneous attitudes: 'Workers—We are with you!' 'Our demands are your demands!', 'Work for Everyone, Bread for Everyone!', 'Let's Dismiss Incompetent Politicians!', 'Into Tomorrow without Those Who Ruined Yesterday!', 'Down with Corruption!', 'Bureaucrats, Hands Off Workers!', 'Enough of Unemployment!', 'Down with the Princes of Socialism!', 'Down with the Red Bourgeoisie!', 'We struggle for a better man, not for a better dinar!, 'More Schools, Fewer Automobiles!', 'Free Information Media!', 'There is no Socialism without Freedom, no Freedom without Socialism!'. And at mass meetings inside blockaded university buildings the refrain of a song composed for the movement on a theme by Mayokovsky captured their spirit:

Of the courage of our fathers we know from books
And their dream is what warms us
But today and beyond is *our* concern:
Left! Left! Left!

While the influence of the international 'new left' and of the 'humanist intelligentsia' in Yugoslav faculties of philosophy was clear, it could also be argued—and would be—that many specific demands, such as immediate full employment, could only be implemented by a return to a quasi-Stalinist command economy, and that the movement therefore played into the hands of Stalinists or 'Rankovićites' in the 'political underground'. But the dominant influence was clearly acceptance of the official LCY programme and of the Party's own recently reiterated criticism of the social and political *status quo*; at least the student élite among the children of the Yugoslav revolution had apparently absorbed some of its ideals and taken them seriously. The conspicuous absence, at least at Belgrade University, of the normally dominant theme of ethnic nationalism in any slogan, demand or speech during the strike was equally significant. It was perhaps the first time in the fifty years since the creation of Yugoslavia that ethnicity had played no role in an important political event.

In reacting to what all realised was a crisis, the officials concerned were forced to reveal more clearly than usual their own political preferences. Some, initially most outspoken in municipal Party, Socialist Alliance and Assembly meetings, clearly felt that a dangerous movement must be suppressed. Others preferred to consider it to be a positive development, arguing that youthful enthusiasm and idealism and the students' specific demands could be harnessed to useful purpose, to implement proclaimed reforms and ideals, and that the process would also integrate the new generation into the existing system. Any other course, they suggested, would only consummate the alienation of that generation, at home as seemed to be happening abroad. In later political reckonings both sides were to remember 'who stood where in that moment of visibility', as one of the participants put it at the time.[71]

Despite this disagreement, a semblance of an agreed strategy emerged and was adhered to during the critical days of the strike, except for that momentary swing towards a harder line before Tito entered the lists at the weekend. The strategy was two-pronged and its success on both counts offered insights into the new style of Yugoslav Communist politics.

First, in order to isolate the students from the workers and avoid the danger of a general strike, as had happened in France only a month earlier, street demonstrations and other activities outside university buildings were banned. Party organisations in factories throughout the country moved rapidly, with the help of what the students called 'lies' about their aims in the press, to summon workers' meetings which dutifully produced suspiciously similar letters and resolutions. Ignoring wider political issues, these agreed with the 'material demands' of the students for better living conditions and for university reform, but condemned their methods and noted that it would be the workers who would have to pay for increased education costs. Student delegates sent to factories in the Belgrade area were, with few exceptions, turned back at the gates, and some 'workers' guards' were formed to repel 'provocateurs' and 'subversive elements'. (In his television address the following Sunday Tito implied that the regime had indeed feared that the strike might spread to industry. Workers had far more to complain about than students, he said, and some officials had been 'shocked' when 'they realised what might happen if the working class were to take certain steps which would not be in harmony with our relations in a socialist society'.)

In the second place, if those urging a 'firm hand' were to be neutralised, it was necessary to manoeuvre the movement into accepting an officially sanctioned institutional and ideological framework. Whether by instinct or design, most Party members at the university had immediately (if in some cases only temporarily) accepted the justice of the student cause, championing the demonstrations and sharing the students' anger over police behaviour, the press and the country's failure to live up to proclaimed ideals. Student leaders were praised for their maturity and devotion to socialism, as demonstrated by the alleged identity of their programme with that of the LCY. Thus the movement was encouraged to keep within the broad limits of what was considered legitimate and acceptable in the post-Ranković atmosphere. Existing institutions like the Student Federation and the university's Party committee also helped channel the movement and then, during succeeding months, to split and thus demobilise it by wooing 'moderate' students and staff and isolating 'extremists', largely identified with the faculty of philosophy.

Hence an important group of Belgrade University Communists, supported by a group in the republican Party apparatus, found themselves behaving—*mirabile dictu*—as contemporary Yugoslav Communist theory said they should behave, and with success: they were decisively influencing events through persuasion and manipulation and not through power, which they temporarily lacked as a minority in a fluid situation. The reasons for this success are worth examining, for they included the only classic advantages of a Leninist Party which official Yugoslav theory had not abjured—organisational monopoly and relative coherence of ideas. The sole university organisations were either Party committees or Party-dominated. Their only rivals were student Action Committees spontaneously springing up during the first two days and with rotating memberships which precluded control by any one group, either Communist or non-Party. Though at first accepted, these Action Committees were under pressure to dissolve themselves by the end of the first week. Their continued existence then became the central issue of the second week, since their potential significance was fully realised by the better trained Marxist-Leninists in the Party.[72]

Secondly, in a situation characterised by ill-defined anger and random political discontent the 'official' university organisations also had a ready-made set of criticisms and demands on which the movement could focus. These demands happened to consist of unfulfilled clauses in the LCY programme, which contained enough participant democracy, personal liberty, social justice and anti-bureaucratic invocations to appeal to any but the most jaundiced young idealist. The student and faculty minority who regarded this as a trick to demobilise the movement were isolated and, lacking organisation or a coherent counter-programme, reduced to political impotence.

Meanwhile, higher Party and State organs were reacting with alarm and a flurry of activity. The Executive Committee and Party Presidency were hastily summoned to a meeting on June 9. Then Tito made his televised appeal to the students and the country, a fireside-chat *tour de force* by an understanding but stern grandfather asking for help to build a better future for his family. He said that the Party summit had been urgently considering accumulated economic and self-management problems since mid-

March, but agreement had eluded them and a Party commission had been appointed to make recommendations, with a mid-June deadline. Now, however, 'events have anticipated us'. It was clear that immediate action must be taken to get the economy moving, to remove obstructionists from the Party, to discipline those violating socialist norms of behaviour, and to help the low income workers who had so far borne the heaviest burden of the economic reform. Such action would fulfil the 'justified' student demands. He too tried to capture the students (successfully for the moment) by claiming that they only wanted what he himself was trying to do:

The revolt was partly a result of the fact that the students had seen that I have often raised those same questions, but that they have nevertheless remained unsettled. This time I promise the students that I am going to call wholeheartedly for the settlement of these problems, and the students should help me.... If I am not capable of solving these problems, I should no longer occupy the place where I am.

At the end of the week the results of the Party commission's hurriedly completed work were published as 'Guidelines for the most important tasks for the League of Communists in developing socio-economic and political relations'.[73] On July 16 the Central Committee met, its 9th Plenum, to evaluate these and the strike and to approve further proposals for Party reorganisation to be presented to the forthcoming Congress, which was postponed until early 1969. The meeting was also used as an authoritative forum to express strong sympathy for the Dubček regime in Czechoslovakia and to warn other socialist States against interfering.[74]

The Guidelines and the Plenum brought no major deviations from the established goals of the economic and political reforms or from the usual list of 'objective' weaknesses and of enemies of self-management. Both attempted to impress by expatiating on almost every Yugoslav economic problem, but usually without specificity, which signalled failure to agree about solutions. There was, however, some minor trimming to indicate that the reformers were beginning to take popular dissent and their intra-Party critics more seriously. Instead of the 8th Plenum's defence of laissez-faire, the Guidelines admitted the need to reform the tax system and other instruments to enable the State to exert some corrective influence over the market, though they were reluctant to go further than absolutely necessary in this direction. They suggested direct multilateral consultations and agreements among 'self-managers' to resolve such problems as employment, income distribution, prices and social services, thus obviating the need for more State intervention in these fields. (Here was the germ of another idea, which was to grow into a full-fledged, formal system of decision-making by 'self-management agreements' and 'social compacts' enshrined in 1971 constitutional amendments and then in the 1974

Constitution.) But if State control might be necessary to prevent 'unjustifiable enrichment' through illegal activities or imperfect competition, there could be no question of *uravnilovka* or 'Mao's equality in poverty', which some students seemed to demand. Even large income disparities, if they reflected differences in skill, productivity or value as judged by the market, were defiantly defended as beneficial and not merely unavoidable 'at the present stage of socialist commodity production'.

The Guidelines and Todorović's keynote speech to the Plenum returned repeatedly to the implications of the Belgrade student strike, which was now regarded as having on balance more negative than positive dimensions. Tito himself had given the signal for a tougher interpretation in a speech to the opening session of a Trade Union Congress on June 26, less than three weeks after his televised eulogy of the movement's 'socialist orientation'. He now said that he stood by what he had said then, but wished to enlarge on his passing allusion at that time to 'alien elements' trying to infiltrate the universities. These elements, with their diverse interests and ideologies, 'seem today to have united' and 'are at one in their effort to create some sort of chaos in our country, or to fish in troubled waters'.[75] Todorović said that the movement was being used by the united opposition of all anti-socialist forces, whom he enumerated: 'counter-revolutionary circles from émigré centres, vestiges of the class enemy, nationalists and unitarists of all shades, Rankovićite, Cominformist and other neo-Stalinist elements, pseudo-liberals and others'. These forces had become aware that the movement's criticism, drawing on the views of certain professors who were describing present Yugoslav policies 'as a path which leads to the dehumanisation of man and social relations and to the restoration of capitalism', represented 'a current which can discredit our socialism better than plain reactionaries and Stalinists can'.[76]

The drafters of the Guidelines and organisers of the Plenum seem to have hoped that an unprecedently frank confession of past failure and detailed but vague promises to do better in future, propagated with great fanfare and accompanied by an upturn in key economic indicators becoming perceptible in mid-1968, would pass for action and thus calm the political atmosphere. In fact an admission of failure without serious remedial action—there were no real policy changes, only a sullen determination to identify all critics as 'objectively' enemies of socialist democracy—seemed singularly unlikely to have the desired effect. In particular the students and their professors had much reason for bitterness. Their own moderation and readiness for dialogue rather than confrontation and Tito's apparent sympathy and promises of satisfaction all seemed cruelly betrayed, the latter a trick to disperse them for the summer holidays before moving against them. By the end of July observers were anticipating a hot time in the quadrangle when the academic year began in the autumn.

Instead, on August 21, 1968, the armies of the Soviet Union and four other Warsaw Pact States occupied Czechoslovakia. The threat to Yugoslavia which seemed to be posed by the invasion and its subsequent justification in the 'Brezhnev Doctrine', proclaiming a Soviet right to intervene in any Communist-ruled State whenever Soviet leaders considered socialism to be endangered there, temporarily silenced the critics and changed their and the regime's views of the outside world and their own situation. One figure sums up the magnitude of the change: in the course of 1968 about 100,000 young people under the age of 25 joined the LCY, nearly doubling the size of that age cohort in the Party. The overwhelming majority of them joined after August 21.

The impact of Czechoslovakia

Yugoslav Government and Party spokesmen and all but the most unreconstructedly anti-Communist or neo-Stalinist among articulate citizenry had repeatedly expressed their enthusiasm over developments in Czechoslovakia under Alexander Dubček's leadership during the first seven months of 1968. The media reported extensively and sympathetically the evolution of Dubček's 'socialism with a human face', and much of the reporting from Prague reflected a search for real or imagined analogies with recent Yugoslav experience, especially in terms of a struggle between 'conservative' and 'progressive' Communist forces in both States. It was pointed out that the Czechs and Slovaks, like the Yugoslavs, had started with a necessary liberalising reform of an obsolete economic system, had then discovered that the new economic model required a 'democratisation' of political life and a new role for the Party as well, and now found themselves struggling to remove those in the Party who continued to disagree with and attempt to sabotage the new course. A further analogy was found in the important role played by solidarity between Czechoslovak writers and the 'technological intelligentsia' in demanding liberalisation. Emphasis was placed on the 'return' to or 'revival' of pre-1948 democratic traditions in Czechoslovakia, after years of disappointment that the only industrially developed Communist-ruled State with a genuine democratic past should have taken so long to move toward 'democratic socialism'.

At the end of April 1968 Tito had visited Moscow, where the situation in Prague and growing Soviet alarm over trends there were among the topics discussed. After the August invasion, he revealed that he had warned the Russians at that meeting: 'Just don't try anything with force, for that would lead to a catastrophic situation'.[77]

During the summer the links connecting Yugoslavia, Romania and Czechoslovakia were reinforced by a series of meetings, culminating in dramatic successive visits to Prague, only a week before the invasion, by Tito and Nicolae Ceauşescu, the Romanian President and Party leader. Western commentators spoke of a revival of the interwar Little Entente, which had allied these same States in defence of their independence and territorial integrity—then against the threat of a Habsburg restoration, now against the threat of a neo-Stalinist one. This was potentially dangerous in view of the Soviet Union's visibly hardening attitude, but Yugoslav leaders afterwards admitted that they never imagined—except for a few anxious days in July, just before the Soviet-Czechoslovak meeting at Cierna—that Soviet reaction could take the form of a sudden military intervention. Like Dubček and many Western observers, the Yugoslavs had focused on two factors which they believed were strong enough to preclude a solution by force: the new Czechoslovak leadership had taken infinite pains not to repeat the mistakes made by the Imre Nagy Government in Hungary in 1956, provoking Russian intervention; and the Soviet regime itself was thought to have evolved too far from Stalinism, to value too highly its remaining influence over key non-bloc Parties, and to be too much interested in East-West détente to dare undertake such a move. Warsaw Pact troop movements along Czechoslovakia's borders were interpreted as no more than a threatening demonstration to put new pressure on the Prague Government.

The invasion of August 21 therefore caught the Yugoslavs by surprise—and on vacation. Members of the Party Presidium and Executive Committee were hastily hauled back from their holidays by jet, helicopter and speedboat to an emergency evening meeting at Tito's retreat on the Brioni islands, where they issued a statement condemning the 'aggression' against Czechoslovakia and the 'trampling of Czechoslovak sovereignty' by armies of five Warsaw Pact States. The full Central Committee assembled in Belgrade two days later and heard Tito—just back from a hasty meeting with Ceauşescu on the Yugoslav-Romanian border—declare that, if Yugoslavia's own independence should now be threatened, 'we shall know how to defend and protect it with all means against whatever side the threat comes from'. Tito also drew a parallel between the invasion, carried out to stop a 'progressive evolution' in Czechoslovakia and prevent its 'rapid' spread to other socialist States, and Stalin's campaign against Yugoslavia: 'The glorious proletarian red flag was dirtied once already in 1948, but we have done much to clean the mud from it. Now it has fallen again. Whether we shall succeed in cleaning it as quickly now—that is a question.'

By mid-October a balanced strategy for a Yugoslav defensive posture in the face of the new threat from the East had emerged. It reflected a careful evaluation of the options for pressure available to the Russians and was designed to check them one by one:

First, encouraged by the mild Western response to the invasion and reckoning that they had already paid a maximum price in terms of world opinion and alienation of key West European Communist Parties, the Russians just might be considering a clean military sweep—while they were at it, so to speak—of the remaining dissident Communist States in Eastern Europe.[78] It was therefore to be made abundantly clear to them that the Yugoslavs, unlike the Czechs and Slovaks, would fight hard and long if their country were invaded. Firm statements to this effect were issued at all levels, backed by mass meetings to demonstrate public support. Some reserves were called up, exposed invasion routes were mined, and paramilitary youth volunteer brigades were organised and trained. In addition to these immediate emergency precautions, the regime undertook a long-range redirection and restructuring of its defence establishment and strategy. An 'All-National Defence' law was rushed through the Federal Assembly. It attempted for the first time in history, according to the Yugoslavs, to codify and institutionalise Partisan-style warfare, integrating regular and irregular armed forces, as a small country's basic strategic defence concept. Under the new law all Yugoslavs between the ages of 18 and 65 were to have their combat assignments: in the regular armed forces; in civil defence and subsequently in sabotage and harassment units in the cities, which would be lost to enemy occupation after an initial defence of the frontiers; or in guerrilla units in the mountains and their supporting village organisations.[79] In short, the Russians were warned that Yugoslavia would become their Vietnam if they attempted a military solution.

A second possible Soviet option was a resumption of Eastern bloc economic sanctions, on the limited scale of 1958-60 if not the total blockade of 1948-54. The Yugoslavs responded on two fronts. They sent up a series of signals to Moscow indicating their desire to maintain normal and expanding economic relations with the East despite deteriorating political relations. As a reserve line, they accelerated efforts to increase trade and credit arrangements with the West, including in particular a commercial agreement with the EEC, already by far their most important trading partner, and new credit lines to the World Bank and the US Export-Import Bank.

Third, on the ideological and propaganda front they rejected the counsel of the cautious, who advised presenting a low-profile target to Soviet bloc polemics, and elected to strike back. When the Soviet press called them 'revisionist' or even 'capitalist', and wrote disparagingly of growing unemployment and inequality and the failure of the reform in Yugoslavia, the Yugoslav press replied by again disparaging the Soviet economy as 'State socialism' and by reporting objectively, for the first time since the early 1950s, on standards of living and wage differentials in the Soviet bloc. Tito himself noted that the Eastern bloc condemned the Yugoslav economic model while their citizens rushed to Yugoslavia, when they could get a passport, to buy the good things of life which that economy produced in quantity and quality unequalled at home. When the bloc press condemned workers' councils as an anarchosyndicalist deviation and the downgrading of the role of the Yugoslav Party as an anti-Leninist hazarding of the whole socialist revolution, the Yugoslavs revived their 1950-52 analyses of the Soviet political system as centralistic-authoritarian and wrote of the stifling lack of individual and enterprise freedom in the bloc.[80]

Fourth, precautions were also undertaken to watch and neutralise the activities of domestic groups or individuals who, for various motives, might be tempted to exploit Soviet pressures—or be exploited by them—in order to discredit Yugoslavia's 'revisionist' reforms and overthrow the reformers from within.

Later, when it became apparent that the invasion psychosis of the autumn of 1968 had been wildly exaggerated if not totally unjustified, and while first inter-State and then inter-Party relations with the Soviet Union were gradually normalised, the last of these precautions remained on the agenda, along with a more explicitly 'all-azimuths' development of 'all-national defence'. The more enduring legacy of Czechoslovakia was to be a renewal of deep suspicions in the minds of many or most Yugoslav leaders concerning Soviet intentions, which again seemed more threatening than the pattern of an American-led imperialist offensive which had preoccupied those same minds only a few months earlier.

The Yugoslav 'political underground' drew its strength from adverse economic conditions, the humbling of the Serbs since July 1966 and nationalist 'excesses' by other nationalities. If the Russians still or again really had designs upon Yugoslavia, whether in terms of short-run pressures or of long-run speculation with the after-Tito-what question, would they not exploit this discontent, attempting to turn the 'political underground' into a Soviet party in Yugoslavia? And was there not much which would lend itself to such a strategy in the platform and ill-assorted philosophies of the underground—the conservatives' nostalgia for a Leninist type of Party, the underdeveloped areas' yearning for a return to distribution by a centrally-planned command economy, the

Serbian nationalists' traditional pro-Russianism and the dissenting students' disgust with the consumerism, inequalities and corruption of market socialism? These things were, after all, the precise targets of the criticisms being levelled against Yugoslav socialism by the Soviet bloc press in the new polemical war which began after the Yugoslavs condemned the occupation of Czechoslovakia.

Certain logical conclusions followed for those who wanted them to. In a 1969 interview with Latinka Perović, the new secretary of the Serbian Party's Executive Committee, the present writer contrasted her now critical attitude towards the Belgrade student movement with her generally positive evaluation of it in a June 1968 speech. 'But that', she replied, 'was before the events in Czechoslovakia. Since last August we must judge these things again.' It must be remembered how strong 'political conservatism' still was and that there were ultra-egalitarian tendencies at the university and in the LCY; 'the ideological horizons' of the people of the past phase of the Yugoslav revolution were still present. 'Stalinism grew out of the nature of the Soviet system, not out of some "cult of the personality"—and we cannot say that we do not still have the preconditions for a Stalinism in our society!'

This judgement and the political values and strategic concepts implicit in it were representative of those who had consolidated their positions in the leadership of the Serbian Party at its December 1968 Congress, and of their like-minded colleagues of the post-Ranković liberal ascendancy in other capitals, especially Zagreb, Ljubljana and Skopje. Equally typical and revealing was her further evaluation of the 'current phase', which she described as 'a hermaphrodite system, moving towards political pluralism within a Socialist Alliance framework'. One saw, for example in the 1969 elections, that there was no longer a central place of decision-making. The question was whether Yugoslavs could accept the consequences of 'our opening to a free struggle among ideas', which also involved one among different interests, 'and, after Czechoslovakia, a struggle between theories'. There would have to be a search for greater tolerance, but if a Czechoslovak type of solution was to be avoided, when it came to 'political actions which divide us', the LCY must have and act according to its own standpoints. 'What is needed is a factor—the League of Communists—which is democratic in structure and decision-making but which knows what it wants and works for it consistently.'

The strengths and weaknesses and the basic ambivalence of the Communist 'Whigs' in the reform coalition were all implicit in statements like this. The strengths included determination and at least tactical consistency deriving from a deep and genuine belief that Yugoslav socialism could and must include progressively more participant democracy, a generally accurate weighing of the motives and strengths of the political forces opposing such an opening to the masses, and greater confidence than most of the older generation of Party leaders in manoeuvring in a more open and pluralistic political system. Their weakness was in failing to analyse fully the implications of the conversion of the LCY from a Leninist cadre Party, a 'party as an organisational weapon', into six federated, democratically structured and numerically large élites, bound by ideology and theoretically enjoying the advantages of 'knowing what they want and working for it consistently', operating in a 'political pluralism within a Socialist Alliance framework'. Success in this endeavour, to paraphrase Peter Blau's description of the dynamics of an ordinary mass party's interaction with society,[81] would destroy what was left of the boundary between the League and other institutionalised aggregations of social interests. In so far as the League, subdivided in six parts, then remained important as something more than *primus inter pares* in the decision-making system—partly because it had previously co-opted most other élites into its membership and partly because of its inter-institutional universality of competence—its primary function would be to serve as a locus for competition and exchange among representatives of functional or ethnic interests whose principal aim would be to win dominant influence over its programme and policies.

If it were thus reduced to the status of a neutral and partly *entideolisierte* market place, or a confederation of six such market places, what would remain of the League's original and ideal function as a pure revolutionary force, above particular interests in theory and in practice encumbered by only a random minimum of unbreakable commitments to other social forces?

Such considerations had an immediate practical relevance, which was one reason for the ambivalence of the reform politicians, however imprecisely they perceived it. On the basis of recent evidence concerning the strengths of the forces and ideas defined as the 'political underground' in the Party catechism, and considering the weakness and immaturity of the 'forces of self-management' catalogued in recent Party documents, it was hazardous to calculate *a priori* that the sum of the complex political equation generated by this process would not after all 'divert the policy of democratisation either towards the conceptions of a bourgeois State ... or towards the restoration of State-bureaucratic or technocratic absolutism'—as the 1968 'Guidelines' had defined the two dangers threatening the Yugoslav experiment. If either of these seemed to be the price of pluralism, who would be the ultimate protectors of the Yugoslav road to socialism, and what would they do then?

7

THE PRICE OF PLURALISM

Dissent revived, and the Croatian strategy

The calm induced in the domestic political atmosphere by the external threat which the Yugoslavs saw in the occupation of Czechoslovakia did not last long. The first dramatic break came while official and public nervousness about immediate Soviet intentions was still at a high pitch and on the very eve of celebrations of the new Yugoslavia's official twenty-fifth birthday, November 29, 1968. It took the form of widespread, apparently well-organised, and sometimes violent demonstrations by Albanians in the Kosovo Autonomous Province, significantly timed to coincide with neighbouring Albania's own National Day, on November 27, and less than a week after the minority's problems had had an unusually open airing at the 6th Congress of the League of Communists of Serbia. Instead of being gratefully satisfied with the considerable increase in equality and personal security which they had enjoyed since the taming of the Province's Serb-dominated UDBa after July 1966, politicised strata of the rapidly growing minority, now nearly 1 million in number, were demanding more of the same and the transformation of their region into a seventh Yugoslav republic in which the Albanians, as the local majority, would in fact be politically dominant.[1] The demonstrations in Kosovo and their echoes in western Macedonia, alarming in scale and in the context of historic Greater Albanian irredentism, also witnessed the return of the national question to centre stage among Yugoslavia's problems. Bakarić's prophecy of March 1966, that nationalism would become the country's 'question number one' if the battle for the reform were not won quickly, was coming true.

There had been a number of other reminders of its continuing centrality during the twenty months since the uproar surrounding the Croatian 'Declaration' and Serbian 'Proposal' of March 1967. Slovenes and Macedonians had pressed vociferously for greater recognition of their languages at the federal level; the results included the introduction of equipment for simultaneous translation in the Federal Assembly after the elections of 1967.[2] In

October 1967 the Croatian Central Committee purged one of its more distinguished members, Večeslav Holjevac, a respected former Major of Zagreb and member of the Croatian Government. He was accused of 'nationalistic deviations' in his leadership of the Centre for Croatian Emigrants, a quasi-governmental institution then considered a nationalist hotbed.[3]

In post-Ranković Serbia the activities of the 'political underground' and the importance of nationalist elements in it made it seem for a time that a Serbian nationalist backlash would present the most serious problem on this front. The Serbian Party leadership, until the November 1968 Party Congress still largely comprised of only relatively uncompromised holdovers from Ranković's day and during 1968 headed by one of these, the former FEC President Petar Stambolić, reacted with demonstrative hyper-sensitivity. At a May 1968 meeting of the republican Central Committee, two members, the historian Jovan Marjanović and the writer Dobrica Ćosić, ventured to criticise manifestations of Albanian and Magyar nationalism in Kosovo and the Vojvodina. Albanian 'nationalism and irredentism' were being openly promoted in Kosovo, they said, and Serbs were suffering systematic discrimination in current employment policies in the Province. As evidence they cited the emigration from Kosovo of an increasing number of Serbs and Montenegrins, 'especially the intelligentsia'. They also expressed concern that a supranational sense of Yugoslav identity was no longer being encouraged, as it should be in order to bring the Yugoslav peoples closer together, and that declaring oneself a 'Yugoslav' in a census or on forms was now actively discouraged. 'Bureaucratic and nationalistic or republican forces' were in fact supporting their own narrow nationalisms under the cover of a struggle against 'unitarism', Marjanović warned. Although both also criticised several specific manifestations of Serbian nationalism, they were condemned by their colleagues for being 'nationalistic' and 'opposed to self-management'; that they were not actually purged from the Central Committee was probably because the Serbian Congress was then only six months away and would provide a less dramatic way to drop them, which it did. Considering the past and later records of both men as genuinely Yugoslav patriots, far less tainted with Serbian nationalism than most members of the Committee, their condemnation seemed—even more clearly than the Holjevac case—an excess of anti-nationalist zeal, or a classic case of scapegoatism.[4]

It is against the background of the apparent intensification of divisive nationalist sentiment—only partly explainable in terms of greater freedom to express such sentiments openly—and of inter-republican tensions and disputes that the behaviour of the post-Ranković leadership is to be understood. They clung stubbornly to as much as they could of the laissez-faire spirit imbuing the 1965 reform, even after the student strike and Trades Union Congress of June 1968 had, each in its own way, demanded action to deal with serious economic problems. They concentrated their attention instead on further reforms of the Federation and the further 'federalisation' of the Party. They did both of these things because they continued to view the continuing resistance to modernisation and pluralism by the remaining bastions of 'bureaucratic centralism' (a label which focused attention on the federal administration and federal Party apparatus) as the Gordian knot which made the solution of all other problems impossible. Only when the knot was cut and these bastions were finally rendered defenceless—by taking away their remaining economic weapons or by manning them with delegates of regionally and functionally plural interests—would the danger of a quasi-Stalinist, centralist, and putatively Serb-dominated authoritarian restoration vanish. Then and only then could the State again intervene in the economy, at appropriate levels from Federation to commune and with modern fiscal rather than administrative instruments, as a stabiliser and corrector of what inter-enterprise 'self-managing agreements' and 'social compacts' could not stabilise or correct. As a leading Serbian politician of this persuasion told the present writer in 1969:

We are not economic illiterates, as some economists suggest. We know what needs to be done and the costs of delay. But we see, as they do not, the *political* dangers of doing it too soon, before both the people and the mentality which could lead us backwards have been thoroughly eliminated, and this is a long process.

At the same time, most of the reformers believed that cutting the Gordian knot of residual centralism was the only way of definitively solving the national question. Its solution in this way, in effect an extension of the policy of killing nationalism with kindness implicit in Yugoslav federalism since 1943, constituted in their eyes the prerequisite of a more open and competitive political system which would not promptly degenerate into sterile interethnic squabbling. Otherwise there would be an eventual return to centralised, authoritarian suppression of centrifugal nationalisms. Still convinced by the classic Marxist argument that national tensions and nationalism will disappear when the economic reasons for them are eliminated, they thought that the nationalists who would inevitably appear on a more open political stage would find no significant following if there were no longer a central pie, whether of funds or of patronage, to quarrel over.

It was only natural, given the personalities of Bakarić's disciples in Zagreb, the special Croatian interest in opposing any Belgrade-based centralism and the role that Croats had already played in drafting the Reform and in overthrowing Ranković, that leadership in articulating and promoting a political strategy to achieve these ends should come from Croatia. It was also for the moment vital to hope of success that it should be so. Until their like-minded colleagues in the new Serbian leadership had consolidated their hold on that republic's Party apparatus, which only happened in November 1968, and as long as these Serbian leaders must contest control of republican and local State apparatuses and Serbian public opinion with those who were sullenly determined to regard Ranković's fall as a Serbian humiliation, only the Croat anti-centralists could lay claim to a constituency so large and united that it demanded attention. The rest must resign themselves to the role of necessary auxiliaries. The fate of Yugoslavia, as always, would ultimately be decided by Serbs and Croats, together or in opposition.

The political strategy of the Croatian leaders during 1967-68 concentrated on two targets.

They urged further decentralisation and also further 'democratisation' of Party and polity. These should be achieved through simultaneous action on four fronts: through constitutional changes which would further emasculate the federal centre (the 1967 and 1968 amendments proved to be only first steps in this direction); by relaxing the rules of 'democratic centralism', permitting minority voices to be heard; through an increased say for ordinary citizens in direct, competitive elections and in distribution of enterprise earnings (which would be larger after further reducing federal taxes and fiscal powers); and through a purge of older Communists unwilling or unable to play by the new rules. Part of their reasoning was certainly based on considerations of personal and Croatian political advantage. Weakening democratic centralism would weaken the remaining power of the federal Party centre over republican centres, while an opening to the masses was expected to strengthen the position of young, 'modern' Communist politicians like themselves, who believed that they knew how to speak the language of the people and how to manage a more open political system. It was also a strategy which enabled them to enjoy and exploit the advantages of labelling their 'unitarist' opponents as old-fashioned, unprogressive, sceptical of socialist democracy and self-management, and unjustifiably fearful of the ability of 'socialist ideas' to triumph in 'an open, democratic political dialogue and confrontation'.

Such people, Tripalo told a Party meeting in Rijeka in January 1968, represented a 'ballast from the past' which included old Partisans 'who do not agree that anything is being done right now... [who] are completely demoralised'; and there is no reason for them to stay in the League of Communists'. They and others still in influential positions, including some who had participated in the coalition which brought Ranković down, were as 'bureaucratic' in outlook as Ranković himself. It was these people who were now blocking further progress:

> Regardless of the fact that there is probably no one personality around which this bureaucratic-conservative opposition could gather, because we are a multi-national country, we should not neglect the fact, Comrades, that in all our republics, including Croatia, there is an ideological-political platform for these forces, for the forces who feel that self-management leads to the collapse of a socialist society, who feel that one should return to the old administrative-bureaucratic and centralist system.[5]

While they pursued these goals affecting State and Party organisation and cadres, the Croatian leadership also vigorously attacked continuing federal control of most foreign currency (a particularly sensitive issue in Croatia, as already described), former federal banks with seats in the capital and former federal funds in their safes (one of the key issues not settled in the 1965 reform), and certain wealthy foreign trade enterprises which had been founded, financed and staffed by Serbian-dominated federal institutions and capital before the reform and which were now exercising what many besides the Croats regarded as an alarming and exploitative country-wide power. The slogans were 'federal-isation of former federal capital' and 'clear accounts' (*čisti računi*), which would allow each republic to see what it was contributing to and getting from the Federation and make appropriate decisions about future contributions.

In advancing all these arguments the Zagreb leadership could claim that they were not only defending the interests of Croatian entrepreneurs and workers, and thus the Croatian nation. Theirs was also a defence of the interests of all 'producers' who, in Yugoslav Communist theory, should have control over the 'surplus value' of their labour which was being 'expropriated' by Belgrade bureaucracy, Belgrade banks and the grasping tentacles of those Belgrade-based foreign trade enterprises.

Implicitly underlying this line of attack were other ethnic and historical considerations. The metaphor for all that was outdated, centralist, and authoritarian was 'Belgrade'. Belgrade, the capital of Serbia. Serbia, whose notorious 'Serbian bourgeoisie' had ruled and ruthlessly exploited richer, more sophisticated Croatia and Slovenia in prewar Yugoslavia, and who had recently attempted a repeat performance with Ranković and a Serbian-dominated Party and police bureaucracy. Serbian politicians, primitive by education, hardfisted by training, and therefore 'neo-Stalinist' or at least 'dogmatic Communist' by definition. Serbian hegemony, exploita-tive and authoritarian, the primary—perhaps the only—reason why

Croatia was not already as rich and democratic as ... Denmark? The Croatian strategy had from the start two faces: one national, one socialist. As early as 1967, before and after the language crisis, the new leadership had become sensitive to the charge that in their opening to the masses in the name of decentralisation they were playing with Croatian nationalism.

Meanwhile, the programme of the LCY and the national interests of the Croatian nation both called for 'decentralisation, de-etatisation, depoliticisation, and democratisation'. There was no contradiction here, and the enthusiastic support of the Croatian masses—which, as in any society, meant the politicised minority that had found means to articulate its feelings—was further proof, if any were needed, that their course was correct. So, too, were their numerous allies in other republics and regions: the Slovenes, whose anti-centralist economic interests were the same; the Macedonians, whose defensive new nationalism and consequent fear of Serbian hegemony had come to weigh more heavily than the financial benefits they had gained as an underdeveloped region from centralised redistribution of national income; and others, even in the new Serbian leadership, whose interests or ideological convictions made them also anti-centralist. With such strength at home and elsewhere in the Federation and with growing self-confidence, Bakarić's disciples pressed their case uncompromisingly and vigorously.

Paralysis in a power vacuum

The strategy devised by the anti-centralist regional leaders was feasible as long as it did not matter very much whether Yugoslavia had a central authority capable of serious activity. Unfortunately for them, conditions fulfilling this requirement prevailed for only a brief period, coinciding roughly with the incumbency of Špiljak's 'do-nothing' FEC, and even then only on the assumption that the post-reform recession would run its course without major upheavals or increased intervention by the State. What ultimately frustrated the purposes of the reformers was that past or new problems, particularly economic ones of a kind requiring sternly-enforced remedies of an all-Yugoslav character, were becoming more serious and would not wait for them to finish the job. When they realised this, a realisation symbolised by Špiljak's replacement after the elections of 1969, they were to find that the particular quality of their partial but still incomplete success would prevent them or anyone else doing anything effective about it.[6]

The upturn in production which began in the third quarter of 1968 continued. The growth rate of Social Product in the four years 1968-71 was again to average 8 per cent per year, with a high of 10 per cent in 1969. Industrial output in these four years grew by 43 per cent, compared with 20 per cent during the quadrennium of the recession; by 1971 it would stand at 674 per cent of the 1952 level. Employment, which had continued to stagnate through 1968, began to rise at an average annual rate of about 4 per cent.

While this was all singularly welcome news, there were serious imbalances, and the usual negative side effects which always accompanied booms were proving even larger and more troublesome than normal. After two years of relative stability, the official cost of living index increased by 5 per cent in 1968, by 8 per cent in 1969, by 11 per cent in 1970 and by 16 per cent in 1971; most observers thought real increases were even higher. The problem of liquidity became so acute that workers in a number of enterprises were forced to go without pay, sometimes for several months. In foreign trade the gap between exports and imports widened until the trade deficit in 1971 reached a record US$1,437 million out of a total turnover of $5,000 million. In the same year the percentage of imports covered by exports fell to 55·5 per cent from 84·7 per cent in 1965 and 73·3 per cent in 1967. Despite a growing surplus in invisibles, particularly tourism and remittances from workers abroad, the balance of payments deficit continued to grow, reaching $434 million in 1971.[7] Meanwhile, with new age cohorts coming into the job market still at postwar maximum size, the renewed increase in employment remained inadequate even to stop the growth in the number of persons forced to emigrate each year in search of work or better jobs, much less to absorb those returning. The official total of Yugoslav *Gastarbeiter* in Western Europe was approaching 800,000 by 1969, nearly 22 per cent of total domestic employment, both public and private. However welcome their remittances, they represented a political embarrassment to a socialist regime, future social problems and hostages to the continuing economic prosperity and racial sentiments of their host countries.

Effective intervention was urgently required and eagerly sought, beginning in 1969, but was not forthcoming. The emasculation of the ability of central apparatuses to make decisions had by then proceeded so far that it was necessary to secure the agreement of most or all regional leaderships before measures affecting general interests could be adopted or enforced. At the same time, the dynamics of the intervening political struggle and the passions it had aroused were making such agreement more difficult to obtain than ever.

Officals of the now virtually autonomous regional and local Party organisations and governments, no longer fearing reprimand or dismissal from the federal centre, were still subject to sanctions or pressures from their peers in their own republics. In the increasingly public political marketplace where federal policy was debated and still sizeable federal funds were collected and disbursed, it was therefore more important than of old that they faithfully represent and be seen to represent the interests of these constituents. At the same time, their leverage in negotiations over these matters would be increased if they could point convincingly to mass support back home. In mobilising and in using such support there was frequently an overwhelming temptation to play the nationalist card, historically the easiest way of arousing popular enthusiasm, while simultaneously frightening one's negotiating partners with the implicit threat that nationalist forces might get out of hand if one's demands were not met.

Thus regional leaders tended with mounting urgency and recklessness to pose as national leaders, defending the interests of 'their' nation against attempted exploitation or domination by others and accepting the help of those whom they chose to define as 'moderate' or 'harmless' nationalists in or outside the Party. The kind of Communists who had been drummed out of office or the Party as recently as 1967 for displaying their nationalism too freely returned to the fray, brazenly stating, publishing and winning applause for sometimes fair but often irresponsible accusations of discrimination against their nation's language, its share of the national income or its representation in Party, State or army cadres, or in employment.[8]

In such an atmosphere it was increasingly difficult to make the necessary concessions to achieve the consensus which a *de facto* veto power had rendered obligatory, or to aggregate opinions on any except an ethnic and republican basis.

In 1970, for example, the Croatian leaders were to propose reforms of the banking, foreign trade and foreign currency systems which were unacceptable to the authorities of at least four other federal units. The Federal Government meanwhile proposed a package of anti-inflationary stabilisation measures which was unacceptable to the Croatian leaders. Nothing was done. The only important measure actually carried through was an unavoidable devaluation of the dinar (in January 1971), which miserably failed to accomplish anything positive that a devaluation should accomplish because it was unsupported by other effective measures. Exports stagnated, and imports increased at an accelerating rate. So did inflation, in defiance of a formal price freeze, the ineffectiveness of which revealed the federal administration's almost total impotence. Similarly without effect was another continuing Croatian-led campaign, for restrictions on the monopolistic behaviour of those notorious Belgrade-based foreign trade conglomerates which were said to be 'buying up the Croatian economy'. Only after Croatian spokesmen on this issue fell from power at the end of 1971 did some Serbian leaders admit that they, too, had been just as troubled by the implications of these monopolies, but had felt unable to say so 'as long as the Croats made the issue into a Croatian national question'.[9]

There was also little possibility of dealing with these issues at the republican level, even when the nature of a problem was theoretically susceptible to solution at that level. The republican and provincial apparatuses, despite their new political weight, lacked commensurate economic power. Monetary and fiscal instruments and two key tax powers (the turnover and capital taxes) remained in the hands of the immobilised federal administration. An important fraction of total investment funds remained in the former 'federal' banks, located in the federal capital, and partly still under federal control. Thus the power of the regional authorities was still almost entirely negative: they could veto but they could not implement policies of their own in the areas in which this now mattered most.

While it was generally agreed as early as 1969 that the situation was becoming intolerable, there was no agreement as to what should be done about it. The dispute was still essentially about the future primary locus of the power to make and implement effective public choices. There was nothing new in this, or even in the basic line-up of individuals and regional-ethnic groups behind alternative solutions. What was new was the *present* locus of such power. It had once been in a definable place, in the federal Party and State apparatuses, and the argument was about whether it should stay there or be decentralised in one way or another. A series of incomplete victories by the 'decentralisers' had now largely destroyed those centres, but without in fact defining the legatees. As a result, power by the late 1960s was nowhere and everywhere, in greater and smaller accumulations, creating a quasi-anarchy of diffused decision-making with reduced responsibility (since anonymous power is irresponsible power) and a free-for-all scramble to collect the pieces. The one thing that was clear, however sincere the reformers had or had not been in claiming the opposite since 1965, was that 'the forces of self-management', now said to be suffering 'a certain stagnation in development', were not yet ready to pick them all up unaided.[10]

There were only three other possible solutions. One could restore the federal centre's power to make binding decisions without a consensus, either arbitrarily or on the basis of some kind of majority vote. One could finish the job of destroying the centre by transferring the remaining instruments of an independent economic policy to the republics and provinces, creating a loose confederation with no country-wide solutions for country-wide problems. Or one could find new modalities for effective decision-making by inter-republican consensus.

The first option, while gaining more secret or 'off-the-record' advocates as the stalemate continued,[11] was still anathema to the reformers and the republican or provincial interests they represented, who had made anti-centralism into an official fetish of such magnitude that no one could for the moment openly advocate a strengthening of the federal apparatuses. It could therefore only be mentioned as an undesirable alternative which might be imposed by events in the absence of any other solution, a consideration which now gave rise to alarmist café talk about a possible military coup d'état or one variant of a scenario for Soviet intervention, à la Czechoslovakia, to 'save socialism' in Yugoslavia.

Some of the reformers pursued the second solution, which in effect meant holding *faute de mieux* to the strategy of the preceding two years. Others pursued the third. In either case, their efforts completed an at most partly conscious and wilful inversion of the rank order of the cardinal political values of the reformist wing of the Yugoslav Party, which were self-management and national emancipation. Such an inversion had already been implicit in the predominant role of republican Party barons in the victorious coalition of 1965–66, and had already begun to receive constitutional sanction in the amendments of 1967 and 1968. Its central feature was a gradual shift from one concept of decentralisation and principle of aggregation to another, which was fundamentally different. The first aspired to pluralistic decision-making through essentially syndicalist or corporativist mechanisms, by delegates of 'working people' grouped according to economic and social functions. The second aspired to pluralistic decision-making on the basis of territorially focused ethnic groups. The first had received its clearest expression in the Constitution of 1963; the second surfaced gradually through amendments to it. The distinction was for some time obscured by the alliance of advocates of both concepts in the struggle against 'centralist unitarism' which characterised the 1960s, and also by the fact that the choice was as unclear in the minds of individual players as their motives were mixed. It has already been suggested that many of them really did see republican and provincial 'sovereignty' as a prerequisite and guarantor of 'self-management' (whether understood as management by managers or really by workers, always an important subdivision), and not as an alternative and an end in itself. Nevertheless, the retreat of the 'bureaucratic centralist' enemy was being marked by institutional changes which seemed to be moving in the latter direction.

The Party Congresses of 1968-69

The 9th LCY Congress, which met in Belgrade during the week of March 11, 1969, was not to be a Congress of compromise, as the 8th had been. The debate would be freer than ever before, and the draft resolutions would be subjected to an unprecedented number of amendments, some of them substantive in nature. There would actually be divisions in the voting on these, occasionally close, and it was publicly admitted that vagueness or platitudinous generalisations in phrasing on certain issues could be correctly interpreted as signifying lack of agreement and specific compromises yet to come.[12] It was nevertheless on balance a Congress of triumph and consolidation for the persons and ideas of the liberalising economic and political reforms which had taken place since the last such gathering in 1964.

It was also unlike the 8th Congress, but like all others since 1948, in being held without the presence of guest delegations from the Communist Parties of the Soviet Union and other Communist States except Romania. The Russians and the others who had participated in the occupation of Czechoslovakia were invited but were still expressing their displeasure over the Yugoslav Party's initial and continuing if gradually less demonstrative disapproval of that action. The Czechoslovak Party itself, with Dubček still formally in charge, timorously if reluctantly joined the boycott and was criticised at home and in Yugoslavia for ingratitude in not defying the Russians on a minor issue and joining the Romanians in Belgrade.

One other side effect of the Yugoslavs' heightened concern with military and ideological defence and search for domestic unifying factors after Czechoslovakia was an elevation of the status of the Party organisation in the Yugoslav People's Army and its representation in higher Party organs. The 9th Plenum of the Central Committee, meeting just before the August 1968 invasion, had decided that army representatives should be included in the Party Presidency which was to be proposed to the 9th Congress. Party members in the army should also have a separate congress, parallel and equal to those of the republican and provincial Parties. The 1st Conference of the LCY in the Yugoslav People's Army was duly held, at the end of the regional series, in February 1969.[13]

As the anti-centralists had intended when they scheduled them to take place first, these republican, provincial, and army congresses and conferences, held between November 1968 and February 1969, were for the first time worthy of greater attention than the federal Congress itself, which was to produce only one important surprise. The regional meetings nominated the people who would comprise the new federal Party organs, and who would receive only formal confirmation at the federal Congress. They also formulated occasionally conflicting standpoints which the subsequent all-Yugoslav meeting would merely co-ordinate and endorse or silently consent to regard as matters of continuing disagreement. In addition, they set a new political style, which was also *mutatis mutandis* to characterise the parliamentary elections of 1969 and in which the reformers sought their own particular reconciliation of the contradictory principles of greater freedom and safety for their own controlling positions.

The first characteristic of the new political style was the atmosphere of open and relatively free debate and criticism, ostentatiously praised as demonstrating that this was now indeed a new kind of League of Communists. The second, imposed by the same people, was the care taken *not* to give the republican congresses a genuinely free choice of candidates, which might have resulted in an excessive dilution of the unified support and unfettered mandate to which the presently dominant liberal faction was aspiring. To this latter end they took special and usually successful pains, primarily by invoking the rules of rotation which had been formally adopted in 1964 but hitherto generally ignored, to prevent the re-election of too many 'well-known veterans of the Revolution', who were suspected of 'conservatism' but whose candidacies were apparently being urged by an alarming number of basic Party organisations.[14]

The consequent turnover in leaderships at almost all levels was staggering in its formal dimensions, as if to make up for remarkably little change during the preceding twenty years. To begin with, an average of over 90 per cent of the delegates to the regional meetings (and in the extreme case of Macedonia fully 97·8 per cent) had never before attended a Party Congress. Of the 297 persons whom these delegates approved as members of the six republican central committees, 69 per cent were new. The turnover was also one of generations: 60 per cent of members of the new central committees were under 40 years of age and 15 per cent were under 30.

The pattern which emerged from nominations for membership in the new federal Party organs and from the election of new regional Party presidents and secretaries was one of little change of political significance in the fiefdoms of the powerful republican barons who had combined to topple Ranković thirty months earlier, and of further adjustments where leaderships associated with the losing side in 1966 had not yet been thoroughly reformed. The most significant changes were in Serbia, where the post-Ranković transformation was now finally complete. The new President of the Serbian Central Committee was Marko Nikezić, a diplomat since 1952, Yugoslav foreign secretary since 1966, and not hitherto in a leading Party post; Latinka Perović, born 1933, became Secretary of the Serbian Executive Committee.[15] As for most of the older generation of the revolution, some were retired, some who had participated in the anti-Ranković coalition were sent to the new federal Party Presidency, and others were relegated to the permanent membership of the presumably less important federal Party Conference (described below), which the Montenegrins explicitly suggested was the right place for these veterans, in order 'to guarantee revolutionary continuity'.[16]

The republican congresses also provided an occasion for reminders that spokesmen for backward regions were still unreconciled to neglect. Complaints and demands for 'compensation for the unfavourable effects of individual measures and relations in an integrated market', particularly articulated at the Montenegrin and Bosnian congresses,[17] were incorporated in the draft resolution to be approved by the all-Yugoslav Congress or in proposed amendments to it. The unresolved and perhaps unresolvable problem of investment and development strategies equally appropriate to underdeveloped and to relatively developed regions was thus carried over to the federal gathering, where these and similar or conflicting proposals became the focus of the most serious and substantive polemics (the label used by *Borba*'s correspondent)[18] and most of the contested votes which enlivened the 9th Congress.

While such exchanges were suggestive of both the more open atmosphere characterising the 1969 Congress and some areas of still unresolved and significant disagreement which surfaced there, the primary purpose of the meeting was to endorse and at one vital point to modify the changes in organisation, personnel and character which the Party had undergone since July 1966.

The provisional changes made by the July 1967 Central Committee Plenum in the structure of basic Party organisations were confirmed in the new Statute. So was the reorganisation of federal Party organs which the old Central Committee had endorsed at its July 1968 Plenum, and which the republican and provincial congresses had anticipated in electing their representatives to them. The Central and Executive Committees of the LCY were abolished and replaced by two new bodies. The first was a new Presidency, at the time of the regional congresses to consist of 5 representatives from each republic, 3 from each autonomous province and 3 from the army, with the presidents of republican central committees as *ex officio* members. The Presidency would be formally responsible between Congresses to the second new body, an annual Conference of 280 delegates. One-quarter of these last had been elected by the regional congresses and were to be endorsed by the Yugoslav Congress; their mandates would run until the following Congress. The other 210 would be elected for each annual Conference by 'communal and other appropriate conferences'.

In this form the new Party centre would have displayed three new features of importance. First, abandoning the principle of proportional representation for the regional Leagues, it would consist in each of its organs of an equal number of representatives from each socialist republic (and a correspondingly smaller number from each of the two autonomous provinces),[19] regardless of population or number of Party members. This could be and generally was interpreted as a further recognition of the 'federalisation' of the LCY. It was also a principle which could be applied to Government organs as well, as in due course it was. Secondly, the Yugoslav People's Army had received a curious sort of formal recognition, through its representation on the Party Presidency alongside the republics and provinces, as a kind of ninth partner in this federation, by definition the only nationally non-specific, 'Yugoslav' one. Thirdly, as though to put a final seal on a 'federalisation' en route to 'confederalisation', there apparently would have been no executive organ of any kind, except perhaps Tito as President of the LCY, at the federal Party centre.

It was this last feature which on second thoughts proved to be too much, at least for Tito himself, leading to the one important surprise of the 9th Congress. It came in a postscript which was not in the distributed text of Tito's opening speech to the final Plenary Session. After consultations with 'the leaderships from all the republics', Tito announced, it had been agreed that a new Executive Bureau should be established above the Party Presidency and that, 'in order to reinforce the centre of leadership in the League of Communists', it should include 'some of the present presidents and secretaries of the central committees or other leading comrades from all six republics'. It would consist of fifteen persons: two from each republic, one from each province, 'and of course myself'.[20] These should include 'some younger comrades ... to ensure continuity, [since] some of us are already fairly along in years'.

Tito insisted, as other Party spokesmen were to do, that the Executive Bureau was not a step backward towards a traditional, authoritarian Politburo, as some might think. Democratisation and decentralisation had already progressed too far for that danger to arise, he said. On the contrary, it was precisely the achieved level of pluralised decision-making and democracy which demanded a strengthened Party centre which would co-ordinate autonomous interests and prevent anarchy by seeing to it that democratically agreed solutions enjoyed uniform country-wide implementation.

The way that he hoped to achieve these aims was clear from

Tito's suggestion that existing Party presidents and secretaries should be sent, and that the press of business would require them to spend most of their time in Belgrade. The Sun King was summoning his barons to his court, away from the local power bases which had enabled them to challenge central authority to what he now considered a dangerous degree. In Belgrade they would be free from direct responsibility to their respective republican Parties, and their roles would make all Yugoslavia their collective concern. Tito clearly hoped that they would be able to reach agreement in this setting and that—at least until new influential regional leaders emerged—the regional Parties would have to obey them.

To avoid tearing up all that the republican congresses had done in nominating candidates for federal Party organs, the Presidency of the LCY, from which the Executive Bureau was to be drawn, was enlarged to 45 members, including 6 rather than 5 for each republic, plus the republican Central Committee presidents *ex officio*. How each region solved the riddle of musical chairs which these last-minute changes posed for them is worth examining, since some of the personnel changes carried out in haste in the back rooms of the 9th Congress were to have important and unforeseeable effects on the future political history of the country.

Only the Croats and Bosnians sent their presidents and secretaries. So Bakarić and Tripalo came; their places in Zagreb were taken by Savka Dabčević-Kučar, aged 46, an economist and Europe's first woman prime minister as head of the Croatian Government since 1967, and by Pero Pirker, aged 42 and Mayor of Zagreb from 1963 to 1967. Bakarić thus did what he had earlier always refused to do—removed himself from day-to-day effective control of the Croatian political scene—but Tripalo continued to spend most of his time in Zagreb as partner and rival of the less able Dabčević-Kučar. Croatia thus fell under the spell of a triumvirate of sometime Bakarić disciples, who were to lack the skill and balance of their master.[21]

The Macedonians sent Central Committee President Crvenkovski, who was replaced by Party Secretary Angel Čermerski. Their second member of the Executive Bureau was Kiro Gligorov, whose entire career had been in federal Party offices, where he had been one of the architects of the economic reform.

On the other hand the Serbian, Montenegrin and Slovenian Parties kept both their recently elected presidents and secretaries at home, partly on the excuse that others were more authoritative comrades than they. One important consequence was that Nikezić and Perović thereby remained in charge of Serbia, where their leadership was to prove as fateful as that of the triumvirate in Zagreb, albeit for different reasons. Five of the six persons delegated to the Executive Bureau by these three republics were logical choices, men already primarily associated with the federal Party apparatus at a high level and with 'progressive' anti-centralist records. Todorović and Miroslav Pečujlić (b. 1929) represented Serbia, while the Montenegrins chose Vlahović and Budislav Šoškić (b. 1925)—in each case exactly fulfilling Tito's criteria, with one leading figure from the old guard of Party liberals and one from the brightest and best of the younger generation. Kardelj was an even more obvious figure for the Slovenes to send, but their second choice came as a surprise. Kavčič, the republic's prime minister and leading politician, was the logical and expected candidate, but was widely rumoured to have angered Tito by refusing—despite a two-hour personal confrontation at the Congress—the elevation to the new Party summit which would have cost him his Slovenian base. In his stead Kardelj's partner was to be Stane Dolanc, then aged 43. Another of the middle generation of 'teenage Partisans', to which Tripalo, Dabčević-Kučar and Šoškić also belonged, Dolanc had joined the Party and the People's Army near the end of the war, in 1944. Since 1960 he had been a functionary of the Slovenian Central Committee, working his way up to membership in it and the republican Executive Committee since 1964. He was virtually unknown in Belgrade in 1969, but his coming there was also to have consequences of then unforeseen magnitude.[22]

Liberal dilemmas and the elections of 1969

The political situation in Yugoslavia after the 9th Congress could be described with a suggestive oversimplification as the situation of the summer of 1962 turned upside down. Then a still ultimately centralised Party and State apparatus was under the predominant control of Party 'Tories' grouped around Aleksandar Ranković, while a 'loyal opposition' took the form of a nascent alliance of Party 'Whigs' with others who believed that their personal or group interests would be advanced by decentralisation and/or liberalisation. In 1969 these same apparatuses, now highly decentralised in an inchoate polyarchy, were largely controlled by that 'Whig'-liberal alliance, while the 'Tories', in opposition, sought to regroup with the conscious or unwitting help of a variety of forces whose interests and/or values had been injured by decentralisation and liberalisation. The factors which undid the ruling group of 1962 had included the failure of their economic policies and nationalism in their own midst, especially Serbian. The rulers of 1969 were also to be undone by flaws in their economic policies and by their own nationalists, especially Croatian, but they had other problems as well.

The elections held in April and May 1969—for the first time since 1963 involving all legislative bodies, a grand total of 620 federal deputies, 2,779 republican and provincial deputies, and 40,279 communal councillors—dramatised one important dilemma confronting the liberal coalition and offered a snapshot view of the Yugoslav political system after two decades of deviation from the Soviet model. They also set a postwar record for openness, number and proportion of contested seats and untoward 'incidents'. For these and other reasons they are worthy of more attention than any other elections in Yugoslav history, at least since dictatorship began in 1929.[23]

Both the procedure and the results presented a series of contradictions. For the first time the voters had a choice of two or more candidates for a majority of the seats to be filled. On the other hand, the nomination process was more complicated and strictly controlled than in 1967, in a blatant effort to ensure that only 'acceptable' candidates would appear on the lists and that the voters' role should thus be restricted to selecting 'the most capable' from among a group of ideological Tweedledums and Tweed-ledees, all of them supporters of the programme of the presently dominant group within the League of Communists. Further, except in Croatia, there was still only one directly elected chamber in each five-chamber Assembly above the communal level, and in the Federal Assembly, after the compromise amendments of 1968, the directly-elected chamber was less powerful than the most indirectly elected of all, the Chamber of Nationalities (see above, p. 228). Even so, a sizeable number of 'undesirable' candidates managed to get themselves nominated, primarily but not exclusively to the directly elected chambers. Some of them were elected, even at the federal level, over officially endorsed opponents and in defiance of energetic campaigns mounted against them by the Party and the Socialist Alliance. Finally and of particular importance, the way the nomination procedure was rigged had interesting and in part unintended and unanticipated consequences, since it tended to produce slates reflecting the kind of interest aggregation normally associated with an effectively pluralistic political system. And it did this, for the first and so far last time, in public.

These contradictions were in large part a result of increasing ambivalence about what they wanted on the part of those who made the rules. With important exceptions, including Kardelj, those now dominant at the federal and republican Party summits had once been genuinely committed to the principle of a more genuine public choice among persons and 'socialist alternatives', but the results of their first, partial step in this direction during the 1967 (see above, pp. 223f.) elections had made them cautious. On the other hand, some more traditional Communists, in principle sceptical of the need for free elections, representative assemblies and other relics of 'bourgeois parliamentary democracy', but pushed out of power since 1966, had discovered that contested popular elections, when relatively uncontrolled, could be to their advantage because they could get themselves elected.

This was at first glance an indeed astounding reversal of fortunes, One way in which the reform elements in the Party had achieved their present relative dominance was by using the parliamentary machinery created by the Constitution of 1963 to bypass the Party machine, then in the hands of Ranković and these same traditionalists, who ignored the assemblies they thought that they still had reason to disdain. To this end the reformers had 'put our boys into the assemblies' (see above, p. 155). They did this at a time when decisions about candidates were still made behind the closed doors of Party and Socialist Alliance committees, where their conservative rivals were generally uninterested in these formerly meaningless parliamentary games, and when the voters were almost always offered only one candidate in direct elections above the communal level. It was the 1967 lesson of Lazarevac and kindred incidents which made them realise that their positions in several regions were now safer in the back rooms than before the electorate, which was frequently displaying a perverse preference for heroes or 'demagogues' rather than more modern, younger exponents of a 'socialist democracy' that sometimes seemed to be leading to political and economic anarchy,[24]

There were other reasons for their ambivalence. While they spoke with apparent sincerity, for example of the need for a 'free struggle of ideas' about 'socialist alternatives' and of the virtues of genuinely contested elections, they invariably hastened to add that the struggle must never degenerate into 'a struggle for power' or into purely 'spontaneous' political behaviour. The first of these aversions, with its apparent contradictions and naiveté, represented vague Yugoslav gropings toward a theory of decision-making through dialogue and consensus, without the special risks of majority rule in a multinational State, and perhaps also a subconscious touch of formally abandoned Soviet concepts of 'conflictless' political life under socialism. The second reflected, in addition to the rationale of traditional Marxist antipathy to 'spontaneity', a genuine conviction that such political behaviour by a largely uninformed, ignorant and apathetic electorate would mean the rule of demagoguery and manipulation by the kind of 'informal groups' who had indeed packed many voters' meetings in 1967. Such a system would be no more and probably less likely to produce really responsive representatives and policies than the much-abused filters of traditional parties, single or plural.

It was in this sense that Firdus Džinić, head of the Institute for

Public Opinion in Belgrade, commented on criticism that the Socialist Alliance was 'usurping the democratic rights of citizens' by playing a central role in the electoral process. This was not so, he told a SAWPY Conference in Bosnia: such a role for the Alliance should be seen instead as a hopeful way 'of ending a vague political situation, of long standing in our country, which has enabled political engagement and action from any starting point, simply by adhering to the general goals of the system'; it should now be possible 'to see more clearly who is coming to the fore, from which positions, and with which concrete goals'.[25] The SAWPY General Secretary, Beno Zupančič, similarly noted that experience in the 1967 elections had included the appearance of 'demagogy' and of a 'false ideal' of the uninformed and unorganised voter's fitness to make intelligent decisions on his own. The Alliance had a duty to protest against (*ograditi se*) 'those known for their dissatisfaction with self-management or, for instance, with the equality of our nationalities and national minorities'.[26]

To square these circles a bewilderingly complicated nomination process was devised. It began with the 'registration' of potential candidates at 'pre-nomination meetings', usually convened by the Socialist Alliance and held in any territorial or organisational unit with a logical interest in proposing candidates to one or several chambers of the various assemblies. These meetings—in villages, enterprises, urban neighbourhoods, a university faculty, a medical centre, a trade union branch, etc.—were open, informal and usually genuinely unguided. Then communal and inter-communal 'nomination conferences', the principal innovation of the 1969 system, were convened in each constituency. Finally, subsequent 'voters' meetings' could under certain conditions add additional candidates.

The rules for the nomination conferences were extremely complicated and designed, *inter alia*, to 'filter out' unwanted candidacies. All names 'registered' at the 'pre-nomination meetings' had to be presented, but none had to be accepted and the conferences could legally produce entirely different lists. Guidelines issued by the Socialist Alliance urged the conferences to nominate at least two candidates for each seat, except in very special cases; the reasons why the majority nevertheless failed to do so, causing apparently genuine consternation in Party and Alliance headquarters half-way through the campaign, were illuminating.

By mid-March the tune being sung at Party and Alliance headquarters had changed. Despite all the controls about which Zupančič and others had been so apologetic, the nomination conferences were not behaving as anticipated. While they were frequently successful in excluding candidates unwanted by the

Party (when the local Party organisation was united, which sometimes seemed more the exception than the rule), they continuously violated two other proclaimed principles. They failed to approve the officially desired percentages of workers, youth and women—which may have shown that the process really was more 'democratic' and representative of voter preferences than previously.[27] More importantly, they also tended to nominate only one candidate for many and often most seats in republican and federal chambers. The response of the authorities, suggesting that their demand for contested elections was sincere, was to plead for subsequent 'voters' meetings' to correct these 'mistakes'. This in effect opened the door to more 'wild' candidates.

The Belgrade daily *Politika*, analysing early results on March 19, was among the first to put a finger on the reason for the insubordinate behaviour of the nomination conferences. According to the electoral law, each potential candidate must receive votes from more than 50 per cent of the delegates at a conference in order to be nominated. *Politika* noticed that each delegate usually came with his own list for most posts, and initially voted only for those on his list. No one could receive a majority. After several futile ballots, bargains had to be struck, usually on the basis of 'I'll vote for your man for this post and you vote for my man for that one'. Alternatively, as weariness set in, there were voluntary withdrawals or better-known names began to accumulate more votes from those who gave up pushing their own favourites. In either case there was eventually a ballot on which one person, but frequently only one, achieved the elusive majority. At inter-communal nomination conferences the problem was further complicated by the necessity to distribute the seats 'fairly' on a territorial as well as functional basis. Once again the delicate balance achieved through lengthy bargaining could be upset if more than one candidate were chosen for a seat, unless of course both came from the same commune.[28]

The process was a little like the bargaining at an American party convention before 'favourite son' candidates are dropped by State delegations, but with two complicating differences: at a Yugoslav nomination conference there were many posts to be filled, each requiring different technical qualifications, and a secret ballot. The first of these differences was important. What was really happening was the kind of 'interest aggregation' referred to above. The proposed candidates in a conference delegate's pocket were those suggested (and then often politically 'filtered') by the group he represented: a teachers' association, an enterprise, an ethnic community, a farmers' co-operative, the commune's veterans, the youth organisation, etc. Bargaining over the slate of final candidates was therefore simultaneously a bargaining among organised interest groups, collectively representing a majority of the citizens, however indirectly and with more or less adequate purification by the Party and Alliance 'filters'. The resulting slate itself generally reflected the relative voting strength of the delegations to the conference, in turn roughly proportionate to the relative numerical strength of these interest groups in the commune.

Proportional representation for important interest groups has always been, to be sure, a serious concern in other Communist-ruled States. In their own period of undiminished Party autocracy the Yugoslavs too saw to it that all ethnic groups, regions, economic sectors and 'currents' within the Party were properly represented, in rough proportion to their political strength in the Party if not to their numerical strength in the country. The difference is in the direction of flow in which the process takes place, and in its private or public nature. It had been and in other countries still was the Party hierarchy which decided who got what, in secret and on penalty of being overthrown by a palace coup if it did its calculations too badly and alienated too many important interest groups. In Yugoslavia in 1969, however, it was at the base—or more accurately, just above the base—that proportions were set by interest group delegates themselves, with the bargaining done, often very noisily indeed, in public. A peculiarly Yugoslav kind of functional and territorial political pluralism had thus been institutionalised and legalised in the electoral process as well as in the structure of the assemblies.

Meanwhile, the process and the results were characterised and enlivened by the bemusing phenomenon of public 'blacklists' of Party members, forbidden to run for office by their own Party organisations, and by not infrequently successful defiance of such blacklisting by both Party and non-Party aspirants to public office.

The institution of Party blacklists undoubtedly had its ironic side. As one of *Borba*'s leading editorial writers pointed out, such black lists were 'not logical':

Now the Party is denying to the voters what it formerly imposed on them ... And what does all this really mean: Individual Communists are being punished, because of their dirty game during the last elections, in that they are being deprived of their right to be elected, but they are, in spite of this, permitted to stay in the League of Communists. It looks as if the League is imposing stiffer political principles on the voters than it prescribes to itself.[29]

Moreover, efforts to impose blacklists frequently ended in a debacle for the Party organisation, with open splits between the Party committee and the communal assembly or other 'socio-political organisations' in the commune and the defiant election of mayors or deputies criticised or even expelled from the Party.

Those whom the Party condemned were accepted by the voters or, for indirectly elected chambers, by the councillors in the communal assemblies.[30]

An examination of some representative cases of such 'undesirable' candidates revealed two basic and overlapping types. The first were fundamentally cases of political in-fighting between factions based on individual personalities, groups or clienteles, normally without identifiable ideological or programmatic distinctions, each seeking to gain or maintain political control of a community. The second and more significant category—'People's Hero' Sredoje Urošević, who repeated his 1967 performance at Čačak by defeating the 'official' candidate by an amazing 79,227 votes to 29,346, was the most publicised example—involved those labelled Party 'conservatives' and alleged to enjoy the support of the 'political underground'. In a case like Urošević's this was said to mean Serbian nationalists, former UDBa men and Ranković supporters, former supporters of the Cominform and other philo-Soviet elements, ex-Chetniks and those who really believed that self-managing market socialism spelled anarchy and neglect of underdeveloped areas, and that Yugoslavia needed a (Serbian) firm-hand rule to hold it together.

Enough such people won to raise again Kardelj's question about the appropriateness of such elections. Even before the results were in, an unsigned and therefore authoritative editorial in *Komunist* of April 10, 1969, referring once more to 'politically dissatisfied people of various colours, [who] have formed a real alliance, ... and sowed doubt about the political line contained in the election platforms', speculated prophetically about the proper conclusion:

It should be emphasised that many opposing views have been expressed—that the nomination of several candidates with the same platform is a remnant of bourgeois parliamentary democracy in our minds and that the whole pyramid of the assemblies—from the commune to the Federation—should emerge from a commune organised on a democratic basis.

The crisis of modernisation

As the 1960s ended the mood and the condition of the Yugoslavs, especially in Belgrade, strikingly contrasted with those of ten years earlier. Then there had been widespread optimism, which ignored warning signals that the boom of the 1950s was coming to an end and with it the post-Djilas political truce. Now the sense of drift and uncertainty of the later 1960s, fortified by the cumulative impact of a freer press on those unaccustomed to printed and televised criticism of shortcomings, had slowly grown from universal pessimism to a *grande peur*, which was at first only partly justifiable on logical grounds, but which was to become a self-fulfilling prophecy.

It seemed in many ways a curious time for such an atmosphere to develop. The Soviet threat, which had appeared so alarming after August 1968, had apparently again diminished to a longer-term speculation with the after-Tito question. The Vietnam war at last seemed to be moving towards some kind of settlement, and East-West détente was again a topic of lively discussion. Even relations with China and its Albanian ally were improving for the first time since 1955.[31] Although Soviet-Yugoslav press polemics occasionally continued at a more subdued level than in 1968-69, a visit to Moscow by Mitja Ribičič as President of the FEC in June 1970 seemed to be moving 'normalisation' along a predictable and comfortable path. Good relations with the other superpower were proclaimed by a two-day state visit to Belgrade and Zagreb on September 30 and October 1, 1970, by Richard Nixon—the first visit to Yugoslavia by a US President. On other fronts, Tito's patient personal advocacy of a third non-aligned summit conference, which he had been urging since February 1968, finally bore fruit in the Lusaka Conference of September 8-11, 1970, which proved that non-alignment was still alive if not entirely healthy. In August the establishment of *de facto* full diplomatic relations between Belgrade and the Vatican was announced, dramatising the remarkable improvement in relations between the regime and the Catholic Church in Yugoslavia which had begun during the reign of Pope John XXIII.

Perhaps most important of all in external relations, negotiations for a long-sought commercial agreement with the European Economic Community were concluded by an agreement signed in Brussels on March 19, 1970. In October Tito toured five of the six countries of the Community—official State visits to the Benelux group and unofficial ones to West Germany and France. This was his most extensive tour of Western Europe, Tito noted in an airport statement on his return, and reflected both Yugoslavia's position as a European State and a new emphasis on its role in Europe. The Community already accounted for 49 per cent of Yugoslav imports and 39 per cent of all exports as well as some 180 licensing agreements, thirty of them for long-term co-operation in technology and production. The 1970 agreement provided for non-discriminatory trade and most-favoured-nation treatment, special concessions to Yugoslav exports of baby beef (an important and lately threatened element in foreign trade), and a permanent Yugoslav-EEC mixed commission. Fears of a West European protectionism which would inevitably drive Yugoslavia into the commercial arms of the Eastern bloc, with all the economic and political implications which this would entail, were thus largely assuaged and participant observer status in Comecon was at least partly balanced by the EEC institutional links.[32]

At home, lively discussion of additional changes in the structure of the Yugoslav State seemed to be moving the country further along the road from federation to confederation, but this would only institutionalise and advance a trend which had been apparent for four years. While these discussions were both a result and an additional cause of tensions and disputes among the Yugoslav nationalities, the tensions themselves were not new or recently created, and the extent to which an increasing number of nationalist 'excesses' represented a genuine worsening of relations or merely greater freedom to express differences openly was still a matter of fair debate. The federal administration was still paralysed and unable to implement measures to deal with critical economic problems, but Yugoslav Governments had muddled through serious economic crises in the past without major disturbances and could reasonably be expected to do so again, once the division of competencies between Federation and republics had been clarified.

While the economy also offered plentiful grounds for concern in governmental or academic circles, its problems—with the admittedly major exceptions of inflation for all and illiquidity for some—were not yet those which directly affect ordinary citizens and cause unrest and political crises. On the contrary, the publicly most striking fact about the economy after 1969 was that the long post-reform recession was over, at least in most sectors. More Yugoslavs were living better than ever before, more goods were available to more people, and the unemployment rate was dropping for the first time since 1965.[33] The press, with ever wider freedom to print almost anything from political criticism and satire to blatant special-interest pleading and extraordinarily shabby pornography, accurately reflected a remarkably high if occasionally challenged level of intellectual and artistic liberty. In politics and the economy the special Yugoslav promotional logjam presented by the Partisan generation had finally come unstuck, permitting new and younger faces to appear in leading roles everywhere and relieving the pent-up career frustrations of those born after 1927.

In such circumstances one might have expected a passive or at most a critical contentment with the existing system on the part of most people, or at least of the growing number who had 'never had it so good' and who included most Yugoslavs whose positions made them eligible to participate in political processes. There was therefore some temptation to agree with those numerous non-Party or non-political Yugoslavs who argued, during the first winter of despair, that the developing atmosphere of crisis was largely artificial, deliberately concocted by otherwise incompetent politicians who saw in such an atmosphere the only way of maintaining their power and status and of avoiding personal political and social redundancy. But there were other genuine grounds for apprehension, one set of them hard and demonstrable and the other soft and unquantifiable but equally real.

With Tito's advancing years, the succession question was being posed with an increasing urgency which no one could know was remarkably premature. It was because of this that a critical conjunction of other challenges loomed larger than it otherwise might have done. Current economic and associated ethnic problems, the paralysis of central apparatuses, the prolonged struggle for the power they had once wielded and foreign pressures and intrigues, also inspired by the presumed proximity of a succession crisis at a time of domestic uncertainty, might have been faced with some equanimity if they had come sequentially. Together, and on top of the succession question, they were more alarming.

What additionally worried ordinary Yugoslavs was less their actual situation than the anxiety born of the unexpected and the unpredictable in that situation. In part this arose from political uncertainty and disappointed political expectations, even if most aspects of this disappointment involved changes that many or most of them should logically have welcomed.

Outside observers of the Yugoslav scene in the years 1970–72 were ceaselessly surprised and a little amused, for example, by the number of non-Communist and even anti-Communist Yugoslav friends who *complained* that today's economic and social chaos and free-wheeling, public political confrontations would not have been allowed to happen in the good old days of Ranković and the partly de-Stalinised but still controlled system of the early 1960s. Such people apparently missed the security of the sinner when the definition and penalties of sinning are known. Others, including many young people and especially students as well as some older Party members and intellectuals, were anxious or angry because of another kind of disappointment. They wanted ideals and a system with a purpose. The LCY used to supply these things, or at least they imagined that it did, but now they saw only crude pragmatism and all but the most admirably stubborn of idealists and true believers among them were tending to seek another faith.

There were others, including less politicised strata, with similarly frustrated but concrete and personal expectations. The system promised, more explicitly and centrally than do Western Welfare States, that there would be jobs and equality of opportunity for all. But its functionaries now openly and candidly warned that many, especially educated youth, had little prospect of an appropriate job in a desirable place, while equality of opportunity was only occasionally more real than the equality of status and cultural levels into which children are born. The system was declaratively a socialist and therefore a *planned* market economy, but managers and technicians were frustrated by endless inflation, instability, chronic illiquidity, more but less coherent State intervention than they needed and constantly changing rules and regulations.

In addition, everyone was frustrated by a 'self-management democracy' which involved endless time spent on interminable discussions at perpetual meetings of innumerable institutions producing an inexhaustible number of decisions ... but little effective action. In part this was because there were too many loci of decision-making, too little co-operation and orderly conflict-resolution and too long an agenda on which more time was allocated to the question of whether a new under-secretary should have a telephone than to a major investment decision. This last type of phenomenon, sometimes deliberately engineered by those who set the agenda, suggested a further reason for the inefficiency of the system and attendant frustrations. Such occurrences indicated and resulted from the fact that members of these self-management bodies were generally not equipped with the education, motivation, and spare time for adequate study required to make the kinds of decisions demanded by the theory and formal structures of self-management. The ideologically inadmissible realisation that this was so and the dynamics of what Marxists call 'the social division of labour' were usually more important than commonly imputed personal power-seeking in the development of strategies designed to keep real decision-making in other hands, originally those of Party politicians and State officials, and now the generally more competent ones of managers and technicians, particularly in big banks and big enterprises. The same realisation also led, as has been seen, to an interest in élites and in élitist theories by philosophers and sociologists, who thereby annoyed practitioners of the art, with good reasons for not wanting the nakedness of the emperor of self-management pointed out or rationalised in this way. Meanwhile, the incongruity between theory and practice in an area touching many lives added to general discontent and malaise, for it was equally if differently distressing to the several million persons who were obliged to devote much time and energy to the often meaningless rituals of self-management and to those who took it seriously as an aspiration if not yet a reality.[34]

Finally, all this and more, including widespread graft and corruption, was known to anyone who read or who listened to the radio or television, since the media, exploiting and jealously guarding an expanding freedom, now told all or almost all. This, too, was a part of the unnerving unexpected; it was very easy to assume that all these disturbing things were just now happening rather than only now being told.

Equally important was the psychological reaction of Yugoslav society to the cumulative impact of rapid social change and to the new quality of individual freedom and responsibility which recent events seemed to be making possible. The amorphous but universal sense of malaise and insecurity which was affecting an increasing number of Yugoslavs was in this sense a reflection of a specific crisis of modernisation and transition. Bewilderingly rapid social change had everywhere engendered a sense of unpredictability. It began with one's own social status and identity, material prospects and relationships to changing social institutions, starting with the family, both nuclear and extended. It was then easily projected to a regime which seemed to have lost its sense of direction, and to an external world full of the alarums and excursions of its own transition from a bipolar world of Cold War into something else, as yet undefined. At the same time, there were also elements of fear and uncertainty in the face of the possibility, which suddenly seemed to have become real, that an ancient Western liberal and Marxist dream of human freedom and responsibility might be realised in greater measure than most Yugoslavs were prepared to cope with.[35]

Postwar Yugoslavia had come far along the road of 'modernisation', whether the concept is measured in terms of per capita or gross national product, industrialisation and urbanisation, changing 'life styles', occupational and social differentiation and specialisation, or pluralism of autonomous but integrated and participant social institutions. Meanwhile, the shape of the political stalemate following the disintegration of the monopoly of political power held by the federal Party and State apparatuses—a development guaranteed by triumphant regionalism founded on ethnic jealousies—meant that no person or group was in a position to call a halt to an increasingly pluralistic reconstitution of decision-making power ... except through a coup d'état or other violent alteration of the balance of forces. Instead, pluralism in one form or another was genuinely supported by regional political leaderships and by powerful economic interests, jealous of their growing effective autonomy and able to defend it. It was also encouraged by still influential individuals at the federal level who had played a leading role in dispersing their own power, whether out of truly 'democratic socialist' convictions, because they were really the agents of the regional or sectional interests which provided their power bases, or because they were reluctantly hoist by their own rhetorical petards after years of lip service to the Party's liberal ideological line.

The conjunction of these developments seemed to have

generated a moment of unique opportunity, a tide to be taken at the flood lest the future of the great experiment should be bound in shallows if not in miseries. When the disintegration of the former monopolistic centre of political power reopened the question of the future locus of public decision-making, the minimum ideological, institutional, and economic prerequisites of greater collective and individual freedom to make and to participate in making a wider range of effective public (and personal) choices had been created. In addition, the political environment at the highest levels of leadership, however unstable, was momentarily favourable for such a mobilisation and expansion of participation.

However, the first reaction of both public and polity was a recrudescence of defensive and exclusive ethnic nationalism, a search for scapegoats for both real and imaginary problems and persecutions, usually among other ethnic groups, and attempts to reconstruct traditional States at republican and provincial levels, with traditional functions and controlled, limited participation, to replace the centralised apparatuses which had been destroyed. This was a reaction which included elements of irrationality, of rational scepticism, and of a preference for the evil one knows. In all three dimensions it reflected the influence of history, as reality and as myth, and of traditional social structures and attitudes. The lesson of Yugoslav history was that the evil one now knew was indeed preferable to evils one had known—fratricide, disintegration of the State, foreign domination, and attempted mutual genocide—which could conceivably recur if the safeguards built into the postwar system were dismantled with the system. More generally, the wisdom of traditional attitudes is that the known is always bad but the unknown is almost certainly worse; among more sophisticated, less traditional elements this had been transformed into a sly awareness that one had learned to operate and do relatively well out of the present system, whatever its defects, and might well lose one's way and do worse in an unknown if theoretically preferable one.

It was also inevitable, in the light of Yugoslav history, that the strong irrational factor in such a reaction to the ordeal of change and in such a flight from freedom should assume the form of nationalism.

The anxiety and lack of confidence which were troubling many or most Yugoslavs by 1970 manifested themselves in many ways, including a marked increase in religiosity among younger people, especially in Slovenia and Croatia, and a growing distrust of foreigners and of one another. Daily life and the press revealed an instinctive search for scapegoats in public and private life: another enterprise or branch or foreign competition; big banks or export-import companies or 'megalomaniacal' investments; the consequences of free enterprise or of State intervention in the economy; the Party, or youth, or intellectuals; 'Cominformists' or 'unitarists' or 'chauvinists'; Soviet agents and/or Western anti-Communists in league with Yugoslav political émigrés; and always and especially some other ethnic group or groups within the Yugoslav community.

This last was by far the most striking aspect of the situation and the principal source of growing alarm about the future of the State and system. In an atmosphere of escalating mutual suspicion and intolerance, epithets with ominous historical connotations were being exchanged with growing frequency and aimed even at regional Party leaderships. Croats were accused of being chauvinists, separatists and, most deadly of all, Ustaša nostalgics. Serbs were charged with unitarist centralism, great nation chauvinism and even Cominformism and neo-Stalinism. Elements on each side were suspected by others of flirting with Soviet support. In Kosovo, demonstrations and sometimes bloody incidents between Albanians and Serbs continued spasmodically through 1969.[36] That same summer the Slovenes, in their own non-violent but outspoken way, precipitated the year's major political crisis and almost brought down the Federal Government, then headed by a Slovene prime minister, with vehement public demonstrations and official protests over alleged ethnic discrimination. The subject was a World Bank loan for the construction of Yugoslavia's first motorways, in the distribution of which the FEC totally ignored Slovenia's manifestly high-priority need for an improved Nova Gorica-Ljubljana artery in favour of less urgent Serbian and Croatian projects. The protesters clearly implied that this was a Serbo-Croatian deal which typically ignored the numerically less significant Slovenes.[37]

The tendency to subsume all other questions and conflicts to the national one and to interpret and simplify every issue in national terms, reminiscent of old Yugoslavia and of the Habsburg monarchy before it and always an important sub-theme in the new Yugoslavia, was again becoming nearly universal. There was thus recreated the atmosphere and intensity of emotion which come to surround the question of nationality when all discontent and every grievance, every perception of injustice, oppression or relative deprivation, is projected as a national issue.

A new Croatian strategy

There were several reasons why this last phenomenon assumed a particularly acute form in Croatia. A thousand years as second-class citizens in someone else's State, combined with the relatively early development of a modern national consciousness and of

sufficient political and social mobilisation to spread this consciousness to wide sectors of the nation, had bequeathed to the present
generation of Croats a kind of collective national paranoia about
efforts to 'de-nationalise' them or keep them in second-class status.
Successive experiences—with Habsburg and Magyar betrayals in
1849 and 1867 and subsequent 'salami-tactic' Magyarisation, with
the betrayal of federalist aspirations in 1918 and subsequent
Serbian domination in the Yugoslav kingdom, and with the
behaviour of Belgrade-based centralism in the first two decades of
a socialist Yugoslavia—had taught them to beware every smallest
encroachment on their national interests and identity, and to see
such encroachments where they were not as well as where they
were. In addition and in contrast to Slovenia and Macedonia, the
population, size and resources of Croatia were a constant reminder
that they might have gone it alone as an independent State if they
had chosen and been permitted to do so. Finally, theirs was also a
multinational republic within multinational Yugoslavia, and the
tendency for most Croatian nationalist leaders to come from
particularly mixed areas or communities was again noticeable in
1970–71.

There was another and purely contemporary reason, derived
from differences in the status and image of Croatian and Serbian
national sentiments after the fall of Ranković. As has been seen,
the expected Serbian backlash did occur and took the form of a
'political underground', defined as an unholy alliance of
Ranković's followers (Ranković himself, ever loyal to Tito, has
made no known political move since his fall) with former Stalinists
and Cominformists, 'new left' students and intellectuals, and even
former royalist Chetniks. For a time it seemed that a 'Serbian
question' was replacing the 'Croatian question' as Yugoslavia's
most urgent national problem. The reasons why this danger never
fully materialised are important and provide an instructive counterpoint to simultaneous developments in Croatia. Because only
Serbian nationalism was identified with Ranković, 'integral
Yugoslavism', conservative Communism and centralism, most
persons rightly or wrongly suspected of overt or covert Serbian
nationalism were gradually removed from leading positions after
July 1966. The new leaders of the Serbian Party after the 1968
Congress were as young and 'liberal' as their counterparts in
Croatia. They also happened to be abler politicians and were by
process of elimination untainted with Serbian nationalism in its
traditional form, which was always 'hegemonistic' and thus
centralist and authoritarian. Here, as in other areas, they displayed
remarkable skill in using the political manipulation and ideological
'open polemics' which were supposed to be a modern Yugoslav
Communist's only legitimate weapons in dealing with opponents,

leaving frustrated Serbian nationalists at least temporarily disorganised and ineffective.

The situation in Croatia was quite different. There Croatian national sentiment and legitimate grievances had powerfully reinforced the resistance to and overthrow of centralist 'unitarism' and were in no way discredited by recent events. Further, many Croats (and some Serbs, another reason for their reconciliation with the new situation) found a new and persuasive argument to back a feeling that the Serbs had won after all. In old Yugoslavia and in the first postwar decades it had often been argued, especially by Serbs, that Serbian Belgrade needed centralised political power to counterbalance the concentration of economic power in Croatian Zagreb. Now the destruction of that 'unitarist' political power of Belgrade seemed a Pyrrhic victory, since the enduring legacy of postwar centralism included the transfer of predominant economic power, in the form of big banks and the headquarters of wealthy insurance companies and of the wealthiest and most powerful commercial enterprises, from Zagreb to Belgrade.

For a time, and especially after their reaction to the 'Declaration' in March and the purge of Holjevac in October 1967, it seemed that the Croatian leadership would prove willing and able to maintain in practice as well as declaratively a struggle on two fronts, against what they chose to consider Croatian nationalism at home and against 'the relics of bureaucratic centralism' in Belgrade. It was the continuing and increasingly intolerable stalemate at the federal centre and one of its consequences, the impregnability of Belgrade-centred economic 'unitarism', that induced a shift in Croatian strategy which altered the balance in Zagreb. The man who proposed the change was Vladimir Bakarić; those who disposed it were his less astute disciples, headed by the triumvirate comprised of Tripalo, Dabčević-Kučar and Pirker. The combination proved fatal to the Croatian strategy and to the post-Ranković order in Yugoslavia as a whole.

The stalemate at the federal centre had continued. The device of the Party Executive Bureau did not become a revival of the once all-powerful and dictatorial Politburo, which many had feared, but merely another forum for non-agreement among republican barons who continued to view their primary responsibility in regional and therefore ethnic rather than in all-Yugoslav terms. Economic and social problems persisted and sometimes grew in magnitude. The apparent incapacity of the system to produce decisions or action multiplied the ranks of the discontented and heartened both non-Communist and intra-Party opponents of the regime. These ill-assorted forces tended to polarise around two extremes:

exclusivist nationalism or neo-centralism. Caught between two fires, the Croatian leadership took a decision during the second half of 1969 to concentrate on the one they considered more dangerous.

Bakarić himself explained the rationale of the choice in a speech to republican Party leaders on December 13, 1969, and even more clearly in his remarks during the 10th session of the Croatian Central Committee a month later. These two events marked the public opening of a new phase in Croatian politics.[38]

Bakarić told the 10th session that he wished to discuss Croatian unitarism as well as nationalism as threats to the line of the Party. The roots of Croatian unitarism lay in the fact that all founders of the Croatian Communist Party, except Tito himself, had been 'Yugoslav nationalists' in their youth and had kept that 'ballast' when they became Communists. Their unitarism was later reinforced by the atrocities of the Ustaše during the war, the 1948-53 Cominform attack on Yugoslavia and the postwar centralist system of Communist rule, which for many years was remarkably successful in providing economic development and political stability. Unitarists therefore represented a strong, permanent current in Croatian Communism, and many of them were in or close to top Party and Government bodies capable of setting policy. But they could return to power only with external help: their strength lay in 'bureaucratic centralism and Cominformism'.

Croatian nationalism, on the other hand, had never been an 'enduring tendency' in the Croatian Communist Party, although individual nationalists had often penetrated it. So could nationalists ever form a Government? No, they were too divided and confused and too discredited by the Ustaša variant. Without direct prospects, traditional Croatian nationalism sought a role inside the League of Communists, on a platform of criticism of Yugoslavia as it was. This was entirely negative. On this basis they were capable only of 'sabotage', but because they had no positive 'real ideology or programme', they were otherwise not dangerous.

The occasion for the December meeting and the 10th session of the Central Committee (January 15-17, 1970) was a series of articles about Croatian nationalism written by a prominent Croatian politician, Miloš Žanko, and published in *Borba*, a 'federal' newspaper considered by the Croatian leadership to be centralist and anti-Croatian. The articles gave a detailed and documented analysis of the increasing activities of Croatian nationalists and suggested that the Party leadership had failed to take more than verbal action against them. Particularly incriminated were the publications and other activities of the Matica Hrvatska, a cultural organisation which had played a distinguished and aggressive role in developing Croatian national consciousness during the 'Slav awakening' and the bitter inter-nationality struggles of the last decades of the Habsburg monarchy. The *Borba* series portrayed the Matica as having fallen into the hands of nationalists and clericalists who were transfor-ming it into a political organisation in competition with the League of Communists.

The 10th session publicly condemned Žanko 'for views and actions ... contrary to the policy and course of the League of Communists'. His articles were interpreted as a malicious effort to discredit and so to overthrow the Croatian Party leadership by labelling it soft on nationalism. Since Croatian Communists and the Croatian public had full confidence in their present leaders, they could only be overthrown through outside intervention. Žanko must therefore be the witting or unwitting agent of such interventionists. Bakarić had already indicated, in his December 16 speech, where they were to be found: in the 'Serbian Čaršija' (a derogatory term for Belgrade coffee-house politics), which he specified did not mean the Serbian League of Communists, and 'in a part of the federal administration' which was attempting to maintain its power and to this end was 'withholding from the public information about the nature of the difficulties facing the country'.

The 10th session was later to become the totem of Croatian Communism and the touchstone of 'progressive' views which qualified both Communists and non-Communists for participation in Croatian politics. The first principle of the 10th session, in subsequent interpretations, was all-out struggle against 'unitarism' and its advocates, considered the principal threats to democratic socialism and Croatian national interests. Croatian nationalism and nationalists, clearly defined and located, were also termed alien and dangerous, but were at present considered a lesser threat. In the name of democracy the struggle against them could employ only 'ideological-political' and indirect weapons: argument and positive action to solve the economic problems and end the 'bureaucratic-centralist' exploitation of Croatia on which nationalism fed. To accomplish the latter purpose allies would be needed and should be sought (without, of course, any compromise of the principles of 'self-management socialism') in mobilisation of the masses, including non-Communists and even sometime nationalists won over by such a programme, and in other republics. The 'Žanko case' had exposed the face of the principal enemy and the fact that he was to be found inside Croatia as well as outside. Among first priorities must therefore be the forging of a monolithic Croatian front, requiring a domestic political house-cleaning; the 'homogenisation of Croatia' soon became a favourite political phrase.

Bakarić's plan at the 10th session[39] seems to have been to evade the deadlock at the Party and State centre and the consequent 'stagnation' in the economy and self-management, both of which were fuelling dissent in nationalist and also in neo-centralist forms. The centre was inactive because of an inter-republican stalemate on basic issues. A republican Party and Government were not so hampered, but needed adequate economic instruments (or 'material means') with which to act, a legitimating constituency and firm unity of cadre and conviction. Croatia, so armed and under progressive Bakarić-trained leadership, could set an example for the rest of the Federation of a successful, modern, democratic socialism. What was new in this strategy was that the effort to reform the system at the federal level was temporarily given up: modern socialism could be built in one republic.

If this was its purpose, there were four weaknesses in the strategy:

1. In the Croatian historical context it would necessarily attract offers of assistance from Croatian nationalists, dangerous allies from the Communist point of view. Bakarić recognised this, but in the event wrongly discounted the danger by arguing that the nationalists were disunited, unorganised and had no positive programme.

2. Because national sentiment and the subordinate status of Croatia for 1,000 years were always very near the surface in most Croats' minds, it would prove temptingly easy to mobilise politically conscious Croats on a national platform. And because years of seemingly empty rhetoric about self-management had left few Yugoslavs (except, oddly enough, in top echelons of the political élite) with a strong belief in its feasibility, it would prove correspondingly difficult to mobilise them on the alternative basis of 'class' or 'self-management'.

3. By increasing the power and prestige of republican apparatuses, and by casting republican leaders in the role of indispensable mediators in the defence of class *and* national interests, the strategy was fundamentally 'anti-self-management' in tendency if not in conception. This may not have worried Bakarić; it was almost always impossible to say whether or not an individual Yugoslav Communist leader was cynical in his obligatory confessions of faith in the feasibility of self-management without political intermediaries. However, the significance of this aspect of the strategy would not be unnoticed by one important social grouping, in addition to the republican Party leaders, who stood to benefit from it. Managers and other members of the new Croatian 'middle class' (a term which came into somewhat apologetic use at about this time) had no love for Belgrade centralism and all that it implied, but equally little desire to live with a literal implemen-

tation of the theory of self-management without intermediaries. Everything in their experience cried out to them that such a system would be inefficient if not absurdly unworkable. Instinct and historic experience also suggested to them that a strong leadership which respected and supported their roles but also enjoyed mass legitimacy—better still, enthusiasm—as a *national* leadership would be the best protection against both Scylla of centralism and the Charybdis of self-management.

4. To avoid compromising alliances with nationalists, to resist the temptation to take the easy road to mass support, and to escape becoming the instruments and guarantors of the rule of a middle-class 'technocracy' would require a high order of political skill, intellect, level-headedness and ideological conviction and consistency on the part of the Party leadership, especially one distracted by and in need of allies in its struggle to push Croatian views about the power and competence of the Federation and further economic reforms in the face of determined opposition in Belgrade and elsewhere. The triumvirate and their friends were convinced that they possessed these qualities in more than sufficient measure, as the self-confidence of their actions and words indicated, but the coming months were to prove that they did not.

For a time political developments at the federal level continued to conform to their highest hopes. Three months after the 10th session, in April 1970, the Yugoslav Party Presidency adopted a resolution recognising the 'sovereignty' of the republics and provinces and defining the Yugoslav State as 'an institutionalised agreement and co-operation among the republics'. The competence of the Federation should be limited to foreign affairs, defence and instruments necessary to guarantee a single market and economic system and ethnic equality. The federal administration and the army should more consistently implement the principle of the 'ethnic key' (strict proportional representation for all nations and nationalities) in personnel policy. Party commissions to watch over the implementation of the resolution were appointed.[40] And in October the Serbian Government and the Presidency of the Serbian Assembly committed themselves to the Croatian view that the residual federal role in financing investments (through the device of extra-budgetary accounts) should be ended once and for all.[41] The Serbian regime was thereafter to insist as strongly as Zagreb on 'clear accounts' in the federal budget.

Towards confederation

The succession question was specifically posed by Tito himself, in a calculatedly offhand manner, during a talk with Party activists in

Zagreb on September 21, 1970. Speculation at home and especially abroad about what would happen to the multinational State when he was no longer there to symbolise and guarantee unity was unhealthy and dangerous, Tito said. To stop it and initiate a gradual transition now, he was therefore suggesting the adoption of a constitutional amendment creating a collegial Presidency to replace him as President of the Socialist Federal Republic of Yugoslavia. It should consist of an equal number of 'outstanding personalities' from each of the country's six republics and appropriate representation from the two autonomous provinces.[42]

The proposal was in one sense only a logical extension to the State apparatus of the device of the Executive Bureau adopted for the Party at the 9th Congress. A reconstitution of other federal State bodies on the basis of republican parity, to conform with the solution adopted for the federal Party bodies at the Congress, was already under consideration. In another sense, however, it was more than that. It openly put the succession question 'on the agenda' and made it the lynchpin of all the other variables in the present, tense Yugoslav equation. It gave primacy among these other variables to the increasingly sensitive question of inter-republican relations and thus to the national question. And through the proposed constitutional amendment it opened the door to other, related institutional changes and thus to broad public discussion of the nature of the Federation itself.

Tito, now 78, continued to enjoy the physical and mental health of a far younger man, as his again frequent and forceful public interventions in the domestic political scene in coming months and his apparent indefatigability during the Lusaka Conference, just before his tour to a series of West European countries and immediately after the Zagreb meeting, were demonstrating. His departure through death or incapacity did not appear imminent. In terms of its timing, therefore, the succession problem as he posed it could be described as a manufactured crisis. It was deliberately provoked by a leader whose advancing years had apparently not dulled his acute political and gambler's instincts, and who had boldly elected to meet the future at a time and on terms of his own choosing, while the threatening elements of that future were still manageable and while he was still there to manage them. The storm clouds had been building up for some time, and Tito had chosen to act like the peasants of his native Zagorje, who fire rockets at real hail-bearing thunderheads in order to precipitate the tempest before the hailstones have grown big enough to destroy their vineyards.

Before the Zagreb meeting, during visits to Split and Zadar on August 28 and 29, Tito had already spoken with a bluntness which was reminiscent of his 1962 Split speech about the difficult situation confronting the Yugoslav economy and Party. The fault, he said, lay in large part with the continuing lack of discipline of some leading Communists and with an improper concept of democracy and of the role of the Party which could be traced all the way back to the 6th Congress in 1952.[43] He was particularly concerned by regional 'political pressures' exerted in the search for solutions to economic and political problems, by which he seems to have meant the Slovenian 'motorway crisis' of the preceding summer, the 10th session of the Croatian Central Committee, and other unpublicised instances.[44]

The hints contained in Tito's remarks about the 6th Congress, republican 'pressures' and his own comprehension of 'the leading role of the Party' were to grow into increasingly explicit threats during the next year. Meanwhile, however, his September suggestion of a collective Presidency indicated that he was still willing to go along with one more try on the path pursued since 1966.

The 1st LCY Conference, meeting in October, followed this lead. Its conclusions dutifully endorsed Tito's proposal and then set it in a broader context, consistent with the Party Presidency's resolution of the preceding spring: 'There is urgent need', the Conclusions stated, 'for a further step in the direction of reconstructing the Federation as a function of the statehood and sovereignty of every republic and the autonomy of the provinces as the basis of the equality of the nations and nationalities of Yugoslavia'.[45] A joint commission of all Federal Assembly chambers was appointed at the end of the same month to draft a third package of amendments to the 1963 Constitution. It was to make another effort to achieve two contradictory objectives at once: to kill particularist ethnic nationalism with one more massive dose of kindness while ending the paralysis at the federal centre by providing new mechanisms for decision-making by inter-regional consensus. The commissions's sub-committees and a co-ordinating committee under Kardelj's chairmanship were all constituted on the basis of republican and provincial parity.

Agreement on a draft took longer and proved more difficult than had been anticipated. The storm precipitated by Tito's proposed answer to the succession question broke with what must have been a wilder display of thunder and lightning than even he could have expected. For seven months the tensions and 'speculations' which he had hoped to dispel grew more rather than less intense. Paralysis of the federal administration continued unabated and was excused (by members of the Government, but not by parliamentary deputies who attacked them for inaction) on the ground that with far-reaching constitutional changes under discussion this was now a lame-duck administration which should not undertake initiatives that would bind the protagonists of next year's new power structure. The interregnum was repeatedly extended by the expanding scope of the changes under discussion and by the failure of the regional chieftains to reach agreement on almost all key issues, including the remaining powers of the Federation, regional-federal relationships and the distribution of powers within the new federal structure.

Tensions among the nationalities were aggravated by a by-product of the level of 'democratisation' already achieved. For the first time in postwar Yugoslavia, institutional changes of manifest importance, changing the nature of the Federation, were not being imposed from above, with only formal public discussion of a *fait accompli*, but were being argued in public and in print before they had even been drafted. Neither the audience nor the participants were prepared for such a procedure. Political leaders offered their views and opening negotiating positions in speeches and articles employing the same vehement style they had been wont to use behind the closed doors of higher Party meetings. Partisan regional newspapers and journals simplified issues and quoted 'opposition' statements out of context with a lively journalistic irresponsibility unknown on the eastern shore of the Adriatic since the war. Unused to a spectacle they had long demanded, the general public reacted with alarm and with displays of nationalism. Some of their leaders, excited by a new kind of political game, responded with an intensified demagogy which others saw as nationalist rabble-rousing.

For some months the embattled national leaderships, preoccupied with tough negotiations, remained curiously deaf to the rising clamour of public alarm and blind to the dangerous potential of licence for 'chauvinist excesses'. Once again it was Tito who proved more responsive to the mood of his peoples than their more direct representatives seemed willing or able to be. In April he paid one of his periodic and tireless visits to the countryside for talks with local leaderships and ordinary citizens, this time to Bosnia, South Serbia and Kosovo, the first and third ethnically mixed regions where the national question was hypersensitive. As the royal progress went on, he became visibly angrier with what he was seeing and hearing. Finally, after nationalist arguments had been aired in front of him at a Party meeting in Priština, he exploded:

We are a socialist community, in which the League of Communists is the ideological-political principle of the entire development. But behaviour in the League of Communists is not good and I am not satisfied. I must say this hurts me terribly. You know that I have long been at the head of the Communist Party and the League of Communists of Yugoslavia. But I think that so far we have not had such a situation as we have today.... But as long as I am in this office, as long as the rank and file uphold me, I shall endeavour to make order in the League of Communists.

If the situation did not improve, he said, it would be necessary to have recourse to administrative measures: 'I know, there will be cries against undemocratic procedures and the like, but is it possible to act otherwise when such behaviour is in question, especially when Communists behave like this?' More immediately to the point, he said that he was going to summon a special meeting of the Party Presidency 'and the most responsible figures in all the Yugoslav republics and provinces', and that 'we will not go our ways until we come to an agreement'.[46]

Meanwhile, six weeks before this outburst, the increasingly acrimonious public debate about the future shape of the Federation had finally been given a set of specific proposals to focus on. The Constitutional Commission and its subcommittees, after being 'locked up' on the Brioni islands for a month in early 1971 in order to isolate the members from publicity and day-to-day pressures from their constituents, had at last produced a draft of nineteen amendments. The draft was accepted by the full Commission at the beginning of March, after consideration by the Party Presidency at its 16th session, thus initiating the formal stage of public discussion required by the Constitution. The package, with a number of changes and the addition of two further amendments, was finally adopted and promulgated only on June 30, 1971, just before the Federal Assembly broke up for its summer recess.

The attitude assumed during the debate by the most important actors, the republican leaders, can only be inferred. In contrast to prevailing practice at the time, their consideration of the amendments was conducted in 'secret sessions', the records of which are still embargoed. In public and published discussions, however, there was a predictable polarisation of views between a portion of Serbian and a portion of Croatian opinion. The extreme among the former was represented by a three-day debate by professors and instructors at the faculty of law of Belgrade University, some of whom bluntly condemned the amendments as the beginning of the end of Yugoslavia. Others were concerned about the fate of Serbs living outside the Serbian Republic.[48] In Croatia a correspondingly extreme position, which proclaimed the amendments to be only the first step towards a full realisation of Croatian 'national aspirations', took shape in the pages of *Hrvatski tjednik*, a new weekly 'cultural' journal of the Matica Hrvatska which soon surpassed *Vjesnik* in circulation. After discussion of the federal constitutional amendments ended, *Hrvatski tjednik* turned with equal passion to an elaboration of the Matica's own proposals for corresponding amendments to the Croatian Constitution. One historically and politically significant demand was for a straightforward definition of the Socialist Republic of Croatia as 'the national State of the Croatian nation'—to which Tripalo was to reply, on behalf of the Croatian Party leadership, that Croatia 'is not only that, beyond any doubt, but also the State of the Serbs in Croatia and the State of the national minorities in Croatia'.[49]

While the final version of the amendments adopted in June ignored criticism of these kinds, it did incorporate both technical and substantive suggestions from sources of greater legitimacy in the Yugoslav system, including the Federal Council of the Trade Union Federation and the 2nd Congress of Self-Managers, which was held in Sarajevo in April. Three of the amendments (XXI–XXIII), which became known as the 'workers' amendments', were of particular interest to trade unionists and to the delegates at the Sarajevo meeting and did not deal with the organisation of the Federation. Unusually obscure in language, even by the standards of Yugoslav Constitutions, the 'workers' amendments' were little understood and generally ignored at the time. Only later did it become clear that they constituted an important historic and philosophical link between the operating principles of social self-management elaborated in the original 1963 Constitution and those which would take new shape with the Constitution of 1974. They marked the first official appearance of a new concept, 'basic organisations of associated labour' (*osnovne organizacije udruženog rada*, OOUR), and a further elaboration of 'communities of interest' (*interesne zajednice*) and of 'self-management agreements' and 'social compacts' (*samoupravni sporazumi* and *društveni dogovori*) as the primary vehicles of further 'de-étatisation' of Yugoslav society. These three articles, Kardelj and Federal Assembly President Milentije Popović said in their authoritative commentaries on the draft amendments, provided a foretaste of further changes which were then expected to take the form of another package of amendments to be completed by 1973. They also represented the survival, during the high tide of almost exclusive preoccupation with the national question, of the second, 'self-management', current in Yugoslav political thought and practice under Communist rule.[50]

Amendment XX presented the basic theme of the remaining eighteen amendments, most of which were to be incorporated with minor changes in the 1974 Constitution. Reversing a basic principle of the 1963 Constitution, it allocated to the republics and provinces primary sovereignty and all powers except those explicitly granted to the Federation by the revised Constitution. These powers in turn were restricted almost entirely to foreign policy, national defence, and measures necessary to ensure a unitary Yugoslav market, common monetary and foreign trade policies, the 'principles of the political system' and ethnic and individual rights.[51]

Even in these areas, decision-making was to be the end product of complicated procedures designed to ensure interregional consensus and in effect recognising the veto right of each federal unit in matters of importance to them. A specific list of subjects on which the Federal Assembly could act only 'on the basis of agreement with responsible republican and provincial organs' included virtually all areas of frequent inter-republican disagreements.[52] In addition, the federal budget would have only customs duties and State tax stamps as direct and exclusive sources of income; the rest of its income, to a ceiling authorised by the republics and provinces, would come from rebated shares of turnover taxes collected by republican and provincial Governments. Republican and provincial parity or the 'ethnic key' would provide the basis for constituting not only the new collective State Presidency but also most other important federal organs and institutions, including the FEC, the most powerful chamber in the Federal Assembly (the Chamber of Nationalities, already so constituted), the Constitutional Court, and the personnel of the ministries. Territorial militia under republican control, created by the new defence law of 1969, received constitutional sanction.[53]

The Presidency of Yugoslavia was to be comprised of three representatives from each republic and two from each province rather than the two per republic and one per province which Tito seems to have envisaged when he made his proposal. The reason for the increase, another token of the sensitivity of the national question within multinational republics, was an objection from Bosnia-Herzegovina, which needed three members in order to ensure representation of each of its three major ethnic groups. The result was to make an unwieldy and generally ineffective body, as was recognised by its reduction in size in the 1974 Constitution from 23 to 9 members (always also including Tito).

The way in which these institutional arrangements functioned during less than three years before they were partly superseded by a new Constitution is more instructive than a detailed examination of their formal powers and relationships, especially since only some of the mechanisms of actual decision-making in this period were in fact anticipated by the amendments. Those which were—the Presidency, the FEC (now also formally constituted on the basis of regional parity and with its members once again in charge of ministries), and the Federal Assembly—in fact proved less busy and effective than partly or entirely extra-constitutional mechanisms, particularly five specialised inter-republican committees and one inter-republican co-ordinating committee which no one had foreseen and which became the most important governmental body of all.

The five committees, only casually authorised by the amendments, were based on five primary areas of remaining federal competence. Each was composed of one representative from each republic and autonomous province, with a member of the FEC as chairman. When these nine people could not agree on some controversial issue, it was referred to the totally extra-constitutional Co-ordinating Committee, composed of the President of the FEC, the presidents of the eight republican and provincial executive committees, eight members of the FEC, and ad hoc additions of other leading political figures. If agreement could not be reached there, the matter was in theory referred on to the collective State Presidency, and back into constitutional channels, but this almost never proved necessary. In the first half-year of the new system, according to one compilation, 92 out of 124 controversial issues were resolved by the inter-republican committees and solutions for the remaining 32 were found by the Co-ordinating Committee.[54]

One incidental effect of this arrangement was to turn the Federal Assembly and Government back into the rubber-stamp bodies which they had been in the early days of the Communist dictatorship, ending a period in which the Yugoslav parliament, unique in the history of legislatures in Communist-ruled countries, had played an important role in the governmental process. The reason was simple. With regional vetoes hanging like a sword of Damocles over the entire process, the legislative or regulatory proposals worked out in the inter-republican committees represented the end-result of a long and delicate process of argument, mutual concessions, and reference back to eight regional capitals (specifically to the republican and provincial governments, therefore without enhancing the powers of the regional assemblies). In these circumstances the FEC, which formally submitted these proposals to the Federal Assembly, and the Assembly chambers which must discuss and vote on them were under tremendous pressure not to dispute or amend and thus risk violating some detail of a compromise solution achieved at such cost.[55]

If this was understandable, what was remarkable was that the system worked at all. The resolution of 134 controversial issues in six months, most of them between December 1971 and March 1972, and including important and emotion-charged questions like the foreign trade and foreign currency systems, price policy and a Five-Year Plan which should have been adopted in 1970, amounted roughly to 130 more resolutions of controversial issues than had occurred in the preceding two years. It was difficult to attribute the change to the arrangements decreed by the amendments, which had really only recognised and institutionalised the confederal structure, with veto powers, which had paralysed central Government since the late 1960s. The primary reason was rather a change in the political atmosphere in the country.

A series of events during the last months of 1971 was to remove from power some of those most responsible for the paralysis of the federal centre in recent years. The same events reminded the rest, and all who valued the recent enlargement of regional autonomy and the greater freedom and more pluralistic and participatory decision-making which had accompanied it, that Yugoslavia's ultimate arbiter still had the power and the will to abolish or at least limit these gains if they appeared to him to be ill used. The reaction of the general public, meanwhile, was also of a kind to remind them that many people, quickly forgetting the disabilities which they had suffered under a centralist and arbitrary Government, would agree with that arbiter's definition of ill-use and applaud drastic remedies which they might later regret. Those cognisant of these warnings that their political values and their own political positions could be threatened included most of the Party and State leaders in at least four republics, who were suddenly eager to make the existing system work in spite of itself.

It was too late. By 1972 the enemies of the divided, demoralised and in one region already politically decapitated liberal coalition had both the *grande peur* and Tito behind them. The crisis which began in Croatia became a crisis of the system.

The road to Karadjordjevo

The meeting of the Party Presidency and other 'responsible figures' which Tito had demanded at Priština was duly convened at the end of April 1971. It met at his Adriatic retreat on the Brioni islands, lasted three days, entered Party history as the 17th session and issued a communiqué of startling blandness. The speeches were not published, which was unusual in current Party practice but justified by Tito, in a May Day speech, on the ground that there had been sharp disagreements at the beginning of the session and that publication would only aggravate tensions. What was important, Tito said, was that complete agreement had been reached before they adjourned. The communiqué listed the points of this agreement: the constitutional amendments had been adequately discussed and should be adopted and implemented without further delay; nationalism and divided leaderships were bad; all other matters of disagreement were negotiable.[56]

One other document was released during the meeting—rather curiously, since it was not a Party but a Government paper, which normally should have been issued from Belgrade. It was designed to put an end to what remains to date the most mysterious chapter of the political drama then unfolding in Croatia.

Three weeks earlier the Croatian Central Committee had issued an extraordinary statement accusing 'certain federal agencies' of a 'conspiracy' to discredit the Croatian Party leadership by concocting evidence of links between them and Ustaše émigrés in Western Europe. The accusation came at a time of rising concern about these émigré organisations and their recruiting efforts among Croatian *Gastarbeiter*. On April 7, two young Croatian emigrant workers had walked into the Yugoslav Embassy in Stockholm and shot down the ambassador. Three days later, as he lay dying, the leading Croatian separatist organisation in Western Europe, whose head had recently claimed to have the backing of the Soviet Union, held a provocative meeting in Munich to celebrate the thirtieth anniversary of the creation of the fascist 'Independent State of Croatia' in 1941.

It now appears that the Croatian leaders' accusations concerning a 'conspiracy' against them had been discussed at the federal Party level in February or March, and that it was agreed that no public announcement should be made until a special Party commission had investigated and reported. The Croatian Central Committee then decided, after an unusual closed-door meeting and for still obscure reasons, to violate this agreement and make the accusation public.[57] Once that had happened the nature of the charges, involving Government agencies, made it necessary to appoint an FEC commission to conduct its own investigation, parallel to that already undertaken by the Party. It was the report of this commission which was released from Brioni, but which only deepened the mystery. It firmly absolved the still unnamed federal agency[58] of any improper behaviour, either collective or individual. But it also agreed and deplored that there had been a conspiratorial effort abroad—source and agents unspecified—to discredit the Croatian leadership by alleging links with the émigrés which did not exist. The incident and its inept handling illustrated the breakdown in mutual confidence and communications between Zagreb and Belgrade and the fraying nerves everywhere, particularly in the Croatian capital.

Later revelations also confirmed that the Croatian leadership was specifically brought to task on other and more general grounds at the Brioni meeting, and that the principal accuser was Tito himself. Slovenian and Bosnian representatives reportedly sought to bring the dispute into the open, and the Slovenes proposed but did not insist on the adoption of a resolution admitting the existence of serious differences 'between the Croatian and Serbian leaderships, and that these must in some way be taken into account'.[59] Tito disagreed. He preferred, characteristically, to keep the quarrel a private matter at the highest Party level and persuaded himself that everyone had learned a lesson, as all humbly said they had, and would mend their ways and resolve their differences. No one was therefore to say or imply that any one republican leadership had been singled out for special criticism.

It was a policy which Tito stuck to doggedly for another seven months. He was encouraged in doing so because the Croatian Party leaders, for reasons of their own although no longer unanimous about anything else, were pursuing the same policy: hiding their internal differences from Croatian and all-Yugoslav public opinion, including Tito, in an increasingly desperate effort to avoid a 'Yugoslavisation' of the Croatian crisis. The combination and its effect on intra-Party and inter-republican relations were to aggravate and prolong the emerging crisis until only a politically violent dénouement was acceptable to Tito. That in turn altered the balance of power in Yugoslavia as a whole.

By early 1971, a year after the Zagreb Central Committee's 10th session, the strategy implicit in that session had produced a mixture of success and failure. Its quality and distribution convinced Tripalo, Dabčević-Kučar and their team that they were on the right track and had accurately defined their enemies and friends. The reorganisation of the Federation and the reduction of its powers were continuing in the desired direction. Croatia was in the throes of a 'national euphoria' (a phrase which was becoming a favourite of the leadership) without precedent since the founding of Yugoslavia. Party leaders in general and Dabčević-Kučar and Tripalo in particular enjoyed a mass popularity which was compared to that of Dubček during the Czechoslovak spring of 1968. Like Dubček, they reacted to the heady wine of such popularity with increased self-confidence and intransigence and soon became, in part at least, the prisoners of the aroused emotions of their mass audience.

In the economic sphere, on the other hand, they had so far failed to impose their views about what they considered vital issues, including reform of the banking and foreign currency systems, curbs on wealthy Belgrade export-import firms and redistribution of former federal assets and obligations. Here they now made a serious tactical error, which was to have ramifying consequences. They pressed their case on each of these issues with an uncompromising vehemence which suggested that all their demands were fundamentally non-negotiable.

There were several reasons for such a stance. These issues involved the essential economic instruments without which the goal of full, effective Croatian political and economic autonomy would not be achievable. Without them the transfer to the republics of responsibility for economic planning and control, sanctioned by the constitutional amendments, would remain empty of meaning. There would thus be no adequate guarantees that the developed north, including Croatia, would not continue to be 'exploited' by the numerically preponderant, underdeveloped south, even in a genuine parliamentary democracy after Tito's departure. It is also reasonable to assume that intoxication with a series of victories in recent battles contributed to the adamance of the leadership. Finally, and of particular importance, they were on these issues for the first time specifically the prisoners of their success in mobilising mass enthusiasm on a national platform and in tolerating support, including the right to exert pressure and to criticise, by nationalist forces outside the disciplinary control of the Party's network of mass organisations. The more they insisted that their position on each issue represented vital Croatian interests, the more a compromise on precisely these issues was impossible.

One consequence was the loss of their allies outside Croatia. Slovene and Macedonian support, in particular, had been important in every fight with Belgrade since the reform of 1965 and the fall of Ranković. For a time, in fact, the Slovenes had seemed the most uncompromising of the decentralisers, as in the 'motorway crisis' of 1969. Afterwards, however, they had drawn in their horns, apparently alarmed by the implications of republican economic autarky for an industrialised region heavily dependent on unrestricted access to markets and raw materials in less developed areas and by the nationalist fellow-travellers being attracted by radical decentralisation, unwanted allies whose growing stength might lead towards separatism or a centralist reaction. Relatively satisfied with achieved levels of decentralisation and further alarmed by the implications of developments in Croatia, the Slovene and Macedonian leaders were increasingly ready to bargain and compromise in order to reach agreements which would get a sufficiently emasculated federal mechanism moving again. Thus the Croatian delegation often found itself a minority of one in inter-republican negotiations.

This isolation affected the Croatian leaders and their strategy in at least three ways. It confirmed them in their feeling that they must have firm institutional guarantees, including a veto right, to protect each republic against being outvoted in the Federation, a view which was pressed with growing emphasis during the public debate on the 1971 amendments. Secondly, it increased the relative importance to them of the mass support they enjoyed inside Croatia and made them more dependent on its maintenance and unanimity; the 'homogenisation of Croatia', implying both the mobilisation of non-Communists and the conversion or silencing of doubters and dissenters within the Croatian Party, assumed an even higher priority than before. Thirdly, the 'internal logic' of both isolation and pretensions to mass support by all Croatians emphasised their role as primarily national and only secondarily Communist or 'class' leaders, further affecting their political style and also, it seems reasonable to assume, their self-image.

A final consequence materialised only after mid-1971 and the adoption of the amendments to the federal Constitution. These, as we have seen, created instruments and procedures for the negotiated resolution of inter-republican disputes. The isolation of the Croats meant that it was extremely unlikely that Croatian views would prevail in such negotiations without the compromises which the Zagreb leadership's domestic strategy had made it increasingly difficult for them to accept. In anticipation of continuing deadlock and the political inexpediency of compromise, they would be tempted to encourage or at least condone extra-constitutional pressures inside Croatia in support of their positions.[60]

The 'clear line of demarcation' drawn at the 10th session between progressive, nationally-conscious Croatian Communism and Croatian nationalism began to evaporate. Basing their opening to the masses on the claim that they were effectively defending Croatian national interests (still equated with all-Yugoslav working-class interests, a less convincing claim since they had lost their allies in other republics), the Croatian Party leaders had left themselves vulnerable to nationalist heckling, to the charge that they were insufficiently vigilant or successful in defining or defending these interests. Responding rhetorically and in action, they placed themselves in a curious position. They had in effect if unintentionally legitimised Croatian nationalism as a political competitor for the allegiance of the 'national movement' which they had themselves invoked, which was now essential to their own legitimacy and bargaining strength, and which they could hold only by outbidding the nationalists on the latters' own ground.

The Croatian 'national euphoria', intensified by isolation and both by the victories and the defeats of a leadership seen as defending national interests, became more exuberant. The national question, always at least the second subject in any conversation with most urban, politicised Croats, was now invariably the first and obsessive subject. The change was atmospheric: an exponential rise in intensity, in the size of the catalogue of real or rumoured wrongs and in the frequency with which they were raised and in detailed knowledge about kinds of exploitation or about the number of Serbs who were directors of Croatian enterprises, commanders of Croatian regiments or to be found in Croatian factories, on Croatian railroads or in the Zagreb police force.

'Nationalist excesses' occurred with growing frequency. They ranged from the midnight destruction of an advertising sign in the Cyrillic alphabet by a gang of youths wearing armbands inscribed with the Croatian national emblem—a red and white checker-board—to demonstrations in which the Croatian flag and coat of arms appeared without the obligatory red star, a political struggle to oust an enterprise director because he was a Serb, a riot after a football victory over a Serbian team, or a village street brawl in an ethnically mixed area. Most were trivial incidents, but they were enough to fire the emotions of peoples only thirty years removed from civil war.

At this point and on this issue the Croatian leadership split.

Seriously contrasting evaluations of Croatian nationalism and its implications for Party strategy apparently first became evident in closed meetings of the republican leadership in February 1971.[61] One group, headed by Dabčević-Kučar, Tripalo and Pirker, continued to maintain that 'nationalist excesses' were marginal phenomena and that the 'national euphoria' was socialist and therefore positive in essence and direction and supportive of the Party's programme and goals. The strategy set at the 10th session, as interpreted by them, should therefore be continued. As for their cautious alliance with 'moderate' nationalists, they argued that it simultaneously strengthened the Croatian bargaining position, facilitated the Party's opening to the masses, contributed to democratisation by permitting more non-Communist but essentially pro-socialist elements to participate in the political process, and isolated 'extreme' nationalists and separatists, rendering them harmless. But another group, including as time went on seven of the nine members of the Executive Committee, argued instead that the escalation of nationalism which had taken place since the 10th session required a thorough review of the Party's tactics.

If statements made by members of the second group after the crisis are complete and accurate, their initial dissent was based on two observations. The first was that the Croatian Party's toleration of nationalist 'excesses', whether or not these were really marginal phenomena, was causing alarm in the rest of the country and among non-Croats (especially Serbs) in Croatia. It thus tended to isolate the Croatian leadership, weakening their bargaining position, and to provoke the 'greater danger' of Serbian nationalism. The second touched on the basic but rarely arti-culated principle on which the Party's continuing claim to ultimate political power in an increasingly pluralistic Yugoslav polity was founded: that dissent and even opposition can be tolerated and can even make a positive contribution, but only as long as they are not organised. It was an infringement of this principle that this group were sensing, and that would eventually bring Bakarić into the lists on their side, when they noted that in the 'national euphoria' individuals who were 'not ours' were coming forward and being accepted by Party as well as populace as legitimate spokesmen and intermediaries. If they were 'not ours', whose were they? [62] The suspicion that they represented organised political forces outside the control of and in competition with the League of Communists, capturing its own network of pre-emptive mass organisations cell by cell and one by one, was to grow with time and with mounting evidence that it might be so. For the Communist mind, even in its open and protestant Yugoslav variant, the mere existence of such forces raises *a priori* suspicions of anti-socialism and images of conspiracy and counter-revolution. It is essential to understand this if the nature and seriousness of the accusations which were to be made at Karadjordjevo on December 1, 1971, and afterwards are to be understood.

Although the second group included a majority of the Executive Committee, their position was far weaker than that of the first. The latter included the Croatian Party's most visible and popular politicians, Tripalo and Dabčević-Kučar, whose formal roles also made them (along with an again ailing and temporarily withdrawn Bakarić)[63] Croatia's most authoritative spokesmen. It also included Pirker, whose position as Secretary of the Executive Committee gave the triumvirate a monopolistic control over communications with subordinate Party organs throughout the Republic, and Marko Koprtla, whose job as Executive Committee member responsible for 'cadre policy' meant control over Party appointments and promotions, once the secret of Ranković's power.

The activities of the Matica Hrvatska provided the primary focus of these initial disagreements within the Party leadership. At its annual assembly in November 1970 the Matica had launched a membership drive and a new programme, in which it was declared to be its right and duty to interest itself in economic and political questions. In March 1971 the first issue of the Matica's new weekly, *Hrvatski tjednik,* appeared. It was a primarily political journal expressing opinions which in an earlier period and a multi-party society would have labelled it as the organ of a National-Liberal party. It was joined a few weeks later by the *Hrvatski gospodarski glasnik* (Croatian Economic Tribune), which expressed the Matica's views on economic problems and theory. In subsequent months the *Hrvatski tjednik's* circulation climbed to over 100,000; the Matica's membership rose from 2,323 in 30 branches in November 1970 to 41,000 in 55 branches and was provided with a vertical hierarchy in the form of 16 'commissions',

33 'initiating committees' and a Zagreb headquarters. It was indeed beginning to resemble a political party of the same semi-illegal type once represented by the CPY.[64]

In April 1971 came the first, and in its consequences most important, capture of a citadel of the Communist establishment in Croatia by an organised political movement whose primary focus of loyalty lay outside the framework of that establishment, in competition with it ideologically and for political domination. It took the form of a faultlessly planned coup against the existing leaderships of the Student Federations at Zagreb University and at the republican level. The Party leadership's acceptance of the coup set a precedent which many later regarded as the first serious and ultimately fatal mistake by the ruling triumvirate, after which they were never again in full control of the situation. The new non-Party and Croatian nationalist leaders of the Zagreb and Croatian Student Federations, Dražen Budiša and Ante Paradžik, were also to organise the student strike which precipitated the dramatic end of the crisis seven months later. It was characteristic of the nationalist movement that Budiša came from Drniš, in the barren Dalmatian hinterland, and Paradžik from Herzegovina, both ethnically mixed districts and traditional breeding grounds for radical Croatian nationalism.[65]

The Brioni meeting of the federal Party Presidency and the circumstances surrounding it ushered in a brief period of public optimism and phony peace on the inter-republican front. During the week following the 17th session Tito delivered two important speeches, one the May Day speech at Labin in Istria and the other at the closing session of the Congress of Self-Managers at Sarajevo on May 8. Like the Brioni communiqué, both were important less for what was said than for their style and impact.

Especially at Sarajevo Tito was in top form. Perhaps it was in part because the Self-Managers' Congress, despite a satirical cartoon in the Sarajevo daily *Oslobodjenje* referring to it as a 'Congress Only of Managers' (*Kongres samo Upravljača* rather than *Kongres samoupravljača*), had proved a forum for constructive criticism of enterprise and economic organisation and policies by workers' representatives apparently untainted by preoccupation with the national question. Tito spoke scathingly about domestic critics, who were not those workers and pensioners without enough to live on who had a right to criticise, but pensioners with large incomes (including 'some generals—I mean retired ones, not on the active list'), who sat in cafés complaining and plotting because they had not realised 'megalomaniacal ambitions to become President of the Republic or at least ministers'. A unity had been achieved at Brioni, he said, which included a guarantee of action against enemies of our socialism. We spoke also of democracy. I think that there, we all together arrived for the first time at a common view that democracy can be—and how—harmful to the development of socialism if it is abused by the opponents of socialism.

After his Istrian speech, he continued, he had read a commentary in a Western newspaper saying that all of this had been heard before, 'that Tito had threatened many times and that he threatens now also, but it is an empty gun and everything will be the same as it was. But now, this will not be an empty gun—we have plenty of ammunition'. There was much more of the same, little that was specific or impressive on the printed page but a popular and even demogogic rhetoric and show of vigour which had an immense impact on the audience, both in Sarajevo and on television.[66]

These details are important for an understanding of what happened next. 'The old magician has pulled another one out of the hat' was the immediate reaction of Tito's English biographer, Phyllis Auty, one of the foreign observers present at the Sarajevo Congress. The change in the atmosphere in Yugoslavia during the following weeks indeed bespoke magic more than it did political realities, which were essentially unchanged. Newspapers and politicians spoke with a new tone and the public mood in Belgrade passed for the moment from alarmist pessimism to an equally exaggerated optimism.[67] It seemed briefly that the worst of the crisis was over. Agreement was reached on several, usually minor, issues which had long been blocked by inter-republican disagreements.

The Croatian leadership did their part. They chose to interpret their return from Brioni publicly unscathed and the decision to proceed with constitutional amendments as personal victories and an endorsement of their basic strategy. In return they knew that they were expected to contribute to a calmer atmosphere and to rendering the central Government again capable of action in its residual spheres of competence, obligations which would require them to show a willingness to compromise on some disputed issues and to take a stronger stand against Croatian nationalism. Croatian leaders spoke of the necessity, now that they had won the system and republican 'sovereignty' they had demanded, to prove that it would work. 'S.R. Croatia is [now] a State', Tripalo told the republican Central Committee on May 14, 'so it is necessary to behave like statesmen'.

The meeting at which he said this, the Croatian Committee's 20th session, had been convened to discuss implementation of the conclusions of the Brioni meeting. One after another the members rose to condemn Croatian nationalism as well as Serbian nationalism, unitarism, étatism in any size or package and other official vices. The tenor was such that the session was soon thereafter condemned by *Hrvatski tjednik* and others, including Party leaders in some districts, as a victory for 'conservative forces' in the Central Committee. Spokesmen and publications of the Matica Hrvatska began to suggest that it would prove necessary to convene an Extraordinary Congress of the Croatian League of Communists to purge these conservatives and fill the Central Committee with 'true representatives' of Croatian sentiment—a threat later to be taken up by some Party leaders.

There were, indeed, significant differences of emphasis among speakers at the 20th session (and—as usual—in the reporting of them in the Zagreb and Belgrade press). Some demanded an all-out political offensive against 'national elements' of all kinds. Others wished to make careful distinctions between 'separatists' and 'chauvinists' on the one hand and those whose 'national euphoria' was being or could be channelled into mass support for 'self-management socialism' and 'the line of the League of Communists'. Several discussed the mass enrolment of new members in the Party which many were insisting on as a natural corollary of what was now being called 'the national mass movement'. For some this was dangerous without careful 'ideological-political preparation' and screening of candidates; for others such caution was itself a sign of old-fashioned, conservative thinking appropriate only to an earlier revolutionary period. Some accused Croatian nationalists of not seeing how much the Party was doing for Croatian interests; others were worried that the Party, in taking this line, was emphasising national over class interests to a dangerous degree. Tripalo replied with what became the basic thesis of the 'mass movement': national and class interests were the same as nation and class had become identical.[68]

At the same time, the triumvirate was already demonstrating that it was not retreating on any fundamental principles. At the 20th session Tripalo again raised the flag of the Croatian demand for a radical revision of the Yugoslav foreign currency system. This now became, somewhat curiously, the cardinal Croat demand, from which the leadership would not budge and on which their alliance with the Matica and other elements of the 'national mass movement' was most firmly founded. If their grievance was real, the solution they proposed was singularly unrealistic.

It was an old argument. At one time the Zagreb Chamber of Commerce had joined those of other major exporting centres, including Ljubljana, Belgrade and Sarajevo, in a joint démarche to the Federal Government, demanding an upward revision of retention quotas (see above, p. 207). Now, however, the Croatian leadership was seeking, in effect, separate republican foreign currency regimes: each should keep what was earned or remitted on its territory, buying and selling as needed on a free all-Yugoslav (in fact inter-republican) currency market. The principal objection to this proposal was that it made nonsense of a unified Yugoslav market in goods and services and could not be implemented without giving rise to equally reasonable supplementary demands which would create a dual-currency system, impossibly cumbersome and more inequitable than the present one. If it were accepted, what, for example, would stop a Bosnian or Serbian firm which sold meat or vegetables to a Dalmatian hotel from demanding payment in the foreign currency which the hotel was 'earning' by serving food to foreign tourists? Or a steel mill in another republic from demanding payment in foreign currency for steel delivered to a Croatian shipyard for a tanker sold to the Japanese? Where would such a process stop?[69]

The Croatian leadership never found a reply. The argument soon became symbolic and emotional rather than practical, and eventually provided the pretext for the student strike which precipitated Tito's coup.[70]

The battle lines within the Croatian Party had now been drawn, although few outside the inner circle and a consistently well-informed Matica Hrvatska executive yet knew it and there was still time and room for change. The political struggle during the next months was focused on three interrelated fronts. The first was the struggle of the triumvirate and their friends, in competition with the Matica and its network, to maintain Party control of the 'national mass movement', preventing 'excesses' wherever possible. The second involved efforts by all members of the Party leadership to find a definition and interpretation of the 'mass movement' and a corresponding programme of action on which they could all agree and operate, thus avoiding a definitive split in their ranks and a struggle for power at the Party summit. The third was marked by a struggle by all concerned to resolve all issues within the boundaries of Croatia, without influence or intervention from outside which might compromise their newly won 'sovereignty' and the principles of confederation—i.e. a struggle to avoid a 'Yugoslavisation' of the Croatian crisis.

By November developments on all three fronts had entered a new phase. On the first the leadership of the 'mass movement' had in effect become a triumvirate-Matica condominium in which the triumvirate were struggling to preserve their autonomy but were increasingly cast in the role of junior partners. On the second the search for unity within the Party leadership had been abandoned and some or all of the triumvirate's group were prepared for open conflict and a decisive political battle to remove the 'factionalist' majority on the Executive Committee and their friends. Knowing this and aware of their weakness, the anti-triumvirate faction was now prepared to invoke outside help by appealing to Tito.

The appropriateness of the word 'struggle' is of central importance. The bare fact that an inability to resolve an initially minor disagreement about political tactics in one vitally important sector had evolved into a struggle for enough power to impose one tactical orientation or the other, and that such a political struggle necessarily involves polarisation, was introducing a new, dynamic factor into an unstable equation. Within the leadership, the group around the triumvirate became increasingly deaf to warnings which they might otherwise have listened to because they were really hearing things they themselves had also said and felt. Their opponents, attention focused on one subject and the political battle associated with it, increasingly saw only what was (from their point of view) negative and dangerous in the 'mass movement'. They thereby failed to give serious thought to the implications of the fact that nationalism was a more powerful mobilising force than the official ideology and practice of 'self-management socialism'.

On the second and third fronts, the story was one of an unending series of indecisive meetings and of declarations and 'action programmes' which were, with one exception, too vague and general to commit anyone to specific action. The battle on the first front (and during the second phase on the second front as well) was fought throughout the Republic, but most intensively in Dalmatia and Slavonia and in Zagreb itself. It included the founding of new Matica branches with pomp and processions, demonstrative celebrations of anniversaries of events or historic heroes in Croatian history, struggles for control of individual Party organisations and town halls, and 'incidents' concerning employment in or control of individual economic enterprises. It was also characterised by a mounting tension between Croats and Serbs in ethnically mixed districts, where both communities were said to be arming themselves in anticipation of a physical show-down.

Articles analysing the ethnic composition of employment in the police, in Government bureaux, in the Party, in enterprise managements and eventually among workers in certain enterprises became numerous, and always the Croats were found to be inadequately represented in their own country. The criterion of the 'ethnic key', accepted in principle for political leaderships and government employment, was applied everywhere, leading to nervousness and 'crises' in economic sectors and enterprises in which, usually for historic or demographic reasons, Serbs were more numerous than their 15 per cent participation in the total population warranted.

In such an atmosphere the Party leadership met, debated and continued to disagree.[71] Then on July 4, an unusually angry Tito descended on the Croatian capital and summoned the Executive Committee and some other Party leaders to a meeting. Typical of the style of the Croatian crisis, there was at the time no mention in the press of this meeting or what transpired there, so that the general public depended on rumours while Croatian Party organisations learned only what individual emissaries from Party headquarters chose to tell them. Since these presented sharply contrasting versions, they only added to the disorientation and confusion which characterised the Party in the countryside in the months to come.

Finally, on May 9, 1972, a text of Tito's remarks at the meeting of July 4, 1971, was published in all major newspapers. It appeared to be a transcript, but was in fact a reconstruction from memory and notes by some who were present—members, needless to say, of the anti-triumvirate group—since it seems that no verbatim record was kept. If the published version is nevertheless assumed to be a reasonable approximation of the words actually spoken, it is a remarkable document.

'This time', Tito allegedly began, 'I am going to speak first. You see that I am very angry. That is why I have summoned you and the meeting won't last long.' The situation in Croatia, he said, was not good. Nationalism had run wild. The only counter-measures taken were useless verbal condemnations, while 'under the cover of "national interest" all hell collects, ... even to counter-revolution.' Relations between Serbs and Croats were bad, and 'in some villages because of nervousness the Serbs are drilling and arming themselves. ... Do we want to have 1941 again? That would be a catastrophe.'

Three separate times in his remarks Tito referred to the international context, the third time apparently confirming earlier and otherwise scarcely credible rumours that he had told the Croats at the Brioni meeting in April that Brezhnev had telephoned to offer Soviet 'fraternal assistance' if he should need it in dealing with the situation:

Others are watching. Are you aware that others would immediately be present if there were disorder? But I'll sooner restore order with our army than allow others to do it.... We've lost prestige abroad and it will be hard to get it back. They are speculating that 'when Tito goes, the whole thing will collapse', and some are seriously waiting for that. The internal enemy has plenty of support from outside. The great powers will use any devil who'll work for them, whether he's a Communist or not.... All kinds of things are being said. Now, among you, it is being said that I invented my conversation with Brezhnev in order to frighten you and force you into unity.

Tito specifically criticised ethnic head-counting of Serbs and Croats in factories ('we will not allow that, and I shall say so publicly'), toleration for 'the transformation of the Matica into a political organisation, to such a degree that ... it has become stronger than you, so you're in no condition to curb it', and the situation at the university. 'Now', he said, 'I seek firm action'.

At the end of the meeting he was again conciliatory. He apologised for such sharp criticism and said that he was pleased to hear that they accepted it and would undertake unified action along the lines he had demanded. He had thought to make a public and open statement of his views, but now he would not need to do that. The outside world expected after Brioni that 'the process of the disintegration of Yugoslavia' would be brought to a halt, and if he were to speak it would be said that Yugoslavia had become non-viable.

Tito's views therefore still unknown to a wider public or in other republics, the crisis and the divisions within the Croatian leadership continued, as did the Matica's activities. The Executive Committee majority acted on the assumption, which some later described as 'naïve' but which may have been calculated, that the entire leadership would fulfil its promises to Tito. The triumvirate and their friends pursued their own course unaltered. There thus developed what was later termed 'two lines and two directives' at Zagreb Party headquarters. This only added to the perplexity of lower-rank Party leaders in the countryside, primarily concerned with political self-protection and therefore increasingly eager to choose the winning side in the struggle which such contradictory instructions suggested was imminent at the republican Party centre. To most of them it must have seemed that the position of the triumvirate, backed by the 'mass movement', Koprtla's control of Party appointments and the growing organisational strength of the 'second party' based on the Matica, was unassailable. They chose accordingly, reinforcing the impression that Tripalo and Dabčević-Kučar commanded the loyalty of almost the whole of the Croatian Party except for 'conservative die-hards' like the majority of the Executive Committee and Bakarić.[72]

Tito, making another of his periodic royal progresses through the countryside in the midst of this ferment, visited parts of Bosnia and then a series of places in Croatia, beginning and ending in Zagreb. Accompanied by the Croatian leaders, he was everywhere greeted with even more enthusiasm than usual, which seemed to document the triumvirate's theses about the existence and quality of the 'mass movement'. His initial reception in Zagreb on September 6 resembled that normally accorded a visiting head of state; a holiday had been declared, and *Vjesnik* claimed that 300,000 Zagrebčani were in the streets to greet him. Back there and in a good mood on the final evening of the tour, he offered a toast to his hosts.

The enthusiasm he had seen reminded him, he said, of the Partisan spirit of the wartime National Liberation Struggle and the first postwar years, with the same positive socialist orientation. Nowhere had he found evidence of nationalist deviations in this enthusiasm, and so he must conclude that reports of 'nationalist excesses' dominating the Croatian atmosphere were exaggerated. He was most pleased with what he had seen and with the attitudes of the people with whom he had spoken.[73]

From the point of view of those demanding a hard line on nationalism, the consequences of Tito's toast were catastrophic. For the next ten weeks their every attempted move in this field would be answered, by the triumvirate, by *Vjesnik* and VUS, and by the student and Matica press, with an argument-stopping 'But Tito said. ...'

Two of the majority group in the Executive Committee, Milka Planinc and Ema Derossi-Bjelajac, later offered an explanation of what was for them otherwise an embarrassing and puzzling lapse by the President. Relying on the promises made to him in July, they said, Tito was attempting to make the task of the Croatian Party easier by expressing full confidence in them and inhibiting the kind of criticism from other parts of the country which had tended to force them defensively to defend their nationalists. Pavle Gaži, an eternally blunt non-professional politician on the Committee, would not take this easy way out: 'We all lied to Tito', he said in December, 'by telling him that the entire leadership was united on his course' when they knew this to be untrue.[74] Some Western commentators have suggested that Tito changed his mind after a visit from Brezhnev, only eight days after the Zagreb toast, or during his own State visit to the United States in November, when additional American financial support for Yugoslavia's liberal economic reforms was not forthcoming.[75]

Tito's apparent endorsement of the triumvirate and their policies disheartened and temporarily demobilised the opposition within the Party leadership and virtually legitimised public attacks on the latter. As autumn came and went the differences within the leadership at last emerged into the open, although spokesmen on both sides continued to maintain that they were neither serious nor concerned with fundamentals.[76]

The mood of the country, the dynamics of the triumvirate's pretensions to mass leadership in Croatia and to progressive leadership in Yugoslavia, and the continuing paralysis of the Federation as a result of Croatia's isolation and intransigent veto (the federal Party Presidency, recognising impasse, did not even attempt to meet for three months) all demanded action and results. But in what direction? The majority of the Croatian Executive Committee, now joined by Bakarić, Sabor President Jakov Blažević and other members of the Party 'old guard', insisted that the first priority must be a 'reckoning with Croatian nationalism' to clear Croatia's good name in Yugoslavia and end the Republic's isolation. The 'mass movement', as articulated by a Matica press now obsequiously trailed by the Party press, demanded the opposite: a cleansing of 'conservatives' and 'unitarists' to achieve unity on a platform of a 'homogenised' Croatian nation in which class and nation should be conterminous; nationalist 'excesses' were still only marginal phenomena of no importance.

The crisis was becoming a purely political one, a struggle for political survival by all the factions. In this situation of *sauve qui peut* the differences of ideological nuance, evaluation of nationalism and its protagonists, emphasis on nation-State or class and tactical orientation which had started the process of polarisation were almost irrelevant.

Despite their mass popularity, the triumvirate and their friends were oddly isolated, without a political apparatus they could confidently call their own and expect to do their bidding. Titular leaders of both the Party and the 'mass movement', they had been struggling since the spring to maintain and enlarge their effective control over both at once, but had only succeeded in splitting the former by tolerating in the latter the increasing activity of non-Party elements and the growing predominance of purely national symbols and demands. As political organisations, despite overlapping memberships at the base and at the top (the trium- virate), there were now really two separate movements with distinct goals and programmes. Each of them was a condominium in which the triumvirate shared power with different people, whose diametrically opposed attitudes and demands for action had hardened on both sides. The further polarisation of previously uncommitted Party members and other politicised Croats, in response to recent events, had left virtually empty any middle ground. They therefore faced a Hobson's choice: to move with the Executive Committee against the Matica and other 'hotbeds of nationalism', or to move with the Matica against the majority of the Executive Committee, Bakarić and the old guard.

A number of factors pushed them, by all the evidence reluctantly, towards the second solution. First among these was a calculus of power too simple and obvious for a man of Tripalo's capabilities to overlook. To go with the Executive Committee and the old guard would not regain their confidence, which was irretrievably lost.[77] Instead, it would mean an implicit admission that the triumvirate had been seriously wrong in their attitude towards and evaluation of Croatian nationalism and the 'mass movement'. In politics such admissions are dangerous for those who make them unless they are otherwise in an invulnerable position, which the triumvirate were not. In addition, they were also conscious of the extent to which Koprtla's personnel policy in combination with the Matica's organisational work and indefatigable agitation and propaganda had been successful. As a result, the Party and State apparatuses in key regions like Dalmatia and Slavonia, which also happened to be the personal home bases of most of the inner group around the triumvirate, were in the hands of the 'movementists'. The triumvirate must have sensed that if they broke with their Matica allies, went over to the 'unitarists' and were labelled 'traitors to the Croatian nation' by the Matica, as Bakarić already had been, the primary loyalty of these people was likely to be to the Matica and not to them. To go with the Executive Committee therefore meant public political isolation and certain defeat, the end of the game.

The alternative also carried clear and frightening risks. If Tito should enter the lists against them, as his attitude during the spring and in July suggested was likely, they were almost certainly lost. Even if he did not, and they won, the process could easily leave them in the position of junior partners in the alliance with the Matica which would then be their chief or only support. But at least there was a chance. Tito's behaviour in September had been encouraging, while Tripalo in particular—according to many reliable witnesses in Zagreb—remained supremely confident that he was cleverer than the Matica's leaders and could master them.

Meanwhile, there was to be one final effort, by both factions in the Party leadership, to evade the triumvirate's fateful dilemma.

On November 5, the Croatian Central Committee, which had met only once since May, assembled in Zagreb for its 22nd session.[78] The introductory speech was a three-hour, 26,000 word 'report' by Savka Dabčević-Kučar. The section which attracted most attention discussed—for the first time at a Central Committee session—the 'mass national movement'. The movement, the report said, had an undoubtedly 'positive socialist orientation' and was a specific Croatian reflection of the 'positive political climate' now existing throughout Yugoslavia. It had its roots in the 10th session, where 'a unity of nation and Party was forged and sturdily grew into a mass political movement'. But some comrades had doubted and criticised that formulation:

Some think that we should behave with reserve towards that mass support or even reject it in the interest of some abstract revolutionary 'purity', which to my mind, incidentally, represents nothing less than sectarianism and fear of the mobilisation of the masses. ... As though our programmatic position that the working people should be active creators of policies were valid only as a proclamation, but that we should not think of making it a reality of life. Or as though we, as a League of Communists, are a closed sect who think that society and the working people exist for us and not we for them.

After two days of debate, in which seventy members of the Central Committee participated, the entire text of this speech was unanimously adopted as the 'conclusions' of the session. According to later testimony, this was a violation of an explicit agreement with Bakarić and the Executive Committee majority, which had stipulated that only the conclusions of the report, without the disputed sections about the 'mass movement', should be voted on and become an official document. The chair also violated another purported agreement, which was that the Central Committee should consider and 'verify' a strongly anti-nationalist and anti-Matica 'Action Programme' which the Executive Committee had drafted on August 2. When it did not appear on the agenda, one member of the Executive Committee, Jure Bilić, attempted to introduce it for discussion but was ruled out of order. At another point Dušan Dragosavac, the Croatian Serb vice-secretary of the Executive Committee, broke ranks with a sharp attack on nationalism and some features of the 'national movement' which was an implicit attack on Dabčević-Kučar's speech. This time it was Bilić, still determined to avoid a public confrontation, who intervened to call his colleague's speech 'unhelpful'. In the general discussion, meanwhile, special emphasis was placed on warnings that Croatian public opinion would not tolerate further delay in the reform of the foreign currency system.

The price of maintaining the façade of unity, to which the Executive Committee had agreed, was therefore a meeting entirely along the lines desired by the triumvirate—a reversal, in effect, of the 20th session's stand on nationalism less than six months earlier. The results would leave the anti-triumvirate group formally committed to the triumvirate's line and thus legitimately subject to charges of factionalism and a violation of democratic centralism if they subsequently continued to criticise the 'mass movement' or Croatian intransigence on issues like the foreign currency system. Their purge would then be a foregone conclusion.

It was at this point, according to Bakarić's testimony,[79] that he and the other anti-triumvirate Croatian leaders decided to go to Tito on his return from a State visit to the United States and Canada. When they did so, Bakarić said, they found that the President, who 'read the press and sensed what was happening', had already decided to move.

Events now moved rapidly towards a climax. Even while the Croatian Central Committee was meeting, *Hrvatski tjednik* published the final text of the Matica's proposed revisions of the draft amendments to the Croatian Constitution and launched a Republic-wide campaign for their adoption. These proposals included a straightforward definition of Croatia as 'the sovereign national State of the Croatian nation' (a formula again criticised, the same day, during the Central Committee's debate), with its sovereignty based on 'the right to self-determination, including the right to secession'. Croatian was to be the sole official language, Croatian authorities would exercise full control over all tax revenues collected in Croatia (with only 'voluntary' contributions to the Federation on the basis of inter-republican agreements), there would be a separate Croatian monetary policy and bank of emission, Croatian recruits with the Yugoslav People's Army would normally serve only in the Republic, and there would be an autonomous Croatian territorial army. A week later the same journal began an open attack on Dragosavac and Bilić. At Matica and students' meetings Croatian membership in the United Nations, a real 'federalisation' of the Yugoslav army, a revision of the Republic's frontiers at the expense of Herzegovina and Montenegro and a separate foreign policy were discussed. Rumours and articles in Croatian émigré journals again spoke—as they had in July and September—of a student or even a general strike, ostensibly in support of the beleaguered triumvirate.

Tito returned to Yugoslavia on November 8. For seven weeks, since shortly after his September visit to Zagreb and the fateful toast, he had been involved almost exclusively with foreign policy, and for most of the past month he had been abroad. He had received Leonid Brezhnev in Belgrade at the end of September and then observed the first major demonstration of the 'all-national defence' concept in manoeuvres near Karlovac in Croatia. Since mid-October he had been to Persepolis, where he exploited the Shah's celebration of Iran's 2,500 years of statehood for an intensive round of talks with other Heads of State and Government assembled there, and then New Delhi, Cairo, North America for the State visits, and London, with only a long weekend in Belgrade between the Eastern and Western trips. It was not a casual exercise in summitry. Brezhnev's diplomatic offensive and the Western powers' response to it, moving towards détente in Europe but not in the Middle East and the eastern Mediterranean, seemed to be leaving the intervening zone which used to be called the Near East—the Balkans—in a precarious limbo. Tito was in search of clarification, support from old friends, and a reassertion of Yugoslavia's attitude towards the tendency of great powers to use small ones as pawns in their games. His mission was not without relevance for the domestic crisis he had left behind, for Yugoslavia was still filled with rumours, some of them quite substantial, that one or both of the superpowers were dabbling in Yugoslav and Croatian politics.

On November 11, three days after his return, the press announced that the President had gone to Bugojno, an isolated place in western Bosnia, for a shooting holiday. One of his visitors there, on November 15, was Dušan Dragosavac, the emissary of Bakarić and the majority of the Zagreb Executive Committee. After listening to him and perhaps to other unidentified callers,[80] Tito agreed to meet with the full Executive Committee. The following night, in Zagreb, Student Federation President Budiša, addressing a university mass meeting attended by two leaders of the Matica Hrvatska, attacked Bakarić by name and issued a blunt warning to the triumvirate. 'If they do not see through a dirty and behind-the-scenes game being played to divide them from the Croatian people', he declared, 'it can happen that they will lose the confidence of the nation'.[81]

On November 17 Tito returned to Belgrade and late on the 22nd he left for Timişoara, in the Romanian Banat, for a preannounced meeting with President Ceauşescu. A few hours earlier some 2,000 students of Zagreb University attended a mass meeting called by Budiša and the Student Federation and tumultuously greeted a proposal that the university should go on strike the next morning over the foreign currency issue. The strike was well organised, with students and professors forcibly prevented from entering their classrooms when necessary. The executive of the Croatian Student Federation called for its extension to the entire Republic, emissaries were dispatched to provincial universities and to factories in the Zagreb area and there was talk of a general strike.

The timing of the students' move took everyone by surprise, since rumours and the émigré press had predicted that the strike would only take place after Christmas, when thousands of emigrant workers, presumably influenced by Croatian émigré organisations and propaganda, would be home for the holidays. The Matica and student leaders, always well informed, apparently knew as the public did not that the anti-nationalist faction in the Party had made its move and appealed to Tito. Time was suddenly short, and the move was made hastily, while Tito was again out of the country. It was clearly a desperate attempt to force the triumvirate and their friends to declare themselves openly and irretrievably, something they had not yet really done. Wavering, divided, preparing for the worst, and ready to move against their Executive Committee opponents, they were still desperately trying to find a middle ground which would enable them to avoid choosing sides for a final battle which would have an unpredictable but in any scenario an almost certainly undesirable outcome. The strike was thus a wild gamble, but those who took it may have reckoned that if even some factories joined them the triumvirate and their Party following would have to, facing Tito with a civil war if he called in the army. The workers, however, did not move, which Tito was to call 'fortunate'.

The moment of truth had come. In the confusion a number of individual Party officials issued ambiguous statements which appeared to approve or at least condone the student action. But the triumvirate, already informed of Tito's intention to call a meeting with them, were immediately aware of what was at stake. One by one Party organisations known to be close to them adopted resolutions condemning the strike as 'an action directed against the policy and course of the League of Communists of Croatia'. Tripalo, in Dalmatia when it began, hurried to join the chorus at a marathon series of meetings, but the students stayed out. On November 29, Yugoslavia's National Day, Tripalo made a speech declaring that 'it would be be necessary to change a thousand leaders in Croatia' to change the Republic's policy,[82] and Dabčević-Kučar went on television with a public appeal to the students to end the strike. Although few in her countrywide audience knew it, the summons to Karadjordjevo must have been in her pocket. She looked ten years older than she had three and a half short weeks before, at the 22nd session.

8

'ONE RING TO BIND THEM ALL'

Karajordjevo and after

On December 1, 1918, the Serbian Prince-Regent Aleksandar Karadjordjević received a delegation from the National Council in Zagreb, a *de facto* Government of the Croats, Croatian Serbs, and Slovenes of the vanishing Habsburg Monarchy, and responded to their urgent request for immediate union by proclaiming in their presence the creation of the Kingdom of the Serbs, Croats and Slovenes, later renamed Yugoslavia. At dawn on December 1, 1971, the fifty-third anniversary of this proclamation, the Croatian Communist successor of the Serbian kings of Yugoslavia was meeting with another *de facto* Zagreb Government, at a former royal hunting lodge which still bore the name of the Serbian royal family, to tell them that their policies and activities were endangering that union and that they must bear the consequences.

Later the same day, after Tito had been closeted with the Croatian leaders for twenty hours, the rest of the Presidency of the LCY assembled at the lodge for what was formally their 21st session and heard him at last make good his threats of the preceding April and July. He disavowed the policies pursued by the Party in Croatia and the leaders who had made them, and he did so publicly: next afternoon, as the Karadjordjevo meeting was coming to an end, Yugoslav radio stations repeatedly interrupted their regular programmes —a highly unusual and thus momentous occurrence—to broadcast his opening statement.

The Party leadership in Croatia, Tito said, had pandered to nationalists and separatists and displayed 'rotten liberalism' in the face of a developing 'counter-revolution'. He granted that most of their complaints about the economic system were justified, particularly those which referred to the foreign exchange system and the 'alienation' from the workers of income and self-management rights by managers and technocrats in banks and big enterprises. But it was impermissible that these should be posed as national questions and that demonstrations and other extra-legal pressures should be encouraged now that the amendments had provided constitutional mechanisms for the solution of such problems.

Equally unacceptable was the view, again expressed during his meeting with the Croats, that 'no one, not even the Presidency of the LCY', had the right to interfere in the affairs of the republican parties: the Party, Tito said in his closing remarks, 'is the one factor which does have the right to undertake ideological-political action in an all-Yugoslav framework'.

He also said pointedly that the primary fault for events in Croatia did not lie in the intentions of the Croatian leaders but rather in an ideological crisis in the Party 'which goes back a long way', and that the crisis and analogous if less extreme deviations by leaderships existed in most other republics. All these phenomena were largely the result of the lack of attention which had been paid to 'Marxist education' in recent years and the toleration of 'anti-Marxist ... and in large part pro-Western' teachers in the schools and universities from which younger Party cadres and the rest of the new generation were coming. All regions therefore had lessons to learn from what had happened in Zagreb. Meanwhile, Tito said, it was now up to the Croatian Central Committee to put their own house in order and to re-establish unity in conformity with the line of the Party.

The triumvirate, after a week of feeble efforts to save their personal positions, told Tito individually that they were resigning. A public announcement nevertheless was delayed until the Croatian Central Committee met on December 12, allowing a wave of demands for their removal to build up from meetings throughout the Republic. On the day of the meeting army helicopters were poised over the city, police in riot helmets were posted at strategic points and Budiša and his colleagues were arrested at dawn. Dabčević-Kučar opened the session and relinquished the chair to read her and Pirker's letter of resignation; Tripalo's letter to Tito resigning from the Executive Bureau and the State Presidency (he held no republican office) was also read. Bakarić and Josip Vrhovec, the latter about to replace Pirker as Secretary of the Executive Committee, asked for the floor to pay tribute to 'a political maturity which facilitates the settlement of topical problems' and to urge that criticism of the failures of those who were resigning should be coupled with appreciation of the positive services which they had rendered. It was a dignified performance by all concerned and a scenario deliberately planned, like the delay in announcing the resignations and as a counterpoint to army helicopters and precautionary arrests, to ensure a smooth transition. The 'cleansing' of Croatia had begun.[1]

In fact the 'mass national movement' collapsed with a speed and completeness which Bakarić and others later admitted was a pleasant surprise. There were sporadic demonstrations in Zagreb on each of the next few evenings, during which 550 persons, mostly students, were arrested and briefly detained. Otherwise no hand was raised to defend fallen leaders and their lieutenants, over 400 of whom had resigned or been dismissed by mid-January,[2] or to protest the banning of the Matica Hrvatska and the arrest of its leaders. In May 1972 the triumvirate were stripped of Party membership.[3] Although many ordinary Croats remained sullen and resentful for many months, most Party members behaved after its 'cleansing' as if nothing had happened, or at least nothing in which they had been involved.

If part of the reason was represented by those army helicopters over the Central Committee building on December 12 or was to be sought in Tito's still awesome authority, another part concerned the personality of the Party as dictated by its middle and lower rank officials, a personality which was not peculiarly Croatian. Speaking of the triumvirate's apparent mass support in the Party at a post-Karadjordjevo meeting on December 10, Milka Planinc, who was to succeed Dabčević-Kučar as President of the Croatian Central Committee three days later, wondered how it could have happened that 'in some places entire Party structures, so to speak, stood up and cheered those who were usurping the Party'. Her answer inadvertently explained the principal reason why the same people were within the week to accept and sometimes even unashamedly to cheer her and the new team, demanding the further disgrace and even imprisonment of their former idols. It also incidentally focused on the central problem, alongside nationalism, besetting the 'Yugoslav road to socialism'.

Their behaviour was that of fortune-hunters and careerists, ... careerists who I would say were not primarily nationalists, if you ask me, but who thought that this was the card on which they would build their careers. Unfortunately, the majority is that way, because we have drawn into the Party the clerk mentality of obedient servants, not people who think and seek answers to the further continuation of the revolution, but obsequious clerks. We must find an answer for this. Without it, if we do not remove such people from the Party, we will not be equipped for the stage that will last even after Tito but on Tito's line. Because we have drawn into the Party pusillanimity, opportunism to the methods of Stalinism, because in some circles honest people simply have not been in a position to stand their ground.[4]

Although Planinc was attempting to suggest, for immediate tactical reasons, that the Party had only recently become characterised by a majority of 'obsequious clerks', the same complaint had been heard before and would be heard again, frequently and in all parts of the country, and always with the same explanation.[5] One of the finer ironies of the situation was that the methods used by the former Croatian leaders to control the Party, methods which were now one of the principal accusations against them, were in fact and always had been standard operating procedures, the glue of Party discipline. The personality of the organisation she was describing was not the recent creation of the latest generation of Croatian Party leaders. It was the creation of Lenin, Stalin, Tito and the dynamics of the revolutions they made, and it was now a major part of the ballast which was threatening to capsize Yugoslavia's valiant experiment with an eventually party-less 'socialist democracy' built on the keel of 'self-management'.

Tito meanwhile elaborated on his reasons for taking forceful action. Events in Zagreb 'and elsewhere', he told the Council of the Trades Union Federation in mid-December, had been moving 'little by little towards a separatist line'. Therefore,

if we had not gone into battle now and stopped that, ... perhaps in six months it would have come to shooting, to a civil war. And you know what that would mean. How could we permit, how could I as head of state and President of the Yugoslav Party permit someone else to come and restore order and peace. I have said that I would never permit that, that I will sooner employ the ultimate means, and you know what those means are.[6]

There were many Yugoslavs, including Party leaders in other republics and significantly numerous erstwhile Croatian supporters of the triumvirate, who were ready to accept these propositions or others as justifying drastic action in Croatia, but who feared the wider consequences of that action. Agreeing that the situation in Croatia and its backlash elsewhere had indeed become a serious threat to the stability of the system, to peace among the nationalities and perhaps even to the unity of the country, such people perceived a danger that measures already taken or contemplated might mean a perhaps irreversible turning back in the country as a whole and not only in Croatia. Achieved levels of pluralistic and participatory decision-making could again give way to the 'firm hand' rule of a centralised, hierarchical and authoritarian Party, with all of its historically known defects in terms of efficiency, honesty, responsiveness and civil liberties.

Most of the senior figures of the Party establishment, including the new leaders in Croatia and the existing ones in Serbia, displayed extraordinary sensitiveness to such fears. They issued repeated warnings against the consequences of any return to 'firm hand rule' or even temporary alliance with 'the defeated forces of centralism, neo-Stalinism, or neo-Cominformism' which were offering their help in the struggle against 'nationalism and chauvinism'. The terms and the context left little doubt, in most cases, of the sincerity of the authors.[7]

A conspicuous exception was provided by Tito himself, although he too said that there should be no 'witch hunt' in Croatia.[8]

Yugoslav Communists who were worried about the wider implications of the purges in Zagreb found particularly alarming his
more emphatic repetition, in his strongest post-purge speech, that
the rot had started with the 6th Congress in 1952, and that he
personally had never liked that Congress.[9] He was to return to this
theme several times in coming months. As *NIN* dared to remind its
readers on reporting the speech on January 26, 1971, in an article
which undoubtedly represented the views and concerns of the then
Serbian leadership, it was the 6th Congress which had first
proclaimed the change in the Party's role from that of a Leninist
Party ruling over the State and society to a Marxist association of
'progressive' Communists exerting influence rather than power in a
'socialist democracy'. If the Yugoslav Party had never become
merely that in practice, the spirit and aspirations of the 6th
Congress had provided the ideological basis for the considerable
degree of decentralisation and pluralisation achieved in recent
years. For those who had dominated the Party establishment since
1966, to call in question precisely that Congress was to call in
question most of the things which distinguished Yugoslav from
Soviet communism.

For several months the omens were mixed. High-level assuran-
ces of no return to the past seemed contradicted by the dimensions
of the purge in Croatia, the escalation of charges levelled against
the purged, arrests of non-Party 'movementists' and the widening
use of other methods and language reminiscent of former times.
The position of liberal leaders in other republics, however much
and publicly they had disagreed with the policies of the Croatian
leaders in 1971, was weakened by the fall of the latter and their
own association with 'rotten liberal' if not 'nationalist' ideas.
Several such leaders were already under pressure before the end of
the year, including Crvenkovski of Macedonia and Kavčič of
Slovenia. Each of these had been criticised by an important fellow
countryman: Crvenkovski (without actually being named) by his
old rival Koliševski for having 'made no small contribution to the
general atmosphere and inflammation of nationalism and chauvinism in Croatia', and Kavčič by Kardelj, who condemned as
'people's capitalism' a proposal by Kavčič that enterprises should
be permitted to sell shares—non-voting but with a variable return
on a profit- and risk-sharing basis—to private Yugoslav citizens.[10]
Kavčič, Nikezić and Perović were also reliably reported to head
Tito's own blacklist because they had initially opposed the
Karadjordjevo decision to denounce the Croatian leaders publicly
and force their resignation, preferring a final warning.

For a time, however, there were no consequences. In 1972
Crvenkovski served as *de facto* Vice-President of Yugoslavia under
the State Presidency's rules of rotation, although he was dropped

from the Party Executive Bureau in January on the pretext that no one should be a member of both these bodies; Kavčič was re-elected as President of the Slovenian Government on February 7, 1972. In Croatia the new leadership continued to support earlier Croatian views on questions of economic and political reform, stripped of arguments betraying national or regional prejudices. The more than tripling of foreign currency 'retention quotas', announced a fortnight after the resignations of the triumvirate, was only the first of the fallen leaders' specific demands to be accepted at least in part after their fall.

At the 2nd Conference of the LCY, which met in Belgrade from January 25-7, 1972, the only organisational change of significance was in the size and membership of the Executive Bureau. It was reduced from fourteen members (plus Tito) to eight, one from each republic and province. With completely new people representing three republics—Krsta Avramović for Serbia, Bilić for Croatia and Todo Kurtović for Bosnia-Herzegovina—nine members of the old Bureau were dropped, clearly for varying reasons. These were Bakarić (hospitalised and more seriously ill than usual) and Tripalo (already resigned), Mijatović and Dizdarević (appointed ambassador to Paris), Pečujlić and Todorović, Kardelj, Crvenkovski and Vlahović. The Bureau was to have a Secretary, a position which was to rotate annually but nevertheless a more powerful one than the monthly chairman it had thus far had. Dolanc of Slovenia, who had impressed Tito with his skilful handling of the December crisis while the Bureau's chairman-for-a-month, was named as the first such Secretary; in violation of the rotation rule he was to keep the job until and after it was made permanent at the 10th Congress in 1974.

All persons with reputations as advocates of republican Party autonomy were thus eliminated from the Executive Bureau. On the other hand, except for Bilić as Croatia's new leading spokesman, Gligorov as an economic specialist of growing authority and Fadil Hoxha as the Kosovar Albanians' perennial representative at the Party summit, the Bureau was now comprised of second-rank political figures. The changes were therefore clearly a compromise between Tito's repeatedly expressed desire for a genuinely powerful new federal Party centre and the determination of Serbian and other republican leaders to defend decentralisation of the Party as far as possible. Tito himself referred to such resistance, specifically in Serbia, in his closing speech to the Conference. He also noted, among 'some other things which perhaps bothered me a little during the discussion', that 'no one mentioned the dictatorship of the proletariat. Many tend somehow to avoid it as they formerly avoided democratic centralism. But the dictatorship of the proletariat exists in our country, as indeed it must.'[11]

The Conference discussion and documents were dominated by two apparently contradictory themes: strengthening Party control and the Party centre, and strengthening self-management.[12] Both were emphasised by Vlahović, who submitted the principal report on the political and ideological situation, and who insisted that the two were reconcilable. The first was in fact a prerequisite of the second, he said, since only a strong, united and politically effective Party could protect self-managers from those who through personal or class ambition or the dynamics of their social roles would continuously seek to usurp the rights and powers of workers. In addition, he continued, the 'workers' amendments' of 1971 must be implemented, fully and promptly. They should then be expanded in further amendments, which would also 'turn indirect democracy into direct democracy' by emphasising the commune and by changing the parliamentary system into the 'system of delegations' long advocated by Kardelj. These forthcoming changes, Vlahović said, would 'definitively dispel the fears, still present here and there', that developments since Karadjordjevo would mean 'a change of course in the development of a self-managing socialist Yugoslavia'.[13]

The same two themes and attempts to reconcile them were to dominate Yugoslav politics during the next two years, until a theoretical synthesis incorporating numerous compromises was institutionalised in a new Constitution and at the 10th LCY Congress, both in the spring of 1974. The process included a major realignment of the forces represented in the Yugoslav political system. This realignment was in part a response to the subtraction from the political equation of Croatia's late leaders, who had been among the principal and most powerful advocates of the liberalising and decentralising reforms of 1965-68. It also, however, represented a new awareness of interests and values and where they coincided with those of others.

Such awareness was apparent in the shift from a national to a 'class' or 'self-management' perspective in attacking the 'alienated centres of financial and political power' found in big business, big banks and enterprise management boards, and thus from the federal Party and State bodies to the 'managerial-technocratic élite' as the principal wielders of such power. Criticism from this perspective had been a major theme of the ideological debate of 1967-68 (see above, pp. 214-21) and of some later writings by Kardelj and others,[14] but had been overshadowed first by preoccupation with the remaining powers of central apparatuses and then by the projection of all problems as national questions. Now, however, the way was open for what was officially described as a struggle on another and currently more pressing front but was in reality the rationale and focus of something more complicated.

The thesis that there was a compatibility and even a necessary connection between more control by a more centralised Party and more rather than less economic and social self-management suggested interesting but different possibilities to a broad spectrum of individuals and social forces.

It was in the first place a formula for a recentralisation and reassertion of Party authority which claimed not to challenge the system's unchallengeable second founding myth of self-management. As such it appealed to those nostalgic for the power, prestige and perquisites of the Party boss and/or the traditional Communist values which had been lost or devalued in recent years. This category included superficially diverse elements: veteran Party conservatives and centralists, youth disgusted with what they took to be the *embourgeoisement* of the Yugoslav revolution, and quondam liberals who were discovering that the conservatives had been right after all when they argued that less Party power was not as nice as more.

To yet another equally heterogeneous group, comprised of people who were simply eager to limit the apparently imminent erosion of achieved levels of pluralistic decision-making, of a market rather than a command economy and of civil and entre-preneurial liberties, the new dual focus offered two quite different potentials. The first was a loophole through *a priori* legitimation of new devices which could be called 'strengthening self-management', the very way in which liberalisation had begun again after 1959. The second was a way of turning an otherwise defensive stance into a positive platform on which these people could accommodate themselves to new conditions and appear as paladins of proletarian interests and true self-management. They could thereby seek renewed contact with the politically conscious members of the working class and its institutions, and new allies among the more moderate of the centralists and Marxist traditionalists, who at least shared their apprehension of a straightforward return to the pre-1965 system. Such a rallying point was especially attractive to many senior and middle-rank Party Whigs of the old coalition and to many socialist entrepreneurs, writers, artists and other intellectuals, all with an interest in saving the savable of the past decade.

Finally, the new platform also suggested a road worth exploring to the genuine ideologues and interest groups of a more literal interpretation of self-management. These, too, had been among the constituent elements of the reform coalition of the 1960s, but had had some disagreements with the others as early as 1966, as we have seen. Now all of their sometime partners seemed to have betrayed them. This was clearest in the evolution of Croatian national and liberal Communism into national-liberalism and possibly even into a kind of fascism based, like the Italian original, on a combination of nationalism and a corrupted socialism defending middle-class interests. But it could also apply to the 'managerial-technological élite' and their political supporters, whose devotion to economic efficiency and 'big systems'[15] had led them to defend industrial and commercial oligopolies, concentration of capital in big banks without 'social control' and centralised decision-making by trained and technically informed professional cadres, all of which seemed to mock any hope of effective participation by workers or their organisations. In the light of such considerations, many of those with a genuine ideological, personal, or group stake in decision-making by people outside both Party-State and managerial bureaucracies were ready for new if desperate formulas.

For at least a few members of this last group, true sons of and true believers in the official ideology and values which had evolved in Yugoslavia since 1949, the kind of Marxian 'unity in contradictions' implicit in the new formula was more than a desperate expedient or good practical politics. It also represented the only remaining hope of optimising the simultaneous development of both socialism and democracy, especially in a multinational State 'which, to reiterate, belongs among the most conflict-prone social and state units in Europe'.[16] Democracy, in their view, would become a myth and a mockery if genuinely polycentric and participatory decision-making and a market economy were abolished. At the same time, the recent ascendancy of particularistic nationalisms and of the 'managerial-technocratic élite' had been salutory reminders that unguided, 'spontaneous' democracy could undermine socialist principles of social ownership and self-management by ordinary people, and would always do so as long as money, education, information and political mobilisation are unevenly distributed. Such distribution, they now believed, inevitably leads to concentrations of power and thereby to the repeated and 'spontaneous' creation of new 'counter-classes'.[17]

Perhaps, therefore, a way out might after all be found in a felicitous combination of the two principles enunciated at the 2nd Conference: keeping plural and autonomous decision-making institutions, a market economy and popular participation, while re-establishing the Party as 'one ring to bind them all', the sole guarantor of unity in a multinational confederation and multi-interest diversity and a counterweight with power to challenge each and every other emerging 'counter-class'. Essentially what such people envisaged, although they could or would not have put it this way, was a deadlock between the Party apparatus and the technological élite, socialism's two 'new classes', competing for the role of its exclusive tutor. Such a deadlock had hitherto been impossible because the Party's vastly greater strength in the regime's early years and its disorientation, disintegration and partial abdication after 1966 had given first one and then the other a dominant position. Now, if the reassertion of Party authority could be limited to creating and not again upsetting such a balance, the tendency of both to seek to dominate the increasingly mature instruments and agents of self-management might be mutually frustrated. The road to the genuine socialist democracy envisaged by Yugoslav theory would then be open.[18]

Meanwhile, the diversity of supporters and aims of the new platform did much to explain why forecasts made by many Yugoslavs and outside observers at the end of 1972—anticipating a speedy and simple return to the system of the 1950's, or perhaps to an analogue of the current Romanian variant of the Soviet one—were not for the moment to be fulfilled. The new vogue for phrases like 'the class basis of conflicting interests', 'new middle strata (or classes) generated under socialism' replacing 'the (temporarily) defeated forces of State-socialist centralism' as the 'counter-class' opposing the proletariat and self-management, and even a superficially Orwellian neologism about 'self-managing democracy as a specific form of the dictatorship of the proletariat appropriate to the present stage of social development' had more dimensions of meaning than appeared at first glance. Such slogans provided all members of this emerging new coalition, as heterogeneous and unstable as the old one, with sometimes literal and sometimes metaphoric emblems of otherwise diverse views, hopes and strategies.

It was also only one of many ironies that the resulting political programme included numerous criticisms, demands and slogans originally proposed from two sources which now competed with 'rotten liberalism' for first place on the programme's list of enemies of Yugoslav socialism. These were the deposed Croatian leadership, whose criticism and demands were now placed in a 'class' context and shorn of those which had aspired to a 'federalisation' of the Party, and the 'Marxist humanist' professors and 'ultra-leftist' students of Zagreb and Belgrade Universities. The latter won no laurels from their long-standing warnings about resurgent nationalism, their permanent conflict with presently or soon-to-be purged leaderships in Zagreb and Belgrade or the unacknowledged acceptance in the new programme of the heart of their criticism of 'social differences', laissez-faire economics, the social structure of the Party and underdeveloped self-management. They continued to be anathema to Tito and like-minded Party leaders because of the other central feature of their criticism, which attacked continuing Party dictatorship and the survival of 'Stalinist dogmatism' in Party thought. They were also no better loved by the beleaguered remnants of their ertswhile protector-critics among more liberal Party leaders and intellectuals, who were bitterly convinced that extremist criticism by the 'Marxist humanists' had been a self-fulfilling prophecy, contributing significantly to the present neo-Leninist if not neo-Stalinist backlash. The demand that the offending professors should be sacked, again made by Tito at Karadjordjevo, was frequently repeated during the following year. Serious Party efforts to remove them from the universities were nevertheless unsuccessful until early 1975, when eight members of the Belgrade Faculty of Philosophy were finally suspended—by an act of the Serbian Assembly of dubious constitutionality—and *Praxis* was forced to cease publication after eleven turbulent years.

October in Serbia

The second chapter of the dénouement of the crisis in Croatia, extending the purge to other republics, was postponed until the autumn of 1972. In part this was because the Party Presidency and other relevant bodies were still largely packed with supporters of these republican leaders, and because the new realignment took time to effect and in fact was still far from complete even then. In part, however, it was also because some of these leaders, Nikezić and Perović in particular, had made themselves additionally difficult to attack through their consistent anti-nationalism and their generally effective demonstration of 'modern' Party tactics, exerting 'influence' through activity, manipulation and a stern approach to *organised* political activity outside Party and Socialist Alliance frameworks. They thereby confined dissent to a largely harmless kind of safety valve and an often helpful source of criticism and new ideas with very infrequent recourse to 'administrative measures', implicitly answering Tito's argument that 'revolutionary weapons' were now essential to unity and the defence of socialism.

When the attack came, its timing and some of its inspiration may also have been affected by considerations of foreign policy and foreign trade on the part of some senior officials, including Tito and Kardelj.

After a second consecutive year of excellent harvests, 1972 was proving to be a reasonably good year economically and particularly in foreign trade. With exports 20 per cent higher in value and imports 12 per cent lower, the former again covered about 75 per cent of the import bill. Invisible earnings reached a record of US$1,560 million, a 23 per cent increase over 1971; $870 million of this total consisted of remittances by Yugoslav workers in Western Europe, and $470 million came from tourism. The net result was a balance of payments *surplus* of about $250 million, the first in twenty-five years except for a modest one of $23 million in 1965.

The changing qualitative structure of Yugoslav exports bore witness to a new level of economic development and the success of postwar industrialisation. In the decade since 1961 raw materials, then already down to 24·7 per cent of all exports, had declined further to 11·2 per cent. Semi-finished goods had also declined further, from 37·6 per cent to 31·8 per cent, while the share of what Yugoslav statistics define as highly finished goods had grown from 42·8 to 57 per cent.[19] Also significant was the list of principal exports and their principal buyers, in 1971 headed by shipbuilding, in which Yugoslavia now ranked tenth in the world, with Britain and the Soviet Union as the leading customers. Others that year included, in rank order of values, copper and zinc products (the USA, Italy and the USSR as principal buyers), machinery and electrical equipment (principally to Comecon, Egypt, India and Indonesia), fresh and tinned meat (the former primarily to Italy, the latter to Britain and the USA), footwear and outerwear, rail and road vehicles and furniture (all to diverse markets), followed by cables and wires and steel products. Serbian-made TV sets were doing well on the West German market.

The assortment was certainly no longer that of a producer primarily of agricultural goods and raw materials, while the distribution of markets cast some doubt on the argument that Yugoslav industrial goods were competitive only in the Soviet bloc and possibly in the underdeveloped world. While this performance in the foreign trade sector might prove temporary—it was assisted by two devaluations of the dinar in 1971 (by 16·8 per cent in January, without effect, and by 18·7 per cent in December) and by renewed efforts at stabilisation launched in October by the FEC—these and other economic indicators seemed to suggest that the agony of readjustment imposed by the reforms of 1965 was at last paying dividends.

Precisely at this moment, however, a number of business as well as political leaders began to lose their nerve. During 1972 several leading personalities from both of these worlds declared privately or publicly that Yugoslavia would never achieve the economic integration into the developed world's 'international division of labour' which had been a primary goal of the economic reforms of the 1960s. The attempt should therefore be abandoned and the system should be reoriented towards the less demanding markets of the Communist bloc. Particularly significant was Kardelj's warning in September 1972 to his fellow Slovenes, who had come closest to the goal:

People who think that the solution is a one-sided link-up with Western Europe or Bavaria and similar ideas spread under the slogan 'our place in

Western Europe' do not at all accept the fact that, despite the economic progress achieved, this type of economic relations could turn Slovenia into a province exploited by West European capitalism. It must also be asked, to what type of political dependence would such a solution lead and how would the East European countries react to such a separatist and anti-socialist orientation?[20]

Kardelj's warning came after a year in which the Soviet Union, for the first time since 1948, had moved into first place among the markets for Yugoslav exports, followed by Italy and West Germany (the traditional best customers and still the chief source of Yugoslav imports), Czechoslovakia and Great Britain. Comecon's share in Yugoslavia's foreign trade consequently rose to 36·1 per cent of exports and 21·1 per cent of imports in 1971, compared to 45·4 per cent of exports and 58·9 per cent of imports in trade with Western Europe and 6 per cent in both categories with the United States.

The increase in trade with the Comecon bloc reflected, as usual, an improvement in Yugoslav-bloc relations. Healing the wounds inflicted by Czechoslovakia had been a slow process, but it seemed to be complete when Brezhnev visited Yugoslavia in September 1971 and responded to Yugoslav pressure by reaffirming both the Belgrade Declaration of 1955 and the Moscow one of 1956.[21] In June 1972 Tito returned Brezhnev's visit, the first time he had been to Moscow since the consultations following the Arab-Israeli war of 1967, and in July FEC President Džemal Bijedić became the first Yugoslav prime minister to attend a Comecon meeting. The way was now clear for a further increase in commercial relations. In September, at the time of Kardelj's speech in Ljubljana and as Tito's attack on the Serbian leaders was beginning, a Yugoslav delegation was in Moscow concluding negotiations for a huge $1,300 million Soviet credit line for the construction of new industries in Yugoslavia. On November 2, after the purges had begun, a subsidiary agreement regulating the use of a first, $540 million instalment of this credit line was signed.

The Western press and other observers promptly perceived a cause and effect relationship between these developments, with the purges as a political *quid pro quo* for Soviet credit.[22] Yugoslav spokesmen naturally denied such a connection, and there is no evidence that they were not telling the truth. On the contrary, if international considerations were an important factor in Tito's moves to reassert centralised Party control over Yugoslav political life, it seems far more likely from his own record and recent statements and the history of the regime that his concern and that of his lieutenants was to leave no serious disunity, internal faction or blatant deviations from their own interpretation of Marxist principles to provide an excuse for foreign intervention 'to save socialism in Yugoslavia' after his departure. This does not mean, however, that the Russians were not as pleased with the fall of former Yugoslav foreign secretary Nikezić, his successor Tepavac and their likeminded comrades as they were by the Yugoslav retreat from an 'anti-Leninist' concept of the Party, or that Tito and the purgers were not aware of this and prepared to exploit it.[23] Nor does it mean that the desire to reorient some foreign trade towards the easier markets of the East, based on a failure of nerve, on fears of EEC protectionism and later on the first signs of economic crisis in the West, were not genuine. It would in any case have been difficult, given repeated declarations of a commitment to good relations by both Yugoslavs and Russians and the needs of the Yugoslav economy, for the Yugoslavs to say no to an ostensibly generous offer.[24]

The course on which Tito was now embarking was in fact explained, and is fully explainable, in the public speeches which he and others had made recently and were now making. The most important of these, which also heralded stages in the final dénouement, were Dolanc's talk with regional Party leaders in Split on September 19, Tito's interview in *Vjesnik* on October 7 and his speech 'to leading functionaries of socio-political organisations of Serbia' on October 16, and a subsequently famous letter which was presented to and signed by Tito and Dolanc on behalf of the Party Executive Bureau on September 18 (the day before Dolanc's Split speech), sent to all Party organisations on October 2, but published only on October 18.[25]

The central message of all these and subsequent statements and of the 10th Congress, which was postponed until May 1974 to give the Party time to accept it, was simple and clear. A newly reunited, recentralised, redisciplined and therefore thoroughly purged LCY must and would reassert effective control over the country's political and economic life. It would do this by reassuming its 'leading role': by having firm and coherent principles, by again playing a decisive role in 'cadre policy' in Government organs and the economy and by firm action, including 'administrative measures' (dismissal or imprisonment) against any and all whom the Party chose to define as 'enemies of our socialist democracy'. It would do this to preserve the unity of the country, its international prestige and creditworthiness and above all the future and progress of self-management.

The Party, it was now said, had virtually abdicated such a role when and because it became disoriented and disunited by 'incorrect views' promulgated at and ever since the 6th Congress[26] and by politically unrealistic and ideologically unacceptable corollary theories now scathingly described as 'anarcho-liberal', or sometimes simply 'liberal'. Such theories, originating in a then correctly 'one-sided' preoccupation with the threats posed by Stalinism and by 'bureaucratic State centralism', had been espoused in latterday form and in varying degrees by political leaders in several republics, but especially in Serbia. In the language of the indictment made in October 1972 and again endorsed by a 'purified' and regenerated Party at the 10th Congress, these erring leaders had held that the further development of social self-management now could and should be characterised by more 'spontaneity' and 'pluralism'—and therefore by a decreasingly political or 'interventionist' role for the Party—if Yugoslavia was to move on towards a genuine 'direct socialist democracy without political intermediaries' in which 'self-managers' and those delegated by them would freely decide on the distribution of national income and other public choices. They thereby overlooked the 'class content' of socialism, specifically in assuming that in what was not yet a classless society the working class could already be equated with Yugoslavs as a whole (which they liked to call 'the working people', an ideological obfuscation later somewhat gingerly blamed on Kardelj himself).[27] Building error upon error they went on to assume that present levels of economic and social development and 'social consciousness' were adequate as a support and guarantor of 'spontaneous' democracy and genuine self-management without the protection of a powerful and active Party.

What happened instead was that such 'liberalism', with its insistence that the Party could warn and advise but must not otherwise interfere in self-management and that the Party centre was no longer entitled to dictate to subordinate Party organs, permitted and encouraged the revival of centrifugal or hegemonistic nationalisms in the multinational State and the rise of a 'technocratic-managerial élite' controlling the economy and 're-privatising' it through 'group ownership'. Therefore, instead of the further expansion of self-management, the gradual relaxation of firm Party control and of centralised Party discipline led to power being grabbed by local politicians who were often more nationalist than Communist, and by 'technocrats' in industry, commerce and banking who admired Western managerial techniques more than they did the Yugoslav working class. The 'liberals' who countenanced these developments, thereby betraying their links with the new 'counter-class' of the 'technocratic bureaucracy', were either unwittingly or consciously and deliberately promoting the restoration of a crypto-capitalist economy and a multi-party 'bourgeois democracy'.

The 'federalisation' of the Party and insubordination to the rules of democratic centralism had enabled such people, allegedly concentrated at the republican level and seldom found in lower

Party ranks, to frustrate implementation of clearly stated and unanimously accepted Party principles and action programmes. This was most conspicuous in recent months in the non-implementation of the 'workers' amendments', which were designed to subject the overweening financial power of those still notorious commercial conglomerates, big banks and insurance companies and the influence of their business partners and investors to 'social control'.

Tito pointedly recalled that most of these 'centres of alienated financial power' were in Belgrade.[28] Implicit in such reminders was the suggestion that the wily Serbs were seeking economic hegemony as a substitute for the political hegemony which they had lost with the dismantling of a unitary State. This was a consideration certain to affect the attitude of leaderships in other republics, even including liberals among them.[29] It was a weighty argument. The magnitude of the wealth of these banks and enterprises and the power implicit in it were not exaggerated by those now seeking the removal of these leaders, as Serbian newspapers close to the Belgrade leadership themselves admitted.[30] Of the country's ten largest banks the first three and the sixth were in Belgrade; with other Serbian banks they controlled 63 per cent of the country's total bank assets, compared to 17 per cent in banks in Croatia (a republic then producing 27 per cent of the Yugoslav Social Product, 30 per cent of its industrial production and 36 per cent of its foreign currency earnings). Four of the ten largest foreign trade enterprises were also located in Belgrade and together had a then annual turnover of 23,500 million dinars (compared to the 2,000 million of Zagreb's one large firm in this sector), realised from involvement in 70 per cent of Yugoslavia's total foreign trade.

What should now ensue was equally clear. There was no need, Dolanc said, for more 'analyses, proclamations, declarations, reports, etc.', since those already on record were correct and provided a more than adequate agenda for immediate action. Nor was there a need for more warnings to those who obstructed such action. Revolutionary breakthroughs required a revolutionary Party, which would prefer to have but would not be inhibited by the lack of a consensus or a majority in the country or even, temporarily, within its own ranks. Power could take care of those problems. Yugoslavs had not heard language like this from official sources for many years, but they heard it now, loud and clear, from Tito and Dolanc. The first step in this direction, they and Kardelj said, must be the removal from leading positions and then from the Party rank and file of those who disagreed.

The first step nevertheless proved momentarily more difficult than its prolegomenon, the removal of the Croatian leaders ten months earlier. Tito was apparently reluctant to summon the Party Presidency and its still putatively liberal majority until he had dealt with the Serbian leadership, whose present stance and control of the numerically largest Party and nation in the Federation made them the key to the entire situation—as he told them on October 16. He was therefore forced to confront the Serbs from an unprecedentedly weak position, without the backing of the Presidency which he had invoked against the Croats at Karadjordjevo and so with no formal authority except his own and that of the Executive Bureau's letter of September 18. The latter, moreover, was arguably a technical violation of the Party Statute, under which the Bureau was responsible to the Presidency in policy matters of such importance. Tito took what precautions he could, especially by packing his meeting with the Serbian leaders (at which he was accompanied by Dolanc and Gligorov) with lower ranking republican and Belgrade city officials whom he expected to be readier to support him than those closer to Nikezić's circle.

It did not work. The meeting, which began on October 9, lasted four days and was then suspended after a majority of those present and declaring themselves had supported their own leaders against Tito, an event unprecedented in the postwar history of Yugoslavia. Tito himself referred to what had happened, in shocked, resentful and threatening words, when the meeting was reconvened on October 16:

I wish to say here that when a Party's line, results, and weaknesses are being discussed, then the number of speakers for or against a certain view is not the decisive factor in revolutionary choice and assessment of which path to take and what is to be done....

I saw at the very start that the discussion was taking a quite different direction from what I wished and which I thought it should take in response to my criticism both before this meeting and in my introductory remarks.... It became clear that not a small number of comrades to whom I listened, I am thinking primarily of leaders, lack virtues such as self-criticism....

And now, here, I have gained the impression that it is not a question of how to remove what is hampering the unity of ideas and action in implementing the general line, but of who will remove whom. Even before we have finished our work, the story began to circulate around Belgrade that those who were criticized had won, and not those who made the criticism, and that these would have to be dealt with ... I think that the majority of members of the LCY and the LCS ... expect something quite different of us....[31]

Publication of this speech two days after it was made and of the Tito-Dolanc letter of September 18 one day later marked Tito's now unavoidable escalation of the crisis. He had in effect issued public orders to Nikezić, Perović and their Central Committee, telling them clearly what he expected them to do. With this simple act, probably the outcome of secret negotiations and still unrevealed mutual concessions during the pause of October 13-15, he had won. Despite his own hurt and astonished recognition in his October 16 remarks that for the first time 'there have been instances of unfavourable and impermissible comment [in the Serbian Party] not only about me as a personality and man, but also not taking account of the fact that I am the President of the LCY and have been for a long time—since 1937', it was still literally unthinkable that anyone should openly oppose him on such a clear-cut issue once it had been publicly stated in this way. Besides, it did not need a long memory to recall his threat to use the army in the Croatian crisis, whether or not he had explicitly repeated it now.

The Serbian Central Committee duly met on October 21, unlike the Croats in analogous circumstances at a closed and unpublicised session, to receive and approve the resignations of Nikezić and Perović. The announcement was delayed for a further three days, possibly in order that it should not be made during a State visit by Queen Elizabeth II, accompanied by numerous foreign journalists and wartime chiefs of the British mission to the Partisans.[32] On October 26, at a second closed session, the Central Committee met again to select new leaders. Its new President was to be Tihomir Vlaškalić, aged 49, a respected professor of economics at Belgrade University and supporter of the economic reforms of 1965 but with little previous political experience. Perović's successor as Secretary of the Executive Committee was Nikola Petronić, aged 37, originally a skilled worker elected to the Serbian Central Committee as recently as July 1971; he was to be dismissed within a year, reportedly for simple incompetence.

On October 30, after a series of further resignations in Serbia and in Slovenia and Macedonia, the federal Party Presidency finally met, dutifully endorsed the Tito-Dolanc letter of September 18, and went on to delegate potentially extensive new powers to its Executive Bureau. Only during the second week of November, however, was the Serbian Central Committee ready to hold two public sessions, lasting four days, at which Nikezić's and other resignations were again accepted to the accompaniment of a chorus of denunciations of their errors.[33]

Resignations of importance during the last days of October and subsequent months included those of Kavčič in Ljubljana, Central Committee Secretary Milosavlevski (a Crvenkovski protégé) in Skopje, the chief and some other editors of *Politika* and *NIN*, Tepavac at the Secretariat for Foreign Affairs, his successors and colleagues in the Vojvodina Party, and many of their close supporters. More surprising and totally unexpected was the resignation from the State Presidency of the redoubtable Koča Popović. He had not been attacked or publicly implicated; nor had he ever been labelled either a 'liberal' or a 'conservative'. His motives remained obscure, but Nikezić had been his deputy and choice as successor at the foreign ministry and his protégé in the Serbian Party.[34] Others far more compromised lingered on at their posts until their terms ended, no longer influential but uncondemned and formally Party members in good standing.

Meanwhile, the Party decks were now clear for the 'ideological and political offensive of the League of Communists' which the Letter of the Executive Bureau and President Tito had proclaimed.

The Constitution of 1974

Yugoslav political life during the year following these events was dominated, in the otherwise preternatural calm which they had imposed, by preparations for the adoption of a new Constitution and for the Party's 10th Congress. During 1973 drafts of the former and of resolutions to be adopted by the latter were prepared, published, discussed and amended. Together with the Congress itself they summarised the state of the country and its socialist system on the thirtieth anniversary of the meeting at Jajce which marked the birth of the new Yugoslavia, of its Communist regime and of the reign of Tito, doyen of world communism, who celebrated his own 82nd birthday on the eve of the Congress.

They also signified the end of a clearly defined chapter in postwar Yugoslav history, coincident in duration with the restored State's third decade. It had begun with a series of bold experiments in further economic and political liberalisation and ended with serious economic problems, a major political crisis and Tito's response, which had taken the form of a Titoist coup against some central elements of what the Western world calls 'Titoism'. The Constitution and the Congress, ending the chapter with their endorsement, institutionalisation and modification of Tito's answer, again postponed the system's frequently heralded 'moment of truth' to what was still the future and not yet history. Contemplating the pronouncement of the Congress and Tito's coup, Western critics and Eastern friends forecast a neo-Stalinist or at least a neo-Leninist restoration. Yugoslav protagonists instead proclaimed a giant step forward towards a true socialist democracy based on universal social self-management. In fact the first paragraphs of the new chapter contained elements of both in another uneasy synthesis of contradictions.

Their fourth Constitution in less than thirty years, promulgated on February 21, 1974, at last gave the Yugoslavs and their love of 'firsts' the world's longest Constitution, surpassing in number of articles and equalling in number of words the previous record-holder, the Constitution of India.[35] Its complexity and the at least initial perplexity and doubts even of most Yugoslav lawyers exceeded its length. Like the 1963 Constitution, but in greater detail, it was a programmatic document as well as a supreme Statute for the Federation. It therefore purported to lay down rules for social organisation of all kinds, for self-management and even for some aspects of inter-personal relationships, as well as the principles of the economic and political systems, division of powers and organisation of the Federation. Among the subjects which the Yugoslavs claimed to be the first to treat in a Constitution were the right of parents to plan the number and timing of their children and the right of all people to a clean and healthy environment, both therefore in theory enforceable before the law.

Most of the changes which it introduced reflected lessons officially learned from recent events, complete with the contradictions implicit in these. The role and responsibility of the LCY were redefined by adding a few but significant words which constituted a more explicit confession of the Party's ultimate power than could be found in any earlier Yugoslav Constitution or in those of other Communist-ruled States.[36] It was additionally specified that the President of the Party would be an *ex officio* member of the State Presidency of Yugoslavia, which was at the same time reduced in size to eight other members, one from each republic and province. Kardelj explained why the Party President was included:

By making this a constitutional principle, we are in fact recognising a reality of our society, namely that the leading ideological and political role of the League of Communists is an essential factor of stability and cohesion in our society.

He said that the question was bound to arise why this provision was being introduced into the Constitution, since the Party had already played such a role without a specific constitutional stipulation. That was true, but there was another 'in this sense new truth'—that in the course of democratising Yugoslav society, which the new Constitution wished to promote, 'some new reactionary or highly conservative pretenders to the leading role in the system of State authority have emerged and are trying to push the League of Communists and the socialist forces onto a side track of our social life …'.[37]

With this exception, for some a contradiction which undid the intent of all the rest but in official Yugoslav eyes its ultimate guarantor, most other changes had one basic theme, which also reflected the lesson of recent events. This was the elaboration of devices designed to break the iron law of oligarchy (in contemporary Yugoslav idiom called the challenge of old or new 'counter-classes') by preventing political or economic power from accumulating in any one or several places. The system thus described therefore included a far more complicated and multi-dimensional version of the American Constitution's 'checks and balances', here including economic and social as well as political institutions. The basis of it all was once again to be the commune, which Kardelj now defined as

a complex social community in which working people ... not some purely abstract working class with abstractly determined ideological and political features, but a quite concretely organised working class ... are associated and organised as self-managers in work organisations and local commun-ities, in other interest communities, and in their socio-political and other organisations.[38]

Changes and modifications in economic organisation and relations between the economic and political systems were focused primarily on what Najdan Pašić in a commentary called 'the basic dilemma of public ownership, which is therefore the basic dilemma of socialism: who controls the great economic power materialised in public property and social capital?' In Yugoslavia the dilemma involved two subsidiary questions: how to avoid the State's doing it, to which the answer in principle had long been workers' self-management; and then, once this answer had been given in practice as well as theory, how to prevent self-management from perverting 'social property' into 'group property' through appro-priation of effective ownership rights by the professional cadres or even the workers who managed it.[39]

The new Constitution sought to answer both of these questions in a variety of ways. It defined 'social property' and its abuses more precisely and made rules to prevent intra-enterprise and inter-enterprise credits or those made by banks and insurance companies from becoming a source of control over income earned by the present or 'past' labour of others. It extended 'de-étatisation' by expanding the area in which 'self-management agreements' among economic units or 'social compacts' involving these, 'self-managing interest communities' and 'socio-political communities' should legislate and collect and dispense revenues in place of the State at any level.[40] 'Self-management courts' were to be created and were expected to take over competence from ordinary (State) courts in many areas of public and private law, although their ultimate jurisdiction was vaguely defined in the Constitution and unclear even to the Yugoslav legal specialists who had drafted the relevant articles.[41] Potentially of particular importance, the new Statute in effect destroyed the enterprise as it had existed since 1950, completing the gradual evolution of 'work units', created in the late 1950s and since 1971 called BOALs (Basic

Organisations of Associated Labour), into the central legal entity
of the economic system.[42] The enterprise remained as the form in
which a contractually integrated cluster of BOALs would normally
appear on the market or be represented in other external relations,
but only on the basis of powers delegated by the otherwise
independent BOALs. Most important of all, all net income from
economic activities was now BOAL income, its use and distribution
with few restrictions under each BOAL's control; the enterprise had
no income of its own.[43]

Within BOALs and enterprises the new Constitution also forbade
the election of managerial and technical staff to workers' councils,
an attempt to reduce their power and separate policy-making from
technical administration. Also indicative of the campaign against
the power of the 'techno-managerial bureaucracy' were two other
changes affecting enterprise directors, one of them representing
renewed aversion to 'capitalist' terminology and the other restoring
a large measure of political control over their appointment. They
were now officially entitled 'individual management organs' and
not directors (only the most striking of many tortuous ideological
circumlocutions in the new terminology),[44] and were again to be
elected, for a renewable four-year term, from a list of one to three
candidates proposed to the workers' council by a commission
comprised of an equal number of enterprise representatives and of
communal assembly appointees. This last was a return to the
system ante-1964 when communal participation in the nominating
commission was eliminated after it was criticised as unjustifiable
political interference in workers' rights.

Analogous efforts were made to control if not to eliminate other
frequently criticised forms of 'monopolistic' or 'technocratic'
economic power. Of basic importance was another reform of the
banking system. Required by provisions in the new Constitution, it
was designed to make the banks at last really responsible to the
BOALs and enterprises which subscribed to their capital and thus in
theory to the workers who produced values rather than those who
administered them, an ideological distinction on which all such
new controls were based. Bank employees were to be excluded
from membership on a bank's credit committee which, like the
bank's assembly, would be comprised of representatives of the
'shareholders'. These in turn would no longer include 'socio-
political communities' (Government bodies), which were now
required to deposit their funds in a regional or the central National
Bank, ending their legal power over commercial ones. At the same
time, all funds earned by a bank through its activites, after a
deduction of commissions to finance the bank's wage and business
funds, would be distributed to the 'shareholders', finally
eliminating the problem of 'anonymous capital' administered by

banks without accountability to anyone. Similar controls were to be imposed on insurance companies, while commercial enterprises were to be forced to share the income as well as the risks of their operations with the business partners whose goods they handled.

Many of these changes had been anticipated by the 'workers' amendments' of 1971, still largely unimplemented. The magnitude of the political struggles which were involved, and which therefore began before promulgation of the new Constitution, is suggested by the fact that in Belgrade alone some 200 enterprise directors were replaced in two years, between mid-1972 and mid-1974, many of them after losing their Party membership. Disagreements, particularly concerning reforms of the banking system and commercial enterprises, continued during discussion of the draft Constitution and after its promulgation. Implementation of the provisions applying to commercial enterprises was still held up in late 1974 because Croatian spokesmen wished to subordinate them more completely to producing enterprises by defining them as a 'service organisation' rather than a 'partner' of the latter.[45]

In the political area *per se* and despite expectations to the contrary since Karadjordjevo, the confederal structure of the State created by the amendments of 1971, recognising the sovereignty of the republics and reducing the Federation almost entirely to an apparatus for agreement among them, was retained. The legislative and executive organs of the Federation kept only the extremely limited areas of competence left to them in 1971, including the same list of subjects on which prior agreement of all eight regions must be obtained. Only their ability to decide and to act in these areas was enhanced. At the same time one purpose of the new structure and base of the now bicameral Federal Assembly (renamed the Assembly of the Socialist Federal Republic of Yugoslavia) was to eliminate the awkwardness of semi-private decision-making by the extra-constitutional 'inter-republican co-ordinating committee' and the special powers this had inadvertently placed in the hands of republican and provincial executive committees. By constituting *both* chambers of the Assembly on the basis of regional parity and the 'delegate system', and with the delegates explicitly responsible to the regional assemblies rather than their executive organs, these bodies could be assumed to represent the same authority to negotiate that the co-ordinating committee had appropriated since 1971.[46]

The most discussed, theoretically significant and cynically greeted change in the political sector was the long-delayed and still partly compromised introduction of the 'system of delegations and delegates' throughout the assembly hierarchy, from commune to Federation. Three-stage elections under the new system, held for the first time in April and May 1974, helped to clarify what its authors had in mind and added to the cynicism of Yugoslavs who remembered the relative free-for-all of 1969.

During the first round 'delegations' of between ten and thirty members were elected by and from about 65,000 BOALs, general agricultural co-operatives, other work collectives, army units, etc. Candidates, in the words of the Constitution, were 'proposed and determined by the Socialist Alliance'. At the same time all voters elected similar delegations on the basis of Yugoslavia's smallest territorial units, the country's 12,000 'local communities' (*mesne zajednice*). In all cases the Constitution further specified that the composition of the delegations 'must correspond to the social composition of the basic self-managing organisation or community concerned'. About 1 million Yugoslavs, or one out of every fourteen of voting age, thus became members of a delegation of one of these two types, with a non-élite majority statutorily assured on each of them. These delegations in turn elected 'delegates' to their respective communal assemblies, where those from the first type of delegation comprised a Chamber of Associated Labour and those from the second type sat in a Municipal Chamber. There they confronted a third chamber, comprised of delegates elected by 'socio-political organisations'—by the Party, the Socialist Alliance, the trade unions, the youth federation, *et al.*—and therefore another striking token of the return to a direct, undisguised political role for the Party and its network of pre-emptive mass organisations.

In the second stage the communal assemblies elected further delegates, from their own ranks, to the appropriate chambers of the now similarly tricameral republican and provincial assemblies. Finally, at the third stage, came the election of delegates to the bicameral Assembly of Yugoslavia: to the Federal Chamber, 30 delegates from each republic and 20 from each province, nominated by all three types of basic delegations, from lists proposed by the Socialist Alliance, and elected by the communal assemblies; and to the Chamber of Republics and Provinces, 12 from each republican assembly and 8 from each provincial assembly, elected by these assemblies from among their own members.[47]

In addition to inter-regional parity in both Federal Assembly chambers, the indirectness of the voter's role at all levels above that of the delegation, and the control exercised at all stages by the Socialist Alliance (and by the Party within the Socialist Alliance), the system displayed two other features worth noting. The first, which was the core of the Kardeljian distinction between a 'delegate system' and a 'representative system', was the (theoretical) direct and virtually day-to-day responsibility of delegates to their delegations and of the latter to the neighbourhood or 'working communities' which had elected them. The Constitution specified that all questions on the agenda of a forthcoming meeting must be discussed by delegates with their delegations, and that the delegates, while not bound to a specific stand or vote in negotiating with fellow delegates, must faithfully seek the solutions agreed on at such meetings. The second feature, reinforced by the requirement that delegates keep their ordinary jobs during their term of office, was the 'de-professionalisation' which it imposed on the assembly hierarchy. The new dispensation guaranteed that no chamber *except* the socio-political chambers would be dominated, as assemblies after 1963 had tended to be, by members of the 'managerial-technological élite' or by professional politicians. Described as an important measure of further 'democratisation', such an arrangement could also be viewed as a further device for control by Party bosses, inspired by unhappy Party experiences with frequently articulate and politically able managers and administrators in the corporate chambers of the old assemblies. Would it not ensure Party domination of legislative bodies in which the majorities would be comprised of inexperienced and otherwise busy part-time parliamentarians, inevitably unable to do their homework on all the complex and sophisticated issues before them? In addition, if all the meetings and consultations required by the system's rules really took place, one might wonder when any Yugoslavs would have time for work or play.[48]

Meanwhile, with a new Constitution placing equal emphasis on both planks of the post-1972 Party platform—on the one hand impressive further development of plural institutions and loci of decision-making and of checks and balances among them, and on the other hand a blatantly increased role for the Party as the one ring to bind them all—the composition and ethos of that Party and the extent of its unity and determination to rule were more important than they had been since 1966.

The 10th Congress

After more than two years of major and often dramatic changes in leaderships and policies, the LCY assembled in Congress at the end of May 1974. The function of the Congress was to survey and endorse the results of these changes and to declare *urbi et orbi* that what *Politika* in 1971 had called 'Yugoslavia's most serious postwar political crisis' was over and that the regime and system were stable and back on their still different but again course-corrected high road to socialism.[49]

The scene, like the event, was in part familiar and in part different. Jamming the parking lot were the same serried ranks of well-polished Mercedes, mostly black and mostly new, which had characterised at least the last four Party Congresses, bringing cynical smiles or puzzled frowns to the faces of foreign observers still naïve enough to imagine that Communist ethics or discretion should discourage such ostentation. But the physical setting was new. In place of the pretentiously austere 'early-socialist' trade union hall on Marx-Engels Square in downtown Belgrade, site of all previous postwar Party Congresses in the federal capital, the 10th Congress was held in a strikingly modern sports centre out near the Pančevo bridge, a modern prefabricated and poly-chromatic sports centre completed in 1973 for a world boxing championship. Whether moving the Party Congress to such a structure was significant was a matter for conjecture, but the explanation offered by press spokesmen was that the sports palace had a far larger parking lot. There were apparently even more Mercedes than there used to be.

The delegates presented the usual picture of the usual mixture of self-confident professional politicians (metropolitan easily distinguishable from provincial), self-important intellectuals and managers and self-conscious members of the working-class, including the obligatory half-dozen peasants in homespun shirts and *opanke*, traditional Serbian shoes with turned-up toes. Published statistics on the social composition of the Congress proudly noted, however, that this time there were fewer represen-tatives of the first two and more of the last of these socialist estates. It seemed to some that there were also more uniforms of the Yugoslav People's Army than at earlier Congresses, reflecting the more precisely defined role of the army in politics which was being formalised in amendments to the Statutes adopted at the Congress and in the new Constitution.

Congressional procedures also followed traditional patterns, beginning with the ceremonial entrance of Tito and his 'closest collaborators', while the delegates applauded, chanted 'Tito-Party', and sang *The International* with the help of two youth choruses. Then came the ritual of the opening plenary session and the discussion in commissions, limited to two days this time, where rank-and-file delegates judiciously interspersed with more authoritative spokesmen have their say and are often outspokenly critical of political and economic performance and even of the details if never the principles of policies. The last day, as always, was devoted to another ritualistic plenary session: reports from the commissions heard and approved, resolutions adopted and new 'leading bodies' elected—all unanimously and in 1974 invariably without further discussion. Finally, the procedure repeatedly interrupted by enthusiastic acclamations and the singing of wartime songs swearing fealty to his person and ideas, Tito was re-elected President of the Party. This time it was 'without limitation of mandate' (i.e. for life), which had also happened, equally for the first time, at his re-election as President of the Republic two weeks earlier.

Tito's own display of energy throughout the four days was a forceful and no doubt in part calculated answer to rumours recently circulated in the Western press that he had suffered a serious stroke and was semi-incapacitated or dying. On the first day he disdained a stool placed by the podium for the reading of his long keynote speech and then sat out the entire eight hours of plenary routine and discussion, listening intently and smoking the thin cigars which had replaced the cigarettes in pipe-shaped holders that were once his trademark. During the next two days he granted non-stop audiences to the more important of the foreign guest delegations, and on Thursday he was back to sit through and participate in the closing plenary sessions with apparently undiminished energy.

Novelties at the 10th Congress included the presence of guest delegations from all the Soviet bloc Communist Parties, only the second time in postwar Yugoslav Party history that they had come. The Soviet delegation, headed by Politburo member A. P. Kirilenko, was listed first among the 98 guest delegations and received as much applause as was otherwise accorded only to representatives of the Chilean and Portuguese Communist and Socialist Parties and the Italian Communist Party. But the Russian visitors were also pointedly reminded by Tito and other speakers that the Yugoslav Party's earnest desire for comradely relations was still conditional, presupposing mutual respect for the legitimacy of separate roads to socialism, the independence of each Party and each socialist State's foreign and domestic policies, the right to disagree and non-interference.

The keynote of the Congress in foreign policy was therefore continuity, with Yugoslavia's traditional non-alignment and precarious defiance of both superpowers intact. Frequent critical references to 'imperialism', meaning the United States, were carefully balanced by equally critical references to 'hegemonism', the Yugoslav code word for the Soviet Union's behaviour towards other Communist regimes and Parties. Despite Tito's observation that the world was in a parlous state, the omnidirectional paranoia recently reviving in Yugoslav press and foreign ministry commentaries on international affairs was temporarily suspended. It would recur again, in renewed suspicion of American activities in the world in general and among Yugoslav émigrés in particular and in the widely publicised trial, in September 1974, of a predominantly Montenegrin group accused of organising a secret congress of an underground pro-Soviet Yugoslav Communist Party and of taking orders from 'Cominformist' Yugoslav émigrés in the Soviet Union and Western Europe. A pre-Congress wave of demonstrations and official protests, inspired by an Italian note which seemed to reopen the question of ex-Zone B of the Free Territory of Trieste, was part of the same atmosphere. Before this faint and curious echo of the great Trieste crises of 1945 and 1953 ended—again through painstaking secret negotiations which finally eliminated the stillborn Triestine mini-State *de jure* as well as *de facto*—there had also been a renewal of polemics with Austria, largely dormant since 1960, over treatment of the Slovenian minority in Carinthia, and with Bulgaria, always viewed as a running dog of Soviet hegemonism, over the never dormant Macedonian question.[50] But if the outside world seemed more than usually threatening, in part perhaps as a device to invoke unity at home, the Congress tried to minimise such worries for the moment.

Another novelty was the universality of Tito's picture, which appeared even on Congress documents and lapel badges, of slogans referring to him, and of often hagiographic references to his person and accomplishments. To be sure, there had always been a 'cult of the personality' surrounding the man who was simultaneously the father of the revolution and the ultimate and sometimes apparently only guarantor of the unity and continuity of both state and system. But at least since the early 1950s Titoist myth and symbols had never been as exaggerated and omni-present as in 1974, and not only at the Congress. There were several possible explanations and all may have been true, including competitive sycophancy designed to flatter an old man who had recently demonstrated his continuing ability to behead courtiers who displeased him, or deliberate manipulation of the chief emblem of Yugoslav and Party unity as part of the present campaign of reunification and retreat from confederation. It may also have been a kind of unconscious reversion to magic, a parading of icons with their intimations of immortality and divine protection and a conjuring with the personification of unity and stability to frighten away the demons of divisive ethnic nationalisms, political pluralism, and foreign intrigues.

If Tito was omni-present, both live and in effigy, many other familiar faces of the preceding decade of Yugoslav politics were missing from the 'leading bodies' elected or confirmed when the Congress ended, although some of them were still to be seen among the delegates on the floor and occasionally at the podium during the debates. In all, according to statistics presented to the Congress, some 143,756 persons had left the Party as a result of expulsion or 'deletion from the records' between December 1968 and December 1973, reducing total membership by 35,000 over the preceding four years, to 1,076,711. The magnitude of the decimation at the top was indicated by the fact that 21 of the 52 members of the Party Presidency confirmed at the 9th Congress had ceased to be members by the time the 10th Congress convened. Two had died. Eight had resigned under attack for serious deviations and seven of them had lost their Party memberships. The remaining eleven had left the Presidency for other reasons, including a January 1972 decision that members of the State Presidency should not simultaneously be members of the Party Presidency—a change of rules affecting six of them. None of this last group had been formally disgraced and many were certainly still in favour, but the changed rules did provide a convenient device for getting rid of men like Crvenkovski, who for some reason did not quite merit purging but whose presence in a powerful post was no longer desirable.

The banished leaders were replaced by a mixed lot, in background, in age, in previous ideological-political position in so far as this was known, and in ability. Only two generalisations could be made. The first was that the median level of political talent they had so far displayed was lower than that of their predecessors, although many had considerable ability as specialists, for example in economics. The second was that almost all, including the most talented, were considered by their fellow Yugoslavs to be *poslužni ljudi* (retainers, or 'in-service people' in the British idiom) and not 'their own men' with an autonomous power base, which their predecessors often had been. In age and previous experience they tended to fall into two groups. Some were young and entirely new to federal politics or to senior decision-making posts in general. Others, like Stambolić and Koliševski (both freshly elected to the new nine-member State Presidency), were over 55 and veterans whose political lives were considered finished after they were retired to the shadows in 1968-69. The average age of the new, twelve-member Executive Committee, for example, was 51 years. Its youngest member was 40 and its oldest was 56. Three of them had not participated in the 1941-45 Partisan struggle and only four were in the Party and the Partisans in 1941, once a kind of union card for jobs at the top of the State or Party hierarchies. Among the non-members of the 'club of '41' was Dolanc, re-elected by the 10th Congress as Secretary of what was again called the Executive Committee and ostensibly *primus inter pares* in the new lieutenancy.

In addition, out in the hall, there were those never formally disgraced but no longer in positions of power. One group, comprised of those only lightly compromised by identification with the liberal policies which the Congress was denouncing, was personified by Todorović. Formally President of the Federal Assembly until his term ended twelve days before the Congress opened and a member of the Party Presidency until a new one was approved at its end, he was appointed to the Commission which prepared the Draft Resolutions under Dolanc's chairmanship but was not expected to and did not receive a post on any of the new leading bodies approved by the Congress. Crvenkovski, there as a simple delegate who did not speak, represented those more seriously compromised, while Vukmanović-Tempo, a simple delegate who inevitably did, represented those who had gone into political limbo in 1968-69 but had not been resuscitated after 1972. The position of such people as Party members formally in good standing, also shared by Koča Popović and others, was of some importance. Like that of Stambolić and Koliševski in 1969, but unlike that of the 'liberals' and 'nationalists' who had been anathematised and deprived of Party membership since 1971, it made an eventual return to the political stage possible, without the embarrassment and difficulty of formal rehabilitation, when and if the pendulum should swing again.

All this did not mean that all Yugoslav leaders associated with the great experiment in economic and political liberalisation of the preceding decade were now out or on the sidelines. In fact the two men most frequently held to have been the key figures in bringing about those events, Kardelj and Bakarić, were still at the top, members simultaneously of the Party and State Presidencies (the 1972 ban on holding both offices having been lifted) and conspicuously more intimate with Tito at recent public occasions than any other leaders except Dolanc. Several other members of the new thirty-nine-member Party Presidency, including Sergej Krajger (otherwise Slovenian Head of State as President of the Republic's Presidency) and Gligorov (otherwise Todorović's successor as President of the Yugoslav Assembly), had also played important and apparently enthusiastic roles in designing and implementing the reforms of the 1960s.

The basic outline of the new course was meanwhile clear enough, in the proclamations of the Congress as it had been in the new Constitution. Yugoslavia was to return to stricter control by a recentralised and re-disciplined Party. The Party's right to 'intervene' in decision-making and selection of officers by enterprises and communities, which had been denied and called outdated and pernicious by many of those purged since 1971, was explicitly reaffirmed. Within the Party itself, whether or not there was to be more genuine participation 'from the bottom upward' in policy-making and more genuine workers at all levels—both of which were once more promised—the other and more commonly observed side of 'democratic centralism'—unqualified acceptance and active implementation of policies and directives issued by higher Party bodies—was to be strictly re-enforced, with passivity as punishable as opposition. 'Liberalism', 'spontaneity', 'pluralism' and 'the federalisation of the Party' were categorically condemned. The advantages of an almost uncontrolled market economy, so uncritically accepted in the later 1960s as to resemble nineteenth-century Manchester-school liberalism, were being subjected to critical re-evaluation. The State might continue to 'wither away', as more of its functions were transferred to the sector described as 'direct social self-management' by 'organisations of associated labour' in collaboration with 'self-managing interest communities', but the Party would not. In brief, Yugoslav socialism would continue to be based on autonomous enterprises and communes and 'social self-management', but with firm Party direction and more economic planning.

It was noteworthy that Lenin's name was invoked more frequently at the 10th Congress and during the months which preceded it than had been customary in Yugoslavia for many years. This, to use a popular Marxist phrase, 'was not coincidental'. It represented a conscious and explicit attempt to return to Leninist principles of Party organisation and Leninist doctrines concerning the role of the Party during the transitional period called socialism. 'The leading role of the Party' was the key phrase, to which recent events had ascribed a new—or more accurately an older—and stricter meaning.

What precisely the new course was to mean for Yugoslav worker-managers, intellectuals, and socialist entrepreneurs nevertheless remained unclear. Authoritative speakers and documents at the Congress continued to insist that there would be no return to the bad old days of absolute Party dictatorship, centralism and a command economy. Such a return, it was said, would not only be ideologically and politically undesirable—since the rationale and purpose of the return to Party rule was more self-management, not less—but also impossible at the present, relatively advanced stage of socio-economic and political development and diffused decision-making. In any case, while Tito, his new lieutenants and the Congress might propose, a more complex equation of social forces would dispose, and even the Party was not as united about the quantity and quality of optimal intervention as the 10th Congress was designed to demonstrate.

Debates at the Congress, particularly those which followed Gligorov's spirited defence of the necessity and virtues of a market economy in his keynote speech to the Commission for Socio-Economic Relations, and the mixed composition of the Party's new leading bodies provided further evidence that many vital questions were still open. It was clearly premature to conclude that a recentralisation of authority within the Party and a verbal reassertion of its ubiquitous 'leading role' must and would mean a thoroughgoing recentralisation of decision-making in Yugoslavia's still highly decentralised economic and political system.

The question was therefore how far Tito and the leadership endorsed by the Congress intended to go and how far they would be able to go in reimposing the Party's authority, and whether they would thereby solve, merely suppress, or even aggravate the problems which had led to Tito's coup.

That Congress and pre-Congress documents and speeches and resolutions all expressly declared that there would be no return to a centralist Party dictatorship, or even to the quasi-centralist one of the 1950s, could of course be discounted as politically necessary rhetoric, self-delusion or wishful thinking. Atmospheric indicators that it could happen or was already happening included the significant revival, constant repetition and tendentious use of certain Marxist terms and arguments which in other times and places had been employed to rationalise Stalinism and which had been purposefully neglected, differently construed or seldom and usually only ritualistically used by Yugoslav Party ideologists in recent years. Even Yugoslavia's own Stalinist epoch, 1945-50, was now described as 'the period of revolutionary étatism', in Marxian language a more positive euphemism than 'the administrative period'. Moreover, while changes in political style and cadres generally affected only Party members and intra-Party life, there were other indications that a harder line affecting all citizens was seriously meant. The muzzling of a press, which by 1971 had achieved a remarkable level of freedom and liveliness, was only one harbinger. There were also the arrest of actively dissident students, intense pressure on university councils to fire professors accused of propagating ideas contrary to the Party line, and directives calling for the ideological purification of teaching staff at all levels. Newspaper stories describing with approval the success-ful intervention of a local Party committee to secure the dismissal of a factory director or a change in enterprise policy were also indicative; such a story would have been reported disapprovingly three years earlier.

The coup which led to these trends was Tito's. He did it because he believed that the system was producing social and economic consequences too much at variance with official or socially accepted norms and expectations, with its own legitimizing myths and with the preservation of his own and the Party's authority to be tolerable for long. Most important of all was his clearly genuine anguish as he contemplated, in his own twilight years, the breakdown of what he now repeatedly and with growing under-tones of sadness and bitterness described as his greatest accom-plishment. This was not socialism or Yugoslavia's unique experi-ment in self-management, themes reserved for his more formal speeches and lectures, but 'the brotherhood and unity of the Yugoslav peoples', the great slogan of the Partisan war.'[51] He had warned and cajoled for years, the urgency growing with each birthday and sign that the national question could shake his system apart, but he stayed his hand until an indomitable political impasse and the escalation of national tensions in 1971 convinced him and others that the change of strategy and policy which he demanded could only come about through a *coup de main*.

So Tito acted. It did not necessarily follow, however, that the solution which he was now offering was particularly relevant or would solve the problem it was supposed to in the way that the author intended. Tito's answer, reduced to its essential core, was little more than a rather simplistic attempt to return to the purity of first principles, to the old myth of a Marxist-Leninist Party's paternalistic and enlightened despotism as the surest diviner and confounder of counter-revolutionaries and the somehow ultimately infallible guardian of socialism, of the interests of the working class, and of the brotherhood and unity of the Yugoslav peoples.

It was additions made by others that were turning this simplistic answer into a more complex one. They included those who produced the new Constitution, incorporating in it new developments and accommodations drawn from the other, democratic 'self-management' strand in the Yugoslav dialectic. They were the people who did not share Tito's views of the principles of the 6th Congress, and people who at the 10th Congress returned (under the rubric of a 'workers' majority') to the theme of the need for a different social composition and 'mentality' in the Party. Their hand was detectable again in amendments to the Party Statutes requiring in significantly firmer and more specific terms than ever before that higher Party organs must respond to initiatives from below.

This is not to say that a more complex equation will prove to be a solution, or even that one exists. Nor do Party platforms and Constitutions produced by Communist Parties have more significance than those produced by parties and politicians of another persuasion. But it did seem to mean that some of the reconstructed Yugoslav Party leadership, strong enough to insert their views into the Party's most authoritative declarations and have them endorsed by the Congress, had accepted Tito's coup in the name of the Party with reservations and for pragmatic reasons. These included recognition that it was the least-risk way out of an impasse and associated crisis which were threatening the stability of the regime, their own positions, and political or socialist values that at least some senior Yugoslav Communists really seem to believe in. The post-purge establishment was therefore apparently still divided between those who saw the reassertion of hierarchical discipline and the Party's 'leading role' as a return to principles of permanent validity and others who saw it as a *reculer pour mieux sauter* which must be carefully limited in scope in order that it should not become permanent. Both groups were influenced in the attitudes they assumed by the interests and roles they felt closest to, by their reading of what was acceptable to those social strata, organised interests and individuals whose at least passive support they considered essential to their own and to the system's survival, and also by ideological preferences.

Yugoslav Party Congresses do not make decisions in the sense of openly debating and voting on disputed issues or electing officers from competing slates or among individuals representing different currents, social forces, or factions within the Party. They do, however, provide a deadline for other forms of debate and decision-making. A Congress must have policies and people to endorse, and these will be influential if not unchangeable in the years immediately ahead. In addition, Party rules and traditions, inherited from a period of revolutionary struggle and kept alive by the mythology of a continuing, merciless struggle with tirelessly encircling and infiltrating 'class enemies' and 'alien ideas', require an appearance and preferably the reality of monolithic unity and its public display at a Congress, when friends and enemies are watching. If there are disagreements within the leadership, the approach of a Congress therefore lends urgency to their resolution. This may be through the triumph of one group (or coalition) and their ideas, in which case the losers will be silenced or removed to avoid the risk of an awkward display of disunity or indecisiveness at the Congress. Alternatively, if no one view has prevailed in time, the same imperatives of unity and decisiveness will produce a programme and slate of officers which experienced observers promptly identify as a compromise and which sometimes only transparently disguises continuing differences. The former type of resolution is, roughly speaking, what happened at the 9th Congress in 1969, when a liberal policy was clearly endorsed, while the latter represents a reasonably accurate picture of the 8th Congress in 1964.

The 10th Congress, on first reading, resembled the 8th. Declaratively a 'Congress of stabilisation' after the traumas, crises and purges of the preceding three years, it really caught a continuing disagreement *in medias res* and produced another compromise. Again as in 1964, the details of agreement and dispute, the precise line-up of protagonists, and hence the consequences of the compromise were temporarily obscure, but the overall balance was clearly lopsided. The difference is that the balance which emerged from the 8th Congress was weighted in favour of Yugoslavia's Communist Whigs, while the 10th left the

Party Tories in by far the stronger position. It is in this sense that the political chapter which opened with preparations for the 8th Congress closed with the pronouncements of the 10th.

9

CONCLUSIONS

History knows few genuine villains but recognises much stupidity, innumerable cases of moral cowardice and ambivalent values, a world full of misinformation and misconstructed or suborned networks for moving information to the places it is needed, and more roads paved with good intentions which have led to hell than have led anywhere else. So it is with the Yugoslav story portrayed in these pages. What is remarkable about it is that a small country, and more specifically a revolutionary party as minuscule as was the CPY in 1940, should have produced so many leaders with such a relatively high level of intelligence, dedication, imagination, and ability to learn from experience and to adapt to change without loss of basic integrity. One is reminded of that remarkable first generation of the American revolution, when another and even smaller emerging nation also produced a disproportionate number of men with a similar combination of vision, intellectual and political abilities, and integrity. In both cases the times in which they lived, their ultimate values and ideologies, and the human and natural raw materials which were their inheritance, all affected by the baggage of historical memories and myths which leaders and followers brought with them, placed limits on their aspirations and ability, testing some too sorely in the trying.

The men around Tito started with an ideology and a mechanism, the Leninist Party, which were appropriate to the carrying out of a revolutionary breakthrough in a social environment like Yugoslavia, but not to a consolidation in accord with all of their own and the ideology's most basic and humanist original principles. Their place in world as well as Yugoslav history was won by the way in which they saw this and attempted to draw conclusions in harmony with those principles. They boldly confronted if they still failed to solve what might be called (in order to emphasise that it is not peculiar to Communist revolutions) the Atatürk dilemma—the familiar dilemma of a revolution based on liberal myths of emancipation, modernisation and democracy, but carried out by a radical minority which has assumed 'temporary' dictatorial powers over a still largely traditional and conservative society in which there is no national consensus in support of the values of the revolution. How can such a minority regime offer its citizens a bona fide, active role in choosing leaders and making other public choices if it has good reason to fear that the results of free choice might threaten other values, policies and the cadre it considers vital to fulfilment of the revolution's goals? Yet how long can it fail to offer such a role if its programme and principles also include participant democracy, and if its repeated declarations on the subject, its hesitant or withdrawn steps in that direction, the institutions it has created and the slow growth of civil and entrepreneurial liberties and of popular political sophistication have all combined to 'transform the illusion of [popular] power into a power of illusion that gradually became a prime mover of developments, animating them from below'?[1]

Confronted by a particularly acute form of this dilemma after 1970, Yugoslavia's Communist leaders, again shedding those among them who were too compromised or too principled to keep their footing during the change of course, found another way to try to square the circle.

The solution they devised, as described in the last chapter of this study, incorporated compromises with old and new social and political forces and seemed almost certain to prove another non-solution which would nevertheless leave a variety of eventual outcomes still possible. The author of this study wrote in 1971 that 'the moment of truth for Yugoslavia's unique and eternally experimental brand of socialism and multinational federalism', so often prematurely announced by many other observers, had finally come.[2] He thereby joined these others in error. Despite a considerable and in most Western eyes deplorable retreat since 1972 from what Western political tradition defines as personal liberty and political pluralism, the Yugoslav story remains a cliffhanger. It is the story of a changing and modernising society whose institutions and systems, and the individuals who run them, are still as likely to succeed as they are to fail in adapting to changing conditions in ways conducive to further modernisation and to the realisation of their own proclaimed principles of self-managing socialist democracy.[3]

The history of Yugoslavia during the quarter-century since the experiment with a 'separate road' began in 1949 has therefore actually 'proved' nothing except the astounding flexibility and adaptability of the Yugoslavs, both leaders and led, and an impatient, apparently inexhaustible and often bewildering willingness to experiment. It does, however—and with great respect for the caveat that all societies and systems are different, that some are more different than others, and that Yugoslavia's are more different than most—suggest some conclusions or hypotheses which might be worth testing elsewhere, particularly in other rapidly modernising societies. Two clusters of these, the choice reflecting the writer's own larger interests, have received particular attention in the preceding pages, although in a narrative history which attempts a synthesis and not a social scientist's analysis of events this has usually been implicit rather than explicit.

First, a compromise economic model, which seeks to gain the incentives and flexibility of capitalism by inserting a few market mechanisms into an otherwise largely unreconstructed 'command economy'—introducing profit-orientation, still largely administered prices which come closer to reflecting relative scarcity values and some independent entrepreneurial decision-making in the enterprise—may be inherently unstable and eventually untenable. Although useful in escaping some of the grosser defects of the pure command model and therefore productive in the short run, it tends to produce a situation in which no agency is capable of coming even close to making fully rational allocative decisions. Entrepreneurs cannot do so because investment decisions are still at most only marginally within their competence, and because signals from the market are too distorted by other remaining administrative controls and the hybrid rationale on which these controls and prices are based for them to be able to make such macroeconomically rational choices. Planners also cannot do so, since they have lost control over several key variables in the equation and must in any case work with the same hybrid, contradictory, and misleading information as the entrepreneurs. The only alternative then is either what Grossman calls recentralisation 'in little steps, virtually unnoticed but important in aggregate impact'[4] (which can mean polycentric recentralisation in a decentralised political system like Yugoslavia's), or a bold and politicaliy and socially hazardous breakthrough to a genuinely free socialist market economy with merely indicative or no planning.

If breakthrough is chosen and goes to the extreme of a 'laissez-faire socialism', which is what happened in Yugoslavia (with the added complication of more but haphazard and irrational residual controls than such a market needed), then such a socialist society is likely to find itself confronting most of the old traditional economic and social problems associated with laissez-faire capitalism. These will include monopolies and their familiar consequences, maldistribution of income and assorted other inequalities which do not necessarily reflect inherent inequalities of personal ability and diligence. The regime, if its ideology, the interests of its rulers or its responsiveness to public opinion suggest that these phenomena are becoming intolerable, may then find Government intervention to tamper with the operation of free enterprise, along lines already followed by many neo-capitalist societies, the best if still inadequate way of coping with these problems. This, too, can be politically hazardous if the political forces and the mentality of the 'command economy' phase are still or again strong.

Secondly, the Yugoslav story as a case study again emphasises the importance to students of modernisation theory of the dynamic relationships and particularly the 'feedback mechanisms' connecting four key variables. These are the specific ideology and consequent style of deliberately engineered social and economic modernisation, the specific quality and discontinuities of the modernisation thereby produced, the altered kind and distribution of the demands which this quality and these discontinuities make on the system and its engineers, and the reaction of the latter to these demands.

The political fall-out from Yugoslavia's series of liberalising economic and cautiously decentralising political reforms and from social modernisation had by the 1960s produced a system which could no longer reasonably be called totalitarian or even a Party autocracy. An impressive number of autonomously organised and institutionally legitimised forces, representing divergent interests and values, most if not all social strata, and most politicised Yugoslavs who had not opted out because of basic ideological dissent, participated in making effective public choices at all political levels from commune to Federation. The result has been defined in this study as a polycentric polyarchy involving a network of élites to which access was usually open to all except a few minorities excluded by geographical, cultural or self- or externally-imposed ethnic or ideological isolation. The emergence and further evolution of this polyarchy provided an interesting and suggestive case study of the circumstances under which and the extent to which a genuine political democracy can develop without a multi-party system.

This kind of political fall-out may or may not be an inevitable consequence of a style and of institutional forms of economic development like those chosen and periodically modified by the Yugoslav regime. There was, however, nothing in the later chapters of the story to suggest that such polyarchic political and economic systems must then inevitably, or even probably, move on towards complete political democracy—either in the classic liberal sense of Government of, by, and for all the people or as the generalised and unfettered social self-management posited by Yugoslav theorists. As the State and the regime began their fourth decade a modest approach to such an ideal outcome was still a possibility, but it seemed more likely that Yugoslavia would become merely another slovenly, moderately oppressive, semi-efficient, semi-authoritarian State run by an oligarchy of contending élites, a society in which many people are free and participant and many are not. Like most States.

NOTES

For particulars of works cited by names of authors and also of LCY Congresses and other official documents, see Select Bibliography.

Abbreviations

AUFS	American Universities Field Staff
CC	Central Committee
CP(Y)	Communist Party (of Yugoslavia)
CSM	*Christian Science Monitor*
EB	Executive Bureau
EC	Executive Committee
FEC	Federal Executive Council
i.a.	*inter alia*
LC(C)	League of Communists (of Croatia)
NIN	*Nedeljne Informativne Novine*
NYT	*New York Times*
PISKJ	Čolaković *et al., Pregled istorije SKJ*
RFE	Radio Free Europe
SAWPY	Socialist Alliance of the Working People of Yugoslavia
Službeni list	*Službeni list FNRJ/SNRJ* (Official Gazette)
STAP	Socialist Thought and Practice
VUS	*Vjesnik u Srijedu*
White Book	*White Book on Aggressive Activities by the Governments of the USSR, Poland, Czechoslovakia, Hungary, Rumania, Bulgaria and Albania towards Yugoslavia.* Belgrade, 1951.

Foreword

1. In a speech during a State visit to Finland, reported by *Borba* (Belgrade), June 2, 1964.
2. The first census in the new Kingdom, in 1921, listed all of these South Slav peoples except the Slovenes together as 'Serbo-Croats' (74·6 per cent of the total population); any further breakdown is therefore an estimate based on a backward projection from post-1945 censuses.
3. A distinction is made throughout this study between 'Serbs', as a national or ethnic group concentrated in Serbia but strongly represented in Bosnia-Herzegovina, Croatia, the Vojvodina and elsewhere, and 'Serbians' as Serb citizens of the former Kingdom and

post-1945 Republic of Serbia. For a famous contemporary Croatian statement of the problem of asymmetrical distribution of economic and political power in old Yugoslavia, see Bićanić 1938; he was then the leading economist of the Croatian Peasant Party.

4. The Ustaša, founded shortly after proclamation of the royal dictatorship, operated from Hungarian and Italian bases and was led by Ante Pavelić (see below). IMRO (the Internal Macedonian Revolutionary Organisation) dated from the first stirrings of anti-Ottoman Macedonian and Bulgarian national consciousness in Vardar Macedonia in the 1890s. It always included both pro-Bulgarian and Macedonian autonomist and proto-nationalist factions; many adherents of the latter became Yugoslav Communists after the CPY declared for an independent or autonomous Macedonia and provided leaders to the fledgling regime in Skopje after 1945. (Cf. Kofos, and Palmer and King.)

Ch. 1: The Birth of a New Yugoslavia

1. Jozo Tomasevich, 'Yugoslavia during the Second World War', in Vucinich (1969), p. 74. Cf. Hoptner (1962), the best and most sympathetic account of the ancien régime's vain efforts to strengthen the country internally and externally during the last prewar years; and Ristić (1966) for the coup of March 27, with an introduction by Vucinich surveying historical interpretations of it.

2. The term *narodna oslobodjenje* may also and perhaps more accurately be translated as 'people's liberation', but the more common version is followed here to avoid confusion. *Narod* means both 'nation' and 'people' in Serbo-Croatian, creating a problem for the translator (see my own deliberately inconsistent 'people's liberation committees' and 'People's Front'), but more importantly for the thinking and perceptions of the Serbs and Croats. Whether, for example, the Croatian *narodni pokret* of 1970-71 (see Ch. 7) was a 'national movement' or a 'popular movement' was not merely a problem for translators.

3. Edvard Kardelj in the first wartime issue of the CPY's *Borba* (Užice, Oct. 19, 1941, reprinted in *Istorijski arhiv KPJ*, i. 1, 1949, pp. 18-20).

4. An adequately detailed, researched and objective ('de-mythologised') study of Yugoslavia's wartime epic as a whole has been curiously slow in appearing, but Jozo Tomasevich's monumental trilogy (vol. i, *The Chetniks*, appearing in 1975) is filling the gap. Sir William Deakin's *The Embattled Mountain* and Tomasevich's contribution to Vucinich (1969) are useful, the first for glimpses of the story's drama and complexity and the second as a good brief analytical summary. Roberts (1973) is impressively researched and does more than its title suggests. The brief account in the following pages is based on these and other standard sources.

5. There did, however, seem a further possibility at the time, namely that Serb-Croat bitterness would be so intense, and royalist sentiment in Serbia so strong, that the reconstruction of a Yugoslav State would be impossible. For the effect on Western Allied thinking and policy, see Auty and Clogg.

6. The exchange took place in Cairo in December 1943, as Churchill was returning from the Teheran Conference and was originally related by the mission chief, Brigadier Fitzroy Maclean (Maclean (1950), pp. 402f). Although Churchill was precisely at this period and throughout 1944 pressing the Americans and his own generals to agree to a landing in Istria as a beach-head from which to beat the Russians to Vienna (an idea which he communicated to Tito during their August 1944 meeting, alarming the latter into a pre-emptive bid for possession of Istria and Trieste)—he never advocated a *Balkan* landing in force. (Cf. Churchill's *The Second World War*, v. 304–14, vi. 50–7, other sources cited in Rusinow (1969), p. 362–4; and Roberts, pp. 168f., 235f., 265).

7. During his consultations with Stalin in Moscow, October 1944, recounted in Churchill, vi. 226ff.; cf. Roberts, pp. 240–3, 266–70; Dedijer (1969), esp. pp. 73–92.

8. The figure accepted by Tomasevich (in Vucinich), p. 101. Marjanović (1962), p. 103, usually a reliable source, gives 130,000 for the enemy force engaged during Weiss I and II. Statistics on the total size of the Partisan forces at various stages in the war also vary and are here taken from an official Party history, *PISKJ* (1963), pp. 312, 355, 384, 401.

9. When the Supreme Command's emissaries focused so prematurely and brutally on a *socialist* revolution that the populace reacted against them, virtually wiping the Partisan movement out of the Montenegrin scene for a full year.

10. Most studies, following Dedijer's authorised biography, published in English as *Tito Speaks* (1953), date Tito's appointment as Secretary-General in late 1937. Auty, in *Tito* (1970), p. 128, convincingly argues from more recent Yugoslav sources a January 1939 date for his confirmation in the post.

11. *PISKJ*, pp. 272–4, 281, 332, which gives the CPY's July 1941 membership as '7–8,000'; almost all other sources give the figure 12,000 for that date. Cf. Avakumović, i. (1964), table on p. 164.

12. 'Why did you become a Communist?' is a question which the present writer has asked of every prewar Yugoslav Party member (most of them from the 1937–41 generation) whom he has known well enough to expect an honest reply. The answer has invariably cited one or both of the motives suggested here.

13. Roberts and Tomasevich (1975) have the last, fully documented words on this thorny subject.

14. Mihailović himself was not captured until March 1946 and was executed, after a trial in which he conducted himself with dignity, the following July.

15. In *The East European Revolution* (1950), pp. 167–229.

16. The Partisan myth as a source of legitimacy is particularly and rightly emphasised by Zaninovich (1960), pp. 44–50.

17. Cf. Adam Ulam's perceptive and prescient description (Ulam, 1952, pp. 102–5).

18. Stepinac's attitude towards and relations with the Pavelić regime is still a matter of dispute but was basically irrelevant to the new regime's purposes in trying him. (He was released from prison in

1951 and lived and died in 1960 in exile in his native village.) Tito's olive branch, offered at a meeting with Church dignitaries in Zagreb on June 2, was reported publicly in *Borba*, June 5, 1945.

19. Quoted in Vucinich, p. 129.

20. *Komunist*, 2/1951, also cited in Hoffman and Neal (1962), p. 92.

21. Cf. Duroselle (1966); also Rusinow (1969), esp. pp. 379–407 and *Whatever Happened to the Trieste Question?* (AUFS, 16/2, Jan. 1969). Agitated Yugoslav Government and public reactions to an Italian note which protested what the Italians viewed as an extension of Yugoslav legal claims to ex-Zone B in the spring of 1974 (when Zone B had been a *de facto* part of Yugoslavia for twenty years) were a reminder that the issue was still revivable. (It also gave Belgrade its joke of the year: 'Who are the world's most musical people? The Yugoslavs, because the Italians send us one note and we can sing variations on it for three months.')

22. *Službeni list*, 10 (1946). The best analysis in English is Hondius (1968), pp. 137–67.

23. Cited in Shoup (1968), pp. 117f., along with other little-known territorial disputes among the republics at the time of their formation.

24. According to tables compiled ibid., pp. 274–9, which are not always accurate, the Federal Government in 1946 included 8 Serbs, 4 Croats, 2 Slovenes, and one each for the Montenegrins, Macedonians, and 'Yugoslavs', plus 2 'unknowns'; the Party CC of 1948 (there is no breakdown for the still quasi-clandestine CC of 1945–8) included 25 Serbs, 12 Croats, 8 Slovenes, 10 Montenegrins, 5 Macedonians, 1 'Yugoslav' and 2 unknowns.

25. A Leninist doctrine according to which Party decisions, in theory democratically adopted after free discussion 'from the bottom up', must then be loyally and unquestionably implemented by all members on the basis of directives 'from the top down'.

26. That the ethnic disproportion in all three bureaucracies continued in later years and as they took in younger cadres was partly a function of 'old boy networks', favouring friends, relatives and hometown youngsters, and partly because in Yugoslavia, as in other societies, economically backward regions with fewer jobs or promotional opportunities tend to send a higher proportion of their sons and daughters into the civil service or the army.

27. An interpretation argued by Halperin (1958).

28. Djilas, who says he was one advocate of Sarajevo, to the present writer.

29. Shoup, Ch. 3, is a meticulously researched survey of early postwar nationalist disturbances, their suppression and other aspects of the national question in this period.

30. The same or similar figures, partly UNRRA and partly Yugoslav calculations, are cited in all standard works (e.g. Hoffman and Neal, pp. 86–9; *PISKJ*, pp. 426f.).

31. Bilandžić (1973), pp. 30f.; cf. Hoffman and Neal, pp. 89–91.

32. Boris Kidrič to the 5th Congress in July 1948, in Kidrič (1960), iii. 332, 349.

33. Cf. Johnson (1972), pp. 35f. and 59f., for arguments from textual

analysis of Yugoslav sources indicating that this really was Hebrang's position, which was obfuscated by later accusations and counter-accusations concerning his role during the war, in 1946 and in 1948.

34. *Law on the Five-Year Plan* (1947). 'Social Product' as measured in socialist countries and encountered throughout this study does not include 'non-productive' activities like health, government, and many services and therefore underestimates GNP, as calculated in the West, by at least 10 per cent.

35. Bilandžić (1969), p. 35; Djilas's boast is quoted by Johnson, p. 36. For the most thorough discussion of Soviet spatial planning theories and Yugoslav practice in this and subsequent periods, see Hamilton (1960).

36. Bilandžić (1973), pp. 64–9, describes the harassment of the peasants and hints that others besides Hebrang and Žujović favoured rapid collectivisation. Cf. Hoffman and Neal, pp. 97f., 270f., and Tomasevich, 'Collectivization of Agriculture in Yugoslavia', in Sanders (1958).

37. Bilandžić (1973), p. 40. Cf. the good, short sketches of the economic system in Milenkovitch (1971), pp. 60f.

38. Only Tito, Djilas, Kardelj, Leskošek and Ranković, the survivors of the group presented to the 1940 Zagreb Conference, were listed in 5th Congress documents as members of the outgoing Politburo (*V kongres KPJ*, pp. 846–56), but Svetozar Vukmanović-Tempo (1971), ii. 4 and 488f., says that he, Pijade, Blagoje Nešković, Žujović, Hebrang, Kidrič and Ivan Gošnjak were also Politburo members just after the war and that he and Žujović attended wartime meetings as though members. Žujović and Vukmanović himself are omitted from other lists (e.g. Ulam, p. 108).

39. Cf. Djilas (1962), Vukmanović, vol. i, Dedijer (1953) and Adamic (1952) for testimony on the way resentment and doubt were reflexively suppressed by the Yugoslavs. The Kremlin 'dossier', literally or as metaphor, is also not a historian's licence, as evidence in these sources and the published Soviet letters of 1948 demon-strates.

40. The Soviet–Yugoslav correspondence of March–June 1948, trans. by Jane Degras and published by RIIA as *The Soviet–Yugoslav Dispute* (1948, later referred to as 'RIIA'), and Dedijer (1953), both invaluably revealing but 'official' and therefore selective, are still the primary sources for all later accounts. Ulam is the best of the early ones and needs remarkably little revision considering the date, anteceding even Dedijer's biography; Hoffman and Neal, Chs. 7–9, is still the best brief survey. Cf. also the good Yugoslav analysis by Pribičević (1972); Armstrong (1951); Halperin, Chs 9–10; Korbel (1951); Maclean (1957), Chs 12–14; Wolff (1956), Ch. 11. Recent Yugoslav memoirs add many interesting details and a few amend-ments but do not change the basic picture or solve mysteries like Stalin's real purpose in urging the Yugoslavs to 'swallow Albania' and conclude an immediate federation with Bulgaria as late as January 1948; the 'missing' letters before March 20; or the full nature of Hebrang's role and motives (the last also unclarified by Milatović (1952)).

41. The most pathetic evidence that the faith was genuine was Pijade's 37-day wait in the bitter cold of a Durmitor winter in 1941 for a promised Soviet arms drop which never came and which could at best have been token, given the range of Soviet aircraft. For this and the whole list, see Pijade (1950).
42. Ulam, p. 103.
43. Cf. Vukmanović's characteristically primitive and simple reaction, recorded in his memoirs, ii. 75-9, 94.
44. A point emphasised by Johnson (1972), Ch. 2 (p. 5), who is interested in proving that 'the statement "It was at least a year [after 1948] before the [Soviet-Yugoslav] struggle was extended to the ideological plane" is factually incorrect'. He therefore stresses some singularly subtle distinctions between Yugoslav and other East European definitions of 'people's democracy' prior to 1948.
45. This and the earlier Stalin-Djilas meeting are described by Djilas (1962), pp. 128-33, 154-68, who adds to Dedijer's (1953) earlier description (pp. 318-33), an admission that a Yugoslav-Albanian unification was indeed being planned in Belgrade and Tirana. The Yugoslavs interpreted Stalin's 'swallow Albania' as a provocation and his insistence on immediate Yugoslav-Bulgarian federation as an effort to penetrate Yugoslav apparatuses by uniting them with already Sovieticised Bulgarian ones. Alternatively, insistence on immediate federation may have been designed to force a Yugoslav-Bulgarian crisis. Negotiations on the issue, begun by Tito and Dimitrov at Bled in Slovenia the preceding summer, had bogged down over Yugoslav insistence that Bulgaria should form a seventh republic in the existing Federation. The Bulgarians were understandably holding out for a separate two-member federation.
46. But which was not the first of the exchange, since the Soviet reply, dated 27 March, begins with a reference to 'your answers of 18 and 20 March' (RIIA, Doc. 2).
47. Ibid., Yugoslav letter (signed by Tito and Kardelj) of Apr. 14, 1948.
48. Dedijer (1969), p. 141, quoting a 1952 conversation with Tito about the draft letter of Apr. 14 (see below, p. 34).
49. Ibid., p. 146.
50. Ibid., p. 152.
51. As translated in RIIA.
52. According to Ranković's report to the 6th Congress, Nov. 1952.
53. *V kongres KPJ*, esp. pp. 5, 844-6, 866.

Ch. 2: The Break with Stalinism

1. Dedijer (1953), pp. 392f. Stalin's ikons and obeisances to them did not disappear until after mid-1949. Cf. Johnson (1972), pp. 67-9, who accepts these later claims that this policy had been 'a directed rather than spontaneous reaction', and who therefore disagrees with the interpretation offered here.
2. Ulam, p. 97.
3. Djilas (1969), p. 29.
4. Dedijer (1969), p. 190; cf. pp. 269-72 and *passim*.
5. Ibid., p. 186.

6. F. W. Neal (1958), pp. 3f.

7. Adamic, pp. 254f., 260; cf. pp. 76, 96, 118-31. See p. 52 n. 57 below.

8. Dedijer (1969), p. 190; cf. Dedijer (1953), p. 348.

9. Dedijer (1953), p. 353.

10. Hoffman and Neal, p. 141n. Cf. Ulam, pp. 126f.

11. *PISKJ*, p. 475. Cf. Kardelj's report to the 5th Congress in *V kongres KPJ*, pp. 573-8.

12. For details of economic and other pressures at this time, see the *White Book*. Cf. Marjanović *et al.* (1973), pp. 258-63.

13. *PISKJ*, pp. 472-4.

14. Cf. Bakarić's veiled doubts expressed to deputies to the Croatian Sabor (parliament) in Dec. 1948, and his strong criticism of forced and *irrational* collectivisation at a Croatian CC Plenum in May 1949 (both in Bakarić (1960), pp. 88-93, 107-14) and Johnson (1972), pp. 76-9.

15. *PISKJ*, loc. cit.; Daniel Ivin, 'Analiza "Pregleda istorije Saveza Komunista Jugoslavije" u vezi sa II i III plenumom CK KPJ u 1949. godini', and Rade Stojasavljević, 'O politici Partije u pitanju kolektivizacije naše poljoprivrede', both in *Putevi revolucije*, 3-4 (1963); Cf. Dedijer (1969), pp. 272f.; Bilandžić (1969), pp. 50-52; Marjanović *et al.*, pp. 271f.

16. S. Popović (1964), p. 14. Other sources give slightly different figures (e.g. Bilandžić (1969), p. 52), reflecting problems of classification.

17. S. Popović (1964) and Bilandžić (1969). Cf. *PISKJ*, p. 479, Hoffman and Neal, pp. 272f., J. Tomasevich, art. cit. in Sanders.

18. Hoffman and Neal, p. 145.

19. Adamic, p. 56. Cf. Kidrič's speech to the Federal Assembly, Nov. 28, 1948, on the economic situation and prospects for Plan fulfilment in 1949, in Kidrič, iii. 453-84.

20. Cf. Bilandžić (1969), pp. 27-31. There is an ironic confirmation of this last assertion in Kardelj's *criticism* (in his report to the 5th Congress in July 1948) of local autonomy left over from wartime organisation and his insistence that it must give way to stricter hierarchical authority (in *V. kongres KPJ*, pp. 557-9).

21. Cf. Dedijer's description of the methods used by Belgrade 'activists' to recruit 'volunteers' for public works (1969, pp. 383f.), and Marjanović *et al.*, p. 270, for data on volunteer labour.

22. Cf. the succinct summary of such defects in Bićanić (1973), p. 64.

23. S. Stojanović, 'From Primitive Towards Developed Communism', (unpubl. paper delivered at the 10th Session, University Internat. Centre for Social Science of Univ. of Belgrade, 1968), pp. 2f. Cf. the same writer's *Between Ideals and Reality* (1973) and Bilandžić (1973), pp. 72-94.

24. The Montenegrin Party predictably reported a far higher rate of expulsions for Cominform sympathies—one out of every six Party members—than any other republic. In Croatia one out of twenty was expelled, in Bosnia-Herzegovina one out of twenty-three, and in Macedonia one out of thirty-one. The Serbian and Slovenian Parties never issued figures (see Shoup, p. 138).

25. Cf. Kardelj's 1953 admission: 'The socialist forces of our country had no source of support [after 1948] except their own working people.

Therefore, all state policies had to have the support of the majority of the people ...' (speech of Nov. 10, 1953, quoted by Johnson (1972), pp. 143f.).

26. Dedijer (1969), p. 392.

27. 225,000 out of 448,175. Cf. Ranković's report to the 5th Congress (*Borba*, July 23, 1948) and Tito's to the 6th Congress (ibid., Nov. 4, 1952).

28. Adamic, p. 115; cf. Bilandžić (1969), p. 53.

29. Dedijer (1969), p. 187. Cf. also Kidrič to Neal in the summer of 1950 (Neal (1958), p. 39n.).

30. Such perceptions are of course difficult to document, and allowance must be made for the propagandistic or cynical manipulative intentions of the actors. The conversations which Adamic had with top and middle-rank leaders in 1949 and the reminiscences of Dedijer (1969) and of Vukmanović (the former an incorrigibly romantic revolutionary and the latter basically too guileless to write a consistently self-serving or dishonest account) are nevertheless convincingly permeated with this ethos. Cf. also Djilas (1969), Bilandžić (1969), pp. 30f., Ulam, pp. 102f. and Djilas, 'Anatomy of a Moral' (in *Nova misao*, 1/54, publ. in English in 1959).

31. Dedijer (1969), p. 391, quoting the stenographic record. Cf. F. W. Neal, *Yugoslav Communist Theory* (AUFS FWN-5-'54).

32. Little has been said by any of the participants about such 'peace feelers', but see Adamic, p. 251 for an account of conversations held in neutral capitals in the early spring of 1949 and cf. Dedijer (1969), p. 190.

33. The note warned that if Soviet citizens were treated in this way, it was proof that the Yugoslav Government was fascist and the Soviet Government 'would be obliged to adopt other, more effective means to secure the rights and interests of Soviet citizens in Yugoslavia' (*White Book*, Doc. 51).

34. All according to Dedijer (1969), pp. 284f. Military demonstrations along Yugoslavia's borders beginning in August 1949 are reported by other sources (e.g. Bilandžić (1969), p. 43, Marjanović *et al.*, p. 261). The documents in the *White Book* (sect. IV) pertain largely to border incidents in later months.

35. Bilandžić, (1969), p. 43.

36. Cf. Rubinstein, pp. 13f., Marjanović *et al.*, p. 261; Dedijer (1969), pp. 277–82.

37. 'Meeting of the Information Bureau of Communist Parties in Hungary in the Latter Half of November 1949', published in the Cominform journal, 1950.

38. See e.g. their probing questions to Adamic shortly after his arrival (Adamic, Chs. 2–5); cf. Dedijer (1969), pp. 269–72.

39. Rubinstein, pp. 12–20; cf. Dedijer (a delegate to the UN) (1969), pp. 337ff.

40. Quoted (*i.a.*) in Neal, pp. 6f.

41. Campbell, pp. 14–29, is the most authoritative and complete study of Yugoslav-American relations in this period as in others.

42. Vukmanović, ii. 125f.; Halperin, p. 174. Nešković returned to his

career as a doctor and was still on the faculty of Belgrade University Medical School twenty years later.

43. Campbell, p. 25.
44. Hoffman and Neal, pp. 419-23.
45. Duroselle, and Rusinow, *Whatever Happened* ...; cf. B. Novak (1970).
46. In a 1968 press conference held while Yugoslavia was alarmed after the occupation of Czechoslovakia, Foreign Secretary Marko Nikezić was asked whether the Yugoslavs might invoke the Balkan Pact against a threat from the East. Smiling and lapsing into English, he replied: 'Old pacts, like old soldiers, never die but quietly fade away'.
47. Campbell, p. 28; cf. Hoffman and Neal, tables on pp. 348f.
48. Cf. Rubinstein, Ch. 1, and Campbell, Ch. 5.
49. With the exception of the Civil War in Spain, in which several of the Yugoslav Party inner circle had participated. This proved a more useful training for the Partisan war in Yugoslavia than for administration, management or innovative theoretical work, but one may speculate that ideas exchanged with non-Communist leftists there could have planted seeds that germinated much later in 'Titoist' theory after 1949. No documentation is available.
50. See e.g. the figures on Yugoslavs brought to the US for technical training under the ICA 'Project Assistance' programme (855 between 1954 and 1959) in Hoffman and Neal, pp. 351f., who note that 'the list of projects and of individuals trained reads like a gazetteer of technical projects and a Who's Who of technical specialists'.
51. Bilandžić (1969), p. 45f.; cf. Pribićević, pp. 50f.
52. The official Plenums of this period were the 2nd (Jan. 28-30, 1949), 3rd (Dec. 1949), 4th (June 1951) and 5th (May 27, 1952).
53. Cf. the similar list in Johnson (1972), pp. 235f., who interestingly downgrades Djilas's importance below that of Bakarić.
54. Adamic, p. 94. Cf. Dedijer (1969), pp. 385-8, and Slobodan Nešovic (1968), pp. 67ff.
55. Djilas (1969), pp. 220-3.
56. Adamic, pp. 102f. Cf. Tito's similar words nearly four years later, in his report to the 6th Congress (quoted by Dedijer (1969), p. 415).
57. Adamic, pp. 120f., where he is paraphrasing rather than quoting directly. His account of his 1949 encounters with Yugoslav leaders deserves more serious study than it has usually enjoyed; other accounts, not available to him at the time, confirm that he was an accurate reporter of conversations to which he had a uniquely privileged access, even if he did not always fully grasp the significance of what he heard.
58. Cf. Milenkovitch (pp. 56f.), who adds that Kidrič's Jan. 1949 position was not accepted in the Soviet Union until 1956. The Kidrič article appeared in *Komunist*, 1 (1949).
59. Djilas, in the first issue of *Partijska izgradnja*, Mar. 1949.
60. As noted by Johnson (1972), p. 95n.
61. Cf. Ivin, art. cit. n. 15 above, pp. 3-4.
62. Marjanović *et al.*, p. 275; *PISKJ*, p. 476; Bilandžić (1969), p. 54; cf. Neal (1958), p. 162.

63. *Komunist*, 4 (1949), p. 39 (also quoted by Bilandžić, (1973), pp. 104f.).

64. In *Komunist*, 5 (1949). It was preceded and heralded by M. Popović's 'O ekonomskim odnosima izmedju socijalističkih država', ibid., 4 (1949).

65. 'Veliki majstori licemerja', *Borba*, Sept. 22, 26, 29, Oct. 5-6, 1949.

66. According to Halperin, p. 110; cf. Johnson (1972), p. 96n., for further evidence. The most thorough and thoroughly documented study of the ideological evolution of these months is Johnson (1972). For articles and speeches assembled for foreign consumption on the post-1950 evolution of the Yugoslav position, see the monthly review, *Questions actuelles du socialisme*, which began publication in March 1951 with contributions by Djilas, Kardelj and Kidrič. Cf. also Neal (1958), Ch. 2; the same author's *Yugoslav Communist Theory* and Halperin, Chs 14-21.

67. The first to so describe the Soviet system seems to have been Djilas, in a Nov. 1950 series of articles in *Borba*. Later the preferred term came to be 'State socialism', a shift which reflected both the milder tone of Soviet-Yugoslav polemics after Stalin's death and a concession to academic (Marxist) arguments that 'State capitalism' was technically incorrect.

68. *PISKJ*, pp. 478f.; Marjanović *et al.*, p. 275.

69. Ibid., Marjanović *et al.*, pp. 272f., and Johnson (1972), p. 177.

70. His evolution is traceable in the articles republished in Bakarić (1960). Johnson (1972), Ch. 8, again provides a useful analysis of the hesitations which marked the regime's reluctant and agonising reappraisal in this field.

71. *PISKJ*, p. 477.

72. The quasi-official Party history (ibid., p. 480) refers to opposition at this time from unnamed persons, presumably in the trade unions, who felt that workers' participation could be achieved as effectively (and with better control?) through a strengthening of the role of the unions as through workers' councils.

73. Djilas (1969), p. 222. Yugoslav sources are inconsistent about which bodies (Government, Politburo, trade unions) participated at what stages—cf. Marjanović *et al.*, p. 274; *PISKJ*, p. 477.

74. In February 1950 the Federal Ministries of Mining and Electrical Industry were abolished; in April those of Agriculture, Forestry, Light Industry, Construction, Trade and Supply. As they received these new responsibilities, the republics simultaneously transferred most of the regional economic branches previously under their control to the counties (*srezovi, kotori*). Cf. *PISKJ*, pp. 477f.; Bilandžić (1969), pp. 54f.

75. Hoffman and Neal, p. 175; Bilandžić (1969), p. 53; Mike Handler in *NYT*, Oct. 30, 1950.

76. *Službeni list*, No. 43/50 (July 5, 1950, Act No. 391). For an analysis of the law see *i.a.* D. Gorupić and I. Paj (1970), pp. 40-2, V. Meier (1956), pp. 102-45 and Neal (1958), pp. 120-6 (who is not always consistent in distinguishing provisions of the original law from later amendments).

77. *Borba*, June 27, 1950.

78. The word 'enterprise' (*preduceće, poduzeće*) is used throughout in its Yugoslav sense, denoting all economic organisations in the socialist sector, whether engaged in production (industrial or agricultural), trade, service or finance. The word 'trustees' is used to emphasise the fact that neither the workers nor the workers' councils formally 'own' the factories in Yugoslavia, although with the development of the system most of the normal attributes of ownership as understood in the West fell to the latter, alone or in collaboration with communal governments. (Cf. the articles by Kardelj, Predrag Vranički, Vučina Vasović, etc. in J. Djordjević *et al.* (1972)).

79. Marjanović *et al.*, p. 276; cf. Meier, pp. 116ff.

80. Cf. an oblique admission that this was indeed one consideration in the quasi-official *PISKJ*, p. 481.

81. In his speech introducing the law, Tito warned that the introduction of self-management would not be easy and that the Party must be under no illusions; nor should they ignore 'the objective conditions of development', especially those which were 'the consequences of backwardness'.

82. Cf. the calculation of shortfalls in achieving planned targets by Ivan Liović in *Putevi revolucije*, 3-4, pp. 337-9; out of Liović's selected list of 32 articles (ranging from coal and iron to soap, beer and cooking oil) only 2 (transformers and lead) had exceeded the plan, 5 had fulfilled between 75 and 90 per cent of their targets and 12 had only managed to achieve 25-50 per cent of their plans.

83. Bilandžić (1969), p. 56.

84. Several Yugoslav economists have told the present writer that they discovered Lange's work (see esp. Lange and Taylor, *On the Economic Theory of Socialism* (Minneapolis, 1938)) only *after* the Yugoslav model of the early 1950s had been developed in principle, but the basic solution which they chose at that time was remarkably similar to his proposals; there is no evidence that Kidrič ever read Lange. Another case of Yugoslavs 'discovering America' for themselves?

85. Cf. *PISKJ*, pp. 484-6, 489-91; Marjanović *et al.*, pp. 277f.; Bilandžić (1973), pp. 114-21; also Kidrič in *Questions actuelles* ..., Mar.-Apr. 1951, pp. 113-18.

86. *Službeni list*, Dec. 30, 1951 (Act No. 569). Analyses of the law may be found *i.a.* in Bićanić (1973), pp. 102-5; in Bilandžić (1967), pp. 75-9 and (1973), pp. 127-40; in Milenkovitch, pp. 81-9, Meier, pp. 129-39 and Pejovich, pp. 13-16, 24.

87. Based on Kidrič's analysis of the 'basic proportions' when the law was introduced, in *Questions actuelles* ..., Oct. 1951, pp. 18-25. Other writers order the proportions somewhat differently (e.g. Pejovich, p. 134). Cf. Kidrič's earlier article 'Teze o ekonomici prelaznog perioda u našoj zemlji', in *Komunist*, 6 (1950), for a halfway point in the revealing evolution of his theories.

88. Pejovich, p. 49.

89. Vukmanović, ii. 153f. (he related the same anecdote earlier, in *NIN*, May 3, 1964).

90. Bilandžić (1967), p. 76.

91. Total US economic aid amounted to $44.8m in 1950, $127.9m in 1951,

$81.4m in 1952 and $122.6m in 1953 (Hoffman and Neal, table p. 348).

92. Bilandžić (1973) pp. 172-81, offers a more detailed, critical analysis of the 1954 reforms. Cf. Bićanić (1973), pp. 105-7, Milenkovitch, Ch. 5, Pejovich, pp. 16, 18-20, 30 and Meier, pp. 139-43.

93. Bićanić (1973), p. 106.

94. Ibid., p. 107. Cf. Bilandžić (1973), pp. 176-81, for detailed analysis of the instruments which assured a 'decisive role of the Federal State organs in administering the national economy'.

95. The account given here is highly abbreviated, omitting many minor experimental innovations and some major but abortive ones, of which the most intriguing was the introduction, in December 1952, of investment auctions as a device for apportioning investment credits (cf. Egon Neuberger, 'The Yugoslav Investment Auction', *Quarterly Journal of Economics*, Feb. 1959, pp. 88-115).

96. Printed as a pamphlet (Kardelj, 1952). It is instructive to compare this work with Djilas (1957); the critiques of the existing system are very similar, and the only real (but vital) difference is in Djilas's pessimistic conclusion of late 1953, that Yugoslavia would escape the fate of the Soviet Union only if the CP dissolved or accepted a multi-party solution.

97. Kardelj (1952), p. 17.

98. Ibid., pp. 28f., 32-4.

99. Ibid., pp. 30f.

100. Ibid., pp. 26f.

101. Cf. Bilandžić (1969), pp. 70-3.

102. For detailed discussions of the 1953 law see Hondius, pp. 192-206, and Hoffman and Neal, pp. 213-24.

103. Hondius, pp. 194-8, and Shoup, pp. 191f. For the subject in general see I. Lapenna (1964).

104. At the same time, however, the republics, in losing some formal but usually fictitious status and authority, in fact acquired more administrative powers. While the legislative competence of the Federation was expanded at the expense of that of the regions, the Constitutional Law stipulated that federal organs should execute federal acts directly only in enumerated areas of exclusive federal competence; execution and administration in all other areas should be by republican or local organs.

105. Cf. Hoffman and Neal, pp. 222f., on this point and the subsequent vicissitudes (until 1962) of the principle and its implementation.

106. Hondius, p. 204, on information provided by federal officials. Cf. Shoup, table on p. 274, dividing the FEC in 1958 by nationality rather than republic of origin and identifying 16 Serbs, 5 Croats, 6 Slovenes, 3 Macedonians and 4 Montenegrins.

107. The CC directive was printed in *Partijska izgradnja*, July 1950; cf. *PISKJ*, p. 494, Johnson (1972), p. 199.

108. *PISKJ*, pp. 495f.

109. Although not publicly stated, that high-level consideration was given to a multi-party solution in 1952 can be inferred from the terms and the detailed argumentation used by Kardelj (see above, p. 68) and others in rejecting the possibility; cf. also *PISKJ*, p. 496. For details

the reader is again referred to Johnson (1972) and Neal (1958), loc. cit. and the sources cited there.

110. As defined, *i.a.*, by G. Ionescu (1967), pp. 60-4.

111. *Borba komunista Jugoslavije ... VI kongres KPJ* (1952), pp. 190-4. Cf. the summary in *PISKJ*, p. 506.

112. Djilas (1969), p. 219.

113. Vukmanović, ii. 159: Dedijer (1969), p. 418, calls Djilas's oration 'perhaps the best speech he ever made'.

114. Tito's interview of Nov. 9, 1951 and Kardelj's even earlier reference to the subject, in a speech of Apr. 27, 1951, are quoted by Johnson (1972), p. 201.

115. The same consensual method had given rise to Tito's proposal, adopted by the 4th Plenum in June 1951, that lower Party organisations should be instructed no longer to treat 'the works of individual leading members of the Party which have a clearly theoretical character' as authoritative documents, requiring study and action, unless 'the CPY expressly passes a resolution to that effect'. It was to be made clear that 'the development of new theoretical views in the CPY unfolds on the basis of discussion and the struggle of opinions' (Resolution of 4th Plenum, *Komunist*, 2-3 (1951)).

116. Quoted in *PISKJ*, p. 508, by Hoffman and Neal, p. 177, and Johnson (1972), pp. 203f.; the first, pp. 502-10, and the last, pp. 203-9, provide useful summaries of the Congress. Cf. Halperin, pp. 173-9, for some eye-witness details and analysis.

117. Hoffman and Neal, p. 208, and Neal's AUFS Reports.

118. After Nešković's resignation the outgoing Politburo consisted of Tito, Djilas, Gošnjak, Kardelj, Kidrič, Leskošek, Pijade and Ranković.

119. *Komunist*, 5-6 (1952), pp. 127f.

120. Djilas (1957), subsequently modified but with essentially the same conclusion in Djilas (1969), which is subtitled 'Beyond the New Class'.

121. See below, pp. 190f., 310f. for critical descriptions by high officials of the 'mentality' of the Party nearly twenty years later. Cf. also the reflections of Djilas, loc. cit., and N. D. Popović (1968), the last a highly prejudiced work by a defector from the regime's sub-ministerial ranks, worth consulting for specific examples drawn from personal experience.

122. Cf. Hoffman and Neal, pp. 183f., Bilandžić (1973), pp. 147f., Johnson (1972), pp. 212f.

123. Kardelj, 'The Role and Tasks of the Socialist Alliance of the Working People of Yugoslavia (Report submitted to the 4th Congress of the People's Front)' official trans. (mimeo., 71pp), pp. 53f.

124. Johnson (1972), pp. 206f., noting that 'these claims went considerably beyond any that had been made at the Sixth Party Congress', thinks that an important 'instrumental reason' for over-emphasising the political importance of SAWPY at its 1953 Congress was the realisation that the 'Communist' in the LCY's name and image made it an inappropriate instrument for their increasingly important relations with social democratic parties and movements in the West.

125. As n. 123, p. 32.
126. *Službeni list* 14 (1953); cf. Hoffman and Neal, pp. 275-7.
127. Ibid., 22 (1953). See Johnson (1972), pp. 188-90, for details of advocacy and opposition and sources, and Bakarić (1960), pp. 349ff., for his continuing advocacy of the private peasant in the name of more rational and larger agricultural production.
128. Of the land thus acquired, 103,500 ha. were distributed to State farms, 70,800 ha. to the surviving SRZs, and 42,600 ha. to OZZS (Sv. Popović, p. 21; cf. 'Agrarian reform in Yugoslavia', *Yugoslav Survey*, July-Sept. 1961; Tomasevich, in Sanders, pp. 179-81).
129. *PISKJ*, p. 524.

Ch. 3: Consolidation and Development

1. Djilas (1969), p. 30. The plenary sessions of Yugoslav Central Committees (federal and republican) are numbered serially, beginning anew after every Congress. The 1st session is always a brief formal one, held as the Congress adjourns to 'elect' an Executive Committee, etc.
2. *PISKJ*, p. 520 (full text in *Komunist*, July 1953).
3. Djilas (1969), pp. 30f.
4. See his second statement to the Plenum, in *Questions actuelles* ... 22 (Jan.-Feb. 1954), pp. 86f. (*Komunist* same date).
5. The most important of this early series was 'Početak kraja i početak', published in his own favourite and new monthly, *Nova misao*, Aug. 1953. Cf. his agreement with Crvenkovski at the 3rd Plenum that this represented the beginning of his 'deviation' from the Party line (loc. cit.).
6. Statement at the 3rd Plenum, loc. cit., p. 4. Hoffman and Neal, pp. 185-95 and Halperin, Chs 25-6 are still the best summary descriptions of the entire crisis.
7. Cf. his own retrospective introspection (in Djilas (1969), esp. the first and last three chapters), including his description of the agony of the night of December 7-8, when he realised where he was going and determined to go on consciously; the clues found in the *Borba* series itself; references to his personal behaviour by Tito and others, including Djilas himself, at the 3rd Plenum; and Vukmanović, ii. 80-95.
8. Most of the entire series, as noted, is in Djilas (1959).
9. The details in Vukmanović's memoirs (ii. 189-95), and Kardelj's speech to the 3rd Plenum (loc. cit., p. 44), are confirmed in general outline but not specifically by Djilas's (1969) scattered reminiscences.
10. Djilas (1969), p. 246. The precise date of Tito's decision to move against him is not recorded in the published sources. Djilas says Kardelj informed him of it three weeks after his decision during the night of Dec. 7-8 (ibid., p. 26), which would mean their conversation which Kardelj identifies as occurring on Dec. 22. Vukmanović (ii. 191) says that at a New Year's Eve party, when he spoke to Djilas about Tito's anger with him, Djilas replied worriedly: 'What do you think, will they go to a plenum?' But Vukmanović also places Kardelj

and Ranković's 'two-day' confrontation with Djilas several days later, after publication of 'Anatomy of a Moral'.

11. Cf. Hoffman and Neal, pp. 189f., for details. Neal was in Belgrade at the time, and his initial account, including an interview with Djilas which was the first obtained by a foreigner after the 3rd Plenum, is in his *Yugoslav Communist Theory* (AUFS, loc. cit.).

12. *Questions actuelles* ..., loc. cit., pp. 16, 6. See below, pp. 182f., 322.

13. Also quoted in Hoffman and Neal, p. 194; cf. the speeches in *Komunist, Questions actuelles* ..., loc., cit. and Halperin, Ch. 26, for an early and sympathetic effort to explain Djilas's behaviour at the Plenum. Djilas's own intimate, but in places still contradictory, explanation and description of his subsequent anguish over and reaction to his performance at the Plenum is in Djilas (1969), pp. 242-50.

14. *Questions actuelles* ..., loc. cit., pp. 11f. Tito used precisely the same argument against the Croatian Party leadership in Dec. 1971 (see Ch. 9).

15. In *Nova misao*, Aug. 1953.

16. Halperin, Chs 27ff., is the most sophisticated and persuasive version of this view.

17. For this background see, *i.a.*, R. Lowenthal (1964), original German ed. 1963, pp. 10-14, 73-6, and Halperin, Ch. 27.

18. The visit is described with varying emphasis and interpretations in Halperin, Ch. 28, Maclean (1957), pp. 439-44, Hoffman and Neal, pp. 424-6, Lowenthal, pp. 14-17, Vukmanović, ii. 231-9; for text of the Belgrade Declaration see Clissold, Doc. 174.

19. Cf. Halperin's argument, loc. cit., that the scene at the airport and what followed was a carefully and jointly prepared scenario designed to conceal the full significance of the visit (a reconciliation of the two *Parties*), and Lowenthal; p. 74, explaining Tito's 'famous scowl' in different terms: In preparing the meeting, Lowenthal says, Khrushchev had proposed to Tito that the Russians should blame their share of the quarrel on Beria and the Yugoslavs *their* share on Djilas; Tito put this idea to his CC, which rejected it on Tito's recommendation. It was therefore Khrushchev's sticking to a formula rejected by the Yugoslavs by blaming 'Beria ... and others' that angered Tito.

20. Clissold, Doc. 174.

21. Ibid., Doc. 179 and pp. 65f.

22. Made on Nov. 11, the Pula speech was not published for five days (*Borba*, Nov. 16, 1956; cf. Clissold, Doc. 181), a delay indicating a concerned debate about its effect. Cf. Clissold, pp. 66-9, Lowenthal, Ch. 4 and Hoffman and Neal, pp. 435-41, for details and somewhat conflicting interpretations of the Yugoslav role in the Hungarian revolution, also found in the voluminous literature on the Polish and Hungarian Octobers and the Soviet response to them.

23. Clissold, Docs 180 and 183.

24. Hoffman and Neal, pp. 444-9, Lowenthal, and Clissold, pp. 70-5 and Docs 189-203, give the most detailed accounts of the second rapprochement and its failure.

25. *PISKJ*, p. 546.

26. This exchange, quoted by Hoffman and Neal, pp. 450f., is especially worth recalling in the light of Khrushchev's particular problems, soon afterwards, with Soviet wheat production.
27. Cf. Campbell, pp. 43-7, and Hoffman and Neal, pp. 426-8, 446, for the ups and downs of Yugoslav relations with the West, and Rubinstein, esp. Chs 2-3, for the emergence of non-alignment in this period.
28. The latter argument, really only speculation, is advanced by Lowenthal. Evidence for the 'high tide' of 1956-57 is scattered and largely indirect, but includes the present writer's interviews with persons sent to prison or to Goli otok, the notorious prison island in the Gulf of Quarnero, in that period.
29. Figures (which vary in detail but not in trend in other sources) from Hoffman and Neal, pp. 196-9.
30. *PISKJ*, p. 540.
31. *Borba*, Mar. 14 and 15, 1956, cited by Hoffman and Neal, pp. 199f.
32. Quoted at length from *Komunist* (Feb. 28, 1958) by Hoffman and Neal, pp. 201-3, who also quote from an earlier issue (May 24, 1957) an instance, described as 'by no means an isolated curiosity', in which 'one same comrade' was simultanously chairman of the economic council of the district (*srez*), of the communal council for planning and finance, of the administrative board of the radio station and of the theatre council.
33. Cf. Bilandžić (1973), pp. 182-4 (in a section significantly entitled 'Insignificant changes in the political system'), Hondius, pp. 211-14, *PISKJ*, pp. 525-8, 537-9 and Leon Geršković, 'Samoupravljane u društveno-političkim zajednicama', in Djordjević *et al.* (1972), pp. 573-95.
34. These figures, available in many sources, are here taken from Bilandžić (1973), pp. 185f. and *PISKJ*, pp. 528-31.
35. The second largest decline was Bosnia-Herzegovina (from 79 to 75 per cent after peaking at 81 per cent in 1954); Macedonia and Montenegro had fallen by one or two points in these four years to 67 and 57 per cent respectively, while Serbia proper displayed a fluctuating but on balance rising curve which had reached 93 per cent by 1957 (calculations of M. B. McDonald (1968), the most convincing study of the problem to date, unmarred by ethnic prejudice or special interest pleading).
36. Crude birth-rates in 1953-54 averaged 23·4 per thousand population in the developed areas and 39·2 per thousand in the underdeveloped areas.
37. In 1953 the less developed republics received no special help except that two of them, Bosnia-Herzegovina and Montenegro, were allowed to rebate to the Federation a lower percentage of the tax on 'accumulation and funds' collected on their territories than the other republics, while all four then classified as underdeveloped (including Serbia) received interest-free credits from their contributions to the federal funds. With the establishment of the GIF in the following year, some resources from the Fund were earmarked for specified projects in Macedonia, Montenegro and Serbia (but not Bosnia), and in 1955 these same republics were granted special 'global allocations' from the GIF. While all of this represented significant efforts to

discriminate in their favour, constantly changing rules did not permit Governments or enterprises in the southern republics to engage in the longer-range planning which their level of development clearly required.

38. Kardelj's speech to the People's Assembly in December 1956 (quoted in part in Lowenthal, p. 86 and Bilandžić (1973), pp. 188f.) explicitly linked the lessons of Hungary to the need for further liberalising economic and democratising political reforms in Yugoslavia.

39. Bićanić (1973), p. 69.

40. Here following the description of the Brioni meeting and its consequences in Bićanić (1973, pp. 76-82), who coined the labels 'global and accumulative industrialisation'; cf. ibid., p. 186, *PISKJ*, pp. 530-2, and J. T. Bombelles (1968), who treats the 1955 shift in priorities as a more important watershed than any previous or subsequent systemic reform until 1965. Vukmanović, ii. 223-31, 339-41, describes the debates leading to the decision and his own overruled disagreement with the abandonment of extensive investment in basic industries.

41. Cf. Bilandžić (1973), pp. 185f., McDonald, pp. 118-21 (for provisions affecting underdeveloped areas), Hoffman and Neal, pp. 305-12 and Bombelles, pp. 76f., 115f.

42. Figures calculated from the Statistical Yearbook 1963 but available in many sources.

43. Cf. Bilandžić (1967), pp. 86-8, *PISKJ*, pp. 535-7 and Marjanović et al., pp. 284-6.

44. Bilandžić (1973), pp. 191-4; cf. Bićanić (1973), pp. 107-10. The reforms of 1958 were embodied in a series of laws and regulations, the most important of which are in the *Službeni list*, Nos. 52/57, 54/57 and 1/58.

45. For principal reports (by Tito, Ranković and Kardelj), the Programme, the Statute, and other selected Congress documents see *VII kongres* ... (1958); for Eng. trans. of the enormously long Programme by Stoyan Pribichevich, see *Yugoslavia's Way* (1958). Cf. also *PISKJ*, pp. 548-61, Hoffman and Neal, pp. 157-70, 205-8 and Bilandžić (1973), pp. 194-6.

46. *VII kongres*, p. 400. Djilas nevertheless haunts this section of the Programme, which included repeated and defensive protests that the Party is 'not a superior elite separated from the people'.

47. Ibid., p. 178.

48. Ibid., pp. 360-4. For a fuller discussion of the 'Yugoslavism' campaign see Shoup, pp. 190-211, occasionally mixing references from the 1950s with others from the attempted revival of the concept in 1962-63 (see below, pp. 134f).

49. The EC of thirteen elected at the 6th Congress had lost Djilas through expulsion and Kidrić and Pijade through death. At the 3rd Plenum, when Djilas was expelled, the secretaries of the three republican CCs who had not been elected to the Yugoslav EC at the Zagreb Congress—Blažo Jovanović of Montenegro, Miha Marinko of Slovenia and Petar Stambolić of Serbia—were co-opted as members. In 1957 Jovan Veselinov replaced Stambolić (who became President

of the Federal Assembly) as Serbian Party head and also joined the EC, making 14 members.

Ch. 4: The Great Debate Resumed

1. Campbell, pp. 42, 125
2. As calculated by Bombelles, pp. 163f.
3. For a breakdown of these aid figures, D. I. Rusinow, *Trade and Aid at the Halfway Point in Developing Yugoslavia* (AUFS,) xi/2, Feb. 1964), p. 23. Cf. Campbell, table on p. 171.
4. Cf. Bilandžić (1969), p. 100 (who sees the resulting bottlenecks as the principal source of the downturn in growth rates in 1960) and Milenkovitch, pp. 169-74.
5. Bilandžić (1967), p. 99.
6. The 1961 reforms, adopted by the Federal Assembly on March 1, are discussed in detail ibid., pp. 94-7; cf. Milenkovitch, p. 123.
7. These are the figures Boris Krajger gave to the CC in July 1962 (see *Fourth Plenum of LCY* (1962), pp. 8ff.). In March 1962 Tito and Kardelj were admitting that the Five-Year Plan must be revised, but in July Minić, as chairman of the FEC Committee for the Plan, called for its abandonment and the drafting of a new plan for 1964-8 (ibid., pp. 81f.).
8. *Osmi kongres SKJ* (1965), i. 89.
9. Reproduced ibid., i. 282-90.
10. Lendvai (1969), pp. 185-7; Vukmanović, ii. 599f. Cf. Shoup, pp. 210, 250, who reports that 'lurid accounts' of the meeting later circulated spoke of Serbs and Macedonians facing each other at pistol point and of Slovenian threats to secede from the Federation. See also references made at the 4th Plenum the following July and at the other, more famous 4th Plenum of July 1966, where Tito regretted the 'papering over' of March 1962.
11. The impact made by this speech—in Serbo-Croatian, *Govor u Splitu*—can be judged by the 1963 Belgrade witticism that recent Yugoslav history would be divided into two eras, ante-GUS and post-GUS.
12. Milenkovitch, p. 265. cf. Rusinow, *Yugoslavia's Problems with Market Socialism* (AUFS, xi/4, May 1964).
13. In *Progres* (Ljubljana), 9/1957.
14. The proceedings are in *Ekonomist* (Belgrade), xi/1-2 (1958). Milenkovitch (p. 122) calls it 'the first large meeting of economists to discuss matters of economic policy'.
15. Vukmanović, ii. 318-22. Cf. his reaction to his exclusion from the Politburo at the 1948 Party Congress (ibid., ii. 98f.).
16. The trade union central organisation thereafter relapsed into a kind of collective schizophrenia, unable to decide whether to follow the lead of Vukmanović's successor and revert to a tamer role, or under the influence of the spirit and cadres of Vukmanović's time to play the part of tribune of the working class—or at least the mouthpiece of the proletarian aristocracy employed in the socialist enterprises.
17. Vukmanović, ii. 326f.
18. Bilandžić (1969), p. 96. Cf. Vukmanović, ii. 327f., for the specific tax

proposals, and Milenkovitch, pp. 105f., for a concise summary of the effects of the reforms of the 1950s on personal incomes and hence worker incentives.

19. Vukmanović, ii. 329.

20. Ibid., ii. 332-7, 377f., is the principal (but always somewhat unreliable) source of most of these details. Cf. Bilandžić (1967), pp. 92f.

21. In 1964 the index of net national product per capita in Italy ranged from 142 in Lombardy to 51 in Basilicata and Calabria, despite years of effort focused on the Cassa per il Mezzogiorno; the corresponding range in Yugoslavia that year ran from 190 in Slovenia to 69 in Macedonia, 68 in Bosnia-Herzegovina and Montenegro, and 35 in Kosmet (McDonald, pp. 10f.).

22. Shoup, pp. 244-6, makes the useful distinction between initially 'localist' or 'particularist' economic interests, nourished by the nature of the quasi-market system and only later through the dynamics of the political process incorporated in national interests, and those which were regional and thus national in origin.

23. McDonald provides the most detailed and best documented account of changing strategies of aid to underdeveloped regions up to 1965 and their effects, or lack of same. Cf. Hamilton; Džeba and Beslač; Milenkovitch, pp. 178-86; Bombelles, pp. 91-101, 156.

24. Bilandžić (1969), p. 95.

25. *Fourth Plenum*, pp. 106, 108. Cf. Vukmanović, ii. 409f., on Tito's dissatisfaction, expressed to him during an interval in the Plenum.

26. Examples are given, *i.a.* by Shoup, pp. 244f.; Džeba and Beslač; and Rusinow, *Lipizzaners Under Socialism* (AUFS, xii/1, Sept. 1965).

27. *Fourth Plenum*, pp. 5-42.

28. Ibid. esp. pp. 130, 125; cf. *Osmi kongres*, i. 80-3.

29. *Fourth Plenum*, pp. 110f.

30. *Yugoslavia's Problems with Market Socialism*, pp. 9f.; cf. Lendvai, p. 187, for a different interpretation in which Tito is still a 'dedicated centralist' and 'the reformists were defeated' if unreconciled to their defeat at the 4th Plenum.

31. A summary of the conference is in *Ekonomist*, xv/3-4 (1962); cf. Milenkovitch, p. 124, who appropriately calls it a 'warm-up' for the Zagreb meeting.

32. The Yellow Book was published by the Federal Planning Institute in 1962 (see bibliography). The White Book was reproduced in *Ekonomski pregled*, xiv/3-5 (1963), a 324-page special issue which also contained material from the January discussion. Cf. also a critical summary of the Yellow Book, ibid., xiv/8, by Sime Djodan and Uroš Dujšin. The Zagreb discussions were published in full in *Ekonomist*, xvi/1 (1963).

33. An aspect emphasised *i.a.* by Bićanić, 'Economics of Socialism in a Developed Country', *Foreign Affairs*, July 1966, pp. 633-50, one of the clearest statements of the matured position.

34. Milenkovitch, pp. 125f., Tito, it was worth noting, also distinguished the two kinds of 'decentralisers' as early as the 4th Plenum and did not much like the second kind (see p. 122 above).

35. *Borba*, Dec. 21, 1963.

36. Ibid., July 25, 1964. Cf. the early warning in *Ekonomska politika*, May 18, 1963.

37. The 'work stoppages' were referred to, still somewhat gingerly, in *NIN* on Feb. 2, in *Borba* on Mar. 29, and then more candidly in *Ekonomska politika* on Apr. 11, 1964.

38. Cf. the tracing of the evolution of the White Book position, primarily in the mass-circulation press, which appeared in *Yugoslavia's Problems with Market Socialism*, pp. 10-15, and the detailed discussion in Milenkovitch, esp. pp. 125-75, which is more technical and based primarily on professional and theoretical journals.

39. The slogan itself was not new, but it was only after November 1963 (see *Ekonomska politika*, Nov. 9, 1963) and with President Tito's brief speech at Niš on March 7, 1964 (*Borba*, Mar. 8), that it was used as a polemical weapon and *the* preferred slogan of reform.

40. The development model of W. W. Rostow (*The Stages of Economic Growth*, Cambridge, 1960) was widely known and discussed in Yugoslavia in this period. 'Take-off in the Rostowian sense', two liberal economists told the present writer on separate occasions in 1963, 'has been achieved'. The importance of $500 per capita national income as a turning point was again being cited at the 8th Congress in December 1964.

41. These are the most relevant figures because they were the ones being used in the debate: e.g. by Vukmanović in his report to the 5th Trade Union Congress on April 20, 1964; by Miko Tripalo in a *Vjesnik* interview on April 12; or in another *Vjesnik* article on March 1, 'Where is the Centre of Unrest in the Market?'.

42. Typical contemporary summaries of these criticisms are an early contribution to the mass media phase of the debate by Gligorov, in *Ekonomska politika*, Dec. 14, 1963, and a succinct statement (in English) by Zagreb economist Drago Gorupić in *Eastern European Economics*, Spring 1964, pp. 55. Cf. also Džeba and Beslač.

43. An early complaint in these terms appeared in *Ekonomska politika*, May 25, 1963, with a table of prescribed prices as a percentage of total income by industrial sectors; by this calculation, 97 per cent of prices were controlled at that time (cf. 70 per cent of *commodities*, the figure normally cited). Cf. Džeba and Beslač, pp. 72f., and Milenkovitch, pp. 227-49, for a detailed and technical discussion of price theory and policy in Yugoslavia.

44. Kardelj, 'Productivity of Labour and Tasks of Work Collectives and Public Organs', series in *Borba*, June 9-12, 1963.

45. An analysis of the extent and disincentive effects of this last aspect appeared in a series entitled 'Clouded Earnings' in *Vjesnik*, Feb. 12-15, 1964. Cf. *Vjesnik*, Mar. 1, calculating the 1964 bill for subventions and subsidies to support uneconomic enterprises at 400 billion dinars, or 12 per cent of planned national income.

46. As will be seen. At the time, however, almost no one seems to have realised the extent to which one essential part of the proposed reform—changes in the price system, sharply raising the prices of agricultural goods, raw materials, and producers' goods in relation to other commodities—would benefit the less developed regions and at least partly counterbalance their losses in other parts of the package.

Cf. Bakarić's admission that this aspect was initially overlooked in Croatia and Slovenia (speech in Sarajevo, in *Vjesnik*, May 29, 1966).

47. In addition to the arguments presented at the Zagreb meeting and elsewhere in 1963, the conservative position continued to be expressed in 1964, *i.a.* at a meeting of Serbian economists in Niš on February 3-4 (summarised by *Ekonomska politika*, Feb. 8) and in subdued and often pessimistic contributions to parliamentary and Trade Union Congress debates in the spring. Cf. also the speech of Slobodan Penezić, the Serbian Prime Minister, at the LCY CC 6th Plenum (*Borba*, Mar. 18, 1964).

48. Meat and higher quality foodgrains, for example, were in short supply because of the general weakness of the agricultural sector and also enjoyed good export possibilities, for balance of payments reasons preferable to domestic consumption as an outlet for any increase in production.

49. McDonald, pp. 158f. and detailed appended tables, provides the last word on this dispute, demonstrating that both sides were right.

50. Hamilton's study elaborates all of these arguments sympathetically and objectively from the point of view of an economic geographer. Cf. Milenkovitch, pp. 181-5; McDonald, esp. pp. 131-57.

51. Quoted by Lendvai, p. 143, a perceptive observer who interviewed leaders on both sides at the time and who noted that 'figures, figures, figures dominate the conversation whenever one travels'.

52. The clearest statement of the 'Danubian concept' was by the Serbian economist Kosta Mihajlović, 'Regional Aspects of Economic Development', in R. Stojanović (1964); of the 'Adriatic concept', by the Croatian economist Bićanić in *Pomorstvo*, 9/10 (1964).

53. Rusinow, *Ports and Politics in Yugoslavia* (AUFS, xi/3, 1964).

54. The agreement was announced on the front page of *Komunist*, but with some delay, on Feb. 6, 1964. Cf. Shoup, pp. 245f., 251f., who probably exaggerates its significance and impact, since it was in fact only one of several now public manifestations of the Serbian nationalist element in the conservative and centralist position, as has been seen. The Belgrade-Bar railway was finally completed in 1975.

55. The articles, two by each man in the form of a dialogue, appeared in the issues of Dec. 6-9. Cf. the good summary in Hondius, pp. 241f.

56. Tito's argument was that 'our cultural life should develop in a Yugoslav framework' because there could not be separate *socialist* cultures for each republic, but the distinction between socialist and national cultures was never clear to anyone.

57. Shoup, pp. 193n., 195n., lists several such articles from this period, while also maintaining that the *Jugoslovenstvo* campaign died after 1958.

58. *Prednacrt Ustava FSRJ* (1962), pp. 120, 247f., quoted by Hondius, pp. 242f. The meeting, on September 20, 1962, marked the opening of public debate on the draft of a new Constitution (see below).

59. See esp. Bakarić's speech to the Zagreb City Committee of the LC, Sept. 17, 1964, and interview in *Ekonomska politika*, Oct. 10, 1964, both in Bakarić (1967), pp. 143-69.

60. Shoup, pp. 217f., 252f.; Rusinow, *The Other Albanians* (AUFS, xii/2, 1965).

61. It would be highly misleading to use a simple ethnic criterion and assume that the Committee elected at the 7th Congress was divided into 6 'liberals' (the Slovenes and Croats), 8 'conservatives' and Tito. The Macedonian (Koliševski) was a conservative, now being challenged from Skopje by Crvenkovski. One of the Croats (Gošnjak) was generally believed to have no political convictions except loyalty to Tito. Of the Montenegrins, Vlahović generally and Vukmanović frequently (as in his trade union role, as described) have taken liberal positions, while Blažo Jovanović was considered a conservative but like an American counterpart, Earl Warren, surprised everyone by handing down generally liberal judgements after he was translated to the newly created Constitutional Court as its first President. The aged Slovene Leskošek had never said or done anything that would justify any label.

Ch. 5: Laissez-Faire Socialism

1. Halpern (revised ed. 1967), pp. 301, 303. JAT had begun using Caravelles in 1963, but some of the pilots were at first so unskilful in handling jet aircraft that the manufacturers feared serious maintenance problems and the pilots were sent back to Toulouse for retraining.
2. Statistics in this section from Rusinow, *Population Review 1970* (AUFS, xvii/1 [1970]), and *Some Aspects of Migration and Urbanization in Yugoslavia* (AUFS, xix/2 [1972]).
3. Between 1945 and 1966 a total of 146,213 students had graduated from originally three and now seven universities, in increasing numbers which had reached a peak in 1963, when there were 12,794 graduates, followed by a slight decline to 11,642 (of whom 3,628 women) in 1966. Other post-secondary schools produced an additional 17,000 graduates in 1966, while 130,000 pupils completed secondary education of various kinds, including *gimnazije* (28,000) and schools for qualified workers (60,000). Although in many areas it was still the case that less than 60 per cent of those who legally should do so were finishing the obligatory eight-year minimum, and in Kosovo only 30 per cent, it was a sign of progress that in a six-year period the number of those completing eight years had increased by 82 per cent, while primary school enrolment increased by 13 per cent and the total number of those of primary school age by less than 3 per cent: more were going to school and more of those who did were finishing. The percentage of Yugoslavs over 10 years of age with less than four years or no schooling declined from 42 in 1953 to 33 in 1961 and 24 in 1971, while the population in that age group grew from 13·4 to 16·7 million.
4. Jon McLin, *Eurovision* (AUFS, West Europe Series, iii/2, Feb. 1969).
5. The greatest circulation, however, was reserved to *Večerne novosti*, the lively evening tabloid in Belgrade which kept its owner, a moribund *Borba*, crippled by its ineradicable image as an 'official' newspaper, in business.
6. Generational boundaries, as here defined, are roughly 1919 and 1928. Birth years of some leading politicians, whom we have met in this

history or soon will, are both illustrative and illuminating. The older group, remarkably clustered, includes Ranković (1909), Kardelj (1910), Djilas (1911), Bakarić and Vukmanović (1912), Todorović (1913) and Vlahović and both Krajgers (1914). Appropriate symbols of the second are Stane Kavčič (1919), Crvenkovski, Marko Nikezić and Kiro Hadživasilev (1921), Savka Dabčević-Kučar (1923), Budislav Šoškić (1925), Tripalo (1926), Pero Pirker (1927) and Miroslav Pečujlić (1929); harbingers of the third include Latinka Perović (1933) and Mirko Čanadanović (1936). Most of an emerging core group of politically influential intellectuals of the period, both 'establishment' and 'Marxist humanist', also belong to the chronologically brief and therefore numerically small but important middle generation.

7. Data in these paragraphs from 'Membership of the League of Communists of Yugoslavia', *Yugoslav Survey*, Nov. 1967. Eight years later and after a different kind of purge, workers comprised 29·1 per cent and peasants 5·6 per cent of Party membership.

8. See 'Financing Socio-Political Units, 1961-67', ibid., May 1968. An instructive contrast can be found in the evolution of American federalism, where an opposite fiscal trend, the gradual concentration of tax powers and revenues at the federal level and the growing relative financial weakness of local and state governments, contributed to the transfer of ever more functions and power to the federal centre. This was in turn, in the opinion of many scholars, a primary reason why local government, seen as at most a boring stepping stone to Washington, is now seldom competently manned. Canadian experience, on the other hand, has been similar to Yugoslav. (Cf. the papers and discussions at a North-American-Yugoslav Seminar on Federalism at Indiana University, Bloomington, 1-7 June 1967.)

9. Cf. several contributions to Djordjević *et al. (1972)*. Andy Roth, 'The Belgrade School System: Managed or Self-Managed?' (unpubl. student thesis, AUFS Inst. for Mediterranean Studies, Rome, 1972) is a fascinating case study of conflicting interests, and results, in this field.

10. 'Prednacrt ustava', reprinted in Bakarić (1967), pp. 39-92.

11. For the draft, *Prednacrt ustava FSRJ*. The authoritative Eng. trans. of the final text is that of Marko Pavičić (published in 1969 with the 19 amendments adopted to that date). See also Djordjević's massive *Novi ustavni sistem* (1964), the standard Yugoslav commentary, and Hondius. Ch. 7, again the best and most complete English one.

12. Hondius, p. 245.

13. Cf. Kardelj (1962), pp. 3, 9, 15, 17.

14. Another important institutional innovation was the establishment of a constitutional court, empowered to pass judgement on the constitutionality of acts of the assemblies, administrative organs, or organs of self-management. These were the first such courts in a socialist country but only the most conspicuous of several breaches of the Marxist principle of unity of power introduced by the 1963 Constitution.

15. Nominated (under the supervision of the Socialist Alliance) by

meetings of voters-at-large in each constituency and elected by communal assemblies, these deputies, unlike those to other chambers, were to be 'confirmed' by popular referendums. See below, pp. 261-6 for the consequences of this peculiar provision.

16. With the 1963 Constitution Kosovo-Metohija ceased to be an autonomous region and was elevated to equal status with the Vojvodina as an autonomous province. In December 1968, by Amendments VII and XVIII, the purely Serbian geographic designation 'Metohija' was dropped as a concession to Albanian national sentiment and the Kosmet became simply Kosovo.

17. A partial exception was the Organisational-Political Chamber, candidates to which had to be members of management bodies of 'work communities' or 'any officer of a socio-political organisation or association', making it in effect and somewhat curiously a Chamber of Managers, Bureaucrats and Politicians.

18. The terminology was as cumbersome in the Yugoslav languages as in the English translation and thus faithfully represented a specific stage in an effort by Yugoslav theoreticians to solve a problem of practical as well as ideological importance. The awkward term 'work community' (*radna zajednica*, cf. *društvena zajednica*) was an attempt to find a portmanteau word to cover everything from a factory or agricultural collective—the 'enterprise' where self-management had begun—to a school, hospital, retail organisation or association of lawyers. Before the next Constitution was drafted in 1973 'work communities' were to become 'organisations of associated labour' (*organizacija udruženog rada*).

19. Kardelj (1962), *passim*. Cf. especially the same (1952) discussed above, pp. 67-9.

20. Rusinow, *A Note on Yugoslavia* (AUFS, xi/5, June 1964), pp. 17f.

21. The debates were reported in detail in the press, including *Borba*, Nov. 20 and 22 and Dec. 7-8, 13 and 21.

22. *Yugoslav Survey*, Oct.-Dec. 1963, p. 2144.

23. Lendvai, p. 96.

24. The preliminary draft of 1962, like the Constitutional Law of 1953, had specified that the President of the Federal Assembly, a post which was to be Kardelj's, should deputise for President Tito during his frequent travels abroad.

25. Under the 1953 Constitutional Law, it will be recalled, the President of the Republic (Tito) presided over the FEC; but the 1963 Constitution (certainly at Tito's request) separated the functions of Head of State and Government.

26. *Četvrti plenum Centralnog komiteta SKJ*, pp. 30, 72f.

27. One of these recently told the present writer that there were two members of the Party old guard whom he had known intimately since early youth, but would never really know: Bakarić and Koča Popović. Both of them were the Communist sons of wealthy or influential prewar bourgeois families—Popović's father a Belgrade millionaire and Bakarić's a Croatian judge with mildly leftwing proclivities who had once been kind to a young Communist agitator in prison named Josip Broz (Auty (1970), pp. 55).

28. When he did go in 1969, believing Croatia to be safe in the hands of hand-picked disciples, disaster ensued (see Ch. 7).

29. Cf. Lendvai, pp. 189-92, whose evaluations of both Kardelj and Bakarić and whose judgement on the latter's importance are very similar. While the views here attributed to Bakarić are clear from his writings, speeches and actions, crediting him with originating them or with 'masterminding the strategy' is usually based, given his preference for anonymous political operations, on hearsay or indirect evidence: it is said to be the case by most other Yugoslavs in a position to know, and if one makes the effort to trace the pieces of the alleged strategy back to their point of origin, either by placing instances of public advocacy of a relevant idea in a chronological series or by identifying the political relationships of the advocates to one another, the thread has a curious habit of leading ultimately to Bakarić.

30. *Službeni list*, No. 52/63.

31. Vukmanović, ii. 444f.

32. Both reproduced, with Tito's closing remarks and the Plenum's conclusions, in *The VIth Plenum of the CC* ... (1964).

33. 'The Basic Directives', ibid., pp. 59f.

34. Vukmanović, ii. 428f.

35. '... nego ni kod nas gore nije sve u redu' (the present writer's notes from the Congress).

36. Bilandžić (1969), p. 102; Stenographic Reports of the Congress (mimeo.) and the present writer's notes; Vukmanović, ii. 428-34, 445-7. Vukmanović's *Borba* series appeared on Feb. 25, Mar. 9 and Apr. 12, 1964.

37. *Borba*, Apr., 17 and 18, 1964.

38. *Službeni list*, No. 23/64.

39. *Službeni list*, No. 31/64.

40. Rusinow, *Yugoslavia Reaps the Harvest of Coexistence* (AUFS, xi/1, Jan. 1964); cf. Rubinstein, pp. 299-303 for the Cairo conference, and Campbell, pp. 49-66 for the attitude of the US Congress, which ultimately led to a ban on even dollar credits for food purchases (in Oct. 1966).

41. Cf. Clissold, pp. 74-7, for a fuller account.

42. It was also characteristically Yugoslav that these speeches and the press campaign accompanying them had almost no noticeable consequences. Nine months later, for example, the Belgrade October Salon, Yugoslavia's most important annual exhibition of contemporary art, contained almost nothing that was not abstract and no one commented.

43. Clissold, p. 76.

44. *Yugoslavia Reaps ...*, pp. 7f.

45. As quoted in *Borba*, May 19, 1963 (see also Clissold, Doc. 208).

46. Cf. 'New Alignment in the International Workers' Movement', *Komunist*, Dec. 12, 1963.

47. *Osmi kongres*, i. 314-35.

48. Moreover, as Kardelj pointedly emphasised in presenting the recommendations of the EC's working group to the Congress, 'most

of the opinions expressed have already been submitted to the Federal Assembly in the form of bills' (ibid., i. 378).

49. *Osmi kongres*, i. 446-8, 726-34.
50. Ibid., i. 343. Much the same wording was repeated in the Congress Resolution.
51. Ibid., i. 345, 411-16.
52. Ibid., i. 362-4.
53. Ibid., i. 366-424.
54. Ibid., i. 644-53.
55. Ibid., i. 667-74.
56. Ibid., i, 617-23. Bakarić himself never spoke at the Congress.
57. Ibid., iii. 2057f.
58. Ibid. i. 432 and 442.
59. See below, p. 221. Eric Bourne had 'heard on very reliable authority that, prior to the Congress, the question of a second party, some kind of 'opposition' group to keep the Government on its toes, was discussed at a very high leadership session' before being rejected (*CSM*, Dec. 26, 1964). Cf. David Binder, *NYT*, Dec. 10, 1964.
60. Cf. Ranković and the Report on the Work of the CC (in *Osmi kongres, i. 19-198*). For criticism of the CC from the liberal side, see Bakarić's conversation at *Vjesnik* on the eve of the Congress (Nov. 12, 1964, in Bakarić, 1967, pp. 171ff.).
61. Binder and Bourne, loc. cit., note 59.
62. Bilandžić (1967), pp. 103-12; cf. George Macesich, in Vucinich, pp. 215-18.
63. *Službeni list*, 12/65 (Mar. 24, 1965), and 'Reform of the Credit and Banking System', *Yugoslav Survey* July-Sept. 1965, which provides useful historical background and interpretation.
64. Early warnings about flaws in the law and their consequences were sounded by *Ekonomska politika*, Nov. 13, 1965 and *Privredni pregled*, Dec. 10, 1965. In view of its major theoretical and practical importance, the law and its implementation have received curiously little attention in most studies of the reform and its aftermath or of Yugoslav economic theory.
65. Cf. *Ekonomska politika*, May 6-12, 1960.
66. The new arrangement did in fact have this last effect, if not in the desired quantity. A random sample of Yugoslav enterprises by the present writer during the winter of 1965-66 revealed that most of those which had profited from changed price ratios or lower taxes were increasing their bank deposits and distributing them with a keen eye for the particular banks whose policies and decisions they might wish to influence. One major Croatian agricultural-industrial combine, for example, had placed the bulk of its free capital in the Yugoslav Agricultural Bank in Belgrade, the source of most of their long-term investment credits, but had reinsured by also 'buying shares' in the republican bank in Zagreb and in the local communal bank. These last were chosen in part because they were respectively the normal sources of short-term credits and of credits for the combine's housing fund and in part 'because it makes political sense'.
67. Conversation with the Bosnian Party *aktiv* in Sarajevo on May 6, reported in *Vjesnik* on May 29, 1966.

68. *Službeni list*, No. 33/65 (July 24, 1965, items 559-66, 568, 597-9, 606, trans. with Krajger's speech by the Joint Translation Service, Belgrade).

69. Ibid., No. 17/65 (described in detail by Gorupić and Paj).

70. Remaining exceptions brought the *average* capital tax level down to 2·8 per cent. Sectors which continued to enjoy a special concessionary capital tax rate of 2 per cent included the production and transmission of electric energy, coal and coke, ferrous metallurgy, agriculture and food processing, and transport. These were generally the same sectors most favoured by changed price ratios.

71. The federal budget for 1966, presented to parliament in early November 1965, called for an increase of 17·5 billion old dinars, primarily because of the increased costs of national defence as a result of the reform (*Borba*, Nov. 4, 1965).

72. IMF Press Release of July 24, 1965, and B. Krajger, loc. cit.

73. Tito speech at Varaždin, Nov. 8 (*Borba*, Nov. 9, 1965), and Macesich, in Vucinich, p. 226.

74. See esp. *Borba*, Oct. 8-9 (the Federal Assembly debate), Oct. 25 (employment trends), and Nov. 9 (Tito at Varaždin); *Privredni pregled*, Nov. 3 and Tripalo (1969), pp. 99-107 (his Zagreb speech of Nov. 16). Cf. Lendvai, pp. 140-3, for revealing interviews in Zagreb, Belgrade and Skopje at this time.

75. *Borba*, Dec. 24, 1965 (emphasis added). The speech was made on December 8 but significantly was not reported in the press for over two weeks.

76. Cf. esp. Popović's interview in *NIN*, Jan. 23, 1966.

77. Cf. the contrasting tones of the Serbian and Croatian CC Plenums, both held on January 7 and with Lukić the principal speaker at the Serbian one, described in *Borba*, Jan. 8, 1966.

78. Kardelj's description (at the 3rd Plenum, ibid., Mar. 13, 1966).

79. Ibid., Mar. 12, 1966; also, with the 'theses' prepared for the Plenum and Tito's opening speech, in *Yugoslav Survey*, Apr.-June 1966, pp. 3569-600. For other Plenum speeches, *Borba*, Feb. 26-27 and Mar. 12-14, 1966.

80. According to Vukmanović, ii. 486f., who also claims that Tito had told him a few days earlier 'that relations between him and Ranković were not good'.

81. Cf. Shoup, pp. 255-7, for detailed speculations about various republican meetings in April and May, including a curious, and for him ominous, mid-March meeting of Serbian and Montenegrin EC members 'for the purpose of establishing broad areas of co-operation between the two republics'.

82. Among the better summaries are Binder's early attempts to piece together the story in the *NYT* (esp. July 8, 1966), and Lendvai, pp. 160-3, both including several still officially uncorroborated but probable details.

83. *Četvrti plenum Centralnog komiteta SKJ*, p. 56.

84. Initial press reports of the Belgrade and Sarajevo meetings were significantly bowdlerized summaries; all three statements are reprinted in full in *Aktuelni problemi sadašnje etape revolucije*.

85. Vukmanović, ii. 489-92.

86. Lendvai, p. 162.
87. Binder in *NYT*, July 16, 1966.
88. *Četvrti plenum*, p. 47.
89. Ibid., p. 57.
90. This discovery was revealed two months later by Miko Tripalo, the Croatian member of the Crvenkovski Commission, in an interview in *VUS*, Sept. 7, 1966.
91. *Borba*, July 6, 1966.
92. *Četvrti plenum*, pp. 93-8 (trans. by M. Pavičić and Mary Rusinow in *Yugoslav Survey*, Oct.-Dec. 1966, pp. 3931-3).

Ch. 6: The Liberal Ascendancy

1. Lendvai, Ch. 3, provides a particularly lucid description of this dimension of the struggle.
2. *Politika*, Oct. 14, 18, 23, 1966 and *Ekonomska politika*, Oct. 29, 1966; cf. also Vukmanović's memoirs, ii. 495-501.
3. One of the best efforts to grapple with this problem at this period is Kardelj's lengthy treatise, *Notes on Social Criticism in Yugoslavia*, originally published in *Sodobnost* (Ljubljana), Nos. 11-12, 1965, and trans. in *STAP*, Oct.-Dec. 1965, pp. 3-61, and Jan.-Mar. 1966, pp. 3-51.
4. 'The Fifth Meeting of the Central Committee of the LCY', *Yugoslav Survey*, Feb. 1967, pp. 31-58 (*STAP*, Oct.-Dec. 1966, pp. 30-59, 160-8).
5. For a cogent exposition of the lesser of these programmes, see Ante Fiamengo, 'From Statism to Self-Management', *STAP*, Jan.-Mar. 1967, p. 57.
6. 'The Fifth Meeting ...', loc. cit., pp. 57f.
7. 'The Seventh Meeting of the Central Committee of the LCY' and 'Theses', *Yugoslav Survey*, Aug. 1967, pp. 33-44 and 66-74. Bilandžić (1969, p. 122) calls this 'the first important organisational change in the postwar development of the LCY'.
8. See Dragomir Drašković. 'Informal Grouping in LC Basic Organisations', *Gledišta*, Jan. 1966; also Stipe Šuvar, 'Informal Groups as Centres of Power in a Self-Managing Society', in Djordjević *et al.* (1972). Cf. the specifically Yugoslav features of the operation of such groups with analogous phenomena in other socialist States described, e.g. by Azrael (1966) and Ionescu (1967).
9. The increasingly worthwhile political pages of leading Yugoslav newspapers and case studies by social scientists in journals like *Sociologija* and *Gledišta* provide the basis for such a description. Specific examples are cited in AUFS, esp. xvi/5-6 (1969).
10. Bilandžić (1969), p. 127 and table. The Statistical Yearbook gives somewhat higher values to almost all the same data. Cf. Rusinow, 'Yugoslavia', in Baklanoff.
11. In the first two years of the reform 716,000 pupils completed the obligatory eight-year primary school, 276,000 completed secondary schooling and 86,000 students graduated from post-secondary schools or universities. The latter two categories represented increases of 42 and 31 per cent, respectively, over the number of

graduates in the last two pre-reform years (1962-64). When they sought jobs they encountered a market in which the number of employed, up 6 per cent in 1964 (the last boom year), grew by only 1 per cent in 1965, fell by 2 per cent in 1966 and another 1 per cent in 1967, and grew by 1 per cent in 1968, when recovery began. See Bilandžić (1969), pp. 130f., and Statistical Yearbook 1970 for all these figures.

12. During the 1961-65 period about 78 per cent of expenditures on education were communally financed, while republican and federal contributions (15-20 per cent) were earmarked almost exclusively for new school construction (*Yugoslav Survey*, Jan-Mar. 1965).

13. Data collected by the writer on visits to Bačka and Baranja. Cf. also Svetolik Popović, 'Agricultural Policy in Yugoslavia', and Milosav Ilijin, 'Co-operation in the Countryside', both Medjunarodna Politika *Studies*, 6/1964 and 7/1965, for the general picture.

14. Halpern, in Vucinich, pp. 338-42.

15. Cf. the findings and conclusions of the Centre for Demographic Research in Belgrade, in Breznik, esp. pp. 73, 331-5.

16. Bilandžić (1969), pp. 126-8, and (1973), pp. 298f. See also Marijan Hanžeković's postscript to Bićanić (1973), pp. 211-38. Other calculations differ in detail but show the same trends (cf. Statistical Yearbook 1965 et seq., and Ivan Maksimović in Broekmeyer, pp. 133-5).

17. Cf. Bilandžić (1969), p. 135: 'In many environments people still think and conduct business as formerly. There is still a strong tendency towards closed enterprises and markets and an autarchic approach in the development policy of individual regions, as well as insistence on large projects of doubtful economic potential, etc. Slowness, uncertainty and inconsistency in the realisation of the purposes of the reform exist. In parts of the economy there are instances of opposition to acceptance of wider responsibility and demands that problems be solved from the centre by old methods.'

18. 'Yugoslavia—Foreign Economic Relations and the EEC', in Baklanoff.

19. Details of the 1967 system in *Yugoslav Survey*, viii/4, pp. 80-2, 91-6.

20. For two recent summaries of the banking problem see Hanžeković in Bićanić (1973), pp. 220-5, and Bilandžić (1973), pp. 295-7; also LCY, *Druga konferencija SKJ* (1972), Kiro Gligorov's speech to the 10th Party Congress (LCY, *Stenografske beleške X kongresa SKJ*), and *Yugoslav Survey*, vii/4).

21. The 'extra-budgetary accounts' were liquidated in principle, after a long political debate, in 1971.

22. For details and sources, see AUFS, xv/1 (Feb. 1968).

23. Ibid. For the CC-LCY's letter to the Czechoslovak CC see *STAP*, July-Sept. 1967, pp. 141-7.

24. Jurij Gustinčič, reporting from the Budapest meeting, in *Politika*, Feb. 28, 1968.

25. *Komunist*, Feb. 22, 1968. The above summary of the Yugoslav attitude to the conference is based on press commentaries during 1967 and on conversations with LCY members in the winter of 1967-68.

26. Summarised by Campbell, pp. 106–11. Cf. the comments in Stephen Fischer-Galati, *The New Rumania* (MIT Press, 1967), and David Floyd, *Rumania: Russia's Dissident Ally* (London, 1965).

27. Rusinow, *The Macedonian Question Never Dies* (AUFS, xv/3, Mar. 1968).

28. This was a series of Mediterranean conferences co-sponsored by the Italian CP and Italian Socialist Party of Proletarian Unity to discuss the recent 'pattern' of intensified 'imperialist' probings into the area (including the Greek coup, the Israeli blitzkrieg against the Arabs, Cyprus and some rumoured plans for a military coup in Italy). The Russians and the French Communists chose to interpret it as anti-Soviet as well as anti-American. The ideologically broader participation of 'other non-aligned and progressive forces', which was the principal Yugoslav interest, also proved difficult to obtain. French Communists objected to the inclusion of Gaullists, Italian Communists to Italian Socialists, Arabs to the Mitterrand group in France and Egyptians and Algerians to the Tunisian Neo-Destour Party. The entire scheme was thereafter permitted to slip unnoticed into the back pages of the press and the marginalia of non-aligned diplomacy. See Josip Djerdja, in *Komunist* ((Jan. 1 and Feb. 1, 1968); also commentaries in *Borba* (Jan. 14 and 20, Feb. 19), *Politika* (Jan. 23, 25, 26), *Vjesnik* (Jan. 20 and 28).

29. Actually a series of amendments to existing laws (see the semi-official commentary by the Yugoslav Bank for Foreign Trade, *Regulations on Joint Investment of Domestic and Foreign Partners in Yugoslavia*, Belgrade 1967).

30. According to still officially unconfirmed but certainly reliable Belgrade rumours. The first formal steps towards a decentralisation of foreign policy were taken in early 1968 with the establishment of republican commissions for foreign affairs, attached to the assemblies of the six republics. No one was quite sure what their role was to be, except for agreement that there could not be six separate foreign policies. But a Canadian diplomat then in Belgrade wondered wryly when Croatia and Quebec would exchange diplomatic missions.

31. Cf. Anatole Shub, 'Letter from Belgrade', *Encounter*, June 1964 and the same writer's 1963–64 newsletters for the Institute of Current World Affairs (New York).

32. Early 'establishment' contributions include some articles and speeches by Kardelj (reprinted in Kardelj, 1964–68) and Bakarić (1967), Djordjević (1964), and several early articles in *Socijalizam*. George Zaninovich, 'The Yugoslav Variation on Marx', in Vucinich, pp. 293–315, analyses many of the relevant ideological positions.

33. Frane Jerman, 'Post-war philosophical trends in Yugoslavia', unpubl. lecture, 1965.

34. Cf. Rusinow, 'Marxism Belgrade Style', *Antioch Review*, winter 1967–68.

35. Enzo Bettiza, 'The Yugoslav Paradox', *Atlas*, July-Aug. 1965. Cf. David Binder, *NYT*, June 14, 1964.

36. See esp. Binder, *NYT*, Aug. 9–10, Sept. 25, 1966; Richard Eder, ibid. Apr. 20–23, 1967 (for Mihajlov's retrial and renewed sentencing);

Eric Bourne, *CSM*, Aug. 15, 1966; and Campbell, pp. 146f., for the most balanced versions.

37. 'The Principal Dilemma: Self-Management or Statism', trans. in *STAP*, Oct.-Dec. 1966, 5-29.

38. Trans. ibid., Jan.-Mar. 1967, 40-9.

39. In *Yugoslav Survey*, viii/3, p. 50.

40. Bakarić's contribution to the polemic is in 'Kakav Savez komunista?' Two competing ideological journals dedicated double issues to this debate at the beginning of 1968 (*Socijalizam* and *Praxis*, both 1/2, 1968). Cf. also Kardelj in *STAP*, 29-30, 1968, and the particularly illuminating polemic between Svetozar Stojanović and Miroslav Pečujlić (in *Socijalizam*, 11/67, 1-2/68) based on Stojanović's 'The Statist Myth of Socialism' (*Praxis*, Internat. ed. 2/67).

41. Speeches made at the meeting of the Zagreb Party's Commission for Ideological Questions were reprinted in eight instalments in *Vjesnik*, May 14-23, 1966; the Sabor debate is reported ibid., June 26, 1966.

42. Publication was in fact suspended for eight months in 1966, a move widely interpreted as a counter-sacrifice to balance the fall of Ranković, but began again early in 1967 with a trilingual international as well as a Croato-Serbian edition and a 47-member Advisory Board recruited from Yugoslavia and from abroad, both West and East.

43. Their battlefields also included officially sponsored symposia, with papers submitted by representatives of both sides, on subjects like 'the LC in conditions of self-management', 'democratic centralism in the context of the reorganisation of the LCY', or 'changes in the character of the working class and its political vanguard'. Nor were the columns of *Socijalizam*, *Komunist* and other 'establishment' journals always closed to 'anti-establishment' writers.

44. In *Komunist*, Jan. 16, 1969 (italics in original).

45. A precise analogue can be found in the polemics among national-liberal parties in the last years of the Habsburg monarchy. Another was the bitterly inter-personal as well as ideologically significant dispute which divided Yugoslav leftists of the 1930s on the subject of the correct Marxist attitude to culture; surviving veterans of this particular polemic and their respective intellectual heirs divided along the same lines again in the first postwar debate on cultural policy and now in the 1960s. (See Lasić.)

46. Cf. also Tripalo, then a Bakarić disciple, who considered it 'great progress' that in the course of 'certain problems in the relationship between the Party and the intelligentsia ... we have by and large not employed administrative measures or withdrawn subventions to journals'. On the contrary, he said, 'the possibility of expressing contrary opinions is one of the prerequisites for an ideological battle with certain standpoints with which we do not agree' (in a Nov. 1967 lecture, reprinted in Tripalo (1969), pp. 259f.).

47. Cf. Boško Šiljegović (member of the CC-LCY and retired Partisan colonel-general): 'Criticism neither is nor can be destructive of the creative process. On the contrary. If viewpoints and principles, even those which were once already checked in practice ..., are not reconsidered and checked again and again, the results will be

stagnation and dogmatism. Criticism and dogma cannot coexist.... We shall gradually have to get used to the fact that progressive, democratic, socialist ideas are not anybody's monopoly' (interview in *Expres nedeljnja revija*, Sarajevo, Jan. 26, 1969).

48. Mito Hadži-Vasilev, in *STAP*, Jan.-Mar. 1967, p. 69; cf. Crvenkovski, 'Divorcing the Party from Power', loc. cit., and Tripalo (1969), pp. 244f., 320-8, for one honest statement of the dilemma.

49. Even before the 4th Plenum Crvenkovski was suggesting that obedience to the majority must be tempered by the realisation that 'at times the minority may prove to be right' (interview in *Borba*, 20 Mar. 1966); cf. also his interviews in *Politika* (Oct. 23, 1966) and *Komunist* (Dec. 14, 1967). Also Tripalo (1969), pp. 254f., 329-32, Šoškić, in *Socijalizam*, 12/1968 and Stane Dolanc (an interesting early liberal statement by Tito's chief Party lieutenant after 1971), ibid., 12/1967.

50. Address to the Conference of the Belgrade Party, Apr. 17, 1967, *STAP*, no. 26.

51. *Foreign Affairs*, July 1966, p. 643.

52. Cf. Kardelj, 'Responsibility for the Elections', *STAP*, Jan.-Mar. 1967.

53. *Yugoslav Survey*, Nov. 1967.

54. Rusinow, *Yugoslav Elections, 1969*, Pt III (AUFS, xvi/6, July 1969), based on Belgrade press reports and personal interviews during 1967. For a nervous reaction to analogous 'conservative' or 'political underground' victories in Croatia, see Tripalo (1969), pp. 256f.

55. The *Deklaracija* was originally published in *Telegram* (Zagreb), Mar. 17, 1967; reactions were published in the daily press during April and May. The significance of the incident and passion of the reaction can only be understood in the historical context of European national movements, for which language was crucially important as the ultimate distinguishing characteristic and legitimation of separate nationhood.

56. Hondius, pp. 324-6, who suggests that the proposal could not be challenged on grounds of nationalism or chauvinism because it came from the one formally multinational republic.

57. Ibid., p. 329.

58. Published as 'Some Questions Relating to the Further Development of the Assembly and Political System' by the Federal Assembly, 1968.

59. The ethnic sensitivities of the Serbs then required another change in the original list, since the Presidents of the Republic and of the FEC were now both Croats; Milentije Popović, like Todorović an anti-Ranković Serbian liberal, therefore became President of the Federal Assembly in place of the original candidate, the Montenegrin Vlahović. Cf. Lendvai, pp. 166-8, who emphasises the role of the national question and the 'Declaration' crisis in these shifts.

60. Bilandžić (1973), pp. 270f.

61. Ibid., p. 274.

62. Mentioned by Todorović in an interview in *Komunist*, Oct. 26, 1967, and confirmed by the 8th CC Plenum on Nov. 23.

63. The other republics retained only one directly elected chamber while turning their Organisational-Political chambers into Chambers of

Communes—except Slovenia, which dropped the fifth chamber altogether. Biennial elections for half of all Assemblymen were eliminated; all members of all chambers would henceforth be elected every four years. For details of a very complicated system, see Rusinow, *Yugoslav Elections, 1969*, Pt I, and S.B. McCarthy, 'Yugoslavia Moves Toward Consociational Democracy' (unpubl. MS., Yale Univ., 1969).

64. *VUS*, Nov., 8, 1967; the first Horvat series in *Vjesnik*, appeared Sept. 15-23, and the Bajt series on Nov. 6-8, 1967.

65. Žarko Božić in *Borba*, Nov. 11. Cf. ibid., Nov. 23; *Svet*, Nov. 18 and Dec. 23; *Ekonomska politika*, Nov. 25; a Slavoljub Djukić-Bajt exchange in *Borba*, Dec. 1, 6 and 8; and Dec. issues of *VUS*. Also the Horvat-Sime Djodan polemic in *Vjesnik*, Oct. 24-8, 1967 and Feb. 23-4 and 27-8, 1968.

66. 'Eighth Meeting of the cc-lcy', *Yugoslav Survey*, Feb. 1968, p. 35; *STAP*, Oct.-Dec. 1967.

67. Cf. the exposé of average and top earnings in banks by Danilo Vuković in *Borba*, Dec. 18, 1967. At the top of the list the Yugoslav Foreign Trade Bank was then paying *average* personal salaries of 2,656 new dinars.

68. 'Eighth Meeting', loc. cit., pp. 33f.

69. As reported in *Književne novine*, May 25, 1968. See also Rusinow, *Anatomy of a Student Revolt*, Pts I & II (aufs, xv/4-5, Aug.-Nov. 1968).

70. See the drafts of early demands and the matured 'Political-Action Programme of Belgrade Students' (June 4), trans. and analysed, ibid., Pt. I.

71. Ibid., Pt II.

72. Cf. the revealing interview (*Borba*, June 22, 1968) in which the Secretary of the Party Committee at the University, Prof. Žarko Bulajić, defended the Committee's 'motives' in assuming the leadership of the student action (quoted in *Anatomy*, Pt II).

73. *Borba*, June 14, 1968 (*Yugoslav Survey*, Aug. 1968).

74. *Borba*, July 17, 1968 (*STAP*, July-Sept. 1968).

75. Quoted at greater length in *Anatomy*, Pt II.

76. *Borba*, July 17, 1968.

77. Ibid., Aug. 24, 1968. For Tito's and other official Yugoslav Party and Government statements about the invasion see *Yugoslav Survey*, Nov. 1968 (*STAP*, no. 31).

78. Suggestions that the Yugoslav authorities had received secret information indicating serious Soviet consideration of such a course were planted on selected Western newspapermen in Belgrade during the winter of 1968-69, but were never confirmed.

79. Cf. A. Ross Johnson, 'Yugoslav Total National Defense', *Survival*, Mar.-Apr. 1973 and Rusinow, *The Yugoslav Concept of 'All-National Defense'* (aufs, xix/1, Nov. 1971).

80. Two 'off-the-record' remarks to the present writer in the autumn of 1968 suggest that this press campaign contained an element of honest re-discovery as well as calculated propaganda. 'We now see', a senior diplomat said, 'that our initial interpretation of Khrushchev's overthrow was essentially correct. It *was* a neo-Stalinist coup d'état'.

A distinguished Yugoslav journalist said in November: 'If we had carried through a consistent Marxist analysis of Soviet society ... we would have known that there had not been and could not have been the fundamental changes in the nature of the regime that we recently thought there had been.'

81. *Exchange and Power in Social Life* (New York, 1964), cited in Jowitt, pp. 8-20.

Ch. 7: The Price of Pluralism

1. Dessa Trevisan in *The Times*, Dec. 17, and Jonathan Randal in *NYT*, Nov. 28 & Dec. 6, 1968. There was no sign, for once, that the Albanian regime in Tirana had anything to do with the demonstrations, nor does it seem likely. Tirana, also nervous about Soviet intentions after Czechoslovakia, was precisely at this time toning down its anti-Yugoslav propaganda and suggesting that Yugoslavs and Albanians had always stood together against common foes. Among the demonstrators students from the new University of Priština again played a conspicuous role.

2. See e.g. Crvenkovski's argument in a 1967 brochure, reprinted in Nikolić and Atlagić, pp. 381-3. Questions asked by Slovene deputies to the Federal Assembly when new 10 dinar notes were found to have omitted the Slovene variant of one word (*Socijalistična* as well as *Socijalistička Republika!*), leading to a reissuing of the offending notes, provided an example of the sensitivities involved.

3. Holjevac had already been in trouble sixteen months earlier, but for a different reason: it was the awarding of prizes to two *Praxis* contributors by another quasi-governmental commission which he headed that led to the June 1966 Sabor debate on *Praxis* (see above, p. 218) at which he was officially censured and removed from the commission.

4. Marjanović is the outstanding historian of recent Yugoslav history belonging to the Serbian Partisan generation; Ćosić is generally considered the best living Serbian writer. Plenum speeches, some of them reported in *Borba*, May 30 and 31, 1968, were reprinted as *14 sednica CK SK Srbije* (1968); cf. also Vucinich, pp. 261, 268, 274f.

5. *Vjesnik*, Jan. 25, 1968 (Cf. his almost identical words to the Macedonian Party *aktiv* two months earlier, ibid., Dec. 1-2, 1967, and the similar if more sympathetic description of the psychology of 'old Partisan' conservatism in Bilandžić (1973), p. 273). The strategy described here emerges clearly from speeches of this period by Tripalo (many collected in Tripalo (1971)), Dabčević-Kučar, *et al.*

6. For one of several earlier complaints 'about a blocked social situation' leaving vital economic problems unsolved and 'half of the work organisations [in Croatia] in a worse position than in 1964', see an angry article by Neda Krmpotić (later a leading journalist of the Croatian 'mass movement'), *Vjesnik*, Apr. 25, 1968. In October 1969, however, Croatian and Slovenian spokesmen (Tripalo and Kavčič in particular) were still insisting that economic problems would be solved if only market laws were really respected (at the 5th Session of the LCY Presidency in Belgrade, reported to *Politika*, Oct. 15, 1969).

7. Compiled from Statistical Yearbook 1972 and 1973; cf. the chapter on Yugoslavia in Baklanoff. From a later perspective it is important to recall that price rises like those recorded here were considered ground for alarm in a period before Western Europe and North America were forced to come to terms with ubiquitous 'double-digit inflation'.

8. Cf. the list of Croatian examples cited in a Dec. 1969 series in *Borba* by a then member of the Croatian CC and Vice-President of the Federal Assembly, Miloš Žanko, who was therefore accused by his Zagreb peers of 'unitarism' and purged in Jan. 1971 (see below). An emerging but always publicly qualified claim to 'national' leadership is traceable in 1967–69 speeches and interviews by Tripalo, Dabčević-Kučar, Kavčič, *et al.*

9. Conversation with the present writer, spring 1972.

10. Hence the increasing popularity of the slogan 'stagnation'. It and others with similar import appear with growing frequency from 1968 in the speeches and writings of leaders at all levels including Tito, but were seldom used before that date.

11. 'We should have democratised our central Party and State apparatuses rather than abolished them', a former senior official of undoubted liberal persuasion (and one of several Partisan generals of Serb nationality who defy the group's primitive and conservative stereotype) grumbled in one such private conversation.

12. *Stenografske beleške IX kongresa*; a one-volume *Deveti kongres saveza komunista Jugoslavije* (1969) contains major speeches, the resolution and new Statute, etc.

13. Briefly reported in *Narodna Armija*, Mar. 3, 1969; cf. Chief of Staff Ljubičić's speech in *Borba*, Mar. 1 and reference to the decisions of the 9th Plenum in *Deveti kongres*, p. 287.

14. Such problems were admitted e.g. in Slovenia, where Miha Marinko, Ivan Maček, Boris Ziherl, Vida Tomšič, Lidija Šentjurc and Viktor Abvelj, all well-known pre-war Communists born before 1914, were added to and again removed from the list of candidates for federal bodies shortly before the Congress (*Borba*, Dec. 10, 1968); also in Montenegro, where the problem was the 'demotion' of Vukmanović, Blažo Jovanović, Veljko Mičunović and CC President Djoko Pajković to membership in the federal Party Conference, bringing protests from Vukmanović and Pajković (ibid., Nov. 13, 1968). For praise of the 'new style' of open debate and 'fewer traditional monologues', see Todorović's wrap-up of the republican Congresses, which also specifically referred to the need to 'guide' the selection of candidates because 'our democracy is new' and so subject to abuse (ibid., Jan. 16, 1969).

15. In Croatia and the Vojvodina there were no changes in the two top posts: Bakarić and Tripalo remained as CC President and EC Secretary in Croatia, as did Mirko Tepavac and Mirko Čanadanović in Vojvodina. In Macedonia and Bosnia-Herzegovina the CCs kept their Presidents (Crvenkovski and Cvijetin Mijatović), but there were new EC Secretaries (Angel Čemerski and Nijaz Dizdarević). In Montenegro Veselin Djuranović moved up from EC Secretary to replace Pajković as CC President. The most powerful Slovenian

politician, Stane Kavčič, preferred to remain Head of Government rather than Party, so Franc Popit moved up from EC Secretary to CC President. Veli Deva remained Party President in Kosovo, but got a fellow-Albanian in place of a Serb as Secretary.

16. During the dispute with Vukmanović and Pajković, cited above.

17. See Djuranović's keynote address to the Montenegrin Congress, quoted in *Politika*, Dec. 13, 1968, and Mijatović's interview, on the eve of the Bosnian Congress, in *Borba*, Jan. 4, 1969.

18. Report on the debate in commissions, Mar. 15, 1969; cf. Crvenkovski's exposition of these disputes in the following plenary session, ibid., Mar. 16, and the *Stenografske beleške*, for both the commission and plenary discussions.

19. In presenting the new Statute to the Congress for approval, Mijatović noted that there had been some discussion of constituting the Conference on the basis of an equal number of delegates from each republic *and* province, but that the commission of which he was rapporteur thought that this needed further consideration (*Deveti kongres*, p. 236).

20. '... i, naravno, ja'. This phrase, from my own taping of the speech, was characteristically modified in the stenographic report to read 'together with the President of the LCY'.

21. The departure to the EB of the Bosnian President and Secretary, Mijatović and Dizdarević, was to be less significant. The riddle of musical chairs was solved in both these republics because Dabčević-Kučar and the new Bosnian Party President, Branko Mikulić, had been elected to the LCY Presidency by their respective congresses; they were now entitled to sit there *ex officio*, thus liberating two Croatian and two Bosnian seats in the Presidency (including each republic's newly created sixth one) to be filled by those selected for the EB.

22. The Vojvodina sent Stefan Doronjski, a Serb, and not Provincial Party President Tepavac, but Tepavac had to leave the presidency two months later when he succeeded Nikezić as Yugoslav foreign secretary; Čanadanović, then only 33 years old, became Provincial Party President, the last link in a chain of protégés and/or successors (Koča Popović to Nikezić to Tepavac in the foreign ministry; Tepavac to Čanadanović in Novi Sad), all of whom would fall or feel obliged to resign in the Serbian purge of October 1972. Kosovo, to complete the list, kept Deva as Party President and sent Fadil Hoxha, ever since the war Yugoslavia's senior Albanian functionary, to the EB.

23. For a detailed analysis and citation of sources see Rusinow, *Yugoslav Elections, 1969*, Pts I-III, based on Yugoslav press coverage, interviews and pre-election and election day trips through Serbia, Macedonia and Kosovo.

24. Thus *Komunist* (on Jan. 2, 1969), referring to the unfortunate experiences of 1967, issued 'directives' for the behaviour of Communists in the 1969 elections. They should be 'neither passive nor tutors', and were 'expected to secure full democracy and at the same time to prevent possible instances of spontaneity'.

25. *Borba*, Jan. 18, 1969.

26. Ibid., Jan. 8, 1969. Several examples of ignorance, lack of interest, and reasons for choosing one candidate rather than another ('I picked the names that sounded nicest'—a student at the political science faculty of Belgrade University!) are cited in *Yugoslav Elections*, Pt. I.

27. One or two newspapers and some SAWPY officials I interviewed admitted that this was the implication of the tendency to bypass youth, workers and women in favour of well-known politicians, energetic directors or engineers or leading doctors or directors of medical centres (as appropriate to the chamber in question). It was obvious and reasonable, they thought, to demand representation by the most able people in their communities, whatever the Alliance guidelines might say about the appropriateness of real 'people's deputies' in a 'people's democracy'. Only old-fashioned dictation of candidates by Party centres could have defied this logic.

28. Specific examples from Bijelo Polje (Montenegro), Stari Grad and Palilula communes in Belgrade, Subotica, Banjaluka and three Serbian inter-communal conferences are examined in *Yugoslav Elections*, Pt II, as are the reactions of SAWPY and the national press.

29. Milan Bajec, in *Borba*, Mar. 1, 1969.

30. Cf. an editorial comment on the implications of these 'debacles' in *Politika Expres* (Belgrade), May 7, 1969.

31. A Sino-Yugoslav trade agreement in March 1969 was followed by the exchange of ambassadors in May and August 1970, ending a ten-year break in diplomatic relations. Albanian leaders spoke of 'good neighbourly relations' and 'traditional' Yugoslav-Albanian comradeship despite Yugoslav 'revisionism' (Enver Hoxha's speech of May 30, 1970), and the Yugoslavs responded with equally cautious warmth (cf. *Vjesnik*, Apr. 25, *VUS*, June 10, *NIN*, June 14 1970).

32. Cf. 'Yugoslavia and the EEC', *Review of International Affairs* (Belgrade), Dec. 20, 1970.

33. After peaking at 331,000 in 1969, the number of registered unemployed declined to 320,000 in 1970 and 280,000 in 1971 (Statist. Yearbook 1972).

34. The literature on Yugoslav self-management is vast. Valuable studies focusing on these later years include many of the contributions to Broekmeyer (1970), among the 1103 pp. of Djordjević *et al.*, and the empirical studies cited in Gorupić and Paj, pp. 52–80, 127–32, 191–223, which provide a useful summary of these. But many of the insights of David and Elizabeth Tornquist (1966) were still valid ten years after their experiences as workers in a Belgrade publishing firm.

35. The principal and admittedly inadequate source for all of these assertions must be the writer's many Yugoslav friends, official but primarily unoffical, whose intimate hopes and fears he shared in those years. But cf. Stipe Šuvar's perceptive argument 'On the Fringe of the Nationality Question', in *Gledišta*, May–June 1971, placing the resurgence of ethnic nationalism in the context of social changes which had led to the decay of *Gemeinschaft* without building *Gesellschaft*; Simić, Hammel and the studies by a Yugoslav-American team of opinion researchers in Barton. The influence of the

titles and arguments of Eric Hoffer's *Ordeal of Change* and Erich Fromm's *Escape from Freedom* on the interpretation offered here is obvious.

36. RFE research reports (Yugoslavia, June 23 and Oct. 14, 1969) based on the Priština daily, *Rilindja*.
37. *Politika*, July 31 and *Vjesnik*, Aug. 2, 1969; cf. Bilandžić (1973), who refers to the crisis as 'threatening the fall of the Federal Government' and thereby 'strengthening the practice of republican pressures for the realisation of their interests'.
38. An edited version of all speeches at the 10th session, with Bakarić's Dec. 13 speech as an appendix, was published by *Vjesnik*, as *X sjednica Centralnog komiteta Saveza komunista Hrvatske*, on Jan. 24, 1970.
39. Although as always difficult to prove from available documentation, there was no informed observer of the Yugoslav and Croatian scene who was not convinced that this session was staged on Bakarić's initiative, and that it was meant to be part of a new master strategic plan concocted in his fertile but as usual impenetrable mind.
40. Cf. Slobodan Stanković, 'Analysis of the Yugoslav Party Presidium Meeting', RFE research reports, Yugoslavia, Apr. 27, 1970.
41. Bilandžić (1973), p. 277, claims that 'this Serbian position finally marked the end of the perennial debate about the economic role of the Federation which had gone on there since 1945'.
42. *Vjesnik*, Sept. 23, 1970.
43. From the speeches as quoted in *Politika*, Aug. 29 and 30, 1970. This was Tito's first critical reference to the 6th Congress which I have found, but he was to return to the theme again after Dec. 1971.
44. Bilandžić, with his access to Party archives, says of this period: 'Hidden from public knowledge, dramatic situations were created, plots were hatched and resolved, all of which created a strained political situation and gave rise to temptations to stop the process [of reform of the Federation] and take the course of the so-called "firm hand" ' (1973, pp. 273f.).
45. *Konferencija Saveza komunista* (1970), pp. 23f.
46. As quoted by Tanjug dispatch from Priština, Apr. 15, 1971.
47. As noted by Bilandžić (1973), p. 286.
48. The fullest account of the meeting was published in the university's undergraduate newspaper, *Student*, Apr. 4, 1971.
49. For an analysis of the style and significance of the journal and the contrasting style of Tripalo and his colleagues, see the present writer's *Crisis in Croatia*, (AUFS, xix/4-7), Pt IV and Perić, who does not make the clear distinctions which existed.
50. Kardelj's authoritative commentary is in his long report to the 16th session of the Party Presidency (in English in *STAP*, Jan.-Mar. 1971, pp. 3-47; cf. *Vjesnik*, Mar. 3, 1971). Popović's is reprinted as a forword to *Komunist's* 1971 ed. of the revised Constitution; cf. also his last speech, made to the Sarajevo Congress three days before his sudden death in April 1971, in *STAP*, Apr.-June 1971.
51. In addition, but only 'when necessary to prevent or eliminate major disruptions in the economy, or when required by the interests of national defence or other extraordinary needs', federal organs could

place temporary limits on the tax powers of republics and communes or block the use of certain funds by enterprises, communities of interest, and socio-political communities (Amendment XXVIII).

52. On the list were the Social Plan of Yugoslavia; the foreign currency and foreign trade systems; the monetary system and monetary policy (for which the National Bank of Yugoslavia would now share decision-making responsibility with newly created National Banks of the six republics and two provinces); the division of income from the turnover tax; and the federal budget.

53. Cf. also 'The Latest Changes (1971) in the Constitution of the SFRY', *Yugoslav Survey*, Nov. 4, 1971; Burks, and Bilandžić (1973), pp. 281-5.

54. Rusinow, *A Note on Yugoslavia: 1972* (AUFS, xix/3, July 1972).

55. Ibid. A point also made later by Kardelj (1973, pp. 105f.) when the 1974 Constitution was being prepared.

56. Eng. version of both communiqué and May Day speech in *Yugoslav Survey*, Aug. 3, 1971.

57. From the Josipović Commission's report and other sources cited in Rusinow, *Crisis in Croatia*, loc. cit.

58. Although generally assumed to be UDBa, one rumour at the time named Military Intelligence as the culprit and Bakarić much later, in a Zagreb TV interview in 1974, dropped what seemed to be hints that 'unitarist' Croats in the Secretariat for Foreign Affairs had been responsible (as quoted in *Politika*, May 15, 1974).

59. Again according to Bakarić, ibid. Cf. also earlier revelations by Ema Derossi-Bjelajac, in a speech at Rijeka on Dec. 10 and by Pavle Gaži at the 23rd session of the LCC-CC on Dec. 12, 1971 (*Vjesnik*, Dec. 12 and 14).

60. This was to be one of Tito's specific charges against them at Karadjordjevo (see below, p. 308).

61. For sources, largely Yugoslav dailies and weeklies during 1971-72 and including the report of an investigating commission headed by Ante Josipović, portions of which were published in the national press after its acceptance by the LCC-CC in May 1972, see the *Crisis in Croatia* series, loc. cit. Cf. Perić, and Lendvai, 'National Tensions in Yugoslavia', Inst. for the Study of Conflict, Study No. 25, Aug. 1972.

62. Both Bakarić and Derossi-Bjelajac placed emphasis on this point (speeches at Virovitica on Dec. 7 and at Rijeka on Dec. 10 in *Vjesnik*, Dec. 9 and 12, 1971).

63. Bakarić as usual was to advertise and exploit his ill-health, but it is interesting to speculate about the impact on Croatian and Yugoslav politics in 1971 of the fact that two of the triumvirate were suffering unpublicised illnesses which are generally thought to affect personality and induce erratic behaviour: Savka as a chronic hypoglaecemic and Pirker to die of cancer soon after his fall from power.

64. A good and remarkably objective account of the Matica's strategy is in Ema Derossi-Bjelajac, 'Karakteristike i dimenzije idejno-političkih devijacije u Savezu komunista Hrvatske', *Naše teme*, Jan. 1972. pp. 9-14; Cf. Perić, *passim*.

388 · · Notes · · [pp. 295-302]

388   *Notes*   [pp. 295-302]

65. Most other leaders of the national movement at the university were also from these districts. The coup is described in detail in *Crisis in Croatia*, Pt III.

66. *Stenografske beleške*, corrected to the original style and wording from the present writer's own notes taken at Sarajevo.

67. Commenting on the change, Frane Barbieri wrote in *NIN* (June 6, 1971) that it was either part of the Yugoslav's 'mentality' or because they had not yet 'become used to an open dialogue' that 'our political mood so frequently swings between extreme optimism and pessimism'.

68. See long excerpts from all speeches, sometimes significantly cut or paraphrased, in *Vjesnik*, May 14-16; cf. what the Serbian press preferred to quote in *NIN*, May 16, 1971.

69. The solution finally adopted—precisely 15 days after the resignation of the Croatian leadership suspended the Croatian veto—was to raise 'retention quotas' from ±7 per cent to 20 per cent in the economy generally and to 40-50 per cent in tourism. In late 1973 a modified inter-bank rather than inter-republican version of the Croatian proposal for an internal foreign currency market, authorised by a July 1972 law (*Službeni list*, 36/72), was opened after a series of delays 'for technical reasons'.

70. For a perceptive description of how the foreign currency problem was 'transformed' from the economic to the national plane, see 'Kontra-revolucija bez krinke', *VUS*, Feb. 2, 1972.

71. The most important such gathering was conducted at the end of June, in two sessions of reportedly bitter and inconclusive debate, at the Villa Vajs, a Party retreat in Zagreb, with Bakarić and Tripalo in attendance. Details in extracts from the Josipović Commission report in *Vjesnik*, May 9, 1972, *NIN*, Dec. 12, 1971, and speeches by Milka Planinc and Ema Derossi-Bjelajac (*Vjesnik*, Dec. 12) and by Antun Biber at the LCC-CC, 23rd session (ibid., Dec. 14, 1971).

72. Bakarić's first public disagreement with his erstwhile protégés came in a late September speech and took the form of a warning that the concept of a 'mass national movement' and the proposed definition of Croatia as 'the national State of the Croatian nation' were ideologically dubious and politically dangerous (as quoted in *Politika*, Oct. 1, 1971). For details of the complex political story of these months, including the curious history of the EC's 'Action Programme' of Aug. 2, see *Crisis in Croatia*, Pts III and IV.

73. *Vjesnik*, Sept. 16, 1971.

74. Speeches ibid., Dec. 12-14.

75. Cf. Slobodan Stanković, 'Yugoslavia-One Year Later', RFE reports, Dec. 8, 1972.

76. Cf. 'Croatian Orientation', *NIN*, Oct. 17, 1971, a particularly useful contemporary survey based on interviews with most of the Croatian leaders and sometimes prejudicially selected quotations from their recent speeches.

77. This was also the view of the Josipović Commission. By the beginning of November 1971, the Commission's report says, 'disagreements about the handling and evaluation of individual political excesses and phenomena had evolved into very differing

views concerning the present situation and perspectives for development in Croatia and Yugoslavia.... Because of this and because of
the undemocratic methods used by those who resigned after the 21st
[Karadjordjevo] session, mutual trust and real faith in the possibility
of any kind of united action had disappeared.'

78. Cf. *Vjesnik*, Nov. 6 et seq.; *NIN*, Nov. 14, *Hrvatski tjednik*, Nov. 12
and references in various speeches after Karadjordjevo, loc. cit.

79. In his Virovitica speech of Dec. 7 (*Vjesnik*, Dec. 8, 1971).

80. None has ever been admitted, but Stoyan Pribichevitch, an American
writer and old friend of Yugoslavia and its Marshal, had a meeting
with Tito on May 12, 1972 and wrote in an article commemorating
the Yugoslav President's 80th birthday (in *NYT*, May 25, 1972): 'In
November [1971] at a secret meeting in Bugojno, Bosnia, Yugoslav
Army leaders showed Tito suppressed TV reels of Croatian
Communist mass meetings, with only Croatian flags and with
Croatian nationalist and anti-Tito slogans, songs, shouts and signs.
Then Tito struck.'

81. *Politika*, Nov. 17, 1971, which also quotes Budiša as repeating recent
maximum student and Matica demands (UN membership, separate
army, etc.) adding that even acceptance of all these demands would
'by no means mean that the struggle for full Croatian sovereignty is
really won and finished'. *Vjesnik* explained the following day that it
had not reported the meeting because it had not been notified to
send a correspondent.

82. Speech at Vela Luka, on Hvar, published in *Vjesnik* on Dec. 1, when
the Karadjordjevo meeting was already under way.

Ch. 8: 'One Ring to Bind Them All'

1. Details of these post-Karadjordjevo events are in *Crisis in Croatia*, Pt
IV.

2. Report to the 5th Conference of the LCC, Jan. 21, 1972.

3. Pirker died of cancer a few months later, aged 45. In 1974 Tripalo,
like Ranković, was living on the large pension earned by his many
years in Party service, and Dabčević-Kučar, only much later removed
from her university professorship, was a member of the Croatian
Government's council of economic advisers.

4. *Vjesnik*, Dec. 12, 1974. Cf. the self-critical remarks of Djuro Kladarin
and Pavle Gaži and the perspicacious analysis of Bilandžić in their
speeches at the Dec. 12 meeting (*Vjesnik*, Dec. 13–15).

5. One example, important because of his role, is Dolanc's comment:
'There is a good deal of opportunism in the basic organisations and
[higher] forums of the Communist League' and that this constituted
'one of the gravest illnesses in our society' (talk with Party members
in Split, Sept. 19, 1972).

6. On Dec. 18, 1971, quoted in *Politika*, Dec. 19. Cf. also his remarks at
Sarajevo and Rudo about the army's responsibility for internal order
and socialism as well as external defence, on Dec. 21 and 22, which
increased domestic and foreign speculation concerning the increasing
political role of the Yugoslav People's Army.

7. 'Our friends in the West', Bilić assured the present writer with

apparent conviction in Jan. 1972, 'need not worry that we will go backwards to a dogmatic Party. We are not social democrats but we are not an old type of Communist Party. Our immovable commitment to self-management is what distinguished us from Eastern types, and we will continue on our own road.'

8. In his closing speech to the 2nd LCY Conference (*Druga konferencija*, p. 14).
9. Speech of Dec. 18 to the Trade Union Council, loc. cit.
10. *Borba*, Dec. 10 and 13, 1971 (*NIN*, Jan. 9 1972), for Koliševski's attacks and Miloslavlevski's and Crvenkovski's responses; *Delo*, Nov. 13 and *Komunist*, Nov. 25, 1971, for Kavčič's suggestion and Kardelj's criticism of it.
11. *Druga konferencija*, pp. 10, 14 (*STAP*, Jan.-Mar. 1972).
12. With a subtheme provided by Gligorov's vigorous defence of the continuing validity of the principles of a market economy, properly but indirectly controlled and planned and with an increasing role for 'self-management agreements' among enterprises replacing State planning (in his major address, *Druga konferencija*, pp. 40-54, and *STAP* loc. cit.) For his identical line at the 10th Congress 15 months later, see below.
13. Ibid., pp. 21-39.
14. See Kardelj (1969).
15. 'Veliki sistemi', a favourite and then positively valued term, particularly in Serbian political and business circles, ca. 1969-71.
16. Bilandžić (1973), p. 293, introducing a final chapter, entitled 'Pressures Towards the Renewal of Capital-Social Relations and Efforts to Open new Paths to the Development of Workers Self-management', which is the most lucid and complete exposition of this position so far to appear in Yugoslavia.
17. Ibid., and for one early exposition of the 'counter-class' concept (already part of the ideological debate of 1967-68) Stipe Šuvar, a new member of the Croatian CC and a rising star among Croatian and Yugoslav establishment ideologists, in *Borba*, Jan. 27, 1972 (also his pre-Karadjordjevo series on the same subject, *Politika*, Nov. 7-9, 1971).
18. Cf, Kardelj's formulation (in Kardelj (1973), pp. 15, 17): 'Any monopoly in disposing with social capital funds also inevitably contains elements of class relationships between the workers and the holders of these monopolistic rights.... What is more,... if the system of economic control based on self-management were to fail, technocracy in our country could grow into an even more powerful factor than in a system of centralised State ownership or monopoly capitalism. For in both these social systems technocracy is in a more or less subordinate and dependent position', since managers must account to 'the owner of capital, whether it is State-owned or privately-owned'.
19. For an alternative calculation, grouping exported goods in accordance with standard international commercial classifications, see Baklanoff, also the source of other figures quoted here.
20. At a seminar for Party workers in Ljubljana, *Borba* (Zagreb ed.), Sept. 20, 1972.

21. *The Star-News* (Washington), Oct. 8, 1971. Cf. Western speculations about a connection between this visit and Tito's apparent reversal of the attitude he had shown towards the Croatian leaders two weeks earlier in Zagreb, p. 301 above.
22. Cf. Stanković, 'New Soviet Credits Indicate Change in Yugoslavia's Foreign Policy', RFE research reports, Nov. 14, 1972.
23. Soviet representatives in Belgrade were bluntly and openly describing Nikezić as a 'notorious Sovietophobe' as early as the spring of 1972.
24. Ironically, little came of the much-discussed and widely-feared Soviet credit line of 1972. Only ten days after the $540 million deal was signed, on Nov. 13, 1972, *Ekonomska politika* was discussing difficulties in finding appropriate users. The agreement was so completely and complexly tied to supplies of Soviet equipment which was either not available or not wanted by the Yugoslav economy that only a fraction of the credit was ever used. A five-year extension of the Yugoslav-EEC agreement in June 1973 was in fact far more significant for Yugoslav foreign trade and domestic investment opportunities.
25. All collected in Dolanc (1972).
26. Tito again returned to this theme in his *Vjesnik* interview, loc. cit. and other speeches of the period. Like his parallel return to the 'dictatorship of the proletariat' theme, his critique was duly echoed by other spokesmen but with sometimes significantly milder interpretations and definitions. (Cf. Dolanc to Ljubljana Party 'activists', *Politika*, Jan. 25, 1973, and Bilić's interview in *Borba*, Feb. 19, 1973.)
27. Cf. Šuvar's comments at a sociological symposium in Opatija, in which he named Kardelj, Bakarić and the now demoted Pečujlić as the sources of this 'confusion' (*Borba*, Feb. 9, 1973), and Kardelj's amendment of his views in a speech one week later (ibid., Feb. 16).
28. In his speech to the Serbian leadership, loc. cit. pp. 86, 94, after hints earlier and elsewhere.
29. Bakarić, for example, was significantly the only veteran member of the Party inner circle other than Kardelj who was specifically named by Tito (in the *Vjesnik* interview, ibid., p. 71) as supporting his and Dolanc's offensive.
30. Cf. articles in *NIN*, Feb. 13, 1972 and in *Ekonomska politika*, Sept. 4, 1972 (a list of banks and assets), with the latter periodical's 248pp. special issue devoted to Yugoslavia's 100 biggest enterprises ('100 najvećih', Sept. 14, 1970) the source of the statistics mentioned here.
31. Dalanc *et al.* (1972), pp. 91–5. While this speech of Tito's was the only one from the meeting to be published, it adequately confirms contemporary Belgrade rumours and later revelations concerning the tone and outcome of the meeting of Oct. 9–12.
32. The State visit was from Oct. 16 to 21, but many of the journalists and others accompanying the Queen stayed on for several days.
33. Nikezić and Perović kept their Party memberships for another 18 months and were expelled only on the eve of the 10th Congress.
34. Among other Belgrade *čaršija* guesses there is one which holds that Koča Popović was reacting to Tito's comment (in his Oct. 7 *Vjesnik* interview, loc. cit., p. 71) that 'among those of us who led the revolution,... there are some others who have come from unhealthy

intellectual environments, the non-socialist intelligentsia'. Another suggested that his resignation at that time and without explanation, coupled with the impossibility of labelling his position within the Yugoslav Party political spectrum, left the man who had already once been vice-president of Yugoslavia as a universally uncompromised 'dark horse' candidate to succeed Tito.

35. Its 406 articles were preceded by 10 lengthy 'basic principles'. The authorised Eng. trans. by Pavičić, published in April 1974, is 293 pages long, including Todorović's 40-page speech introducing it to the Federal Assembly. Cf. Kardelj's authoritative commentary (1973)(also in *STAP*, May-July 1973) unfortunately often as obscure as the Constitution itself; Miodrag Jovičić, 'Novi ustav SFRJ od 1974—Njegova svojstva i karakteristike' (pre-publication MS. 1974); and a helpful 132pp. commentary in *Yugoslav.Survey*, Aug. 1974.

36. The new Statute decreed that the Party, '*as the conscious champion of the aspirations and interests of the working class,*... shall be the prime mover *and exponent* of political activity aimed at safeguarding and further developing the socialist revolution and socialist social relations of self-management, and especially at the strengthening of socialist social and democratic consciousness, *and shall be responsible therefor*' ('Basic Principles' VIII; italics indicate additions to otherwise identical wording in the 1963 Constitution); a similarly expanded definition of the Socialist Alliance, its own political role enlarged and made more explicit, also included references to the 'leading role' of the Party in this mass organisation.

37. Kardelj (1973), pp. 114f. and 100-2.

38. Ibid., pp. 102, 116. The present writer's more detailed analysis of this system is in *The New Yugoslav Constitution* (AUFS, xxii/1, 1975), which includes references to additional Yugoslav commentaries and primers for 'self-managers'.

39. Belgrade lecture on the new Constitution to American law students, organised by the AUFS Center for Mediterranean Studies, July 1974.

40. See above, pp. 237, 284, for earlier and the glossary in *Yugoslav Survey*, Aug. 1974, pp. 121-32 for current, definitions of these terms. 'Interest communities' now included 'local communities' (*mesne zajednice*, hitherto largely non-functioning sub-divisions of communes), communities of education and health and various organised citizens' interest groups, including consumers and recently even environmentalists.

41. Conversation with one of the principal drafters, Belgrade, Aug. 1974.

42. Stages in this evolution were marked by the Basic Law on Economic Organisations of 1965, which granted some rights to the 'work units', including 'internal economic accounts, by amendments to this law in 1968 (*Službeni list*, 32 and 48/68), which introduced the term 'organisation of associated labour' and gave the work units independent legal status; and by the 'workers' amendments' of 1971. Cf. T. Eger, 'Das ordnungspolitische Grundgefuge der sozialistischen Markwirtschafts Jugoslawiens', in Hamel, and *Yugoslav Survey*, loc. cit., 15-26.

43. The Constitution was silent on the obviously vital question of the

conditions under which a BOAL could secede from an enterprise because agreement could not be reached in time.

44. And a literal translation of *inokosni poslovodni organ* (arts. 100ff.). Pavičić translates this as 'individual business executive', which is kinder to English-speaking readers but loses the full flavour of the circumlocution inherent in the original, apparently invented because *direktor* was now thought to have bourgeois-technocratic connotations.

45. Late 1973 complaints that 'resistance' to bank reforms 'is still strong' came, *i.a.*, from Gligorov and a Belgrade factory director, Milan Dragović (in *NIN*, Nov. 18 and *Komunist*, Nov. 19). See above, pp. 173–6 and 208f. for the 1965 banking reform and its consequences.

46. See above, p. 285f. for the post-1972 system of extra-constitutional rule by committee, and Kardelj's comments (1973), pp. 104–14. The specialised inter-republican committees created in 1971 remained to perform the same function of co-ordinating regional views in less important areas in which the FEC was empowered to act without the authority of the Assembly.

47. Thus a Party member trade unionist, for example, was involved in the process at several points and in different roles: in electing all three kinds of delegations (and three kinds within the third category, Party, trade union, and Socialist Alliance members) and in influencing candidates through the Socialist Alliance; at the other extreme a peasant who was not a member of a co-operative was involved at only one point: electing his *mesna zajednica*'s delegation.

48. The Yugoslav press was soon reporting the failure and practical difficulties of delegates' regularly consulting their delegations as required by the Constitution (e.g. 'Da li se otudjuju delegati?' in the Zagreb *Borba*, Jan. 27, 1975.).

49. The following is based on my *Yugoslavia's Return to Leninism* (AUFS, xxi/1, June 1974), an eyewitness report supplemented by the *Stenografske beleške* of the Congress.

50. See *Politika*, Sept. 21, 1974, for reports of the trial of the 'Cominformists'. Kardelj himself went to Moscow to see Brezhnev just before the public announcement (*Komunist*, Sept. 16, 1974), but apparently did not get a response of a kind to dissuade the Yugoslavs from publicising the incident. The disputes with Italy over Trieste, with Austria over Carinthia and with Bulgaria over Macedonia were the daily fodder of the Yugoslav press for most of the year.

51. He returned to this theme after 1970 with such (growing) frequency that specific citations would inevitably be too selective to communicate the emphasis he placed on it, or his increasing sadness and bitterness. The best archive is in any case not his printed words or major speeches but Yugoslav TV's detailed and candid newsreels of his 'royal progresses' of these years, a multitude of informal meetings with communal and loocal Party leaders, workers' councils, youth delegations, etc. It was through these that all who watched the eight o'clock *Dnevnik* could become acquainted with another Tito, a personality halfway between the one who appears on formal and public occasions and the one glimpsed in the less sycophantic memoirs of those who are or have been in his inner Party circle.

Ch. 9: Conclusions

1. Lendvai, p. 96.
2. *The Price of Pluralism* (AUFS, xviii/1, July 1971).
3. Cf. the optimistic conclusions and forecasts in Johnson (1974).
4. Gregory Grossman, 'Economic Reforms: A Balance Sheet', *Problems of Communism*, Nov.-Dec. 1966.

SELECT BIBLIOGRAPHY

Note: For reasons of space, with a few exceptions this bibliography is confined to works cited or drawn on in writing this book; hence it excludes some basic classics, especially for the pre-1941 period.

I. YUGOSLAV OFFICIAL AND PARTY SOURCES

LEAGUE OF COMMUNISTS OF YUGOSLAVIA (congresses and other sessions, official documents, listed in chronological order).

Istorijski arhiv KPJ. Belgrade, 1949.

V kongres KPJ. Belgrade, 1949.

Borba komunista Jugoslavije za socijalističku demokratiju, VI kongres KPJ. Belgrade, 1952.

VII kongres: stenografske beleške. Belgrade, 1958.

Yugoslavia's Way. The Program of the League of Communists of Yugoslavia. New York, 1958.

The Fourth Plenum of the League of Communists of Yugoslavia. Belgrade, 1963.

The VIth Plenum of the Central Committee of the League of Communists of Yugoslavia. Belgrade, 1964.

Osmi kongres SKJ—Stenografke beleške. 3 vols. Belgrade, 1965.

14 sednica CK SK Srbije. Belgrade, 1968.

Deveti kongres Saveza komunista Jugoslavije. Belgrade, 1969.

Stenografski beleške IX kongresa (mimeo). Belgrade, 1969.

X sjednica Centralnog komiteta Saveza komunista Hrvatske. Zagreb, 1970.

[I] *Konferencija Saveza komunista Jugoslavije*. Belgrade, 1970.

Druga konferencija Saveza komunista Jugoslavije. Belgrade, 1972.

Službeni list FNRJ [SFRJ]—(Official Gazette).

Yugoslav Federal Executive Council. *The Constitution of the Socialist Federal Republic of Yugoslavia: Constitutional Amendments*. Belgrade, 1969.

— *Ustav SFRJ; Ustavni Amandmani*. Belgrade, 1971.

— *The Constitution of the Socialist Federal Republic of Yugoslavia*. Belgrade, 1974.

Federal Institute of Statistics, Belgrade (Savezni zavod za statistiku). *Statistički godišnjak FNRJ (SFRJ)*, 1963 et seq.

— *Demografska statistika 1967*. Belgrade, 1970.

— *Statistički prikaz razvoja poljoprivrede 1950-1971*. Belgrade, 1973.

Federal Planning Institute (Belgrade). *Uzroci i karakteristike privrednih kretanja u 1961 i 1962 godini*. Belgrade, 1962.

White Book on Aggressive Activities by the Governments of the USSR, Poland, Czechoslovakia, Hungary, Rumania, Bulgaria and Albania towards Yugoslavia. Belgrade, 1951.

II. OTHER WORKS

Adamic. Louis. *The Eagle and the Roots.* New York, 1952.
American Universities Field Staff, Fieldstaff Reports, Southeast Europe
  Series, vols i and ii (1953-54) reports by Fred Warner Neal, and vols.
  xi-xxii (1963-75) reports by Dennison I. Rusinow.
Armstrong, Hamilton Fish. *Tito and Goliath.* London, 1951.
Auty, Phyllis. *Yugoslavia.* London, 1965.
— and Clogg, Richard, eds. *British Policy Towards Wartime Resistance
  in Yugoslavia and Greece.* London, 1975.
Avakumović, Ivan. *History of the Communist Party of Yugoslavia.*
  Aberdeen, 1964.
Azrael, Jeremy. *Managerial Power and Soviet Politics.* Cambridge, Mass.,
  1966.
Ban, Milenko. *Naselja u Jugoslaviji i njihov razvoj u periodu 1948-61.*
  Belgrade, 1970.
Bakarić, Vladimir. *O poljoprivredi i problemima sela.* Belgrade, 1960.
— *Aktuelni problemi sadašnje etape revolucije.* Zagreb, 1967.
Baklanoff, Eric, ed. *The Mediterranean and the EEC.* Alabama, 1976.
Barton, Allen, *et al.* eds. *Opinion-Making Elites in Yugoslavia.* New York,
  1973.
Bass, Robert and Marbury, Elizabeth. *The Soviet-Yugoslav Controversy
  1948-58.* New York, 1959.
Bićanić, Rudolf. *Ekonomska podloga hrvatskog pitanja.* Zagreb, 1938.
— 'Economic Growth under Centralized and Decentralized Planning in
  Yugoslavia', *Economic Growth and Cultural Change,* Oct. 1957.
— 'Economics of Socialism in a Developed Country', *Foreign Affairs,*
  July 1966.
— *Economic Policy in Socialist Yugoslavia.* Cambridge, 1973.
Bilandžić, Dusan. *Management of the Yugoslav Economy 1945-66.*
  Belgrade, 1967.
— *Borba za samoupravni socijalizam u Jugoslaviji 1945-69.* Zagreb,
  1969.
— *Ideje i praksa društvenog razvoja Jugoslavije 1945-73.* Belgrade,
  1973.
Bombelles, Joseph T. *Economic Development of Communist Yugoslavia
  1947-64.* Stanford, 1968.
Breznik, Dušan, ed. *Migracije stanovništva Jugoslavije.* Belgrade, 1971.
Broekmeyer, M. J., ed. *Yugoslav Workers' Self-Management.* Dordrecht,
  1970.
Burks, R. V. *The National Problem and the Future of Yugoslavia.* Rand
  P4761, 1971.
Campbell, John C. *Tito's Separate Road.* New York, 1967.
Čolaković, Rodojub, *et al.,* eds. *Pregled istorije Saveza komunista
  Jugoslavije.* Belgrade, 1963.
Clissold, Stephen. *Whirlwind: An Account of Marshal Tito's Rise to
  Power.* London, 1949.
— ed. *Yugoslavia and the Soviet Union 1939-73.* London, 1975.
Damjanović, P. *Tito na čelu partije.* Belgrade, 1968.
Deakin, F. W. *The Embattled Mountain.* London. 1971.
Dedijer, Vladimir. *Tito Speaks.* London, 1953.

— *The Beloved Land.* London, 1961.

— *Izgubljena bitka J. V. Staljina.* Sarajevo, 1969.

Djilas, Milovan, *The New Class: An Analysis of the Communist System.* London, 1957.

— *Anatomy of a Moral; the Political Essays of Milovan Djilas.* London, 1959.

— *Conversations with Stalin.* London, 1962.

— *The Unperfect Society: Beyond the New Class.* New York, 1969.

— *Memoir of a Revolutionary.* New York, 1973.

Djordjević, Jovan, *Novi ustavni sistem.* Belgrade, 1964.

— *Socijalizam i demokratija.* Belgrade, 1964.

Djordjević, Jovan *et al.,* eds. *Teorija i praksa samoupravljanja u Jugoslaviji.* Belgrade, 1972.

Dolanc, Stane, *et al. Ideological and Political Offensive of the League of Communists of Yugoslavia.* Belgrade, 1972.

Duroselle, Jean-Baptiste. *Le Conflit de Trieste.* Brussels, 1966.

Džeba, K. and Beslać, M. *Privredna reforma-što i zašto se mijenja.* Zagreb, 1965.

Erlich, Vera St. *Family in Transition: a Study of 300 Yugoslav Villages.* Princeton, 1966.

Fisher, Jack C. *Yugoslavia: A Multinational State.* San Francisco, 1966.

Ginić, Ivanka. *Dinamika i struktura gradskog stanovništva Jugoslavije.* Belgrade, 1967.

Gorupić, Drago and Paj, Ivan. *Workers' Self-Management in Yugoslav Undertakings.* Zagreb, 1970.

Halperin, Ernst. *The Triumphant Heretic.* London, 1958.

Halpern, Joel. 'Peasant Culture and Urbanization of Yugoslavia'. *Human Organization,* Summer 1965.

— *A Serbian Village.* New York, 1958; rev. ed. 1972.

Hamel, H., ed. *Arbeiter selbstverwaltung in Jugoslawien.* Munich, 1974.

Hamilton, F. E. I. *Yugoslavia: Patterns of Economic Activity.* London, 1968.

Hammel, Eugene A. *The Pink Yo-yo.* Berkeley, 1969.

Heppell, Muriel and Singleton, F. B. *Yugoslavia.* New York, 1961.

Hoffman, George, ed. *Eastern Europe; Essays in Geographical Problems.* London, 1971.

Hoffman, George W. and Neal, F. W. *Yugoslavia and the New Communism.* New York, 1962.

Hondius, Fritz W. *The Yugoslav Community of Nations.* The Hague, 1968.

Hoptner, J. B. *Yugoslavia in Crisis 1934-41.* New York, 1962.

Horvat, Branko. *An Essay on Yugoslav Society.* White Plains, 1967.

— *Towards a Theory of a Planned Market Economy.* White Plains, 1969.

Ionescu, Ghita. *The Politics of the European States.* New York, 1967.

Jelavich, Charles and Barbara. *The Balkans in Transition.* Berkeley, 1963.

Jelić, Borivoj. *Sistem planiranja u jugoslovenskoj privredi.* Belgrade, 1962.

Johnson, A. Ross. *The Transformation of Communist Ideology. The Yugoslav Case, 1945-53.* Cambridge, Mass., 1972.

— 'Yugoslav Total National Defence', *Survival,* Mar.-Apr. 1973.

— *Yugoslavia in the Twilight of Tito.* The Washington Papers, 1974.

Jovanović, Vladimir. *OOUR.* Belgrade, 1974.

Jowitt, Kenneth. *Revolutionary Breakthroughs and National Development: The Case of Romania.* Berkeley, 1971.

Kardelj, Edvard. *Socialist Democracy.* Belgrade, 1952.

— *Socialism and War, A Survey of the Chinese Criticism of Coexistence.* 1960, publ. in English, London, 1961.

— *On the Principle of the Preliminary Draft of the New Constitution of Socialist Yugoslavia.* Belgrade, 1962.

— *Problemi naše socijalisticke izgradnje,* vols. 6/7. Belgrade, 1964-68.

— *Raskršća u razvitku socijalističkog društva.* Belgrade 1969.

— *Osnovi uzroci i pravci ustavnih promena.* Belgrade 1973.

Kerner, Robert J., ed. *Yugoslavia.* Berkeley, 1949.

Kidrič, Boris. *Sabrana dela.* 4 vols. Belgrade, 1960.

Kofos, Evangelos. *Nationalism and Communism in Macedonia.* Salonika, 1964.

Korbel, Josef. *Tito's Communism.* Denver, 1951.

Lapenna, Ivo. *State and Law in Soviet and Yugoslav Theory.* New Haven, 1964.

Lasić, Stanko. *Sukob na književnoj ljevici 1928-52.* Zagreb, 1970.

Lederer, Ivo. *Yugoslavia at the Paris Peace Conference.* Yale, 1963.

Lendvai, Paul, *Eagles in Cobwebs.* London, 1969.

Lowenthal, Richard. *World Communism.* New York, 1964, orig. Germ. ed. 1963.

Macesich, George. *Yugoslavia; The Theory and Practice of Development Planning.* Charlottesville, Va., 1964.

Maclean, Sir Fitzroy. *Eastern Approaches.* London, 1949.

— *Disputed Barricades.* London, 1957.

Marjanović, Jovan. *Ustanak i Narodno-Oslobodilački Pokret u Srbiji 1941.* Belgrade, 1963.

— *Guerra popolare e revoluzione in Jugoslavia.* Milan, 1962.

— et al. *30 Godina socijalističke Jugoslavije.* Belgrade, 1973 (an updating of the same authors' *25 Godina socijalističke Jugoslavije*). Belgrade, 1968.

McDonald, Mary B. *Economic Development in the Backward Regions of Yugoslavia 1953-64.* Unpubl. D.Phil. thesis, Oxford 1968.

McVicker, Charles P. *Titoism, Pattern for International Communism.* New York, 1957.

Meier, Viktor. *Das neue Jugoslawische Wirtschaftssystem.* Zurich, 1956.

Milatović, Mile. *Slučaj Andrije Hebrang.* Belgrade, 1952.

Milenkovitch, Deborah D. *Plan and Market in Yugoslav Economic Thought.* New Haven, 1971.

Miller, Margaret, et al. *Communist Economy Under Change.* London, 1963.

Neal, Fred Warner (see also American Universities Field Staff). *Titoism in Action: The Reforms in Yugoslavia after 1948.* Berkeley, 1958.

Nešović, Slobodan. *Moša Pijade i nejegovo vreme.* Belgrade, 1968.

Nikolić, M. and Atlagić, D., eds. *O nacionalnom pitanju.* Belgrade, 1967.

Novak, Bogdan. *Trieste 1941-54.* Chicago, 1970.

Novak, Viktor. *Magnem krimen.* Zagreb, 1948.

Organization for Economic Co-operation and Development. *Economic Survey of Yugoslavia.* Paris, May 1963 et seq.

Palmer, Stephen E. Jr. and King, Robert R. *Yugoslav Communism and the Macedonian Question.* Hamden, Conn., 1971.

Pattee, Richard. *The Case of Cardinal Aloysius Stepinac.* Milwaukee, 1953.

Pavlowitch, Stevan K. *Yugoslavia.* New York, 1971.

Pejovich, Svetozar. *The Market-Planned Economy of Yugoslavia.* Minneapolis, 1966.

Perić, Ivan. *Ideje 'masovnog pokreta' u Hrvatskoj.* Zagreb, 1974.

Pijade, Moša. *About the Legend that the Yugoslav Uprising Owed its Existence to Soviet Assistance.* London, 1950.

Popović, Nenad D. *Yugoslavia-The New Class in Crisis.* Syracuse, 1968.

Popović, Svetolik. *Agricultural Policy in Yugoslavia.* Belgrade, 1964.

Pounds, Norman J. G. *Eastern Europe.* Chicago, 1969.

Pribičević, Branko P. *Sukob Komunističke partije Jugoslavije i Kominforma.* Belgrade, 1972.

Radio Free Europe Research Reports.

Roberts, Walter. *Tito, Mihailović and the Allies 1941-45.* Rutgers, 1973.

Royal Inst. of International Affairs. *The Soviet-Yugoslav Dispute.* London, 1948.

Ristić, Dragiša. *Yugoslavia's Revolution of 1941.* Univ. Park, Pa., 1966.

Rubinstein, Alvin Z. *Yugoslavia and the Nonaligned World.* Princeton, 1970.

Rusinow, Dennison (see also American Universities Field Staff). 'Interpreting the Yugoslav Reforms', *The World Today*, Feb. 1967.

— 'Marxism Belgrade Style', *Antioch Review*, Winter 1967-68.

— *Italy's Austrian Heritage.* Oxford, 1969.

Sanders, Irwin T., ed. *Collectivization of Agriculture in Eastern Europe.* Lexington, 1958.

Seton-Watson, Hugh. *The East European Revolution.* London, 1950.

Shoup, Paul. *Communism and the Yugoslav National Question.* New York, 1968.

Shub, Anatole. Newsletters. Inst. of Current World Affairs (New York), 1962-63.

— 'Tito on a Tightrope', *The Reporter*, 31 Jan. 1963.

— 'Letter from Belgrade', *Encounter*, June 1964.

Simić, Andrej. *The Peasant Urbanites.* London, 1973.

Spulber, Nicholas. *The Economics of Communist Eastern Europe.* Cambridge, Mass., 1957.

Stojanović, Radmila, ed. *Yugoslav Economists on Problems of a Socialist Economy.* New York, 1964.

Stojanović, Svetozar. *Between Ideals and Reality.* London, 1973.

Tomasevich, Jozo. *Peasants, Politics and Economic Change in Yugoslavia.* Stanford, 1955.

— *The Chetniks.* Stanford, 1975.

Tornquist, David. *Look East, Look West; the Socialist Adventure in Yugoslavia.* New York, 1966.

Tripalo, Miko. *Bez kompromisa, u ostvarivanju samoupravnog socijalizma.* Zagreb, 1969.

— *S poprišta.* Zagreb, 1971.

Ulam, Adam. *Titoism and the Cominform.* Cambridge, Mass., 1952.

Vinterhalter, Vinko. *Životnom Stazom Josipa Broza.* Belgrade, 1968.

Vucinich, Wayne S., ed. *Contemporary Yugoslavia.* Berkeley, 1969.
Vučković, Milos. 'The Recent Development of the Money and Banking System of Yugoslavia', *Journal of Political Economy* (Chicago), Aug. 1963.
Vukmanović-Tempo, Svetozar. *Revolucija koja teče.* Belgrade, 1971.
Ward, Benjamin. 'Workers' Management in Yugoslavia', *Journal of Political Economy*, Oct. 1957.
Waterston, Albert. *Planning in Yugoslavia.* Baltimore, 1962.
Wolff, Robert Lee. *The Balkans in Our Time.* Cambridge, Mass., 1956.
Zaninovich, M. George. *The Development of Socialist Yugoslavia.* Baltimore, 1968.

III. PERIODICALS

Published in Belgrade unless otherwise noted

Ekonomska politika
Ekonomski Pregled (Zagreb)
Gledišta
Hrvatski tjednik (Zagreb 1971)
Književne novine
Komunist
Narodna Armija
Naše teme (Zagreb)
NIN—Nedeljne Informativne Novine
Nova Misao (1953-4)
Partijska izgradnja
Privredni pregled

Privredni vjesnik (Zagreb)
Praxis (Zagreb)
Questions actuelles du socialisme
Review of International Affairs
Socialist Thought and Practice (abbreviated *STAP* in footnotes)
Socijalizam
Sociologija
Stanovništvo
Svet
VUS—Vjesnik u Srijedu (Zagreb)
Yugoslav Survey

INDEX